Catholicism and Communit

This is a groundbreaking study of the political, religious, social and mental worlds of the Catholic aristocracy from 1550 to 1640. Michael Questier examines the familial and patronage networks of the English Catholic community and their relationship to the later Tudors and Stuarts. He shows how the local history of the Reformation can be used to rewrite mainstream accounts of national politics and religious conflict in this period. The book takes in the various crises of mid- and late Elizabeth politics, the accession of James Stuart, the Gunpowder plot, religious toleration and the start of the Thirty Years War and finally the rise of Laudianism, leading up to the civil war. It challenges current historical notions of Catholicism as fundamentally sectarian and demonstrates the extent to which sections of the Catholic community had come to an understanding with both the local and national State by the later 1620s and 1630s.

MICHAEL C. QUESTIER is Senior Lecturer in History at Queen Mary, University of London. He has published *Conversion, Politics and Religion in England, 1580–1625* (1996).

Cambridge Studies in Early Modern British History

Series editors

ANTHONY FLETCHER

Emeritus Professor of English Social History, University of London

JOHN GUY

Fellow, Clare College, Cambridge

JOHN MORRILL

Professor of British and Irish History, University of Cambridge, and
Vice-Master of Selwyn College

This is a series of monographs and studies covering many aspects of the history of the British Isles between the late fifteenth century and the early eighteenth century. It includes the work of established scholars and pioneering work by a new generation of scholars. It includes both reviews and revisions of major topics and books, which open up new historical terrain or which reveal startling new perspectives on familiar subjects. All the volumes set detailed research into our broader perspectives and the books are intended for the use of students as well as of their teachers.

For a list of titles in the series, see end of book.

CATHOLICISM AND COMMUNITY IN EARLY MODERN ENGLAND

Politics, Aristocratic Patronage and Religion, c. 1550–1640

MICHAEL C. QUESTIER

CAMBRIDGE
UNIVERSITY PRESS

CAMBRIDGE UNIVERSITY PRESS
Cambridge, New York, Melbourne, Madrid, Cape Town, Singapore, São Paulo

Cambridge University Press
The Edinburgh Building, Cambridge CB2 8RU, UK

Published in the United States of America by Cambridge University Press, New York

www.cambridge.org
Information on this title: www.cambridge.org/9780521860086

First published 2006
This digitally printed version 2008

A catalogue record for this publication is available from the British Library

Library of Congress Cataloguing in Publication data
Questier, Michael C.
Catholicism and community in early modern England : politics, aristocratic patronage and
religion, *c.* 1550–1640 / Michael Questier.
p.   cm. – (Cambridge studies in early modern British history)
Includes bibliographical references and index.
ISBN-13: 978-0-521-86008-6
ISBN-10: 0-521-86008-3
1. Catholic Church – England – History – 16th century.   2. Catholic Church – England –
History – 17th century.   3. England – Church history – 16th century.   4. England – Church
history – 17th century.   I. Title.   II. Series.
BX1492.Q47   2006
282′42′09032 – dc22   2005024106

ISBN 978-0-521-86008-6 hardback
ISBN 978-0-521-06880-2 paperback

CONTENTS

ILLUSTRATIONS

PREFACE

This book has been a long time in the making. It would never have appeared at all if it had not been for the considerable kindness of so many friends. In particular Pauline Croft read the entire typescript (more than once) and made numerous invaluable suggestions. Rivkah Zim shared her understanding of the aristocracy during this period; Simon Healy provided essential advice on early modern parliamentary procedure; and I am exceedingly grateful to Simon Adams for allowing me access to his utterly encyclopaedic knowledge of sixteenth-century politics. Most helpful also were Geoff Baker, Caroline Bowden, Thomas Cogswell, Ginevra Crosignani, Richard Cust, Andrew Foster, Gabriel Glickman, Paul Hammer, Matthew Piggott, Glyn Redworth, Geoffrey Scott and Margaret Sena. And I am indebted to Peter Lake for discussions of many of the topics and themes in this volume.

One of the advantages of doing any species of local history is that it allows one to see at first hand some of the places and things in which one claims to be interested. I would like to thank Richard Clark of Battle Abbey school for discussing the architecture and history of the abbey with me, and also Helen Atkins of Firle Place for her assistance with the records of the Gage family. Timothy McCann and Christopher Whittick, local history supremos respectively in West Sussex and East Sussex, were exceptionally helpful in guiding me to sources that I would, without doubt, never have discovered on my own. I would like also to record my thanks to *Historical Research* for allowing me to use material previously published in that excellent journal, and to Michael Watson and Linda Randall of Cambridge University Press, and also to the Marc Fitch Fund and the Isobel Thornley Fund for financial assistance towards the costs of publication.

Another debt of gratitude is owed to Geoffrey Holt and Thomas McCoog, the guardians of the Jesuit library and archive in Mayfair in London. It is a tribute to their tolerance that I was allowed to use their archival resources to complete a study of Catholicism in the early modern period, a significant proportion of which is concerned with hatred (expressed by both Catholics and Protestants) of the Society of Jesus. Ian Dickie, at the Westminster Cathedral

Archives, has had to put up with listening to stories about the Jesuit archive in a different part of town and yet still allowed me to take liberties with his archival holdings (and with his photocopier).

My last debt is to the Tudor and Stuart seminar at the Institute of Historical Research in London. In the context of a crumbling and decaying, and frequently deeply depressing, higher education system in twenty-first-century Britain it is reassuring that some things, and notably the seminar, have not changed. One former convenor of the seminar liked to think that the compensation for a lower standard of living in London academe was a higher standard of thinking. Whether or not this is true, the seminar, with its intellectual solidarity and sheer unpretentiousness, has been for many of us the centre of the early modern historical world (at least in London). Had I not been privileged to attend it, and had it not been for the many friends whom I have met there, I would, without question, never have had the incentive to carry on.

In a recent overview of the Reformation period Peter Marshall suggested that I had misunderstood the nature of the post-Reformation Catholic community in England, in particular in my belief that there was no such unitary thing as Catholicism during the period. After a certain amount of bad-tempered huffing and puffing I am bound to say that, at least in some respects, I now agree with him. The contours of this volume owe a lot to his thoughts. It is, as its title indicates, written also with an eye to John Bossy's *English Catholic Community 1570–1850* of 1975. The whole project is, in some sense, a response to that extraordinary book, even though it is not really in disagreement with any aspect of what Professor Bossy said. (I am, in fact, still thinking about the general thrust of Bossy's argument and, in a perplexed state, will probably go on doing so.) But I recognise that, probably misled by the weight of both early modern polemics and also by more modern historical establishment-centred accounts of the Church and religion during the later sixteenth and early seventeenth centuries, I have not previously acknowledged sufficiently the coherence of the early modern Catholic community (although coherence does not necessarily mean harmony), and I have done my best, therefore, both to adjust my own perspective and also to reignite the debate about the religious politics of the period which Bossy pioneered over thirty years ago.

NOTE ON THE TEXT

In the text, dates are given Old Style (unless otherwise indicated) but the year is taken to begin on 1 January. The place of publication of printed works cited is London unless otherwise stated. Original spelling in all quotations from early modern manuscripts and printed works has been retained (except for 'than', which frequently appears in them as 'then'; and, also, i is transposed to j, and u to v, where necessary in order to conform to modern usage). Contractions have been silently expanded. Capitalisation has been modernised and punctuation has been partly modernised.

ABBREVIATIONS

AA	Anthony Maria Browne, second Viscount Montague, 'An Apologeticall Answere of the Vicount Montague unto Sundrie Important Aspersions in the Seven Reasons, and some other partes of a Letter of a Namelesse Author cov[e]red under the Letters A.B.' (Gillow Library MS, on microfilm at WSRO)
AAW	Archives of the Archdiocese of Westminster
ABSJ	Archivum Britannicum Societatis Jesu
Adams, 'Protestant Cause'	S. Adams, 'The Protestant Cause: Religious Alliance with the West European Calvinist Communities as a Political Issue in England, 1585–1630' (D.Phil., Oxford, 1973)
Akrigg, *Southampton*	G. P. V. Akrigg, *Shakespeare and the Earl of Southampton* (1968)
Albion, *CI*	G. Albion, *Charles I and the Court of Rome* (1935)
Allison, JG	A. F. Allison, 'John Gerard and the Gunpowder Plot', *RH* 5 (1959–60), 43–63
Allison, QJ	A. F. Allison, 'A Question of Jurisdiction: Richard Smith, Bishop of Chalcedon and the Catholic Laity, 1625–1631', *RH* 16 (1982), 111–45
Allison, RS	A. F. Allison, 'Richard Smith, Richelieu and the French Marriage. The Political Context of Smith's Appointment as Bishop for England in 1624', *RH* 7 (1964), 148–211
Allison, RSGB	A. F. Allison, 'Richard Smith's Gallican Backers and Jesuit Opponents', I (*RH* 18 (1987), 329–401), II (*RH* 19 (1989), 234–85), III (*RH* 20 (1990), 164–206)

List of abbreviations

Anglia MS 1	Letters of the Jesuit general, Muzio Vitelleschi, to members of the English province (summaries at ABSJ, XLVII/3 (vol. I: 1605–23), XLVII/4 (vol. II: 1624–32) and XLVII/5 (vol. III: 1633–41))
Anstr.	G. Anstruther, *The Seminary Priests* (4 vols., Ware and Great Wakering, 1968–77)
Anstruther, *Vaux*	G. Anstruther, *Vaux of Harrowden* (Newport, 1953)
APC	J. R. Dasent *et al.* (eds.), *Acts of the Privy Council of England 1542–1628* (46 vols., 1890–1964)
ARCR	A. F. Allison and D. M. Rogers, *The Contemporary Printed Literature of the English Counter-Reformation between 1558 and 1640* (2 vols., Aldershot, 1989–94)
ARSJ	Archivum Romanum Societatis Jesu
Bellenger, *EWP*	D. A. Bellenger, *English and Welsh Priests 1558–1800* (Bath, 1984)
Berry, *Sussex*	W. Berry, *County Genealogies: Pedigrees of the Families in the County of Sussex* (1830) (copy at WSRO annotated by J. Comber)
BIHR	*Bulletin of the Institute of Historical Research*
Bindoff, *HC*	S. T. Bindoff (ed.), *The House of Commons 1509–1558* (3 vols., 1982)
BL	British Library
Bodl.	Bodleian Library, Oxford
Bossy, 'Character'	J. Bossy, 'The Character of Elizabethan Catholicism', *Past and Present* 21 (1962), 39–59
Bossy, *ECC*	J. Bossy, *The English Catholic Community 1570–1850* (1975)
Breight, 'Caressing'	C. Breight, 'Caressing the Great: Viscount Montague's Entertainment of Elizabeth at Cowdray, 1591', *SAC* 127 (1989), 147–66
BS	*Biographical Studies*
Challoner, *Memoirs*	R. Challoner, ed. J. H. Pollen, *The Memoirs of Missionary Priests* (1924)
Cockburn, *Kent Assizes: Elizabeth*	J. S. Cockburn (ed.), *Calendar of Assize Records: Kent Indictments: Elizabeth I* (1979)

Cockburn, *Surrey Assizes: Elizabeth*	J. S. Cockburn (ed.), *Calendar of Assize Records: Surrey Indictments: Elizabeth I* (1980)
Cockburn, *Surrey Assizes: James I*	J. S. Cockburn (ed.), *Calendar of Assize Records: Surrey Indictments: James I* (1982)
Cockburn, *Sussex Assizes: Elizabeth*	J. S. Cockburn (ed.), *Calendar of Assize Records: Sussex Indictments: Elizabeth I* (1975)
Cockburn, *Sussex Assizes: James I*	J. S. Cockburn (ed.), *Calendar of Assize. Records: Sussex Indictments: James I* (1975)
Codignola, *CHL*	L. Codignola, trans. A. Weston, *The Coldest Harbour of the Land: Simon Stock and Lord Baltimore's Colony in Newfoundland, 1621–1649* (Montreal, 1988)
CRS	Catholic Record Society
CRS 1	*Miscellanea I* (CRS 1, 1905)
CRS 2	*Miscellanea II* (CRS 2 1906)
CRS 4	*Miscellanea IV* (CRS 4, 1907)
CRS 5	J. H. Pollen (ed.), *Unpublished Documents relating to the English Martyrs* (CRS 5, 1908)
CRS 10–11	E. H. Burton and T. L. Williams (eds.), *The Douay College Diaries* (CRS 10–11, 1911)
CRS 18	M. M. C. Calthrop (ed.), *Recusant Roll No. 1, 1592–3* (CRS 18, 1916)
CRS 21	J. H. Pollen and W. MacMahon (eds.), *The Ven. Philip Howard Earl of Arundel 1557–1595* (CRS 21, 1919)
CRS 22	*Miscellanea XII* (CRS 22, 1921)
CRS 37	W. Kelly (ed.), *Liber Ruber Venerabilis Collegii Anglorum de Urbe: Annales Collegii Pars Prima: Nomina Alumnorum I. A.D. 1579–1630* (CRS 37, 1940)
CRS 39	L. Hicks (ed.), *Letters and Memorials of Father Robert Persons, S.J.,* I (CRS 39, 1942)
CRS 41	L. Hicks (ed.), *Letters of Thomas Fitzherbert 1608–1610* (CRS 41, 1948)
CRS 51	P. Renold (ed.), *The Wisbech Stirs (1595–1598)* (CRS 51, 1958)
CRS 52	A. G. Petti (ed.), *The Letters and Despatches of Richard Verstegan (c. 1550–1640)* (CRS 52, 1959)
CRS 53	C. Talbot (ed.), *Miscellanea* (CRS 53, 1961)

CRS 54–5	A. Kenny (ed.), *The Responsa Scholarum of the English College, Rome* (2 vols., CRS 54–5, 1962–3)
CRS 56	E. E. Reynolds (ed.), *Miscellanea* (CRS 56, 1964)
CRS 57	H. Bowler (ed.), *Recusant Roll No. 2 (1593–1594)* (CRS 57, 1965)
CRS 58	P. Renold (ed.), *Letters of William Allen and Richard Barret 1572–1598* (CRS 58, 1965)
CRS 60	A. G. Petti (ed.), *Recusant Documents from the Ellesmere Manuscripts* (CRS 60, 1968)
CRS 61	H. Bowler (ed.), *Recusant Roll No. 3 (1594–1595) and Recusant Roll No. 4 (1595–1596)* (CRS 61, 1970)
CRS 64/68	A. J. Loomie (ed.), *Spain and the Jacobean Catholics* (2 vols., CRS 64, 68, 1973, 1978)
CRS 71	H. Bowler and T. McCann (eds.), *Recusants in the Exchequer Pipe Rolls 1581–1592* (CRS 71, 1986)
CRS 74–5	T. M. McCoog (ed.), *English and Welsh Jesuits 1555–1650* (2 vols., CRS 74–5, 1994–5)
CSPD	R. Lemon and M. A. E. Green (eds.), *Calendar of State Papers, Domestic Series* (12 vols. (for 1547–1625), 1856–72)
CSP Rome	J. M. Rigg (ed.), *Calendar of State Papers, relating to English Affairs, Preserved Principally at Rome* (2 vols. (for 1558–78), 1916–26)
CSP Scotland	J. Bain *et al.* (eds.), *Calendar of State Papers relating to Scotland and Mary Queen of Scots 1547–1603* (13 vols., Edinburgh, 1898–1969)
CSP Spanish	M. A. S. Hume (ed.), *Calendar of Letters and State Papers relating to English Affairs, Preserved Principally in the Archives of Simancas* (4 vols., 1892–9)
CSPF	J. Stevenson *et al.* (eds.), *Calendar of State Papers, Foreign Series, of the Reign of Elizabeth* (33 vols. (for 1558–96), 1863–2000)
CSPV	H. F. Brown and A. B. Hinds (eds.), *Calendar of State Papers, Venetian Series* (11 vols. (for 1581–1625), 1894–1912)

Davidson, RC	A. Davidson, 'Roman Catholicism in Oxfordshire from the Late Elizabethan Period to the Civil War *c.* 1580–1640' (Ph.D., Bristol, 1970)
Devlin, *Life*	C. Devlin, *The Life of Robert Southwell* (1956)
DNB	*Dictionary of National Biography*
Dockery, *CD*	J. B. Dockery, *Christopher Davenport* (1960)
ER	*Essex Recusant*
ESRO	East Sussex Record Office
Foley	H. Foley, *Records of the English Province of the Society of Jesus* (7 vols., 1875–83)
FSL	Folger Shakespeare Library
GEC	G. E. Cokayne, *The Complete Peerage* (13 vols., 1910–59)
Guilday, *ECR*	P. Guilday, *The English Catholic Refugees on the Continent 1558–1795* (1914)
Hamilton, *Chronicle*	A. Hamilton (ed.), *The Chronicle of the English Augustinian Canonesses Regular of the Lateran, at St Monica's in Louvain* (2 vols., 1904–6)
Harris, 'Reports'	P. R. Harris, 'The Reports of William Udall, Informer, 1605–1612', part I, *RH* 8 (1965), 192–284
Hasler, *HC*	P. Hasler (ed.), *The House of Commons 1558–1603* (3 vols., 1981)
HEH, BA	Archive of Webster of Battle (Henry E. Huntington Library, Los Angeles)
Hibbard, *CI*	C. Hibbard, *Charles I and the Popish Plot* (Chapel Hill, 1983)
HJ	*Historical Journal*
HMC	Historical Manuscripts Commission
HMCA	S. C. Lomas (ed.), *Report on the Manuscripts of the Earl of Ancaster* (HMC, 1907)
HMCD	E. K. Purnell *et al.* (eds.), *Report on the Manuscripts of the Marquess of Downshire* (5 vols., HMC, 1924–8)
HMCS	M. S. Giuseppi *et al.* (eds.), *Calendar of the Manuscripts of the Most Honourable the Marquess of Salisbury* (24 vols., HMC, 1888–1976)
Hope, *Cowdray*	W. H. St John Hope, *Cowdray and Easebourne Priory in the County of Sussex* (1919)

HPT	History of Parliament Trust
HR	*Historical Research*
HRO	Hampshire Record Office
Hughes, *HSJ*	T. Hughes, *History of the Society of Jesus in North America* (4 vols., 1908), vol. I
Hughes, *RCR*	P. Hughes, *Rome and the Counter-Reformation in England* (1942)
Hyland, *CP*	St George Kieran Hyland, *A Century of Persecution* (1920)
JBS	*Journal of British Studies*
JEH	*Journal of Ecclesiastical History*
Larkin and Hughes, *SRP*, I	J. F. Larkin and P. L. Hughes (eds.), *Stuart Royal Proclamations: Royal Proclamations of King James I 1603–1625* (Oxford, 1973)
Larkin, *SRP*, II	J. F. Larkin (ed.), *Stuart Royal Proclamations: Royal Proclamations of King Charles I 1625–1646* (Oxford, 1983)
Law, *AC*	T. G. Law, *The Archpriest Controversy* (2 vols., Camden Society, second series, 56, 58, 1896–8)
LJ	*Journals of the House of Lords*
LM	Loseley Manuscripts
LMA	London Metropolitan Archives
Loseley MSS	'The Manuscripts of William More Molyneux, Esq., of Loseley Park, Guildford, co. Surrey', *Seventh Report of the Royal Commission on Historical Manuscripts*, part I (report and appendix) (1879), 596–681
LPL	Lambeth Palace Library
Lunn, *EB*	D. Lunn, *The English Benedictines, 1540–1688* (1980)
Lunn, 'Opposition'	D. Lunn, 'Benedictine Opposition to Bishop Richard Smith (1625–1629)', *RH* 11 (1971–2), 1–20
McClure, *Letters*	N. E. McClure (ed.), *The Letters of John Chamberlain* (2 vols., Philadelphia, 1939)
McCoog, *Society*	T. M. McCoog, *The Society of Jesus in Ireland, Scotland, and England 1541–1588: 'Our Way of Proceeding?'* (Leiden, 1996)
Manning, *Religion*	R. B. Manning, *Religion and Society in Elizabethan Sussex* (Leicester, 1969)

Milton, *CR*	A. Milton, *Catholic and Reformed* (Cambridge, 1995)
Milward I	P. Milward, *Religious Controversies of the Elizabethan Age* (1977)
Milward II	P. Milward, *Religious Controversies of the Jacobean Age* (1978)
Morris, *Troubles*	J. Morris (ed.), *The Troubles of our Catholic Forefathers* (3 vols., 1872–7)
Mosse, *ME*	N. Mosse, *The Monumental Effigies of Sussex (1250–1650)* (Hove, 1933)
Mott, HR	A. Mott, 'A Dictionary of Hampshire Recusants: Tempo Eliz' (typescript at ABSJ)
NAGB	M. Questier (ed.), *Newsletters from the Archpresbyterate of George Birkhead* (Camden Society, 5th series, 12, 1998)
NCC	M. Questier (ed.), *Newsletters from the Caroline Court, 1631–1638: Catholicism and the Politics of the Personal Rule* (Camden Society, 5th series, 26, 2005)
NDNB	*The New Dictionary of National Biography*
n.p.	no place (of publication)
OFM	Order of Friars Minor
OSB	Order of St Benedict
Paul, HR	J. E. Paul, 'The Hampshire Recusants in the Reign of Elizabeth I with some Reference to the Problem of Church Papists' (Ph.D., Southampton, 1958)
Peckham, 'Institutions'	W. D. Peckham (ed.), 'Chichester Diocese Institutions, 1560–1658' (typescript at WSRO, Miscellaneous Papers 1096)
PRO	Public Record Office (National Archives)
Questier, LF	M. Questier, 'Loyal to a Fault: Viscount Montague Explains Himself', *HR* 77 (2004), 225–53
Questier, PM	M. Questier, 'Catholicism, Kinship and the Public Memory of Sir Thomas More', *JEH* 53 (2002), 476–509
RAF 3/4	Battle Abbey: Account of the Steward to Lady Montague 1597 (Raper & Fovargue, solicitors, Antiquarian Collection, Box 3/4)
RH	*Recusant History*
Roundell, *Cowdray*	C. Roundell, *Cowdray* (1884)

SAC	*Sussex Archaeological Collections*
SAS	Sussex Archaeological Society
Sharpe, *PR*	K. Sharpe, *The Personal Rule of Charles I* (1992)
SHC	Surrey History Centre
SJ	Society of Jesus
Smith, *Life*	L. P. Smith (ed.), *The Life and Letters of Sir Henry Wotton* (2 vols., Oxford, 1907)
Southern, *ERH*	A. C. Southern, *An Elizabethan Recusant House Comprising the Life of the Lady Magdalen Viscountess Montague (1538–1608)* (1954)
SR	*The Statutes of the Realm* (11 vols., 1810–28)
SRS	Sussex Record Society
SRS 19–20	E. H. W. Dunkin (ed.), *Sussex Manors, Advowsons, etc., Recorded in the Feet of Fines . . .* (SRS 19–20, 1914–15)
Stone, *CA*	L. Stone, *The Crisis of the Aristocracy* (Oxford, 1965)
TD	M. A. Tierney, *Dodd's Church History of England* (5 vols., 1839–43)
Traherne, *SC*	J. M. Traherne (ed.), *Stradling Correspondence* (1840)
TRHS	*Transactions of the Royal Historical Society*
VA	Vatican Archives
VCH Surrey	H. E. Malden and W. Page (eds.), *The Victoria History of the County of Surrey* (4 vols., 1902–67)
VCH Sussex	W. Page *et al.* (eds.), *The Victoria History of the County of Sussex* (9 vols., 1905–97)
VCH Wiltshire	R. B. Pugh *et al.* (eds.), *A History of Wiltshire* (17 vols., 1957–2002)
Watson, *Decacordon*	William Watson, *A Decacordon of Ten Quodlibeticall Questions* (1602)
WSRO	West Sussex Record Office

1

Introduction

This book started out as a proposal for a doctoral thesis on the post-Reformation experiences of one aristocratic family – namely the Brownes who dwelt during this period principally at Cowdray in West Sussex, Battle Abbey in East Sussex and in their Southwark residence, Montague House, which was situated in St Saviour's parish on the south bank of the Thames. (The head of the Browne family during Mary Tudor's reign, Sir Anthony, was promoted to the peerage in 1554 as Viscount Montague.) These were the sort of people whose lives and careers could be used, I thought, to explore certain central themes within the social history of the aristocracy of the period, especially with reference to political ideology and religious belief. For the Browne family was predominantly and often openly Catholic in its religious inclinations.

At the time that I was commencing research, however, this topic looked potentially rather unfashionable. It was the 'popular' rather than the blue-blooded variety of English Catholicism which was then attracting Reformation historians' attention. Popular conservatism, we are still told, is the key to explaining why the English Reformation failed in its purpose of transforming the English Church into the godly and pious institution which some Protestants wanted. Indeed, popular residual Catholic sentiment would have had even more clout after 1559 had the natural leaders of Catholicism, the high-born, particularly the peerage, not been vertebraically challenged. But they did nothing to crystallise and express that popular defiance which perhaps could, with proper direction, have completely halted the Reformation in its tracks. If, as has been estimated, approximately 20 per cent of the aristocracy remained Catholic in this period,[1] it must have been the least important 20 per cent. And their Catholicism can stand only as an index for their irrelevance. They were generally deprived of high office, but, not having the zeal of humbler Catholic folk, they were not usually called to account

[1] Lawrence Stone estimates that in 1641 about one fifth of the 121 peers could be described as Roman Catholic, Stone, *CA*, 742. See also Allison, *QJ*, 139.

for their religious opinions in the way that many recusant nonconformists were when they were hauled before the judges of the ecclesiastical and the secular courts.

It was therefore something of a worry to me that, since the project was concerned, initially at least, with the first Viscount Montague and his grandson and heir (who succeeded to the title as the second viscount), the thing might end up being called 'a tale of two nobles', or that, reflecting on their (apparent) withdrawal from the national stage, some wit might suggest that the first and second viscounts were an example of, using John Bossy's famous phrase, 'inertia to inertia in three generations', without there even being an active generation in the middle! Therefore, the preliminary work which I had done on the project I simply put aside, thinking that one day it might become an article in a local history journal.

But, as the years went by, I kept coming across references to this family, stories told and opinions voiced about them, and not just them but a wide variety of people with whom they were connected in various ways (by blood, marriage, tenurially, through patronage and service and even purely through ideological affinity). Although I was stumbling across bits and pieces of information and evidence essentially at random, it began to look as if there was something amounting to a fairly significant social entity which, for shorthand purposes, I decided to call an 'entourage' (grouped around the leading members of the family).[2]

I began to hope that by pursuing this entourage in some depth, even by resorting from time to time to some of the methodology of microhistory,[3] it might be possible to take an identifiable unit or nexus of individuals within the English Catholic community and ask a series of questions about it. For example, what political opinions did they hold? What were their attitudes on a range of questions such as nonconformity? How did the patronage structures work which allowed for the support of the Catholic clergy? Why was Catholicism so factionalised? What structures of authority for preserving Catholicism were created among such people? In particular, how did these Catholics understand the relationship between themselves and the

---

[2] By 'entourage' I mean something broader and looser than the patronage and clientage structures which have been discussed in such detail by, for instance, historians of early modern France. See e.g. S. Kettering, *Patrons, Brokers and Clients in Seventeenth-Century France* (Oxford, 1986), chs. 1–3, for an elaborate theorisation of the forms of patronage in France during this period. As Paul Hammer notes, the 'terms "following" and "followers" are imprecise, but suggestive, words'. The second earl of Essex's '"following" consisted of (primarily) men who were either his servants, clients (those linked to him by some significant patronage tie), relatives or close friends. Very often, individuals qualified as followers under more than one of these categories', P. Hammer, *The Polarisation of Elizabethan Politics* (Cambridge, 1999), 269. For differences between Lord Burghley and the earl of Essex about how a following or entourage should be constructed, see *ibid.*, 298.

[3] See C. W. Marsh, *The Family of Love in English Society, 1550–1630* (Cambridge, 1994), 10–14.

regime? And what was the nature of their relationship with the Church of England? The interaction of the Catholic community with the outside world, or, rather, the rest of English society, was something which Professor Bossy's justly famous magnum opus, *The English Catholic Community 1570–1850*, for methodological reasons, did not fully address. In some very real sense Catholicism did become, as Bossy argued, 'sectarian'. But Bossy developed this concept by writing about his topic from within. He specifically said that he was not interested in the 'relation of minority to majority, considered either as State or as Church, but with the body of Catholics as a social whole and in relation to itself'.[4] But this did not mean that the relationship of minority to majority could or should not be considered. Indeed this aspect of the topic positively invited study since one of the consensuses of recent Reformation scholarship has been that there was a good deal more interaction between people of supposedly hermetically sealed religious traditions than we had previously thought. Thus, by indulging myself in telling a story about a specific bit of the early modern Catholic community in which I was interested, I hoped to be able to narrate something which was not only about that community, at least not as it has traditionally been understood.

It is not surprising, of course, that, within the small-ish world of late sixteenth- and early seventeenth-century English gentry/aristocratic Catholicism, people tended to know other people. Methodologically, there was clearly a danger that what started out as a study of one relatively coherent family unit might become a mêlée of stray remarks about everyone who had even the slightest connection with anybody else within this comparatively narrow universe of individuals. There was also a risk that one would attribute impulses, attitudes and ideas exclusively to this group which were much more widely shared and held by other people, people about whom one knew next to nothing simply because they did not figure in the sources upon which one was relying.

On the other hand, I was sure that one could do more here than write a connected series of biographical sketches. For while at certain points in the period all we can find out about these characters is the absolute minimum of scattered biographical detail, at other times the aristocratic entourage's political and religious identity converged with and influenced, in quite significant ways, the wider Catholic community. Many of the well-known factional divisions and inclinations within the early modern Catholic community can be found being played out within this particular aristocratic following, as Catholics argued with each other about what Catholicism in post-Reformation England should be like. While there was often, as we might expect, a close fit between what clergy and laity within this aristocratic entourage thought and wanted, it was by no means guaranteed that

[4] Bossy, *ECC*, 5.

they would always agree. In the early seventeenth century we can find clerics within this entourage making a bid for influence and authority in a fashion which many other Catholics, lay and clerical, looked at askance. It seemed to me that what one had here was an often fairly coherent and quite sizeable slice of the English Catholic community, and a window potentially on to the whole of it.

I also hoped to do something which might be regarded as methodologically and historiographically innovative. As I have already suggested, a good deal of the current historiography of post-Reformation Catholicism in England tends to adopt a worm's-eye view of the beast. It has been defined almost exclusively as a popular response to the official Reformation, a response which was sulky and negative, enunciated by the 'people' who lived mainly in a series of shattered parochial rural idylls. For the Tudor State had systematically attacked, sequestrated and/or destroyed the forms and accoutrements of traditional religious practice.[5] Here 'Catholicism' and 'popular' are almost interchangeable terms. In contrast to this 'popular' groundswell of opinion, the actual Catholics whose names appear in the indexes of most of the volumes which deal with ecclesiastical politics in this period look like an ill-assorted and rather paltry lot – a few peers and gentry, a few seminary priests and the odd, sometimes very odd, conspirator. As I have intimated at the start of this chapter, historians have often defined what happened to English Catholicism by looking at these individuals in the context of the massed ranks of conservative plebeians. Here was the interpretative key necessary to explain why neither achieved anything: elite Catholicism was inept and detached from reality; popular Catholicism was inert and leaderless. And, in consequence, Catholicism after 1559 rapidly became a spent force.

Our entourage-based view of Catholicism does not fit this model at all. It wants, instead, to look from the top down as well as from the bottom up, and outwards as well as inwards. It is necessary to do this if we want to understand why some contemporaries continued to see Catholicism as a dynamic and threatening ever-present religious and political force or movement. To do this we have to know what the Catholics in our entourage said to each other, which of them spoke to each other and especially which ones did not, what they wrote and published, what forms of patronage were exercised among them, what the patrons among them wanted from their clients, and how their clients responded, and how these Catholics positioned themselves in relation to the regime and the State (both local and national).[6]

---

[5] E. Duffy, *The Stripping of the Altars* (1992); D. MacCulloch, *Tudor Church Militant* (1999).
[6] See S. Kettering, 'Patronage in Early Modern France', *French Historical Studies* 17 (1992), 839–62. Kettering notes that the word 'patronage' in English has meanings which the French version of the term does not possess (even though the literature on patronage and clientage

Now, in an ideal world, one might have extended one's research to more members of the Catholic aristocracy. But the surviving papers for most Catholic aristocratic families of the period are extremely limited. About some leading Catholic clans, such as the Barons Windsor, almost nothing is known. Obviously, for them, as for most landed families in this period, trawls through the Public Record Office's archives of chancery, exchequer and other government departments might turn up some material, but it would for the most part be about their economic and legal concerns and interests, not their politics or their religion. (To base a study on such sources would certainly tell one relatively little about such people's Catholicism.) Thus it seemed sensible to fix upon one specific entourage where it might be possible to reconstruct in some detail both the web of relationships between its members and also its political and religious concerns; an entourage which was clustered about a great man or men whose patronage, protection and company were consistently sought by a variety of people whose own paths and politico-religious interests crossed and collided in a variety of ways.

For my purposes the ideal entourage turned out to be the one with which I was already familiar – namely the following of the Viscounts Montague of Cowdray. Here there appeared to be an extremely wide set of marital relationships and ideological affinities, in some sense national in scope (since they were not restricted by county boundaries), perhaps even international (if one takes into account the entourage's clerical members' friends and contacts abroad). The entourage was also usefully decentred, in that what it stood for was not any single belief, objective or programme. Precisely because it was not a univocal and unidirectional entity, it might allow one to glimpse what a quite major section of English Catholicism was like, and what factors and characteristics enabled contemporaries to identify people as Catholics in the post-Reformation period.

This approach was suggested, in fact, by a throw-away comment in an essay written by Professor Bossy, an essay which I read years ago while I was still an undergraduate. In a survey of Jacobean Catholicism he remarked, commenting on Lawrence Stone's account of noble religion, that the Catholic aristocracy played 'a comparatively passive role' in the history of the Catholic

in early modern France seems now to be greater than the equivalent work on these things in early modern England). However, as Kettering observes, one of the principal meanings of the word is a 'system of personal ties and networks'. In the English context, that might be taken to denote 'an individual relationship, multiple relationships organized into networks, and an overall system based on these ties and networks', *ibid.*, 839. Such a definition is particularly relevant to the workings of post-Reformation aristocratic Catholicism because it is not dependent, for its evidence, on the kinds of activities, principally office-holding and appointments to office, which have frequently supplied the raw data for analysis of patronage and clientage systems. For the problems experienced by historians in locating evidence of patron and client networks, see *ibid.*, 842.

community. In particular he noted that 'it might be argued that the Catholicism of the earls of Worcester was as much an effect as a cause of its popularity among the gentry and people of Monmouthshire'.[7] This idea was sparsely footnoted but intriguing. Obviously, what he meant by 'passive' was that the peerage was at best a buffer zone to protect the Catholic community from the predatory hand of government. Meanwhile the character of the community was formed among the gentry class by both the 'active' and the 'quiet', with the clergy primarily and necessarily serving those gentry once their own larger ambitions of exercising a restored clerical authority had been frustrated by those same gentlemen who had no wish to see clerics lording it over them. I was not entirely sure how 'passive' the Catholic aristocracy were. But the idea of interplay between patrons and clients helping to define what Catholicism was, and how it was perceived, seemed interesting, perhaps crucial, and worth further exploration and more time than Bossy could give it in a short essay for a Macmillan 'Problems in Focus' volume.

So what I had conceived originally as a study of a minor south-coast aristocratic family became, instead, an attempt to recover a series of political *démarches* within Catholicism between the Reformation and the civil war, and to chart some of the responses to major issues which were thrown up by, and were directly concerned with, or touched upon, the problem of Catholicism, issues such as non/conformity, the succession to the throne, allegiance and loyalism, intra-Catholic division over ecclesiastical issues (notably over hierarchy and discipline), sacerdotalism and the 'triumph of the laity', and also the coming of 'Laudianism', or at least the series of policy innovations which some historians have identified as radically changing the face of the Church of England during the 1630s.

It would, of course, have been possible to deal with Catholic attitudes to allegiance, the succession and so on, in a purely thematic way. But I have chosen to pursue them within the context of a particular Catholic 'entourage' because I did not want to see these things only, as it were, in the abstract. The dearth of source material generated by as well as about Catholics has often meant that such issues are, by default, discussed in a thematic manner. But, at the end of it all, it frequently remains a problem to say which Catholics held this or that view on all or any of the above questions, or whether such views were, in fact, merely being attributed to them by others. I wanted to set the whole thing in the context of a specific Catholic group of people talking to and about each other, bound and linked to each other by various

---

[7] J. Bossy, 'The English Catholic Community 1603–1625', in A. G. R. Smith (ed.), *The Reign of James VI and I* (1973), 91–105, at p. 102. For other instances of the opinions expressed within a patron's clientele helping to shape the opinions of the patron, see e.g. S. Adams, 'A Godly Peer? Leicester and the Puritans', *History Today* 40 (1990), 14–19; Hammer, *Polarisation*, 78–81.

ties (of kinship, ideology etc.). And I wanted to see how Catholics' ideas were discussed inside a large clientage/patronage network, and to see what such a network thought and did in particular circumstances.[8]

Clearly, not all human life was here, and not even all of the post-Reformation English Catholic community. The Brownes and their friends were not necessarily representative of all other Catholics. But by describing how such an entourage was built up, and how it intersected with other parts of the community, I believed and still think that it is possible to contribute to a description of how Catholicism evolved in later sixteenth- and early to mid-seventeenth-century England, and why at particular times it was so politically 'hot', when, on many modern historical accounts of the 'seigneurial' (or gentrified) and marginalised Catholic community, it should have been nothing of the kind.

There have been some outstanding studies of patronage networks among English Protestants of the period.[9] Clearly in the patronage stakes Catholics generally had a lot less to play for. Catholic clergymen were not eligible for university posts, for official Court chaplaincies, indeed for any Church-of-England benefice. In addition, lay Catholics who were recusants were barred from holding public office. Those who were tainted by suspicion of Catholicism were liable to lose official posts and employment in both the local and national State. It is extraordinary, however, that, for example, no systematic study has been undertaken of which Catholic clerics were attached to which lay patrons. It is often not known even which houses and households they lived in. Even where this is known it is generally assumed that their residence in those houses and households was an ideologically neutral event (i.e. that they were there simply to carry out the functions of a priest) even though it is evident from many sources that clergy frequently attached themselves to those patrons with whom they were ideologically in sympathy. In England, those Catholic clergy who had an impact on public opinion were invariably those who had powerful patrons. By incorporating those patrons back into the picture, and by identifying how they and their clients talked not just to each other but also to curial officials in Rome, to foreign diplomats and notables and especially to the papal nuncios in Paris, Brussels and other places, and to local and national representatives of the English/British State, it seemed possible to give both definite social shape, and even, in places, a narrative form (and thus, perhaps, a degree of coherence) to the lives of some of those Catholics who tend otherwise to be discussed

---

[8] Kettering remarks that kinship and patronage were 'essential to the diffusion of information and ideas' among the French provincial nobility, Kettering, 'Patronage in Early Modern France', 842.

[9] See e.g. K. Fincham, 'William Laud and the Exercise of Caroline Ecclesiastical Patronage', *JEH* 51 (2000), 69–93.

in the thematic abstract and are mentioned, if they are lucky, only in the footnotes of monographs.

Thus, while it would be difficult to pretend that this social entity, this Catholic aristocratic entourage, was itself the Catholic community, it is, I claim, nevertheless, possible to read off from its view of itself and the world, an account of Catholicism during the period, or rather, how Catholicism was understood and discussed by a range of contemporaries (both Catholics and Protestants). For the fact that traditional parish worship was largely ground out at the root by a series of reforming Tudor regimes did not mean that Catholicism died the death as a public and political issue. Contemporaries talked endlessly about Catholicism (or 'popery'), its political inclinations and significance, the vicissitudes of the pan-European 'Protestant cause' and the real or imagined threat from its diametrical opposite, the 'Catholic cause'. The connection between the danger from an international Catholicism and the existence and activities of actual English Catholics was a source of constant contemporary comment.[10] English Catholic polemicists and ideologues, often with powerful foreign patrons, developed coherent and sometimes perilous lines of thought on major political issues – for example (during Elizabeth's reign) the unsettled question of the succession, the problematical topic of when and how far it was legitimate to resist sovereign authority and the issue of toleration.

The drive for toleration was carried on with even more vigour after the accession of James Stuart, a king whose dynasty's claims to the English throne many English Catholics had long reckoned to have supported. After his accession, they loudly and continuously reminded him that this had been so. James's European dynastic ambitions for his own house, principally a marriage for his heir with either the Habsburgs or Bourbons, meant that the 'Catholic issue' was given renewed political vigour in the middle and at the end of his reign. And, under Charles I, while it is possible to overestimate the extent to which actual Catholicism infiltrated the Court, many contemporaries perceived a link between the regime's ecclesiastical projects and the infiltration of popish Catholicism into the bowels of the regime and State. There were violent anti-Catholic scares throughout the period, and notably after 1637.[11] The crisis leading up to the civil war was perceived by many Protestants to be the product of a popish plot, and, as Thomas Cogswell has remarked, by their reckoning this would have been 'at least the third' time since the beginning of the seventeenth century that a popish

---

[10] For very sensible remarks on this topic in a seventeenth-century context, see M. Braddick, *State Formation in Early Modern England c. 1550–1700* (Cambridge, 2000), 325.

[11] R. Clifton, 'The Popular Fear of Catholics during the English Revolution', *Past and Present* 52 (1971), 23–55; *idem*, 'Fear of Popery', in C. Russell (ed.), *The Origins of the English Civil War* (1973), 144–67.

plot had been concocted in order to overthrow the commonwealth.[12] During the civil war, Catholics heavily engaged themselves for the crown. Virtually to a man those Catholics who took part in armed conflict were royalists. A glance at the pages of the heralds' visitations, printed by the Harleian Society, reveals numerous members of the Catholic gentry who are recorded as having been slain at one or other of the civil war's various battles. Catholics recalled and eulogised their co-religionists who suffered in the king's service.[13]

It is worth pointing out here that I have, throughout, decided deliberately to privilege evidence of kinship networks. Clearly this might be regarded as a somewhat tendentious methodological approach.[14] After all, the mere fact of kinship can be precisely that – a mere fact. On the other hand, the fact that so many of the Catholics dealt with here were indeed related by blood or marriage does in itself put a specific gloss on the nature of the Catholic 'community' in this period. Catholics tended to portray themselves as being a 'gathered' community of all right-thinking people who had a conscience in matters of true religion and the courage to express it. The post-Reformation/pre-civil-war Catholic community has since that time often been presented by historians in the same way. Instead, the suggestion here will be that contemporaries might well see the Catholic community as a series of entourages and networks, often factionally aligned internally, whose ideological concerns inflected the more basic fact of their blood, kin and client relationships.[15]

THE FATE OF THE RECORDS

Where, then, should one look for evidence of all this? As we have already noted, remarkably little material on the Catholic aristocracy actually survives, at least in the form that such records were originally kept.[16] And there is even a dearth of archival material for the family at the centre of this study – the Brownes of Cowdray.

---

[12] T. Cogswell, 'England and the Spanish Match', in R. Cust and A. Hughes (eds.), *Conflict in Early Stuart England* (1989), 107–33, at pp. 128–9. The other two 'plots' were the Gunpowder conspiracy and the Spanish match negotiations of the early 1620s. See Hibbard, *CI*.

[13] See ch. 15, pp. 499–507 below.

[14] See, however, D. Smith, *The Stuart Parliaments 1603–1689* (1999), 87; J. T. Peacey, 'Led by the Hand: Manucaptors and Patronage at Lincoln's Inn in the Seventeenth Century', *Journal of Legal History* 18 (1997), 26–44.

[15] See Kettering, *Patronage, Brokers and Clients*, 33, 73, for the functional relationship between kinship, patronage and clientage.

[16] A number of Catholic noble families' papers were destroyed in the civil war, for example in the sieges of the Paulets' residence at Basing and of the Arundells' castle at Wardour.

In the late eighteenth century a series of mishaps conspired to wipe out both the family's title and much of its memory. In the late summer of 1793 the eighth viscount, George Samuel, took it into his head to go on a jolly jape of a boating trip and try to 'shoot the falls' at Laufenburg on the Rhine. He proceeded to take himself and a friend and an unfortunate dog to a watery grave despite the best efforts of the local authorities and an old family retainer to prevent him. (His heir, a distant relation, died without issue and the title became extinct.) Shortly before the drowning incident, the family's palace of Cowdray was destroyed by fire, on 24 September 1793. (See Figures 1 and 2.) Workmen who were completing alterations and repairs to the building had taken to burning charcoal in an improvised carpenter's shop in a tower above the north gallery, in 'the midst of all the shavings and chips which strewed the floor'. Several of the staff were soused on that particular night, and they were quite unable to form a chain to pass water buckets up from the river.[17]

In fact, the muniment room (in the Kitchen Tower) which housed the family's records was not destroyed in the blaze. But nothing was done to preserve the papers there. In 1834 they were noted to be 'lying in heedless heaps on the floor, or . . . scattered on the shelves' while a few of the more important documents 'more ancient, and known by their rightful owner to be more curious than the rest' were set aside in some rudimentary kind of exhibition for the multitude to come and look at. Actually, visitors carried away quite a lot of deeds and manuscripts, and others were used 'as wrappers, or for kindling fires'. The scandal was remarked on even by a pupil at the

---

[17] Hope, *Cowdray*, 26; Roundell, *Cowdray*, 100–2, 123, 127. A separate stone building near to the main house contained a fire hose and buckets, but the key was missing, and further delay was caused as those servants who were not fully intoxicated tried to get the door off its hinges. After the fire the house was plundered for building materials, *ibid.*, 131, 130. Catholic tradition claimed that these events were the fulfilment (albeit rather late) of a fire-and-water curse allegedly pronounced in 1538 (in the abbot's hall at Battle) by an ejected monk on Sir Anthony Browne, Henry VIII's boon companion, abbey-plunderer and new owner of the dissolved Battle Abbey, J. Gillow, *A Literary and Biographical History, or Bibliographical Dictionary of the English Catholics* (5 vols., 1885–1902), V, 82. Lady Montague, the mother of the eighth viscount, and a convinced Protestant, by contrast blamed both Providence and one Higgeson, the supervisor of the carpenters, Roundell, *Cowdray*, 129. According to a contemporary, had not the steward at Cowdray wrongly addressed his letter describing the fire – to Lucerne as opposed to Laufenburg – the eighth viscount might have returned to England and not launched himself over the fatal waterfall, *ibid.*, 126, 132. To add insult to injury, the family's splendid funeral monument was removed in 1851 from Midhurst parish church and placed in Easebourne priory church (simply to make more space at Midhurst). (See Figures 3 and 4.) In the course of the move the monument was badly damaged, Mosse, *ME*, 72. For the monument as it originally stood at Midhurst, see Hope, *Cowdray*, plate 52. The monument was structurally mutilated by the diminution of its plinth, the removal of its four massive obelisks (one at each corner), its emblazoned shields and some of the kneeling figures around it; and by altering the position of the structure, i.e. turning it into a mural monument and rearranging the position of its three central figures, B. W. Greenfield, 'The Wriothesley Tomb in Titchfield, Hants: Its Effigial Statues and Heraldry', *Proceedings of the Hampshire Field Club* (1889), 65–82, at p. 66.

Figure 1. The ruins of the palace of Cowdray (east range), the residence of the Browne family (Viscounts Montague), near Midhurst, West Sussex. The palace was badly damaged by fire on the night of 24 September 1793.

Figure 2. A view of the west range of the ruined palace of Cowdray, including the chapel.

Figure 3.   Marble and alabaster monument to Sir Anthony Browne, first Viscount
Montague, in Easebourne parish church (St Mary). The monument's original
arrangement was changed, and its structure damaged, when it was moved to
Easebourne from Midhurst parish church in the nineteenth century.

Figure 4. Detail of the first Viscount Montague's two wives (Jane Radcliffe and Magdalen Dacre) on the funeral monument in Easebourne parish church (St Mary).

grammar school in Midhurst. In 1863 Sir Sibbald Scott noted that he had been able to root around in the 'parchments and papers' of the family in the same muniment room, still decaying and mouldering with the effects of the weather, damp and passing jackdaws. From his description, the really serious loss would appear to have been not so much estate documents but rather the 'piles of letters to and from different members of the family'.[18] By circuitous routes a few clutches of papers have survived, but comparatively little overall, and distressingly little for the mid- to late sixteenth and early seventeenth centuries.[19]

Furthermore, any kind of family archive which might have remained at the family's Southwark residence, Montague House (see Figure 5), was lost during the civil war when the family's property was sequestrated. (Montague House was demolished in the nineteenth century.)[20]

We are left, therefore, with very scattered and uneven evidence for these people. A few contemporary printed books mention them in passing. There

[18] A. A. Dibben, *The Cowdray Archives: A Catalogue* (2 vols., Chichester, 1960), I, xxviii–xxix.
[19] *Ibid.*, xxix–xxxii, describing the papers in question.
[20] F. T. Dollman, *The Priory of St. Mary Overie, Southwark* (1881), 29.

Figure 5.   A view of Montague House looking towards the gateway, 1827 (by John Chessell Buckler (1793–1894)).

are references to them in the archives of local and central courts, but these are often of little real significance, at least for the topics under discussion here. Some estate material survives. But for the purposes of an account of aristocratic politics and patronage the subsistence of court rolls is frankly not a great deal of help. They tell one little of the sort of thing which can be gleaned only from personal correspondence. For the Browne family there really is very little left, of a personal nature, for the later sixteenth and early seventeenth centuries – a few speeches, a few letters (many, however, of the formal variety), one hagiography, one translation each by the first and second viscounts, and in the second viscount's case a couple of tracts, including a massive 701-page disquisition (on Catholic ecclesiastical controversy in the early Caroline period) which must be in the running for a prize for the most boring book ever written. There is a detailed set of rules and orders drawn up in 1595 by the young second viscount setting out in wearisome detail how his domestic servants were supposed to cater to his every need. As virtually the sole surviving account of what went on inside Cowdray, it seems to tell us little more than that he scaled the late-sixteenth-century peaks of jumped-up blue-blooded household fussiness and pretension.[21]

Yet, for my purposes, all was not quite lost. For it appeared still possible to follow up, as I hope to show, from a series of scattered and sometimes unlikely sources, the opinions and fortunes of such people, and to recover the mental worlds and kinship groups which these families inhabited.

RECAPTURING THE CATHOLIC COMMUNITY

Originally, in order to describe the Brownes, I had envisaged a modified form of county study. Here, by establishing the local structures of Catholicism (particularly in the parts of Sussex and Hampshire where the Brownes and many of their relatives were domiciled), I hoped to be able to reconstruct the shape and extent of these families' influence. But immediately it was clear that there would be real difficulties, not only because of the limited nature of the relevant material in the appropriate county record offices but also because of the traditional format of the county study for this period, particularly the kind which deals with or concentrates primarily on Catholicism and Catholic reactions to the Reformation.

In the first place, county studies are generally the product of comparative analyses of series or runs of administrative records. What one has in the average county study is an account of how the shire's natural governors kept at least a semblance of order and discipline in and through the

---

[21] S. D. Scott, '"A Booke of Orders and Rules" of Anthony Viscount Montague in 1595', *SAC* 7 (1854), 173–212.

commission of the peace, and the deputy and lord lieutenancies. The end product tends to be a story of how consensus and peace were maintained (at least in the absence of too aggressive an interference from outside by central government, or the advent of, say, a civil war). In the case of Sussex, for example, two (very good) county studies took more or less this form – Anthony Fletcher's *Sussex 1600–1660* and Roger Manning's *Religion and Society in Elizabethan Sussex*. Fletcher's work is structured so that it does not focus primarily on the divisions among the gentry which ecclesiastical issues could cause. Manning concentrates on office-holders and administration, and produces a narrative of a gradual political acquiescence and indeed anaesthetisation of the Catholic gentry through exclusion from office (unless they conformed and in the process abandoned their Catholicism). Both argue, in effect, that Catholicism was expunged from the county virtually as the end product of administrative commonsense. Prudent provincial government could hardly be expected to countenance Catholics in office. Manning does, admittedly, describe very well the extent of the hostility between conservative and reforming Protestant religious outlooks in Elizabethan Sussex. But there is often a sameness and uniformity about the county-study method of establishing people's religious positions and this sometimes tends to obscure them. Again, this is partly the product of the limitations of source material.

For example, one well-known county-study approach to the detection of shifts in religious opinion and culture is the statistical analysis of the religious preambles in last wills and testaments. Conservative modes of bequeathing the soul (for example by requesting prayers to saints and the Virgin) have been contrasted with the supposedly 'Protestant' expression, in the preamble, of trust in Christ's merits alone. Several county studies, while conceding that the general unrepresentativeness of the will-making population is something of a problem, have examined these soul bequests in order to determine, at some level, the course of the Reformation. Thus Christopher Haigh argues that, in Lancashire, mid-sixteenth-century Catholics' wills show signs of theological ignorance which left them and their religion 'vulnerable' to the attacks of university-trained Protestants. 'Two prominent gentlemen hoped to be saved by the merits of Christ but asked for prayers for their souls, as did the rector of Ashton, who ought to have known better.' 'A Manchester merchant left his soul to God, the Virgin and the saints, but trusted to find salvation through Christ's merits.'[22]

It is very difficult, however, to extrapolate confidently from such formulae to conclusions about the exact nature of people's beliefs, and also the pace

[22] C. Haigh, *Reformation and Resistance in Tudor Lancashire* (Cambridge, 1975), 194. Cf. M. L. Zell, 'The Use of Religious Preambles as a Measure of Religious Belief in the Sixteenth Century', *BIHR* 50 (1977), 246–9. See also C. Litzenberger, *The English Reformation and the Laity* (Cambridge, 1997), 168–87.

and causes of religious division, without having a pretty good idea of who the people involved actually are and also some other evidence of what they actually thought. Just by way of one example, the first Viscount Montague, who died in 1592, and was one of the most overtly Catholic members of the peerage (though never subjected to legal sanctions for nonconformity), wrote a will which used (so-called) 'Protestant' terminology, for he affirmed his belief in the redemptive work of Christ 'by the which onlye I hope to be saved, and assuredlie truste to be one of his Elect', though at the same time he protested that he lived and died 'a true member of and in the unitie of his Catholicke Churche'.[23] Unless we assume that the ageing peer had, like the rector of Ashton, become theologically confused, we may have to adopt a more sophisticated mode of analysing how Catholicism, as a species of religious sentiment, was expressed.

The methodology of many self-consciously Catholic county studies under-taken in recent years is not necessarily any help here either. A popular Catholic historiographical approach to the recovery of the Catholic presence in a particular shire has been the 'recusancy thesis'. MA and Ph.D. disser-tations on Catholic recusancy usually go in exactly the opposite direction to Manning's and Fletcher's approach. They describe the formation of clear blocs of Catholic religious opinion and allegiance. In an effort to reclaim the Catholic past, they emphasise the Catholic presence in the county at the expense of its context, and take recusant separatism as the norm for Catholics when we know that, very frequently, it was not. 'Recusant his-tory' is overly reliant for its source material on the usually undifferentiated lists of people who were recorded by the authorities as having transgressed the penal statutes which demanded conformity to the Church of England. As often as not, we do not know much else about the people on these lists. Inevitably the Catholic community, as portrayed in such studies, itself takes on a uniformity which is extremely hard to reconcile with many contempo-raries' accounts of the variegated nature of Catholicism.

There are, it should be said, honourable exceptions to this perhaps rather sweeping generalisation about recusant historians. For example, both John Aveling and Alan Davidson envisaged post-Reformation Catholicism as a nebulous and complex structure. Both understood the intricacies of the fam-ily relationships and networks, particularly at gentry level, which it inhab-ited.[24] But, in general, the recusancy study, which to some extent was always

---

[23] PRO, PROB 11/81, fo. 163v; J. J. Goring, 'Wealden Ironmasters in the Age of Elizabeth', in E. W. Ives, R. J. Knecht and J. J. Scarisbrick (eds.), *Wealth and Power in Tudor England* (1978), 204–27, at p. 219.

[24] See J. C. H. Aveling, *Post-Reformation Catholicism in East Yorkshire 1558–1790* (York, 1960); *idem, The Catholic Recusants of the West Riding of Yorkshire 1558–1790* (Proceed-ings of the Leeds Philosophical and Literary Society, Literary and Historical Section, X, pt 6, Leeds, 1963); *idem, Catholic Recusancy in the City of York 1558–1791* (1970); *idem, Northern Catholics* (1966); Davidson, RC.

in danger of becoming the prisoner of its own specialised sources, has not been able or even attempted to determine accurately, for example, to what political ideas the wider Catholic county community (as opposed to Catholic polemical writers and ideologues) subscribed, or to whom it looked for leadership and assistance, or how it was politicised internally, and especially why it was so factionally divided.

What we need, clearly, is a less constrained approach to the study of early modern English Catholics. Thus, although the focus of this book is, in parts, quite heavily county-based, it is not exclusively so. Catholic families did not always find that their interests and ideas were compatible. Of particular interest here, then, is the way in which the frictions between different Catholic clerical factions became embedded within family networks which, in turn, underwrote and amplified such quarrels.

Again, all of this is not without its methodological difficulties. For, although many of the people in this book were *habitués* of Tudor and Stuart high society and the Court, the reconstruction of their world involves dredging up the names of many people who were outside the political and social mainstream in their own time, and are outside, too, the modern historical narratives which cover this part of the early modern period. Only to the few readers who already boast a specialism in this subtopic of early modern ecclesiastical studies will these names be familiar. Other readers will reckon that they have not heard of them before and may think that they are unlikely to come across them again. And yet here, I think, there is often such a close fit between the shadowy existence of these individuals and the main outlines of the history of English Catholicism (which itself intersects at certain points with the mainstream political narrative of the period) that it may be worth the effort of identifying and describing them.

So how will our conclusions about the post-Reformation Catholic community differ from those reached by other county studies of Catholicism during the Reformation? Some localist accounts of Catholicism in this period have described it through a narrative of virtually terminal decline. Haigh's Lancashire and its popular religious culture constituted a bastion against puritan evangelism, but that culture's resistance to the Reformation was not sustained. A. L. Rowse argued that Cornishmen were prominent in the seminarist experiment initiated by William Allen, for in 'the first years the Cornish contingent in the [Catholic] college at Douai was notably large', but he intended to describe 'its gradual diminishing by persecution and financial exhaustion at home'.[25]

By contrast, the recovery of the Catholic networks at the heart of this study will suggest that in several significant senses English Catholicism

[25] Haigh, *Reformation and Resistance*; A. L. Rowse, *Tudor Cornwall* (1940), 355–6.

was not in its death throes. In fact, if we look at the ecclesiastical culture of late sixteenth- and early seventeenth-century Sussex, the Catholic parts of the county were becoming, arguably, much more Catholic; or, rather, the Catholicism of those families who espoused and entertained recognisably Catholic opinions was becoming more sharply defined. This may have been simply because Sussex was not Cornwall or Lancashire. But should similar work, one day, be done on other Catholic patronage networks in other counties, it will be interesting to see whether these judgments are confirmed.

In addition, I hope that this will change some of our understandings of the shape and nature of the pre-civil-war Catholic community. Broadly speaking, there are currently two possible interpretative lines about Catholicism in (partly) Protestantised post-Reformation England. The first is, as we have already seen, that reasonably swiftly a mass Catholic culture was whittled down to a tiny gentrified minority which had access to the Catholic sacraments dispensed by seminary priests (replacements for the ageing Marians who had separated or part-separated from the Church of England). Some historians, such as William Trimble, have seen this Catholicism as virtually identical to the victimised religion which fell prey to the State's intolerance.[26]

The second line (not entirely distinct from the first) is that the vast majority of the population remained something close to Catholic, at least in the sense that the 'people' were not Protestantised. (Elizabethan Protestant/puritan complaint literature dwelt almost obsessively on residual 'popery' among the bulk of the population.) However, this popular Catholicism lost its Catholic edge precisely because of the gentry's selfish appropriation and monopolisation of the sacramental services of the seminary priests. As a result, popular conservative religious attitudes were at last converted into a conformist component of the Church of England. Haigh calls it 'parish anglicanism'. These 'parish anglicans' had 'not been moved by the evangelistic fervour of the Protestant Reformation – indeed, in the sense that they knew little of doctrine and rejected justification by faith and predestination, they were not Protestants at all'. Yet they were 'no longer Catholics', for they had been 'neglected by the missionary priests, and they attended the services of the Church of England'.[27]

Stated bluntly in this way, these interpretations have a tendency to mislead. In the first place, this is because their *terminus ad quem* is usually 1603.

---

[26] W. R. Trimble, *The Catholic Laity in Elizabethan England 1558–1603* (Cambridge, Mass., 1964).

[27] C. Haigh, 'The Church of England, the Catholics and the People', in C. Haigh (ed.), *The Reign of Elizabeth I* (1984), 195–219, at p. 219.

For Haigh's Lancashire, Manning's Sussex, Wark's Cheshire[28] and most of the unpublished dissertations on recusancy written during the 1960s and 1970s, the end of the story is fixed by the death of Elizabeth. The Catholics' inability to convert her or unseat her meant that they had failed in their effort to overturn the established Protestant religion and culture of the Church of England. But a perspective which looks forward from 1603 as well as back from that date makes the whole picture look very different. For the accession of James Stuart was seen by many religious engagés, Catholics as well as Protestants, as ushering in a new era – an era in which much of the agenda of uniformity and conformity would be up for negotiation and amendment. Viewed from this perspective, 1603 looks more like the start of a new chapter than the dragging out of an old one.[29]

THE CATHOLIC ARISTOCRACY AS PATRONS AND LEADERS

Another and more fundamental reason why some of these older interpretations and approaches to the topic need revising and updating is that they leave us without any sense of the structures which underpinned Catholicism, or of how different kinds of patronage operated among those who identified each other as Catholics or were perceived as Catholics by those who were not in sympathy with them.

In fact, historians such as Trimble tend to imply that there were no such structures. In his version of the story, a weak and bullied Catholic laity, unable to withstand official harassment, and ideologically all at sea, had no leadership. He concludes that the position of Catholics in late Elizabethan England was quite 'anomalous'. His evidence is drawn almost exclusively from the records of the State Paper office and the privy council registers which do frequently suggest a harassed and clueless Catholic minority manipulated and terrorised by a powerful government machine. For him, this evidence 'forms a pattern which shows, as the whole reign of Elizabeth manifests, that the Catholics were leaderless and that their well-being depended completely upon the policy of the government and the frame-of-mind of individual officials'. For Trimble, the only kind of evidence which would suggest that the Catholics were climbing out of their government-dug elephant trap was signs of action. And, as far as Trimble could see, there were hardly any such signs. The penning of loyalist tracts which rejected the prospect

---

[28] K. R. Wark, *Elizabethan Recusancy in Cheshire* (Manchester, 1971).
[29] For an admirable account of contemporaries' uncertainty about how far James I's accession caused discontinuity in official attitudes to Catholicism, see J. Watkins, '"Out of her Ashes May a Second Phoenix Rise": James I and the Legacy of Elizabethan Anti-Catholicism', in A. Marotti (ed.), *Catholicism and Anti-Catholicism in Early Modern English Texts* (1999), 116–36.

of Elizabeth's deposition and of forcible national re-Catholicisation was a mark of understandable and inevitable Catholic 'disillusionment'.[30]

Trimble was, of course, attempting a comprehensive overview of Catholicism during the Elizabethan period. But versions of this argument have surfaced even in studies of individual prominent Catholics. H. S. Reinmuth's account of Lord William Howard of Naworth is a good reconstruction of the social circle of an avowedly Catholic noble. In Reinmuth's view, a major aspect of Howard's success in life was to die, if not exactly peacefully in his bed (because he expired in 1640 shortly after being forced to flee the advancing Scots), at least, then, not on the scaffold. But this meant surrendering any thought of being a Catholic leader. The most that he could do was to offer some measure of protection to individual Catholics, people such as the Cornish man Nicholas Roscarrock, whom Howard was able to accommodate in a menial position in his household. As a result of the limitations imposed on nobles such as Howard, there 'never was a Catholic community in England during this period, but rather a number of . . . Catholic enclaves, plus looser associations of related Catholics, and isolated individuals'. Although Reinmuth did not, like Trimble, see the subservient position of the Catholics as dependent 'upon government policy *per se*', it was nevertheless traceable to 'the impact of recusancy laws upon each individual'. For 'isolated persons easily fell victim to the authorities'. The only relief came when prudent but wealthy Catholics such as Howard could, because they enjoyed some measure of protection from the penal statutes, offer limited security and solace to a few individuals who managed to reach the safe haven of a great family's estates.[31]

Great men who were not overtly Catholic could interfere with and deflect the impact of the laws against recusancy for the benefit of their own retainers. In 1593 the earl of Shrewsbury instructed Sir Thomas Williams to protect the earl's servant Nicholas Williamson, who was a recusant, from arrest. (The earl needed Williamson's experience in order to deal with disputes over fishing in the River Trent.)[32] But the whole point is that such peers were not seeking to circumvent the law on conformity for the benefit of Catholicism or the Catholic community, and were certainly not trying to disrupt the general working of the burgeoning legal code against recusant separatism.

The prevailing picture that we have, in existing scholarship, of post-Reformation Catholicism (drawn mainly from the records of recusant nonconformity) is indeed of isolated and segregated enclaves. Lawrence Stone

---

[30] Trimble, *The Catholic Laity*, 171, 253–4.
[31] H. S. Reinmuth, 'Lord William Howard (1563–1640) and his Catholic Associations', *RH* 12 (1973–4), 226–34, at pp. 231–4.
[32] PRO, SP 46/49, fo. 111a.

comments that such enclaves were a product of the combination of aristocratic and gentry patronage and of the recusancy statutes.

The geographical pattern of seventeenth-century Catholicism, which was a rural not an urban movement, was consequently determined in large measure by the attitude of a handful of leading families in each county. What in the early years of Elizabeth had been a widely diffused scatter of passive conservatives had by the end of the reign become a series of isolated little pockets of dedicated recusants, each one centred around and dependent upon a great house.

He rehearses a series of well-known facts and figures in order to show how tiny groups of recusant Catholics were huddled around large aristocratic and gentry establishments all the way from Barwick in Yorkshire to Kesteven in Lincolnshire. (He might also have mentioned Cowdray and Battle in Sussex.)[33]

The corollary of keeping one's head down in this way was surrender of the political initiative. Albert Loomie, who did write about Catholic leadership and action (political, spiritual and literary), confined his account to the Elizabethan exiles in Spain and Flanders. And a central plank of his general thesis about these Elizabethan Catholics was that although from time to time a prominent Catholic peer, 'an earl of Westmorland, the wife of Northumberland, a Lord Dacres, Lord Paget, a Lord Morley . . . needed and ambitioned to acquire a large clientèle among the *émigrés*', nevertheless 'they failed to rally any noticeable influence among their compatriots' even outside the country, let alone in it.[34]

Reinmuth is surely right to stress the limits of the protection that a noble such as Lord William Howard could afford to his fellow Catholics. Even around Midhurst, the Brownes' Catholic neighbours could not necessarily count on the influence of the leading local Catholic peer to shield them

---

[33] Stone, *CA*, 733. See also S. J. Watts (with Susan J. Watts), *From Border to Middle Shire: Northumberland 1586–1625* (Leicester, 1975), 84–5; Bossy, *ECC*, 175–7. Fletcher notes that 'once gentry support was lacking in a parish the recusant tradition quickly failed', A. Fletcher, *Sussex 1600–1660* (1975), 98–9. Battle (where the dowager Viscountess Montague lived until 1608) had many Catholics in the 1590s but only six recusants in 1626. In both 1676 and 1767, Tisbury (where the well-known Catholic family of Arundell was resident) and nearby parishes had nearly half the Catholics in Wiltshire, and in 1839 more than three-quarters, *VCH Wiltshire* XIII, 243; J. A. Williamson, *Catholic Recusancy in Wiltshire 1660–1791* (1968), 182. The fact that there was a Catholic patron in a particular parish did not, however, mean that there would necessarily be a group of recusants gathered around him. At Etchingham there were only four recusants though the Catholic Robert Tirwhit was the patron and the rector was the often-in-trouble and allegedly popish William Holland, W. C. Renshaw (ed.), 'Ecclesiastical Returns for 81 Parishes in East Sussex Made in 1603', *SRS* 4 (1905), 3–17, at p. 9. Sir George Browne, son of the first Viscount Montague, had acquired the patronage of several East Sussex parishes, e.g. St Thomas à Becket, Brightling and All Saints, Hastings, but there were no recusants there, and only two women recusants in Folkington (where he was patron as well), *ibid.*, 6, 10.

[34] A. J. Loomie, *The Spanish Elizabethans* (New York, 1963), 95, and *passim*.

from the depredations of government agents and informers. While, as we shall see, certain people who were in good odour with the family did look to it from time to time for assistance, local recusants could not guarantee that such protection would be forthcoming. Particularly in the early seventeenth century the second Viscount Montague did appear rather powerless. Priests such as Benjamin Norton who wrote up accounts of the casual violence offered to Catholics in the area sometimes said that their only recourse was self-help. Of one predatory sweep carried out in 1610 Norton noted how local Catholics were subject to the crudest kind of harassment. This included seizure of moveable (usually agricultural) goods. Most submitted, but Anthony Williamson, a recusant who had property in Easebourne, near Midhurst, and held land by 'demise and grant of Anthony Viscount Montague', did not. When 'they wold have had Anthony Williamsons, and his mothers cattel', 'he sware . . . that they shold pay dear for them'. 'They drew ther woepons thrise one at the other' and, 'at the last, one of the knaves diswaded his fellow from dealing with such a murtherous minded man'.[35] But the viscount either would not or could not turn out in order to protect his tenant.[36] In fact, from the evidence unearthed by Roger Manning in star chamber cases between 1609 and 1618, it looks as if there was an undercurrent of popular hostility to the second viscount in West Sussex. At around this time there was a series of attacks on Montague's deer parks. Some of those involved in these quasi-popular and semi-public rapes of his estates were those who, Manning shows, had a history of antagonism towards the Browne family, had taken part in similar poaching in the 1590s, and certainly seem to have believed that they could act with impunity against the Catholic viscount's officers.[37]

Nevertheless, as John Bossy's work has shown, one should not simply write off the influence of the wealthy laymen in the Catholic community. Indeed, a crucial part of Bossy's thesis about the development of Catholicism in late sixteenth- and early seventeenth-century England was the reassertion

---

[35] *NAGB*, 92; BL, Additional MS 39415, fo. 26r.

[36] Likewise, in the Brownes' London parish, St Saviour's, there were several recusants in the 1580s, indicted for their separatism, but there is no evidence that the first viscount did anything to assist them, Hyland, *CP*, 379–88. One exchequer case records that the second Viscount Montague did, in fact, intervene to prevent the confiscation of livestock which were stated by the sequestrators in November 1614 to belong to one Clarissa Hunt of Woolavington, PRO, E 368/555, mem. 187a. But such interventions seem to have been rare. See also Williamson, *Catholic Recusancy*, 230.

[37] R. B. Manning, *Hunters and Poachers* (Oxford, 1993), 223–4; ch. 8, p. 238 below. Manning suggests that Catholic gentry and peers were peculiarly vulnerable to poaching, since 'there was a certain amount of truth in the popular perception that Catholic possessors of hunting franchises and well-stocked deer parks lacked the political influence with juries, local magistrates, and crown ministers successfully to prosecute those who raided their game reserves', *ibid.*, 220.

of the power of the gentry over the often politically radical ambitions of some of the Catholic clergy. Bossy's work showed how important, politically, lay patrons were within the community, something which contemporary clericalist narratives often try to cover up.[38]

So, in what did aristocratic leadership consist? Stone's thesis about the social role of the aristocracy claims, rightly I am sure, that the aristocracy functioned as a crucial vehicle for the entrenchment of particular religious attitudes which had an oppositional flavour and which challenged aspects of the Elizabethan establishment of religion. Peers were protected from official wrath against dissent by their exalted social status. Also, because they had so much to lose, it was pointless for them to be so openly adversarial as to risk total forfeiture of office, property and influence.[39]

Stone draws a distinction between conventional attitudes to religion (as a bulwark of order) and the attitudes, which Stone holds to be sincere, of a significant minority of peers who were in some measure dissenters. 'It is very significant that of the 30 peers who between 1558 and 1641 showed signs in their wills of strong religious feelings, no fewer than 7 were recusants or schismatics, and 12 were puritans or puritan sympathizers.' That 'the Catholics were inspired predominantly by ideological consider- ations is proved by their readiness to take the financial and other conse- quences of recusancy', though recusancy here is a problematic term since nonconformity was only very rarely detected and punished amongst the aristocracy.[40]

In fact, declares Stone, the peers were uniquely placed to shape the coun- try's religious geography. 'Given the preponderant authority of the aristoc- racy in the countryside in the early years of Elizabeth, the success of the Anglican settlement depended very largely on their active co-operation or passive acquiescence.' They were able to punish or protect dissenting clergy, to prevent or allow, or even encourage, risqué sermons, and to crack down on or turn a blind eye to lay nonconformity. The preponderance of Catholic peers in the North in the 1560s, not just the future rebels Westmorland, Northumberland and Dacre, but others too, such as Wharton and Lumley (and even the earls of Derby and Shrewsbury), made it difficult to enforce the settlement there. By contrast the great puritan peers were domiciled largely in the South. So, although we should give due weight to the clerical activists, it was the consciences of the peers which dictated, to some considerable degree, 'the religious configuration of seventeenth-century England'. It was the oppositional temperament of 'a handful of magnates on either side which

---

[38] Bossy, 'Character'; *idem*, 'Elizabethan Catholicism: The Link with France' (Ph.D., Cam- bridge, 1961).
[39] Stone, CA, 724.   [40] *Ibid.*, 727.

allowed Catholicism and Puritanism to dig in and take root' in a society which otherwise was 'tepidly conformist'.[41]

While Stone's puritan aristocratic patrons held positions of vast authority, his Catholic peers, almost to a man, did not (or found themselves forced to choose between their Catholicism and their offices). Yet those who were known Catholics were not necessarily deprived of influence. If Claire Cross's description of the establishment of the third earl of Huntingdon is anything to go by, we should not underrate the impact of such a self-conscious social and political unit as the noble household, even if it was a Catholic one.[42] Cross stresses that an establishment such as Huntingdon's was a combination of a seminary, a finishing school and a university college where future great divines might start their careers. In such households, the 'leaders of the coming generation were moulded'. As Cross emphasises, only scraps of information about the household remain, but 'quite enough evidence survives to show the surprising extent of the household's influence'. Huntingdon offered shelter to puritan ministers such as Anthony Gilby who 'helped transform the household' in Ashby-de-la-Zouch 'into a Protestant seminary in miniature'. Cross charts the spread of a particular brand of Protestant piety outward from this household in the shape of some of its one-time inhabitants, e.g. Sir Thomas Posthumous Hoby's famously pious wife, Margaret Dakins, who had served Huntingdon's countess.[43] In a great establishment some of the household servants would themselves be drawn from the gentry. Such service attracted the 'good lordship' of the great man and employer, just as it also reflected the power, authority and general presence of the lord. The lord's servants wore his livery, an emblem of their own authority and credit in his service.[44]

The same might be true for Catholic, or predominantly Catholic, aristocratic establishments. According to the Jesuit John Price (the encomiast of George Talbot, ninth earl of Shrewsbury), Shrewsbury's household operated like a miniature ideal commonwealth. 'There was noe place for drunckards, or otherwayes disorderly persons, in soe much that it was every where taken for a patterne of all good order and vertue.' Price had heard William Petre, second Baron Petre 'affirme that hee did willingly admitt the

---

[41] *Ibid.*, 729. For the fourth earl of Derby's alleged hindering of the legal process against Catholics (even while posturing as an enforcer of it), see D. Flynn, *John Donne and the Ancient Catholic Nobility* (Bloomington, 1995), 163–5.

[42] For the importance of the large noble household in France as a focus for the dispensing of patronage, see S. Kettering, 'Patronage and Kinship in Early Modern France', *French Historical Studies* 16 (1989), 408–35, at p. 418.

[43] M. C. Cross, *The Puritan Earl* (1966), 22–8; *idem*, 'Noble Patronage in the Elizabethan Church', *HJ* 2 (1960), 1–16, at p. 2.

[44] B. Coward, *The Stanleys, Lords Stanley and Earls of Derby 1385–1672* (Manchester, 1983), 85, 86–7, 88.

refuse of my lord his house into his [own] service, and that haveing admitted some of them, hee found them to bee preciouse jewells in his familye'.
Talbot 'had excelent orders which to each servant were notifyed before his
admittance and monthly by his steward read to his whole family and if
any order were not dewly observed strict chardge was given them' for their
'reformacion'.[45]

Of course, in the post-Reformation period, the Brownes could not aspire
to the dizzy political heights of influence and authority garnered and exercised by peers such as Huntingdon. Nor would the Brownes' household be
anything like as big. The earl of Derby's household in 1590 employed 145
people, and the earl of Rutland's had 194 in 1612.[46] The second Viscount
Montague's 1595 book of orders shows him, by contrast, employing about
fifty servants.[47] For Coward, the 'household of an earl could be the focus of
the personal and political ambitions of a whole county'.[48] Less powerful and
wealthy peers could hardly hope to emulate the greater ones in this respect.
And their servants were unlikely to aspire to or attain the authority and
prestige that attendants of a truly great landed family such as the Stanleys
might do. But such lesser ennobled families as the Brownes did not necessarily underestimate their own standing and achievements. We have a 1775
list of the portraits and paintings which hung in the rooms of the Brownes'
palace of Cowdray before it was destroyed by fire in September 1793. The
chief pieces represented a tradition of martial and diplomatic service to the
Tudors. In the 'Eating Parlour' there hung a painting 'of the landing of Henry
8 at Calais whither he sailed in a ship with sails of cloth of gold and landed'
on 14 July 1544 in order to go to the siege of Boulogne. The siege was commemorated by another painting in the same room. Sir Anthony Browne (see
Figure 6), the father of the first Viscount Montague, had played a prominent part in this expedition. There was also a painting of the coronation
procession of Edward VI, where Browne, who was both standard bearer
and master of the horse, had been present. In the same room there was a
painting of 'the sailing of the fleet from Portsmouth whither Henry 8 went

---

[45] B. FitzGibbon, 'George Talbot, Ninth Earl of Shrewsbury', *BS* 2 (1953–4), 96–110, at p. 104.
[46] Coward, *The Stanleys*, 92. For an analysis of aristocratic household sizes in the second half
of the sixteenth century, see S. Adams (ed.), *Household Accounts and Disbursement Books
of Robert Dudley, Earl of Leicester, 1558–1561, 1584–1586* (Camden Society, 5th series,
6, 1995), 29–30. Adams's figures show that the size of such households tended to fluctuate,
as one might expect, according to the political importance of the peer in question. For the
second earl of Essex's household, see Hammer, *Polarisation*, 298. For the structure of and
also the changes in the size of noble households during this period, see K. Mertes, *The
English Noble Household 1250–1600* (Oxford, 1988), esp. chs. 1–3 and pp. 187–93. For
comparative figures from France for the same period, see S. Kettering, 'The Patronage Power
of Early Modern French Noblewomen', *HJ* 32 (1989), 817–41, at pp. 819–20.
[47] Scott, '"A Booke of Orders and Rules" of Anthony Viscount Montague in 1595'.
[48] Coward, *The Stanleys*, 85.

Figure 6. Portrait of Sir Anthony Browne (d. 1548). The style of the painting is French and it may represent him in his role as a diplomat in France.

to attend its equipment in person 1512'. The 1775 list records that there were several other, though by that date badly damaged, paintings of various sieges 'up in different parts of the hall'. In the 'dressing room' there was a depiction of the battle of Pavia, the famous imperial wipe-out of the French, probably an enjoyable sight and spectacle for the virulently Francophobe Sir

Figure 7.   Portrait of Sir Anthony Browne, first Viscount Montague,
by Hans Eworth, 1569.

Anthony Browne and his imperialist son, the first viscount.[49] There was also, in the 'gallery', a portrait of Sir Anthony Browne which commemorated his standing as proxy for Henry VIII during the ceremony of Henry's marriage to Anne of Cleves.[50]

These pictorial reminders of the Brownes' service to the crown in the first half of the sixteenth century probably indicate that the family continued to remember its former power, and perhaps aspired to it again. In a valedictory speech to his friends and family at West Horsley in Surrey, shortly before his death, the first Viscount Montague, literally in the same breath as he declared his Catholicism for all the world to hear, added that his family had been fortunate in that 'it pleased the kinge', Henry VIII, 'to be so good and gratyous to my father and me as to rayse us up to a place of honnor'. Montague also believed that he had personally 'donne her Majestie', Elizabeth, 'good service bothe beyonde the seas, and else wheare. I stoode her in somme steede (as she knoweth) in Quene Maryes dayes, when I was of the pryvye councell and lyvetennaunt of the sheare where I dwelt.'[51]

The Brownes did not achieve high office again after the first viscount lost his seat on the privy council at Elizabeth's accession (at least not until the fourth viscount briefly served as lord lieutenant of his county during the reign of James II). But this did not prevent them from harbouring political opinions and aspirations. That they lacked 'official' positions of authority, nationally and, eventually, even in their own county, certainly did not mean that they could not exercise authority and influence within the Catholic community.

---

[49] BL, Additional MS 5726 E. 5, fos. 20r, 22r. W. H. St John Hope argues that Sir Anthony Browne was responsible for this series of paintings commemorating his career, even though he died on 28 April 1548, not much more than a year after Edward's accession, Hope, *Cowdray*, 91.

[50] The grumpy Horace Walpole, chronicling his August 1749 tour of Sussex which he found a 'great damper of curiosity', recorded nevertheless that it was worth seeing Cowdray; and Walpole was 'much pleased with . . . [the] whole length picture of Sir Anthony Browne in the very dress in which he wedded Anne of Cleves by proxy. He is in blue and white, only his right leg is entirely white, which was robed for the act of putting into bed to her. But when the king came to marry her he only put his leg into bed to kick her out', Hope, *Cowdray*, 26; BL, Additional MS 5276 E. 5, fo. 22r. This portrait was destroyed in the 1793 fire, Hope, *Cowdray*, 22.

[51] Questier, LF, 250–1.

2

The local setting

In what kind of environment did the self-consciously Catholic entourage of the Browne family originate and develop? What was the local context for the expression of the conservative and Catholic opinions and influence of the interrelated families grouped around the Brownes of Cowdray and Battle in Sussex? One of the consistent themes of the more recent tranche of local studies which deal with the English Reformation in the provinces is that the split between a supposedly more backward/conservative/Catholic North and a more progressive/Protestant South has been overdone. Put bluntly, what it means, according to Christopher Haigh, is that many English counties were more like Lancashire than everyone has thought. He suspects that 'the contrast is between Lancashire and what the conventional wisdom tells us happened elsewhere, rather than between Lancashire and what actually took place in the rest of England'.[1] And, indeed, we know from the famous 1564 survey of justices of the peace that there were significant numbers of mislikers, i.e. Catholics or conservatives, among many of the shires' natural governors.[2] There were also widespread deprivations and resignations of conservative/Catholic clergy after the 1559 settlement.[3] Even if the mislikers and malcontents were not going to turn the clock back to before 1559, things were unlikely to be reformed as fast as the reformers would have wished.

It may be worth reconstructing the local Reformation context of the aristocratic conservatism and Catholicism which form the focal point of this study. Many of the people whom we will be looking at either lived or had property in or around the county of Sussex and its borders. So it may serve a purpose to review briefly the character and working of the Reformation

---

[1] C. Haigh, *Reformation and Resistance in Tudor Lancashire* (Cambridge, 1975), vii.

[2] M. Bateson (ed.), 'A Collection of Original Letters from the Bishops to the Privy Council, 1564 . . .' (*Camden Miscellany* IX, Camden Society, new series, 53, 1893).

[3] Haigh, *Reformation and Resistance*, 215; T. J. McCann, 'The Clergy and the Elizabethan Settlement in the Diocese of Chichester', in M. J. Kitch (ed.), *Studies in Sussex Church History* (Chichester, 1980), 99–123.

in this region in order to gauge something of the nature of our Catholics' reaction to it.

One curious aspect of the Catholic reaction to the English Reformation is the apparent combination of lethargy and radicalism. One often wonders how far the patterns of rural life were really disrupted by the occasional interventions of Protestant officialdom in the day-to-day administration of the Church, particularly if revisionist historians are right that, after the initial shock of the Elizabethan settlement, there was no particularly consistent Protestant evangelisation and schooling of the populace. And yet, from time to time, even in an apparently rather sleepy county community such as Sussex, there could erupt violent political and religious passions. Conspiracies against the regime might be, indeed were, discovered and punished; and contemporaries could discern a link there, as elsewhere, between, on the one hand, separatist and semi-separatist Catholicism and, on the other, political opposition to the Elizabethan regime.

Thus it may be worth trying to explain how the uneven pace and character of the Elizabethan Reformation could provoke Catholics sometimes to exhibit both a loyal or at least a quiescent face, and, at other times, one that was much less so.

Most accounts of the Elizabethan Reformation in Sussex agree that it did not exactly go through the county like a dose of salts. The 1564 survey of the county's JPs and the 1569 visitation (after Bishop William Barlow's death) of the diocese of Chichester are snapshots of the lack of success on the part of the reformers in the county (if by 'success' one understands the rooting out of opposition to the thrust of the Elizabethan settlement's religious reforms).

In 1564, Barlow's report on the justices claimed that the shire was reasonably calm. Parishes had unenthusiastically started to use the new order of service, but he feared 'secrett practises which perhappes myghte breake oute into open violence'.[4] There were too many prominent gentlemen who were known to harbour deep misgivings about the government's ecclesiastical programme.

By 1569, it seems, things had got worse. When Archbishop Matthew Parker's commissaries carried out their visitation of the diocese in that year, they painted a very bleak picture. Attempts to remove the rood from local churches had provoked people to paint 'there in that place a cross with chalk', i.e. where the rood had been, and even 'upon the pulpit and communion table in despite of the preacher'. It was not uncommon to find that chalices were still in use, and it was believed that the Mass would one day be restored.

The stipulated quarterly sermons were often not preached, in part because there were not enough preachers, not even in the cathedral (where only four

---

[4] McCann, 'Clergy', 99, citing Bateson, 'A Collection of Original Letters', 8–11.

out of thirty-one prebendaries were resident). Some who technically could preach would, if they were ever given the chance, preach for the other side. Parker's commissaries referred here to some of the Marian clergy whom we shall meet again later, men such as the notorious David Spencer of Clapham. These Marians who had kept their livings were 'hinderers of the true religion, and do not minister'. They were maintained by gentry families such as the Poles, Palmers, Gunters and Gages. This was the kind of association of magistracy/gentry and ministry that Protestant higher authority did not want. 'In the parish of Racton', for example, 'they have no churchwardens, clerk or collector for the poor, because of Mr Arthur Gunter, who rules the whole parish'. There was also illicit literature, printed overseas, circulating in the parishes. In particular, 'certain parishes keep Dr [Nicholas] Sander's book called *The Rock of the Church*, wherein he doth not account the bishops now to be any bishops'. Exiles were being financially supported by 'exhibition' which 'goeth out of the shire and diocese unto them beyond the seas', for example to the inflammatory Romish writer Thomas Stapleton, 'who being excommunicated by the archbishop did avoid the realm'. There were altars, images and other 'popish ornaments' 'ready to be sett up for Mass again within 24 hours' warning', as in 'the town of Battell' (where the first Viscount Montague had one of his two principal estates in the shire – Battle Abbey) as well as 'in the parish of Lindfield where they be yet very blind and superstitious'.[5] And there were unlicensed schoolmasters. One of these schoolmasters, Edward Terry, resided at Battle and was, allegedly, the cause of a lot of the Catholic disaffection there. The report noted that 'in the town of Battell, when a preacher doth come and speak anything against the pope's doctrine they will not abide but get them out of church. They say that they are of no jurisdiction', because the dean of Battle exercised peculiar jurisdiction there, 'but free from any bishop's authority'. 'The schoolmaster is the cause of their going out, who afterwards in corners among the people doth gainsay the preachers. It is the most popish town in all Sussex.'[6]

But was the county actually on the verge of revolt? If so, why was nothing done? The problem was that things said in a report to government could not so easily be said in a corner of Sussex where the old order was not locally understood as an overt and illicit challenge to higher authority. Anthony Garnett, one of the Brownes' chaplains, was informed by Robert Porter from Battle in June 1570 that 'my lord byshopp of Chechester', the recently appointed and very godly Richard Curteys, was 'with us on Frydaye laste and prechyd with us hem selfe and offryd to sett with us in that order as he

---

[5] McCann, 'Clergy', 100–1, citing PRO, SP 12/60/71.
[6] McCann, 'Clergy', 100–1, citing PRO, SP 12/60/71. For Battle's status as a peculiar, see *VCH Sussex* IX, 111.

dyd in hys dyosys abowte us'. Porter said that they had by 'fayre meens usyd our speche to hem and declaryd how our lybartye of our towne had byn ever in tyme paste usyd by hys predessessors that were byshoppes before hem', 'to the wyche sayeng he usyd us verye corteslye and sayd yf we had such a lybartye he wolde not seke to breke yt'. In fact he 'gave us daye' to bring '[our] recordes before hem . . . for the testemonye of our lybartye' before 'Michaelmas Daye next'.

Curteys was, of course, like the 1569 visitors, well aware that Battle was not a leading centre of godly reformation. For 'there had byn manye yll wordes as we understande reportyd to hem of our towne before he came to us'. But Porter was pleased to record that before Curteys 'departyd the towne agayne, he lykyd so well of us that I suppose yll reportes made to hem agayne here after wyll scante bere anye credett with hem'. Two of Curteys's imps, 'Vynall and Benett, were erneste before hem to breke our custom of our churche for our fower asystens to bere no suche actoryte as they claymyd'. Yet, alleged Porter, Curteys had 'answeryd them the order was good and that yf he had to do here to vyssyt he woulde alow yt and no other because of our custom being so long contenwyd'. There were other matters which had to be sorted out before the high commission and 'we delyvered hem a copye of the artycklles at Battell', and 'my lord [Montague] and we are mutche beholdyng to Mr Doctor Bartlye'.[7]

Clearly Curteys, who subsequently fought and lost a really bitter battle with those Sussex gentry whom he accused of popish nonconformity,[8] was unlikely to be in sympathy with the kind of people protecting Battle's ecclesiastical liberties, especially after the 1569 report had discovered or confirmed their popish tendencies. But there was evidently nothing that he could do at that point when faced with a consensus that the established order in that part of the county was merely traditional.[9]

Sussex was not the only south-coast county to contain bastions of conservatism. Bishop Robert Horne complained to Sir William Cecil about the Winchester diocese in early 1570 that something should be done about the papistical faction who 'stamp and stare' at the northern rebels 'and crieth out at their lewde entreprice', and at its failure. 'Most assuredly they looked and were in good hope in all this countrey (I mean the papists), what so ever they sayde, that the matter wolde have gone otherwise.' Horne believed the queen should do something 'to alter this religion and that with her owne handes'.[10]

---

[7] BL, Additional MS 33508, fo. 23r–v. Robert Porter appears as a witness to a deed of November 1569 settling part of Montague's estate on his children, WSRO, SAS/BA 41. For Porter's property at Battle, see HEH, BA 56/1618, 1617, 1623, 1624.
[8] See Manning, *Religion*, ch. 5. See also ch. 5, pp. 151–3 below.
[9] BL, Additional MS 33508, fo. 23r–v.   [10] BL, Lansdowne MS 12, no. 31, fo. 74r–v.

What did all these accounts of widespread and popular resistance to the Elizabethan Reformation add up to? Was this just the inevitable naysaying of the dyed-in-the-wool conservatives who frequently but ineffectually howled at every sign of change? Or was this a serious challenge to a regime which was finding that, although it had made the royal supremacy its flagship ecclesio-ideological policy, it could not impose godly Protestantism on the parishes?

In fact the amount of active popular resistance (outside the northern counties in 1569–70) seems to have been limited in its scope. Certainly there were Marian clerics in Sussex, such as David Spencer, who stayed in their parishes and were known to be no supporters of the 1559 settlement.[11] But other Marians simply upped sticks and went. For instance, Thomas Stapleton, who was noted as an exile in the 1569 visitation, moved to Louvain and eventually to a chair at the seminary at Douai. Edward Godsalve, prebendary of Ferring, also went abroad and took up a teaching appointment at Antwerp. Others, whom one might have expected to put up more vigorous resistance, such as some of those who eventually gathered around the Brownes, did not – for example the first Viscount Montague's chaplains Alban Langdale and Anthony Clerke. After 1559 they lived almost entirely private and retired lives.[12]

Taking the diocese of Chichester as a whole, therefore, the picture painted by the 1569 visitation simply does not seem to have translated immediately into any organised form of political resistance. Deprivations, exile and deaths seem to have effected a thorough clearing out of the county's Marian ecclesiastical establishment. Timothy McCann shows that 'the large number of clergy who were deprived of their livings or who resigned them, left ample room for the reforming clergy when they began to issue forth from the universities, and the passive resisters who stayed in their livings did not have the strength or the influence to form a "Catholic party" to oppose them'. At the same time 'many Catholic gentry were already withdrawing from parish life, and concentrating their religious activities within their own households'.[13]

Were the Sussex Catholics similar, then, to Diarmaid MacCulloch's Suffolk Catholics, who were afflicted by 'a passivity which was to prove the deathblow to the seminary priests' efforts to spread the faith outside the narrow confines of the established recusant estates'?[14]

---

[11] For Spencer's blatant and adversarial Catholicism, and his contact with and financial support of religious exiles, see McCann, 'Clergy', 112.

[12] *Ibid.*, 105–6. Langdale, however, became briefly involved in 1580 in the controversy over recusancy and conformity. See ch. 5, pp. 162–4 below.

[13] McCann, 'Clergy', 114–15.

[14] D. MacCulloch, 'Catholic and Puritan in Elizabethan Suffolk: A County Community Polarises', *Archiv für Reformationsgeschichte* 72 (1981), 232–88, at p. 261.

Perhaps, but Catholics in the upper reaches of provincial society could sometimes appear distinctly dangerous. The Ridolfi conspiracy was largely Sussex-based. In the wake of the Edmund Campion affair, leading Sussex Catholics (the heads of the Gage and the Shelley families) were arrested, as were several men in the entourage of the second earl of Southampton whose principal seat was at Titchfield, just over the border in Hampshire. (See Figure 8.) The earl had many links with West Sussex Catholic families as well as with the Hampshire ones.[15] In September 1583 the exile Charles Paget returned briefly into the county from France in connection with the Throckmorton plot. The discovery of the conspiracy led to the downfall of the eighth earl of Northumberland (who lived at Petworth).[16] William Shelley, Northumberland's retainer, was the principal Sussex gentleman to suffer personal ruin because of the plot.[17]

Not surprisingly, when the war against the Spaniards began, the southern coastal counties were watched closely for signs of disaffection, and were policed thoroughly as one invasion scare succeeded another. There was constant anxiety about what was happening in the Channel and about how well coastal defences were being maintained. The execution of the priests William Marsden and Robert Anderton on the Isle of Wight in April 1586 was a high-profile event. The regime modified its usual propaganda pitch of claiming that it prosecuted such people only for treason and not for religion. They were condemned not only because they would not explicitly repudiate a papally sponsored invasion but also because they would not promise not to meddle with the religion established by law. The regime's proceedings against them were vindicated by a royal proclamation.[18]

In early June 1586 the earl of Sussex informed Lord Burghley that an insurrection in Hampshire, 'a certeine mutenye and assembly to be shortlie practized within this shire', was in train, and was to take place with a 'fyring of the beacons'. Ten days later the earl claimed that this was part of some kind of concerted action across several shires 'as yt was in King Edwards tyme'. He had taken swift action to repress this alleged rebellion. Significantly he believed that various recusants, whom he did not name but who had been egged on 'by the perswasion of forrayne rebelles and fugitives', were privy

---

[15] Robert Persons, 'Of the Life and Martyrdom of Father Edmond Campian', *Letters and Notices* 11 (1876–7), 219–42, 308–39, and 12 (1878), 1–68, at vol. 12, p. 52.

[16] L. Hicks, *An Elizabethan Problem* (1964), *passim*, though the actual purpose of Paget's visit is much disputed; cf. D. Flynn, *John Donne and the Ancient Catholic Nobility* (Bloomington, 1995), ch. 7.

[17] For the Throckmorton conspiracy, see C. Read, *Mr. Secretary Walsingham* (3 vols., 1925), II, 381–6; J. Bossy, *Under the Molehill* (2001). For suspects from the Sussex–Hampshire border region, including George Brittaine and Nicholas Wolfe, see PRO, SP 12/167/59.

[18] *APC 1586–7*, 58–9; Anstr. I, 8–9, 218; P. L. Hughes and J. F. Larkin, *Tudor Royal Proclamations* (3 vols., 1964–9), II, no. 680.

Figure 8.   The gatehouse of Titchfield Abbey, near Fareham in Hampshire.

to this 'rebelliouse conspiracie' and that they now 'prepared themselves to flye beyonde sea, and to cary with them their goods, and other matters'. The earl had given instructions to arrest those whom he suspected of organising this flight abroad. After he had established which ship at Portsmouth was to be used, he laid a trap to catch them in the act as they started to embark.[19] Three days later, on 16 June, the priest Martin Array, a frequenter of Sussex gentry houses (notably the Carylls'), and the Catholic gentleman Gervase Pierrepoint were interrogated concerning this supposed conspiracy.[20]

Shortly after this, at the end of August 1586, the sheriff of Hampshire was being warned about the danger of a French incursion; he was told to prepare to defend Portsmouth.[21] (Late summer of 1586 saw Lord Buckhurst responding to a false invasion scare when ships were spotted off Brighton.[22]) In early September, official payments were being secured for Sir Thomas Heneage to fund a private search by a cleric, one John Paine, to arrest certain seminary priests along the coast of Sussex and Hampshire.[23] In February 1587 the privy council moved to confiscate the arms and armour of the young earl of Southampton at his palatial residence of Titchfield Abbey. This was done in order to prevent them getting into the wrong hands, 'the rather in respecte of the doubtfullnes of theis times of some forraine attempts that might be intended upon the seacoast of that shire', and especially at Portsmouth.[24] Early in 1588, recusant gentlemen in the region started being interned.[25] In late July 1588 there were worries about the defence of Hastings because so many of the town's mariners were at sea with the lord admiral.[26] October 1588 saw a treason trial of four Catholic clergymen at Chichester, two of whom recanted after sentence was passed against them.[27]

Jeremy Goring stresses that the regime 'did not need to be reminded that the Sussex coast was exceptionally vulnerable to enemy attack', though the Spanish threat was not limited to that part of the coast. A security report in 1587 had revealed how the natural defencelessness of the coast was made worse by the lack of military provision there.[28] Curtis Breight argues that the royal progress through the area which included the well-known visit to

[19] BL, Lansdowne MS 50, no. 19, fo. 43r, no. 20, fo. 45r, no. 21, fo. 47r.
[20] *Ibid.*, no. 72, fos. 155r–v, 156r, printed in J. Strype, *Annals of the Reformation* (4 vols., Oxford, 1824), III, appendix, p. 153; Anstr. I, 11; Cockburn, *Surrey Assizes: Elizabeth*, nos. 1333, 1422. Array had been arrested in London on 7 June. For Pierrepoint, one of the Jesuit Robert Persons's associates, see McCoog, *Society*, 143; PRO, SP 12/167/59, fos. 144v, 145r.
[21] *APC 1586–7*, 212. [22] J. Goring, *Sussex and the Spanish Armada* (Lewes, 1988), 3.
[23] *APC 1586–7*, 220.
[24] *Ibid.*, 340. For disarming of recusants in Sussex, see also BL, Harleian MS 703, fos. 21r, 67v.
[25] Manning, *Religion*, 146–7. [26] *APC 1588*, 201, 203.
[27] L. J. Ward, 'The Law of Treason in the Reign of Elizabeth I 1558–1588' (Ph.D., Cambridge, 1985), 289; Anstr. I, 94.
[28] Goring, *Sussex and the Spanish Armada*, 5–6; M. A. Lower (ed.), *A Survey of the Coast of Sussex Made in 1587* (Lewes, 1870).

Cowdray in August 1591 was (although the queen's actual destination was Portsmouth, where she hoped to meet the French king Henry IV) in part an intimidatory exercise designed to teach a lesson to the region's Catholics. (It was, says Breight, also designed to counter disaffection caused by troop levying in Sussex in 1589–90. This had bred discontent because so few of the recruited men had returned alive.[29])

Recusancy commissioners were operating in the shire in 1592, in pursuance of the 1591 proclamation. They were ordered by the privy council to start locking up papists, in private houses if necessary. The council cited 'the notable backwardnes and defeccion in religion of late nowe growing generallie amongst' the queen's subjects 'especiallie sithence the last libertie and leave graunted to such principall persons as were formerlie committed'.[30] In early September 1592 Buckhurst was being lectured by the council about recent reports of a great number of ships in the Channel. They were believed to belong to the Spaniards and Spain's French Catholic allies. It was expected that they would attack the Isle of Wight or one of the Sussex maritime towns.[31] In October of the same year, Sussex, like other shires, found its JPs being instructed to signal publicly their loyalty by taking the oath of supremacy. The council noted how it was known that 'divers persons doe occupie the office of justices of the peace who do not repaire to theire churche or chappelles accustomed'. Their wives and children allegedly refused on principle to come to divine service, 'a matter not agreable with the vocacion of any that ought to inquire of suche offendours and to reforme the same'. Unless such matters were remedied, the justices in question, 'without delaie', should cease to be justices.[32] A stream of privy council orders came in 1593 that the shire's governors should keep up to date about papist exiles and illicit books and should check on people coming from abroad.[33] The Jesuit Robert Southwell, an East Anglian man who had many relatives in West Sussex and East Hampshire,[34] wrote what, during the war years, must have seemed an exceedingly inflammatory tract, his *Humble Supplication*. It

---

[29] Breight, 'Caressing'. See ch. 5, pp. 169–76 below.

[30] BL, Harleian MS 703, fo. 68r; Hughes and Larkin, *Tudor Royal Proclamations*, III, nos. 738, 739.

[31] *APC 1592*, 160.   [32] *Ibid.*, 255–6; BL, Harleian MS 703, fo. 69v.

[33] BL, Harleian MS 703, fo. 72r–v.

[34] Southwell was first cousin of Anthony Copley (the Copleys of Horsham were prominent Sussex Catholics), and his sister Mary married the recusant Edward Banester of Idsworth in Hampshire who also had Sussex estates. He was closely associated with the Cotton family (George Cotton was his mother's cousin) which held property at Warblington and Funtington, Devlin, *Life*, 5, 7, 10, 15, 215. His eldest sister and brother married respectively a nephew and niece of the second earl of Southampton. Southwell said his first Mass in England in Montague House in Southwark with various members of the Cotton and Banester families attending, *ibid.*, 15, 108–9, 152.

defended the Babington plotters. It appears to have circulated in manuscript around the region. He was executed in February 1595.[35]

In August 1595 a report voiced worries yet again about the vulnerability of the coast to invasion. For the city of Chichester was in a 'ruinous estate', and the 'late incursion of Spaniards into Cornwall suggests as well for that 500 men armed, ordered and appointed, might land and, in despite of the city and the help of the country, there set it on fire'. Something ought to be done to fortify Chichester properly. The same report complained also about the 'transportation' out of the realm 'of iron ordnance, cast-iron and wrought-iron'.[36] There was an invasion scare in 1596, and another in 1599 when it was believed that the Isle of Wight would be taken and, from it, galleys would be sailed into Chichester harbour.[37]

It is easy to see how, in these fraught times, those who did not adequately disguise their Catholicism could be regarded with suspicion. And it was quite easy for the authorities to believe that Catholic resentment of the regime might bleed into and inform more general political disobedience. While many conservative gentry families were outwardly conformist, others did not display that level of quiescence which was necessary to escape the attentions of the local authorities. In June 1585 a Sussex gentleman called Robert Threele was alleged to have said that 'the queene is an hoore, yea and an arrant hoore'.[38] And in the mid-1580s and up to and around the time of the Armada we find the assize judges dealing also with cases of what looks like popular discontent. In February 1586 Jeremy Vanhill of Sandwich, a labourer, was condemned for saying in April 1585, 'shyte uppon your queene; I woulde to God shee were dead that I might shytt on her face'. Sometimes this discontent seems to have had 'Catholic' overtones, even if we cannot always locate the discontented individuals at the heart of the

[35] *Ibid.*, 249. Southwell claimed that the plot was more the government's attempt to entrap the conspirators than 'any device of their owne', Robert Southwell, *An Humble Supplication to her Maiestie* (n.p. [printed secretly in England], 1595, n.d. [1600–1]), 31–2. Robert Gage, executed for his part in the plot, was one of Southwell's cousins, Devlin, *Life*, 110. The authorities in Hampshire tried to prevent the circulation of Southwell's work in manuscript. John Wilkinson of Winchester, an undersheriff of Southampton, testified in late 1602 that in March 1596 he had found two seditious books in the possession of the recusant Richard Baker (described as 'servant or baylyf' to the recusant Thomas Pounde) 'which books weare first made', as Henry Henslowe, another Catholic, told Wilkinson 'by a Jesuite or seminary priest that was executed at Tyborne for treason'. Wilkinson took this to mean Southwell. Henslowe had liked what Southwell had written so much that 'he got a coppie of yt', and 'out of that wrote the said ii bookes and comended them to his frindes as matters of greate worthe', PRO, E 133/10/1517, fos. 1r, 2r.
[36] *HMCS* V, 323. For Sussex's importance in the manufacture and export of iron ordnance, see H. Cleere and D. Crossley, *The Iron Industry of the Weald* (2nd edition, Cardiff, 1995), 170–2.
[37] Goring, *Sussex and the Spanish Armada*, 17–18.
[38] Cockburn, *Sussex Assizes: Elizabeth*, no. 1006.

Catholic community. In February 1589, John Gardener of Canterbury, a yeoman, was indicted for saying in November 1588 (a politically sensitive time!) that 'the pope and his religion must needes have good succes heare in Englande, for that theire religion ys good'. When he was informed of the defeat of the Armada, he 'saide that it was lyes'. And, of the recent execution at Canterbury of the priests Christopher Buxton, Gerard Edwards and Robert Wilcocks, he said that 'the Jesuitts that suffered latelye . . . were better than the Protestants and died better than they woulde doe'. In the same sessions, the Kentish yeoman William Simpkins was indicted for saying that he would fight against the queen's troops.[39]

Sometimes, those who were pursued for sedition and disloyalty were known Catholics, or were close to well-known Catholic families. At Easter 1592 Henry Collins, one of the leading Sussex recusant John Gage's retainers, was arrested, allegedly for plotting to kill the queen.[40] James Gildridge, whose brother Lancelot was closely connected with the Gages, was in 1596 suspected of espionage. There were family links between the Gildridges and the Darells in Lamberhurst on the Kent–Sussex border (through Henry Collins, who married Lancelot Gildridge's daughter). The Darells were rounded up in early 1597 for their offensive political murmurings in late 1596, i.e. during the invasion scare at that time.[41]

At this time also, in Etchingham parish, William Holland, the minister there, was showing an extraordinarily unwise sympathy for the Spaniards. Holland was a Lincolnshire man who undoubtedly had some connection with the ironmaster-patron of the living, Robert Tirwhit. Tirwhit came from the Catholic Lincolnshire family of that name. It was said that on May Day 1596 Holland declared that 'if the Spaniard[s] should come it were best to yield to them'.[42] One of Henry Darell's servants spread a false rumour that

[39] Cockburn, *Kent Assizes: Elizabeth*, nos. 1479, 1757; Anstr. I, 60–1, 109, 381. Although we can only guess at the exact motivation for these seditious remarks, it may be worth locating them in the context of the wider commercial and mercantile doubts about the wisdom of the war. See P. Croft, 'Trading with the Enemy 1585–1604', *HJ* 32 (1989), 281–302, esp. pp. 300–2.

[40] PRO, SP 12/243/45, fo. 150r. In April 1601 we find John Gage (the younger) helping to extricate Collins from the full burden of his recusancy penalties, PRO, E 368/543, mem. 235a.

[41] *APC 1596–7*, 422, 424, 430, 432, 436, 438. For James Gildridge, who was freed after interrogation, see *APC 1595–6*, 420, 496. For the connections between thè Gildridges and the Gages, see PRO, STAC 5/N2/32, STAC 5/N5/7. Thomas Gildridge witnessed a change of overseer in the will of John Gage (the elder) in 1599, PRO, PROB 11/93, fo. 344r.

[42] Cited in J. Goring, 'The Reformation of the Ministry in Elizabethan Sussex', *JEH* 34 (1983), 345–66, at p. 358; Cockburn (ed.), *Sussex Assizes: Elizabeth*, no. 1760. The strongly Protestant Thomas May of Pashley alleged that Holland was 'a sedicious quarrelinge and a contentious fellowe', PRO, REQ 2/106/21, mem. 2a. Holland was, temporarily, exonerated. In November 1597, the privy council decided that it did not credit the new accusations against him by one Welshe that Holland 'should use certaine lewde speeches unto him to wish that

the Spaniards had landed, and it was alleged that the news was greeted with enthusiasm by Lady Montague's servants.[43]

Even if there was apparently no overt religious basis for some similar outbursts (as for example when, in July 1598, Henry Daniell of Ash said that 'he hoped to see such warre in this realme to afflicte the rich men of this countrye to requite their hardnes of hart towards the poore', and that 'the Spanyards were better than the people of this land and therefore he had rather that they were here than the rich men of this countrie'), the fact remained that aggressive politicised Catholicism could sometimes appear to be glossing and representing popular political disquiet.[44]

It is also interesting to observe that although the indictments for sedition and seditious words at the assizes tended to be of those below gentry status, the authorities clearly felt that the unwise and inflammatory words of servants and tenants reflected the opinions of their gentry masters and landlords. The servants of the Darell family were, with their master Henry Darell, dragged in during early 1597 for their reported comments in 1596 (when, as we have just remarked, the family was subject to arrest and interrogation). Ellen Usher had wished that 'the queene were as old agayne as she is'. Joan Gurr hoped the queen would be either converted or confounded. And Thomas Waters, Darell's bailiff, was also charged with 'very undutifull speeches and behavior'.[45] At Midhurst, under the eye of the Brownes, Thomas Cholcroft said he wished that those who did not hate Elizabeth were all hanged. In February 1600 the yeoman Henry Elliott of West Firle (the stamping ground of the Gage family) was sentenced to the full treason penalties for predicting that the queen's troops would be thrown out of Ireland.[46]

wee were all of the old religion', *APC 1597–8*, 118. But Holland was accused of uttering more turbulent speeches at Christmas 1602, BL, Harleian MS 703, fo. 115v, shortly before one of his Catholic recusant parishioners, Henry Whiting, was indicted, in February 1603, for seditious words spoken on the previous 13 January. (Whiting eventually conformed before Bishop Lancelot Andrewes at Greenwich Palace chapel in 1606 after a recusancy conviction in 1605.) See BL, Harleian MS 703, fo. 129r; Cockburn, *Sussex Assizes: Elizabeth*, no. 2093; PRO, E 368/522, mem. 211a. Once again, however, Holland seems to have got off the hook. The Catholic Booth family of Whatlington, near to Battle, appears to have come into the county with the Tirwhits. William Booth was a conformist whose conformity certificate issued by Samuel Harsnett describes him as being 'sometymes of Kettlebye', in co. Lincoln, where, indeed, he was also indicted for his nonconformity in 1592, PRO, E 368/541, mem. 108a; CRS 18, 153; PRO, PROB 11/149, fo. 260v (will of William Booth, dated 1 December 1609 with probate issued in 1626).

[43] See ch. 7, pp. 221–2 below.   [44] Cockburn, *Kent Assizes: Elizabeth*, no. 2589.

[45] *Ibid.*, nos. 2455–7; *APC 1596–7*, 422–3, 423–5. Thomas Harris, vicar of Lamberhurst, had alleged 'the treasonable disposicion of the said Dorell, both by maintenance' of an alleged seminary priest, 'and by certaine traiterous speeches . . . that ar said to have proceeded from some of his familye', *APC 1596–7*, 423.

[46] Cockburn, *Sussex Assizes: Elizabeth*, nos. 1857, 1887.

THE ENFORCEMENT AND LIMITS OF THE LAW AGAINST CATHOLIC NONCONFORMITY

We might imagine that in the mid-Elizabethan period, and particularly during the later 1580s and early 1590s, the plethora of rumours about conspiracies, and the constraints on what could be publicly said and done, imposed by the war against Spain, would have made life virtually impossible for Catholics, particularly if they had openly separated from the Church of England.

Yet within the county of Sussex, as indeed elsewhere, Catholicism was not wiped out or driven underground. In part this was because the Elizabethan State, like all early modern States, did not have the administrative resources at its disposal to coerce and repress dissent in ways available to modern governments. But it seems to have been more than a mere lack of administrative capacity and clout which was responsible for this. Certainly many contemporaries detected the shadowy influence of unseen webs of corruption impeding the proper enforcement of religious conformity. The earl of Pembroke puzzled in August 1590 over what should be done concerning those untrustworthy persons who sat on the council in the Marches in Wales, for whereas Lord Burghley

doth wish me to use the service of some of the councel in the Marches, whom I shal like best, I am sorry to write it, but most sory to find it, that (the justices excepted) there is not one of them whom I may employ in these causes. For either they be coldly affected in religion, of kinred or alliance to persons accused, or otherwise so qualified, that I have smal hope to do good by their means.[47]

Conversely, for those within the governing elite in a shire or municipality to stand out against the general sense of their own kinship group on such matters could be most uncomfortable. Henry Hastings, earl of Huntingdon, wrote to Burghley in late July 1592 that his trusty agent Henry Sanderson deserved Burghley's favour for otherwise he would not be able much longer to dwell in Newcastle. Sanderson was 'greatlye envyed theare of those which carrye the best cowntenans, and of sum I knowe ys so depelye hatyd, as he walkyth not wythout sum daunger', only for his good service to the queen, which the admiring Huntingdon had never expected he would have performed thus because he was not only born in the town but also 'ys greatelye lynkyd theare in bludde with dyverse that are not so well affectyd as he hathe shewyd hym selfe to bee'.[48]

While most leading Catholics' Catholicism was so well known that any nonconformity on their part could not but be interpreted as popish recusancy, in other cases of alleged delinquency it might well be harder to prove that

---

[47] BL Harleian MS 6995, no. 34, fo. 10r.   [48] *Ibid.*, no. 76, fo. 89v.

suspected Catholics were deliberately transgressing the recusancy statutes.[49] In other words, a determined round-up of a county's Catholics for their (alleged) recusancy would require a certain amount of ideological vigour as well as bureaucratic efficiency.

Not, of course, that some ideologically vigorous and bureaucratically efficient officials were not willing to try. It is instructive to see which local Sussex notables, wearing JPs' hats, dealt most consistently with Catholics. Many of those who engaged in this work seem to have been convinced and dedicated Protestants as well as reliable public servants. Significantly, the fact that many of them had Catholic relatives in their extended or even immediate families does not seem to have blunted their effectiveness. The longest serving and leading factotum in Sussex was Sir Walter Covert of Slaugham. Some of the Coverts of Slaugham were Catholics,[50] but Sir Walter was not. Anthony Fletcher charts his still vigorous service in local government early in Charles I's reign, which gives one some idea of what Sir Walter (born in Edward VI's time) must have been like as an Elizabethan justice.[51] The Sussex puritan minister William Attersall's commentary on the Book of Numbers was dedicated to Covert and to his first wife Jane. Attersall confessed that Covert did not 'neede . . . any helpe or furtherance from mee in the race of godlinesse wherein you runne'. But he hoped that when Covert had time to spare from 'waightier affaires' he would 'vouchsafe to peruse this commentary, or at least some part of it' (the book has 1,271 pages of small print in double columns!).[52] Covert served on virtually every commission sent into the county, and was an active deputy lieutenant.[53]

Covert's wife Jane was the daughter of Sir John Shurley of Isfield (another of whose daughters married James the son of Sir John Rivers of Chafford in Kent).[54] This marriage created one of the few really strong Protestant gentry nexuses in Sussex. (William Attersall, Covert's admirer, was beneficed at Isfield.[55]) Covert served on recusancy commissions with John Shurley of the Friars, Lewes, founder of a cadet branch of the Isfield Shurleys.[56] Sir John Shurley of Isfield's mother was Anne, a daughter of Nicholas Pelham

---

[49] See M. Questier, 'Conformity, Catholicism and the Law', in P. Lake and M. Questier (eds.), *Conformity and Orthodoxy in the English Church, c. 1560–1660* (2000), 237–61.

[50] In October 1577 a list of recusants compiled by Bishop Curteys included Edward Covert of Twineham who appears to have been the half-brother of Walter's father, Richard Covert of Slaugham, who died in September 1579, PRO, SP 12/117/15, fo. 36v.

[51] A. Fletcher, *Sussex 1600–1660* (1975), 176, 178–80, 188, 190, 195.

[52] William Attersall, *A Commentarie upon the Fourth Booke of Moses called Numbers* (1618), sig. A5v.

[53] See BL, Harleian MS 703.   [54] Hasler, *HC*, III, 379; Berry, *Sussex*, 65.

[55] Peckham, 'Institutions', 273.

[56] PRO, E 368/473, mem. 32b, E 368/503, mem. 105a, E 368/505, mem. 41a; Hasler, *HC*, III, 378.

of Laughton. Thomas Pelham, son of Sir Nicholas, was a regular recusancy commissioner; and his brother Edward served in this capacity as well.[57]

Another of Attersall's dedicatees was Sir John Rivers of Chafford, whose son, James, as we noted above, married a daughter of Sir John Shurley. Sir John Rivers was a baronet and served on the commission of the peace in Kent.[58] He was the son of George Rivers (a JP in both Sussex and Kent) who led the search of the Darell family's residence of Scotney Castle (see Figure 9) at Christmas 1598 in an unsuccessful attempt to arrest the Jesuit superior Richard Blount.[59] He also led the commission which, on 27 January 1601, effected a major sequestration of Henry Darell's estates.[60] And he cooperated with the very Protestant Sir Thomas May in an unsuccessful attempt early in James's reign to break up the dowager Viscountess Montague's Catholic network.[61] Rivers and May also served on the recusancy commission which, in August 1601, enquired into the estates of the ageing Elizabethan Catholic exile John Leedes of Steyning.[62]

Rivers married Frances, a daughter of William Bowyer. The Bowyers were a Sussex family which had recently arrived in the county from London. Thomas Bowyer of Leythorne was son-in-law to the Marian exile Alexander Nowell.[63] Bowyer was a zealous recusancy commissioner,[64] though his anti-Catholicism may have been increased by bitter land disputes with the Catholic (though conformist) Sir John Caryll of Warnham.[65] Bowyer was the prosecuting counsel at the 1588 treason trial in Chichester of four Catholic clergymen which we have already mentioned. Bowyer's son Thomas married Anne, the daughter of Adrian Stoughton of West Stoke. Stoughton's father Thomas was a known Catholic or Catholic sympathiser (a 1564 'misliker') and had been comptroller of the household to the twelfth earl of Arundel.[66] Adrian Stoughton, however, was a vigorous JP entirely in sympathy with Bowyer and the others who took on the main burden of dealing with recusant nonconformity.[67] Among those with whom Stoughton was to be found assessing Catholic estates was the future judge Richard Lewkenor of West

---

[57] PRO, E 368/496, mem. 85a (a recusancy commission on which Sir Walter Covert and John Shurley were also serving), E 368/503, mem. 105a, E 368/505, mem. 41a, E 368/509, mem. 176a. For Edward Pelham, see PRO, E 368/541, mem. 125a. There was also a William Pelham who served as a recusancy commissioner, PRO, E 368/496, mem. 85a.

[58] See William Attersall, *The Conversion of Nineveh* (1632).

[59] Hasler, *HC*, III, 294–5; J. Comber, *Sussex Genealogies (Lewes Centre)* (3 vols., Lewes, 1933), 226; *APC 1598–9*, 283, 323; Foley III, 486. He had also been involved in the proceedings in January 1597 against the Darells, *APC 1596–7*, 422.

[60] PRO, E 368/540, mem. 198a; PRO, E 377/9.

[61] Southern, *ERH*, 53; *HMCS* XIX, 97; ch. 7, p. 229 below.

[62] PRO, E 368/507, mem. 56a.   [63] Hasler, *HC*, I, 474.

[64] See e.g. PRO, E 368/460, mem. 17a.

[65] Hasler, *HC*, I, 474; PRO, STAC 5/C48/3, STAC 5/C56/15.

[66] Hasler, *HC*, III, 452–3, 453–4; PRO, SP 12/217/1.

[67] See e.g. PRO, E 368/501, mem. 60a.

Figure 9. A view of the ruins of Scotney Castle, near Lamberhurst, Kent, showing the fourteenth-century Ashburnham tower, the rebuilt south wing and the roofless remains of the east range.

Dean; Lewkenor was Stoughton's uncle.[68] The Lewkenor family, particularly the Tangmere/Selsey branch, had Catholic-conformist associations. (Thomas Lewkenor was one of the principal conservative gentry opponents of Bishop Curteys in 1577.) But Richard, Thomas's younger brother, showed no such tendencies. He was the presiding judge at the 1588 Chichester treason trial. He had also helped to investigate the fag-end of the Throckmorton plot.[69] In March 1603 he lamented to Sir Robert Cecil that the Welsh people were so given over to superstition and papistry.[70]

---

[68] Hasler, *HC*, II, 474. Adrian Stoughton's father, Thomas, had taken, as his second wife, Edmund Lewkenor's daughter Elizabeth, *ibid.*, III, 453; PRO, E 368/460, mem. 17a. Ironically, Stoughton can be found in 1607 acting as legal counsel to the second Viscount Montague, PRO, C 2/James I/K6/35, mem. 6a. Richard Lewkenor also functioned as a man-of-business for the Browne family, and he was prepared to offer privately his legal services to Catholic/conservative gentry. We find him acting on behalf of Edward Bellingham when in September 1587 the latter took on the undersheriff John Mynors over the alleged non-payment of Edward Banester's recusancy debts, PRO, STAC 5/M19/33, mem. 2a.

[69] Lewkenor examined Edward Poe, servant to the Catholic Anthony Fortescue, in the wake of the arrest of the earl of Arundel, BL, Egerton MS 2074, fo. 2r (20 April 1585).

[70] *HMCS* XII, 680.

There were other local public servants whom we can identify as convinced and active Protestants. One man who came into the county through marriage (to the daughter of Richard Bellingham of Hangleton) and sat as MP for Shoreham (in 1604) was Sir Barnard Whetstones, a former follower of the earl of Leicester. He had been a soldier in the Netherlands, and had seen action at Zutphen. He was a kinsman of William Fleetwood, the famous anti-popish recorder of London. His brother was George Whetstones – a literary man and, like Barnard, a client of the earl of Leicester; he published a vindication of the State's proceedings against the Babington plotters.[71] Barnard served on the Sussex commission of the peace from 1601 onwards. As one might expect, he was named to recusancy commissions as well. In January 1610 he headed one which hit many of the tenants and retainers of the now deceased dowager Viscountess Montague in the Battle area in East Sussex.[72] He himself speculated in the recusancy business, and he took over the estates of the Banester family of Idsworth.[73] Other regulars in the trade in recusants' estates included people such as Henry Shelley,[74] William Goring, Sir Benjamin Pellatt,[75] Richard Blount of Dedisham[76] and Sir Thomas Eversfield.[77]

It might be imagined that, with a vanguard of the godly thus ensconced in local office, those who were known Catholic nonconformists would inevitably have been subjected to the full rigour of the laws against their style of religious profession. But, in practice, this was not always what happened. For even the most godly of Protestants recognised that there was a large and intractable grey area between full nonconformity and full compliance. In 1587 Sir Francis Walsingham sent directions from the privy council to the deputy lieutenants in the shires concerning what was to be done about recusants and church papists. The Sussex deputy lieutenants had reported that 'there is greate varietie of papistes within the said shire'. Some were

[71] T. C. Izard, *George Whetstone* (New York, 1966), 2, 6, 7.

[72] PRO, E 368/541, mem. 124a.

[73] M. Questier, 'Sir Henry Spiller, Recusancy and the Efficiency of the Jacobean Exchequer', *HR* 66 (1993), 251–66, at p. 263; Alan Davidson, unpublished HPT biography of Sir Barnard Whetstones; HRO, 44M69/L61/52. In the 1604 parliament, Whetstones was on a commission for the suppression of popish books, as well as one for the enforcement of attendance at church.

[74] I.e. Henry Shelley of Patcham whose second wife was Jane, daughter of Richard Bellingham, Hasler, *HC*, III, 375. Shelley may be identified with the MP for Steyning in 1586, the main Protestant member of the Warminghurst family of that name. He also had a Patcham cousin of the same name who signed a Sussex puritan petition in 1603. See Davidson, unpublished HPT biography of Henry Shelley of Warminghurst.

[75] For Pellatt, see *VCH Sussex* I, 227; PRO, E 368/559, mem. 4a.

[76] Richard Blount was involved in Peter Wentworth's failed bill on the succession in 1593, Hasler, *HC*, I, 450. For his service on recusancy commissions, see e.g. PRO, E 368/496, mem 85a, E 368/503, mem. 105a.

[77] PRO, E 368/559, mem. 261a.

'notable recusants, and have bene presented, and stande indicted therof'. There was to be no hesitation in proceeding against these people. But 'other some there be that refuse not to come to churche once a moneth, or nowe and then', but yet they would 'neither take the oathe, communicate, nor have their children christned, other than in secret corners . . . and besides are knowen to favour and geve countenance to papistes, entertaining them, goeing and coming to theire houses verie often'. Ideally, these too should be locked up, though only if sufficient proof of their misdeeds was forthcoming. There were others who 'make curtesie to take the oathe and yet doe come to the churche, and observe an outward shew of obedience to her Majestie's proceedinge' (whom local officers nevertheless believed would 'prove bad subjects in tyme of neede'), and others still who conformed completely, but it was known, on the grapevine, and indeed it was evident from the 'course of theire life', that this was a sham and that they were 'notable papistes'. Also there were those who were habitual noncommunicants. Walsingham, however, directed that such people were 'not to be dealte withall'. Even in 1587, political circumstances might dictate a stand-off. It was simply not possible to imprison all the usual suspects.[78]

Furthermore, not all guardians of public conformist standards, even those men of clear and robust Protestant character, were on exactly the same ideological wavelength. For example, Bishop Richard Curteys's anti-Catholicism was utterly uncompromising. In a sermon at Paul's Cross on 4 March 1577 Curteys alleged that

the papists were wont to say that this [i.e. Protestant] religion would bring in infidelitie, but most falsely and most untruly: marrie, what want of discipline hath done and may do, that is another point. Neither hath there beene, nor is, nor can bee any fault in the religion, for it is the sincere religion that Christ Jesus left to his Church. But surely the remisnes of magistrates either hath done or may doo much harme. Many there be that make little account of common praier, and as little of the word or of the sacraments. Not surely, because they want [i.e. lack] zeale and religion altogither, but either they beare themselves of the losenesse of the time, or of the countenance of some great persons upon whome they depend.

Curteys may have been thinking here of the aristocratic and other patrons in his own diocese who protected Catholics. Curteys's perception of the dangers of half-hearted reform and lack of vigilance was focused on a loosely defined but very broad concept of popery. He worried that 'there be divers partlie irreligious, and partlie papists and spies to[o], that few or none dare controll them, without greater danger to the controller than to the controlled. These

---

[78] BL, Harleian MS 703, fo. 52r, printed in W. D. Cooper, 'Certificate concerning the Justices of Peace in Sussex in 1587 . . .', *SAC* 2 (1849), 58–62, at pp. 60–1.

talke their pleasures of Christian preachers and ministers, and jest at common praier and at sermons, and at every good thing.'[79]

This sermon coincided almost to the day with the beginning of the notorious incident in March 1577 for which Curteys is chiefly remembered – his disastrous confrontation with conservative and Catholic gentry in his diocese and the failure of his strong arm tactics to make them conform. (It was preached, in fact, only forty-eight hours after the date on which Curteys's gentry opponents were supposed to have appeared in the Chichester consistory court in order to make a grovelling submission to his authority.[80])

Curteys was not the only anti-papist in the 1570s Chichester episcopal administration. But not all the members of that administration were zealous in the same way. For example William Overton, who became treasurer of Chichester Cathedral in March 1567 and was a close associate of Bishop Barlow, Curteys's predecessor, seems to have been less uncompromising than Curteys. (Overton was also Barlow's son-in-law, and believed during his father-in-law's tenure of the bishopric that he might succeed him.) Before Curteys was appointed, Overton wrote, in effect, to warn Sir William Cecil against Curteys, who was at that time the dean. Overton remained the focus of the anti-Curteys faction.[81] In a sermon preached at the East Grinstead assizes in either 1579 or 1580 Overton warned his hearers to resolve the current discords in religion and politics, Church and State. And his sermon may have contained a coded criticism of Curteys's overkill against the partially conformist conservative gentry in 1577. For Overton admonished the auditory that, as for the discord troubling the Church,

heere is a great controversie or question amongst men, whence these troubles of the Church shoulde arise, and who are the chiefe authoures of them. And the controversie resteth speciallye betweene the Catholikes and us, I meane the papistes and us. And heere, when I speake of papistes, you may not take me that I meane everye one that is not throughly resolved in every poynte of religion. For there may be many whose eyes God hath not yet opened, but will do when it shall please him, and yet in the meane time are good subjectes to the queene and necessarie members of the common wealth, whome we must not despise but pray for. But under the name of papistes, I comprehende those whyche cleave altogither unto the pope and papacie, and by open worde and writing mainteyne the usurped authoritie of the bishop of Rome, contrary to the word of God and the lawes and statutes of thys realme.[82]

---

[79] Richard Curteys, *Two Sermons Preached by the Reverend Father in God Richard Bishop of Chichester, the First at Paules Crosse. The Second at Westminster before the Queenes Maiestie* (1584), sig. Civv–vr; M. Maclure, *Register of Sermons Preached at Paul's Cross 1534–1642*, rev. P. Pauls and J. C. Boswell (Centre for Reformation and Renaissance Studies, Occasional Publications no. 6, Ottawa, 1989), 57.

[80] Manning, *Religion*, ch. 5.   [81] *Ibid.*, 58, 67, 69.

[82] William Overton, *A Godlye and Pithie Exhortation, Made to the Iudges and Iustices of Sussex, and the Whole Countie, Assembled Togither, at the Generall Assises* (1580), sig. Bvr–v.

Overton's effort was still an anti-popery sermon, and (though he also castigated 'the puritanes') he went on at some length about the dangers of half-heartedness in confronting popery, and of the 'calves of Bason abroade, which since they suckte the bull that came from Rome have given over all obedience and allegiance both to God and the queene'.[83] An assize sermon was not the occasion for moderation and half-measures. Still, Overton seems to be defining a slightly different popish enemy from the one which Curteys had recently excoriated. It looks as if a veneer of conformity might satisfy Overton, whereas for Curteys even the slightest evidence of nonconformity was enough of an excuse for going in hard against those whom he suspected of malignancy (even though many of them were basically conformist).

So there might well not be complete unanimity among those whose religion should technically have made them enthusiastic co-workers in the enforcement of godly conformity. Furthermore, although, as we have just rehearsed, the principal commissions which dealt directly with recusant sequestrations were generally headed by convinced Protestants, by no means the whole of the county commission of the peace was so minded. And, indeed, on recusancy commissions, we occasionally find people such as Sir Thomas Leedes, whose family was heavily Catholicised.[84] Amazingly, George Gunter, from the sometimes flagrantly Catholic family of that name, was named as a recusancy commissioner in October 1602.[85] There is even an 'Edward' Pelham named on a similar commission of August 1593, and this may well refer to the lawyer Edmund Pelham of Catsfield (knighted in 1604) who was regarded by some as a protector of Catholics in East Sussex and very thick with the dowager Viscountess Montague.[86] We also find listed for the same duty Francis Neville (of Sidlesham, and later of Chichester), a brother-in-law of Sir Lewis Lewkenor (the Jacobean Court's master of ceremonies) who arranged that Neville should be returned as MP for Midhurst. Neville had been suspected of Catholic nonconformity in 1579. He also made two very Catholic-looking marriages, the first of which was to Mary, daughter of Thomas Lewkenor of Selsey.[87] Yet another puzzling choice as a recusancy commissioner was Thomas Bishop of Henfield. He was appointed as sheriff of the county in 1587, and was in charge of making the recusant 'light horse' scheme work.[88] At other times he was reluctant to enforce privy council orders against Catholics, and (in 1582) he had been criticised for his

---

[83] *Ibid.*, sig. Diir, Divv.
[84] See PRO, E 368/538, mem. 99a (an enquiry held at Chichester on 10 October 1609 by Leedes and John Morley into the property of the recusant James Rootes of Priesthawes).
[85] PRO, E 368/509, mem. 176a.
[86] PRO, E 368/541, mem. 125a. Edmund Pelham was also referred to as 'Edward' in contemporary documents, Hasler, *HC*, III, 192–3.
[87] Davidson, unpublished HPT biography of Francis Neville.
[88] Manning, *Religion*, 141; Hasler, *HC*, I, 439; PRO, E 368/509, mem. 107a.

leniency by Bishop Curteys.[89] In May 1594 it was reported by an informer that one John Bamford (who allegedly had a son who was a priest) was a recusant, and lived with 'Mr Bishop, a justice of the peace', at Henfield.[90] Bishop's second marriage, in 1589, was made into the Catholic family of Weston, resident at Sutton in Surrey.[91]

Naturally, the appointment of Sir Thomas Bishop as a JP is far from inexplicable. He was part of the Sackville interest in the county. He made his way in county government and administration because he was associated with the rising star of the Sackville family.[92] This career path could evidently be combined with a flexible conscience. Here, then, we seem to have additional evidence to substantiate Roger Manning's thesis that Catholicism was expunged gradually as the logic of getting on with serving the crown dictated a gradual move towards conformity even by those who were initially out of sympathy with the Elizabethan settlement. This is what made it possible for people such as Bishop and Leedes to cooperate with convinced Protestants such as Bowyer and Stoughton.[93]

However, the lack of a uniform, united and univocal front against Catholicism may have allowed not just the survival but also the opportunity for the expression, even if covertly, of Catholic religious identity and opinion. Ironically, by displaying a measure of conformity in obedience to the law, some Catholics may have been able to preserve their identity completely contrary to the intentions of many in the national and local State who saw them as a threat. These conformists played a series of games in which they balanced their (often known) Catholicism against their interpretation of conformist obedience to the law.

Let us look briefly at the Carylls (of Warnham, Shipley and Harting). The Caryll family tree contains a galaxy of Catholic stars – mostly local ones – Cotton of Warblington, Gage of Bentley, Ford of Harting and so

---

[89] Manning, *Religion*, 141–2, 146.   [90] *CSPD 1591–4*, 510.

[91] Hasler, *HC*, I, 439. Both of Bishop's parents were regarded as Catholics. His father had come into Sussex as a servant of Sir William Shelley. Sir Henry Weston in 1559 had married Dorothy, the daughter of Sir Thomas Arundell of Wardour Castle. This marriage would have tied him in with the Catholic families, including the Wriothesleys and, later, the Brownes, who were or subsequently married into the Arundell family. Weston was named on a 1574 list of alleged supporters of Mary Stuart. He was a friend of Sir Thomas Copley, a Catholic exile, Hasler, *HC*, III, 604–5.

[92] For the Sackvilles, see below in this chapter, and see also ch. 3, pp. 83–7 below.

[93] As we rehearsed briefly in the previous chapter, Manning argued that, by degrees, governance in the county was restricted to conformists. This explains how Catholicism came to be no longer the religion of the majority of the gentry by the end of Elizabeth's reign. See Manning, *Religion*, 259 (table iv, part i). Ronald Fritze discerned a similar alteration in the opinions of the Hampshire office-holding class, R. H. Fritze, '"A Rare Example of Godlyness amongst Gentlemen": The Role of the Kingsmill and Gifford Families in Promoting the Reformation in Hampshire', in P. Lake and M. Dowling (eds.), *Protestantism and the National Church in Sixteenth-Century England* (1981), 144–61, at p. 144.

on. Their eligibility in the marriage market took them, however, as far afield as Lancashire. Bridget Caryll married William Molyneux, eldest son of Sir Richard Molyneux, of Sefton, and remarried Richard Radcliffe of Newecroft. (Lord Burghley's *aides-mémoire* in the early 1570s on the state of Lancashire and Cheshire, particularly about the Catholic activism around the earl and countess of Derby, carefully noted 'Richard Ratcliff that married young Mollyneux's wife that was Mr Carrell's daughter'.[94]) The informant Malivery Catilyn, who was a veritable mine of intelligence on Catholicism in and around the Hampshire/Sussex border region, alerted Sir Francis Walsingham in April 1587 to a Catholic safe house in Richmondshire where one of the Carylls could be found.[95]

On the other hand, the Carylls were not usually prosecuted as recusants in the way that other leading Catholic families were. Edward Caryll (knighted in May 1603) was regarded as a recusant by Bishop Curteys (and was actually presented as such in 1580). But thereafter this was not the opinion of the rest of the county. Curteys himself had to admit that, when leaned on, Caryll was ready to conform. Caryll had even agreed to come to prayers at Curteys's episcopal palace.[96] He had been sheriff of the county in 1571, and was on the Sussex commission of the peace in the 1580s and then again during the 1590s.

Many of the Carylls' connections were with Catholic families which also had pronounced conformist tendencies. For example, the conformed recusant Francis Nash of Horsham, whose property was marked down for sequestration by Sir Walter Covert at an exchequer recusancy commission hearing at Lewes in October 1610,[97] and who came to submit before Archbishop George Abbot in Lambeth Palace chapel in 1611, appointed Sir John Caryll (the younger) as the overseer of his will, and he bequeathed an annuity or rent charge of £16, 'due unto mee out of a piece of land called Scenches, lyinge and being in the parish of Warnham and Rusper', 'to Sir John Carrill . . . whome I am most bounde unto', and also £4 to Caryll's son John and forty shillings to Caryll's daughter Mary.[98]

This did not mean, however, that the Carylls were simply and spinelessly compliant. In 1587 Edward Caryll appears to have been temporarily

[94] *HMCS* I, 576.   [95] PRO, SP 12/200/44, fo. 78v.
[96] R. B. Manning, 'Catholics and Local Office Holding in Elizabethan Sussex', *BIHR* 35 (1962), 47–61, at pp. 58–9.
[97] PRO, E 368/539, mem. 147c.
[98] PRO, PROB 11/125, fos. 263v–264r. In fact, Abbot noted on the certificate which he issued to Nash and another conformed 'recusant', Ralph Coote, that '(by witnesses as well as their own protestations) theye never weare recusants of any sorte but have from tyme to tyme heeretofore repared to divine service in there parish church and receaved the holy sacrement in all dew conformitye'. Nash also left a bequest to his parish church in Horsham, PRO, E 368/542, mem. 137a; PRO, PROB 11/125, fos. 263v–264r.

removed from the commission of the peace because of his known adherence to Philip Howard, earl of Arundel, of whose estates he was steward in the 1580s and in whose will he was named as an executor.[99] Edward's name had already come up, with George Cotton's, in 1583 during the investigation of the Throckmorton plot. They were alleged to have helped Lord Paget and Charles Arundell flee overseas. Caryll and a servant, John Michell, were examined, and Caryll was then imprisoned in the Tower.[100] But, quite extraordinarily, he was restored to the Sussex commission of the peace in 1591.[101] In January 1593 Edward Caryll and Sir John Caryll were named as 'fit' to serve the queen. Sir John Caryll of Warnham had been sheriff of Surrey and Sussex in 1588. As Manning notes, Sir John was more openly Catholic than his uncle Edward at Harting, and though he conformed temporarily in the early 1580s and received his knighthood from Elizabeth in 1591 (at Cowdray), he was immediately named again as a recusant in 1592. He was cited, though not necessarily convicted, as a recusant in the early years of James's reign. He had, in fact, been receiving communion in the Brownes' parish of St Saviour in Southwark during the late 1590s.[102]

Manning believed, rightly, that the Carylls were able to hold public office because they were 'much more flexible' than 'their more stubborn cousins', the Gages and the Shelleys.[103] But this does not quite capture the somewhat precarious balancing act performed by the Caryll family – almost a flouting of the regime's prescriptions for dutiful conformist behaviour.[104]

Part of this rather unblushing refusal to submerge themselves into a truly undifferentiated conformity was, ironically, their refusal to withdraw from the parish in the way that Catholic polemical conduct books for the gentry generally insisted was both necessary and logically consistent. For example, it was a contemporary casuistical question among the Catholic gentry whether they should exercise their rights of presentation personally, and indeed there is relatively little evidence that Catholic patrons of Church-of-England benefices did use such rights, even to present sympathetic, or at least moderate, clergymen with whom they would be on good terms. The Carylls,

---

[99] J. Mousley, 'Sussex County Gentry in the Reign of Elizabeth' (Ph.D., London, 1956), 217. Lord William Howard's eldest son Philip married Mary, daughter of Sir John Caryll of Harting.

[100] PRO, SP 12/164/23, fos. 36r, 37v, 38r. Michell was mentioned in Caryll's will, PRO, PROB 11/115, fo. 467r.

[101] Manning, 'Catholics', 59.

[102] *Ibid.*, 59–60; LMA, P92/SAV/190, p. 22, P92/SAV/192, p. 18.

[103] Manning, 'Catholics', 58. John Caryll of Warnham was noted in 1582 to have been 'twice indited and sithence [to have] brought certificat that he hath bene at the church', CRS 53, 5.

[104] It is worth noting that by the 1630s the Carylls of Warnham were compounding for recusancy, William Prynne, *The Popish Royall Favourite* (1643), 7–8.

however, seem to have brought a relative of theirs, Richard Buckenham, to the rectory of Harting (where he remained from November 1611 until his death in 1628).[105] (Buckenham was a protégé and kinsman of Samuel Harsnett.[106]) It is possible that some Sussex Catholics may have been on good terms with Harsnett when he came to the diocese as bishop of Chichester.[107] After Buckenham the rector was Thomas Caryll, who had held the vicarage between 1612 and 1614. He came from the Tangley branch of the Caryll family in Surrey; and he became one of Archbishop Abbot's chaplains. But he was evidently acceptable to the Carylls at Harting.[108] Now, those being presented to Caryll livings were not crypto-papists, but this does suggest a retention of control over the parish by a known Catholic family in a way which some contemporaries would undoubtedly have considered a bit odd.

At Shipley, South Harting and Warnham there were erected splendid Caryll monuments.[109] Monuments, to be sure, were very fashionable, and these could be taken as just that, fashion accessories of a wealthy local family. But, on another level, Catholic monuments such as these might have been regarded as rather intrusive. At Shipley the Caryll monument is stuck (monstrously, perhaps, to someone who found Catholics offensive) in the chancel. It spelled out the family's principal Catholic alliances. It noted that the wife of Sir Thomas Caryll (d. January 1616) was a Tufton, and that two of his daughters married into the Catholic peerage, to Molyneux and Morley.[110] The Caryll monument at Warnham, by contrast, is placed in the chapel on the north side of the church, and is relatively small.[111] (See Figure 10.) But it is not exactly uncontroversial. It records the death in 1613 of Sir John Caryll and then launches into an encomium of his wife Mary, the daughter of George Cotton of Warblington. The Cottons of Warblington were an out and out Catholic family. In mid-1613 there was a relatively major county political scandal involving the family. The houses of the Cottons were searched for evidence that John Cotton (formerly an associate of Edmund Campion, and brother of Mary Caryll) had written a seditious pamphlet called 'Balaam's Ass'.[112] The contemporary impact of the Warnham monument depends, of

---

[105] Thomas Caryll of Warnham (d. 1563) had married Dorothy, daughter of Thomas Buckenham of Norfolk, Berry, *Sussex*, 359; Mosse, *ME*, 186.

[106] K. Fincham, *Prelate as Pastor* (Oxford, 1990), 143n, 159–60, 196.

[107] I am grateful to Kenneth Fincham for this suggestion.

[108] Berry, *Sussex*, 358. Oddly, as Matthew Reynolds has pointed out to me, the presentation, made via Sir Garrett Kempe of Slindon, an occasional conformist, was overturned, on grounds of simony, and (by 1632) another cleric was presented instead.

[109] See Mosse, *ME*, 102–3, 185–7. The Caryll monument at South Harting is badly damaged.

[110] *Ibid.*, 151.   [111] *Ibid.*, 186.

[112] *NAGB*, 227–9. In August 1580 John Caryll and his wife had fled across the Sussex/Hampshire border to take refuge with the Cottons as Bishop Curteys tried to enforce conformity on the Sussex Catholic gentry, Manning, 'Catholics', 59–60.

Figure 10.   Alabaster funeral monument to Sir John Caryll (d. 1613) in the parish church (St Margaret) at Warnham in West Sussex. The monument is situated within the Caryll family chapel on the north side of the church.

course, on when it was actually put up in the church, but the significance of the Cotton name could hardly have been lost on the average local observer.

The fact that the Carylls had invested in some kind of uneasy conformist accommodation with the local State did not mean that there was no place around them for covert expressions of Catholicism. The seminarist William Forster who arrived at Rome in 1606 stated that he was the 'son of a noble father who owing to circumstances is now steward of Sir John Caryll in Sussex' (i.e. Sir John Caryll of Warnham).[113] Forster's mother, 'a puritan', had separated from her husband because he was a Catholic.[114] It appears that the formative experiences which led to Forster's training for the ministry came out of an intense sense of religious division which he experienced within his own family, perhaps fuelled rather than toned down by living within the Caryll orbit. Forster's clerical contacts before he left to train for ordination were with the Jesuits, notably Nicholas Smith SJ (at one time a chaplain to a branch of the Copley family of Roughey and Horsham). Forster himself went on to join the Society of Jesus in October 1609. Also, as Manning points out, Sir Edward Caryll's daughter Mary became a nun, and his son Sir Thomas kept a Jesuit chaplain.[115]

Considering that the Jesuits were so often associated by contemporaries with the worst excesses of popery, it is at first surprising that a conformist family such as the Carylls should have consorted with them. But consort they did. In addition to the Warnham Carylls' employment of Nicholas Smith SJ, we know that John Curry (who became a Jesuit in 1583) was in August 1580 reported to be with one of the Carylls in Hampshire.[116] Martin Array, who was subsequently the pro-Jesuit archpriest George Blackwell's proctor in Rome during the appellant controversy, was resident at one of the Carylls' houses in Sussex in 1584.[117] In 1611 it leaked out that Sir John Caryll in Chichester was sheltering the Jesuit Ralph Bickley.[118] In fact, it seems that the family was positively and ideologically aligned against those Catholics who looked askance at the influence of the Jesuits in England. The anti-Jesuit secular priest Benjamin Norton, who was attached to the clerical circle around the second Viscount Montague at Cowdray, tended to snigger

---

[113] CRS 54, 163. Sir Robert Cecil received a report from one Peter Hardy in late 1603 who claimed that he had been told by someone who believed that he, Hardy, was a Catholic, that if he felt threatened and was in the region of the Sussex coast he should go to 'Sir John Carrell at the Friers', i.e. the Grey Friars, which was leased by Sir John from the Chichester city corporation. At the Grey Friars he should ask for either one Mr Thomas Collbet, or 'Mr Lawrence Foster', evidently William Forster's father, and they would introduce him to the priest who was resident there, one Thomas Smith. Hardy introduced himself into the Caryll household, and attended Mass several times there, and also at the Cotton residence in Warblington, PRO, SP 14/5/24, fo. 54r; BL, Additional MS 5706, fo. 45v.
[114] CRS 54, 163.   [115] Manning, 'Catholics', 59; CRS 74, 102.
[116] *CSPF 1579–80*, 389.   [117] Anstr. I, 11.   [118] *NAGB*, 226.

whenever he heard distasteful or scandalous news about the Carylls. For example, in May 1609 Norton reported that one of the Carylls' servants, who had publicly expressed the wish 'in fervency and zeele' to 'dye a Protestaunte', proceeded to get 'drunke in the lorde, and fell downe' two flights of stairs and died the next morning and 'before dinner hee stuncke untollerablye'.[119] It is not unreasonable to read into this a sneer at the conformist character of the Caryll family and household. (Some Catholic secular clergy took such conformity to be a sign of typically Jesuit/ed casuistical laxity and cynicism towards the duty of Catholics to avoid the scandal caused to the community by any failure to separate unequivocally from the Church of England.)

In other words, what we have here is a partially conformist family which maintained its links with the establishment but did not, by that token, gradually slip into 'mere' conformity. Nor did the Carylls lose touch with the rest of the Catholic community, even if, undoubtedly, some of the Catholic community would dearly have loved to lose touch with them. The Carylls did not therefore conform to any conventional Catholic occasional conformist stereotype. They appeared to give a measure of conformist obedience with one hand and then take it back with the other. This suggests that the range of options open to a large, wealthy and influential family was much wider than most of the Catholic casuistical treatises on non/conformity allowed. In the Carylls we seem to have a family which was shielding its Catholic characteristics and inclinations behind some kind of local and social consensus that their limited, even minimal, compliance should permit them to escape the law's penalties against popish recusancy, although well-informed Protestants would certainly and justifiably have regarded them as popish.

The chance survival of records concerning the Carylls means that we know more about them than about many other Sussex Catholic families during this period. But there were others whose opinions and demeanour were similarly complex.

Members of the Leedes family, which we have already come across, were, by turns, willing conformists and religious exiles.[120] Sir Thomas Leedes, with his very Catholic wife (from a Yorkshire family also called Leedes),[121] went abroad to Louvain, allegedly for religious reasons but also because he had

---

[119] *Ibid.*, 44.

[120] In the early seventeenth century the Leedeses were closely connected with Sir Edward Francis, the Percies' estate manager. Sir John Leedes (the son of Sir Thomas Leedes) had a room at Petworth, G. R. Batho (ed.), *The Household Papers of Henry Percy Ninth Earl of Northumberland (1564–1632)* (Camden Society, 3rd series, 93, 1962), 120. Francis acted as a trustee in trying to sort out the debt problems of Sir Thomas, PRO, C 2/James I/ G2/4.

[121] See PRO, E 368/526, mem. 177a.

accumulated so many financial debts.[122] He was the son of an exile and a recusant. Though he was regarded in the 1590s as papistically inclined, he nevertheless conformed.[123] Perhaps the Leedes family's links with the house of Wriothesley, and particularly with the third earl of Southampton, influenced him.[124] As his son Thomas, a future Jesuit, narrated it, Sir Thomas was a 'schismatic' for some time, although his wife was always a Catholic. He was 'first created a knight of the Bath' at James's coronation, and then was made 'praefectus . . . totius provinciae'. He 'gained a great repute for prudence and equity'. But 'by the pious importunity of his wife, and, indeed, moved by divine impulse, he at length determined as soon as possible to embrace Christian liberty. Having arranged his family affairs, he went into voluntary exile in Louvain, and thus chose a port of salvation.' The younger Thomas claimed that in about 1607 Sir Thomas, 'out of fear of the penal laws and of the earl of Salisbury, persuaded me to frequent the Protestant churches'.[125]

Sir Thomas's conformist tendencies in England may not have been purely cosmetic. For example, he was present in the chapel of Samuel Harsnett's episcopal residence in Chichester when the well-known Sussex recusant William Thatcher made his official show of conformity there on 23 March 1612.[126] And, as we have already noted, he served as a recusancy commissioner.[127] He may have believed that it was possible for Catholics to live within the ecclesiastical establishment and reject outright recusancy.

But Leedes's disillusionment set in rapidly after Salisbury's death. In mid-October 1613 his wife obtained a pass to go to join him at Spa in Flanders.[128] His letters soon made it clear that he was at enmity with Archbishop Abbot. In February 1614 he wrote to William Trumbull, 'you ask my opinion of the distribution of offices among the lords, but my retired life intends no State business, being thereunto called by the undeserved affronts of my lord of Caunterbury heretofore unjustly cast over me'.[129] In fact, even before Sir Thomas's eventual departure abroad, his family seems to have been rediscovering some of its Catholic roots. By 1610 the younger Thomas had been reconciled to the Church of Rome by the Jesuit Michael Walpole, with (Thomas

[122] *HMCS XII*, 176; *CSPD 1603–10*, 411; PRO, C 2/James I/L3/16, C 2/James I/G2/14; PRO, E 112/45/140.
[123] *CSPD 1591–4*, 504, 510; Manning, *Religion*, 158. Sir Thomas obtained a discharge, as a conforming heir, from the exchequer's claims on his father's property after John Leedes's death, PRO, E 368/525, mem. 237a.
[124] *HMCD IV*, 247, 351, 469. [125] Foley I, 247; CRS 54, 287; Anstr. II, 188.
[126] PRO, E 368/550, mem. 118a. [127] PRO, E 368/541, mem. 114a.
[128] *APC 1613–14*, 234. There is evidence, in the records of the exchequer, of a hardening of the regime's attitude towards Catholic recusancy following Salisbury's death, M. Questier, *Conversion, Politics and Religion in England, 1580–1625* (Cambridge, 1996), 137. I am grateful for advice on this point to Pauline Croft.
[129] *HMCD IV*, 316, and *passim*.

claimed) Sir Thomas's full approval; the way was open for him to go abroad
to enrol in a seminary.[130] Another of Sir Thomas's children, Edward, became
a Jesuit as well.[131] And the Jesuit general's letter book in 1622 records that
permission was given for Sir Thomas to be buried in a Jesuit church.[132]
Sir Thomas, who is mentioned in the annual letters of the Jesuit college in
Louvain in 1618, was a benefactor of the Sodality of the Immaculate Conception of the Blessed Virgin Mary (recently established in the college), of
which Sir Thomas was the first prefect. He presented it with a silver chalice
and paten.[133] Secretary of the same confraternity was Sir Ralph Babthorpe.
Babthorpe, Leedes, Sir Edward Parham and Sir William Roper were the subject of an attempt in mid-1615 by the regime in England to get them to return
home. Evidently there was some real irritation at their Catholic posturing
in the Low Countries. Sir Ralph Winwood informed Trumbull on 11 May
1615 that 'the less you have to doe with thys kind of men', i.e. such men
as Leedes, 'the better service you shall doe his Majesty, for howsoever he
doth temporyse him selfe, and pretends the Spaa [*sic*] waters, yet I heare of
what carige hys wyfe ys, who trotts up and downe at all processions and
hawnts all pilgrimages, and omitts noe superstition that may stain and dis-
honor her cowntrye'. It was also believed that Leedes was seeking a military
commission in Flanders.[134]

In other words, we can see how the variegated and inconsistent religious
culture of a post-Reformation county such as Sussex could allow for the
expression of a whole range of styles of Catholicism.

Also, in many Sussex families, disagreements about religion and politics disrupted the conformist culture which the representatives of the State
desired to maintain. The powerful family of Lewkenor encompassed a wide
variety of opinions. As we have already seen, the leading lawyer Richard
Lewkenor was a bastion of order and authority against the dangers of
incipient popery. Yet so many of his family connections were, covertly or
overtly, Catholic. His brother Thomas Lewkenor of Tangmere, MP in 1586
for Viscount Montague's borough of Midhurst, was an opponent of Bishop

[130] Foley I, 247–8.
[131] In the 1630s Edward Leedes became notorious for his writings against the Jacobean oath
of allegiance, Foley I, 251–63; AAW, A XXVII, no. 153, p. 465, XXVIII, no. 220.
[132] ARSJ, Anglia MS 1/i, fo. 151r.   [133] Foley I, 246.
[134] *HMCD* V, 214, 296. The priest Robert Pett noted on 8/18 May 1615 that the four gentlemen had 'all avoyded the citation by absenting them selves, and soe cunningly' was
the business 'hindered that the poore pursivant was made dronke and in his dronkenes
was committed to prison by the magistrate and before he could agayne obteyne his libertie the parties had all convayed them selves away', AAW, A XIV, no. 113, pp. 356–7,
no. 119, p. 371. Henry More SJ claimed that James backed down in the face of Spanish diplomatic pressure, and the Louvain authorities expelled the pursuivant, Foley I,
246–7.

Richard Curteys, and was very hostile to efforts to restrain Catholicism.[135] Another brother, Edmund, became a seminary priest. He had formerly been a tutor to the future Jesuit John Gerard. He hoped, as it was reported in 1601, that the schemes of Sir Robert Cecil to control the succession would be defeated, and, as for James Stuart, it would be possible to 'wrest the sceptre out of his hands'.[136] Lewis Lewkenor, one of Thomas's sons, had an extraordinarily chequered career. After serving as a Spanish pensioner and mercenary he returned to England in the 1590s, conformed and wrote government-sponsored material against the Spaniards. He subsequently acquired an influential position at the Jacobean Court. Then, as the prospect of a successful Anglo-Spanish dynastic treaty approached in the late 1610s, he converted, it seems, back to Catholicism.[137] George Lewkenor of Chichester and his family were recusants in James's reign.[138] John Colpes, Sir Richard Lewkenor's brother-in-law, had a son who was a notable recusant, though he eventually conformed.[139]

Thus, even if the head of a particular gentry or noble family might very much have liked to see and sustain an outwardly conformist front among his relatives, he might find that this was not always possible.

The greatest Catholic 'conformist' in the county was, in fact, the first Viscount Montague himself. It appears that he never subscribed to many of the Counter-Reformation ideals which are generally assumed to have been at the core of the Elizabethan Catholic movement. Traditionally he has been accounted a 'loyalist'.[140] But in his entourage and household there were people whom the regime believed were not as loyal as their master.[141]

Montague's friend Sir Thomas Sackville, Lord Buckhurst, whose daughter married Montague's grandson and heir (the second viscount), was one of the mainstays of county government. But even the Sackville family's outward

---

[135] Hasler, *HC*, II, 475. One of Thomas Lewkenor's daughters married Francis Neville who, as we saw, in the late 1570s was suspected of recusant tendencies.

[136] Anstr. I, 210; *CSPD 1601–3*, 37.

[137] A. J. Loomie, *The Spanish Elizabethans* (New York, 1963), 10–11, 117–18; *CSPD 1581–90*, 603–4; CRS 52, 219; Lewis Lewkenor, 'The Estate of English Fugitives under the King of Spaine and his Ministers. Containing Besides, a Discourse of the Sayd Kings Manner of Government, and the Injustice of Many Late Dishonorable Practises by Him Contrived', in A. Clifford (ed.), *The State Papers and Letters of Sir Ralph Sadler* (2 vols., Edinburgh, 1809), II, 208–33; unpublished HPT biography by Alan Davidson of Lewis Lewkenor; CRS 68, 105. One of his sons became a Jesuit. Another son of Thomas Lewkenor, Samuel, also subsequently an MP, had Catholic sympathies.

[138] *CSPD 1603–10*, 359. See also WSRO, Ep. I/17/16, fos. 10r, 11v.

[139] PRO, C 142/223/64; *VCH Sussex* IV, 123; BL, Additional MS 39414B, fo. 50v; *NAGB*, 92, 95. John Colpes (the younger) assisted George Arden, mayor of Chichester (and son of the MP Lawrence Arden) against his opponents in the city during James's reign, some of whom accused Arden of being popishly inclined, PRO, STAC 8/22/12, mem. 6a.

[140] A. Pritchard, *Catholic Loyalism in Elizabethan England* (1979), 44–9.

[141] See ch. 5, pp. 176–8, and ch. 6, pp. 197–206 below.

face as a pillar of the establishment was not entirely unproblematical. Their Catholic associations were far from purely passive ones, at least in the case of Thomas Sackville, Lord Buckhurst's youngest son (brother-in-law to the second Viscount Montague). He, like Buckhurst's son-in-law Sir Henry Glemham, became involved in some rather questionable intrigues in Rome as the death of the queen approached.[142] (Many of Buckhurst's household and family were Catholic, probably more than is generally realised.[143])

It is easy to see, from this rather brief glance at leading, though ideologically very diverse, lights in the local Catholic firmament in Sussex, why the whole question of occasional conformity, or 'church papistry', as some contemporaries chose to call it, was so crucial.

KINSHIP NETWORKS IN EARLY MODERN ARISTOCRATIC AND GENTRY LOCAL POLITICAL CULTURE

If, then, Catholics continued, even while they were excluded from holding office, to maintain a visible presence within a locality, and were not merely a small and huddled group of put-upon and persecuted nonentities, it must be worth investigating the nexuses between the major Catholic families in the region. What sort of fit was there between, on the one hand, the alleged influence and power of the spider's web of popery detected by Protestant polemicists and the regime's more ideologically committed agents and, on the other, the actual connections and communication between Catholic social and kin networks? Inevitably, any answer to this question involves a good deal of speculation. Undoubtedly, in many cases, marriages between families which we describe as 'Catholic' may have been entered into for reasons which had nothing to do with religion. Indeed, sometimes the label 'Catholic' which we assign to a family is a guess based in part or whole on its having contracted a marriage with another family which we also call 'Catholic'.

But the policy on the marriage market of some of the leading Catholics of the period was to arrange clearly Catholic matches for their children, often outside their own county.[144] A brief glance at the heralds' visitations

---

[142] *HMCS* XII, 309–10, 565–7; Hasler, *HC*, II, 196; A. J. Loomie, 'Spain and the English Catholic Exiles' (Ph.D., London, 1957), 535–6. Thomas Sackville went abroad with Sir Henry Neville, the future Baron Abergavenny, who married Thomas's sister Mary. Neville had Catholic sympathies and, though in the 1606 session of parliament he helped to draft a Commons address for the better execution of the recusancy statutes, in the 1610s he became a professed Catholic. He married into the Vaux family of Northamptonshire. See the HPT biography of Neville by Alan Davidson.

[143] See ch. 3, pp. 85–7 below.

[144] See e.g. H. S. Reinmuth, 'Lord William Howard (1563–1640) and his Catholic Associations', *RH* 12 (1973–4), 226–34, at pp. 229–31, concluding that Howard's 'marriage arrangements for his children may be explained by geography, strengthening the family's

for major post-Reformation Sussex families such as Browne (Viscount Montague), Caryll, Gage, Copley, Shelley and Thatcher seems to provide evidence of a Catholicised clan mentality.[145] Some of the most powerful Catholic gentry connections were to be found in the familial links between those who owned property on both sides of the Hampshire/Sussex border, for example the Poundes, Cottons and Chaddertons, and the Poles, Henslowes and Cuffaulds.[146] The kin relationships and marital alliances within and between the major Catholic gentry families can be followed up in the numerous mentions of each other in last wills and testaments and other legal documents.[147]

Let us consider, then, the principal aristocratic power blocs in and around the county. Taking 'Catholic' to mean politically and religiously 'conservative', it is evident that Catholic political influence was shared at the start of Elizabeth's reign between several aristocratic families with interests in the county.[148]

After the virtual collapse of the former Howard interest (with its huge share of the county's parliamentary representation) around the time of Henry VIII's death, the leading aristocratic figure in Sussex was Henry Fitzalan, twelfth earl of Arundel. Arundel is now a somewhat forgotten figure, remembered, if at all, primarily as one of Elizabeth's lesser suitors. Yet R. J. W. Swales has demonstrated that, mid-century, he was a very ambitious courtier with a predatory territorial and political agenda. He was a privy councillor in 1546. The number of his manors in Sussex increased from thirty-five in 1525 to forty-nine by 1547. He continued to purchase property and acquire offices (such as the stewardship of the Petworth honour).[149] Though temporarily eclipsed under Edward,[150] he became Mary's lord steward of the household.

One of the key features of mid-century Sussex politics was the Marian religious reaction. Swales suggests that the domination of the county by Lord Thomas Seymour after the breaking of the Howards created a temporary but

---

position in the North', and also as a series of alliances 'with several [other] Catholic families'. With one exception he 'provided his sons and daughters with both Catholic and royalist connections'.

[145] The strength of such links is suggested by the seminarist John Copley's replies to the questions put to him in 1599 by the authorities of the English College in Rome, CRS 54, 21–2.

[146] See Mott, HR, *passim*.   [147] See e.g. Manning, *Religion*, 156–7.

[148] As Roger Manning points out, there was in Sussex 'an over-abundance of peers that was unique among English counties', peers who were principally resident in (even if not equally distributed throughout) the county and were politically active there, Manning, *Religion*, 221. As well as Montague, Buckhurst, Arundel, Lumley and de la Warr, there was the earl of Northumberland at Petworth. Also, the Hampshire-based earl of Southampton's interests stretched into Sussex.

[149] R. J. W. Swales, 'Local Politics and the Parliamentary Representation of Sussex 1529–1558' (Ph.D., Bristol, 1964), 13, 20.

[150] Though he was instrumental in putting down the civil unrest in the county during 1549 he was imprisoned by John Dudley, duke of Northumberland in late 1551, *ibid.*, 19.

polarising imbalance. The Catholics came back all the harder at Mary's accession. This stimulated the growth of alternative Catholic power structures to Arundel's. Sir Anthony Browne, created Viscount Montague by Mary, started a rapid rise to prominence in the county. He became lord lieutenant in 1558. With his father-in-law Sir John Gage and other members of the Gage family he was one of the agents of the Marian reaction. Sir John Gage was a friend and colleague of Sir William Fitzwilliam, earl of Southampton, whose estate had fallen to Southampton's stepbrother, Sir Anthony Browne (the first viscount's father).[151]

In turn this Marian assertion of Catholic power in Sussex led to another reaction on Elizabeth's accession. Sir Richard Sackville was the queen's cousin, and the Sackvilles came to dominate county politics in a way that Arundel soon no longer could (even though, as Swales points out, the Sackvilles had been Arundel's dependants).

Although Montague may have been on the outer fringes of the plots from 1569 to 1572, those principally damaged by the revelations about Catholic support for the duke of Norfolk were Arundel and his son-in-law Lord Lumley who also had interests in the county.[152] Roger Manning argues, undoubtedly correctly, that the difference in fortunes between Catholic aristocratic blocs led to conflict between them, with the new nobility of Sackville and Montague winning out over the old nobility – Arundel and Lumley. Montague and Arundel were, it seems, probably somewhat (if not irretrievably) opposed politically in 1559 and 1560 over foreign policy questions. Arundel isolated himself by trying to thwart the regime's intervention in Scotland. Montague collaborated with the regime's policy here by serving as envoy to Philip II to persuade the Spanish Court to support Elizabeth's policy against the French in Scotland.[153] In Manning's words, the conservative and Catholic peers were 'hopelessly divided among themselves and given over to factional rivalries'. The regime could divide and rule and thus keep the peace. In the process it effected 'a gradual transfer of power from the old Catholic nobility and their followers to the new Protestant aristocracy', notably when the lord lieutenancy was, in November 1569, conferred on Buckhurst and Montague (though, of course, Montague was not a Protestant) and Lord De La Warr, who had laid evidence against Lumley for conspiracy in the run up to the 1569 rebellion.[154] In July 1572 Montague wrote to William More at Loseley

---

[151] For recent research on Sir John Gage, see D. Potter, 'Sir John Gage, Tudor Courtier and Soldier (1479–1556)', *English Historical Review* 117 (2002), 1109–46. Potter plays down the extent of Montague's political influence in Mary's reign, *ibid.*, 1144.

[152] See Manning, *Religion*, 226–7.

[153] S. Alford, *The Early Elizabethan Polity* (Cambridge, 1998), 177–8. See ch. 4, pp. 130–6 below.

[154] Manning, *Religion*, 221, 222, 223 n. 1. Manning argues that 'although the White Horse, the Fitzalan badge, still commanded a following in Sussex, the source of Arundel's power was essentially royal service and not feudal loyalty', *ibid.*, 225.

concerning reports that a servant of his, Philip Mellersh, had been defaming Arundel and Lumley.[155]

Montague may simply have been doing his best to preserve peace and harmony in the county. But the tension and dislike between these peers went back a long way. In June 1563 Arundel had written from Nonsuch to Sir William Cecil concerning the purchase of the manor of Godalming. Arundel very much wanted to buy this manor from the queen. He believed that he could offer more than Montague would be able to pay for it. Arundel fumed that, as for Montague, 'hee hath, by his father, his unkel [Sir William Fitzwilliam] and hymself, sukked a gret deal of land' from Elizabeth's father, brother and sister, 'without geving any thing to them' in return. 'First, his unkel had all that hee lyved on' from Henry VIII, 'saving the lands of Cowdray that he bought of the heirs, which passed not four score pounds'. 'Sir Anthonye Browne had all that hee lyved on of King Henry freely; and of the yong king Edward, what hee would choose; yea, that which the king his father would never have left.' Also, 'this man had, of the queen that last was, a hundryd pounds land of that hee wold choose, for service yet to come (to speke yt merilie). Now then methinkyth hee hath no wrong, in consideration, that hee hath layd out no monie for hyt, nor the queen passyd the book for his assurance.'[156]

In Manning's analysis, the regime's easily realised objective was to set Catholics against each other without alienating the loyalists among them. This would keep 'the Catholic gentry politically quiescent'.[157] In the election contest over the knights of the shire in October 1584 the opposition to Buckhurst's nominations, led by Herbert Pelham and George Goring, came from the remainder of the Fitzalan faction. But it failed in the face of Buckhurst's dominance in the east of the county and Montague's in the west. Montague, however, was not reappointed as lord lieutenant, and the transition was finally made from an era of Catholic aristocratic authority to a Protestant/conformist one with Buckhurst now ruling supreme.

And yet it is possible to make out a case that this carefully crafted gradual extinction of aristocratic Catholic influence in the county is not the whole story. For, while Catholic peers were formally excluded from county government, this did not mean that their entourages' Catholicism was necessarily neutralised or sanitised.

For instance, the following of Henry Wriothesley, second earl of Southampton (which extended into Sussex from across the border in Hampshire) was politically quite radical. One of the earl's first cousins was a gentleman called Thomas Pounde. Pounde's trials and tribulations are known to us principally because of his association with the missionary Jesuit

---

[155] Loseley MSS, 624.   [156] BL, Harleian MS 6990, fo. 59r.
[157] Manning, *Religion*, 224.

and martyr Edmund Campion, executed in December 1581. Pounde, who became a Jesuit though not a priest, took part at this time in theological debates with the noted London ministers Henry Tripp and Robert Crowley. Pounde had, indeed, been a thorn in the side of authority in Hampshire for years as he promoted resistance to the ecclesiastical settlement in the county. In 1586 it was reported that he was voicing tacit approval of Spanish aggression towards Elizabeth: 'the causes' that 'forren forces' had come against the queen 'was by reason of robberyes and pyracies'. Much later, in 1606, he admitted that, in 1586–7, he had kept a picture of Mary Stuart on the wall of his prison chamber.[158] Catholic clergy in the Southampton retinue included John Butler who was sought in connection with the Babington plot in 1586.[159]

Among other families attached to the earl of Southampton's following which produced out-and-out recusants were the Chaddertons of Portsmouth (who also held property in Sussex) and the Cottons of Warblington. Henry Chadderton was a friend of Elizabeth Shelley, wife to Sir Thomas Guildford and sister-in-law therefore to Mary Wriothesley, her brother William Shelley's first wife.[160] Chadderton (who converted to Catholicism through the agency of Thomas Pounde) was, from his own account, a mocker and scorner of the authorities in Sussex before he eventually left to train for ordination on the Continent.[161] His father was godfather to the priest John Pounde who was the Jesuit Thomas Pounde's brother.[162] Gilbert Wells (of Brambridge)'s sister Gertrude married William Stanney of Eston in Sussex, and she remarried Henry Chadderton's brother Thomas.[163] Thus Chadderton's brother was (probably) stepfather of the Jesuit Thomas Stanney. Stanney, who entered the Society in 1589, had been in England since the mid-1580s. Gilbert Wells, brother of the celebrated martyr Swithin Wells, was, with Thomas Dymock, an executor of the second earl of Southampton's will of June 1581. Swithin had once been the earl's tutor. Dymock was

[158] Foley III, 595, 615. See ch. 5, pp. 157, 159–60 below.
[159] *CSPD 1591–4*, 502; Anstr. I, 59. In Southampton House in London, Butler occupied the chamber next to that of Robert Gage who was executed in 1586 for his part in the plot.
[160] CRS 54, 53; Berry, *Sussex*, 62–3.
[161] CRS 54, 52ff; Anstr. I, 68; Bindoff, *HC*, I, 606. Chadderton was named Henry after the second earl of Southampton. Chadderton's reconciler was a priest called Richard Stephens, formerly Bishop John Jewel's secretary. Stephens was the ecclesiastical companion of the Catholic Court party of the later 1570s. He had reconciled some of them to the Church of Rome. He was resident with Lady Guildford, Anstr. I, 334–5. As Mott notes, Campion was believed to have confessed that 'one Stephens' brought Pounde 'to speak with Campion at Throgmorton House in London', and 'Pounde directed Campion by a token' to Thomas Dymock, the second earl of Southampton's servant, in order that Campion should speak to the earl himself (though whether such a meeting actually took place is unknown), Mott, *HR*, 541; Foley III, 650.
[162] CRS 54, 53.   [163] Mott, *HR*, 471.

arrested, with Swithin, after the exposure of the Babington plot.[164] Agnes Mott speculates that Henry Wells, another brother, probably lived at Titchfield, where the earl had his principal residence in the county, Titchfield Abbey.[165]

Although the young third earl of Southampton divested himself of his Catholicism before James's accession,[166] the Cottons still regarded themselves as part of his affinity and their oppositionism got them into trouble in the middle of James's reign when, as we have already noted, John Cotton was accused of writing the inflammatory tract called 'Balaam's Ass'. He was arrested as he made his way to Southampton House (where Catholic clergymen were still made welcome despite the third earl's 'puritanism') to take refuge.[167] The third earl had been closely associated with Robert Devereux, earl of Essex. Essex himself attracted something of a Catholic following in the run-up to his apocalyptic showdown in 1601 with his opponents on the privy council. It seems likely that some of the Catholic affinity of the Wriothesley family looked also in that direction, for example the priest Simon Fennell (formerly resident with Jane Shelley, wife of the Throckmorton conspirator William Shelley), who was often at Southampton House, and who also found a welcome with the keeper of the Wardrobe and future chancellor of the exchequer, Sir John Fortescue, another (though low-key) supporter of the earl of Essex.[168]

---

[164] Paul, HR, 105; HRO, 5M53/282.

[165] Mott, HR, 473. In August 1587 it was reported to Lord Burghley that Gilbert Wells's brother Henry was resident in Purbeck; Purbeck was the birthplace of the Jesuit Thomas Stanney, HMCS III, 279; Mott, HR, 471. For Swithin Wells's active links with other Catholic families in the region, see his confession (dated speculatively to 1587) of his recent movements. He made abode at Weton in Berkshire at the house of Francis Parkins, his nephew, before Christmas, and, among other residences, visited Mr Coles's house in the parish of Berington. Then he went to his cousin George Cotton at Warblington, to Anthony Kempe of Slindon, and to the Shelley family at Michelgrove, PRO, SP 12/206/77, fo. 167r. Mott, HR, 489, notes, from Richard Challoner's martyrology, that Stanney was 'soon after his coming into England . . . conducted by Mr Wells down into the West of England, and settled there in the house of a certain gentleman' in which place, Stanney, by catechising, brought hundreds to the Catholic faith. In 1588 George Cotton and Gilbert Wells were both prisoners at Wisbech Castle, Mott, HR, 473. George Cotton was a close neighbour of Thomas Pounde and they were associated in Catholic proselytising, Foley III, 576–7. Cotton was, with other gentlemen, arrested in early 1603 as the authorities pre-emptively immobilised possible exploiters of any uncertainty over the succession, HMCS XII, 676.

[166] As G. P. V. Akrigg notes, the Southampton household continued to have Catholic associations. In January 1605 John Chamberlain recorded that popish books had been confiscated in Southampton House. Akrigg remarks that when the third earl 'could do a good turn for his former co-religionists by the discreet use of his influence, or by taking nominal possession of estates that Catholic families such as the Uvedales and Philpots had forfeited to the law, he did so', Akrigg, *Southampton*, 180–1.

[167] HMCA, 355–81.

[168] HMCS IV, 402–3; Anstr. I, 115; PRO, SP 12/248/95, 102. Fennell also had ties with Viscount Montague's household and at one time was able to move around Sussex by donning Montague's livery, PRO, SP 12/248/99.

Of course, the entourages of both the second and third earls of Southampton might be thought rather volatile and unrepresentative. But, as this study hopes to show, the following of the Viscounts Montague in the later sixteenth and early seventeenth centuries was, if not quite so mercurial, at least as complex and extensively networked as that of the Wriothesleys, and it similarly created routes for the expression and dissemination of Catholic ideas and aspirations.

CONCLUSION

We should not lose sight of the fact that there was a real struggle between Catholicism and Protestantism in post-Reformation England. But only a small part of that struggle took place within the weird world of the spies, professional intelligencers and plotters whose activities have traditionally filled the pages of histories of post-Reformation English Catholicism. At the same time, the complexities of Catholicism and Protestantism (so multifaceted that it is virtually impossible to talk coherently of single phenomena called 'Catholicism' and 'Protestantism') meant that there was never any straightforward battle between the regime and some unitary dissident Roman Catholic bloc. Sometimes Catholicism showed itself perilously uncompliant. At other times it could almost merge with the established order of things. There were many possible positions in between. That there is no one adequate description of what Catholicism was like perhaps tells us, paradoxically, what Catholicism was like – not a uniform entity but a conglomeration of social attitudes, political allegiances, parish frictions, marital links and patronage/clientage connections. After 1559 there were many aspects of what historians have chosen to term Catholicism, often fragmented and subfragmenting – conservatism, clericalism, several species of political dissent, evangelical (or at least evangelising) fervour, loyalism, church papistry, separatist recusancy and so on. One cannot describe, therefore, the development of dissenting Catholicism as nothing more than a retreat into a seigneurial and virtually dormant existence, or even a 'parish Anglicanism' which was merely a cover for a Catholicism which dared not, or could not be bothered to, speak its name. There was certainly no single social or political or religious structure which we can label exclusively as Catholicism. But certain patterns of behaviour, informed by particular political, social and religious structures, often looked to contemporaries like Catholicism (though they frequently disagreed about how to describe it, just as they disagreed about how it should be treated and dealt with).

Here it makes sense, I think, to try to resurrect a range of contemporary Catholic existence and experience through the exploration of the people and connections within a specific entourage (involving patron-and-client, kin, tenurial and other relationships). In the first instance I have concentrated on one specific, though extensive, aristocratic entourage, namely that of the Browne family. But I have attempted to recover this entourage not so much for the purpose of writing a family history but rather to find a way into a world of aristocratic political and ecclesiastical thought and experience, in order to see how far the entourage's concerns, opinions, character and aims confirm or question traditional narratives and descriptions of the post-Reformation Catholic community in England.

3

The emergence of a Catholic dynasty: the Brownes of Cowdray

The Browne family was very much a newcomer in the ranks of the sixteenth-century nobility. But the Brownes had, for some years, been notching up marriages with peerage families, old and new, and continued to do so. Elizabeth, the eldest daughter of Sir Anthony Browne, Henry VII's standard bearer who had died in 1506, married Henry Somerset, earl of Worcester. Lucy, the second daughter, married Sir Thomas Clifford, the third son of the earl of Cumberland; and the third daughter, Anne, married Charles Brandon, duke of Suffolk.[1] As the family rose to prominence, the aristocratic marital networking carried on. Sir Anthony Browne (Henry VII's standard bearer's son), who was a close friend of Henry VIII and father of the first Viscount Montague, remarried, shortly before his death, Elizabeth, daughter of the ninth earl of Kildare. The first viscount himself married first the daughter of Robert Radcliffe, earl of Sussex,[2] and secondly Magdalen, daughter of Lord William Dacre of Gillesland. Mary, the first viscount's sister, married Lord John Grey of Pirgo, son of the marquis of Dorset.[3]

What was the family's aristocratic self-image? The Brownes, perhaps wisely, hardly ever spoke explicitly about their ambitions and their view of themselves. And on many contemporary political questions they may actually not have had a great deal to say. In the British Library's Harleian manuscripts, however, there is a hastily drawn pedigree, dating from 1615, of the Brownes and their relatives.[4] The pedigree traces, as the catalogue states, related descents of 'Spencer, Marshall, Bruer, and de Cardurcis, Tiptofte, de Clare, Badelesmere, Wentworth, Montacute [Montague], Mount-Hermer, Holland, Neville, and Stoner'. It seems to tell us something about the Browne family's

---

[1] For the Brandon marriage, which was an utter disaster and ended with Anne Browne's early death, see S. Gunn, *Charles Brandon, Duke of Suffolk c. 1484–1545* (Oxford, 1988), 28.

[2] Berry, *Sussex*, 354.

[3] J. Nicholls, *The Progresses and Public Processions of Queen Elizabeth* (3 vols., New York, 1823), I, 93–4.

[4] BL, Harleian MS 1195, no. 1, fo. 1v. The pedigree ends with the second Viscount Montague, who is described as 'the Lord Montacute now living 1615'.

self-image (in the early seventeenth century) within the web of marital relationships that the family inhabited, although we do not know who actually
compiled it. With its emphasis on the fifteenth-century Neville antecedents
of the Viscounts Montague, the pedigree proclaims an essentially, or mainly,
Yorkist identity for the family (even though Richard Smith, Lady Magdalen
Browne's chaplain, described her husband, Sir Anthony Browne, as 'the issue
of the most famous Marquess Montague (who descended both of the house
of Lancaster and of the most ancient nobility of England)'.[5] It declares the
importance of the (otherwise, one might think, rather tangential) relationship of the Browne family to the Nevilles of Brancepeth (who obtained the
title of earl of Westmorland), the Montagues, earls of Salisbury, and the
successor by marriage to the title of earl of Salisbury, namely Sir Richard
Neville, whose daughter Cicely married Richard, duke of York (and gave
birth to the future Edward IV), and whose son, the earl of Warwick, was the
'kingmaker'.[6] The pedigree descends through the political dynasties of the
Nevilles and Plantaganets down to Lucy,[7] third daughter of John Neville,
marquis of Montague, brother of the 'kingmaker', who was, with the 'kingmaker', killed at the battle of Barnet in 1471. She took as her second husband
Sir Anthony Browne, grandfather of the first Viscount Montague. (Her first
husband was Sir Thomas Fitzwilliam of Aldwark, near Rotherham, and her
son by this marriage was the Fitzwilliam earl of Southampton whose death
brought the Cowdray estate to the Brownes.[8]) Among the paintings recorded
as hanging at Cowdray in 1775 was a set of pieces, apparently all by the
same artist, of the 'Neville family, Lords Raby and earls of Salisbury and
Marquis Montague whose daughter and coheir Lucy married Sir Anthony
Browne about the year 1480'.[9] And on the magnificent funeral monument of
the first viscount and his two wives (see Figures 3 and 4), constructed during
the second viscount's lifetime, the link with the Nevilles is clearly spelt out:
'as he was noblye descended from the Ladye Lucye, his grandmother, one of
the daughters and coheyres of Lord John Nevill, Marques Montague; so he
was perfectly adorned with all the virtues of true nobilitye'.[10]

---

[5] Southern, *ERH*, 14. For the complex fluctuations in the support shown by leading noble
houses, such as the Nevilles, for the rival sides during the Wars of the Roses, see J. Gillingham,
The Wars of the Roses (1981).
[6] Around 1730, George Vertue noticed the portraits at Cowdray of Richard Neville, earl of
Salisbury, and Warwick the 'kingmaker', and observed 'here are pictures belonging to the
Nevils, from thence to the Fitzwilliams and lastly the Mountacute Browns', K. A. Esdaile
et al. (eds.), *Vertue Note Books* (Walpole Society, 6 vols., Oxford, 1930–55), II (vol. 20),
81, 82.
[7] Given in the pedigree as 'Margaret'.   [8] Bindoff, *HC*, II, 142, 145.
[9] BL, Additional MS 5726 E. 5, fo. 22r.
[10] Mosse, *ME*, 72–3. See also S. Adams, 'The Patronage of the Crown in Elizabethan Politics:
The 1590s in Perspective', in S. Adams, *Leicester and the Court* (Manchester, 2002), 68–94,
at p. 73.

Sir Anthony Browne's decision to plump for the title of Montague itself made a rather direct contemporary political statement. It recalled one specific political tradition which the now deceased Henry VIII had particularly feared and loathed. It remembered the partial extirpation by Henry of the Pole family. Henry had at first tried to placate the Poles. Margaret Pole, daughter of the duke of Clarence and mother of the future cardinal, Reginald Pole, had been restored to the Salisbury title. And her eldest son, Reginald's brother Henry, became Baron Montague. The countess was appointed governess to Princess Mary. Not surprisingly the Poles aligned themselves against the divorce and were sucked into the treasons of the late 1530s with ghastly and fatal results.[11] The choice of the Montague title in 1554 was a reference, therefore, to a recent Henrician political martyr. It may conceivably have been a self-association with the imminent return to England of Reginald Pole, the great enemy of Henry's massive ecclesiastical pretensions.

The importance of the title is reflected in the suit which Viscount Montague brought against Sir Edward Montague (knighted in 1568). The viscount alleged that Sir Edward was using the arms of John, marquis of Montague

> whose right heire so farre as concerneth his armes and parte of his landes the said Viscount Mountague by descent is from the Lady Lucye, eldest daughter of the five daughters of the said John, Marques Mountague, and doth beare the same without a difference, as also the coate armes of Mounthermer, earle of Gloucester whose heire also by the said marquis the said viscount nowe is.

The viscount protested that Sir Edward should be called to show just cause 'whie hee ought to beare the same', and, since the viscount reckoned he could not, forbear to do so henceforth.[12]

Of course, the Brownes' political significance might be thought to have diminished to virtually nothing after Viscount Montague lost his privy council seat following Mary Tudor's death.[13] But it is worth speculating how the various marital connections of the family might have continued to confer a political character and identity on the Brownes' entourage. To do this, it will be necessary to retrace in some detail those connections, even if the names in question are often far from household ones in other accounts of the period. But, in the absence of any real surviving archive of personal papers

---

[11] Bindoff, *HC*, III, 115.

[12] BL, Additional MS 38139, fo. 185v. Sir Edward Montague replied that 'the said viscount is not right heire (so farre as concerneth the armes of the howse of Mountague) vizt not right heire to Allice sole daughter and heire of Thomas Mountague, earle of Sarum'. See also Godfrey Goodman, ed. J. S. Brewer, *The Court of King James the First* (2 vols., 1839), II, 109.

[13] See ch. 4, p. 117 below.

and correspondence, this series of links is, by default, the only way initially to grasp the contours of the Brownes' circle and following, and the potential extent of their patronage network.

Merely to recount, however, to the last degree, who was married to whom in this extended aristocratic clan would be both painfully boring and arguably pointless since the end product would be little more than a narrative of interlocking family trees. At the best of times, discussion of genealogy can be extremely convoluted and off-putting. Linda Peck has rightly remarked that within the 'small *élite*' of 'as highly structured a society as sixteenth- and seventeenth-century England', 'almost everyone was related to someone else of standing if not *everyone* else (even if not interred next to them)'.[14]

What I am interested in is what the 'who-was-married-and-related-to-whom' evidence actually meant to those who were locked into these structures. Sometimes there is virtually no indication that a major marriage alliance between aristocratic families had any immediate significance. At other times, even very indirect and distant family connections can be shown, by a chance remark or incident, to have been immediately relevant, even crucial to the functioning of a family and its dependants. Now, one might imagine that predominantly Catholic kin networks were of little political relevance in the post-Reformation period anyway, since such connections could never have been anything more than a linkage of the politically dispossessed. But the reader must temporarily suspend disbelief for a time and accept that the kinship networks, which David Cressy, for one, has demonstrated were so fundamental to early modern understandings of the family, functioned in the same way for Catholics as for others, and, indeed, were particularly important to Catholics for whom they represented a means of investing in the social and political establishment from which in many senses they were excluded. As Cressy comments, in this period 'affinal and consanguinal ties alike provided a basis for sympathy, linkage and collaboration'. Kinship 'involved a range of possibilities' which 'began with acknowledgement, advice and support, stretched to financial help and career encouragement, and also included emotional comfort and political solidarity'. Most of the modern academic debate about the extent of kinship awareness in the early modern period is about how far such awareness existed below the level of the gentry. However, the evidence uncovered in the course of this debate, by historians such as Cressy, also reaffirms how strong kinship ties were at

[14] L. L. Peck, 'Goodwin *v.* Fortescue: The Local Context of Parliamentary Controversy', *Parliamentary History* 3 (1984), 33–56, at p. 44. See also W. Hunt, *The Puritan Moment* (1983), 220.

the social level of the gentry and above. The gentry, Cressy remarks, 'were chronically fascinated by family history and often knew their lineage and blood ties across several degrees and generations'.[15]

We have a few surviving accounts by contemporary Catholics of exactly how pivotal kin networks were for them, and how these networks were informed by their religion. Thomas Meynell of North Kilvington in York-shire, whose father, Roger, was attainted for his part in the 1569 rebellion, himself experienced imprisonment and sequestration for his recusancy in Elizabeth's reign.[16] He wrote an account of his family (in his 'book of evi-dences', which John Aveling calls 'a typical product of the contemporary interest in genealogy and medieval descents').[17] This account deliberately tied in his Catholicism with his family connections and associations. It was virtually a roll-call, in fact, of northern dissident Catholicism. Having already depicted an intensely Catholic kin circle established by his own marriages and those of his immediate forebears (with families such as the Greens, Pudseys, Lawsons, Cattericks, Thwaiteses, Inglebies, Stapletons, Lamberts, Radcliffes, Fenwicks and Constables – 'there was ever an ancient league of friendshippe betwixte the Constables of Burton Constable and mine aunces-ters'), Meynell said he would 'set downe such names as I am the nearest allied unto, and do most affect, especially sich as I have had no occasion to nominate before', including, *inter alia*, other 1569 rebel families such as the Tempests.[18]

If we were, in the absence of this manuscript genealogical account written by Thomas Meynell, to trace out all Meynell's connections by marriage, as he does, this would look like mere antiquarianism. And yet his account of his kin makes it clear that even relationships which technically were rather distant (for example his first wife's brother's daughter's marriage into the Catholic Thatcher family in Sussex) were an intense and immediate reality for him (and perhaps also for those whom he named).[19] Meynell's account is phrased in terms of religious purity (his daughter Elizabeth, he says, 'is a virtuous maide', and she 'consecrated hir virginitie to pure divinitie') allied to social exclusivity and a perceived right to constant upward social mobility;

---

[15] D. Cressy, 'Kinship and Kin Interaction in Early Modern England', *Past and Present* 113 (1986), 38–69, at pp. 48, 49.

[16] See J. C. H. Aveling, *Northern Catholics* (1966), 74–5, 125–7, 145–6.   [17] CRS 56, xix.

[18] *Ibid.*, 4–9, 11. As Aveling notes, the Meynell family's 'alliances had an increasingly Catholic core, but still stretched out to cover many church-papists and Protestants who were "dear friends"'. He was on particularly good terms, however, with those who were zealous Catholics, such as William Middleton of Stockeld, the Lascelles family of Brakenbrough, the Gascoignes of Barnbow and the Pudseys, *ibid.*, xx–xxi.

[19] *Ibid.*, 8.

he proudly and regularly drops names of leading northern noble families to which he was allied.[20]

It was easy for contemporaries to see how those Catholic family affiliations could translate into practical political realities. For example, when Catholic gentry families clubbed together to fight off predatory recusancy commissioners, this was a demonstration of how blood and marital kinship could take on a serious local political significance. A recusancy commission's enquiry into Meynell's own landed property was stymied by a less than impartial jury. To some this resembled political conspiracy as much as mere social cohesion and gentry class solidarity. According to a report delivered to Bishop Tobias Mathew, the wrong sort of people sitting on the recusancy commission's jury (rigged by a new precept delivered to the commissioners after a perfectly good and reliable jury had been empanelled) had included 'manie . . . frends' of Meynell and another recusant, Christopher Conyers. Among these friends was George Holtby 'who marryed Mennells syster and is a nere kynsman to Holtbye the seminarie priest', i.e. the notorious Jesuit Richard Holtby.[21]

MARRIAGE ALLIANCES AND THE BROWNES

The crucial and defining marriage compacts entered into by the first Viscount Montague were with the Dacre and Dormer families. Both these families were, by and large, Catholic and were opposed to most of the Reformation's processes. The Carthusian Sebastian Newdigate, brother of Jane Dormer, was executed in 1535 for denying the supremacy.[22] Ironically, Jane's husband Robert was one of the hostile jurymen selected by Cromwell to sit in Westminster Hall in May 1536 and to condemn the alleged accomplices of Anne Boleyn.[23] As is well known, the Dacre family got involved, with disastrous results, in the latter stages of the 1569 northern rising. Magdalen Dacre had been taken by the first Viscount Montague as his second wife (after the death in 1552 of his first, Jane Radcliffe). In the hagiography of Lady Magdalen, written after her death by her chaplain Richard Smith, Smith noted that 'whiles she was a married woman she fell into an extreme and continual grief and affliction of mind upon the ruin of her family, procured, as she sometimes said, by him in whom she had placed the hope of best relief thereof'. This was an acid reference to the duke of Norfolk, who had

[20] *Ibid.*, 8.
[21] *Ibid.*, 47–8. For another instance of a recusancy commission being subverted by sympathetic gentry relatives, see J. A. Hilton, 'Catholic Recusancy in County Durham, 1559–1625' (M. Phil., Leeds, 1974), 130, 133.
[22] Bindoff, *HC*, II, 52, III, 12.   [23] E. W. Ives, *Anne Boleyn* (Oxford, 1986), 385.

through his own family marriage policy alienated his Dacre relatives before the rebellion began.[24] (Viscount Montague, her husband, had allegedly tried to dissuade Leonard Dacre from becoming embroiled in the rebellion.[25])

Smith claimed that God's compassion had served to cure Lady Magdalen of her 'melancholy affliction' after physicians and friends had failed. For she had a dream in which God granted her effectual and inward consolation on condition of performing 'a very pious action', which was no sooner performed than 'she was instantly cured of that affliction of mind, which no human art, medicine, or counsel could prevail in'.[26]

This may be a coded way of telling us that she decided it was prudent to shelve any thoughts of revenge against those whom she held responsible for the destruction of the Dacre inheritance. In any event, she was herself largely sheltered, it seems, from the possible retribution which the regime could have inflicted on her for her Catholic inclinations. Other members of the Dacre family were not quite so quiescent, prudent or fortunate. Francis, one of the brothers of the rebel Lord Dacre, became a wandering malcontent.[27] After he failed to recover his property, in part because of the opposition of Lord William Howard, Dacre left the country for Scotland.[28] He vowed loyalty to Elizabeth but consorted with virtually anyone who would promise to restore to him, when the queen should die, that which he considered rightfully his. One of those whom Dacre approached for aid and hospitality after reaching Spain in 1592 was a leading member of the other noble house with which the Brownes contracted marital alliance, namely Jane Dormer, duchess of Feria, a focus and magnet for English Catholic exiles. Dacre had formulated a proposal for a Spanish landing in the West of Scotland – a prelude to an armed invasion across England's northern border with the aim of raising Dacre retainers and sympathisers. Dacre was, however, eventually dropped by the duchess, and was kept at arm's length also by the former Marian privy councillor Sir Francis Englefield. This may have been because Dacre too openly supported the claims of James VI. (Englefield was one of the leaders of the Hispanophile party among the English Catholics, people who were less than whole-hearted champions of James's rights.)

---

[24] Southern, *ERH*, 52. Smith's work is based, as he says, on the oration which he 'uttered before a great audience at the funeral of Lady Magdalen', *ibid.*, 3. For the marriage policy of Thomas Howard, duke of Norfolk towards the Dacre daughters, his wards, see *The Lives of Philip Howard, Earl of Arundel, and of Anne Dacres his Wife* (1857), 172–4.

[25] *HMCS* I, 557; ch. 4, p. 144 below.   [26] Southern, *ERH*, 52.

[27] See also ch. 7, pp. 222–8 below.

[28] *CSPD Addenda 1580–1625*, 208–10 (an account of the disorders committed in Morpeth in April 1587 by the supporters of Francis Dacre and Lord William Howard when Dacre turned up there and attempted to enforce his rights). See also BL., Cotton MS Caligula D I, no. 105, fo. 281r (Dacre's letter of 25 July 1588 to Secretary Walsingham, complaining of his property vexations). See also *CSP Scotland 1589–93*, *passim*; CRS 60, 91.

The Brownes' connections with the Dormers who stayed in England were very differently inflected. The Dormers in Buckinghamshire were on good terms with the Russell family (earls of Bedford) and seem to have enjoyed a large measure of protection in consequence. Sir William Dormer (d. 1575) of Heythrop and Wing, father of the duchess of Feria, had married (as his first wife) Mary, the daughter of Sir William Sidney of Penshurst. Dormer was known to be a 'hinderer' of Protestant religion in the 1560s. He was named on a 1574 list of alleged supporters of Mary Stuart, although in 1570 Englefield had claimed that Dormer was 'beset with heretics and breathing their spirit'.[29] Dormer was elected knight of the shire for co. Buckingham in 1571 with the second earl of Bedford's support.[30]

The Dormers were, it seems, never dealt with in the post-Reformation period for their Catholicism. This may have been simply because they eschewed the unwise exploits of some of the Elizabethan Catholics. Sir Robert Dormer was overtly loyalist.[31] The Brownes secured, therefore, for their son and heir a match with, in effect, another protected Catholic family. The first viscount's son Anthony[32] married Mary, daughter of Sir William Dormer (by Anne Catesby, his second wife). Their son became the second Viscount Montague when he succeeded his grandfather (who was himself predeceased by his son Anthony a few months before his own death). In addition, Elizabeth, the first viscount's daughter by his Dacre marriage, married Sir Robert Dormer, Sir William Dormer's son. (She was thus the second viscount's aunt.) The references in the Catholic secular clergy's early seventeenth-century correspondence to the activism of the 'old lady Dormer' testifies to the continuing influence over the clan that the first viscount's redoubtable daughter retained into her old age.

There was also a series of other influential sub-connections between the two families. The Dormers were on good terms with the Fortescue family in Buckinghamshire. The leading light of that family in the 1590s was the chancellor of the exchequer, Sir John Fortescue. A good many of his kin were Catholic, and one branch was closely allied with the Pole family in Sussex. (Sir Anthony Fortescue of Racton, comptroller of the household to Cardinal Pole, married Katherine, one of Sir Geoffrey Pole's daughters.) In the seventeenth century one of the Fortescue family, George, a man of letters, friend of Galileo Galilei, and grandson of Sir Anthony Fortescue and

---

[29] Hasler, *HC*, II, 49. For the monuments to the Dormers in Wing parish church, see Figures 11 and 12.

[30] Bedford appears to have secured the seat of Tregony for Dormer's son, Robert, in the same parliament, Hasler, *HC*, II, 49.

[31] *HMCS* IX, 332. Jane Dormer, duchess of Feria had an aversion to the Jesuit Robert Persons, and tended to align herself with the Catholic exiles who opposed the Jesuits, AAW, A IX, no. 69.

[32] By his first (Radcliffe) marriage.

Figure 11.   Funeral monument to Sir William Dormer (d. 1575) and his family
in Wing parish church (All Saints), Buckinghamshire.

Figure 12.   Funeral monument to Sir Robert Dormer, first Baron Dormer (d. 1616) and his family in Wing parish church (All Saints), Buckinghamshire.

Katherine Pole, was heavily involved with the clergy chaplains and clients
of the second Viscount Montague in defending the newly acquired episcopal
authority of Lady Magdalen's former chaplain Richard Smith.[33] As we have
seen, the first Viscount Montague was himself kin to the Pole family. The
Poles gave their support and patronage to several of the second Viscount
Montague's chaplains.[34]

Another family in between the Dormers and the Brownes was that of
Pelham. Dorothy Catesby, who was Sir Robert Dormer's mother, remarried
Sir William Pelham, a client and field commander of the earl of Leicester. Sir
William had been involved in Wyatt's rebellion. However, his half-brother,
Sir Edmund Pelham, who, like Sir William, held legal office in Ireland, was
reckoned to be a close associate of Lady Magdalen and was sympathetic to
her Catholic predilections. Sir Edmund's own wife, Eleanor Darell, was a
Catholic recusant. He may have been some kind of occasional conformist.
He was named as an executor in the first viscount's will.[35] In November 1613
Edward Bennett, Lady Dormer's chaplain, recorded Sir William's widow's
death and noted that 'they say a great estate is fallen to . . . Sir Robert
Dormer'.[36]

The marriage of the Dormers into the very Catholic Constable family of
Burton Constable, itself a constant object of suspicion to the authorities
in the 1580s and 1590s, created a line of communication up country, an
elongated support network along which Catholics could travel all the way
from Cowdray in Sussex to Holderness in the East Riding.[37]

The Brownes' crucial marital alliance, however, as far as their local power
base in Sussex was concerned, was with the well-known and eventually ultra-
Catholic family of Gage. The first viscount's mother was Alice, daughter of
Sir John Gage, the great trader in dissolved monastic institutions' property in
Surrey and Sussex.[38] The Dissolution was a trail of destruction and tenurial
upheaval from which the Brownes, partly through Sir John Gage's help (since
he was a commissioner for the dissolution of Battle Abbey), also profited.[39]

Sir John Gage was one of the most important Henrician politicians in
Sussex. He was a friend of Sir William Fitzwilliam whose entailed estates

[33] AAW, A XXII, no. 69, XXIV, no. 3; Mott, HR, *sub* Fortescue; Allison, JG, 58–9.
[34] See ch. 10, pp. 325–7 below.
[35] Berry, *Sussex*, 314–16; Hasler, *HC*, III, 192; WSRO, SAS/BA 67.
[36] AAW, A XII, no. 195, p. 435.
[37] See the unpublished HPT biography by Simon Healy of Sir Henry Constable of Burton
Constable. Sir Henry Constable's heir, who became Viscount Dunbar, remained a supporter
of those English secular clergymen who most strongly opposed the Jesuits, AAW, B 27,
no. 107.
[38] Bindoff, *HC*, II, 181. Montague was the overseer of Sir Edward Gage's will of December
1565, ESRO, SAS/FB 7/4. Montague owned property in the Gage family's heartland of West
Firle, ESRO, SAS/FB 13/4.
[39] For Sir John Gage's alabaster tomb in the parish church at West Firle, see Figure 13.

Figure 13.   Alabaster tomb chest of Sir John Gage (d. 1556) in the Gage family
chapel in West Firle parish church (St Peter), East Sussex.

came to the Brownes by inheritance. Gage succeeded Fitzwilliam as chancellor of the duchy of Lancaster. He was also comptroller of the royal household. Gage opposed Henry's divorce of Katherine of Aragon,[40] and was a central figure in the conservative reaction against Thomas Cromwell. In Edward's reign he quarrelled with the duke of Somerset, and did not support him against the earl of Warwick, though Gage and Somerset had once been fellow warriors in Henry's military machine. (Gage had fought against both the Scots and the French.) Sir William Paget took Gage's place as comptroller of the royal household and as chancellor of the duchy.[41] As we have already noted, Sussex was dominated by Lord Seymour after the Howards' political disaster of 1546–7. So the stage was set for a Catholic renaissance and reaction as soon as Mary succeeded Edward. Gage and his Browne relatives, marginalised though never quite politically eclipsed under Edward, now moved centre stage. Gage became Mary's lord chamberlain. (He somewhat ingloriously confronted the Wyatt rebels at Charing Cross.)[42]

Sir John died in 1556 but the Gages remained, as a glance at their pedigree reveals, integral to the group of families which we tend to associate with the core of Sussex/south-coast gentry Catholicism, notably the Shelleys, the Copleys, the Guildfords, the Pordages, the Thatchers, the Darells, the Kempes, the Mores, the Ropers and the Crispes, as well as to several instantly recognisable Catholic gentry families further north, for example the Oxfordshire Belsons, the Essex Bendloweses, the Stradlings of Glamorganshire[43] and so on. The Gages certainly stayed close to their Browne cousins. Edward Gage, Sir John

---

[40] Bindoff, *HC*, II, 180.   [41] *Ibid.*, 180.   [42] *Ibid.*, 181; ch. 2, pp. 61–2 above.

[43] Sir Thomas Stradling had acquired various manors in Sussex in 1550, and one in 1555 from Henry Fitzalan, earl of Arundel, who was his political patron, SRS 20, 441, SRS 19, 183; Bindoff, *HC*, III, 394. Sir Thomas sat for East Grinstead in October 1553 and for Arundel in April 1554, and was integral to the Marian Catholic reaction in Sussex. In 1561 he was imprisoned in the Tower for having disseminated copies of a picture of a cross which had miraculously, it was alleged, appeared in a tree damaged by a storm, *CSPD 1547–80*, 176. The story was included in Nicholas Harpsfield's *Dialogi Sex*. (Harpsfield was part of the Pole–Roper family network.) In January 1574 Viscount Montague wrote to Sir Edward Stradling, Sir Thomas's son, about a proposed marriage between one of Montague's friends, Robert Giles, and one of Stradling's sisters, who was a religious exile in the Low Countries. An undated letter written on the same topic from John Gage in Liège to Sir Edward Stradling ('my verie lovinge brother') advertised him of the 'good fortune to yow and your howse, a happie match beinge concluded betwine your syster Mrs Wenchliane Stradlinge and a most deere frinde of mine, Mr Robert Gyles', Traherne, *SC*, 138, 221–2.

The closeness of the Stradling family's link to the Brownes through the Gages is demonstrated by the first viscount's reference, in a letter of May 1583 to Sir Edward Stradling, to 'my cosyn your wiefe', Anne, daughter of Sir Edward Gage. In the same letter Montague appealed to Stradling to assist him over a debt contracted by one Christopher Morgan, cousin to William Carne (presumably a relative of Sir Edward Carne, Montague's fellow ambassador to Rome in 1555). Morgan functioned as Montague's receiver. Sir Edward Carne's father, Hywell, was based near Cowbridge, close to the Stradlings at St Donats. See Traherne, *SC*, 139–40; PRO, SP 12/269/69, fo. 97v. Christopher Morgan may have been a relative of Thomas Morgan (Mary Stuart's servant) and the priest Roland Morgan, Thomas's

Gage's grandson, was executor to the first Viscount Montague. In November 1592 Bishop Anthony Bickley and other recusancy commissioners were instructed by the privy council to release Edward Gage from house arrest for a month 'forsomuch as the said Mr Gage is about matters of accompt and other important business to attend on the funerals of the late Lord Viscount Mountague'.[44] Edward Gage had been allowed out of prison in June 1581 at Montague's own behest to see to the affairs of the recently deceased Henry Wriothesley, second earl of Southampton (Montague's son-in-law), to whom Gage was also an executor.[45] (The second Viscount Montague was named as the sole overseer of the will of John Gage, the long-term recusant who died in 1598. Gage bequeathed him a 'standing cup with a cover of silver and gilt' as a 'poor remembrance of my goodwill'.[46])

The Gages therefore occupied an important space in the web of relationships between the Brownes and their great neighbours to the west, in Hampshire, the Wriothesley earls of Southampton. The Gage connection with the Wriothesleys seems to have been maintained after the death in 1581 of the zealously Catholic second earl. In June 1586 Gervase Pierrepoint confessed that, in the course of his recent travels (which had aroused the regime's suspicions), 'he had been to Mr Edward Gage at his lodging in Southampton House' in London where he found Gage, his wife and his sister Mary

---

brother, Anstr. I, 235. It was alleged also that Sir Edward Stradling's daughter, who married Robert Giles, was part of the notorious Charles Paget–Thomas Morgan faction, aligned with exiles such as the Welsh ecclesiastical careerist Owen Lewis, *HMCS* IV, 6–9. Stradling was also on good terms with Lord Buckhurst, who addressed Stradling as 'cousin' because of Buckhurst's kinship to Stradling's wife, Anne, Traherne, *SC*, 51–2; ESRO, SAS/G 21/47. Katherine, wife of Sir Thomas Copley, also addressed Stradling as 'cousin' (her sister-in-law Margaret was John Gage's second wife), Traherne, *SC*, 223–4. And, in the 1560s, Sir Edward Stradling's sister, Damasyn (d. 1567), was a companion to Jane Dormer, duchess of Feria, *ibid.*, xxi, 342–4. Stradling was 'steward generall' of John, Baron St John's property in Wales, and carried on in the same capacity to John St John, who inherited the title from his father in April 1582 and who addressed Stradling as his 'very good cosen'. The elder Baron St John married Catherine, the daughter of Sir William Dormer, *ibid.*, 124, 125, 127. Anthony Kempe of Slindon addressed Sir Edward Stradling as 'brother'; Kempe had married Margaret, Sir Edward Gage's daughter, in 1569, *ibid.*, 216–17; Berry, *Sussex*, 295.

[44] *APC 1592*, 329.

[45] *Ibid.*, *1581–2*, 93, 296, 376–7. The second earl's funeral appears to have been an openly Catholic affair. Robert Glover, Somerset herald, had to write to the earl of Leicester, on 24 January 1584, to vindicate himself from a charge of popery against him owing to his involvement in the funeral proceedings. Glover claimed that 'even from the bottome' of his heart he did 'detest and abhorre all papistrie', and he acknowledged the queen as 'chiefe and supreme gouvernour' of the Church of England. But in a marginal note he said he had heard that Leicester had been informed that he, Glover, kept company with papists 'and that my behaviour at the late erle of Southamptons funeralles shewed me to be such a one', BL, Cotton MS Titus B VII, no. 7, fo. 14r; B. W. Greenfield, 'The Wriothesley Tomb in Titchfield, Hants: Its Effigial Statues and Heraldry', *Proceedings of the Hampshire Field Club* (1889), 65–82 at pp. 68–9; Bodl., Ashmolean MS 836, fos. 395r, 427r.

[46] Bindoff, *HC*, II, 179; ESRO, SAS/FB 11/12.

Banester.[47] The third earl of Southampton was, in turn, one of Edward Gage's executors.[48] William Shelley (Edward Gage's brother-in-law) had taken as his first wife, Mary, the second earl of Southampton's sister.[49]

The second earl, Henry Wriothesley, had married the first Viscount Montague's daughter Mary. Montague stood surety for his errant son-in-law in the early 1570s when the regime became fed up with Southampton's involvement in the recent conspiracies focused on Mary Stuart and the duke of Norfolk. The association between these two south-coast families went back into the Henrician period. Sir Anthony Browne, Montague's father, had been one of the religious conservatives of the 1540s, and had been closely associated with Earl Henry's father Sir Thomas Wriothesley and Bishop Stephen Gardiner. (Sir Thomas was Gardiner's protégé.) Among Sir Thomas's other children was Mabel who married Sir Walter Sandys. Sandys's aunt Mary had married Sir William Pelham, father of the occasional conformist Sir Edmund Pelham who was such a good friend to Montague's second wife, Lady Magdalen.[50] Another of Henry Wriothesley's sisters, Elizabeth, had married Thomas Radcliffe, Lord Fitzwalter, who succeeded in 1557 to the earldom of Sussex, thus establishing another kinship link between the Wriothesleys and the Brownes, since Montague's first wife, Jane, was a daughter of Robert Radcliffe, first earl of Sussex.[51]

Hovering between the two clans of Browne and Wriothesley in the 1560s we find, as well as the Gages, people such as the courtier, masque organiser for the young queen, and future lay Jesuit, Thomas Pounde. He was, as we noted in the previous chapter, a first cousin of the second earl of Southampton, whose marriage to Mary Browne took place in Montague's residence in Drury Lane on 19 February 1566.[52] (The dowager countess of Southampton did not, however, approve of the match.) Sir William Cecil was there. There was an entertainment organised by Pounde, who made a poetic 'oration' (which, it has to be confessed, is utterly atrocious) in order to accompany 'a brave maske out of the same house all on great horses at the marriage of the young earl of Southampton to the Lord Montagu's daughter about Shrovetyde'. The oration which Pounde composed for the occasion ran (unfortunately) to eighty-seven verses.[53]

---

[47] BL, Lansdowne MS 50, no. 72, printed in J. Strype, *Annals of the Reformation* (4 vols., Oxford, 1824), III, appendix, p. 153.

[48] PRO, PROB 11/123, fo. 420r.

[49] Berry, *Sussex*, 62–3; PRO, SP 12/117/15. William Shelley's nephew, Sir John, was another of Edward Gage's executors, PRO, PROB 11/123, fo. 420r.

[50] Mott, HR, *sub* Sandys and Wriothesley; Berry, *Sussex*, 316.

[51] GEC XII/i, 524. Radcliffe's second wife was Frances, daughter of Sir William Sidney of Penshurst, Kent.

[52] For the marriage settlement, see HRO, 5M53/184, 198.

[53] Mott, HR, 533–4; Bodl., MS Rawlinson Poet. 108.

Apparently the Wriothesley–Browne match was initially a matter of some passion, and the union between the two houses seemed assured. But in the end the marriage turned out to be a catastrophe. It has been suggested that Shakespeare's Capulet–Montague saga in *Romeo and Juliet* is based on the fraught relationship between these two noble houses. But in the real-life version it was the lovers who became murderously hostile. Their families, by contrast, tried to maintain an air of dignity and detachment. The second earl got it into his head by the end of the 1570s that his wife was a rampant adulteress. He therefore removed his heir from her, putting him in the care of his faithful steward, Thomas Dymock.[54] (The second earl's furious jealousy may also have been a source for Shakespeare's *Othello*.[55]) This feud and division accompanied the religious radicalisation of the second earl. He became a Catholic activist just at the time when Catholic seminarist clericalism was itself becoming radicalised. He was on the fringes of the Persons–Campion agitation in 1580–1. As we observed in the previous chapter, his following was much more provocatively Catholic than Montague's. Significantly, Montague's unfortunate daughter, the second earl's wife, insisted that she herself was a conformist.[56] The subsequent coolness between the two families may have contributed to the different religio-ecclesiastical paths which they pursued. The Brownes adopted a consciously moderate, sometimes even compliant, Catholic approach, at least until the mid-1590s. The Wriothesleys, in the person of both the second and the third earls, took a far more extreme and oppositional course – the second earl in a Catholic mode, and the third earl in a Protestant one.[57]

In the east of the county, the first Viscount Montague constructed a very different marriage alliance, namely with the Sackville family. A match was arranged for his grandson, the young man who would inherit in 1592 as the second holder of the title. Sir Thomas Sackville, Baron Buckhurst was the principal power in this part of the land. The marriage cemented the long-standing political compact between Buckhurst and the first viscount.[58] Buckhurst was a cousin of the Surrey family of More of Loseley, with whom Montague, as a substantial landowner in the county, particularly in and

---

[54] Akrigg, *Southampton*, 13–15; Mott, HR, 533–4. Cf. *Romeo and Juliet*, ed. B. Gibbons (Arden edition, 1983), 31–2 n. 2, noting that 'the Montagues and Capulets had been of special interest to the family of the [third] earl of Southampton, Shakespeare's patron', since the time (1572) that George Gascoigne had been employed by the first Viscount Montague to write a masque for the marriage of his son Anthony and his daughter Elizabeth; Hasler, *HC*, II, 172; Berry, *Sussex*, 354–5.
[55] Mott, HR, 540. [56] Paul, HR, 150; ch. 5, p. 162 below.
[57] As Simon Adams points out, the third earl of Southampton's 'personal religious position' was far from clear, though, politically, he followed the second earl of Essex, Adams, 'Protestant Cause', 118.
[58] See ch. 2, p. 63 above.

around Guildford, also had an extremely good working administrative and personal relationship.[59] Sir William More was a very active and godly JP, and was one of those relied upon to implement the famous 1591 proclamation against recusants and seminary priests. He became an enthusiastic prosecutor of recusants, and regarded Rome as 'that Anti-christian and malignant Church'. But this did not seem to affect adversely his friendship with Montague and his family.[60] Much of the building material for the rebuilding of Sir William's house at Loseley near Guildford came from the dismantling of the Waverley Abbey property which had been granted to the Browne family after the Dissolution.[61]

It is worth noting that the first viscount and More could swap godly providentialist apophthegms without the slightest confessional inflection. In early April 1576, when Montague was informed about the death of More's son-in-law, he sent his condolences and advised him to 'receive and use these God his works to his pleasing and your own commodity'.[62] In May 1587 he wrote to More that he believed he had great cause to laud and magnify the mercy and power of God for allowing More's daughter to escape from the dangers of childbirth. He rejoiced with More as much as if the girl had been his own, 'esteaminge my selff partaker with yow eyther of your good or evill happes than I doo to any . . . man in Ingland'. And then,

as no momentt of tyme ever . . . was or shalbe wherin the superabondauntt goodnes of God is not to be magnifyed, so have I even at this instantt receaved word thatt my dawghter [Elizabeth] Dormer is well deliveryd of a joyly boye, att the first despeared of, and now (God be praised) a goodly child and to him I refer his increase and continuance.[63]

In grief as well as joy, Montague could perform the same style of religious discourse with someone who technically should have regarded him as an agent of the Romish Antichrist. In 1590, when More's daughter and grandchild both died, Montague offered his heartfelt condolences.

---

[59] See Loseley MSS, 627, 626, 629, 630, 631, for Montague's cooperation with Sir William More during the early and mid-1570s in the administration of Windsor Forest. In 1576 Montague recommended his Catholic relative William Dawtrey to More for the post of undersheriff of Sussex and Surrey, R. B. Manning, 'Catholics and Local Office Holding in Elizabethan Sussex', *BIHR* 35 (1962), 47–61, at p. 55. Montague relied on More to look after his son-in-law, the second earl of Southampton, when the regime put him under house arrest at Loseley in the early 1570s.

[60] See Loseley MSS, 637; Hyland, *CP*, *passim*, and esp. pp. 202–3, 300. In August 1586 Richard Young passed on Sir Francis Walsingham's 'hearty thanks' to More for searching Francis Browne's house at Henley Park, presumably as a consequence of the Babington plot enquiries, Hyland, *CP*, 188. More's attitude to Browne was, however, far from hostile, and Montague was grateful to More for his benign custody of his brother.

[61] *VCH Surrey* II, 623.   [62] SHC, LM, 6729/8/59 (transcript at SHC).

[63] *Ibid.*, 6729/8/103.

Now (my deere frend) hathe God made triall of yow. Now dothe he examine your constancy and obedience to his will. Now hathe he throwin yow in to the furnace of greff and adversitye by the greatest wor[l]dely losse yow might have, and to trye yow to be (I trust) pure golde in my sight by conforminge your will to his who disponit omnia suaviter.[64]

A similarly cordial relationship was maintained by Sir William More with the second viscount.[65]

Significantly, the Sackville affinity was riddled with Catholics. In many ways, this was ironic. Buckhurst was a joint author, with the Protestant zealot Thomas Norton, of a stage play (*Gorboduc*) concerning the succession, and was himself a cousin of the queen. His father, Sir Richard Sackville, had been a political supporter of the duke of Northumberland and had signed the piece of paper which attempted to secure the succession for Lady Jane Grey.[66] But Buckhurst mixed easily with those whose views were rather different from his own. One such was his own wife Cecily, daughter of the Kentish Catholic Sir John Baker.

Buckhurst himself was undoubtedly conformist in the fullest sense of the word. The Jesuit author of the early seventeenth-century life of Philip Howard and Anne Dacre recalled Buckhurst's comment on the offer made by the queen to the imprisoned Philip that he would be allowed to see his relatives again if he conformed. 'A very worshipful gentleman who was present at this passage' when Philip refused the offer 'has often averred it [the offer] to be true' and 'I do the more easily believe it in regard the Lord Buckhurst ... told the same in substance to his son-in-law the Lord Antony, [second] Viscount Mountague, from whose mouth I heard it.' Buckhurst condemned 'the good earl of much want of wisdome and discretion for not accepting so great and gracious a favour, as he esteemed that offer to have been'.[67] But there was no reason why religion should have been a bone of contention between Buckhurst and the first viscount. The viscount remained a conformist for most if not all of his life, in spite of his general reputation as a supporter of the old religion. Buckhurst protected Catholics such as Anthony Kempe (his fellow MP for Westmorland in 1558),[68] and offered patronage to a Sussex Catholic gentleman, one John Threele, who sought to become a sub-warden of the Fleet in 1594.[69]

[64] Loseley MSS, 644; SHC, LM 6729/8/104, 114. Montague also sent More pre-Reformation religious songs, FSL, L.b. 562, 563.
[65] Loseley MSS, 654.
[66] R. J. W. Swales, 'Local Politics and the Parliamentary Representation of Sussex 1529–1558' (Ph.D., Bristol, 1964), 39. See the *NDNB* article on Sir Thomas Sackville by Rivkah Zim.
[67] CRS 21, 331. [68] Bindoff, *HC*, II, 460.
[69] *HMCS* V, 29, 127. It appears that Threele not only kept this position but was advanced to be the warden of the prison, BL, Harleian MS 7042, fo. 227v; E. D. Pendry, *Elizabethan Prisons and Prison Scenes* (2 vols., Salzburg, 1974), II, 204.

Buckhurst's patronage of such people may, in fact, have had absolutely nothing to do with religion.[70] But there is architectural evidence which suggests that his massive house of Knole had a receptacle constructed in it, before his death, in order to protect Catholic clergy from arrest.[71] In early 1584 one Humphrey Cartwright was being held in prison because he had become 'a Catholyk in the Lord Buckhursts house by reading Catholik bookes'.[72] Robert Persons briefly turned to Buckhurst for help after being ejected from Balliol College. Persons noted that he returned to London and put himself under 'the protection of my Lord Buckhurst by meanes of the Culpepers and Sydneys (of whome I had 2 or 3 for my schollers in Oxforde)'.[73] In a polemical tract of 1592, Richard Verstegan, one of Persons's closest friends, gave Buckhurst a good write-up. Verstegan alleged that Lord Burghley was allowing books to be printed (at a time when Philip II was engaged in military action against the Turks) which declared that it was better to fight against Catholics than against the Turks. Then a minister, 'in a sermon at Paules crosse, affirmed that it was a more better acte to assist Turks than papistes. For the which woordes, the Lord Buckhurst the same day reproved him at the shirif of Londons table', although the minister stiffly stood his ground 'and had (as it seemed) learned his lesson of the superintendent of Winchester', Bishop Horne, 'who published in a printed booke that it was better to sweare unto the Turk and turkery than unto the pope and popery'.[74]

Buckhurst's son and heir was Robert Sackville. Robert's first wife was Lady Margaret Howard, eldest daughter of the fourth duke of Norfolk. In 1587 she was still being warned not to associate with seminary priests and Jesuits.[75] Robert was being relatively openly talked of in the early years of James's reign as a collector of funds for the Catholic clergy,[76] even though in Jacobean parliaments he was named to committees which dealt with the problem of recusancy.[77] In July 1604 Francis Tresham claimed that Robert

[70] See Manning, *Religion*, 240. An informer against John Threele claimed that Sackville was 'abused by this mans hypocrisy' and would 'shew him no favour' if he 'did know his disposition', BL, Harleian MS 7042, fo. 227v.
[71] M. Hodgetts, *Secret Hiding Places* (Dublin, 1989), 106.
[72] Davidson, RC, 673. Buckhurst sent three sons to Hart Hall in Oxford, an establishment which was known to have a Catholic ethos, *ibid.*, 658–9.
[73] CRS 2, 23.
[74] Richard Verstegan, *A Declaration of the True Causes of the Great Troubles, Presupposed to be Intended against the Realme of England* (Antwerp, 1592), 20–1. For the significance of the comparisons between Catholics and Turks, see H. van Nierop, 'A Beggars' Banquet: The Compromise of the Nobility and the Politics of Inversion', *European History Quarterly* 21 (1991), 419–43, at pp. 431–2.
[75] PRO, SP 12/200/59.
[76] AAW, A VIII, no. 168, p. 661. One of the other collectors of funds named in this manuscript was a Hampshire recusant called Hoord. Dorothy Hoord, from the same family, had been placed in service with Robert Sackville's wife, Margaret, by Lady Magdalen, Viscountess Montague. (She had at one time waited on Anthony Browne's wife Mary.) See CRS 21, 45.
[77] See the unpublished HPT biography of Robert Sackville by Alan Davidson.

Sackville more or less admitted that the anti-recusancy legislation (which passed into law as 1 James I, c. 4) of that session was a bad mistake.[78] In a scandalette just before James's accession, Buckhurst had been accused of financial corruption (particularly the sale of crown lands and the with-holding of funds from the war in Ireland) and, with his heir Robert, his daughter Anne Glemham, and several of his servants, of tending towards popery.[79] And then there is the weird story of Thomas Sackville, the youngest of Buckhurst's sons, openly Catholic and recusant, apparently interfering in the political negotiations and horse-trading which went on in Rome before the accession of James VI,[80] and the even weirder (and impossible-to-prove) tale of Buckhurst (now earl of Dorset) being reconciled to the Church of Rome shortly before his death.[81]

One can see therefore that the Brownes were at the centre of a num-ber of marriage alliances with clans which had significant Catholic associ-ations. However much social, economic and local political considerations must have supplied the motivation for the creation of this web of relation-ships, it appears that such unions were clearly informed and inflected in part by the known Catholic characteristics of these families.

When we look at the extended Browne genealogy, we observe other mar-riages where shared Catholic views certainly influenced and reaffirmed the religious temper of the whole clan. For example, Viscount Montague's sis-ter Lucy married Thomas Roper of Eltham and Canterbury, the son of Sir Thomas More's famous son-in-law, 'son [William] Roper'. A William Roper, perhaps Thomas Roper's own son William, is to be found witnessing a deed for the first viscount in 1586.[82] In the early seventeenth century, the Rop-ers and the Mores were at the heart of the clerical entourage of the second Viscount Montague.[83]

Just as important was the Brownes' link with the west-country family of Arundell. The main Catholic branch of the Arundells in the mid-Elizabethan

---

78 PRO, SP 14/8/126, fo. 246r. Tresham had witnessed a conversation between one of the Gage family and Robert Sackville (now styled Lord Buckhurst). Gage 'told him that he much merviled that such severe lawes were in makinge against recusantes, when they had been promised farr better, and since had given no cause to deserve the contrary. But as yow punishe us so the puritanes will in time growe to punishe yow.' It appeared to Tresham that 'my lord of Buckehurst was of the [same] opinion' as Gage.

79 *HMCS* XII, 565–7. See ch. 8, p. 263 below.

80 A. J. Loomie, *Toleration and Diplomacy* (Philadelphia, 1963), 12.

81 Rivkah Zim has suggested (in her *NDNB* article on Sir Thomas Sackville) that the story is a fabrication.

82 WSRO, SAS/BA 63. Later, in the seventeenth century, there would be another Browne–Roper marriage when the fifth Viscount Montague's sister, Elizabeth, married Christopher Roper, Baron Teynham.

83 See chs. 7–10 below. The Mores were also networked into the Gage family, the Brownes' cousins. Christopher Cresacre More married Elizabeth Gage, daughter of Thomas Gage of West Firle, D. Shanahan, 'The Family of St. Thomas More in Essex 1581–1640', *ER* 2 (1960), 76–85, at p. 85.

period was located at Lanherne. Lady Magdalen's chaplain, Richard Smith, noted that while she was a maid of honour at Mary Tudor's Court she had received a proposal of marriage from Sir John Arundell before she finally plumped for Sir Anthony Browne. Sir John Arundell, 'commonly for his great wealth and authority called the Great, who afterward under Queen Elizabeth suffering long imprisonment for the Catholic faith died a glorious confessor . . . was so inflamed with chaste affection towards this lady that he would never desist to solicit her, till he understood that her espousals with another were published'.[84]

However the principal Browne–Arundell link was established via marriage with a scion of the Arundells of Lanherne resident at Chideock and Wardour. Mary Wriothesley, the first Viscount Montague's granddaughter, in mid-1585 married Sir Thomas Arundell, future first Baron Arundell of Wardour, nephew of the Charles Arundell who had been at the centre of the Elizabethan Catholic Court faction which supported the project to marry the queen to the Valois duke of Anjou.[85] Charles Arundell's father, Sir Thomas Arundell, executed in March 1552, had a half-sister, Mary, whose first husband was Robert Radcliffe, earl of Sussex, father of the first Viscount Montague's first wife. And then, in the seventeenth century, Mary, the eldest daughter of the second Viscount Montague, made a second marriage to William Arundell of Horningsham, the first Baron Arundell's second son. In December 1621 Edward Bennett, the Dormers' chaplain, sent his brother news of the bridegroom 'Mr William Arundell, by whom I have been very kindly interteyned'.[86]

In some ways the Arundells' Catholicism was a good deal more pronounced than the Brownes'. The Elizabethan regime's onslaught against Catholic dissent in the later 1570s could be said to have begun with the extraordinary incident when the Cornish county community fractured as the seminary priest Cuthbert Mayne was arrested at the residence of Francis Tregian. This was, according to A. L. Rowse, an attempt by the county's Protestant coastal gentry, led by Sir Richard Grenville, to take out their inland gentry enemies. Sir John Arundell was imprisoned.[87] Shortly afterwards, Charles Arundell went into exile when the Catholic faction at the

---

[84] Southern, *ERH*, 14.

[85] On 18 February 1601 Sir Thomas Arundell wrote to Cecil his observations on the earl of Southampton's treason and fall, and said that he could 'not but greeve for beeinge allyed to one that hathe so fowlye blotted his alleageance and that to sutch a princes[s]', Bodl., Ashmolean MS 1729, no. 100, fo. 189r.

[86] AAW, A XVI, no. 75, p. 254. The Arundell family had connections by marriage with the Fortescue family of Salden, Buckinghamshire, at whom we have already briefly glanced for their links with the Poles. Edward Gage of Bentley, the first Viscount Montague's friend and executor, was (with Lord Henry Howard and Lord William Howard) executor to Sir Matthew Arundell, brother of Charles, PRO, PROB 11/93, fos. 81r–82r.

[87] A. L. Rowse, *Tudor Cornwall* (1940), 333, 344–7 362–3, 367–9. Rowse describes the Arundell family as the mainstay of Catholicism in Cornwall, *ibid.*, 342.

Elizabethan Court collapsed after the failure of the proposed Anjou match. Arundell may have contributed some of the material in the notorious sour-grapes commentary on the Catholics' defeat at Court, a commentary which was known to contemporaries as 'Leicester's Commonwealth'.[88] Wardour remained, however, a centre of excellence for Catholic activism. Sir John Harington's *Metamorphosis of Ajax* was set among the Arundells at War-dour Castle (see Figure 14). (Harington was an admirer of Edmund Campion and his literary work.[89])

Sir Thomas Arundell's ambitions took him to serve in the English regiment in Flanders.[90] He had, late in the queen's reign, got into hot water over his acceptance of an imperial title.[91] In the new reign (shortly after he was created Baron Arundell of Wardour) he infuriated both the king and the earl of Salisbury when, in August 1605, he arrived in Flanders, as Sir Thomas Edmondes reported, 'to be colonel of the English regiment which hath lately been levied . . . to the number of 1,500 men'.[92] Henry Howard, earl of Northampton wrote to Edmondes on 10 October 1605, 'I am sory for the folly of my cosin the Lord Arundell who by addinge one absurdity to another hath by circles of error plunged himself into the most just indignation of the king.' In particular, the appointment of the recently reprieved traitor Griffin Markham as Arundell's lieutenant 'hath more vexed . . . the king than his former presumption in embarkinge expressely against the kings commaundement in one of his owne vessells to the scandale of his hows and the haserde of the treaty' of 1604 with Spain.[93] Arundell escaped recall to England only through 'the archdukes entreaty' and James's desire to 'prevent all bruits abroad of any jealousys between the princes'.[94]

Arundell subsequently spent a good deal of his time reassuring anyone who would listen of his untarnishable loyalty.[95] One of the ways in which

[88] *The Copie of a Leter, Wryten by a Master of Arte of Cambridge* . . . (Paris [?], 1584); D. C. Peck, *Leicester's Commonwealth* (Athens, Ohio, 1985).

[89] G. Kilroy, 'Paper, Inke and Penne: The Literary *Memoria* of the Recusant Community', *Downside Review* 119 (2001), 95–124, at pp. 102–3; *idem*, 'Eternal Glory: Edmund Campion's Virgilian Epic', *Times Literary Supplement* (8 March 2002), 13.

[90] P. Croft, 'Serving the Archduke: Robert Cecil's Management of the Parliamentary Session of 1606', *HR* 64 (1991), 289–304, at p. 295; D. Lunn, 'Chaplains to the English Regiment in Spanish Flanders, 1605–06', *RH* 11 (1971–2), 133–55, at pp. 136–7.

[91] Bodl., Ashmolean MS 1729, no. 99, fo. 187r; Lunn, 'Chaplains', 137.

[92] *HMCD* II, 428; Croft, 'Serving the Archduke', 295.

[93] BL, Stowe MS 168, no. 41, fo. 169v; Croft, 'Serving the Archduke', 295.

[94] BL, Stowe MS 168, no. 54, fo. 221r–v.

[95] Arundell recounted to the earl of Salisbury in 1606 that 'in my first travels I was persuaded by the duke of Guyse that then was to offer my services to his Majesty's mother [Mary Stuart], which I did, yet with a reservation of my allegiance to our late queen'. Mary Stuart 'graciously accepted' but Secretary Walsingham got hold of the letter, 'whereupon I was banished out of the Court for 13 months, and the displeasure which ensued thereof was so great that, being still reputed Scottish, I was debarred from all those favours whereby I might have advanced my fortunes had not my zeal to his Majesty's title procured me this disgrace', *HMCS* XVIII, 377.

Figure 14.   The ruins of Wardour Castle, Wiltshire. A view of the damage caused by the gunpowder mines laid under the castle walls during the civil war.

he did this was to posture, apparently with some conviction, as an enemy of the Jesuits and, by implication, of a brand of extremist Catholicism which had no place in the Stuart polity. His nomination of the Benedictine John Bradshaw as 'chaplain major' to his soldiers was a clear snub to the Society in Flanders. The Society had previously been almost the sole source of spiritual counsel to the regiment's men. Bradshaw was known to have been favourable to the appellant clergy (bitter enemies of the Jesuits), and was rumoured now to be an agent for the regime in England.[96] Even the Spanish overhaul of their Low Countries forces in mid-1606, which led to the cashiering of Arundell and his replacement by Sir Thomas Studder, could be construed as a Jesuit plot to eject those in the regiment who claimed that their first loyalty was to the Stuart regime. Arundell returned to England with his reputation intact, perhaps even enhanced.[97] In 1606 he assured the earl of Salisbury that the Jesuits in Flanders 'left the regiment destitute of any priest . . . by reason that I would not admit any of the Jesuited sort'.[98]

Arundell remained politically vigorous, clearly trading off his self-fashioned 'loyal Catholic' image. He was a quite active figure in the early 1620s, much more so actually than his cousin the equally loyal and equally Catholic second Viscount Montague. Arundell agitated to be allowed some measure of influence over the negotiations for the proposed Anglo-Spanish dynastic treaty (by which Prince Charles would wed the infanta Maria). He hawked himself about as a middleman to broker a toleration for James's Catholic subjects, without which the marriage could not proceed.[99]

Both the Brownes and the Arundells also contracted clearly Catholic and socially illustrious marital unions with the Somerset family. The first Viscount Montague's aunt Elizabeth had married, as we noted at the start of this chapter, Henry Somerset, second earl of Worcester (and the second viscount's heir Francis would, in 1637, marry a daughter of Henry Somerset, fifth earl of Worcester).[100] And the Somersets contracted a high-profile (though frequently acrimonious – at least between the in-laws) marriage with the Arundells. Blanche Somerset (fifth daughter of Edward Somerset, fourth earl of Worcester) wed Thomas Arundell, the future second Baron Arundell. (She became a lady of Anne of Denmark's privy chamber.)[101]

---

[96] Lunn, 'Chaplains', 139–40, 142.   [97] *Ibid.*, 143, 146, 148, 149–50.
[98] HMCS XVIII, 376.   [99] See ch. 12, pp. 389–90 below.
[100] Berry, *Sussex*, 354. The marriage between Francis Browne and Elizabeth Somerset was a prominent alliance of two major Catholic aristocratic families. The ceremony took place in the chapel of the papal agent George Con, Albion, *CI*, 163.
[101] H. Payne, 'Aristocratic Women and the Jacobean Court, 1603–1625' (Ph.D., London, 2001), appendix. For the long-running acrimony between Baron Arundell, his son and the earl of Worcester over the property arrangements connected with the marriage, see BL, Additional MS 38170, fos. 115r–133r; PRO, SP 16/25/106, fo. 143r, SP 16/30/86, fo. 134r.

The Arundell–Somerset marriage of 1606 was recognised as a classic case of the phenomenon analysed by Sandeep Kaushik, the kind of match between prominent Catholic families which could be read by contemporaries as an aggressive assertion of their political and religious identity. On 12 July 1606 Salisbury wrote to Sir Thomas Edmondes that, although the king had a good opinion of Baron Arundell's loyalty (Arundell was still at that time in Flanders), the regime could hardly ignore that 'by the consent of friends of both sides it is not unknown to him that his son had licence to seek the earl of Worcester's daughter in marriage'. What with 'the clouds hanging over his actions', and 'the suspicion that the mother of the lady and parents of the gentleman had an intention in this conjuncture to knit friendship with the knots of the Romish religion', it was inevitable that the king

straight fell upon that particular of his dislike of such a marriage as would give reputation to that cause which is so contrary to his profession in this State, she being the daughter of so great a councillor and one so much favoured by him, professing plainly that it would never be acceptable unto him except he might see some hope of their inclination to hearken to better instructions.

The earl of Worcester, 'being a wise man, frees himself from that infection and valuing his Majesty's favour before any other thing, became not only a stranger to the desire but directly forbad the proceeding'. But it did no good because 'the young couple . . . serving one of the poetical gods (to which I believe Lord Arundel himself ere now has been content to confess himself a servant) have clapped up the marriage privately' (though Cecil admitted that the couple would, in the end, escape the consequences of this rush of youth).[102]

Across the water, in Ireland, the first Viscount Montague's sister Mabel had married Gerald FitzGerald, eleventh earl of Kildare. The marriage ceremony took place in the chapel royal at the end of May 1554. (The viscount's father, Sir Anthony, had wed, in 1542, the young Elizabeth, 'Fair Geraldine', daughter of the ninth earl of Kildare.)[103] Richard Nugent, fourth Baron Delvin, who was the first viscount's great-nephew (i.e. his sister Mabel's grandson), subsequently kept in close contact with the Brownes. In 1584 Delvin and his wife were staying in Montague Close (and probably in Montague House itself) in St Saviour's parish in Southwark, as was the countess of Kildare herself.[104] This branch of the Irish nobility had effectively turned loyalist.

For the rise of the Somersets as the leading aristocratic family resident in South Wales and the Marches in the early seventeenth century, see Hibbard, *CI*, 153–4.

[102] *HMCS* XVIII, 200–1, 207, 218. See also S. Kaushik, 'Resistance, Loyalty and Recusant Politics: Sir Thomas Tresham and the Elizabethan State', *Midland History* 21 (1996), 37–72, at pp. 42–7.

[103] Bindoff, *HC*, I, 518; N. Williams, *Henry VIII and his Court* (1971), 224.

[104] Foley VI, 712; LMA, P92/SAV/184, p. 19.

William FitzGerald, the thirteenth earl of Kildare, was drowned while crossing to Ireland in April 1599 to assist the earl of Essex's vain attempt to quell
the rebellion of the earl of Tyrone.[105] We know that, in the early seventeenth
century, some of the stories about Catholic martyrs which the Brownes'
clergy repeated in their letters came through Delvin.[106] One of the principal informers against the Browne entourage at this time, John Bird, noted
that Montague's sister, the countess of Kildare, was a virulent papist and a
harbourer of rebels.[107]

Of course, not all such families' marital alliances were dictated by religion,
or even necessarily by politico-ideological sympathy. One match where it is
difficult to discern any particular ideological slant, or even to work out what
was the motive for it in the first place, is the second marriage of the first
viscount's sister Mary to the unsuccessful soldier Sir Henry Capel of Hadham
in Hertfordshire. She had herself formerly been married to Lord John Grey
of Pirgo.[108] The Capels seem to have been a strongly Protestant family. Sir
Arthur Capel dreaded his son's departure on the grand tour because of the
danger of sickness, death and also because, by 'the wycked prests and Jesuites
in those forrane partes, he maye be perverted to the idolatrous Romane
relygion', for 'he is very younge and they [are] subtyle and industrious'.[109]
Mary's first marriage, to Lord John Grey, son of the marquis of Dorset, is
also difficult to interpret, though it would seem to fit with the first viscount's
remarkably good relations with Robert Dudley, earl of Leicester.[110] (On
receiving the news of Leicester's death in 1588, Montague lamented the
passing of 'my good lord and kinsman'.[111]) Lord John Grey was the uncle of

[105] *GEC* VII, 240.   [106] *NAGB*, 146–7.
[107] *HMCS* XVII, 476. See ch. 8, pp. 262, 271 below.   [108] See Hasler, *HC*, I, 534.
[109] J. B. Calnan, 'County Society and Local Government in the County of Hertfordshire,
  c. 1580–*c*. 1630, with Special Reference to the Commission of the Peace' (Ph.D., Cambridge, 1979), 74.
[110] Admittedly, the Spanish ambassador, Alvaro de La Quadra, bishop of Aquila, remarked in
  February 1563, as the parliamentary clamour for a settlement of the succession was reaching
  new heights, that Montague and others 'follow Lord Robert and the earl of Huntingdon'
  (Dudley's brother-in-law and one of those who had a claim to succeed Elizabeth) 'rather out
  of fear than affection', *CSP Spanish 1558–67*, 297. On 12 March 1565, however, Guzman
  de Silva observed that Dudley, now earl of Leicester, was 'very friendly' with Montague.
  Later, in December 1567, he noted that Leicester was in communication with Montague
  over the negotiations for the archduke's marriage suit to the queen, and that Leicester had
  'always been friendly' to Montague, *ibid.*, 407, 690.
[111] SHC, LM 6729/8/108. Montague's relationship to Dudley came through the duchess of
  Northumberland, who was Montague's cousin (for which point I am grateful to Simon
  Adams). For the many instances of cooperation between Montague and Dudley in the
  administration and stewardship of royal property in Surrey, see Loseley MSS, *passim*. In
  April 1561 Montague had been one of those who helped to scupper Dudley's ardent pressing
  of his ongoing suit to marry Elizabeth, S. Doran, *Monarchy and Matrimony* (1996), 51.
  Shortly before, Dudley wrote Montague 'a very loving letter with many promises'. For
  Montague's reply, see Longleat House, Dudley papers DU I, 62, fo. 191r. Whatever the

Catherine Grey. She was released from imprisonment in the Tower into his custody in 1563.[112] But Grey's vehement opposition to any kind of alliance with the Habsburgs (as manifested by his denunciation of the 'Pagetyan' faction in 1560 over a proposed Habsburg match for the queen) would presumably not have gone down well with his imperialist brother-in-law, the first viscount.[113]

In other cases of marital alliance, the mere fact of sharing the same religion did not necessarily make for close feeling and understanding. As we have already seen with the disaster of the Browne–Wriothesley marriage, even marital union between self-consciously Catholic families did not always result in consistent empathy and political and social closeness. Jane, the second viscount's sister, married into the very Catholic family of Englefield. She wed Francis,[114] the nephew of Sir Francis Englefield, the once influential Marian privy counsellor, religious expatriate and one of the key members of the 'Spanish' faction among the Elizabethan Catholic exiles.[115] We might have expected that this union would consolidate the Catholic bloc of families at the centre of which the Brownes were now positioning themselves. However, relations between the Brownes and the Englefields early in the seventeenth century seem not to have been close, and at times were really acrimonious. In September 1617 the second Viscount Montague was in dispute with Englefield over the title to a property in St Saviour's parish, on which stood a 'die-house' 'from whence great annoyance commeth to Winchester House' and to the marquis of Winchester. (Montague's daughter Mary, by now married to William Arundell, was the widow of Lord St John, son and heir of the marquis.)[116] The 'die-house' in question may be the same as the

promises were, they did not immediately work, *CSP Spanish 1558–67*, 195. But a year later Montague, with the duke of Norfolk, and opposed by the earl of Arundel and the marquis of Northampton, petitioned instead that the queen should now marry Dudley, Doran, *Monarchy*, 58. When Montague's daughter, the widowed countess of Southampton, wanted to contest the, to her, intolerable provisions of her deceased husband's will, she turned, apparently with Montague's approval, to Leicester, Akrigg, *Southampton*, 18–19.

[112] S. Adams, 'The Release of Lord Darnley and the Failure of the Amity', in M. Lynch (ed.), *Mary Stewart* (Oxford, 1988), 123–53, at p. 133. Z. Dovey, *An Elizabethan Progress: The Queen's Journey into East Anglia, 1578* (Stroud, 1996), 132, notes that Lord Grey's lenient treatment after the Wyatt rising (when his brothers, Henry, duke of Suffolk, and Thomas, were executed) was due to his wife's access to the regime through Viscount Montague.

[113] S. Alford, *The Early Elizabethan Polity* (Cambridge, 1998), 77–8. See also N. Jones, *Faith by Statute* (1982), 14; C. Read, *Mr. Secretary Cecil and Queen Elizabeth* (1965), 128.

[114] The Catholic lawyer Edmund Plowden obtained the wardship of the younger Francis (having also obtained control of the family property which had been forfeited to the crown). Plowden informed Francis in 1583 that 'my old Lord Mountague . . . hath offered me for you 2000[li]', Davidson, RC, 62–3; G. de C. Parmiter, *Edmund Plowden* (1987), 149–50.

[115] It was reported in May 1594 that Philip Roper of Eltham (a relative of the Brownes through the marriage of Thomas Roper of Eltham and Lucy Browne) and Francis Englefield were consorting together in and around Southampton House, PRO, SP 12/248/116, fo. 250v.

[116] Loseley MSS, 673.

property mentioned in the attempted parliamentary settlements, by private bills in 1621 and 1624, of Montague's debts, debts which had arisen in part because Englefield had defaulted as a trustee of property which Montague had tied up in order to pay his obligations and provide dowries for his daughters.[117] Englefield's dereliction of duty led to the bringing of a chancery suit, on the basis of an earlier chancery decree of 1618, by William Arundell in October 1622 against various tenants of Montague House and of properties in Montague Close.[118]

In the seventeenth century there may have been something of an ideological rift between the Brownes and another Catholic family with whom the first viscount had arranged a marriage alliance, the Lacons of Kinlet in Shropshire. Sir Francis Lacon of Kinlet married the first viscount's daughter Jane.[119] Sir Francis was some kind of conformist Catholic, or rather an Elizabethan recusant who conformed early in James's reign.[120] He was in good odour with the Jacobean regime.[121] What may have caused a rift with the Browne family was the fact that in the early seventeenth century much of

[117] BL, Harleian MS 6847, no. 4, fos. 20v–21r ('An Act for the settling of certain manors and lands of the Viscount Montague towards payment of his debts, or raising his daughters fortunes'); ch. 11, p. 359 below. The act notes that Englefield had been replaced as a trustee because he had refused to comply with an order made in chancery to provide accounts and settle the affairs of the trust. The bill stipulated that, if he now refused his cooperation, Montague could 'have his accion against him as bailiff . . . and proceed therin and have judgment and execution therupon for arrerages and damages'. For the bill, in April 1624, which tried to sort out the business, see WSRO, SAS/BA 75; PRO, C 89/11/76; PRO, C 54/2637/17.

[118] PRO, C 2/James I/A1/6. Arundell claimed that the tenants in question had 'contrived emongest themselves divers and sundrie secret estates', taking advantage of Englefield's obstinacy, and knowing that Arundell and his wife had 'noe estate in lawe' by which they could enforce actions for waste or breach of covenant or take benefit of forfeitures for non-payment of rent. The Arundells were still pursuing their rights in 1626, PRO, C 3/394/40.

[119] Sir Francis Lacon was one of the witnesses to the first Viscount Montague's will, WSRO, SAS/BA 67. See also Hasler, *HC*, II, 427.

[120] PRO, SP 14/28/122. i. See the unpublished HPT biography of Sir Francis Lacon by Simon Healy.

[121] Late in Elizabeth's reign, some extraordinary accusations of political disloyalty were made against him by Valentine Thomas, but they do not seem to have been taken seriously. (Thomas Wright, the ex-Jesuit, in the aftermath of the earl of Essex's rebellion in 1601 referred to Lacon as a 'special man'.) In early 1606, however, the earl of Salisbury regarded Lacon as reliable, and willing to do (unstated) service to the regime, even though in late 1605 Lacon was recruiting soldiers for the archduke, an exercise in which some of the leading English Jesuits were also known to be active at this time. Simon Healy has demonstrated, however, that Lacon used his military contacts, at Salisbury's direction, to expose a projected Catholic conspiracy, hatched in the English regiment in Flanders, to betray Dutch fortresses to the Spaniards and to assassinate James. So it was not surprising that he should have been regarded as a loyalist, PRO, KB 8/54; *HMCS* XVIII, 28; PRO, SP 14/15/95; Healy, unpublished HPT biography of Lacon. This explains the crown appointment (he was sheriff of Shropshire in 1612) and the parliamentary seat which he was able to acquire, Davidson, *RC*, 72. Lacon was, however, named in the Commons's 1624 petition against recusant office-holders.

the entourage and extended family of the Brownes leaned towards that side of the Catholic community which opposed the influence of the Jesuits while, ironically in the context of Lacon's vaunted loyalism, it looks as if the Kinlet household may have been pro-Jesuit or 'Jesuited'. Thomas Lacon, Sir Francis's brother, was named early in James's reign as the patron of the firebrand Welsh Jesuit Robert Jones.[122] Jones seems to have lived with Sir Francis as well. In or around 1605 an informer, one Griffeth, claimed that the Catholics in the region were on the verge of rebellion, and that their belligerence was fired by the Jesuits and their supporters. Among 'the lay men that runne this course with the Jesuits' was 'Mr Lacon', i.e. Roland Lacon (who died in 1608), 'and his sonne Sir Francis, with whome Jones the Jesuit resydeth'.[123] Sir Francis rode with the Jesuits John Gerard, Henry Garnet and John Percy, and the Gunpowder plotters Sir Everard Digby and Ambrose Rookwood, on the notorious August 1605 pilgrimage to Holywell.[124] The intelligencer William Udall reported on 28 July 1606 that another of the Gunpowder plot suspects, the Jesuit Oswald Tesimond, was now 'at this present at M. Lacon's [house] at Kinlett in Shropshire'.[125]

Just as the Brownes established links through marriage with other Catholic families outside the immediate boundaries of their own region, so Catholics from other parts of the country can be found making contact with the Brownes in their own home territory. Some of them, for example the first viscount's servant Richard Lambe, travelled considerable distances to serve the Brownes.[126] The recusant Frankes family's transmigration to Midhurst from Yorkshire was presumably influenced by a desire to enter the viscount's entourage. One of the witnesses who put their signatures to a deed for the first Viscount Montague in 1586[127] was one Edward Rookwood. He was probably a member of the Rookwood family of Suffolk, perhaps the Edward Rookwood of Euston whose wife Montague referred to as his niece 'Ruckwood' in May 1587 when he wrote to Burghley on her and her husband's

---

[122] PRO, SP 14/14/40; cf. PRO, SP 14/7/50, fo. 140r. Thomas Lacon married Mary Thimbleby, from the Society-oriented Irnham family, Robert Tresswell, ed. G. Grazebrook and J. P. Rylands, *The Visitation of Shropshire . . .1623* (2 vols., 1889), II, 308.

[123] AAW, A VII, no. 108, p. 563.

[124] M. Hodgetts, 'Shropshire Priests in 1605', *Worcestershire Recusant* 47 (1986), 24–36, at pp. 24, 31.

[125] Harris, 'Reports', 217. More confusing, though, is the claim in 1609, also from Udall, that Sir Francis, now in charge of the Kinlet household, was harbouring Thomas Wright, the ex-Jesuit who seems to have been a loyalist (and supporter of partial conformity). He was basically acceptable to the leading secular clergy who opposed the Society, *ibid.*, 219. Udall, however, also reported that there had been some kind of rendering or public performance of the scandalous and scurrilous tract *Prurit-anus* at Kinlet, of which it was believed, at that time, that both Thomas Wright and his Jesuit brother William were the authors, *NAGB*, 61–2.

[126] See ch. 6, p. 205 below.   [127] WSRO, SAS/BA 63.

behalf; her husband was at that time imprisoned for debt in the Gatehouse gaol in London.[128]

Among other well-known recusants who were drawn out of their own counties to move into the Browne family circle were the Tirwhits of Kettleby in Lincolnshire. Sir George Browne, the eldest son of the first viscount and Magdalen Dacre, married Mary Tirwhit, a daughter of Sir Robert Tirwhit of Kettleby.[129] Sir Robert himself married Elizabeth Oxenbridge, also from a Sussex/Hampshire family. Their son William, a recusant, was lord of the Sussex manor of Etchingham. Etchingham was a parish which was noted in this period for some stubbornly recusant Catholic inhabitants.[130] William's grandson (also William) married Catherine Browne, a daughter of the second Viscount Montague.[131] The elder William Tirwhit, along with Francis Browne (the first viscount's brother), was among the number of the Catholic notables who drew up the famous Catholic toleration petition of 1585. The petition was delivered directly to the queen's hands by Richard Shelley of Warminghurst, an act which was so politically offensive that Shelley was locked up for most of what turned out to be the short remainder of his life.[132]

Thomas Middlemore, a scion of a well-known Elizabethan Worcestershire recusant family, was another Catholic who is known to have moved into East Sussex and into the Brownes' Catholic orbit. We find occasional references to 'Tom Middlemore' in the correspondence of the Sussex Catholic clergy who were in the Brownes' entourage in the early seventeenth century.[133]

A slightly different, and possibly much more influential, infusion of potentially Catholic blood into the county and into the Brownes' circle had occurred when Henry Clifford, second earl of Cumberland, decided to place

---

[128] BL, Lansdowne MS 53, no. 44, fo. 92r; Foley III (pedigree between pp. 788–9). Edward Rookwood, son of Nicholas Rookwood of Euston, Suffolk, took as his first wife Elizabeth Browne, daughter of William Browne of Elsing, a brother of the first Viscount Montague. See also CRS 54, 338. In March 1601 Edward Rookwood, his wife Elizabeth and other family members, described as of St George's parish in Southwark, were indicted for recusancy, though one of his servants entered a deposition that Edward had attended church in the previous month, Cockburn, *Surrey Assizes: Elizabeth*, nos 3114, 3115.

[129] See CRS 54, 241.

[130] See ch. 2, pp. 40–1 above. C. W. Field suggests that the Tirwhits' Sussex residence was Mountfield Park rather than, e.g., Glottenham Castle, another of their properties, or in Etchingham itself. Mountfield is very close to the Brownes' residence of Battle Abbey, C. W. Field, 'The Kent/Sussex Border at the Change of Religion', *Catholic Ancestor* 5 (1994), 109–19, at p. 112.

[131] *NAGB*, 265–6.

[132] R. B. Manning, 'Richard Shelley of Warminghurst and the English Catholic Petition for Toleration of 1585', *RH* 6 (1961–2), 265–74, at p. 270. When the Oxenbridge family deserted Brede Place, it was managed by, among others, the first Viscount Montague and Sir Robert Tirwhit (d. 1572); Field, 'The Kent/Sussex Border', 110. For the Shelley family wall brass in Warminghurst parish church, see Figure 15.

[133] *NAGB*, 95. See also CRS 60, 145.

Figure 15. Detail from the Shelley family wall brass in the chancel of
Warminghurst parish church (the Holy Sepulchre). Among the children of
Edward Shelley (d. 1554) represented here are Edward and Richard. The younger
Edward was executed on 30 August 1588 for harbouring the priest William Dean.
Richard died in prison after presenting the 1585 Catholic toleration petition to
the queen.

his eleven-year-old heir, the future third earl, George Clifford, with the
Brownes (already kin to the Cliffords via Sir Anthony Browne's sister Lucy's
marriage to Henry, first earl of Cumberland's brother Thomas) for educational purposes. The second earl of Cumberland probably had Catholic
inclinations or at least no Protestant ones. Lady Anne Clifford recounted that
the boy was 'bred up there for a while so that he might see the renowned
Queen Elizabeth and her Court and the City of London and the southern
parts of England', and, one might assume, live in a Catholic though technically conformist environment. Montague was one of the earl's executors.
Immediately after the 1569 rebellion, George Clifford was removed from
the Brownes' care and was placed with the Russells. (Nevertheless in August
1585 a spy in France thought that the third earl, with other peers, was
too close to Catholic activists for his own good; the 'papistes have to there
frendes in the Courte of England the lorde of Cumberland', as well as 'the
lorde of Rutland, the Lorde Compton [and] the Lorde Morley. The lordes

of Comberland and Rutland' were 'moche labored' by the priests John Ballard and Christopher Dryland.)[134] Anne Dacre, second wife of the second earl of Cumberland, afforded protection to her brother-in-law Sir Alexander Culpeper who was forced to fly to her on occasion when troubled for his Catholicism, as he did occasionally to his other sister-in-law Lady Magdalen, Viscountess Montague, and her husband, the first viscount.[135] We find Francis Dacre, the viscountess's Catholic-exile brother, talking in a letter of December 1595 to his daughter Eleanor about his nephew, Francis Clifford, future fourth earl of Cumberland, and describing him as one of his dear friends.[136] Though Dacre had rather predictably failed to persuade George Clifford to defect to Spain, as the 'privateering earl' cruised off the Spanish coast in the early 1590s,[137] it was reported in March 1603 that Dacre and his nephew Francis were hopping backwards and forwards over the border with Scotland as James VI's transition to sovereign status in England was being effected. A border commissioner noted on 31 March that 'this day, with 6 servants, Mr Francis Dacre [came] into this county; and this night Mr Francis Clifford is here with me at Carlell, upon his journey towards the king'.[138] In the early seventeenth century we find some of the Clifford family still scattered around the Brownes' network of friends, especially Henry Clifford who wrote a series of informative newsletters from Antwerp to Rome at the end of James's reign.[139]

The process of attraction and immigration into the ambit of the family worked in reverse as the offspring of the remarkably fecund first viscount and his eldest son and grandson (the second viscount) fanned out across the country. Sir George Browne eventually emigrated to Great Shefford in Berkshire where he married into the Catholic family of Bridges.[140] Sir Henry Browne eventually settled at Kiddington in Oxfordshire. His second wife was Elizabeth Hungate of Saxton, widow of Sir Marmaduke Grimston; her sister

---

[134] R. T. Spence, *The Privateering Earl: George Clifford, 3rd Earl of Cumberland, 1558–1605* (Stroud, 1995), 17–18; BL, Harleian MS 290, fo. 157r.

[135] C. Buckingham, 'The Troubles of Sir Alexander Culpeper of Goudhurst', *Cantium* 2 (1970), 5–8, at p. 5: G. de. C. Parmiter, 'Sir Alexander Colepeper of Bedgebury', *RH* 19 (1989), 364–85, at pp. 366, 367. For Culpeper's funeral monument in Goudhurst parish church, see Figure 16.

[136] *HMCS* XIII, 547.   [137] BL, Harleian MS 7042, fo. 223v.   [138] *HMCS* XV, 20.

[139] Hamilton, *Chronicle*, II, 134–5, I, 127–8; AAW, B 47, nos. 70–1, 73–83; AAW, B 27, nos. 8, 14, 21, 27, 33, 48, 56, 64, 72, 77, 84, 88.

[140] Thomas Dodwell noted in 1584 that 'Mr Bridges of Shifford, iiii myles from Abington, beinge a schismatik, his wief a recusant, keepeth one Hawkins continuallie in his howse, beinge a seminarie preist, and receiveth any priest that will come', and that 'Mr George Browne, sonne to my Lorde Mountagewe, remaininge in the same howse, keepeth one [Samuel] Twiforde, a preist, in the habit of a servinge man', PRO, SP 12/168/34, fo. 81r. Malivery Catilyn described Bridges as a 'great practiser with the [Catholic] fugytives', PRO, SP 12/190/62, fo. 130r.

Figure 16.   Effigies (on the Culpeper family monument in the parish church of
St Mary, Goudhurst) of Sir Alexander Culpeper and Anthony Culpeper.

Mary married the recusant Catholic Richard Cholmeley of Brandsby.[141] In Cholmeley's marvellously informative day-to-day diary we find many references to his friendship with Sir Henry. Cholmeley was extremely grateful to Sir Henry for standing surety with Cholmeley's father-in-law in order to discharge a debt incurred by Cholmeley for his recusancy. When Cholmeley took the oath of allegiance in July 1607 before the exchequer baron Sir James Altham and Serjeant Edward Phelips he noted that 'Sir Henry Browne was with me'. (Sir Henry had himself conformed in 1607 before he left the Brownes' estate at Battle.) Browne and Cholmeley were appointed as supervisors of William Hungate's will.[142] Sir Henry evidently made frequent trips to Yorkshire to visit the Cholmeley family. On 12 January 1619, Cholmeley noted that 'Robert Hungate my uncle did entertayne Sir Henry Brown, his lady, children . . . , I, my wife, Benedict Stapleton, etc. and other freinds from Monday night till Wednesday noone.' During the rest of the year Cholmeley frequently recorded the social and familial contact which he enjoyed with Sir Henry Browne and his wife. On 16 August, for example, Sir Henry and 'his lady, children and famulye came to Brandesby from Saxton. He, his lady, Peter Browne, Francis, Mary, [and] Helen Mudd' left only on 13 September.[143] Shortly afterwards Cholmeley noted that the sheriff had got a 'return' against him of £360 'last vacation for kepeing servants and sojowrners when Sir Henry Browne, his ladye, children and servants lyved at my howse which I stayed and must of necessitie plead to in discharge this tearme next following'.[144]

The Brownes, as we have noted, contracted more than one marriage into the Dormer family in Buckinghamshire. One of Anthony Browne's daughters, Dorothy, married Edmund Lee of Stanton-Bury in the same county. Edmund Lee's brother, Roger, was a Jesuit, and another sister, Eleanor, married John Lenthall of Latchford. The Lenthalls (although they were a Jesuited family) were, it seems, good friends of the Dormers.[145]

CATHOLIC POLITICS, FAMILY POLITICS

But, one might ask, so what? How far *did* Catholics' awareness of the kin structures to which they belonged affect their social, religious and political identity? Probably such awareness rested for the most part on a series of shared assumptions which were not normally articulated, and were even

---

[141] *NAGB*, 67.
[142] *The Memorandum Book of Richard Cholmeley of Brandsby 1602–1623* (North Yorkshire County Record Office Publications no. 44, 1988), 26–8, 48, 44, 156; Cockburn, *Sussex Assizes: James I*, nos. 90, 91.
[143] *The Memorandum Book of Richard Cholmeley*, 178, 180.   [144] *Ibid.*, 193–4.
[145] *NAGB*, 101; Foley I, 456; Davidson, RC, 138–43, 392–5.

less frequently written down. But, all the same, they were very real. We have already rehearsed Thomas Meynell's proud recollections of his illustrious kin network. And every now and again correspondence survives which shows how tight and deeply felt these family relationships, even some of the more distant ones, could be. In a clutch of mid-1620s letters, written by Thomas Roper, a cousin of the English secular clergy's agent in Rome, Thomas More, and a relative by marriage of the Browne family, we get a sense of the range and intimacy of the network of which Roper was a part. In one letter, of 10 June 1625, written to the new clergy agent Thomas Rant, shortly after More's death, Roper notes that he has received Rant's packet of letters and has distributed them as requested, in particular 'my cosen Brownes letter unto Mr Cape' (a servant of the second Viscount Montague) and 'Mr Musket' (the secular priest George Fisher, who was also a relative of several of Roper's friends). Having dealt with recent political events, and in particular the imminent arrival in England of Charles I's bride Henrietta Maria, Roper retailed gossip such as that 'neere Burforde in Oxfordesheere on the 6th of May there was suche a storme of hayle, rayne, thunder, lightninge and winde about 4 in the afternoone as the like never did happen'. One 'Mrs Kenion', probably a relative of the priest Edward Kenion who was one of the second viscount's chaplains, 'neighebour to my cosen Greenewoode, brother in law to my deceased good cosen [Thomas] Moore, thinkes she had in hir courte 40 loades of haylestones some as bigge as egges, some as waulenuttes which remayned unmelted some weekes'. And this brought down such a deluge from the hills (1625 was a very wet year) that her barn was flooded out and it 'carried the corne in the flower beinge 3-quarters cleane a way and bare a waye the mayde and had like to have driven hir into the river'. 'One that was lookinge to my cosen Greenewoodds sheepe reported to see hayle stones' which were 'thicke as a barley corne endwayes and all ragged about as it were the wheele of a watche'.[146]

In a homely and familiar letter of this kind, filled with images such as that of the hapless maidservant carried bodily away by a torrent of water, we get a sense of the awareness of kinship and also of shared religious heritage among people who were part of a very widely dispersed nexus of cousins. Roper had written in October 1624 to Thomas More that 'I doe not heare any suche thinge here as you write concerninge my cosen George Gage' (i.e. the son of Edward Gage, first cousin of the Elizabeth Gage who had married Cresacre More) 'who hathe lived this quarter of [a] yeare in Wayles with his sister Stradlinge'. (George's sister Elizabeth had married Sir John Stradling of St Donats, Glamorganshire.) Roper added that they were

[146] AAW, B 47, no. 188, fo. 213r.

here amonge us . . . very litle spoken of, and that which is with you reported is not beleeved here by any. The lady is in the Lowcountreys and I thinke you will see hir shortely where you are, so you see they are very farre distant one from the other. There was in deede a great speeche of a likinge betweene him and my cosen Thatcher['s] widdowe which was Treshamme,

a reference to Anne Tresham, the widow of William Thatcher whose mother, Mary, was a daughter of Sir Edward Gage as well, 'but that would be no great fortune to him'.[147] He kept More informed about the health, evidently not very good, of his 'Awnte Mallory'.[148] A matter of some family mirth in March 1625 was the news that 'some have an intention to propose a marriadge betwene my cosen Frances Browne and my brother Anthony. I know not how my brother will relishe the notion for he doth not yet know of it.'[149]

We might imagine, however, that all Catholics would know and perhaps associate with each other, and intermarry, and witness wills for each other and so on, simply because that was the obvious thing to do in the face of the hostility of many of their neighbours. Here was the mechanism by which Catholicism would separate and withdraw from the rest of the world, becoming, in the process, the 'English Catholic community' of John Bossy's wonderful book of that name.[150] Indeed, we might assume that the Catholic laity, celebrated in mainstream historical narratives for their passivity and 'do-nothing' attitudes, would have used the comfortable and enclosing screen of kinship alliances to draw apart from the rest of society, a society which, we have been taught, subscribed so readily to the Protestant values of anti-popery. Out of mere commonsense and a desire to maintain the internal cohesion of their families, would the Catholic community also not have been essentially unpolitical? In particular, would the majority of the laity not have kept out of the occasional but embarrassing high-profile quarrels between those small and embittered factions of clergymen during, for instance, the notorious appellant controversy? How could it possibly benefit the majority of lay Catholic Englishmen to excite Protestant hatred by meddling in politics in the way that had brought the Jesuits Europe-wide opprobrium? And why should lay Catholics divide among themselves when this would inevitably weaken them and leave them open to Protestant ridicule? Indeed, one reading of Professor Bossy's account of the 'triumph of the laity' among English Catholics by the end of Elizabeth's reign, with leading gentlemen such as Sir Thomas Tresham offering to do a deal with the State on behalf of the

---

[147] AAW, B 27, no. 10; Berry, *Sussex*, 294–5. John Thatcher (the elder) of Priesthawes had married Anne, the daughter of Sir John Gage (Sir Anthony Browne's father-in-law).
[148] See e.g. AAW, B 47, no. 176, fo. 201r.
[149] AAW, B 47, no. 178, fo. 203r.   [150] Bossy, *ECC*.

community whereby gentry patrons would choke off the capacity for political activity on the part of the clergy, is that there was a lay consensus that the kin and patronage networks of the Catholic community should not be prostituted to clerical strife. And, indeed, relatively few laymen seem to have got consistently and directly involved in such intra-Catholic disputes.

But it is also possible to argue that the Catholic community was politicised in part precisely because the patronage dispensed by the aristocracy and gentry reflected and reinforced the divisions within the community. This can be demonstrated, briefly, by looking at the disjunctures between the Brownes and some other significant Catholic kinship networks. There were those with whom the Brownes did not seem to correspond and associate (even when there had formerly been associations and connections between them). For example, in the major intra-Catholic ideological confrontation of the period, between those who by and large supported the ecclesiastical strategies and political objectives of the religious orders (notably the Jesuits), and those who believed that these strategies and objectives were likely to damage the Catholic community's coherence, it is obvious that, even in the apparently socially harmonious Sussex gentry community, there was a series of glass walls separating some Catholic families from others. These walls may have been invisible to those not finely attuned to the political workings of the Catholic community, but they were very real ones all the same.

Take, for instance, the Darell family, with extensive land holdings and divided into several branches in East Sussex and West Kent. In the mid-sixteenth century they had been linked with the Brownes. (Thomas Darell of Scotney was one of the servants of Sir John Gage and was appointed as understeward to Sir Anthony Browne when Browne took the stewardship of the Sussex estates of the duchy of Lancaster.[151]) By the late sixteenth century the Darells had developed a distinctively Jesuit family tradition. Much later, in October 1757, John Darell SJ (who was rector of the Jesuit college at St Omer) sent a kinsman an account of the authorities' efforts, over one and a half centuries before, to arrest Richard Blount SJ at Scotney Castle when the Jesuit made a celebrated escape across the moat.[152] The account showed, John Darell thought, 'what a good understanding there was betwixt' the family of Darell and 'the family of Ignatius, of above one hundred and

---

[151] Swales, 'Local Politics', 11. Thomas Darell's son, George, sat in parliament in 1547, 1553 and 1554, with Sir John Gage's patronage, for East Grinstead and Lewes, *ibid.*, 98; Bindoff, *HC*, II, 19–20.

[152] See ch. 2, p. 44 above. Blount did not return to Scotney after this event, but his connection with the family did not cease. One of Henry Darell's children, Richard, was placed at St Omer, and then at the English College in Rome, through Blount's good offices, CRS 54, 267.

eighty years date, continued almost uninterrupted down to our days, there
being now actually at the same seat of Scotney a son of Ignatius, a priest of
the Society of Jesus, at the same house where the first provincial', i.e. Blount,
was 'secured and saved'.[153] One of the first Elizabethan Jesuits, John Curry,
was there for a time, and so was the priest Oliver Almond who was respected
by the Society and who later resided with Lord Stafford.[154]

Admittedly, there is no evidence of any ingrained or constant hostility
between the Darells and the families who were most closely associated with
the Brownes.[155] What there was not, however, was the intimate contact
which we might expect between two leading Catholic families in the same
county. And it seems that the principal reason for this may have been that,
while the Darells became thoroughly Jesuited, the Brownes, as we have
already remarked, frequently extended their patronage to clergy who, from
time to time, entertained serious doubts about the motives of the Jesuits and
their patrons.

There were several other Sussex Catholic families who were not inward
with the Brownes, and for much the same reason. As we saw in the previous chapter, the Brownes' priest Benjamin Norton made sniffy remarks
about the Jesuit-orientated Carylls. There was clearly also a lack of ideological affinity between the Brownes and the Cottons of Funtington and
Warblington, although the Cottons' Hampshire residences were very close
to Cowdray.[156] The Cottons' connections were primarily with the Wriothesley family. This meant that they were partly within the Brownes' orbit,
because of the marriage between the first viscount's daughter and the second
earl of Southampton. And two of the Cottons, Richard and John, witnessed
the first viscount's will, while Roger Manning identified (on the basis of
Richard Topcliffe's exhaustive enquiries) the existence of a route for priests
to pass between Warblington Castle (see Figure 17) and Cowdray, set up by
the Jesuit Robert Southwell.[157]

By the early seventeenth century, however, the Cottons had a clear prefer-
ence for Jesuit chaplains. Thomas Lister SJ was resident with the Cotton family in 1603, and, at other times, the Cottons entertained the Jesuits William

[153] Foley III, 482.
[154] BL, Lansdowne MS 72, no. 67, fo. 184r; PRO, SP 12/268/82; AAW, A XVI, no. 138, p. 545.
[155] In fact, as we saw above, Sir Edmund Pelham, Lady Magdalen, Viscountess Montague's
close confidant, had married into the Darell family. See also ch. 7, p. 221 below.
[156] In 1560, George Cotton, a future recusant, was had up for loose talk with Arthur Gunter
of Racton about the prospects for a marriage between the twelfth earl of Arundel (the first
Viscount Montague's leading rival in the shire) and the queen, and what a shame it was that
Mary Tudor had never got around to executing Lord Robert Dudley, who was Montague's
cousin, Mott, HR, 131–5, 136.
[157] WSRO, SAS/BA 67; Manning, *Religion*, 157; Devlin, *Life*, 218–19.

Figure 17.   The ruins of Warblington Castle, the residence of the Pole family. The castle was largely destroyed in the civil war. Only one of the octagonal turrets of the gatehouse survives, with part of the abutting wall.

Baldwin and Thomas Singleton. In 1606, the Suffolk-born former chaplain
to the Jesuit-favouring Darell family, George Jetter, 'a low man with a yel-
low beard', was a chaplain at Warblington.[158] In 1613, the search of the
rooms of John Cotton, one of the sons of George Cotton of Warblington,
turned up evidence of his dealings with the Jesuit Francis Young (formerly
a tutor employed by the Dormer family).[159] He had also been in correspondence with Henry Chadderton, who had, as we saw, been recruited into
the faith by the Jesuit-inclined members of the earl of Southampton's circle. 'Of all sorts of papists', John Cotton 'most affecteth the Jesuits, and
readeth their books, being much delighted with' the leading Jesuit writers
James Gretzer and Martin van der Beeck (Becanus). Formerly he had 'had
acquaintance' with the executed traitor and Jesuit superior Henry Garnet.
Cotton 'had two or three rich copes of his, which he lost upon Garnet's
apprehension'.[160] Some of the information against Cotton was volunteered
by the priest John Copley. Copley had at one time been a chaplain in the
Cotton household but took a dislike to the prevailing ecclesiastical and political temper there. (Before denouncing Cotton, Copley had departed to take
up a more congenial chaplaincy at Cowdray. He shortly thereafter joined
the Church of England.)[161] In mid-1615 there was a falling out between
the second Viscount Montague and Richard Cotton, apparently over some
arrangement made concerning the placement of Cotton's son in the viscount's
household. The Brownes' priest Robert Pett wrote to Thomas More from
Brussels in June 1615 to say that 'Mr Richard Cotton passed this way the
weeke past towards the Spawe, accompanied with his brother Henry and
sonne Edward.' Cotton told Pett that there was 'some discontent betwixt
my Lord Montague and him self about his little sonne Thomas who is alsoe
now agayne from my lord (I hope tyme will weare out that discontent betwixt
them)'.[162]

The issues which served to characterise and politicise contemporary
Catholicism were embedded, therefore, within the family networks which
provided the essential stuff of the Catholic community. Far from silencing
and preventing the famous, though (by historians) largely discounted and
ignored, spats between different Catholic clerical factions, the patronage
networks on which those factions relied actually underwrote and amplified
such quarrels. As we shall see in subsequent chapters, the same networks
served as essential sounding-boards for the airing of those factions' views.
Without them, those views would probably not have made it into the public

---

[158] Hodgetts, *Secret Hiding Places*, 113; Foley III, 501: Anstr. I, 189–90; BL, Lansdowne MS
72, no. 67, fo. 184r.
[159] CRS 54, 8. See ch. 2, p. 53 above.   [160] *HMCA*, 381–2.
[161] *NAGB*, 137, 140, 157, 228. See ch. 11, pp. 367–8 below.
[162] AAW, A XIV, no. 118, p. 369. See also *HMCD* V, 350; AAW, A XV, no. 142, p. 381.

sphere at all. In addition, our exploration of some of these networks will show how a range of politico-ecclesiastical issues were debated and hammered out between Catholics and Catholics as much as between Catholics and Protestants. A recovery of these webs of patronage and empathy, it will be argued, is essential for writing and interpreting an important section of the ecclesio-political narrative of the post-Reformation period in England.

4

The Brownes, Catholicism and politics until the Ridolfi plot

Let us start with a basic question. How did the family and entourage of a successful service noble (the first Viscount Montague) become, in the later sixteenth century, associated with a strain of Catholicism which was so critical of the regime of Queen Elizabeth, the daughter of the sovereign whom Sir Anthony Browne (d. 1548), the viscount's father, had served through thick and thin?

If we want to reassemble and sketch out the Brownes' mid- and later sixteenth-century reputation for Catholicism there are worse ways to start than by trying to recover the formative political experiences of Sir Anthony Browne (the future first viscount). In all probability, he was heavily influenced by the fact that his father, Sir Anthony, Henry VIII's standard bearer, master of the horse and roving military supremo, was an unashamed Francophobe.[1] Partly as a consequence of his dislike of the French, the elder Sir Anthony did not conceal his disapproval of the king's decision to cast aside Katherine of Aragon. He was hauled over the coals in June 1536. He openly stated that he had never considered Henry's divorce to be a lawful separation. He was quizzed as to 'whye he should have such affection' to Princess Mary, whose restoration to the succession was currently at issue, following the execution of Anne Boleyn, although Mary was refusing to submit to the king's demands. He disingenuously replied that 'he was only moved thereunto for the love he beareth to the king, for he never receyved lettre, message, token or recommendacions from her, ne hath sent her any'. And, when Browne was asked whether, if the current queen (Jane Seymour) had a daughter, he would want Mary to be preferred before her, he said, presumably biting his tongue,

---

[1] For Browne's military career, see Bindoff, *HC*, I, 518–21. He helped to suppress the Pilgrimage of Grace; and he served against the Scots in 1542, and went to France in 1544. For his Francophobia, see *ibid.*, flaunted in the face of the French on more than one diplomatic mission.

Figure 18.   Funeral monument to Sir Anthony Browne (d. 1548) in the parish
church (St Mary) in Battle, East Sussex.

that he never imagined any such thing, since the Seymour marriage was
'undoubted'.[2]

Though the elder Sir Anthony was one of the first of the privy council
to accept the earl of Hertford's authority as lord protector after Henry's
death, he now made no secret of the fact that he was wedded to an old-style
politico-religious conservatism and was, on most tests, a Catholic in matters
of religious belief. His will directs that Masses and dirges should be said
for the benefit of his soul.[3] More controversially, though, he had been on
the fringes of the Prebendaries plot against Archbishop Thomas Cranmer.
(One of his chaplains was examined concerning it.) He had also made an

---

[2] BL, Cotton MS Titus C VII, no. 94, fo. 187r–v; J. Brewer *et al.* (eds.), *Letters and Papers,
Foreign and Domestic, of the Reign of Henry VIII* (21 vols., 1862–1932), X (1887), 475–6.
I am very grateful to Simon Adams for assistance with this point.

[3] Bindoff, *HC*, I, 520. For notes on the funeral arrangements of Sir Anthony Browne, see
Bodl., Ashmolean MS 818, no. 5, fos. 12r–13r. For his tomb in Battle parish church, see
Figure 18.

unsuccessful effort to get Henry to place Bishop Stephen Gardiner on the council of regency.[4]

Sir Anthony's son, the future first Viscount Montague, did not conceal, during Edward VI's reign, that he believed the times were out of joint. Although he had been knighted at Edward's coronation, in March 1551 he was actually imprisoned in the Fleet for hearing Mass in the presence of Princess Mary. The regime of John Dudley (his kinsman) apparently tried to buy him off.[5] A number of appointments came his way and also a seat at Petersfield for the March 1553 parliament. But there is no evidence that he made any substantial concessions to the regime on the issue of religion.[6]

The memory of this early stubbornness was retained and celebrated within the Browne family. Richard Smith, the viscount's widow's chaplain, recalled in the early seventeenth century that Montague from early on espoused a 'love of God's worship and religion'. When Edward VI

(or rather others in his name), abolishing the religion of his predecessors as another Jeroboam, had erected a new altar and set up golden calves – I mean a new worship, or rather superstition – and almost all people, either for affectation of novelty or for fear of punishment, flocked to that new and enormous superstition, this pious youth would not stain himself with such heinous crime, but like another Tobias sought out the service of God practised by his parents, and both devoutly and publicly and with due reverence frequented the same.

It was for this that he ended up in the Fleet prison, but he still continued to make his stubborn resistance clear by 'adorning his chamber with tapestry', and resolved 'rather with Daniel to live in prison than to abstain from the divine service of his God'. In fact, noted Smith, he had successfully urged his father to vote against the Edwardian legislation on the Church. 'For when his father by the impious advice of some others, for to avoid the offence of heretics, was persuaded to absent himself from the parliament that day when under Edward the Sixth it was consulted of changing religion', the younger Sir Anthony 'never desisted till by prayers, tears, and such other reasons as he could, he had wrought his father to go to the parliament and courageously to give his voice for the true religion'.[7]

Whether or not Smith was exaggerating the young man's zeal for the 'old religion', Sir Anthony predictably rallied to Mary at the celebrated showdown with Lady Jane Grey. He sat again for Petersfield in the first Marian

[4] Bindoff, *HC*, I, 520. For the relationship between Sir Anthony Browne and Stephen Gardiner, see G. Redworth, *In Defence of the Church Catholic* (Oxford, 1990), 108, 113, 198, 209–10, 237, 242, 245.

[5] He had served with Dudley in the military force which suppressed Kett's rebellion (for which point I am indebted to Simon Adams).

[6] Bindoff, *HC*, I, 514.   [7] Southern, *ERH*, 17–18.

parliament, and then as knight of the shire for Surrey in April 1554. Following a diplomatic blunder whereby he was appointed master of the horse to Philip II and immediately dismissed when Philip brought his own household to England, he was in September elevated to the peerage. The title he chose, i.e. Montague, as we have already seen, spoke political volumes.[8] His investment took place at Hampton Court on 2 September 1554. The witnesses at the occasion were Bishop Stephen Gardiner, Sir John Gage (Gardiner's political ally during the factional disputes in the privy council during this year),[9] the marquis of Winchester (a friend of Montague's deceased father but with whom Montague would later on become rather less friendly),[10] John Russell, earl of Bedford and William Somerset, earl of Worcester. After a procession of various lords came Sir Anthony 'in jackett of whyte sylver', flanked by the earl of Worcester and Edward Fiennes, Lord Clinton, to both of whom the new peer was kin. Then, all the lords standing, save the kneeling Sir Anthony, 'Mr Garter delivered his pattente to the lord chamberlayne Sir John Gage who delivered it to the quene.'[11] In 1557 Montague became a privy councillor.[12]

Several Sussex Catholics had profited from their public support for Mary as she thwarted Northumberland's bid to wrest the succession from her. Lord De La Warr got a pension. Arundel was created lord steward of the royal household. Sir John Gage became Mary's lord chamberlain and received large land grants after the Jane Grey episode and again in 1554 after the Wyatt rebellion. Catholics now entirely dominated the county's administration and parliamentary representation.[13] Some had established links with Mary before her accession. Anthony Kempe of Slindon had been in her service since 1550. His second marriage was to Sir Edward Gage's daughter Margaret.[14] Kempe was something of a Court favourite, and was used as a diplomatic agent to the Spaniards. In 1554 he became an 'aid of the chamber' to King Philip (as did another Sussex Catholic, Richard Shelley, and also James Bassett, Bishop Gardiner's servant, who married into the Roper family).[15]

Though it did not take long for divisions in the Catholics' ranks to appear (Arundel was incensed in 1554 at Sir John Gage who had stolen a march on him in the county through a land grant),[16] Montague distinguished himself by beating down heresy. Thomas Paynell, an Augustinian friar and former chaplain to Henry VIII, dedicated to Montague his corrected version of Alexander Barclay's translation of Sallust's history of the Jugurthine wars;

[8] See ch. 3, p. 70 above.   [9] Bindoff, *HC*, II, 181.   [10] Loseley MSS, 616, 618.
[11] BL, Additional MS 6113, fos. 137v, 138r.   [12] Bindoff, *HC*, I, 515.
[13] R. J. W. Swales, 'Local Politics and the Parliamentary Representation of Sussex 1529–1558' (Ph.D., Bristol, 1964), 20–1.
[14] Bindoff, *HC*, II, 460.   [15] *Ibid.*, II, 460, I, 392–3.   [16] Swales, 'Local Politics', 40.

and in his dedication he praised Montague for, among other things, his vigour against Protestants. To his 'great renown and eternal fame', he had 'at all tymes, and against all the rablement of heretykes, sustained, and most constantly and Christianly avaunced the Catholyke fayth of our saviour and redemer Jesus Christ'.[17]

Not surprisingly, prominent gentry in alliance with the Brownes were enthusiastic to join in the campaign for reform and purification of the Church. James Gage, the brother of Sir Edward and son of the lord chamberlain, was later branded by John Foxe as a persecutor. The interrogation of the Sussex Marian martyr Richard Woodman, in whose misfortunes James Gage figured prominently, receives extensive treatment from Foxe.[18]

In the House of Lords, Montague was named in 1555 to a committee for the bill to punish exiles.[19] The Lady Chapel in Montague's parish church of St Saviour in Southwark, next to Montague House, was used as a spiritual courtroom in January 1555 for trying Protestant heretics (the first such trial under the revived heresy statutes). Stephen Gardiner and Edmund Bonner presided over the proceedings.[20] Montague had also been on the welcoming committee at Dover, with Bishop Thomas Thirlby, in November 1554 for Cardinal Reginald Pole. The new peer thus signalled his affection for the Pole family to which he was related, and with whose political cause he sympathised (even though Pole did not demonstrate quite the same imperialist inclinations that Montague liked to display).[21]

Richard Smith's life of Lady Magdalen recalls that when 'under Queen Mary the true religion did flourish again, none was more studious' than Viscount Montague

---

[17] Alexander Barclay, *The Conspiracie of Catiline . . . with the history of Iugurth* (1557), sig. Yviiir. I am grateful to Peter Lake for this reference. In June 1557, Montague surrendered appropriated rectories in order to found chantries at Midhurst and Battle, J. J. Scarisbrick, *The Reformation and the English People* (Oxford, 1984), 134. The queen's licence for these foundations was obtained on 12 June 1557, but nothing was done to finalise the arrangements before Elizabeth's accession, *VCH Sussex* IV, 78.

[18] S. R. Cattley (ed.), *The Acts and Monuments of John Foxe* (8 vols., New York, 1965), VIII, 333–77. In an undated Elizabethan petition by one John Trewe of Hellingley for compensation against James's brother Sir Edward, the latter was complained of for his malice, in particular that he was 'an extreme persecutor of the gospel' who unlawfully had Trewe pilloried in Lewes and Hailsham, and 'caused his ears to be barbarously cut', Loseley MSS, 665. For the Marian proceedings against heretics in Sussex, see A. S. Gratwick and C. Whittick, 'The Loseley List of "Sussex Martyrs": A Commission of Enquiry into the Fate of their Assets and the Development of the Sussex Protestant Martyrology', *SAC* 133 (1995), 225–40.

[19] Bindoff, *HC*, I, 515.

[20] I. Darlington, *Bankside: The Parishes of St Saviour and Christchurch, Southwark* (Survey of London, 22, 1950), 8.

[21] T. F. Shirley, *Thomas Thirlby* (1964), 138. For Pole's letter of September 1554 to Montague from Brussels, see BL, Additional MS 25425, fo. 304v.

to advance the Catholic faith. For which his zeal and other virtues worthy of such employment he especially was chosen of that queen to go ambassador to the pope and, desiring pardon of the schism past, to promise future obedience in the name of the whole kingdom. Which he performed to his everlasting praise, the honour of his nation, the glory of God, and the applause of the Christian world.[22]

This was Montague's crowning political achievement of the reign. He travelled to Rome in the company of Thirlby (who had been a diplomatic colleague of Montague's father, way back in 1533,[23] and a long-term ambassador at the imperial Court, and had been present to witness the glory of the imperial victory at Mühlberg) and Sir Edward Carne. Together they represented clergy, lords and commons.[24] Montague's role in securing, under the most difficult circumstances, the reconciliation of the realm to the see of Rome lived on in the family's collective memory. It was evidently a key component of their Catholic identity. Montague's embassy was acclaimed on the family's funeral monument in the church at Midhurst (see Figure 3).[25] (This monument was erected during the early seventeenth century when the first viscount's grandson and heir was posing as an essential conduit for negotiations between the Holy See and English Catholics.)[26]

The decision to dispatch the three men was taken in early 1555.[27] An account of their journey was written by one of Thirlby's servants who was distinctly unsympathetic to Roman Catholicism.[28] The servant's travel journal ridiculed the rigmarole and ceremonial used among the curia and cardinalate in Rome. It recounts how the new pope, Marcellus (successor to Julius III), died on 1 May 1555, before they arrived. At or on the way to Perugia they heard of the election of a new pope, the appalling Caraffa, who took the name of Paul IV. Caraffa was the imperialists' worst nightmare. This was something which the ambassadors could hardly ignore, and

---

[22] Southern, *ERH*, 18–19.   [23] Shirley, *Thomas Thirlby*, 142.

[24] T. M. McCoog and L. Lukács (eds.), *Monumenta Angliae III* (Rome, 2000), 177. Montague and Thirlby joined up with Carne on their journey to Rome, BL, Harleian MS 252, no. 15, fo. 62r. T. F. Shirley portrays Thirlby as essentially a moderate, following the commands of the Marian regime to enforce the reaction against Protestantism out of obedience rather than actual enthusiasm, Shirley, *Thomas Thirlby*. But he rejected the Elizabethan settlement of religion in 1559 (see below in this chapter). For Carne, see Bindoff, *HC*, I, 586. Carne's son Thomas was on a 1574 list of supporters of Mary Stuart and was noted in the 1577 survey of nonconformist Catholicism to have been a recusant since 1559, Hasler, *HC*, I, 556.

[25] Mosse, *ME*, 73: 'this honrable man in the yere 1553 was imployed by Q. Marie in an honrable ambassage to Rome with Doctor Thyrlbie Bisshope of Elye which he performed to his greate honor and commendation'.

[26] See ch. 3, p. 69 above and ch. 11, pp. 341–2 below.   [27] Shirley, *Thomas Thirlby*, 142.

[28] He noted that in Perugia 'we saw a speciall relicke forsoth of our ladies ring', the cult and adoration of which he regarded with much scepticism, BL, Harleian MS 252, no. 15, fo. 64r.

they were not allowed to forget it by some of their hosts along the way. 'The great peeces of ordinaunce and small shott, shot of[f] bravely', and there were 'great fireworkes, besides in the ayre'. The cause of the Perugians' 'great joy', sniggered Thirlby's servant, 'was sposed [*sic*] to be because the pope was French in hart, and enimy to the emperor, not withstanding he was a Neapolitan before borne'. In Perugia, on 26 May, 'trumpitteres and drumme[r]s came to visite' Montague and Thirlby, 'and begann to play. But answeare was sent from the lordes, that looke with what freindship they were received and lodged with the like they should receive ther reward.' Then the Perugians 'departed in great despite and anger, strikking upon their drumme heades as hard as they could lay on'. An encounter with the 'vicelegate' in Perugia, who tried to repair the diplomatic damage, was met with a similar stony response from the English party. Via the town of Foligno they arrived at Spoleto where the narrator observed 'the people are very proud and beggerly and of no civillitie, great boasters, but of noe activity, and much given to secret murther' as well as various forms of unnatural vice.

Having arrived in Rome, Montague and Thirlby found that 'great provision' had been made for them 'in the pallace of St Marke'. On 'the eight[h] day at night' the ambassadors 'were sent for and had secret audience' with the pope. At this stage, despite all the inevitable tensions, everything was still being done to jolly along their mission. On 9 June the newly created Cardinal Caraffa, the pope's nephew, dispatched gifts to them. And on the following day 'the lords went to the Courte, accompanied' by various 'bishops, noblemen and gentillmen'. At their meeting with the new pope, Thirlby made an oration. Afterwards 'all the Englishmen of the lords trayne were called for, and came within the rayles to kysse the popes holynes foote', and to receive the pope's blessing. On 11 June more meetings followed with specific cardinals. (Thirlby's servant was slightly losing interest in the diplomatic process by this stage and was more preoccupied, for example, with the 'live ostridge' that he saw 'at the ca[r]dinall of Pisa his howse', from which creature he 'plucked a white feather'.)

On 12 June, in a display of pro-imperial sentiment, the English diplomatic party 'heard a dirge Masse at the Spanish church, for the emperors mother', Joanna the Mad. More meetings with cardinals followed, 'at a place called Bellvidre', and they had another audience with the pope. On 16 June the English diplomats dined with the pope at the palace of St Mark. After dinner they went to visit the cardinals whom they had not spoken with before. And, 'the same night, they toke there leave of the pope who gave my Lord Montague a table diamond with a ringe estemed at 2000 crownes', and presented Thirlby with 'a crosse of gold'. They 'made great bonefyers', related Thirlby's servant, 'because we ware reconciled to the Church of

Rome'. Off Montague and Thirlby went, leaving Carne behind as resident ambassador.[29]

After the return from Rome (via Brussels to meet with the emperor),[30] Montague and Thirlby were the chief mourners at Bishop Gardiner's funeral. (They were also executors of his will.) Gardiner's corpse initially lay in the Southwark church of St Saviour,[31] the Brownes' parish church. They joined the funeral procession as the body was taken for burial to Winchester Cathedral.[32]

Back in his county Montague continued to function as a bastion of law and order. A privy council letter of 8 March 1556 thanked the lord chamberlain Sir John Gage 'for his travayle used in the searching out of the aucthours of certain sedytious billes lately cast abrode in sundrye partes of the countye of Sussex'. And he was asked 'to contynue his diligence in that bihalfe, in whiche matter the Lord Mountague is also written unto to travaile the beste he can'.[33] On 13 April, Montague was commended 'for sending out of two suspecte personnes that woulde have passed into Fraunce in the costes of Sussex', and for his strict dealing in apprehending 'offendours within that shire'.[34]

Montague also demonstrated his military prowess. (He was responsible for mustering men for anticipated military action on the northern border and for service in France.[35]) Montague distinguished himself at St Quentin in 1557 and saw service at Calais as lieutenant general of the army, under the earl of Pembroke.[36] In early 1558, Montague's duties as lord lieutenant in Sussex included responsibility for defending the coast.[37] When Sir Nicholas Pelham (whose brother William had been involved in the Wyatt rebellion) refused in summer 1558 to start mustering men for the war, he was given a dressing down by Montague; he was then locked up in the Fleet until he agreed to comply.[38] Paynell's dedication of his version of Barclay's translation of Sallust's Jugurthine history asked rhetorically, 'what practike feat of war, what instrument or warlike engin is ther that ye moost finely and exactlye

---

[29] BL, Harleian MS 252, no. 15, fos. 49r–73v (quotations at fos. 63v–64r, 64v, 65r, 66r, 67v). See also Shirley, *Thomas Thirlby*, 147–50. The death of Joanna, Charles V's mother and queen of Castile, was politically significant since it cleared the way for Charles to abdicate in favour of Philip. I am very grateful for this point to Pauline Croft.

[30] Shirley, *Thomas Thirlby*, 151.

[31] Gardiner's residence, Winchester House, was in Southwark.

[32] F. T. Dollman, *The Priory of St. Mary Overie, Southwark* (1881), 13.

[33] *APC 1554–6*, 245.   [34] *Ibid.*, 262.

[35] *A Calendar of the Shrewsbury and Talbot Papers in Lambeth Palace Library and the College of Arms* (2 vols., 1966–71), II, 73; SHC, LM 6729/8/1–2.

[36] Bindoff, *HC*, I, 515. This fact was, like Montague's embassy to Rome, recalled on the family's monument at Midhurst, Mosse, *ME*, 73.

[37] Bindoff, *HC*, I, 515.   [38] *Ibid.*, III, 81. Pelham was released in August.

can not handle?'. Montague's martial valour and learning went hand in hand with his zeal for the 'true religion'.[39]

THE ACCESSION OF ELIZABETH

The new regime of November 1558 was a shocking setback to the chief supporters of what, on many accounts, had been a self-confident and extremely aggressive administration poised, for all the disappointments and reverses, military and otherwise, of Mary's last year, to consolidate its power. As Robin Swales has it, 'although Catholics continued to hold local government office' in Sussex, the Gage family and the earl of Arundel 'suffered a serious decline', and the Sackvilles began their phenomenal rise to power.[40] Montague came off badly. Many other Marians seemed able to make an accommodation with the new regime, but he, apparently, would not. He (along with Lord Hastings, Lord Rich and Lord Paget) was dismissed from (or rather, not retained on) the reconstituted privy council while others such as the earls of Arundel, Derby and Pembroke kept their places.[41]

Crucially, Montague was the only temporal peer to oppose the passage of the final Elizabethan supremacy bill in the 1559 parliament (though he was one of nine temporal peers who voted against the accompanying bill for uniformity).[42] He was also the only one to oppose the dissolution of the new religious houses.

Now, in many ways, the hostility of a respected though not first-rank peer such as Montague to aspects of the government's legislative programme may look heroic but pointless. Was it not almost the last respectable gasp of the old order? Surely the regime must have allowed it simply because it seemed prudent to give a bit of air time to someone who was already on the fast track to old buffer status? And, since his opposition was couched in the language of obedience and respect, could this not also be taken to mean that Catholics such as Montague were accepting that they had lost both the battle and the war? There was, we might think, nowhere left for them to turn. Their 'loyalty' was mere compliance, as the regime expertly fitted the

---

[39] Barclay, *The Conspiracie of Catiline*, sig. Yviiir–v.   [40] Swales, 'Local Politics', 22–3.

[41] N. Jones, *Faith by Statute* (1982), 32–3; D. Starkey, *Elizabeth* (2000), 241–2. Starkey reconstructs the context of Elizabeth's words to her sister's privy councillors on *c.* 25 November 1558 (not, in fact, 17 November) when she intimated that some of them were metaphorically for the chop. I am grateful to Simon Adams for the redating of Elizabeth's speech.

[42] J. E. Neale, *Elizabeth I and her Parliaments* (2 vols., 1953–7), I, 75, 80. See Jones, *Faith by Statute*, 72–3, for a list of these peers – William Paulet, marquis of Winchester, Francis Talbot, earl of Shrewsbury, Henry Parker, Baron Morley, Edward Dudley, Baron Dudley, Thomas Wharton, Baron Wharton, Richard Rich, Baron Rich, Edward North, Baron North, Henry Stafford, Baron Stafford and Viscount Montague.

ether mask which asphyxiated the old religion's more vocal and influential supporters.

Admittedly, Montague's and his friends' interventions never really looked like stopping the religious settlement of 1559, though he and his political allies seriously disrupted the course of the regime's legislative programme. But another look at the parliamentary speech which he wrote and delivered as a critique of the decision to impose the royal supremacy and religious uniformity must call into question any account of him as a merely 'loyal' peer.

The first reading of the supremacy bill took place in the Commons on 9 February, and the second on 13 February. Norman Jones has deftly retraced the complex process whereby the crown introduced its programme on religion into the 1559 parliament before the expected prorogation at Easter. There were three days of debate on the bill (13–15 February) and charge was taken of it, at committee stage, by Sir Anthony Cooke and Sir Francis Knollys. Then a bill entitled 'the boke for common prayer and mynystracion of sacraments' was introduced and read, swiftly followed, on 21 February, by another supremacy bill which now included the liturgical legislation (in effect, provision for uniformity). Two days later it was passed in the lower house.[43]

The debate in the Commons had been anything but peaceable, but the Lords was where the bill really ran into trouble – in fact from the very moment of its first reading on 28 February.[44] Following its second and very delayed reading (on 13 March) it was considered in committee (a committee staffed by the marquis of Winchester, the duke of Norfolk, the earls of Westmorland, Shrewsbury, Rutland, Sussex and Pembroke, Viscount Montague himself, the bishops of Exeter and Carlisle and Lords Clinton, Morley, Rich, Willougby and North).[45] Here it was effectively destroyed – sliced and de-boned by its opponents.[46] Allegedly Montague got entangled, at some point, in a slanging match with the strongly Protestant earl of Bedford. As we saw, not all the members of the party which had gone with Thirlby, Carne and Montague to Rome in 1555 had been friends to Rome and Rome's religion. Picking up, perhaps, on stories which may have been circulated by some of those who returned from this diplomatic mission, Bedford enquired whether Montague and his friends had been offered personal services by Rome's sex industry at the curia's expense. Montague hotly denied it.[47]

---

[43] Jones, *Faith by Statute*, 88–9, 90, 93–4; Starkey, *Elizabeth*, 280.

[44] Jones, *Faith by Statute*, 96.   [45] *Ibid.*, 99; Starkey, *Elizabeth*, 280.

[46] Jones, *Faith by Statute*, 99; E. Jeffries Davis (ed.), 'An Unpublished Manuscript of the Lords' Journals for April and May 1559', *English Historical Review* 28 (1913), 531–42, at p. 538. Jones notes that 'the earl of Pembroke, the earl of Shrewsbury, Viscount Montague, and Lord Hastings staunchly supported the bishops' in their opposition, Jones, *Faith by Statute*, 100.

[47] Jones, *Faith by Statute*, 100. As Simon Adams has pointed out to me, Bedford was not a member of the Lords' committee on the bill, so it is not clear when his exchange with Montague took place.

The revised version of the legislation was completely unacceptable to the regime, though the real opposition had been (only) to the proposals for altering the liturgy and imposing uniformity. Indeed the revised bill passed the Lords. It repealed the Marian heresy legislation, offered the queen a form of ecclesiastical supremacy and denied the authority of the pope within the realm. Jones concludes that 'the committee members had refused to grant Elizabeth clear recognition of her claim to be supreme head of the Church of England'. Among the temporal peers only Montague and Shrewsbury voted against the bill after its third reading on 18 March 1559.[48]

Montague had, however, combined with Nicholas Heath, archbishop of York, to deliver a devastating indictment of crown policy on the Church.[49] T. E. Hartley conjectures that the speech which Montague prepared was intended for the debate which began on 13 March, the date of the second reading of the bill which had come up, in heavily amended form, from the Commons. We do not have any direct contemporary evidence that it was actually delivered verbally and in full.[50] But, in the early seventeenth century, Richard Smith recalled the speech in such a way as to make it clear that Montague's oration was set forth in spoken form. Montague had exhorted the lords 'not to permit themselves to be carried away with every wind of new doctrine, nor to dissolve that which themselves so very lately had ratified and with solemn ceremony had promised inviolably to observe: not to abolish that religion, wherein all their Christian ancestors lived with such splendour and died with such piety'.[51]

The speech is often described as the discourse of a moderate man, someone who was quintessentially loyal.[52] In this, Montague is thought to have been similar to Archbishop Heath, his good friend, who spoke five days afterwards (in the third reading debate of 18 March) against the proposed legislation.[53] After his deprivation, Heath was treated leniently and allowed to retire.[54] As Roger Manning describes the viscount's speech, 'Montague did not argue

[48] *Ibid.*, 101, 102–3.   [49] *Ibid.*, 100; Starkey, *Elizabeth*, 280.

[50] T. E. Hartley (ed.), *Proceedings in the Parliaments of Elizabeth I* (3 vols., 1981–95), I, 4–5, 7–11. As Hartley comments, Montague was on the committee to consider the supremacy bill, but the House of Lords' journal 'provides no corroborative evidence' that his speech and that of Archbishop Heath 'were delivered, as opposed to being merely prepared, though the probability must be that they were'.

[51] Southern, *ERH*, 19.

[52] Montague voted in favour of the bill to restore first fruits and tenths to the crown (1 Elizabeth, c. 4), whereas all the lords spiritual voted against it, Neale, *Elizabeth I and her Parliaments*, I, 45.

[53] Hartley, *Proceedings*, I, 4.

[54] See A. Pritchard, *Catholic Loyalism in Elizabethan England* (1979), 41–9; Neale, *Elizabeth I and her Parliaments*, I, 65. For Montague's long friendship with Heath, see Loseley MSS, 632–3; SHC, LM 6729/8/71; R. B. Manning, 'Anthony Browne, 1st Viscount Montague: The Influence in County Politics of an Elizabethan Nobleman', *SAC* 106 (1968), 103–12, at p. 111.

that Protestantism was false; rather he viewed it as a novel doctrine which should not be forced on a people who had not resolved the truth of that doctrine in their consciences.'[55]

This, arguably, is not the only way that Montague's 1559 address can be read. As Conrad Russell has emphasised, political ideas depend a lot for their effect on the way that they are aired. Without the context, it is often difficult to understand the public impact which political speeches had on their hearers: 'the reasons why people in politics do or do not annoy each other are often ones which cannot be recorded on paper' and a speech 'delivered with the head in the brief' will have a totally different public effect from the 'one . . . delivered with waves of anger which the audience reciprocated'.[56] But it seems clear that Montague's words were not a quiet and dignified critique, a mere caveat. It was unlikely, in any case, that a former privy councillor, a stalwart representative of some of the Marian regime's most radical policy lines, would, politically, just curl up and die. The problem is that the terms 'loyalist' and 'moderate' are often used by historians to mean 'not politically active'. Opposition to the royal supremacy was never confused, during Elizabeth's reign or indeed for a long time thereafter, with political inactivity. Of course, Montague did not actually call for a Catholic uprising. Nevertheless, it is far from obvious that Montague's oration would have been taken as a token of quiet obedience.

He began respectfully, with a mass of ingratiating and disingenuous verbiage, a not uncommon way of velveting over a verbal iron fist:

My lords, loath I am to speake and much afraide, waying reverently the matter nowe in hande, both for the weight thereof, and also remembring the person whom yt seemeth to touche therwith, not willing to impugne the judgment of others which have spoken therein, whom otherwise I honour and love, considering also myne owne insufficiency in all respectes to speake in so great a matter and case of such importaunce to those in whom I doubt not either certeyne wisdome and knowledge, nor zeale to the true religion of Christe.

In fact, he said he heartily wished that someone else might have taken on the burden of expressing dissent, but they had not.

At last Montague got to the point. He wished his auditors to consider

the matter in hande, to the body wherof exhibited unto us I have to speake and not to the particularitie of the title, which only toucheth the Scripture, carying awaye by generall wordes the whole estate of Christs religion. For as in the first parte the supremacie is only intreated of, even so in the bodie of the bill, all that ever was made for the defence of the faith against the malignitie of wicked heresies, are wholy repealed, and the confusion lately used in religion, newly receaved and established:

[55] Manning, *Religion*, 229–30.
[56] C. Russell, *The Causes of the English Civil War* (Oxford, 1990), 185.

the Masse abrogated, the sacrifice of the Churche rejected, the sacramentes pro-
phaned, the holie aultars destroyed, temples vyolated, mariage of preistes allowed,
their children made legitimate; lybertie given to them by purchase or other meanes to
procure to their posteritie, lands and hereditamentes, and thus I conceive the effect
of this bill.

In case they had not got the message, he emphasised 'therfore nowe have I
to saye that I must speake for the staye of the whole state of religion, which
this byll carieth awaye dyrectly with yt'.

At this point he paused and admitted, 'yet am I two wayes much afrayed,
the one by speaking to offend those whom I most desyre to please, the
other and cheife, by not speaking, to offend my conscience, and therby God
himself'. But he reassured himself that he was justified in speaking his mind
since the parliament house was a place

wherin all men are bounde to discharge themselves, not only by yea and naye, but
also as occasion serveth to further and advaunce all those thinges that sounde to the
honour of God and wealth of the realme, and to hinder, let and be against all such
thinges wherin God or his Churche might bee dishonored or our countrye hyndred.

What, then, was his prescription for the good of the commonwealth in the
matter of this bill? After more verbiage about how well he had informed his
own conscience, he stated bluntly why he could not accept this measure. It
was because of the respect which he had for the religion 'which I professed
in my baptisme, wher I was made a member of Christs misticall bodie, and
vowed to beleeve the holy Catholique Churche, as the spowse and only
beloved of Christe, by unitie in the which I am to bee saved or damned'.
Over it no temporal governor could preside. And even where princes had
presumed to do this in other countries, particularly Germany, it was still not
the custom to grind out the Catholic faith at the root.

As for the Church of Rome, he remarked on his recent embassy to the
Holy City: 'at Rome yt is said I did or might see much abhomination . . . :
truly my lordes I thinck I knowe that synne is greatly encreased in the whole
worlde, and doth in manner overflowe all nations', but, for his own part, he
had seen no more than a few 'unworthie' cardinals. He could not accept that
the reconciliation to Rome formalised by that embassy was 'not well donne'.
He further argued that he could not believe 'thatt all the worlde is damned,
saving a fewe that beleeve and professe this newe doctrine, unknowne to
the Churche, but by condempnation therof: in the which they never agreed
among themselves, but have spent more mens lyves in their controversies,
and all against the truthe of the Churche', though he softened the starkness
of this statement by saying that he made it out of mere conscience, and
believed simply that they should 'remayne in unitie, with Christs Churche
and . . . [their] neighbours'.

If this had been just a matter of Montague's religious sensibilities, his love of the old order of things and, perhaps, a certain pique at what people had been saying about his embassy to Rome, then it could all be taken as in some sense 'moderate'. But that was not all. In his very next sentence, he made it plain that it was not just a matter of doctrine. For he was also 'almost as hardly driven by duty to my prynce and countrie, whom I doo and ought to honour, serve and humbly obaye'. He was 'fearfull of the sure and quyett estate of my soveraigne and countrye'. Again he claimed that he said this only because he felt it was his duty to the queen, and parliament was the place to say it. Nevertheless the 'matter here offred be as evill an advise as all her enemyes can imagine to give her and her realme'.

Here are the first stirrings of the consistent and increasingly violent line in the Catholic polemic of the Elizabethan period that the queen was being led into evil/Protestant courses by those who posed as her friends but covertly sought her ruin. Montague thought that this unilateral action was insane because 'in chaunging of religion we condempne all other nations, of whom some be our fryndes and many our enymies, open and auncyent, who long tyme have and no doubt doo expect an opportunitie to annoy us'. The pope, 'hearing' that the English were 'by schisme devided from the Churche', might 'proceede to the excommunication of the realme, which we knowe hath followed others in the like case'. 'Howe enjoyeth the kynge of Spayne Navarra? Ys yt not by sentence of excommunication? And therby aucthoritie given to him to possesse the same that coulde by strong hand obtayne yt? Howe came Naples from the auncyent goverment to the hands of their enemyes?' And then there was the dreadful example of King John. 'To what extremitie was he dryven by the like attempt in religion?' In other words, this unilateral change of religion would, thought Montague, create enemies and the grounds for enmity where none previously existed, and give an immense ideological advantage to a foreign foe which, if Catholic, would be able, for propaganda purposes, to allege that the English nation was in schism. If, by contrast, a foreign and Catholic nation was inclined to friendship, it might be discouraged by the fact of that schism. He said also that this throwing off of unity was a sure fire way to destabilise the kingdom internally.

Ad[d] to this our owne weaknes and povertie, at home: mens myndes discontented, great somes of mony dewe, and more of necessitie demanded; and cheifly remember the evill nature of our people that alwaies uppon a little libertie are readie to rebell, and dare doo any thinge, and every man followe his owne waye, which thing if yt doo happen (as to[o] often of late yt hath donne) who seeth not the perrill of the realme almost inevitable?[57]

---

[57] T. J. McCann, 'The Parliamentary Speech of Viscount Montague against the Act of Supremacy, 1559', *SAC* 108 (1970), 50–7; Hartley, *Proceedings*, I, 7–11.

All in all, this was as thorough an indictment of the regime's policy as it is possible to imagine. It anticipates, as we have just suggested, some of the later 'evil counsellor' polemic (notably the *Treatise of Treasons* of 1572) in which it was claimed that the queen was being inveigled and lured to her political doom by malign and Machiavellian advisers.[58] For their own ends they were imperilling the queen's safety and the commonwealth. In particular, these polemics alleged, the Protestant Reformation was like a Trojan horse, introduced by stealth into the English Church to advance the careers of these Machiavels and to destroy their enemies. (One of the effects of the reform was to alienate and antagonise foreign Catholic powers.) Montague's speech predicts all of this. He did not name names, but his meaning was all too clear. And his speech's peroratory claim that the queen, at her accession, had invited noble councillors such as himself to speak their minds, openly and honestly for her benefit, would not have softened the blow.[59]

Montague's and Heath's handiwork compelled the regime to go back to the drawing (or drafting) board on this aspect of its legislative programme. When the bill passed by the Lords in March was returned to the Commons it was unsatisfactory to many of the members who were desperate to destroy the Marian settlement. It was unacceptable also to the regime, which could not politically afford a half-way house. In fact the Commons did pass the bill, but the regime resolved to try again. On 24 March (according to the duke of Feria) it was decided to keep the parliament in being.[60] A new attempt was made when parliament reconvened after Easter.

Montague's persistence in opposition was now futile. He continued to resist but, as we know, by means of a rigged clerical disputation on religion and through simple *force majeure* the two final bills of supremacy and uniformity went through after the members reassembled in early April. After the supremacy bill was passed in the Commons on 13 April and was taken to the Lords, Montague was, as we have remarked already, the only temporal peer to dissent, though the spiritual peers held out. The House approved the final version of the measure on 29 April. Montague was also the only temporal peer to join the bishops in voting against the bill annexing monasteries, chantries and other religious houses to the crown (1 Elizabeth I, c. 24).[61]

Others who similarly opposed the regime's line, such as Montague's diplomat colleague Bishop Thirlby, were now dealt with. Even if Thirlby

---

[58] See [John Leslie], *A Treatise of Treasons against Q. Elizabeth, and the Croune of England* (Louvain, 1572).
[59] McCann, 'Parliamentary Speech', 56; Hartley, *Proceedings*, I, 10; Starkey, *Elizabeth*, 241–2.
[60] Jones, *Faith by Statute*, 103, 117; *CSPV 1558–80*, 52.
[61] Jones, *Faith by Statute*, 123, 130, 134, 139–40, 143–4, 165. Simon Adams has suggested to me that the purpose of the disputation, and particularly of the refutations made during it of arguments against the prayer book, was to persuade the lay peers to support a uniformity bill.

had dallied with the Edwardian regime, and had been a close friend of
Cranmer, he was an inner-circle member of the Marian government (and
was an executor of the queen's will). He had been out of the country when
the queen died – engaged in negotiation with the French in order to try to
get Calais back. But when he returned and the oath of supremacy was put to
him, he refused it, was deprived and actually preached against it. (This led to
his incarceration in the Tower in June 1560, from which he was transferred
to reside with Archbishop Matthew Parker for the rest of his life. He died in
1570.)[62]

THE ISSUE OF LOYALTY

This episode, however, was, in political terms, the start of something, not the
end of it, and whatever the something was, it was not particularly moderate.
Of course, Viscount Montague was happy to promote and embellish his
reputation as a moderate man. Even at the end of his life he was still to be
found lecturing audiences on how it had always been possible for him to
be both a good Catholic and a loyal subject.[63] But, if we look to the later
sixteenth and early seventeenth centuries, we can see how his reputation
had been deliberately constructed by others as much as by himself. One
famous instance of the viscount's behaviour as a good Englishman is his
alleged appearance at Tilbury in 1588. Here he is supposed to have turned
out at the head of a force of almost 200 mounted troops, accompanied by
his sons, to defend the queen whom he had so faithfully served for so long.
But this display of loyalty, whether it actually occurred or not, is known
only from an account in a pamphlet which was penned by Lord Burghley.
At best it was a piece of spin, playing up the English Catholics' allegedly
'loyal' response to the Spanish threat.[64] This was a way of countering the
recent inflammatory 'copies' of letters printed by Catholic activists which
urged Catholics to throw off their allegiance, for example William Allen's
*Copie of a Letter . . . concerning the Yeelding up, of the Citie of Daventrie,
unto his Catholike Majestie, by Sir William Stanley* (published in 1587)
which praised Sir William Stanley's defection to the Spaniards in the Low
Countries. The regime's tactics seem to have worked to some degree. When

[62] A. Jessopp, *One Generation of a Norfolk House* (1879), 117.
[63] SHC, LM 1856; Questier, LF; ch. 5, p. 176 below.
[64] William Cecil, *The Copy of a Letter Sent out of France to Don Barnardino Mendoza, Ambassador in France for the King of Spain, Declaring the State of England* (1588). For the detection of the pamphlet as a forgery, see C. Read, 'William Cecil and Elizabethan Public Relations', in S. T. Bindoff, J. Hurstfield and C. H. Williams (eds.), *Elizabethan Government and Society* (1961), 21–55, at p. 45. See also S. D. Scott, '"A Booke of Orders and Rules" of Anthony Viscount Montague in 1595', *SAC* 7 (1854), 173–212, at pp. 180–1; Manning, *Religion*, 229–30; Breight, 'Caressing', 150.

Richard Topcliffe's men were making their investigations in Aston Rowant in Oxfordshire at the end of August 1589 they found and arrested (on suspicion of being a priest) an individual called Randall. He was resident in the house of one Mr English (a servant of Sir Christopher Hatton). When interrogated by Sir Francis Knollys, Randall denied that he was a priest but admitted his recusancy. He said, nevertheless, that 'he was of my Lord Mowntague his secte and as redye [a] man to fyghte agaynste the Spanyards as my Lord Mowntague was'.[65]

The problematic nature of the first viscount's political loyalty was pointed up also by the way that different Catholic factions themselves subsequently tried to recruit him. During the appellant controversy, Montague was cited as a paragon of virtue by the priest William Watson. Watson argued that a Jesuit-sponsored Spanish invasion would be an overthrow of the whole commonwealth, not a conversion of the realm, and that the Spaniards admitted as much. The invaders would spare the Catholics no less than Protestants or puritans. Watson recorded that 'in the case proposed' of what Catholics should do in the face of a foreign invasion under a Catholic banner,

the old Lord Mountacute of worthie memorie . . . gave a no lesse Catholike than loyall answere . . . saying to this effect: that if the pope himselfe should come in with crosse, key and gospell in his hand, he would be readie with the first to run unto his Holines to cast himselfe downe at his feete to offer his service unto him in all humblenes of hart, and what not to shew himselfe a dutifull childe. But if, in steede of comming in solemne procession with crosse, booke, praiers and preaching, he should come in a sounding royall march with heralds of armes, with banners of blood displaied, with trumpets, alarum, pikes, harquebuse and men of armes all marshald in rankes set in battell aray, then would he be the first man in the field armed at all points, to resist him . . . To the like end did his brother in law the ever honorable [Francis] Dacre his words tend even in the middest of his prince and countries enimies,

in other words while Dacre was in Spain in the early 1590s.[66]

Watson and others were using the viscount's own pronouncements to assemble this picture of him. In his valedictory speech to his relatives and friends at West Horsley in 1592, Montague had protested

that yf the pope or the kinge of Spayne or anye other forreyne potentate shoulde offer to invade this realme, for anye cawse whatsoever, I woulde be one of the fyrst that shoulde beare armes agenst him or them for my prynce and cowntrye to the

[65] Davidson, RC, 260-1.

[66] Watson, *Decacordon*, 176-7; P. Holmes, *Resistance and Compromise* (Cambridge, 1982), 202. In 1620, Thomas Gainsford's 'Vox Spiritus' has the ghost of Sir Walter Raleigh reminding the count of Gondomar of William Watson's words about Montague's determination to resist a papal invasion: if the pope 'cam with Peters sword and colors displayed to depresse the renowne of England', Montague 'would . . . be the first man . . . [to] trample his triple crowne in the dirte', BL, Harleian MS 7187, fo. 25r-v. I am very grateful to Thomas Cogswell for this reference.

uttermost of my power. And yf I shoulde knowe that anye of youe my bretheren or childeren shoulde concent unto anye suche thinge, as to joyne with pope or forreyne potentate, I woulde be he that should fyrst present youe or anye of youe to the quene and her cowncell.[67]

But what do we mean by 'loyalty' here? The two cases – of a pope appearing at e.g. Portsmouth or Dover with a cross, a key and a copy of the New Testament, or, alternatively, with a large army – were equally improbable scenarios. When the supreme pontiff decided to intervene in English domestic political affairs (as, for example, in 1570 when Pius V issued the bull *Regnans in Excelsis*) he, of course, resorted to declarations or rulings on such matters which relied for their force on the complex amalgam of spiritual and political authority which many contemporaries understood to be uniquely located in the papacy. Montague, and others, would then have to decide where they stood. In any case, the whole thrust of Catholic political thought on the issue of loyalty and resistance tended to confuse and obscure the issue of exactly what a 'good' Catholic was supposed to think on the question of political fidelity to sovereign authority. Furthermore, Watson, like other appellant polemicists, was using the Jesuits as an archetype of political Machiavellianism to justify his own peculiar brand of political activity. Watson and his friends described themselves, by contrast, as merely 'loyal', as they sought to work themselves into the good graces of James VI, whom they recognised as Elizabeth's rightful successor. In other words, the memory of Montague as a loyalist was being incorporated for tactical reasons into Catholic tolerationist discourse. But this did not mean that all Protestants simply believed these Catholics' professions of loyalty, or accepted their accounts of recent political history and their constructions of the reputations of figures such as Montague. (Watson's citation of Francis Dacre as a faithful subject of the queen was highly tendentious. Anyone who knew anything about anything would have been aware that Dacre was not, in fact, regarded by the State as a loyalist.[68])

Not to be outdone, however, the other/'Jesuit' side in the appellant dispute sometimes tried to claim Montague for itself, or at least to speak well of him. Robert Persons declared in 1606, in his *Answere to the Fifth Part of Reportes Lately set Forth by Syr Edward Cooke* (a work which strongly defended the recently executed Henry Garnet SJ), that Queen Elizabeth had been 'drawne to many things against her owne inclination', and made 'much resistance . . . at the beginning . . . to admit any change of religion'. She would 'often speake bitterly and contemptuously' against the Protestant 'innovators' in religion who were wrecking the English Church. She would

[67] SHC, LM 1856, 3; Questier, LF, 252–3.
[68] See ch. 3, p. 99 above and ch. 7, pp. 222–7 below.

say such things 'in secret' to 'certaine noble men whom she knew to be Catholicke'. Among these nobles was the loyal and dependable 'old Lord Montague', who was regarded by the queen as a friend, and was here portrayed implicitly by the Jesuit as in sympathy with the Catholic enemies of the appellant priests.[69]

As late as March 1612 the leading Catholic secular clergy were still collating evidence that the first Viscount Montague had been the kind of Catholic who deserved toleration from the State. John Jackson had consulted with the ageing Marian priest Alban Dolman about the issue of a restoration of local episcopal rule over English Catholics. Dolman told Jackson that the college of cardinals had, after Elizabeth's accession and the deprivation of the Catholic episcopate, considered the issue of restoring episcopacy in England. But some Catholics, including Montague, had 'thowght it fit to be stayed tyll they had the opinions of the confessours that at that tyme wear in prison' in England, 'of whom some wear bishops'. Montague and the others who advised caution did so also because 'they wold not in those dowbtfull tymes (hooping and dayly expecting a change) exasperate the State against those they had in prison'. Dolman also said that 'going to church' would have 'been declared by publick decree unlawfull had not the said Lord Montague hindred it, for [fear of] exasperating the State (forsoth)'.[70]

But stories such as Jackson's were being circulated in the mid-Jacobean period at the same time as one powerful faction among the English clergy was lobbying Rome for the restitution of Catholic bishops in England. They were trying to get Rome to alter its settled policy of governing English Catholics by direct rule from the papal curia. They were not merely celebrating the wisdom of a long-deceased Elizabethan peer. Memories of this leading Catholic lord (whose grandson was, in the Jacobean period, a prominent patron of this pro-episcopal lobby) as a moderate and restraining influence within the Catholic community, who also had a great respect for the persecuted Marian episcopate, were likely to be exploited by those clergy who wanted to mount a convincing show of temporal loyalty to the Jacobean regime while pressing Rome to make a major alteration in the structure of the English Catholic community.

So while Montague never rose, like his Dacre relatives, in revolt against the crown, nor, it seems, was ever directly and irrevocably involved in

---

[69] Robert Persons, *An Answere to the Fifth Part of Reportes Lately Set Forth by Syr Edward Cooke* (St Omer, 1606), sig. Zz2v.

[70] *NAGB*, 144. Jackson was evidently referring to the tentative airing of proposals in 1561 about the need for the papacy to take disciplinary action against the queen. Among those to be consulted were the Marian bishops, now mostly incarcerated, McCoog and Lukács, *Monumenta Angliae* III, 548–9. Thomas McCoog suggests that among those whom Cardinal Morone, Pole's friend, approached was, perhaps, Montague himself, *ibid.*, 545–6.

and committed to any of the well-known Catholic conspiracies against Elizabeth, this did not mean that he and his immediate family and entourage were completely clear of all suspicion. Indeed, not long after the accession, Montague was on the fringes of the unrest about the issue of the succession. In August 1559 news came from Flushing via Sir Thomas Chaloner that there was a Spanish scheme to abduct Lady Catherine Grey and use her as a potential candidate for the throne should anything happen to Elizabeth. (The Spaniards feared that Henry II would exploit a succession crisis to make England a satellite State by installing Mary Stuart on the throne.) Among those who were suggested by the plotters as go-betweens to make contact with Catherine Grey was Montague's wife, Lady Magdalen.[71] Lord John Grey of Pirgo, Catherine's uncle, was Lady Magdalen's brother-in-law. He subsequently showed himself as a fringe supporter of Catherine's claim.[72]

The principal Catholic candidate in the early years, however, was the countess of Lennox. As Susan Taylor notes, the scares about political Catholicism in the early 1560s were frequently the product of the Lennoxes' ambition.[73] (The Catholic focus moved exclusively to Mary Stuart only after her marriage to Lord Darnley, the countess's son.) Taylor speculates that prosecutions in Yorkshire in 1562 for hearing Mass and the like were pro-voked by the culprits' contact with the Lennoxes.[74] Some members of the Lennox faction may also have had links with the Pole family, notably Arthur Pole, who was detected for intrigues in 1562 and 1566.[75] After the arrest of Francis Yaxley, who was caught up in these manoeuvres, some of Montague's

---

[71] M. Levine, *The Early Elizabethan Succession Question 1558–1568* (1966), 13–15. See also M. J. Rodríguez-Salgado, *The Changing Face of Empire: Charles V, Philip II and Habsburg Authority, 1551–1559* (Cambridge, 1988), 323–4. The scheme does seem inherently rather weird, and if it ever had been seriously entertained it appears that the Spaniards lost interest after Henry II's death in July 1559. But Levine remarks that Robert Hogan's account of the plot, the only extant source for it, is 'believable', *ibid.*, 14. (Hogan was in the service of Philip II until the 1570s. His brother William served Robert Dudley, earl of Leicester. I am grateful to Simon Adams for this information.)

[72] Levine, *The Early Elizabethan Succession Question*, 55, 63, 69–72.

[73] S. E. Taylor, 'The Crown and the North of England, 1559–70: A Study of the Rebellion of the Northern Earls, 1569–70, and its Causes' (Ph.D., Manchester, 1981), 84; Levine *The Early Elizabethan Succession Question*, 8–9. The countess of Lennox was the daughter of Henry VIII's sister, Margaret Tudor, by the earl of Angus.

[74] Taylor, 'Crown', 124–5, 127, 128, citing *CSPF 1562*, 240.

[75] The Poles and the Fortescues were investigated in 1562 concerning Arthur Pole's contacts with Mary Stuart and an odd scheme to surrender to the Scottish queen Arthur's claim to the English throne (he was a nephew of Cardinal Pole) in return for the dukedom of Clarence, Levine, *The Early Elizabethan Succession Question*, 46, 49. He was arrested with his two brothers and his brother-in-law Anthony Fortescue as they were embarking for France, *CSP Spanish 1558–67*, 259–60, 262, 275, 278–9, 292–3; PRO, KB 8/40; PRO, SP 12/17/18, SP 12/283/76. Susan Taylor notes that Pole, who married a sister of the earl of Northumberland, was still in the Tower in 1566, 'when he joined Lady Lennox in sending messages from the Tower to Darnley in Scotland, promising to resign all his claims and to come to Scotland if he escaped', Taylor, 'Crown', 130.

correspondence with Yaxley was discovered. This would at the very least have alerted the regime to Montague's connection with these people.[76]

Montague, however, stood out from much of the Catholic crowd in one important respect. He was still, to some extent, an insider, even though he had lost his place on the privy council and had done his best to obstruct the new settlement of religion. He was, even now, potentially suitable for crown service, both on diplomatic missions to foreigners (particularly the Habsburgs) and, of course, in his own county. He was never manoeuvred into the suicidal oppositionism of his friend the earl of Northumberland. Nor do we have any evidence that he was in sympathy with Catholic exiles. And he was a relative and friend of the queen's favourite, Lord Robert Dudley. The regime could not easily disregard or discount him.

DIPLOMATIC SERVICE AND DOMESTIC OPPOSITION

From the first year of the new reign, the first Viscount Montague was involved in the negotiations for a dynastic match between Elizabeth and the archduke Charles of Austria. Because of his imperialist connections and inclinations he was an obvious man to have to follow diplomacy of this kind. In December 1559, Montague reported back to the queen on the course of his discussions with the imperial ambassador, Casper Brüner, Baron von Rabenstein. Montague carried the queen's rebuff to the ambassador. But he may have relished telling the queen that the ambassador had given a dire warning, which he swore to be true, 'that the queen and all England is [*sic*] in no small peril, yea and the very person of the queen'. There, temporarily, Brüner had

---

[76] Yaxley had started out in public life as secretary to none other than Sir William Cecil, Bindoff, *HC*, III, 680. Until 1559 he had been a clerk of the Signet. After Mary's death it seems that he developed Hispanophile traits. He was certainly regarded by the Spaniards as a Catholic. This led to a period of imprisonment in early 1561. In February 1562 his involvement with the countess of Lennox over the proposal to marry Mary Stuart to Darnley resulted in his incarceration in the Tower, though he was released by August 1565 when he went off to become Darnley's secretary, PRO, SP 12/14/32. For the Lennoxes, see S. Adams, 'The Release of Lord Darnley and the Failure of the Amity', in M. Lynch (ed.), *Mary Stewart* (Oxford, 1988), 123–53. For Yaxley's problems concerning the countess of Lennox, see PRO, SP 12/14/51, SP 12/21/55, SP 12/23/6. See also Bindoff, *HC*, III, 680–2; W. J. Tighe, 'Courtiers and Politics in Elizabethan Herefordshire: Sir James Croft, his Friends and his Foes', *HJ* 32 (1989), 257–79, at pp. 260–1, noting that Yaxley was a member of Lord Robert Dudley's early patronage circle. (Wallace MacCaffrey claims that Yaxley was an intermediary between Dudley and various Catholics, including Montague, who had been privy councillors under Mary, W. MacCaffrey, *The Shaping of the Elizabethan Regime: Elizabethan Politics 1558–1572* (1969), 73. But, as Simon Adams shows, Yaxley's association with Dudley was limited, S. Adams (ed.), *Household Accounts and Disbursement Books of Robert Dudley, Earl of Leicester, 1558–1561, 1584–1586* (Camden Society, 5th series, 6, 1995), 78, 80.) In the 1580s the priest John Boste, who had lived for a short time in Montague's household, was noted to have among his own circle of contacts Montague's porter, who had once served 'Mr Yaxlie of Yaxlie Hall in Suffolke', CRS 5, 65.

clammed up, but Montague had urged him to specify 'by any mean which way this peril doth grow to her Majesty's realm and chiefly her person'. And the ambassador revealed that 'there hath been talks and devices in no small places for dividing Scotland and England. For the person of the queen's Majesty, I know it hath been offered and is that she shall be slain, which offer of both, how they have been taken, I know not, but sure I am, they have been made.' Montague demanded again who it was who thus threatened the queen. The ambassador said the queen herself ought to know and that she was blamed for the troubles in France.[77]

Whether Elizabeth even faintly intended to marry the archduke we may doubt (particularly when she and Dudley were besotted with each other). But it can be argued that Elizabeth was here contemplating and pre-empting the policy-making initiatives which Stephen Alford attributes almost wholly to Cecil in late 1559/early 1560 – in other words trying to attract Spanish support by dangling herself as a marital prospect, and anticipating the forthcoming struggle against the claims of Mary Stuart, French ambition in Scotland and potential papal hostility. In these circumstances, Montague's assistance might prove invaluable. The Elizabethan regime needed the diplomatic services of those whom the Habsburgs could trust. And Montague had, after all, served (very) briefly as Philip II's master of the horse while the king was in England.

As Stephen Alford has explained in some detail, an international agreement was required as a matter of some urgency after Elizabeth's accession. Something had to be done about the challenge to the English queen's title posed by the charismatic Mary Stuart. There were signs of French hostility to Elizabeth as well.[78] Any potential danger from the Spaniards, as much as the actual danger from the French, needed to be deflected. One of the measures taken to strengthen Elizabeth's international position was to send, in early 1560, Montague and Sir Thomas Chamberlain to Spain. Their orders were to alert the Spaniards to the French military incursion into Scotland and to secure Spanish assistance to prevent any violation of the northern border. Their function was, in other words, to make sure that the Spaniards did not disrupt whatever English policy towards Scotland turned out to be – a strategy which shortly crystallised as and in the treaty of Berwick of 27 February 1560 (ratified by Elizabeth in March) – namely the ejection of the French from Scotland. They also 'sought to induce his Majesty to persuade the king of France to pardon the Scottish rebels and Lutherans', and to restore Calais.

The official aim of the embassy was thus to persuade Philip that the English were concerned primarily with defending their border (though the Berwick

---

[77] *HMCS* I, 161; S. Haynes, *A Collection of State Papers* (1740), 233.
[78] S. Alford, *The Early Elizabethan Polity* (Cambridge, 1998), 71–2.

treaty contained a commitment to send English troops to Scotland) rather than asserting some kind of imperial authority over Scotland or, even worse, trying to promote the spread of heretical Protestantism there.[79]

The bishop of Aquila, Alvaro de La Quadra, wrote from London to Philip in late January 1560 to tell him of the impending departure of the diplomatic party. Montague had managed to get a letter to him to say that he was acting under duress. Montague complained that he had never been allowed to visit the bishop 'except in company with those who came'. Montague added that, if he had not been leaned on, he would never have undertaken 'so troublesome and unjust an embassy as that which he bears, but that as he is accredited to your Majesty, on whom the hope of the country rests, he endures it with all patience'. He was particularly grieved that he was accompanied by some fellow, whom he did not name, 'whose sole purpose' was 'to spy upon him'. Quadra rejoiced, however, that Montague was one who had acted 'undoubtedly the most honourably of any man of his quality in our time'.[80] Quadra reported in early February that Montague and Chamberlain had departed in order to embark at Plymouth.[81] He reaffirmed that Montague was not a free agent and had even claimed that 'if it were not for going to offer his respects to your Majesty and informing you about things here, he would rather lose his head than accept an office from the queen'.[82] Quadra informed Philip, as if he could not have guessed it, that Montague and Chamberlain had been instructed that 'if they are approached on the religious question' they must 'fence and temporise'.[83]

Montague and Chamberlain were instructed to do their best to take the religious heat out of the Scottish question. The French designs upon Elizabeth's title were not to be tolerated. An imminent invasion across the northern border was to be feared. It was absolutely imperative to act now for 'with a small power, partly by sea and partly by land, she can, at the outset, do more with 1,000 men to hinder them' than after three or four months with '5,000 or 6,000'. In any case the Scottish lords had petitioned for aid against the French. Having said that the English intention was to go ahead come virtually what may, the ambassadors were to reassure Philip

---

[79] *Ibid.*, 72–4; *CSP Rome*, I, 17; *CSPV 1558–80*, 173–4; BL, Cotton MS Vespasian C VII, no. 33, fo. 107r–v; *CSPF 1559–60*, 318–20.

[80] Bindoff, *HC*, I, 515; *CSP Spanish 1558–67*, 121. It is just possible that Montague was trying to cover himself both ways, i.e. to facilitate his mission in Spain by making the Spaniards think that he was not a free agent. However Quadra also reported that Montague was urging that Philip should receive him in private, *ibid.*, 124.

[81] On 11 February, Montague and his fellow ambassador Sir Thomas Chamberlain were still at Plymouth trying to organise the journey, *HMCS* I, 179.

[82] *CSP Spanish 1558–67*, 124. On 19 February, Quadra noted that they had left the capital '20 days ago' but had not 'embarked yet for want of a vessel', *ibid.*, 131.

[83] *CSP Spanish 1558–67*, 124.

that Elizabeth was 'determined to refer' to Philip's 'wisdom and friendship her further proceedings against the French in Scotland, so as the French king will forbear to seek the conquest of that realm and the invasion of England'. It would be good if Philip could persuade Francis II to this effect.[84]

As for the delicate question of what Montague and Chamberlain should do in Spain when they were faced with the issue of hearing divine service, the queen

wisheth that they might live in liberty from offence, as other ambassadors do here, so yet if the said ambassadors shall find no such licence nor grace, but shall see any danger to the contrary, she is pleased to remit all pains and censures of her laws, either ecclesiastical or temporal, for all things to be done by them, whereunto they shall be occasioned for avoiding of danger.

But, and this must have been particularly noticed by the openly Catholic Montague, she 'doubteth not in the consideration of any one of them but that they will not willingly herein commit anything against the usage and laws of this realm'.[85] No wonder that Montague thought he was being tested.

Presumably Montague must have been persuaded not just that it was better for him politically to do the regime's bidding but also that his involvement in what, as Alford says, was a crucial piece of early Elizabethan diplomacy, the establishment of a coherent 'British' strategy to deal with the issue of potential encirclement, would allow him to influence the general direction of government policy, and help to define where the true interests of the State and the new regime lay, namely in good, perhaps even (for the queen) sexual, relations with the Habsburgs. From the regime's angle, it was definitely better to have him inside rather than outside the proverbial tent. And others of his kin were also involved in the Alfordian 'British' project. Lord Admiral Clinton, who by May 1560 was warning Cecil about the military problems which the English campaign was experiencing in Scotland, had married Montague's stepmother, Elizabeth FitzGerald.[86]

The embassy, from Montague's perspective, must initially have seemed like rather a success.[87] On 10 April Montague and Chamberlain reported from

---

[84] *CSPF 1559–60*, 316, 317.   [85] *Ibid.*, 318.

[86] Alford, *Early Elizabethan Polity*, 80; Berry, *Sussex*, 354. Cf. Loseley MSS, 624. On the other hand, Montague's brother-in-law, Lord John Grey of Pirgo, who was a friend of Cecil, was warning Cecil at this time against those who wanted a marriage alliance between Elizabeth and the Habsburgs. (Discussions for a match with the archduke Charles had been opened in the middle of the previous year.) Grey lambasted these people as 'arche practesers agaynst God', Alford, *Early Elizabethan Polity*, 77–8; HMCS, I, 212.

[87] On 30 March 1560, the Venetian ambassador Paulo Tiepolo had reported from Toledo that both ambassadors were 'much dissatisfied' because they had not yet been granted audience. One of them (Tiepolo did not specify which) 'complained that they had lodgings unbecoming their official character, and that many things are disseminated through the Court', by the French, 'against their queen'. The French had endeavoured 'to make her appear culpable of

Toledo that Philip had proved amenable to 'compounding all things in this case'. He had laboured with the French to desist from meddling with the issue of Mary Stuart's title to Elizabeth's throne. The French king 'would leave the queen's title and style, using the arms only in the nether quarter of his wife's arms', although Francis II was not prepared to ignore the issue of religion in Scotland. (The Spaniards did not think that he should.) But Francis was 'content to revoke his extraordinary power in Scotland, reserving a small garrison for four holds only'. Philip thought the current French civil broils made this a good time to do a deal, and the English should really get on with it, 'lest in sending to and fro to him the opportunity might be lost, and the French king, finding his tumults appeased, would stand firmer in the matter'. Montague's and Chamberlain's report harps on the theme that Montague had himself emphasised in his recent performance in the House of Lords – the danger incurred by the unilateral English declaration of religious independence from Catholic Christendom. The French had spread about the Spanish Court 'slanderous bruits, imputing the cause of all their tumults to the English as fautors of the Protestant religion' because they knew that this was the one thing likely to move Philip in their favour.[88]

Philip, evidently, was still inclined towards a balancing act of sorts. As Alford points out, part of his response to the news that Elizabeth's envoys were on the way was to pre-empt them by the dispatch of a diplomat, Philippe de Staveles, sieur de Glajon, who conveyed the king's desire to set all to rights and to resolve grievances and injuries on both sides.[89] As Geoffrey Parker notes, Philip's preoccupations in 1560 were primarily with the Turks and the Djerba expedition.[90]

Philip's reply was, however, not exactly what the English wanted to hear. Diplomatically, Glajon was told by Cecil that the French had only themselves to blame for what was about to hit them. A month later, the English military machine was besieging Leith. The ultimately rather lack-lustre English campaign compelled the negotiations which led to the Treaty of Edinburgh. Philip's considered response to Montague and Chamberlain was delivered by way of Spanish diplomatic representatives in London who were thought to be in cahoots with the French embassy there.[91] The French did indeed

the commotions in France' (i.e. the conspiracy of Amboise), and it appeared that Philip was feigning 'indisposition' in order to avoid receiving them, though Tiepolo denied it, *CSPV 1558–80*, 178. The next day, however, the king granted audience to them, and they were 'much satisfied', *ibid.*, 186.

[88] *HMCS* I, 205–6.

[89] *CSPF 1559–60*, 427; *CSPV 1558–80*, 186; Alford, *Early Elizabethan Polity*, 78. Staveles was a councillor of State to Philip II in the Netherlands.

[90] G. Parker, *The Grand Strategy of Philip II* (1998), 118–19, 152–3. I am very grateful to Pauline Croft for this reference.

[91] Alford, *Early Elizabethan Polity*, 79–80.

seem to be coming to an understanding with the Spaniards.[92] Montague and Chamberlain also related, on 29 April, a conversation which they had had with the imperial ambassador to the Spanish Court, Nicholas, baron von Polweiller. He had told them that George, count of Helffenstein, who had been negotiating the archduke's marriage to Elizabeth, had now given up and was leaving the country. He then blurted out that there was a conspiracy to assassinate the queen and Dudley.[93]

Even less welcome would have been the news (dispatched on 19 May, though it only confirmed what Glajon would say) of their interview six days earlier with Philip. Philip merely insisted that Glajon and Quadra were carrying out his instructions in getting the queen to come to an agreement with the French. He maintained that he had her best interests at heart. But he then undercut his professions of deep affection by announcing that Glajon was carrying Philip's assurance that 'he would lend his' ships 'to the French for the suppression of the rebels in Scotland'. This, Philip said, was done only for 'her better surety and satisfaction rather than for the French' (an odd way of construing military assistance) because this would remove the French excuse for continuing their power in Scotland any longer than was necessary in order to see peace and harmony restored! Montague and Chamberlain had politely pointed out 'that the Scots were not rebels', and actually the 'French' action in Scotland was only for the greater glorification of the house of Guise under the pretext of assisting Mary Stuart. Rather, if Elizabeth should detect any sign of the Scots being so bold as to defy their lawful queen in the slightest thing, she personally would go and settle the problem; no need for the French to worry their heads about it therefore. Philip considered this response and then sent back essentially the same answer via the duke of Alva. Alva assured them that it was best to let Philip's 'vassals' into Scotland if they did not want the French to establish themselves there. Montague and Chamberlain could only reply much as they had before. This course of action would simply allow the French to carry out their wicked intentions. Montague, Chamberlain and Alva continued to argue, at cross purposes, for an entire two hours. Alva drifted, they thought, off his brief, saying that Elizabeth was in peril; she ought to marry; she ought not to alter things as they were when she acceded – particularly not religion – 'to the misliking of the world'. They should beware how even a medium-sized invasion force could stir up the queen's realm if it came through the badly defended south coast, towards

---

[92] *HMCS* I, 232. See *CSPV 1558–80*, 196, for Tiepolo's account (26 April) of how Montague and Chamberlain believed that, in spite of Philip's professed goodwill towards Elizabeth, the French were prevaricating, 'endeavouring not only to cajole and deceive the queen whilst they are making preparations for war, but also to justify their cause with the Catholic king by . . . making it appear that the wrong is on the side of the queen of England'.

[93] *CSPF 1559–60*, 601–2; BL, Cotton MS Vespasian C VII, fo. 120r.

the Isle of Wight or Dover for example, as Montague should well know. Alva said quite a lot else, even arguing that a little alteration of Mary Stuart's 'arms and title' should remove all cause of offence. Chamberlain and Montague reiterated, as if it were necessary, 'thus the queen may perceive how many mislikings the king of Spain and his have had with her proceedings'.[94]

Subsequently, on 20 June, they wrote in haste to assure Elizabeth that Philip could be relied on for support. 'For more ample signification of his good will', he would send 'in three or four days' one of his chamber servants, John Pacheco, to offer guidance on the forthcoming treaty with the French and the Scots. Spanish advice that only if the French then overstepped the number of troops allowed them should the 'queen . . . seek to expulse the same' may, however, have rung a bit hollow – merely criticising a likely-to-bolt horse rather than suggesting how to shut the stable door.[95]

Almost immediately Montague set out for home.[96] Elizabeth's letters revoking his commission had been written on 10 May, saying merely that, since Philip had remitted the issue into the hands of his 'ambassadors on both parts', there was no reason for Montague to linger in Spain. There is no implied suggestion that Montague was thought to have failed or to have been irresponsible.[97] But perhaps Montague was telling the truth when he wrote to Cecil on 17 June 1560 of 'his joy' at receiving 'hir Majesties letter for his revocacion'. Now at last he might take his 'leave of the king' and leave behind the new and sole ambassador, Sir Thomas Chamberlain, 'whom his Majestie favourablie received'.[98]

---

[94] *CSPF 1560–1*, 63–7. They said, however, that Alva had intimated that he thought that, if the queen could eject the French from Scotland 'without asking further counsel or aid', she might as well do it. See also Tiepolo's dispatch of 26 May, *CSPV 1558–80*, 211–12. Cf. Tiepolo's report of 13 May, *CSPV 1558–80*, 204–5, stressing that Elizabeth had 'as much suspicion of . . . the Spaniards as . . . of the French', especially after it appeared that Philip might intervene militarily in Scotland.

[95] *HMCS I*, 236–7; Haynes, *A Collection of State Papers*, 328–9; *CSPF 1560–1*, 138; *CSPV 1558–80*, 224. In subsequent years the ambiguous outcome of Montague's negotiation was remembered and cited as a reason for not cooperating with the Spaniards. Bernardino de Mendoza reported to Philip in June 1580 that, in an audience with Elizabeth concerning her aid to the Dutch rebels, it had been put to him that at her accession Montague had been sent to 'confirm the treaties' between herself and the Habsburgs 'although the alliances between England and your Majesty referred only to the House of Burgundy', but 'this your Majesty had neither accepted nor refused; and it was therefore considered that the queen was free from any obligation under the treaties, and was at liberty to help the Netherlands and prevent the French from taking possession thereof', *CSP Spanish 1580–6*, 33.

[96] BL, Additional MS 39866.   [97] *CSPF 1560–1*, 35.

[98] BL, Cotton MS Vespasian C VII, fo. 121r; *CSPF 1560–1*, 122–3. Tiepolo reported, however, that Philip had 'complimented him verbally' before his departure, and 'gave him a handsome present'; and the Venetian remarked also that 'this nobleman favoured the Catholic party in England' and never consented to 'anything that was enacted against it'; and, as a result, in Spain 'he is greatly loved and esteemed by all who know him', *CSPV 1558–80*, 224.

We may speculate that, for all Montague's irritation at the use of him to allure and fob off the Spaniards, he did in some sense wish to see this branch of the new regime's policy succeed. If he actually believed that Mary Stuart and the ambitions of her Guise relatives ought to be resisted, it would help to explain his reputation for 'loyalty' to Elizabeth and his refusal (as far as we can tell) at any point to lend his voice to the cause of the Scottish queen.

However, by April 1561, Quadra was telling Philip that he had (as part of his attempt to work with Dudley to restore some form of Catholicism in the English Church) been in touch with leading Catholics, including Montague and Nicholas Heath. He informed them that Spain's amity with Elizabeth did not mean that the Spaniards had abandoned the English Catholics' cause.[99] In that month Cecil used the arrests of former Marian councillors to put an end to Quadra's plans.[100] Some of the English Catholics in Rome, notably Morris Clenock (actually a Welshman), now said that the papacy should proceed immediately against Elizabeth, excommunicate her and absolve her subjects from their obedience to her. As evidence for his opinion, Clenock cited the fact that Montague had recently been imprisoned (in October 1561), an event noticed also by Quadra.[101] There do not seem to be any other references to his being incarcerated. (Only a few months earlier, the queen had provided a christening present for one of Montague's younger daughters, a 'guilt cup with a cover'.[102]) If he was put under restraint, it may conceivably have been connected with the proceedings against Francis Yaxley, though Yaxley's involvement with the countess of Lennox was only formally enquired into several months later.

Montague returned to the parliamentary arena in early 1563 in order to trumpet loud and clear yet again his opposition to government policy on religion. The parliament saw the introduction of a bill (which became 5 Elizabeth, c. 1) entitled 'for the assurance of the Quenes Majesties Royal

---

Richard Smith's early-seventeenth-century account of Montague's embassy to Spain did not even specify what its purpose was. Smith concentrated instead on Montague's remarkable chastity in a hot country such as Spain. During his time there he fell 'into a most perilous and molestful disease, and the physicians gave judgment that he could not recover unless he had the company of a woman', and, as luck would have it, 'there lying directly over against his lodgings' was 'a most beautiful English quean, who by all lascivious allurements endeavoured to induce him to lewdness', but not even the advice of his doctors could tempt him to lechery. Smith emphasises here the link between Montague's sexual purity, his Catholicism and his rejection of the Edwardian and Elizabethan settlements of religion, Southern, *ERH*, 17.

99 *CSP Spanish 1558–67*, 192. At this point, Quadra was taking Dudley's side over the issue of whether he might marry the queen, MacCaffrey, *The Shaping of the Elizabethan Regime*, 78–80; Longleat House, Dudley papers, DU I, no. 62, fo. 191r.
100 MacCaffrey, *The Shaping of the Elizabethan Regime*, 80.
101 McCoog and Lukács, *Monumenta Angliae III*, 552.
102 J. Nicholls, *The Progresses and Public Processions of Queen Elizabeth* (3 vols., New York, 1823), I, 128.

Power over all Estates and Subjectes within her Highnes dominions'. Its basic function was to increase the penalties for refusing the oath of supremacy and to compel a lot more people to take the oath than had previously done. As Jones describes it, 'this act made it praemunire and, ultimately, treason either to claim that the pope had any authority within the realm or to refuse the oath of supremacy'.[103] Its penalties for denial of the supremacy were clearly aimed at, among others, the remaining imprisoned bishops, the focus of Catholic political resistance to the will of the crown.

Whoever was responsible for the measure,[104] there was opposition from the lawyer Robert Atkinson in the Commons and from Montague and Northumberland in the Lords.[105] Atkinson argued, when the bill came before the Commons in March, that the extant act of supremacy was sufficient. This bill would unnecessarily raise more Catholic hackles. Better the situation in Germany where there was even cohabitation in some regions. Atkinson resorted to a kind of ecumenical reverie. 'Let us therefore, for the honour of God, leave all malice, and, notwithstanding religion, let us love one another; for it is no point of religion one to hate another.'[106] The Commons, however, passed the measure by 186 votes to 83.[107]

The earl of Northumberland spoke against the bill in the Lords in January, though it was not yet before the House. As reported by Quadra, Northumberland said that the bill was 'neither just nor desirable'. The 'heretics' 'should be satisfied to enjoy the bishoprics and benefits of the others without wishing to cut off their heads as well'. He said that 'when they had beheaded the clergy they would claim to do the same to the lay nobles, and he was moved by his conscience to say that he was of opinion that so rigorous an act should not be passed, in which opinion he had no doubt all or a majority of his fellow lords would join'.[108]

Montague was equally forthright. The bill as it stood was not 'possible', 'commodious, apt and fit to be put in execution'. Then he put, in a particularly virulent form, the conundrum about whether the Catholics' perceived offence, delineated in the bill, was to do with treason or religion. He would discuss, he said, whether it was 'good that a law be made whereby it shall

---

[103] Jones, *Faith by Statute*, 171.
[104] Jones argues that the original bill was heavily altered in committee, but that 'the bill first introduced by the government was the harsher of the two, and ... the new bill was softened in order to win support from the Catholic laymen in the Lords', *ibid.*, 171–3; cf. Neale, *Elizabeth I and her Parliaments*, I, 117.
[105] Simon Adams has pointed out to me that Northumberland had been absent in the North during the 1559 parliament.
[106] Neale, *Elizabeth I and her Parliaments*, I, 117–19; TD II, cclv. The emperor, Ferdinand I, was, at this point, trying to prevail upon Elizabeth to grant a form of toleration along these lines. I am grateful to Simon Adams for this point.
[107] Jones, *Faith by Statute*, 174.   [108] *CSP Spanish 1558–67*, 294.

be commanded, under pain of death, that the papists, with oath, confess the doctrine of the Protestants to be true and evangelical'. Whereas Atkinson had, in effect, said that, if the papists did offend, their offence was already suitably and sufficiently punished by existing legal and judicial provisions, Montague went a lot further. The law was not necessary

> forasmuch as the Catholics of this realm disturb not, nor hinder the public affairs of the realm, neither spiritual nor temporal. They dispute not, they preach not, they disobey not the queen, they cause no troubles nor tumult among the people: so that no man can say that thereby the realm doth receive any hurt or damage by them.

Even more barbed was Montague's comment that 'they have brought into the realm no novelties in doctrine or religion'. Should the bill be passed, as it was pretty obvious it shortly would be, 'it shall be contrary and repugnant unto all laws of men, natural and civil' and would not deserve even to have the name of 'law'.

Here we see the leading Catholic 'moderate' of the period getting rather close to justifications for civil disobedience – in the sense of denying the State's capacity to make law (or at least this kind of law) in this context or the right to enforce it. He insisted that this measure would be a 'penal statute to force the subjects of this realm to receive and believe the religion of the Protestants upon pain of death'.[109]

This, naturally, was precisely what Montague's political opponents would have disavowed. One MP in the Commons, in a scathing commentary on Atkinson's words, denied that this was a spiritual matter at all, merely temporal; and he asked whether it was right for a man to 'have conscience in cases of treason'.[110]

Montague hammered on, harking back to the theme of his 1559 oration against the original supremacy measure: 'the doctrine of the Protestants doth repugn unto all the ecclesiastical state of England that were present at the last parliament, and holdeth contradiction with all provinces of Christendom'. 'It repugneth' not just to 'the doctrine of all the parliaments past', but also to 'all general councils'. There was no certainty in Protestant doctrines; they were just opinions. This was, in effect, to denounce the Protestant religion as heresy.

In this context, his subsequent 'moderate' points, in whatever way he expressed them, could only be understood as dripping with intense and bitter irony: 'now, to turn to my purpose, I say that, since the doctrine of Protestants is so uncertain (leaving to call it false)', there is 'no reason nor justice that doth permit or suffer that men should be forced to take it for

---

[109] TD II, ccli–cclii.   [110] Neale, *Elizabeth I and her Parliaments*, I, 119.

certain and true and sure, and affirm the same'. Hence the bill laid before the House was neither just nor reasonable. He moved on to suggest that the law might be unworkable, unenforceable or even cause civil strife. With a final swipe, probably at those around him whose expressions betrayed either cynicism or contempt, knowing that he was not exactly backing a winner, he urged that, although 'the greater part of the assembly of the lords, and the higher House, was of the mind and opinion that the law ought to be made', the bishops, *parti pris* as they were, all being Protestants, should not be allowed to vote at all. He even questioned their competence to enforce temporal penalties in this respect, which should be a matter for secular judges alone. In a final peroratory thought, he counselled his auditory that 'since it belongeth to the said lords not to endanger their lives and goods, if any war should happen within the realm, or with their neighbours', they should 'take good heed, and not suffer themselves to be led by such men that are full of affection and passions, and that look to wax mighty, and of power, by the confiscation, spoil and ruin of the houses of noble and ancient men'.[111]

For Peter Holmes, both Atkinson's and Montague's speeches in the 1563 parliament were 'very little different in tone and content from the orations of Catholic prelates' made in 1559.[112] For Holmes this was a tone and mind set of compromise rather than outright resistance. And, of course, Montague was clearly not 'resisting' the regime's authority in the way that some Catholics eventually would. One has to ask, though, whether his perceived 'moderation' was the product of what he said or of the political circumstances which conspired to prevent any kind of effective challenge to the regime at this point and allowed the regime to construe his protests as 'moderate'.

Whichever is the case, Montague was soon back in his shire, at Cowdray, not entirely living up to the regime's customary expectations of a leading man and county administrator. On 26 June, Quadra noted on the subject of the forthcoming Newhaven expedition that, 'with a view of justifying this enterprise, they are thinking of sending ambassadors to your Majesty and to the duchess of Parma'; Sir Henry Sidney had refused to go to Philip, so 'they have appointed Viscount Montague'. He did not go. Perhaps he actually refused, no longer having the stomach for selling the regime's more offensive policies to his own natural friends abroad.[113]

On 17 July 1563 he wrote to the privy council concerning 1,000 men whose levy from the county had been demanded for the supply of the Newhaven expedition. Montague was not a happy man. He thought that

---

[111] TD II, cclii–ccliii, ccliii, ccliv.
[112] Holmes, *Resistance and Compromise*, 177.   [113] *CSP Spanish 1558–67*, 337.

such a levy would have a bad effect on the shire. He also had misgivings about the whole concept of interfering in France's civil dissensions. The project to assist the Huguenots had been launched in October 1562 without proper thought and adequate planning. By this stage it was looking demonstrably ridiculous.[114] (In fact, by the time that Montague was contesting the council's order, the decision to surrender was already imminent.[115]) At the direction of the council, he said, the county had recently assembled 600 soldiers and had sent 200 of them to Portsmouth as well as 100 'pioneers'. But then he received a 'straight commandment'[116] from 'Mr Vicechamberlain', i.e. Sir Francis Knollys (whose furious interventions in the recent parliamentary debate over the new statute on the supremacy Montague would presumably not have forgotten),[117] to 'send forth 600' more 'than was before appoyntid, besides a number of pioners which be daylye taken up here by his commission'. Montague had 'immediatelye writen to all the justices to send forthe undelayed . . . those 400 which remayne of the 600 by the first order appoyntid and also to muster and gather together another 600 to folow the rest if they have not other advertisement to the contrarye'. So, said Montague, he had carried out the government's order as best he could. But he doubted whether the vice-chamberlain had had detailed 'knowledge of suche numbers of men as have before within this yere bin sent to Newhavin owt of this shier at sondry tymes'. Would the privy council like to consider whether it was still a good idea to depopulate the county? For if this great number should be rounded up and carted off, the rest would be left much weakened and unfurnished 'bothe of strength and also for helpe to take upp tharvest now in hand'. It was, however, entirely up to the council, if that was what they really wanted.[118]

Montague continued to be sent abroad on the regime's business. In 1565 he was dispatched, along with Nicholas Wotton and Walter Haddon, to Bruges on an embassy to formalise the restoration of trade with the Low Countries following the embargo of 1563.[119] It was made clear that Montague was

---

[114] For the Newhaven expedition, see R. B. Wernham, *Before the Armada* (1966), 265–7; W. MacCaffrey, *Elizabeth I* (1993), 79.

[115] MacCaffrey, *Elizabeth I*, 79. The conditions for the surrender of the besieged and plague-ridden Le Havre, where the English were holed up, are dated 28 July 1563, *CSPF 1563*, 480–1.

[116] BL, Harleian MS 6990, no. 21.

[117] Knollys spoke in the debate in the Commons after Cecil and 'said this business must be settled sword in hand, and not by words, and that he would be foremost in the struggle', Neale, *Elizabeth I and her Parliaments*, I, 119–20.

[118] BL, Harleian MS 6990, no. 22, fo. 45r.

[119] MacCaffrey, *The Shaping of the Elizabethan Regime*, 184; Wernham, *Before the Armada*, 282–3. Cardinal Granvelle, who had sparked the tit-for-tat mutual embargoes of trade between England and the Netherlands, was recalled by Philip in 1564, and trade began again in November of that year.

'assigned by her Majestie to be the principall minister of this colloquie'.[120] It made sense to send a Hispanophile such as Montague. He would be recognised as sympathetic. And he was likely to get results, or, as the commission put it, to preserve the ancient 'amity' established between the progenitors of Elizabeth and Philip. Montague, however, revealed to the Spanish ambassador a certain irritation and incomprehension on his own part: 'I cannot understand these people; they cannot endure me and yet they send me to do their business for them.' He believed that 'we are in the midst of troublous times'.[121] While in Bruges, in late July 1565, he wrote to William More, and did not disguise his glee at the Spaniards' triumph in June against the Ottomans (in the relief of Malta). Montague had sent 'from tyme to tyme the true newes in pryntt' though he expected that More had already heard it. Montague's missive dealt with the viciousness of the Ottoman assault on the castle of St Elmo. 'With great slaughter they toke it' after 'five attempts'. But 'in the verey instaunt the king of Spayne his armye landid and without intermission of tymes assaulted itt agayne and recovered itt, nott leaving a Turk within itt alive'.[122]

For some reason this bout of negotiating was suspended rather quickly – from 29 September.[123] From Bruges, Montague wrote to William More at Loseley on 4 September thanking him for some personal favour he had performed. By 26 November he was writing again to More from Guildford manor.[124] But this commercial diplomatic mission was renewed in the following year.[125] On 23 June 1566 Montague's servant and surveyor Roger Brinkborne wrote to More concerning certain business which Lady Magdalen had been badgering him to do for her husband. Montague had

---

[120] See BL, Harleian MS 36, no. 16, fos. 63r–73r; BL, Sloane MS 2442, fos. 28r–33r. For the correspondence generated by the mission, see BL, Additional MS 48011, fos. 1r–71v, Additional MS 48007, fos. 86r–92v, 98r–125r. Walter Haddon was already well known for his anti-papal polemical tracts on precisely the topic (the royal supremacy) which tended to raise Montague's blood pressure, Milward I, nos. 68–77. It cannot have been all that happy a partnership. See L. V. Ryan, 'The Haddon–Osorio Controversy (1563–1583)', *Church History* 22 (1953), 142–54, at p. 143.

[121] BL, Sloane MS 2442, fo. 28r; Bindoff, *HC*, I, 515; *CSP Spanish 1558–67*, 407. At this time, Guzman de Silva reported to Philip II that not only was Montague 'held in high esteem by Catholics' but also that 'he appears to be greatly attached to your Majesty', *ibid*.

[122] Loseley MSS, 618; *CSPF 1564–5*, 391, 418, 554.

[123] BL, Cotton MS Galba C II, no. 78, fo. 274r (new foliation).   [124] Loseley MSS, 618, 619.

[125] See BL, Cotton MS Galba C II, no. 78, fo. 274r (Elizabeth's instructions to Montague, Wotton and Haddon, dated 26 March 1566). Elizabeth's commissioners were instructed to get back to Bruges as soon as possible and start talking again, *ibid*., fo. 274r–v. They were ordered 'either freendly and neigbourly to conclude a contynuance of the auncyent commerce and entrecours, or if the contrary shall succeed, the world shall manifestly perceive that the default therof shall not proceede of us. And in this manner you may make thentrey into this second treaty.' These instructions specify the issues to be settled. For the progress of the negotiations, see BL, Cotton MS Galba C II, no. 100, fo. 371r. One of the major issues was piracy, *ibid*., fo. 372r.

by this stage finally ended the trade negotiations and left for Spa where he planned to stay for a month.[126]

In parliament in late 1566 Montague exerted himself as a busy working peer. At the end of October he participated in a conference with the Commons concerning a petition to be presented to Elizabeth on the difficult issues of the succession and her possible marriage.[127] He was named to committees which considered a series of bills.[128] In November he took part in a Lords' debate and voted in a division over 'the petition presented to parliament by the Protestant bishops respecting their confirmation', as the Spaniard Guzman de Silva described it. Montague, with several Catholic peers (Windsor, Morley, Westmorland and Northumberland), and also with his brother-in-law (by his first wife) the earl of Sussex, voted against it.[129]

THE 1568 POLITICAL CRISIS AND THE 1569 REBELLION

If the first Viscount Montague was the loyalist everyone claimed that he was, then he should have come down firmly on the side of the regime as it confronted the malcontents and Marians in the North at the end of the 1560s.[130] And, in fact, just before the rebellion proper broke out there in late 1569, Montague seemed to get the official nod of approval as he and Buckhurst supplanted the Arundel–Lumley axis in Sussex when they were appointed, rather than the two latter peers, as joint lords lieutenant of the county.

As is well known, a coalition against Cecil had started talking to the Spaniards who were increasingly irritated by the affronts offered over such matters as the seizure of the bullion ships in Plymouth in November 1568. Cecil was under threat from various people, including the earl of Leicester. But Guerau de Spes interpreted this also as the opportunity for a Catholic reaction in which almost every peer who was not a paid-up member of the

---

[126] Loseley MSS, 619. The Browne family's funeral monument at Midhurst recites that Montague was sent, in 1565 and 1566, 'to the duches of Parma then regent of the Low Countries', which mission, as with the 1560 embassy to Philip II, 'he effected both wiselye and honrablye to the service of God his prince and countrie', Mosse, ME, 73.

[127] LJ I, 639.

[128] LJ I, 653, 655, 658, 662, 669. Montague was involved in the passage of a private bill which dealt with the day on which the weekly market was held at Battle in Sussex. The day was changed from Sunday to Thursday, a measure which Geoffrey Elton describes as 'devout', G. R. Elton, The Parliament of England 1559–1581 (Cambridge, 1986), 128, 129, 225. See also R. M. Warnicke, William Lambarde: Elizabethan Antiquary 1536–1601 (1973), 19.

[129] CSP Spanish 1558–67, 596.

[130] In late 1568 the Spanish ambassador, Guerau de Spes, seemed to be using Montague as a mediator to make contact with the earl of Sussex (though King Philip later informed Spes that he should exercise caution in dealing with the earl), CSP Spanish 1568–79, 83.

Protestant club might be included.[131] The Florentine banker Robert Ridolfi was the go-between for the duke of Norfolk's and the earl of Arundel's dealings with the Spanish embassy. There was a proposal for arresting Cecil. But Cecil discovered the scheme and he undermined it through an appeal for unity. Leicester's hesitations made concerted action impossible. And Elizabeth made it clear that she would not sacrifice Cecil.[132] Leicester then became, allegedly, the driving force behind the proposals for Norfolk to marry the Scottish queen as a means of settling the succession.[133]

The irrepressibly (and unreasonably) optimistic Spes seriously believed, however, that he would shortly witness a Catholic reaction which would rival the accession of Mary Tudor. And he thought that conservatives such as Montague would be at the heart of it. The Spaniard reported in almost salivatory mode that 'they brought the bishop of Ross here before the day of the intended arrest (of Cecil) in order that he might be a witness of it. Lord Montague and the earl of Northumberland, as well as other Catholic gentlemen, knew of the matter and came hither in consequence.'[134]

By June 1569 Spes was making lists of the nobility who, he thought, would form a coalition around Norfolk. Arundel and Lumley were the hard men behind the duke[135] but their project would 'be aided' by Montague as well as the earls of Northumberland, Derby, Cumberland, and Lords Dacre and

---

[131] Spes's optimism about English Catholics was, however, never shared by Philip or Alva, N. Williams, *Thomas Howard Fourth Duke of Norfolk* (1964), 151.

[132] *Ibid.*, 146–8. Some historians speculate that Ridolfi at some point became a double agent and betrayed Norfolk's plans, Parker, *Grand Strategy*, 160.

[133] Williams, *Thomas Howard*, 149–50.

[134] *CSP Spanish 1568–79*, 167. Simon Adams has pointed out to me that Spes was under house arrest between January and July 1569, and his information during this period was supplied by Ridolfi.

[135] As early as March 1569 the French ambassador Fénélon was claiming that it was principally Arundel and Lumley who were in league with Norfolk to deprive Cecil of his place, and restore Catholicism. In August 1569 Spes recorded that Lumley and others had told him that they were ready to fight in order to force through the Howard–Stuart marriage project. A second string of peers (Derby, Shrewsbury, Pembroke and Northumberland) was also involved, Taylor, 'Crown', 142. Taylor argues that Williams (Williams, *Thomas Howard*, 150–1) is wrong to suggest, or at least the French and Spanish diplomatic reports do not bear out his contention, that Norfolk was in total ignorance of the schemes of Arundel and Lumley to work for a change of religion. To gain support for the marriage project, Taylor suggests (citing *CSP Spanish 1568–79*, 158), Norfolk was probably prepared to give conservatives such as Arundel and Lumley the impression that he was willing to consider a change of religion and both were convinced that they could convert him. That was the basis on which they gave their support for the marriage scheme. After the duke left the Court on 16 September, now in something of a quandary about what to do, he was informed by Arundel that their league was in peril, but Lumley, apparently, advised Norfolk to seize the Tower. Both Arundel and Lumley then caved in, and Norfolk soon followed them, Taylor, 'Crown', 148ff, 158. In fact, Arundel's and Lumley's schemes were betrayed by William West, Lord De La Warr, Manning, *Religion*, 226. After the northern rising, Arundel was placed under house arrest at Nonsuch, where he stayed until 1572, following Norfolk's decapitation. Lumley was let go and, for a time, simply carried on plotting, though later

Morley 'and many other Catholics'. Spes airily opined that if only the rightful heir, Mary Stuart, were free, even the French would cooperate.[136] Months after the 'arrest' scheme ran out of steam, Spes was still convinced that the impetus for a declaration of Mary's right to the throne was unstoppable, and that Norfolk would succeed in his ambitions. Montague was supposedly hand in glove with these people 'and they all assert that, if they succeed, religion shall be restored'.[137]

Spes claimed at the very beginning of December 1569 that Montague and his son-in-law Southampton had consulted with him about whether they should join the rebellion or simply defect to Alva's forces in the Low Countries. For once, Spes was short on suggestions and told them that he 'could not advise them' until he 'had due instructions to do so'. Just over two weeks later Spes sent word that they had tried to get across the Channel but were forced back by inclement weather and had been ordered to justify themselves at the Court. Nevertheless, although the now rather perplexed Spes had no explanation for this, Montague had been appointed 'governor of Sussex'.[138]

One possible interpretation of what Spes observed is that Montague was steering very close to the oppositional limits without having any real desire to get involved on Norfolk's behalf. The duke, who was not, by any definition, a Catholic, had, after all, mulcted Montague's wife's family, at least to their way of thinking, over the wardship arrangements for the Dacre children.[139] In fact, Montague wrote to discourage Leonard Dacre from assisting the rebels in late 1569. The bishop of Ross alleged that, as the rebellion was in train, the earl of Southampton twice sent an envoy, George Chamberlain, to see Ross in order 'to know the fate of that rebellion and to tell him that Leonard Dacre had been with the Lord Montagu to require assistance for the rebels, and that Lord Montagu had persuaded' Dacre to 'forsake the matter'. Another man, 'Taylor of Todcastle', said that Dacre came to Montague 'to pray him to persuade the earl of Cumberland to be of that faction'. Evidently it did no good. Dacre's own rebellion disastrously misfired after the main rising had itself failed.[140] As Roger Manning comments, 'Lord Montague

he developed a talent for ingratiating correspondence, particularly with Sir Robert Cecil, *HMCS, passim*. Lumley became a friend of Anthony Watson, bishop of Chichester, who seems to have served at one time as Lumley's chaplain, BL, Lansdowne MS 45, no. 61, fo. 130r; *HMCS* VI, 265. (In 1581 Watson had been instituted to the rectory of Cheam in Surrey on Lumley's presentation, *DNB, sub* Watson, Anthony.) Lumley, however, accumulated a mix of Catholic clerics around him, including the appellant priest Cuthbert Trollopp and the future Jesuit George Keynes, who served as his secretary until Keynes entered the Society, PRO, SP 12/284/52, SP 12/154/62; Foley V, 279; CRS 75, 221–2.

[136] *CSP Spanish 1568–79*, 158.　　[137] *CSP Spanish 1568–79*, 183.
[138] Bindoff, *HC*, I, 515; *CSP Spanish 1568–79*, 214, 218.
[139] *CSP Spanish 1568–79*, 167; ch. 3, pp. 73–4 above.
[140] Manning, 'Anthony Browne', 106; *HMCS* I, 557.

narrowly escaped implication' in the subsequent Ridolfi plot, but 'it would have been hard to identify his interests with those of a Howard or a Percy', though this did not stop William Barker and Edmund Powell in late 1571 claiming, under interrogation, that Montague had indeed approved of the proposed marriage alliance between Norfolk and Mary Stuart; and Ridolfi confessed the same.[141]

The *Treatise of Treasons* (published in 1572), a wide-ranging tract which combined a justification of the duke and the Scottish queen with a vicious attack on Cecil and Sir Nicholas Bacon, pointed to the ancient nobility and said that their credit and fortunes were threatened by the insidious effect of the caterpillars of the commonwealth which had sought to monopolise Elizabeth for their own benefit and did it in part by attacking Catholics and Catholicism. Along with the persecuted duke, the author urged his audience to consider 'the unjust captivitie of the earles of Arundel, Worcester and Sowthampton' and 'of the Lordes Cobham and Lumley'.[142] Montague, like Southampton, could hardly call his nobility ancient (though, as we saw in the previous chapter, his title recalled his Neville lineage). But the point was that peers such as Montague could be represented as giving good counsel to their sovereign precisely because, unlike Machiavellian evil counsellors, they were not on the make and, crucially, were not prepared to prostitute religion to 'policy'. They would not, like Cecil and Bacon, the bad apples of the *Treatise*, mislead the queen on the religious issue for their own advancement. And they would not stir up conflict abroad, and so could be relied on to keep the realm out of disastrous foreign wars, particularly war with Spain.

As we have already remarked, it appears that Montague was not really a devotee of Mary Stuart. There is certainly no evidence that he regarded Mary's claim to the throne as superior to Elizabeth's.[143] He was appointed as a commissioner for Mary's trial in 1586.[144] (He made strong hints in his 1592 speech to his friends at West Horsley that he had not been committed to any particular successor to Elizabeth and that had included the Scottish queen.[145]) He was, therefore, clearly distinguishable from peers such as Lumley, although, according to Spes in April 1570, it was 'feared' that Cecil would 'have Lord Montague arrested'.[146]

---

[141] Manning, 'Anthony Browne', 106; *HMCS* I, 526, 542. See *CSP Rome*, I, 347, for Ridolfi's claim that Montague, with other Catholic nobles and gentry, would take part in the 'enterprise'; and *ibid.*, 400, for the duke of Norfolk's listing, in March 1571, of Montague among those whom he believed supported him. The regime evidently took these allegations seriously enough to collate them, PRO, SP 12/85/64. Montague had made a substantial settlement of property in Sussex on various of his siblings and children by a deed dated 1 November 1569, WSRO, SAS/BA 41. The proximity of this disposition of his estate to the time of the northern rising may not have been a coincidence.

[142] [Leslie], *A Treatise of Treasons*, fo. 123r.

[143] I am grateful to Simon Adams for discussions of this point.   [144] GEC IX, 99.

[145] SHC, LM 1856; Questier, *LF*, 253.   [146] *CSP Spanish 1568–79*, 242.

On the other hand, enough of Montague's relatives were involved around the fringes of both the northern rising and the Ridolfi plot to make his position more than a little awkward. Southampton had undoubtedly waded quite far into serious political disobedience. It was at Southampton's palace at Titchfield that Norfolk's supporters assembled before Leicester betrayed their project to the queen.[147] Southampton had met the bishop of Ross, Mary's agent, in May 1570, encountering him in the twilight in the Lambeth marshes, shortly after John Felton had publicly and fatally displayed the bull of excommunication on Fulham Palace's gates. 'I pray yow tell me', asked the earl, 'what think yow of this bull, that is now publist abroad, whether . . . the subjects of this land may, with save [i.e. safe] conscience, obey the quene as our righteous princess?' They were observed, however, and Southampton was arrested, confined to Loseley (under the eye of William More)[148] and badgered into a not particularly enthusiastic show of religious conformity.[149] In September 1570 Spes was still fantasising that, although Norfolk appeared to be deprived of all sense of purpose and motion, 'Montague, Southampton, Lumley, and Arundel and many others, the moment the Lancastrians take up arms, will join them or act'; Spes believed that Sir Thomas Stanley, the second son of the earl of Derby, seriously proposed to raise Lancashire in revolt in Mary Stuart's cause.[150] Independently, it seems, Montague's second son, Sir George Browne, was entangled in the Ridolfi scheme.[151] In September 1571 the full extent of Southampton's dealings with Ross came to light as the Ridolfi conspiracy unravelled, and off he went to the Tower.[152] The man whom Southampton had sent to meet Ross in late 1569/early 1570 on two separate occasions was, as Southampton himself confessed in November 1571, George Chamberlain, his father-in-law Montague's own servant.[153]

In mid-May 1571 one John Hall was arrested at Leith by some inquisitive Scots. He sang like a canary, confessing that he had, after a spell at Gray's Inn, entered the service of the earl of Shrewsbury for approximately

---

[147] Mott, HR, 536–7; Williams, *Thomas Howard*, 159.
[148] Akrigg, *Southampton*, 10; Loseley MSS, 623; Hyland, *CP*, 136–41. A letter from Montague to William More of 5 September 1570 thanked More for trying to obtain Southampton's freedom, and on 31 October 1570 Montague, from Cowdray, was still enquiring from More whether there were any hopes of Southampton's release, Loseley MSS, 623; Hyland, *CP*, 141–2, 143; FSL, L.b. 577.
[149] Hyland, *CP*, 144–5; FSL, L.b. 577.   [150] *CSP Spanish 1568–79*, 274.
[151] Manning, 'Anthony Browne', 106.   [152] Akrigg, *Southampton*, 9–10.
[153] *HMCS* I, 562, 557; Bindoff, *HC*, I, 615–16. George Chamberlain, a friend of Alvaro de La Quadra, had been locked up briefly in 1562 for his correspondence with Catholics abroad, particularly his relative Jane Dormer, *ibid.*; *CSP Spanish 1558–67*, 241. He is recorded in household lists as still being at Cowdray on 18 January 1570, BL, Additional MS 33508, fo. 32r. His brother William Chamberlain was a gentleman-servant of Southampton himself, Davidson, RC, 112; HRO, 5M53/262.

six years (until about 1567). He quitted Shrewsbury's service, however, because he 'misliked my lord's marriage with this wife, as divers others his friends did'. He believed he had left Shrewsbury with a good reference, but he was mistaken. Shrewsbury thought ill of him. Anyway, that did not stop him being '"promovit" to my Lord of Montacute's service', in March 1568, 'wherein he continues as yet undischarged'. Despite his denials, his interrogators established that he then went on his travels, through Staffordshire, Lancashire and even into Scotland, as he got embroiled in some of the northern gentry's intrigues on behalf of Mary Stuart.[154] These people, it emerged, had been actively speculating about the possibility of helping the Scottish queen to get back to Scotland.[155] Hall then admitted that there was something going on, but he said that neither the bishop of Ross nor Montague approved of the scheme. Apparently the regime was convinced that the viscount had not been fully committed to it.[156]

A great deal of this depends on how one reads the famous attempt to hitch Norfolk, the premier peer of the realm, to Mary Stuart, the leading contender to succeed or perhaps even to displace Elizabeth. Clearly, Spes's view of the world was not necessarily that of the privy councillors and peers with whom he corresponded. On the face of it, at least if we give credence to Norfolk's own self-justifications,[157] what happened was that the duke's desire to serve the realm's best interests became temporarily confused with his own self-interest. He then failed to take decisive action during the summer of 1569. He did not give a lead to the councillors who were in favour of the marriage scheme. Unable to consult the earl of Sussex who was resident in the North as lord president, he was then outwitted by the earl of Leicester. He eventually fell foul of Cecil and the queen who knew more or less what he was doing and interpreted his refusal to explain himself as a sign of disloyalty.[158] In the end Norfolk was guilty primarily of a colossal deficiency of leadership, though Stephen Alford would want to stress that many of Norfolk's contacts, including Leicester, had no interest 'in any sort of project which could not have underpinned the stability of England, the Scottish regency and the security of Protestantism'.[159]

There is a gap, however, between, on the one hand, the story line in which a scheming cabal of peers hatched plots for the sudden arrest of Cecil and the marriage of the duke to Mary Stuart, and, on the other, the account

---

[154] *HMCS* I, 499–501.
[155] For the conspiracy to free Mary Stuart from Chatsworth, see D. Durrant, *Bess of Hardwick* (1999), 74.
[156] *HMCS* I, 541. For the arraignment of John Hall and Francis Rolston, see J. Bellamy, *The Tudor Law of Treason* (1979), 65–6.
[157] Alford, *Early Elizabethan Polity*, 200.
[158] This is the line put forward by Williams, *Thomas Howard*, 154–63.
[159] Alford, *Early Elizabethan Polity*, 201.

of Cecil at odds on some policy issues with his privy council colleagues but nevertheless still managing to talk to them about what the regime's line should be on issues such as the succession and foreign policy. Alford does quite a lot to bridge this gap: the Norfolk 'crisis' can be construed as simply a 'dynastic' alternative to Cecil's 'British' policy. This was another and in essence a perfectly respectable way of relieving the twin headaches of Mary Stuart and the succession. 'The planned Howard–Stuart match was not pure conspiracy', says Alford.[160]

Undoubtedly this was how Norfolk himself saw the issue, though this line was given a fiercely anti-Cecilian slant by the bishop of Ross, or whoever it was who penned the *Treatise of Treasons* of 1572. And it is evidently impossible to describe Norfolk's shenanigans as merely a Catholic plot, or even as a Catholic plot fronted by a dupe of a Protestant peer. If Norfolk had really been a covert Catholic leader he could hardly have cooperated with Leicester, or have had the support of Sir Nicholas Throckmorton who acted as go-between for the duke and the earl in the scheme for the duke and the Scottish queen to marry and for her to be restored to her Scottish throne.[161] The hard line 'Catholic' proposals, some of which eventually emerged as the northern rising, were formulated without Norfolk's full knowledge or collaboration. In particular, the disenchantment of Arundel, Lumley and Northumberland with Norfolk's non-Catholicism was, apparently, what instigated the proposals for Mary's release and the ousting of Elizabeth. Here, Norfolk would also marry Mary, though such a scheme now had a completely different political meaning from the one originally intended by Norfolk himself.[162]

On the other hand, the whole thing was still a catastrophe for those who failed to win the argument. Even if, as Alford argues, 'the Norfolk plan – before Ridolfi and without agents – was not a serious grievance for Elizabeth', and the main charge against him was breaking his oath as a privy councillor,[163] the fact remained that some Catholics (even while Norfolk himself maintained his Protestant credentials) had entirely broken ranks with the political establishment. After this, for many of them, there was no going back. Some of the government's propagandists, such as Thomas Norton, pointed this out.[164] Though it appears the queen was herself often

---

[160] *Ibid.*, ch. 9 (quotation at p. 199).   [161] Williams, *Thomas Howard*, 149–50.

[162] *Ibid.*, 150–1. For the fullest account of how the various schemes which led up to the rising were developed, see Taylor, 'Crown'.

[163] Alford, *Early Elizabethan Polity*, 202. It should be pointed out, however, that Norfolk had never really been trusted by the queen; and the queen shared Cecil's deep distrust of Mary even if, famously, Elizabeth did not agree with him about what should be done to render Mary harmless.

[164] See e.g. Thomas Norton, *A Warning against the Practises of Papistes* (1569).

opposed to draconian legislation designed to root out the Catholic menace, the parliament of 1571 passed statutes which were intended to do just that. The place and role of a 'bluff' and 'outspoken' Catholic man (as Manning describes Montague)[165] were going to get a good deal more precarious and difficult.

[165] Manning, 'Anthony Browne', 106.

5

The Brownes, Catholicism and politics from the 1570s until the early 1590s

After the trauma of the 1569 rebellion, Montague may have hoped to limit the reaction against his co-religionists. In early April 1571 he was present in parliament at a conference between the two Houses on a bill concerning religion. The bill enforced attendance at church more strictly and, crucially, compelled reception of communion.[1] In April and May he was nominated to sit on a committee with, among others, the earls of Huntingdon and Bedford to consider the bill which became 'An Acte agaynst Fugytyves over the Sea', and also, in May, the treasons bill which became 'An Acte whereby certayne Offences bee made Treason'.[2]

In some ways it is curious that Montague should have been charged with overseeing a bill which enforced full ecclesiastical conformity, though he was himself a conformist and, in any case, the bill failed because Elizabeth vetoed it. Perhaps Montague intervened in order to stymie the passage of this legislation. There are vague ambassadorial reports which suggest that some of the peers objected to provisions in the bill which intruded on noble privilege in this respect (although there is no direct indication that Montague was among them).[3] When the bill received its third reading in the Lords, four Catholic peers (Worcester, Southampton, Windsor and Vaux) voted against it, but Montague did not.[4] In fact, on this occasion, he was not present in the House at all. (This is one of the very few days in this session in which he was noted as being absent.) It is worth noting also that he was absent for the whole of the 1572 parliament, and so did not take any part in the debates about Mary Stuart and the duke of Norfolk. We do not know why. It may have been, as we have already remarked in the previous chapter, because he felt no personal or political affection for the Scottish queen. Or it could have been because he had no wish for his style of Catholicism to be recruited into the service of the Stuart cause.

---

[1] *LJ* I, 672; J. E. Neale, *Elizabeth I and her Parliaments* (2 vols., 1953–7), I, 192–3.
[2] *LJ* I, 679, 681, 683, 692, 697; *SR* IV, 526, 531.
[3] Neale, *Elizabeth I and her Parliaments*, I, 212–16.   [4] *LJ* I, 688.

In the 1576 parliament he was back again, though his active role seems to have been rather limited.[5] He may have been turning his attention instead to his obligations as a local governor in his home counties of Sussex and Surrey. He was diligent about his duties in regulating forest matters in Surrey, especially in Guildford Park, though in *c*. April 1573 he surrendered to the earl of Leicester his charge of the walks in the Surrey 'ballywyck' of Windsor forest.[6] He was also involved in the regulation of the Sussex grain trade. In May 1573 he wrote to advise Lord Burghley concerning the amount of grain being exported out of the county, particularly from Chichester. With Buckhurst, he was responsible for civil defence.[7] In mid-July 1573 his son-in-law, Southampton, who had been released from the Tower into the custody of William More, was discharged from house arrest with More and allowed to reside at Cowdray, where Montague ensured that he kept out of trouble.[8] Periodic bouts of illness did not seem to diminish Montague's capacity for business, even though in early November 1573 he had to forgo a social engagement at Loseley because he was too sick to travel.[9]

In summer 1577 it was expected that Elizabeth would visit Cowdray. On 4 July Buckhurst wrote to the earl of Sussex in order to ascertain when the queen was going to appear at Lewes, for he had 'sent into Kent, Surrey and Sussex for provicion', but he was finding 'all places possest by my lord of Arrundell, my Lord Mountague and others'.[10] The queen never actually made it into Sussex, apparently because of the threat of plague.[11]

Where we might expect to find more evidence of Montague's presence in Sussex, though in fact we do not, is in the resistance in the county to the zealotry of the irascible Bishop Richard Curteys.[12] Curteys's undoubted enthusiasm for using the episcopal machinery of discipline and correction to enforce conformity cannot now easily be traced because of the patchiness of the relevant records.[13] As early as 1575, however, the privy council agreed that he might usefully deal individually with those who were suspected of

[5] *Ibid.*, 733.
[6] Loseley MSS, 625, 626, 630–1; SHC, LM 6729/8/39, LM 6729/3/82. Leicester was constable of Windsor Castle and the forest bailiwicks seem to have been under his control. (I am grateful to Simon Adams for this point.) For Montague's responsibility for Guildford Manor, the queen's property, see SHC, LM 6729/8/57.
[7] PRO, SP 12/91/31, 40; PRO, SP 12/108/5.
[8] Hyland, *CP*, 147. Southampton's wife Mary (Montague's daughter) came to Cowdray as well. Southampton's heir, the future third earl, was born at Cowdray in October 1573, *ibid.*, 148–9. Southampton already had rooms available to him at Cowdray. In around 1570 we find Anthony Garnett making payments to a workman to put in a 'bay for my lord of Southamptons chamber', BL, Additional MS 33508, fo. 54r.
[9] Loseley MSS, 626.   [10] BL, Cotton MS Titus B II, no. 167, fo. 356r.
[11] J. Nicholls, *The Progresses and Public Processions of Queen Elizabeth* (3 vols., New York, 1823), II, 60–2; M. H. Cole, *The Portable Queen* (1999), 190.
[12] See CRS 54, 54.   [13] Manning, *Religion*, 79.

Catholicism. In the end his campaign was deferred until April 1577 when, on two separate days in that month, he, in high-handed fashion, simply summoned all those whom he suspected to appear before the consistory court in Chichester Cathedral. In particular he went after three people – Sir Thomas Palmer of Parham, Thomas Lewkenor of Selsey and Richard Ernley.

The show trials (on 2 and 17 April),[14] where Curteys demanded of those who turned up whether they were fully conformist, whether they possessed Catholic books and so on,[15] did not go well, at least for Curteys. The gentry took their case initially to Palmer's patron, the earl of Arundel, and it ended up in front of the privy council. Palmer protested that he, Lewkenor and Ernley were fully conformable, and had taken the oath of supremacy, but, in spite of this, Curteys was ordering them to appear before him yet again.[16]

The story of the set-to between Curteys and the gentry, and his humbling and virtual suspension from his office, has already been narrated in some detail by Roger Manning. From our perspective, what is curious is Montague's apparent silence. Maybe he was influenced by Palmer's attachment to the earl of Arundel who, as we have seen, was probably not Montague's friend.[17] Or, perhaps, Montague was not inclined to take the side of people who were so potentially radical as to challenge a bishop in his own diocese. It is possible that Montague was wary of aligning himself with something that could develop into a full Catholic confrontation with the regime, though in the end it was Curteys who lost out, leaving at least some of his gentry enemies to pose and posture as the supporters of authority and stability in the county.

However, the issue of order and stability raised other, secular matters which had already caused bad blood between Curteys and the gentry. Here Montague might well have had an opinion to express. One of the charges levelled against Curteys was that he had interfered in the grain trade and its regulation,[18] where Montague had a definite interest.[19] Thomas Lewkenor said that Curteys was behind the unlawful movement and sale of corn by his own servants. Allegedly his men had accepted bribes to give transport licences to others who wanted them. But he had refused a licence to Lewkenor, so Lewkenor said, even though Lewkenor already had a form of licence from the privy council to transport grain.[20] Curteys responded with a tit-for-tat accusation that the Lewkenor family was profiteering unlawfully in the grain trade. However Lewkenor *et al.* replied with the charge that Curteys had

---

[14] Cf. *ibid.*, 86.   [15] PRO, SP 12/111/45.
[16] PRO, SP 12/112/13, fo. 36r; Manning, *Religion*, 87–8.
[17] Bindoff, *HC*, III, 53. Palmer's Stradling in-laws, however, were a family with which Montague recognised kinship through the Gages.
[18] Manning, *Religion*, 93–4; PRO, SP 12/112/31.
[19] See *APC 1554–6*, 272.   [20] Manning, *Religion*, 99.

crossed Montague in this matter. Palmer, Ernley and Lewkenor signed an affidavit testifying to Curteys's corrupt practices over grain. They said that the previous year Curteys and his chancellor, Henry Worley, had licensed a man from London named Pope 'to transport a quantitie of wheate notwith-standinge that the Lord Mountague hearinge of the ladinge of the same had written to his lordship to staie the said corne and not to suffer the same or any other to passe' until Montague and the other commissioners had dealt with it.[21]

THE ANJOU MATCH

At the end of the 1570s, the regime suffered the massive public relations cri-sis of the Anjou match. The proposal for the ageing queen to wed the duke of Anjou brought about an impasse in government as Elizabeth, apparently determined to marry, clashed with Protestant courtiers who were equally determined to prevent her. Clearly, Catholics such as the first Viscount Mon-tague were not directly involved, although other Catholics, such as the charis-matic Jesuits Edmund Campion and Robert Persons, may well have tried, in 1580, to exploit the political divisions caused by the proposed dynastic union.[22] But Montague's brand of 'loyalist', but also, one suspects, often

---

[21] PRO, SP 12/112/31, fo. 126r. Curteys replied that in fact it was Ernley rather than Worley who had joined with Curteys to give Pope (a West Sussex, not a London man) a licence to transport 'an hundred quarters of grayne to some port within the realme'. This was something 'whereof Mr Thomas Lewkenour . . . lykes very well and penned a certayne lettre about the same to my Lord Montagewe', as Curteys recalled, 'in Mr Gardener his house in the Close of Chichester'. Montague had found no fault with Pope's 'transportacion' of grain but, insisted Curteys, raised objections to a completely different 'quantity of grayne' undertaken by one Ralph Chantler and other citizens of Chichester, PRO, SP 12/112/33, fo. 134r. Chantler was, as Manning shows, one of Curteys's enemies, and a suspect in the April 1577 attempted purge of Catholic nonconformity, Manning, *Religion*, 85n, 93n, 243. In other words Curteys was trying to enlist Montague on his own side in this dispute.

[22] T. M. McCoog, 'The English Jesuit Mission and the French Match, 1579–1581', *Catholic Historical Review* 87 (2001), 185–213. The exact chronology and mechanics of the process by which the Jesuits Robert Persons and Edmund Campion came to be dis-patched to England have yet to be established. Thomas McCoog has speculated that there was a bout of excited message-sending from somewhere within the Elizabethan Court telling pro-active Catholic elements at Rome that now was the time to stir the pot. McCoog suggests that such messages could even have come from the earl of Oxford, one of whose servants, Luke Astlow, had been a friend of Persons in Padua, *ibid.*, 207. Campion had dedicated a seventeen-page poem on the history of the Church to Montague before he, Campion, removed himself from Oxford and went to Ireland, G. Kilroy, 'Paper, Inke and Penne: The Literary *Memoria* of the Recusant Community', *Downside Review* 119 (2001), 95–124, at p. 101; *idem*, 'Eternal Glory: Edmund Campion's Virgilian Epic', *Times Literary Supplement* (8 March 2002), 13; BL, Additional MS 36529, no. 13, 'Nascen-tis Ecclesiae generatio prima . . .'. Kilroy notes that the poem is a product of Campion's Oxford years (1566–70); it 'compares the transitory glory of the empire of Rome with the eternal glory of the Church of Rome', Kilroy, 'Eternal Glory'. Kilroy suggests that the

critical and irritable, Catholicism was still an issue here because there was a concerted attempt at this time by a Catholic Court faction to seize the day and use the match to purge the regime of some of its more Protestant members. The French diplomatic service in the shape of Michel de Castelnau, seigneur de Mauvissière, availed itself of the members of this faction, notably Henry Howard, the earl of Oxford and Charles Arundell.[23]

John Bossy suggests that Mauvissière also went outside the small coterie of Court papists in order to canvass a wider spectrum of English Catholic opinion. Bossy says that Montague would have been the obvious point of contact, though there is no direct evidence that any such contact took place. As Bossy notes, Montague's kin relationship with the earl of Sussex (one of the principal Court supporters of the marriage), through Montague's long-deceased first wife (Sussex's aunt), would have made this a sensible move.[24]

Diplomatic evidence indicates that, faced in October 1579 with a council which would not unite behind her own clearly indicated determination to press ahead with the allegedly ugly but apparently not entirely undesirable French prince, the queen considered admitting four leading Catholics to the council in order to get her way.[25] One of these was Montague. Another was Montague's friend, the Master of the Rolls, Sir William Cordell. Cordell, a Marian privy councillor, and a known Catholic,[26] was a friend of Edmund Campion.[27] This, of course, is not to say that Cordell was some kind of

---

manuscript got into the hands of Sir John Harington via Sir William Cordell, one of the visitors of St John's College, and a friend of both Campion and Montague (see below in this chapter).

[23] J. Bossy, 'English Catholics and the French Marriage 1577–1581', *RH* 5 (1959–60), 2–16, at pp. 5–7. For the earl of Oxford, see A. Nelson, *Monstrous Adversary* (Liverpool, 2003).

[24] Bossy, 'English Catholics', 5, 13 n. 18.

[25] *Ibid.*, 7, 13 n. 17, 14 n. 27 (citing PRO 31/3/27, fo. 407r: Mauvissière to Henry III, 29 October 1579); McCoog, 'The English Jesuit Mission', 192–3. Simon Adams has pointed out to me that the source of this evidence was the archbishop of Glasgow and ultimately Mary Stuart herself.

[26] See e.g. Cockburn, *Sussex Assizes: Elizabeth*, no. 350.

[27] Cordell had been an executor, with Montague, of Mary Tudor's will, and Cardinal Pole's as well, PRO, SP 12/1/32, fo. 69r; Hasler, *HC*, I, 657. He was himself close to the Roper family. He and William Roper had been visitors of St John's College, PRO, SP 12/80/11, 12, where, in the 1560s, they would have known Campion. See R. Simpson, *Edmund Campion* (1896), 10–16. When the principal of Gloucester Hall in Oxford, the Catholic Henry Russell, was ejected, he took up the post of steward at Cordell's family pile – Melford Hall. Russell had been a friend of Campion at St John's. He was among the congregation at Lyford where Campion was arrested in 1581. It was also alleged that Russell and the president of St John's, Francis Willis, had themselves harboured the Jesuit, M. Hodgetts, *Secret Hiding Places* (Dublin, 1989), 54–5, 79. The link with Roper would obviously have tied Montague and Cordell together because of the Roper–Browne marriage connection (Montague's sister Lucy married Thomas Roper of Eltham), Berry, *Sussex*, 354; Bindoff, *HC*, I, 702–3. Cordell was also kin to Francis Yaxley, the Suffolk political meddler who was mixed up in the early 1560s with the countess of Lennox's faction, PRO SP 12/13/12, 14. It appears that Cordell was caught up in the wake of the Yaxley investigation, PRO, SP 12/21/55,

Catholic 'sleeper' at the heart of the system. The wide range of his political contacts – particularly with Sir Nicholas Bacon – suggests rather the opposite.[28] In 1578, when the queen visited him during her East Anglian progress, no mention was made of his religion, while other Catholic gentry families were ritually humiliated for theirs.[29] And he retained his post until his death in 1581. However he was explicitly recognised as 'Catholic' in a way that many other 'conservatives' were not.[30]

Montague's and Cordell's rumoured promotion would have been an extraordinary political comeback. And indeed nothing came of the proposal.[31] But the point was that Montague, Cordell and the other known Catholic whose appointment to the council was allegedly considered at this time, namely the eighth earl of Northumberland, were conformists. They were the sort of people whose links with Campion were unlikely to become overt. They might even defuse the threat implied in the kind of evangelical campaign which the Jesuit started conducting in mid-1580. At the same time, they were not 'mere' conformists. And the fact that such people were being drawn into the Anjou political crisis, or at least were rumoured to be involved, was a measure of the crisis's potential to alter substantially the established ecclesiastical and political order.

In 1581 Montague can be found protecting Catholics who were suspected of fraternising with Campion, in particular Sir Alexander Culpeper, Montague's wife's brother-in-law. Culpeper, who was already being harassed by the high commission, had been hauled in on 8 September 1580 (not long after Campion's arrival, as Culpeper himself noted). Culpeper point-blank refused 'to goe to church' and 'was . . . commited close prisioner at Caunterburie' in December. He was summoned again after three months to appear at Ashford. With other recusants he was locked up until Whitsun 1581 when, 'upon the counsells lettres procured by my good Lord Mountague', he 'was dismissed upon a band of a thousand poundes'.[32]

---

fo. 105r. Nevertheless Cordell in December 1569 dutifully subscribed the oath for uniformity of worship, PRO, SP 12/60/62. i. Montague was also a trustee of Cordell's flagship charity – his hospital at Long Melford, BL, Lansdowne MS 66, no. 50; LPL, MS 671 ('The Ordinances, Statutes and Rules for the Good Government of the Hospitall of the Blessed Trynitie of the Foundation of Sir William Cordell . . .').

28 See R. Tittler, *Nicholas Bacon* (1976), 104, 113, 164, 229.

29 Z. Dovey, *An Elizabethan Progress: The Queen's Journey into East Anglia, 1578* (Stroud, 1996), 42–3; Cole, *Portable Queen*, 142.

30 Cordell was the dedicatee of the Catholic Ferdinando Poulton's *An Abstract of all the Penall Statutes* (1577), sig. Aiir–ivv.

31 Simon Adams doubts whether there was really anything very much behind such rumours. I am grateful to Dr Adams for his advice on this point.

32 C. Buckingham, 'The Troubles of Sir Alexander Culpeper of Goudhurst', *Cantium* 2 (1970), 5–8, at p. 6. Culpeper had been knighted by the queen during her 1573 progress into Kent, Nicholls, *Progresses*, I, 334.

It must be significant that several of the principal Sussex Catholic gentry who, as Culpeper records, were incarcerated at this time were close to Montague. For example, John Gage was put in the Fleet in August 1580 – though it appears that Montague did not intervene on his behalf.[33] In fact, on 8 September 1580 Lorenzo Priuli, the Venetian ambassador in France, believed that Elizabeth had imprisoned various gentry and even 'noblemen', whom 'she either knows or suspects to be Catholics'. Priuli claimed that among them was Montague himself, 'who was a long while in her service' and who 'always feigned not to be a Catholic'.[34] On 21 August, the Spanish ambassador Bernardino de Mendoza had informed his royal master that official letters had been dispatched to the earls of Northumberland, Worcester and Southampton, as well as to Montague, five (unnamed) barons and three hundred gentlemen, ordering them into confinement in preselected 'castles and strongholds'.[35] There is no other evidence that Montague was actually locked up at this time. He was present for most of the 1581 parliamentary session but seems to have done little there. Unpleasant official glances at him may have made him watchful, whereas his son-in-law Southampton was, as usual, much less circumspect.

But even if Montague and his entourage did contemplate trying to interfere in the Anjou match, it became virtually impossible for them to present a united front. The blazing family row over Montague's daughter Mary's split with her husband Southampton was beyond remedy. Indeed the quarrel reached its climax in March 1580 just before the Jesuits appeared in England. The outraged and self-pitying countess's letter to her father, Montague, listing the slights and cruelties which she had suffered at the hands of her husband, is dated 21 March. She was now under virtual house arrest and had been forcibly separated from her son.[36]

This may partly explain why Montague seems never to have been involved with Campion directly,[37] while the earl of Southampton probably was.[38]

---

[33] Bindoff, *HC*, II, 179. Gage procured his own release on bail but was subject to further constraints and harassment.

[34] *CSPV 1558–80*, 646.

[35] *CSP Spanish 1580–6*, 50. It appears that Mendoza was directly in contact with Montague in April 1582, *ibid.*, 348.

[36] Akrigg, *Southampton*, 13–14. Akrigg notes that Montague is not mentioned in the main body of Southampton's will. There was, however, some gesture towards a reconciliation in a codicil which bequeathed to Montague 'a George and a Garter', probably those of the first earl of Southampton, 'of the value of fourtie poundes in token of perfect love and charitie betwene us', *ibid.*, 17–18.

[37] Montague's former servant, George Chamberlain, who had gone into exile after the northern rising, provided assistance for Persons and Campion to cross to England in mid-1580, Bindoff, *HC*, I, 616. Chamberlain supplied Persons's captain's uniform 'of buff laid with gold and with hat and feather suited to the same', CRS 39, xv.

[38] Akrigg, *Southampton*, 15. See below in this chapter.

Robert Persons hinted at this when he recalled that, in addition to the refusal of the French diplomats to assist the English Catholics, 'one thing [which] also increased the difficulties of Catholikes at this tyme . . . was the falling out betweene the earle of Southampton and the Lord Montacute, about the earles wife, which was daughter to the lord, and put away by the earle, as suspected of incontinency'.[39] As we have already seen, the earl of Southampton's entourage was a good deal more radical than Montague's, even though there was undoubtedly some overlap between them. Thomas Pounde, Southampton's first cousin, became one of Campion's publicists.[40] Had the earl not died in October 1581 there might have been a severe retribution exacted against him and his circle after Campion was finally brought to book. Imprisoned with John Gage was William Shelley of Michelgrove who, though primarily a retainer of the earl of Northumberland, was probably closer to his Hampshire kinsman, Southampton, than he was to Montague.[41] After the discovery of the Jesuit secret press at Stonor Park, on which Campion's *Decem Rationes* had been printed, Persons fled to Michelgrove *en route* to the Continent.[42] It is perhaps significant that Persons did not go via Cowdray when one might have expected him to have had access there through the good offices of Montague's chaplain and steward, Anthony Garnett, who was formerly master of Persons's Oxford college, Balliol,[43] and also through Montague's gentleman-servant, Thomas Fitzherbert, whom Persons knew and trusted.[44]

RADICAL AND 'MODERATE' CATHOLICISM IN THE 1580S

It is worth, at this point, trying to bring out some of the contrasts between 'moderate' and 'extremist' or 'radical' Catholicism in this period. The historiography of the 'Catholic' issue has always tended to confirm this division between the supposedly 'loyal' majority and the 'disloyal' minority. For the closest that the history of early modern English Catholicism generally gets to genuine excitement is in the storytelling about the Catholic conspiracies of the period. Some of the most commercially successful books written

[39] CRS 2, 183.

[40] The agent for Pounde's entry, as a layman, into the Society of Jesus was the Wiltshire Jesuit Thomas Stephens, who was probably a relative, perhaps a brother, of the society priest and spiritual mentor of the Court Catholics, Richard Stephens, Bishop John Jewel's former secretary, Anstr. I, 334; Bossy, 'English Catholics', 2–3.

[41] Manning, *Religion*, 155.

[42] CRS 39, xxxix.

[43] Garnett was succeeded as master in 1563 by Robert Hooper. Thus Garnett and Persons would not have overlapped at Balliol, A. Kenny, 'Reform and Reaction in Elizabethan Balliol, 1559–1588', in J. Prest (ed.), *Balliol Studies* (1982), 17–51, at pp. 20, 21, 22.

[44] See ch. 6, p. 197 below.

on the topic have enthralled readers by recreating the shadowy intelligence communities serviced and relied on by the likes of Sir Francis Walsingham, the earl of Essex and Sir Robert Cecil. They weave ever more complex Le Carré-esque webs around the 'plain-man's' narrative of the Catholics' schemes put about by the regime following their 'detection'.[45]

This can be quite exciting stuff, but the piling up of conspiracies and sub-conspiracies (most of which seem to come to little or nothing)[46] has meant that the famous Catholic plots of the period, notably 'Throckmorton' and 'Babington' in the 1580s, 'Squire' in the 1590s and, in James's reign, the Bye and the Gunpowder conspiracies, often appear to be so weird that it is far from clear what they have to do with what one imagines might be Mr Average Catholic's practice of his faith. Mark Nicholls suggests that the early Jacobean treasons were not even '"leftover" disturbances characteristic of an earlier age'; in fact they were not typical of anything. He argues that 'treason, whatever the deeper social impulses that may or may not have played their part, remained a personal crime, committed by individuals with often the pettiest, most idiosyncratic of motives – on occasion, indeed, with no perceptible motive at all'.[47] For Vincent Burke, only a few priests committed acts of political subversion. And he argues that 'those involved in the Catholic conspiracies must . . . be regarded as distinct and separate from the recusant body as a whole just as their behaviour and activities were governed by different laws'. The government's reaction was 'based more upon a misreading of the situation than upon any threat represented by Catholicism'.[48] Robin Clifton, likewise, has suggested that it was only 'the immense shadow and not the substance of English Catholicism which frightened Protestants, for by the early seventeenth century recusancy was remarkable chiefly for its weaknesses'. The Catholics in the early Stuart period had 'lost morale', were 'reduced in numbers', 'resigned to defeat' and weakened by 'factional disputes'.[49]

---

[45] See e.g. C. Nicholl, *The Reckoning* (1992).

[46] Peter Holmes concludes that Elizabeth was not in much personal danger from the actual conspiracies which were raised in Mary Stuart's interest, P. J. Holmes, 'Mary Stewart in England', in M. Lynch (ed.), *Mary Stewart* (Oxford, 1988), 195–218, at pp. 198–9. John Bossy, whose recent *Giordano Bruno and the Embassy Affair* (1991) and *Under the Molehill* (2001) are out on their own as reconstructions of what was happening in the 1580s' intelligence community, concludes rather differently that, with the Throckmorton plot at least, the intelligence arm of the English privy council was fighting a real threat.

[47] M. Nicholls, 'Treason's Reward: The Punishment of Conspirators in the Bye Plot of 1603', *HJ* 38 (1995), 821–42, at p. 842.

[48] V. Burke, 'Catholic Recusants in Elizabethan Worcestershire' (MA, Birmingham, 1972), 231, 229, 226. J. A. Hilton comes to similar conclusions concerning Durham Catholics, J. A. Hilton, 'Catholic Recusancy in County Durham, 1559–1625' (M. Phil., Leeds, 1974), 85.

[49] R. Clifton, 'The Popular Fear of Catholics during the English Revolution', *Past and Present* 52 (1971), 23–55, at pp. 34–5.

Nicholls is certainly right about the oddness of the early Jacobean treasons. But how far should we subscribe to the idea that, in the mid-Elizabethan period, there was an absolute and clear distinction between Catholicism of the 'moderate' and of the 'radical' kind? How far should we separate out, on the one hand, the politics and experiences of the entourage of an avowedly 'moderate' peer such as the first Viscount Montague and, on the other, the opinions of those whom the State tended to regard as political firebrands?

The activism of Catholic radicals was something which Montague would never explicitly endorse. But the divisions between different expressions of Catholicism in this period were distinctly porous, something which the polemicising and publicising of Edmund Campion and Robert Persons made very clear.[50]

And it is not too difficult to find Catholics with radical, or at least disruptive, tendencies in Montague's kin circle. One such was Thomas Pounde, first cousin of Montague's son-in-law, Southampton. Pounde was reckoned to be so dangerous by the regime of Elizabeth and, later, by that of James I, that he was kept in prison more or less continuously for thirty years. His flagrant and outrageous challenges to the local State in Hampshire over religion were an extraordinary departure from his courtier careerism of the 1560s.[51] Pounde's activism was channelled into the Campion dispute as he liaised between the Jesuits and a wider public. Whatever one makes of the famous story of the leaking of Campion's 'Brag' (the Jesuit's pithy written challenge to the regime),[52] Pounde was the means by which Campion's challenge was widely dispersed.

He also took on, in a much-publicised disputation, conducted by way of manuscript challenge and reply, the puritans Henry Tripp and Robert Crowley. While Pounde was in the Marshalsea prison he engaged Crowley in a dispute over the 'Six Reasons', a discourse written by Pounde which made use of, and further popularised, Campion's 'Brag'. Crowley printed Pounde's reasons, along with his own reply to them. The regime noted in January 1581 how the 'Brag' was spreading in particular through Hampshire, Pounde's home county.[53] Aping Campion, Pounde had written his own challenge in

---

[50] See P. Lake and M. Questier, 'Puritans, Papists and the "Public Sphere" in Early Modern England: The Edmund Campion Affair in Context', *Journal of Modern History* 72 (2000), 587–627.

[51] For Pounde's alienation from the Court, conversion to Catholicism, entry into the Society of Jesus and increasingly overt challenges to the local State in Hampshire, see Foley III, 573ff; ch. 2, pp. 63–4 above.

[52] McCoog, *Society*, 146; Foley III, 631.

[53] McCoog, *Society*, 146, n. 61; PRO, SP 12/144/31; Mott, HR, 225. See also *HMC, Report on Manuscripts in Various Collections* III (1904), 5–8; Robert Crowley, *An Aunswer to Sixe Reasons* (1581), which contains an appendix in which is printed Henry Tripp's 'breefe aunswer' to Pounde; Milward I, 56–7; ch. 2, p. 64 above.

the form of a 'petition' in September 1580 addressed to the privy council.[54] Following this spate of polemical activity he was consigned to higher security gaols away from London, first at Bishop's Stortford and then at Wisbech.[55] On 4 August 1581, the council instructed the authorities at Wisbech Castle to examine the incarcerated Pounde. It noted that the Jesuit Thomas Stephens had 'brought the said Pounde to speak with Campian at Throckmorton House in London, and further that Pounde directed Campian by a token to' the earl of Southampton's trusted servant, Thomas Dymock, 'to speak with the earl' himself.[56]

Looking, from a Hampshire perspective, at the connection between the earl of Southampton's Catholic entourage and the Campion agitation, what seems to have happened is that disaffected Catholics, grouped around a disaffected peer, used the arrival of the Jesuits to pursue their own agenda. This involved a public challenge to a crowd of godly ministers and ecclesiastical officials whom they had been baiting for years.

The same thing seems to have happened in some Sussex and Surrey parishes as well. In 1580–1 Campion's endeavours were clearly stirring up prominent conservative Sussex churchmen, for example, Stephen Vallenger and perhaps also Henry Shales who emerged as the foe of the puritans in East Sussex in 1583.[57] In July 1581 Martin Clipsain, until recently the curate of Merrow in

---

[54] Foley III, 632–3.   [55] *Ibid.*, 593–4.   [56] *Ibid.*, 650.

[57] Vallenger was prebendary of Selsey, and was not finally deprived until 1582, T. J. McCann, 'The Clergy and the Elizabethan Settlement in the Diocese of Chichester', in M. J. Kitch (ed.), *Studies in Sussex Church History* (Chichester, 1980), 99–123, at pp. 106–7. He was condemned to the pillory and suffered the amputation of his ears for having publicised Campion's cause. See A. G. Petti, 'Stephen Vallenger (1541–1591)', *RH* 6 (1961–2), 248–64, esp. pp. 251–6, suggesting that Vallenger may have been the writer of some of the material in Thomas Alfield's *A True Reporte of the Death and Martyrdom of M. Campion Iesuite and Preiste* . . . (1582). Vallenger was indicted for being 'author and spreader' of the book, PRO, E 178/2978. For Shales, rector of Hangleton, see Manning, *Religion*, 193. In *c.* March 1583 a group of puritans brought charges against him and five other ministers in the Church court sitting at Lewes. In a sermon Shales had called his opponents the 'new brotherhood, the brotherhood of separation, the separated brethren, private spirits, this new faction', PRO, SP 12/159/14, fo. 68r. See also PRO, SP 12/159/15, 16. A paper written by William Fulke and John Still answers the propositions of 'one Shales' on certain theological topics. In reply to the third proposition alleged to have been stated by Shales, namely 'that yt is not to impeach the trueth of the humanitie of Christ, to saye that concerning his sowle he did not growe in the gyftes of the spyrite', Fulke and Still say: 'we doe thinke yt a false judgment and contrarye to the Scriptures which we doe fynde disputed and maynteyned by the scholemen of the Church of Rome, and lately renewed in the wrytinges of the Jesuites, as Campian, Dureus and others', PRO, SP 12/146/78, fo. 149r. In the judicial hearing of March 1583, one of Shales's puritan opponents, William Jackson, alleged that Shales 'either is yet, or at least hath bene professed or appointed to one of the seminaries of Rome or Reames within thease foure, five or six yeares last', and had received money 'for his chardges'. And during that time he had either said Mass or helped a priest to say Mass, PRO, SP 12/159/14, fo. 67r. The real accusation was that Shales had taught erroneous doctrine, for example the existence of purgatory, and had said that Scripture and preaching were not essential to faith,

Surrey, a couple of parishes away from Montague's residence at West Horsley, was being enquired after because, during a discussion in the previous Lent concerning benefices in the Church of England, he had said that 'he hoped to see the world change very shortly'.[58]

As far as we know, Montague steered well clear of such people, or at least tried in public to distance himself from the adventurism of such Catholics as his son-in-law and his associates who were going out of their way to goad and provoke the regime. On the other hand, Montague was named at this time on a list of leading financial backers of the seminarist clergy, a list compiled by an informer.[59] And it is worth noting that some of Montague's more immediate relatives (in addition to his wayward son-in-law Southampton), notably his daughter Elizabeth and her husband Robert Dormer, definitely did not keep clear of the Jesuits and seminary priests. They were among those who entertained Campion.[60] One of the Catholic gentlemen who was dealt with because of his contacts with Campion was, as we have already seen, Sir Alexander Culpeper, Lady Montague's brother-in-law.[61] Among those who harboured Robert Persons's printing press was Francis Browne, Montague's own brother. The press was reassembled in Browne's house (according to Antony Allison, in whichever part of Montague House in Southwark that Francis occupied) in order to publish the reply to the ministers William Charke and Meredith Hanmer who had attacked Campion in print.[62]

The famous Synod of Southwark in July 1580, where the Jesuits discussed knotty issues of conscience with established Catholic clergymen such as George Blackwell, was held in the parish of St Saviour, at an unspecified house by the river, in other words very close to Montague House, again, perhaps,

---

ibid., fo. 67v. In a sermon, preached at the Church of St Michael in Lewes on 16 February 1583, he allegedly said the Fathers were necessary for understanding Scripture. This could be taken as a reference to the sixth of the principal heads of argument in Campion's *Decem Rationes*, *ibid.*, fo. 68r. In a statement of 18 April 1583, Shales denied everything, PRO, SP 12/160/12.

[58] Clipsain had been ordained during Mary's reign. A deponent witnessed that Clipsain would often say 'that prayer was good for the dead', Hyland, *CP*, 329–30. See also FSL, L.b. 212.

[59] D. Flynn, *John Donne and the Ancient Catholic Nobility* (Bloomington, 1995), 103, 214, citing PRO, SP 12/168/31. Flynn points out that this list also included the fourth earl of Derby who was involved in proceedings against Catholics undertaken by the high commission, so its accuracy may not be guaranteed.

[60] See ch. 6, p. 187 below.   [61] See p. 155 above.

[62] McCoog, *Society*, 153; ARCR II, no. 612; William Charke, *An Answere to a Seditious Pamphlet Lately Cast Abroade by a Iesuite* (1580); Meredith Hanmer, *The Great Bragge and Challenge of M. Champion a Iesuite* (1581); Robert Persons, *A Brief Censure uppon Two Bookes Written in Answere to M. Edmonde Campions Offer of Disputation* (1581); CRS 39, xxxiii. According to Manning, Francis Browne 'sheltered the first printing press of the Jesuit Robert Southwell in St Mary Overy', R. B. Manning, 'Anthony Browne, 1st Viscount Montague: The Influence in County Politics of an Elizabethan Nobleman', *SAC* 106 (1968), 103–12, at p. 110.

in one of the buildings which surrounded Montague's riverside residence.[63] It is not improbable that Francis Browne had something to do with it.

One of the crucial questions discussed at this meeting was whether Catholics were morally obliged to renounce completely the worship of the established Church, in other words to become recusant separatists.[64] The decision that uncompromising recusancy was to be reckoned as the norm for conscientious and true Catholics when confronted by an increasingly angry regime over where their obedience lay was not necessarily welcome to Montague. He was and remained a conformist. And yet, ironically, the process of hammering out the line that Catholics should take on this issue took place within the Southwark heartland of Montague's own following.

The conformist culture of much of Montague's immediate household and entourage is well known. In fact, the central intra-Catholic recusancy debate of the period was conducted by Robert Persons and his associates with a Catholic opposition which included, and for a time was even centred on, Montague's long-serving chaplain Alban Langdale, the former archdeacon of Chichester who had been ejected from his benefices in 1559.[65] Montague's unfortunate daughter, the estranged wife of the earl of Southampton, assured the earl of Leicester that, as for her young son, if he refused conformity it was not her fault. For 'truly, my lord, if myself had kept him, he should in this house [Cowdray] have come to it [common prayer] as . . . my father', Viscount Montague, 'and his doth'.[66] In summer 1586, at a huge wedding celebration at Cowdray, the bishop of Chichester, Anthony Bickley, was himself invited to preach in the chapel.[67] In early 1592 Montague positively boasted that he exerted no pressure on his servants even to profess Catholic beliefs, let alone separate from the Church of England.[68] Some of Montague's family, including his son Henry Browne and (ironically) his brother Francis Browne, and even some of his better-known Catholic servants, such as John Shelley of Mapledurham, from time to time displayed a conformist streak.[69] And Richard Smith's biographical account of Lady

---

[63] McCoog, *Society*, 143–6.   [64] CRS 39, xviii–xx.

[65] Langdale wrote a manuscript treatise in favour of occasional conformity. See A. Walsham, *Church Papists* (1993), 55, 56, 60. Robert Persons and George Blackwell, in a quandary as to what library resources to use to answer Langdale, travelled all over London and finally 'went over the river to Southwarke and procured to have a sight of Mr Doctor Langdales library, who was absent in the country with the Lord Montacute', and found Langdale's books and 'also the same places . . . marked which were alleadged in the pamphlet', CRS 4, 5; CRS 2, 180.

[66] Paul, HR, 150.

[67] Raphael Holinshed, ed. A. Fleming, *Chronicles of England, Scotland and Ireland* (6 vols., 1807–8), IV, 901. I am grateful to Rivkah Zim for this reference.

[68] See ch. 6, pp. 193–4 below; Questier, LF, 252.

[69] Richard Young informed Sir William More in early August 1586 that Francis Browne had conformed to some extent: 'I am very glad that other men's harms make Mr Browne wary. I

Magdalen explicitly says that both Montague and his wife conformed, though Smith blamed this on the advice which they received from Alban Langdale, 'a learned and pious man indeed, but too fearful, who, supposing it expedient something to give to the time, durst not determine such a fact to be sin'.[70]

But, as Alexandra Walsham has pointed out, it is a mistake to cast all those who argued in favour of occasional conformity as spineless and weak. As we shall see, though Langdale's life was undoubtedly quieter than that of many seminarists, that did not necessarily make him *ipso facto* lazy or spineless. Indeed, in the Marian period he had had a reputation, like his master, as a hammer of the heretics. Langdale had been one of the inquisitors who interrogated Archbishop Cranmer.[71] He had been one of Montague's agents in the Marian attempt to extirpate heresy from Sussex.[72] He had taken a leading role in the proceedings against the Sussex heretic Richard Woodman.[73] And he had taken part in the Westminster disputation of late March/early April 1559, where Catholic divines made a last-gasp stand against the incoming Protestant doctrines and liturgical practice.[74] Langdale had been a close associate, and fellow college member at St John's, Cambridge, of

---

pray God all others may reform themselves according to her Maj[esty's] laws', Hyland, *CP*, 188. He had recently agreed to compound for his absence from church, *ibid.*, 306. Henry Browne, who was noticed for recusancy in 1581, seems to have exhibited signs of conformity at that time, Loseley MSS, 636; SHC, LM 6729/8/83; Hyland, *CP*, 387. Francis and Henry Browne can be found listed in the Southwark sacramental token books during the 1580s and 1590s, LMA, P92/SAV/184, p. 19, P92/SAV/187, p. 19, P92/SAV/190, p. 23, P92/SAV/191, p. 11. For John Shelley, see ch. 6, pp. 188, 195, 204, 205 below.

[70] Southern, *ERH*, 19–20. Smith's story that after Langdale's death another clergyman reproved Montague for his conformity, and Montague changed his ways, is not reliable. According to Robert Persons, Langdale permitted Montague 'to have English service in his house for his servants, though [he] himselfe went to Masse', CRS 2, 180.

[71] Walsham, *Church Papists*; McCann, 'Clergy', 104–5; ch. 6, pp. 184, 186, 190 below. Langdale also published a polemical work against Nicholas Ridley, *CSP Rome*, I, 65; Alban Langdale, *Catholica Confutatio impiae cujusdam determinationis D. Nicolai Ridlei . . . post disputationem de Eucharistia in Academia Cantabrigiensi habitae . . .* (Paris, 1556).

[72] Langdale had been presented to the archdeaconry of Chichester by Montague himself in February 1555, Peckham, 'Institutions', 184.

[73] Woodman was arrested in June 1554 by, among others, John Ashburnham and 'Master Culpeper', presumably Alexander Culpeper, subsequently Montague's relative by marriage. Involved in his questioning was John Fawkener, whom Jeremy Goring identifies as a retainer and friend of the Gage family, J. J. Goring, 'Wealden Ironmasters in the Age of Elizabeth', in E. W. Ives, R. J. Knecht and J. J. Scarisbrick (eds.), *Wealth and Power in Tudor England* (1978), 204–27, at p. 219. Woodman's third examination was conducted in front of Langdale and James Gage, son of the former lord chamberlain, Sir John Gage, at Montague House in Southwark on 12 May 1557. His fifth examination was also conducted in front of Langdale, this time in Montague's parish church in Southwark, watched by 300 people, S. R. Cattley (ed.), *The Acts and Monuments of John Foxe* (8 vols., New York, 1965), VIII, 332–3, 337, 352, 367.

[74] PRO, SP 12/3/51; W. P. Haugaard, *Elizabeth and the English Reformation* (Cambridge, 1968), 102–4; Holinshed, *Chronicles of England, Scotland and Ireland*, IV, 183.

the Marian Catholic cleric Henry Comberford.[75] Comberford seems to have been a nephew of Sir Anthony Fitzherbert, and certainly occupied a Fitzherbert living at Norbury in Derbyshire. William Fitzherbert, father of the future seminary priest, martyrologist and Jesuit, Thomas Fitzherbert, was a servant of Montague at Cowdray, as for a short time was Thomas himself.

It looks as if the first viscount may have favoured a compromise position on the question of recusancy. In one Catholic manuscript casuistry treatise, the issue of nobles accompanying the queen to chapel as part of their service at court is cited, including the case of Viscount Montague who, it seems, had gone so far as to accompany the queen to the chapel royal, though the treatise stresses that he did not stay for the service.[76] But he freely associated with others who were prepared to push the boundaries of Catholic critiques of the Elizabethan settlement's conformist culture a good deal further. In other words, what we have here is less a thoroughly conformist and obedient peer, meekly complying with the spirit as well as the letter of the regime's directions, and more a great man presiding within his extended entourage over a number of different views about nonconformity, and endorsing a position (as rendered by his senior chaplain) which, though it might be described as partially 'conformist', was not, of itself, simply and merely compliant. Langdale's arguments fed into a sometimes acrimonious debate within the Catholic community about how to maintain and preserve Catholicism in the face of the Protestant State.

What must have helped to make Montague's attitude to conformity acceptable, and served to shelter those within his entourage who were less conformist than he was, was the far less loyal disposition of other Catholics even in Montague's own county during this period. For Sussex was one of the principal locations of what we know as the Throckmorton conspiracy, a plot which developed during 1583 in the wake of the failure of the proposals for the queen to marry the duke of Anjou. John Bossy's marvellous recent book on the plot concludes that the scheme for the duke of Guise to come ashore in Sussex (in the Arundel region) with an army of 5,000 men was at least a credible plan, even if the other half of the design, a landing in Lancashire by the Spaniards, was essentially a fantasy. The Sussex branch of the plot was 'a relatively modest and precise idea, and if a Catholic rising in the region could be expected not altogether unpromising'. Only Guise's increasing preoccupation with French politics and lack of time meant that

---

[75] For Langdale's ties of affection with other Sussex clergy, see McCann, 'Clergy', 105.

[76] Bodl., MS Jones 53, fo. 205r; P. Holmes, *Resistance and Compromise* (Cambridge, 1982), 105.

the soldiers gathered in Normandy were never used. Bossy comments that 'it was a fairly near thing'.[77]

The main Sussex victims of the plot's exposure were the earl of Northumberland, living at Petworth, and his gentleman-retainer William Shelley of Michelgrove. Subsequently, in April 1585, Philip Howard, earl of Arundel was forced into an ill-timed flight, was arrested and vanished finally into the Tower, never to regain his freedom.[78] Arundel's attempt to escape abroad instigated a series of local inquiries as the authorities tried to find out how many were implicated in the bid to get him out of the country, and to establish what might have been his future plans had he been successful.

A thorough investigation by the regime of how many guilty men there were in Sussex and Hampshire who knew of the earl of Arundel's intentions flushed out many of the leading Catholics in the region who still sympathised with the Howard cause and the remnant of the Court faction which had been undone by the failure of the Anjou match. Among those who were named in the investigations were local men such as Anthony Fortescue, his servant Edward Poe, George Fortescue, Alexander Cuffauld, Geoffrey Pole, Edward Caryll and the priest Ralph Bickley.[79]

What is significant, for our purposes, is that there is virtually no sign that Viscount Montague or any of his relatives and close friends were involved, though of course his wife Lady Magdalen was the countess of Arundel's sister.[80] And even those Sussex gentry whom we know to have been only tangentially involved in the Throckmorton plot, for example the Darells of Scotney, were those who had little if any connection with the Brownes.[81] Admittedly, the ambassador who was dispatched by the duke of Guise to

---

[77] See Bossy, *Under the Molehill*, 75–7; S. Carroll, *Noble Power during the French Wars of Religion* (Cambridge, 1998), 188–92; Flynn, *John Donne*, 106–7, 117–19, 221. For the conspiracy which preceded the Throckmorton plot, a scheme cooked up by Robert Persons, members of the Guise family, Claude Matthieu SJ and others, and which was also supposed to take effect through a landing on the Sussex coast, though a larger invasion force was to move into England through the Scottish border region, see P. Hughes, *The Reformation in England* (3 vols., 1954), III, 320–2.

[78] For the legal proceedings against Arundel, see F. A. Youngs, 'Definitions of Treason in an Elizabethan Proclamation', *HJ* 14 (1971), 675–91, at pp. 687–9.

[79] Many of the interrogations are preserved in BL, Egerton MS 2074.

[80] For allegations that the countess of Arundel was deeply implicated in the Throckmorton plot, see PRO, SP 12/164/9, SP 12/170/20, 23. Charles Paget, who supposedly came back to England in September 1583 to consult with Sussex Catholics over the planned incursion into the county by the forces of the duke of Guise, was blamed by some, notably Robert Persons, for aggravating the marital difficulties of the earl of Southampton and Montague's daughter, though taking into account the characters of Southampton and Montague's daughter, any contribution which Paget made to the acrimony was probably superfluous, Stonyhurst, MS Anglia II, no. 46, fo. 167r. Paget was an executor of Southampton's will, and his brother, Lord Paget, was one of the overseers, Akrigg, *Southampton*, 16.

[81] See PRO, SP 12/170/103; ch. 3, pp. 104–5 above.

Rome in August 1583 was told to say that among those in England who might be relied on to support the enterprise were 'many gentlemen . . . such as the earl[s] of Rutland, Shrewsbury, Worcester, Arundel, Viscount Montague, and others'.[82] But this, in Montague's case at least, was apparently mere wishful thinking.[83] When later on, in 1586, Mendoza was listing for King Philip's benefit all the leading Catholics who might be relied on to take part in a Catholic rising he included 'Lord Montague and all his house, which is the principal family in Sussex and has a great following'. But Philip annotated the memorandum that, though 'he was my master of the horse' back in the 1550s, and was a good Catholic, he was 'not very determined'.[84] As we have already observed, it seems fair to speculate that Montague, a known Catholic peer, enjoyed a charmed life in part because he was known not to be a supporter, in any active sense, of Mary Stuart. Perhaps he even positively disliked or at least distrusted those among his co-religionists who had yoked their fortunes to the dynastic ambitions of the Scottish queen and the Guise family.

Montague seems, however, to have continued to inhabit a kind of political no-man's-land. It is not obvious that he or his friends reaped any substantial reward for having remained loyal during the Throckmorton affair. In July 1585 Montague and Buckhurst were not reappointed to their former joint tenure of the lord lieutenancy of Sussex.[85] Lord Howard of Effingham, a privy councillor, received the commission. Montague, as a noted Hispanophile, can hardly have been regarded as a supporter of the queen's intervention on the side of the Dutch. In a letter to Sir William More on 29 June 1585, Montague referred contemptuously to the diplomatic access to the queen currently enjoyed by 'these states as wee tearme them'.[86] In August 1586, however, Buckhurst (who had become a privy councillor in February 1586) was nominated to serve with Howard. And they held jointly the lord lieutenancy of the county until the end of the reign. (Buckhurst made strenuous efforts to raise the county militia in late summer 1586 to deal with the 'brute of an arrivall of forren enemies upon the co[a]sts of Sussex', in the

---

[82] *CSP Spanish 1580–6*, 504.

[83] In August 1583 Montague expressed his contentment to Sir William More that Elizabeth still held him in high regard, although he was far from keen to appear at Court, SHC, LM 6729/8/89, 92.

[84] *CSP Spanish 1580–6*, 604.

[85] The lord lieutenancies became permanent only in 1585. Sackville and Montague were not, therefore, in any sense dismissed from this post. I am grateful to Simon Adams and Rivkah Zim for advice on this point. Manning, however, speculates that Buckhurst's career could have been temporarily impeded at this point by the scandal of his daughter-in-law Margaret Sackville's Catholicism and her association with the countess of Arundel, Manning, 'Anthony Browne', 111.

[86] SHC, LM 6729/8/98.

form of 'fiftie ships hovering to and fro before Brighthemston'.[87]) Montague was not similarly summoned to join Buckhurst in this honour. This could be just because, as Manning has argued, the 1580s saw the gradual removal in Sussex (as well as in other counties) of Catholics from local office at a time when these posts were going to those who, even if they were not clearly Protestants, had shown themselves to be enthusiastic conformists, or at least more enthusiastic than Montague. (We may assume that, even if he did not openly flout the act of uniformity's provisions, he would have refused to take the oath of supremacy.) Or it could have been a question of age. He was no longer a young man, though he was to live for another seven years. (He was virtually inactive in the 1585 parliament though he attended in the Lords on most days. There is certainly no indication that he tried to impede the anti-Catholic legislation of that session.) Or it could have been simply that Howard and Buckhurst, as privy councillors, outranked him.

Montague was barely touched by the 1586 Babington conspiracy which finally brought down the Scottish queen. And, as we have already noted, he was appointed as a commissioner for her trial in the same year.[88] His only close relative who became a casualty of the Babington affair was Robert Gage from the Haling branch of the Gage family of West Firle.[89] Montague was absent from both the parliamentary sessions of 1587 and 1588. (In the first his proxy was given to the earls of Warwick and Leicester, and in the second to Lord Burghley.[90])

Nevertheless, Montague remained comparatively active in his shire. On 21 August 1587 the privy council wrote to thank him for the speed with which he had travelled to the coast on hearing reports that foreign ships had been sighted. And, as we saw, if we believe Burghley's pamphlet *The Copy of a Letter Sent out of France to Don Barnardino Mendoza*, in the Armada

---

[87] Holinshed, *Chronicles of England, Scotland and Ireland*, IV, 901. In fact the vessels were Dutch merchant ships. But the news of this threatened incursion temporarily interrupted the large wedding feast at Cowdray taking place 'at the same time that this rumor of tumult was so rife'. The 'earle of Worcester, the countesse of Southampton, the Ladie Marie Arundell, the Ladie Greie sister to the . . . Lord Mountague, with divers other knights, ladies, gentlemen and gentlewomen of great traine and attendance' were present; and 'it was thought there were not ten gentlemen of Sussex, which might dispend two hundred pounds lands by yeare, that were absent' and 'there supped (as it was said) fifteene hundred people in and about the said house'; and 'the beere tap never left running, during the space of foure daies', *ibid.*, 901–2. (I am very grateful to Rivkah Zim for this reference.)

[88] GEC IX, 99; ch. 4, p. 145 above.

[89] George Whetstone, *The Censure* (1587), sig. F3r. The Haling branch of the Gage family is recorded in May 1559 as possessing a 'mansion house' in St Mary Overy, Southwark, ESRO, SAS/G 21/40. The only servant of Montague who was alleged to have been involved in the conspiracy was Robert Barnes, but the accusations against him seem to have been aired in the 1590s rather than at the time that the conspiracy was revealed, PRO, SP 12/248/105, 105. i.

[90] *LJ* II, 127, 145.

crisis of the following year the old man gallantly turned up at Tilbury in order to defend the realm.[91] Buckhurst had to warn the council in mid-1588 that Montague's influence in the county could not be ignored and that his followers and retainers could not simply be removed from their posts and employments.[92]

But if, in the mid-1580s, there were no signs that Montague was himself politically disaffected, there were indications that his immediate entourage was becoming implicated in oppositional activity, though they did not suffer for it in the same way as the relatives and servants of peers such as Arundel and Northumberland. We have already seen how Montague's brother Francis was frequently at the centre of sometimes quite radical Catholic political action. Some of Montague's retainers such as Robert Barnes were clearly taking risks about whom they associated with. The priest John Owen, one of the Catholic clerics who was finally put on trial for treason in 1588, was believed in 1585 to be in touch with some of Montague's household servants.[93] Owen confessed that he had left London in February 1585 in order to make contact with Montague's attendants at Hampton Court park. He was then arrested in Winchester, at the house of Mary Warnford. Having been exiled in September 1585, he almost immediately made his way back into the country. In early 1586 he was arrested again, this time at Battle (where the Brownes had their principal family residence in East Sussex).[94] A mid-1580s list of servants in Montague's employ is contained

---

[91] Bindoff, HC, I, 515–16; ch. 4, p. 124 above. Whether he went to Tilbury or not, in late July 1588 Montague could be found loyally mustering men to fight off the Spaniards. He reported to the privy council that, hearing that the beacon on Portsdown was ablaze, he thought it his duty to send a note of the number of servants he had in readiness. He wanted to know whether these should be retained for the defence of the Sussex coast, as he had not received orders to wait upon the queen's person as others had done. He had assembled 20 demilances, 60 light horsemen, a number of arquebusiers and bowmen, and also 100 pikemen, 77 'calleverers', 24 'halberdes' and 12 'partisans'. These may have been the basis of the troop which Montague allegedly paraded at Tilbury, though, as Curtis Breight points out, he was omitted from the formal command (of 23 July) to various peers to attend on the queen with their men. Though Montague's offer here may have been accepted by the council, he was told he would not be leading his own troops. He may even have been temporarily placed under a form of restraint. An information supplied from London said that on Monday 26 August Montague had been 'ordered to remain under arrest in his own house', PRO, SP 12/213/11, fo. 27r; CSP Spanish 1587–1603, 420; Breight, 'Caressing', 164 n. 19, citing APC 1588, 170, 174–8, 194, 232.

[92] Manning, 'Anthony Browne', 109.

[93] Anstr. I, 254. Agnes Mott speculated that there was a family connection between the Owens of Godstow and the Hampshire recusant Thomas Owen of Ellsfield who was probably the father of the Elizabeth Owen who married Montague's servant John Shelley of Mapledurham, Mott, HR, 377.

[94] PRO, SP 12/177/3; Anstr. I, 263; M. Hodgetts, 'The Owens of Oxford', RH 24 (1999), 415–30, at p. 419. Under interrogation Owen confessed that, after the Parry plot broke, he came out of London with William Bray and one 'Brierton' (perhaps the priest John

in the State papers for this period. The list specifically accuses them of being popishly affected, and it probably includes those whom Owen had been seeing.[95]

So, the display put on for the queen when she stayed at Cowdray during her progress through the region in summer 1591, with its implicit claims that Montague was still looked to by many of the county's leading gentry families, could not but have been taken to insinuate and perhaps proclaim that, even in his old age, he regarded himself as entitled to occupy a position of influence and honour in local society; a position which, to his mind, may have been jeopardised by some of the events of the previous decade.[96]

THE QUEEN VISITS COWDRAY

The splendid entertainment provided at Cowdray in August 1591 for the queen on progress was one of the last big social occasions of the first Viscount Montague's life. He was evidently determined to bask in the favour of his queen. Surrounded by his extended family, he would play host not just to Elizabeth but to the Court and privy council as well. His entertainment of her would be a visible demonstration of how the entourage of a great Catholic lord could be as firmly a part of late Tudor society as the following of any other wealthy and respected peer. Perhaps not surprisingly there was no mention made of religion while the queen was there. But it appears from the elaborate spectacles and displays put on for the queen's benefit that the viscount intended to show off to best advantage the mechanisms and functions of a (Catholic) commonwealth in miniature.

Elizabeth arrived at Cowdray with a large train on Saturday 14 August 'where upon sight of her Majestie, loud musicke sounded, which at her enteraunce on the bridge suddenly ceased'. One of the viscount's retainers, dressed in armour and 'standing betweene two porters, carved of wood', 'holding his club in one hand, and a key of golde in the other', made a speech. On this and subsequent days, several of Montague's servants took their turn to dress up in funny costumes and perform in front of the queen.

Lister alias Bruerton). They travelled from Putney Ferry to Kingston, then to Hampton Court Park and there met servants of Lord Montague, Anstr. I, 263; PRO, SP 12/177/3. Owen carried on to Guildford in the company of one of Montague's servants, Hodgetts, 'The Owens', 418.

[95] PRO, SP 12/195/107. The dating of this list in *CSPD* to 1586 is provisional. Several of the people on it were, in mid-1593, marked down by the privy council for arrest, *APC 1592–3*, 400, 406; ch. 6, pp. 199–200 below.

[96] There is no evidence that Montague was embittered by not being reappointed as lord lieutenant of his county. Victor Stater has argued that the lieutenancy was a matter of enormous social cachet and that to forfeit it inevitably meant a loss of face in the county community, V. L. Stater, *Noble Government* (Athens, Ga., 1994), 17–18. But this, as Simon Adams has suggested to me, may have been more of a seventeenth-century concern.

On the Saturday, a 'porter' expatiated on the similarities between the walls of Cowdray and the walls of Thebes:

the walles of Thebes were raised by musicke; by musick these are kept from falling. It was a prophesie since the first stone was layde, that these walles should shake, and the roofe totter, till the wisest, the fairest and the most fortunate of all creatures, should by her first steppe make the foundation staid; and by the glaunce of her eyes make the turret steddie. I have beene here a porter manie yeeres, many ladies have entred passing amiable, manie verie wise, none so happie.

On the off chance that the queen should have failed to spot how much her loyal subject, Viscount Montague, esteemed her, the porter proclaimed that 'as for the owner of this house, mine honourable lord, his tongue is the keie of his heart; and his heart the locke of his soule. Therefore what he speakes you may constantlie beleeve; which is, that in duetie and service to your Majestie, he would be second to none; in praieng for your happinesse, equall to anie'.[97]

The Sunday of the queen's visit was dominated by council business. Lord Buckhurst was in attendance. The council dealt with a series of issues, criminal, commercial and political – including the interrogation of the puritan Peter Wentworth.[98]

Early on Monday morning, 16 August, Elizabeth 'took horse with all her traine, and rode into the parke, where was a delicate bowre prepared, under the which were placed her Highnes musitians'. They serenaded her, and at the same time a 'nimph' presented the queen with a cross bow so that Elizabeth could at her leisure slaughter a number of deer which had been penned in within range. (Elizabeth scored at least three; Montague's sister, Mabel, countess of Kildare, tactfully bagged just one.) Just in case the queen's lust for blood had not been satisfied, Sir Henry Browne organised an evening entertainment in which 'sixteen buckes' were attacked by greyhounds.[99]

On the Tuesday the queen dined at Easebourne priory (see Figure 19), close to Cowdray, 'where my lord himselfe kept house'. In the evening the entertainment became more fanciful. She listened to a flattering oration by someone dressed as a pilgrim. The 'pilgrim' then conducted 'her Highnes to an oke not farre off, whereon her Majesties armes, and all the armes of the noblemen, and gentleman of that shire, were hanged in escutchions most beutifull, and a wilde man cladde in ivie, at the sight of her Hignesse spake as followeth'. 'Mightie princesse', he said, pointing to

---

[97] *The Speeches and Honorable Entertainment Given to the Queenes Maiestie in Progresse, at Cowdrey in Sussex, by the Right Honorable the Lord Montacute. 1591* (1591). For the text, see Breight, 'Caressing', 160–3.

[98] *APC 1591*, 386–95, 413; *DNB, sub* Wentworth.

[99] Breight, 'Caressing', 160–1; R. B. Manning, *Hunters and Poachers* (Oxford, 1993), 3, 201.

Figure 19.   A view of the eastern range and chapter house of Easebourne priory.

this shire shrunke in a tree; that what your Majestie hath ofte heard off with some comfort, you may now beholde with full content. This oke, from whose bodie so many armes doe spread, and out of whose armes so many fingers spring, resembles in parte your strengthe and happinesse. Strength, in the number and the honour, happinesse, in the trueth and consent. All heartes of oke, than which nothing surer, nothing sounder. All woven in one roote, than which nothing more constant, nothing more naturall. The wall of this shire is the sea, strong, but rampired with true hearts, invincible, where every private mans eie is a beacon to discover, everie noble mans power a bulwarke to defende. Here they are all differing somewhat in degrees, not in dutie, the greatnes of the branches, not the greenesse. Your Majesty they account the oke, the tree of Jupiter, whose root is so deeplie fastened, that treacherie, though shee undermine to the centre, cannot finde the windings.

In consequence, the queen's enemies are powerless. For the viscount

and all these honourable lords, and gentlemen, whose shieldes your Majestie doeth here beholde, I can say this, that as the veines are dispersed through all the bodie, yet when the heart feeleth any extreame passion, sende all their bloud to the heart for comfort; so they being in divers places, when your Majestie shall but stande in feare of any daunger, will bring their bodies, their purses, their soules, to your Highness, being their heart, their head, and their soveraigne.[100]

These were more than political sweet nothings. At this time the notorious 1591 proclamation against Catholic separatist clergy and their harbourers was being devised. (It would be issued on 18 October.)[101] Soon the machinery of government would start to enforce it and revamp the recusancy system in order to maximise and streamline the mulcting of the queen's nonconformist Catholic subjects. The proclamation was also a major polemical discourse on how such Catholics fell short of the loyalty which they owed to the queen. It claimed that the Catholic seminaries had assured Philip II that 'though heretofore he had no good success with his great forces against our realm, yet if now he will once again renew his war this next year there shall be found secretly within our dominions many thousands . . . of able people that will be ready to assist such power as he shall set on land'.[102] The proclamation elicited furious replies from two Catholic polemicists abroad, Robert Persons (who was named and vilified in the proclamation) and Richard Verstegan.[103] Montague and his family may have been getting their own coded and 'moderate' reply in early.

On Wednesday 18 August, another day of quite heavy government business, the council dealt with the issue of politically offensive writings discovered in the house of the Catholic Sir Thomas Fitzherbert at Norbury. It also issued a licence to allow Montague's cousin, John Gage of West Firle, to

---

[100] Breight, 'Caressing', 161.
[101] P. L. Hughes and J. F. Larkin, *Tudor Royal Proclamations* (3 vols., 1964–9), III, 86–93.
[102] *Ibid.*, 88–9.   [103] Milward I, nos. 419–24.

travel from his house at Leyton in Essex down to Sussex on family business, following the death of his brother.[104] The court was in a festive spirit. As the printed account of the occasion relates, 'the lords and ladies dined in the walkes', and 'feasted most sumptuously'. Music was laid on for their entertainment, and the queen went to a fishpond where she was addressed by an 'angler' (who doubled as a political commentator). The 'angler' initially took 'no notice of hir Majestie'. Instead he indulged with a 'fisherman' in a bit of informed social reflection, larded with specific commonwealth complaints. Following this exchange of words, he turned to address Elizabeth. 'Envie stands amazed at your happines', he proclaimed. Then he launched enthusiastically into a round of loyal speechification. 'There bee some so muddie minded, that they can not live in a cleere river but a standing poole, as camells will not drinke till they have troubled the water with their feet; so they can never stanch their thirst, till they have disturbed the state with their trecheries. Soft, these are no fancies for fisher men.'

A dish of fish is an unworthie present for a prince to accept: there be some carpes amongst them, no carpers of states; if there be, I would they might bee handled lyke carpes, their tongues pulled out. Some pearches there are I am sure, and if anie pearche higher than in dutie they ought, I would they might sodenly picke over the pearche for me.[105]

There was more official business to attend to by 20 August when another council meeting took place. By 22 August the Court was in Chichester; then it moved on to Titchfield and Southampton.[106]

Traditionally, and unsurprisingly in view of the succession of cloying speeches to which the queen was subjected at Cowdray, this visit has been construed as a loyalist bonding session between Elizabeth and some of her most dependable and faithful Catholic subjects. It would seem to have confirmed, therefore, Montague's status as one of the few tolerated Catholic lords of the period (though in fact there were others who were equally if not more condoned and countenanced, notably Edward Somerset, fourth earl of Worcester).

Recently, however, Curtis Breight has reinterpreted this event. He argues that Montague was already in a highly invidious position in Sussex after being stripped of the lord lieutenancy of the county. Breight takes a much more serious view of the faint ripples of discontent which can be detected within the Montague entourage, and states that he had been involved in

---

[104] *APC 1591*, 396, 402–3. On 10 January 1591 both Gage and Sir Thomas Fitzherbert had been sent to the Tower, to be kept 'close prisoners'. Fitzherbert died there on 2 October 1591. Gage must have been released before his case was dealt with by the council at Cowdray, *APC 1590–1*, 207; BL, Lansdowne MS 65, no. 14, fo. 45r.
[105] Breight, 'Caressing', 162.   [106] *APC 1591*, 404, 413. See Nicholls, *Progresses*, III, 96–8.

'literally treasonous activities'. He was a 'discontented Roman Catholic lord in a heavily Catholic region of the country'. This was, of course, a period of international crisis, with a war not going particularly well for the queen's troops and their friends across the Channel in Normandy and Brittany. So, he claims, this progress had a didactic political purpose in Sussex even though the actual destination of the 1591 progress was Portsmouth, where the queen intended to inspect the defences, and hoped to meet Henry IV – an encounter which, in the end, did not occur. One of the functions of the 1591 progress was, argues Breight, to scrutinise 'an influential yet suspected lord, a potential abettor of native rebellion in support of a Spanish invasion . . . for signs of disloyalty'. Breight notes that there had been signs of discontent in Sussex before 1591 over the levying of troops there for service abroad. Now there was discontent again because of heavy recruiting.

In this context, Breight maintains, Montague could not really be construed as a loyalist and the regime had no intention of giving him credit for being one. Breight suggests therefore that the Cowdray entertainment itself contained a series of coded messages which stressed Montague's and Cowdray's independence and even implied a hint of threat to, or at least distance from, the queen.[107]

It is possible that Breight may have slightly overstated the case.[108] There are signs, in fact, in the late 1580s and early 1590s that Montague was maintaining his lines of communication with the Court. In August 1590 Montague acted as a go-between for his grandson the third earl of Southampton and Lord Burghley's granddaughter.[109] In June 1591, shortly before the royal progress reached Cowdray, we find Montague, from Battle, thanking Lord Burghley for favours done on behalf of his son and brother. He referred to 'the honorable shew and usage of my poore boye Herry [Henry Browne] my sonne lately attendinge upon your lordship bothe in heringe his sute and yeldinge to him your honorable and true advise, and (as itt pleased yow) allowaunce of the maner of his information, nott by himselff arrogantly', but through 'others of more sufficientye'. Montague's brother William Browne had also, the viscount said, been shown the lord treasurer's favour, apparently to obtain freedom from some kind of restraint imposed upon him.[110]

---

[107] Breight, 'Caressing', 147, 148, 149, 150; Cole, *Portable Queen*, 161–2. For the war in northern France, see P. Hammer, *The Polarisation of Elizabethan Politics* (Cambridge, 1999), 104.

[108] See Questier, LF, 236.   [109] PRO, SP 12/233/71, fo. 124r–v.

[110] BL Lansdowne MS 68, no. 10, fo. 20r. Late in James's reign we find the Spanish ambassador Gondomar reporting that James had ticked him off for shaking George Villiers's hand violently in order to aggravate the discomfort from some injury which he had already suffered to one of his fingers. James remarked 'I remember hearing that Lord Montague once did the same to Lord Treasurer Burghley when he had the gout', S. R. Gardiner, *Prince Charles and the Spanish Marriage* (2 vols., 1869), I, 314. We do not know when

The visit to Cowdray in 1591 concluded with a ceremony at which knighthood was conferred on George Browne (Montague's second son), Robert Dormer (Montague's son-in-law), Henry Glemham (Lord Buckhurst's son-in-law, who subsequently came into question for his dealings with Catholics), John Caryll, Henry Goring and Nicholas Parker. Henry Goring was the son of Sir William Goring of Burton. He was a thorough Protestant. Breight argues that both Goring and Parker 'were not merely Protestants – they were agents of the government who would shortly be appointed to the new commission of the peace in 1592'. These were men 'who would soon be hounding the recusant friends, neighbours and retainers of Lord Montague'.[111] It is certainly true that Parker was no friend of the papists and their clergy (though in 1586 his mother-in-law was noted as a recusant).[112] He was one of those named to the Sussex commission for recusants and seminary clergy in August 1592, as was the recently knighted Sir Henry Goring.[113] And Goring was among those who received letters in June and July 1593 from the privy council to support Richard Topcliffe's drive against the Montague network, after the first viscount's death, and to arrest a set of named individuals, including the deceased viscount's Marian chaplains Robert Gray and Francis Rydell.[114]

But, in fact, in the appointments to specific exchequer recusancy commissions which I have traced for this period, Sir Henry Goring does not seem to figure at all, and Sir Nicholas Parker only very rarely. (They were, apparently, not enthusiasts like Sir Walter Covert.) Parker showed complete equanimity in early June 1603 when he was ordered to see that his fellow knight at the 1591 ceremony Sir George Browne took the oath of supremacy as a precondition of his being admitted to the Sussex commission of the peace, even though Browne refused.[115] In fact the only overt unpleasantness at Cowdray during the queen's stay occurred between Sir Robert Cecil and the zealous Protestant Sir Thomas Sherley's son.[116]

---

this incident was supposed to have taken place (or even that it was definitely a reference to the first viscount rather than to his grandson the second viscount) but it may well point to the continuation of a slightly tense but far from entirely hostile relationship between the once powerful member of the Marian administration and Elizabeth's great lord treasurer. As early as 1572 the author of the *Treatise of Treasons* had mocked Cecil's affliction, in that 'for every one least thwart of his superiour', he 'faineth either to be sicke for sorow, or lame of the goute', [John Leslie], *A Treatise of Treasons against Q. Elizabeth, and the Croune of England* (Louvain, 1572), sig. i2v.

[111] Breight, 'Caressing', 159.
[112] In July 1584 he had tried to prevent the escape abroad of one of the Norris family, Sylvester, a future priest and Jesuit, who was being harboured among the Catholics in East Sussex, Anstr. I, 255–6; Hasler, *HC*, III, 173.
[113] BL, Harleian MS 703, fo. 69r.
[114] *APC 1592–3*, 328–9, 400, 406; ch. 6, pp. 199–200 below.
[115] CRS 60, 145–6, 147.   [116] *CSPD 1591–4*, 105.

So one should perhaps not overstate the confessionally informed tension at Cowdray in the summer of 1591. But one has to say that Breight must be correct to stress that the elaborate speeches and displays in front of the queen were not mere pleasantries. Breight points to the initial greeting by an armed man, in front of a literal castle – Cowdray was not a mere folly; it was militarily defensible. He also stresses the violent and ironic content of the classical and other allusions which were voiced by Montague's men.[117]

Conclusive backing for Breight's basic position is supplied by Montague's asides in his valedictory speech to the Surrey gentry at West Horsley a few months later. There he recalled the recent progress and how he had been so honoured by the queen's presence. But he angrily remarked that 'yt hath bene told her Majestie that yt was dawngerous commynge for her to my house, and she was advysed at her peryll to take heede howe she cam to me to Cowdrye this sommer past'. And when she had been at Loseley in early August, as a guest of the More family, she was warned that 'I was a dawngerous man to the State, and that I kept in my house syx score recusantes that never cam to churche, a wonderfull untruthe.' 'But', muttered Montague darkly, 'I know the reporter thereof well inoughe.'[118]

Montague did not divulge the name of the informer. But there undoubtedly were intelligencers and spies at this time who were saying that, whatever the loyal disposition of the viscount himself, there were others at Cowdray who were suspect. Robert Hammond, a shadowy figure, wrote to Lord Burghley in late 1591/early 1592, shortly after the Court had left Cowdray and shortly before Montague addressed his friends in the Surrey county community at West Horsley. Hammond claimed that he had information about papists in Sussex. He said that about three weeks before Easter 1591 he had thought to renew his acquaintance at Lord Montague's and found himself welcome to William Cockerell, the 'cheifest Catholique' among Montague's servants.[119] At Cowdray he met many recusants 'whose secret malice to her Majestie and [the] State I can well witnes'. Cockerell and Anthony Browne, the viscount's eldest son, with Montague's connivance, were, said Hammond, plotting to get one of Anthony's servants out of prison.[120] Around Easter 1592, Montague's cousin, John Gage, on whom the council had looked so kindly when they assembled at Cowdray, came in question over his yeoman

[117] Breight, 'Caressing', 150–2.
[118] SHC, LM 1856; Questier, LF, 251; Cole, *Portable Queen*, 196. For the manuscript of Montague's speech at West Horsley, see Figure 20.
[119] William Cockerell was named, in a set of accounts drawn up in 1597 for Lady Magdalen Browne, dowager Viscountess Montague, as her servant and bailiff for the Battle estate, ESRO, RAF 3/4, fos. 1r, 12r.
[120] BL, Lansdowne MS 99, no. 60, fo. 163r–v.

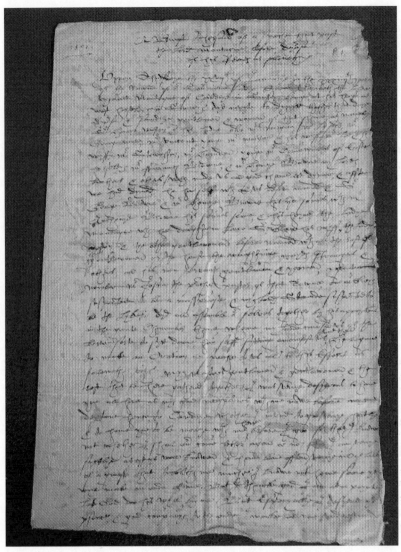

Figure 20. First page of 'A Breefe Rehersall of a speeche that past the Lord Montague before dyverse of his frendes as followeth' (Loseley MS 1856, Surrey History Centre, Woking). The first Viscount Montague spoke the words recorded here to his relatives, household staff and friends at West Horsley on 27 January 1592.

servant, Henry Collins of West Firle. Collins, a staunch Catholic, had, allegedly, wanted to kill the queen.[121]

As we shall see, Montague's death in October 1592 would allow the authorities to open up and rummage around in, if not exactly a can of radical Catholic worms, at least an aristocratic entourage which was still politically active. There may not have been crowds of plotters and assassins haunting Southwark, Cowdray, Midhurst and Battle. But the Brownes' entourage had not been reduced to a politically quiescent band of rural rosary-sayers. We can see here the essential rightness of Breight's dictum that the 'conditions of Catholic survivalism in the late 16th century' were rather problematical.[122]

CONCLUSION

This admittedly rather vignette-ridden survey of the apparently decreasing political influence of a later sixteenth-century peer and his friends confirms, perhaps predictably, that this section of the English Catholic community felt no pressing need to confront the regime in the way that several Catholic engagés of the period did. For a good deal of the period the first Viscount Montague's own political preferences were at least compatible with the regime's, particularly his desire during the early years of Elizabeth's reign to see good relations maintained with the Habsburgs. Enough of his friends and relatives were sufficiently highly placed at the Elizabethan Court to mean that he would never become a complete 'out'. He was on the fringes of the courtier Catholic group which backed the Anjou match. But he did not get mixed up in the largely disastrous Catholic sulk which followed the failure of the proposed Anglo-French treaty, and he avoided the dreadful retribution which was visited on some of his co-religionists. Also, his attitudes to the issue of ecclesiastical conformity differed greatly from those of the often inflammatory seminary priests who, during the 1570s, started to return into the country from Catholic colleges on the Continent. His concerns were simply not theirs.

At the same time, Montague's own 'moderation' did not mean quiescence. And those around him were not necessarily as 'moderate' as he was. The Catholicism of his entourage was not entirely clear of those qualities which made the Elizabethan Catholic movement a matter of concern and anxiety for many Protestant contemporaries.

We have, of course, relatively little evidence of what Montague actually thought about many political issues. Those Catholics whose opinions we know in greatest detail were those who went into exile to enjoy the

---

[121] *CSPD 1591–4*, 282.   [122] Breight, 'Caressing', 157.

freedom of being able to castigate the regime from a safe distance. But even if Montague's views on such things were less flagrant and eye-catching than some Catholics' condemnation of the regime's heresy and its war against Spain, he nevertheless represented a standing critique of some of the Protestant norms and orthodoxies which were enshrined in the established Church via statute, and in a raft of other government policies.

One way of probing a bit further into the Catholicism of this 'loyalist' peer is to look in more detail at his entourage. In the next chapter I want to reconstruct bits of it as best I can, not just to say who fulfilled which domestic functions around their lord, and which servants were responsible for looking after the Brownes' landed estates, but also how the viscount and his family may have been influenced, on certain key politico-ecclesiastical issues, by particular people close to them. I would also like to analyse how the membership and ideological tenor of this aristocratic affinity started to change after the viscount's death in late 1592. In particular, I want to trace (in chapters 7, 8 and 9) the metamorphosis of the entourage, through the circle around the dowager viscountess, Lady Magdalen, into the much more clericalised following of the second viscount, a very different man, in many ways, from his grandfather. The second viscount was a peer who was also recognised as a major Catholic figure, leader and patron, but one who had a much more distinctive, and sometimes aggressive, programme and world view.

The transmutation of that entourage coincides with some of the major alterations in the structure and character of post-Reformation Catholicism, changes which have often been abstracted entirely out of their immediate social and political context and hence have tended to be ignored by many historians of the period.

It is, as we observed above, something of a historiographical commonplace nowadays to say that Catholicism in post-Reformation England retreated into the houses of wealthy patrons. The seminarists preferred a quiet life with the gentry rather than keeping the faith alive among the peasantry by tramping the North Yorkshire moors, or the Lancashire fells, or anywhere that the peasantry were likely to be found. But a view of the circle and entourage of the Browne family in the late 1580s and early 1590s may suggest that this is a false perspective (and, I suspect, studies of most of the entourages of the Catholic aristocracy and major gentry of the period would show the same). Looking at late Tudor and early Stuart Catholicism from within the Catholic community, rather than from outside via the bureaucratic records of Church courts, exchequer agents and high commissioners, provides us with a more accurate perspective on the transformations that were taking place within the community at that time, even if the central tenets of Catholic faith and practice expressed by such people no doubt stayed basically static.

Exploring a specific aristocratic entourage, such as this one, helps us to understand how Catholicism, often understood to have expired in a kind of inertia towards the end of the century, continued to be recognised as a politically focused and ambitious force, retaining a coherent programme or set of programmes and representing an oppositional stance on a number of political, ecclesiastical and religious issues.

6

The entourage of the first Viscount Montague

THE FUNCTION OF THE ENTOURAGE

Recent research has emphasised, perhaps largely as we might expect, that the early modern aristocratic entourage tended to contain a variety of views and opinions. Its ideological tenor was not simply dictated from the top down by the great man or men at its centre. As we have already observed, John Bossy interprets the late Elizabethan and Jacobean earls of Worcester's Catholicism as the product of an environment in the borders of Wales which caused the earls to adopt a series of attitudes which, taken together, looked to contemporaries like Catholicism.[1] Stuart Carroll has traced in minute and fascinating detail the workings of the institution of the family council which influenced the political decisions of the great men among the extended Guise family in sixteenth-century France.[2] Carroll argues that even in the case of the Guise, frequently seen as the spearhead of an, above all else, ultra-Catholic reaction to the fragmentation of royal power during the Wars of Religion, the family's strategy was 'primarily concerned with family interest and not blinded by devotion to family dogma'. For this reason they 'protected their Calvinist kinsmen and employed Calvinist servants on their estates'. As Carroll emphasises, 'at the core of an affinity the nobleman was surrounded by his most trusted friends, servants and kinsmen'. These were the people who 'gave counsel and dominated the household'. But there were others who also might exert influence, particularly 'the judicial and administrative officials who administered the patrimony and constituted the military ret-inue which followed the patron'. Carroll stresses that 'the wider affinity of the patron was dynamic and fluid in its composition, consisting of clients, neighbours, vassals, *amis* and allies who were largely autonomous of his control'.[3]

[1] J. Bossy, 'The English Catholic Community 1603–1625', in A. G. R. Smith (ed.), *The Reign of James VI and I* (1973), 91–105, at p. 102. See ch. 1, pp. 5–6 above.
[2] S. Carroll, *Noble Power during the French Wars of Religion* (Cambridge, 1998), 53–7.
[3] S. Carroll, '"Ceux de Guise": The Guise Family and their Affinity in Normandy, 1550–1600' (Ph.D., London, 1993), 2, 13; *Idem, Noble Power*, esp. pp. 2–7. For a late medieval perspective

Of course, the Catholic members of the English aristocracy in the later sixteenth and early seventeenth centuries were not overmighty power brokers and courtiers, with huge military retinues, striking terror equally into the hearts of the regime and their Protestant neighbours (in the way that, for example, the Guise sometimes did across the Channel). The entourages of families such as the Brownes did not resemble the huge quasi-royal administrative structures which existed to advise the Guise family and do its bidding. And they simply did not have the reserves of rewards, for doling out to clients, which the really politically powerful possessed in abundance.

It is not, however, inherently unlikely that even relatively small entourages, such as the first Viscount Montague's, might, in some respects, function in a similar way to the much larger structures which Carroll describes so well. In the first place, as Mark Greengrass has argued, it is possible to describe client networks by using the term 'affinity' (as, indeed, does Carroll) rather than 'clientele' in order to convey (as Sharon Kettering describes them) the 'emotional and affective elements' rather than the 'materialism' of such relationships.[4] In other words, the lack of formal material rewards could be supplemented or compensated by ideological affinity. And this may well have been the case in families such as the Brownes.[5] Secondly, the family would inevitably act as a repository of a number of different ideological views, and its 'Catholic' character was going to be both formed and affected by advice-giving, relationships and friendships, and even basic socio-economic interests, which were not, in a strict sense, generated by any one particular political or religious issue. As Carroll says, the lord's 'need to confer with clients, followers, servants' and so on 'allowed the lord to come into contact with a variety of opinions and experiences'. Our knowledge of the 'structure of factions and followings' among the aristocracy should be used to test and interpret bare political narratives.[6]

In fact, in the case of the post-Reformation Catholic aristocracy, who were excluded from most of the political activity in this period which

---

on aristocrats' recourse to their affinities for counsel, see C. Rawcliffe and S. Flower, 'English Noblemen and their Advisers: Consultation and Collaboration in the Later Middle Ages', *JBS* 25 (1986), 157–77.

[4] M. Greengrass, 'Noble Affinities in Early Modern France: The Case of Henri I de Montmorency, Constable of France', *European History Quarterly* 16 (1986), 275–311; S. Kettering, 'Patronage in Early Modern France', *French Historical Studies* 17 (1992), 839–62, at p. 851.

[5] However, as Kettering herself observes, 'ideology and self-interest' were not necessarily opposed, and 'self-interest' may 'occasionally have determined an individual's ideological commitment', Kettering, 'Patronage in Early Modern France', 860.

[6] Carroll, *Noble Power*, 53–4, 7. For a discussion of baronial household councils in England, for which there is, however, relatively little surviving evidence, see K. Mertes, *The English Noble Household 1250–1600* (Oxford, 1988), 126–31.

conventionally supplies historians with their narratives, the reconstruction of their entourages may be virtually the only way to say what they were 'doing' or, at least for the purposes of this study, to recover what their 'Catholicism' meant to themselves and their contemporaries. The first Viscount Montague had made his views about the bills for uniformity and supremacy crystal clear in the parliaments of 1559 and 1563. But, after that, he adopted a studiously conformist pose, a pose that he maintained even in the face of hostile criticism.[7] Only by reassembling his entourage can we say anything in particular about the sharper edges of his reputation for Catholicism and what effect that reputation had, even while he, personally, seems often to have kept quiet.

Now, having a wide variety of friends with different ideological views may not necessarily have influenced a great patron in his religious opinions one way or the other. The earl of Essex had an extraordinary mix of papists and puritans within his clerical following,[8] but it is not always clear exactly how far these people moulded, dictated or influenced his judgment on religious issues. At some point late in Elizabeth's reign, Essex's companion Henry Wriothesley, third earl of Southampton, abandoned his family's Catholicism. He took on the role of one of Simon Adams's 'political puritans', and espoused the pan-European Protestant cause. However he retained, among his friends, Catholics who had been attached to the Wriothesleys in the late sixteenth century, families such as the Cottons and the Leedeses. As Barry Coward has shown for the Stanley earls of Derby, their social circle was so huge, and their determination not to fall off the fence, on which it made sense for a great northern peer to sit, so strong that it is difficult to describe the family as holding or adhering to one specific creed or persuasion rather than another.[9]

Among the tenants of the Viscounts Montague, one has to admit, it is usually difficult to discern clear ideological patterns. Occasionally one can trace names, on deeds and leases, of people who were Catholic nonconformists or church papists. For example, one such clearly Catholic family which had a long-term tenurial association with the Brownes was that of Coldham of Midhurst, Stedham and Waverley.[10] These were, at best,

---

[7] Questier, LF; ch. 5 above.

[8] See A. J. Loomie, 'A Catholic Petition to the Earl of Essex', *RH* 7 (1963), 33–42; P. Hammer, *The Polarisation of Elizabethan Politics* (Cambridge, 1999), 89–91, 174–8.

[9] B. Coward, *The Stanleys, Lords Stanley and Earls of Derby 1385–1672* (Manchester, 1983). See also David Smith's account of the clerical patronage of the fourth earl of Dorset, D. L. Smith, 'Catholic, Anglican or Puritan? Edward Sackville, Fourth Earl of Dorset and the Ambiguities of Religion in Early Stuart England', *TRHS*, 6th series, 2 (1992), 105–24.

[10] PRO, C 142/350/4; PRO, E 368/462, mem. 85a; *VCH Sussex* IV, 83; SRS 19, 111; WSRO, SAS/BA 36; *VCH Surrey* III, 19; SHC, LM 6729/8/106; HEH, BA 68/27, 33.

minor (or parish) gentry, but they were, it seems, closely connected with their great neighbours.[11] We can sometimes find evidence that the Brownes may have gone out of their way to render favours and assistance to such people. For instance, in the mid-1580s we run across an aggrieved gentleman called Richard Houghton who was seeking redress against the first viscount. Houghton testified that in 1584 he had, as part of a land deal, surrendered a lease of the manor of Stedham so that Montague could purchase the estate. Houghton believed that Montague had agreed to grant him a new lease of the property, but Montague seems to have changed his mind and sold the fee simple of the house and land to his friend William Coldham.[12]

A sensible place to start looking for evidence of the ideological tone of the first viscount's household is Montague's patronage of Marian clergymen. During the viscount's life, his household's clerical requirements were met exclusively, or almost exclusively, by clergy ordained before 1559 who had partly or wholly separated from the Church of England.[13]

The cleric at Cowdray whom we know most about was Alban Langdale, the former archdeacon of Chichester and the scourge of Protestants in Chichester diocese.[14] He had also been a chaplain to the Wriothesleys.[15] There were other formerly prominent clergymen at Cowdray whose function was, however, as much domestic as clerical. Anthony Garnett was one such. He served as Montague's secretary and household steward (and, we may be sure, his chaplain as well) for over twenty years – 'right worshipfull steward of

---

[11] William Coldham (the younger)'s son and heir, Richard, married into the Gage family of Croydon (Montague's relatives), Berry, *Sussex*, 2. An exchequer enquiry of 22 September 1610 into the estate of the recusant John Browne of Chichester (i.e. one of Anthony Browne's sons, who married Anne Gifford and was a leading Sussex recusant, Berry, *Sussex*, 254) revealed that his manor of Waverley in Farnham had been tenanted, among others, by John Coldham of Midhurst (i.e. a son of Richard Coldham), PRO, E 368/543, mem. 83a; *VCH Surrey* II, 624. Richard and William Coldham witnessed deeds drawn up for the first Viscount Montague, WSRO, SAS/BA 49, 51.

[12] PRO, C 2/Elizabeth/H6/8, mem. 1a; PRO, C 142/350/4.

[13] The seminary priest John Boste may have served him for a short time, CRS 5, 65; Anstr. I, 43–4. (Boste apparently remained a friend of Montague's brother Francis, *HMCS* IV, 432, 420–1; see below in this chapter.) And, according to the informer Thomas Dodwell in February 1584, the seminary priest John Long was entertained at Cowdray, and also the seminarist Robert Nutter, Foley VI, 721, 724. Topcliffe claimed that the Jesuit Robert Southwell had been at Cowdray during 1590, though there is no indication whether this is true or that Montague knew about it, Devlin, *Life*, 219.

[14] See ch. 5, p. 163 above.

[15] One of Langdale's close friends was the prebendary of West Firle and Wightring, Anthony Clerke, an ex-Carthusian who after deprivation in 1562 also went to Cowdray. Clerke's will bequeathed 'unto my said good lorde and master the Viscounte Montague a paynted image which I have of the late virtuos quene of godly memorye Quene Marye whose sole God pardone', T. J. McCann, 'The Clergy and the Elizabethan Settlement in the Diocese of Chichester', in M. J. Kitch (ed.), *Studies in Sussex Church History* (Chichester, 1980), 99–123, at pp. 105–6, 109.

the household' as George Cotton called him.[16] He had formerly been master of Balliol (and, before that, a chaplain of the earl of Northumberland).[17] He came to Cowdray after being levered out of his Oxford post. We find his name on household memoranda and shopping lists which he compiled in his capacity as Montague's steward. He seems to have divided his time about equally between Cowdray and Battle.

Another of the first viscount's Marian clergy, whom we meet in company with Garnett, was Robert Gray. He had for a time worked as a private tutor in the houses of some of the more politically suspect members of the Catholic community in the Midlands, such as Nicholas Langford of Longford in Derbyshire, and William Bassett of Blore in Staffordshire.[18] Gray confessed on 29 August 1593 that the now deceased viscount had been prepared to admit other Marian clerics to Cowdray, in particular Alban Dolman and another priest called Jackson.[19] Gray had socialised with them. They 'dined in his chamber and slept there one night, three or four years ago'.[20]

There were yet other Marians who served as chaplains to Montague, such as William Purphett, but we know virtually nothing else about them.[21] This patronage of Marian priests seems to have gone on right up to the end of Montague's life. When George Cotton of Warblington visited Montague House in Southwark in 1592 to hear Mass, accompanied by other Catholics

[16] BL, Additional MS 33508, fo. 11r. As Kate Mertes notes, in medieval and early modern aristocratic households, 'chaplains often served as treaurers and stewards', Mertes, *The English Noble Household 1250–1600*, 25.

[17] A. Kenny, 'Reform and Reaction in Elizabethan Balliol, 1559–1588', in J. Prest (ed.), *Balliol Studies* (1982), 17–51, at p. 20. Francis Babington had been imposed on the college as master by the visitors, but in 1560 he became rector of Lincoln and the vice-chancellor of the university. He was succeeded as master of Balliol by Garnett, and Garnett was replaced in 1563 by Robert Hooper. At the end of Garnett's life there may have been a falling out between him and Montague. A letter of May 1589 from Garnett to Sir William More claims that he has been dismissed by Montague. However, even in this letter which laments that in 'thes my decaying dayes' he has been 'forsaken and dismissed', Garnett says that Montague 'is (of him selfe) the most lovinge, kynd, faythfull and noble gentleman in this age livinge' and that the fault lay in others who 'labored his lordship therunto'. And, in July 1590, we find Garnett writing on Montague's behalf to More concerning the viscount's travel arrangements, Loseley MSS, 646, 648; SHC, LM 6729/10/75, LM 6729/8/112; Hyland, *CP*, 209. See also SHC, LM 6729/8/80; TD III, cciii; ch. 8, pp. 234, 237, 248–9 below.

[18] In 1593 Robert Gray confessed to Richard Topcliffe that he had said Mass at Longford in Derbyshire for Langford's wife, *CSPD 1591–4*, 380–1. Langford conformed in 1594, Hasler, *HC*, II, 489; PRO, E 368/500, mem. 186a. His name can be found in the Southwark sacramental token books for 1599 and 1600, at which time he was staying in Montague Close, LMA, P92/SAV/192, p. 18, P92/SAV/193, p. 21.

[19] Jackson may be the man identified by Anthony Tyrrell in September 1586 as 'Jackson, priest in Queen Maries time' in the household of the Suffolk recusant Michael Hare, PRO, SP 12/193/13, fo. 20r. Dolman had formerly served in the household of Lord Morley, where he was arrested in April 1574 for saying Mass, Raphael Holinshed, ed. A Fleming, *Chronicles of England, Scotland and Ireland* (6 vols., 1807–8), IV, 324.

[20] *CSPD 1591–4*, 380.

[21] M. O'Boy, 'The Origins of Essex Recusancy' (Ph.D., Cambridge, 1991), 213 n. 2.

from the Sussex/Hampshire border region, including Edward Banester and his wife, Mass was recited by a 'Mr Wilson'. Wilson was, apparently, not a seminarist but a Marian priest who had been in the household of the ageing dowager countess of Pembroke as late as 1586.[22]

Robert Gray himself claimed in 1593 that the first viscount 'would not have any Jesuits or seminary priests brought into his house'.[23] William Clarke alleged in 1603 that the Jesuits had cast forth 'invectives against my old Lord Mountacute when hee lived'.[24] This may conceivably have been because of Montague's policy of not granting patronage and access to the new clergy.

It is not exactly clear why Montague refused, in general, to deal with seminarists. Was it mere caution on his part? Some Catholics, we know, took the Elizabethan regime's hostility towards seminarist clergy very seriously. Edward Jones, who had served at one point in the Tichborne household in Hampshire, confessed in June 1586 that 'my old master Mr Tichbornes father', Peter Tichborne (father of the traitor Chideock Tichborne), even though he had served spells of imprisonment for his Catholic opinions, was 'allwayes . . . timerouse of the law', and 'wolde never [allow] any of theise persons', i.e. seminary priests, 'to have any enterteignment in the howse, by reason of the lawe'.[25] Montague's cousin John Gage of West Firle, a leading recusant, also seems to have entertained only Marian priests, for example Robert Manners who was noted in his company in 1588.[26] The first viscount may have looked askance at the political radicalisation of the Catholic community which was evidently desired and promoted by many of the seminarists and especially by some of the Jesuits.

Alternatively, it may have been because he liked to be surrounded by men of his own age, of some status and influence, people he was familiar with and whom he respected – Langdale and Dolman for example. (In January 1585 Charles Paget informed Mary Stuart that Dolman was 'of comely personage, and when attired like a gentleman of good calling, as commonly, one would esteem him a justice of the peace'.[27])

---

[22] Foley I, 383; Morris, *Troubles*, II, 157. The dowager countess, Anne (Compton), seems to have been a visitor at Montague House. Thomas Phillips, one of a number of purchasing agents for the first viscount in London, reported on 22 June 1570 that 'the lady of Penbroke', whose husband had died in March 1570, 'departed from my lordes house uppon Wensday at nyght last', BL, Additional MS 33508, fo. 12r; GEC, X, 409.

[23] *CSPD 1591–4*, 381.

[24] William Clarke, *A Replie unto a Certaine Libell* (1603), fo. 17v.

[25] PRO, SP 12/190/50, fo. 112r; Mott, HR, 429.   [26] CRS 22, 128.

[27] *HMCS* III, 89. Paget's associate Thomas Morgan informed Mary Stuart in January 1586 that, now she was to be taken to Tutbury, a castle 'under the guard of Lord St John', she might be interested to know that Dolman, not a seminary priest but 'a grave man, and one that hath great acquaintance and credit among the Catholics of that realm', also had a 'particular familiarity . . . with some nigh in blood to the Lord St John'. For the 'better service' of both God and Mary herself, Dolman had been persuaded to return to England, *HMCS* III, 129. In September 1586 Anthony Tyrrell said that Dolman was currently among

But, whatever the precise nature of Montague's opinions about the clergy who were fittest to serve his ecclesiastical needs, the wider Montague entourage was not a seminarist-free zone, as the case of the Dormers shows. In February 1584 the renegade Catholic Ralph Betham confessed that, back in 1581, he had been present at a Mass said by the Dormer priest William Harris in the house of Edward East of Bledlow. (Betham was one of Harris's converts.) Betham had seen Harris 'with Campyon (who was afterwarde executed) at one Mr Robert Dormers house at Wynge in Buckyngham sheere'. Harris brought 'Campyon thither' as Betham had been told by his sister, who was one of Elizabeth Dormer's servants. 'They dyd counterfayte that Campyons name was one Foster' and then 'they had Masse there'. Campion preached a sermon to them. Elizabeth Dormer, Montague's daughter, was present. Betham could not be sure that her husband had been at the Mass, although he had entertained Campion and Harris at his own table.[28] Robert Gray claimed that 'when Lord Montague and his lady were at Wing, with Sir Robert Dormer, who married their daughter Elizabeth, about St James's tide 1590', the same William Harris 'was also there, who had been much with Lady Babington',[29] 'and dined and supped in Sir Robert Dormer's house, and had a chamber' where Gray 'daily conversed with him, as did also the Lord and Lady Montague and their daughter the young Lady Dormer'.[30]

---

the clergy in Cambridgeshire and was a 'provinciall over the rest', PRO, SP 12/193/13, fo. 20v. In the 1590s Dolman was always regarded as a fautor of the anti-Jesuit or 'Scottish' faction, which insisted that it, unlike the Jesuits, had proper respect for the established order and traditional social hierarchies. Dolman had sufficient prestige to be elected as one of the two arbitrators, both Marian priests, who were called on to pacify the disputes between the seminarist clergy at Wisbech Castle in the mid-1590s, CRS 51, *passim*.

[28] PRO, SP 12/168/25. ii, fo. 52r–v. Betham's sister Sybil was in the service of Elizabeth Dormer at the time that Campion visited the family. Betham noted that Harris had also been with the East family (of Bledlow), into which Montague's gentleman-servant Thomas Fitzherbert had married. Betham had himself been reconciled to the Church of Rome at the house of Edward East at Cockthorpe, co. Oxford. Among the clerics he subsequently met was Richard Norris, a fellow of Trinity College, Oxford, who was later placed, as a tutor, with the Owens of Godstow, one of whom, the priest John Owen, as we saw, was on the fringes of the Montague circle in the 1580s, Anstr. I, 254; ch. 5, pp. 168–9 above. Norris was the brother of the future Jesuit Sylvester Norris, whose travel arrangements to the Rheims seminary were made via the Sussex yeoman recusant Henry Norton of Westham. Norton was an innkeeper and brewery owner at Pevensey and was reported as being on the edge of the group of Catholics in East Sussex in the 1590s who looked for protection to the dowager Viscountess Montague, Anstr. I, 254; BL, Lansdowne MS 82, no. 49, fo. 103v; CRS 71, 128; CRS 18, 326; CRS 57, 170; PRO, E 368/491, mem. 150b, E 368/521, mem. 280a, E 368/519, mem. 147d; ch. 7, p. 228 below.

[29] Margaret (Croker), wife of Sir William Babington, was one of Edmund Campion's hosts and a leading Oxfordshire recusant, Davidson, RC, 155.

[30] *CSPD 1591–4*, 380. Gray refused to say whether Harris had celebrated Mass there or not, but there is no indication in Gray's confession, as Godfrey Anstruther seems to assume, that Harris had ever frequented Cowdray or Battle during Montague's lifetime, Anstr. I, 150. For Harris, formerly a fellow of Lincoln College, Oxford, see Davidson, RC, 406–8. Robert Dormer was knighted at Cowdray in August 1591. See ch. 5, p. 175 above.

Among the other seminarists who milled around the fringes of Montague's household was the priest Simon Fennell. Dressed in Montague's livery, he was transported about the region by Montague's gentleman-servant, John Shelley. Fennell was a Sussex man and formerly a pupil of Robert Persons at Balliol. He was welcomed at various Sussex, Surrey and Hampshire gentry residences, including the Shelleys' at Mapledurham, and the Copleys' at Gatton.[31] And when Fennell left the country for Ireland, travelling in the company of the future appellant priest William Watson, also a frequenter of the Copleys' residences, it is possible that he may have been making for the house and protection of Montague's sister, the countess of Kildare.[32] Fennell eventually moved into the archpresbyteral system of government which, as we shall see, relied heavily on the patronage of the second Viscount Montague.[33]

There were, of course, other members of the Browne family who were enthusiasts for the new seminarist style of Catholic clericalism. As we saw in the previous chapter, Francis Browne sheltered the secret press on which the Jesuits' unlicensed and inflammatory tracts were published in 1580 and 1581.[34] When Campion was preaching his last sermon at Mrs Yate's house at Lyford, on 16 July 1581, Persons was staying at Browne's house at Henley Park, whence he eventually fled to the Shelleys at Michelgrove and then across to France.[35] Browne was caught up in the troubles of the priest Edward Osborne. Osborne had performed a high-profile celebration of the Mass in the Fleet prison, an event which brought Sir Thomas Tresham and Lord Vaux to trial at the Guildhall. Osborne's arrest came in the wake

---

[31] *CSP Scotland 1585–6*, 651, 653; Anstr. I, 115. He had once been with the Tichbornes, and was later supported by Jane, the wife of William Shelley of Michelgrove, *HMCS* IV, 402–3. The priest Fennell may have been the man of the same name who acted as a trustee of some of the Gage family's property in 1577 (SRS 19, 129; ESRO, SAS/G 35/14), and may also have been the 'Fennyx' or 'Fennell' who came with George Fortescue to Anthony Fortescue's house, just before Easter 1585, on their way to Boarhunt (the Henslowes' residence) or to Titchfield to see 'the executors of the sayde late erle of Southampton' and 'to receyve their annuyties then due' (though the regime suspected they were, in fact, trying to assist the earl of Arundel's flight abroad), BL, Egerton MS 2074, fo. 3r. Fennell appears to have been a member of the second earl of Southampton's entourage until the earl died in 1581. Fennell then went abroad to train for the priesthood (he was ordained in May 1583) and returned in sufficient time to risk getting caught up in the fallout from the Throckmorton plot. Francis Shaw, the renegade priest, informed the regime in 1593 that 'Fennell the prieste doth use to come very muche to Mr John Fortescue his house', PRO, SP 12/238/62, fo. 88r, SP 12/193/13, fo. 21v. Sir John Fortescue (chancellor of the exchequer)'s brother, Sir Anthony, married Katherine, daughter of Sir Geoffrey Pole. Sir Anthony's eldest son, who was accused of helping the earl of Arundel to flee the realm in 1585, had a second son, John, the one cited by Shaw as the harbourer of Fennell, Davidson, RC, 131–2.

[32] Subsequently another priest, Francis Barnaby, who was, like Watson, one of the appellants, became her chaplain, Anstr. I, 23.

[33] Anstr. I, 115; CRS 54, 168.   [34] CRS 39, xxxiii.

[35] Morris, *Troubles*, II, 14; CRS 2, 30.

of Richard Topcliffe's sweep for the dispersers of Thomas Alfield's printed defence of Campion.[36] Topcliffe had uncovered these clerical rituals also at Lady Vaux's lodgings in the Brownes' Southwark parish, St Saviour's, and at Francis Browne's own lodgings in Montague Close.[37] Topcliffe noted that a seminarist called Bayard resorted 'to Mr Brownes house at St Mary Overies' and said Mass there.[38]

After the arrival of the Jesuits Robert Southwell and Henry Garnet, Browne became their patron as well.[39] The (admittedly often deluded) Anthony Tyrrell said that Browne as well as 'his brother', presumably referring to another of the viscount's many brothers, 'were altogether governed' by William Weston SJ and a priest called John Cornelius. Tyrrell claimed that these Catholic clergymen had 'been by their [the Brownes'] means conveyed to sundry noblemen'.[40] Weston's contact with Francis Browne may have been facilitated by Browne's second marriage – to one of the Tempest family. An informer in April 1586 recorded that he knew several priests in London, including Weston, who commonly frequented the house of the widow Tempest 'nowe wyef of Mr Francis Browne'.[41] The same source claimed that Cornelius was 'moste accompanyed with Mr [Francis] Gower, servant to the Lord Montague and often lodged with the sayd Gower within his lordes house at St Mary Overies'.[42] Cornelius was, as Tyrrell observed, an effectual proselytiser – 'the fittest man for to preach before ladies and gentlemen, both for his sweet and plausible tongue, and for that he could best counterfeit simplicity'.[43] But he was probably on the radical wing of the seminarist movement. He was certainly an exorcist, and was remembered, in the martyrological narrative assembled by the Sussex cleric Thomas Manger, as a severe ascetic and a visionary.[44] In late 1593 Francis Browne was believed to make 'grett accompte' of John Boste. (At this time, Boste was public enemy number one in the North parts. He was arrested and executed in 1594.)[45] We do not know exactly what the nature of the relationship was between Francis Browne and his brother the viscount. We do know, however, that in

---

[36] PRO, SP 12/152/54, fo. 97r. Osborne buckled under the regime's interrogations and its threats of torture. He recanted his Catholicism and gave evidence against his former patrons Vaux and Tresham, Anstr. I, 262.

[37] PRO, SP 12/152/54, fo. 97r; Hyland, *CP*, 306.

[38] PRO, SP 12/152/54, fo. 97r; Anstruther, *Vaux*, 141.   [39] Devlin, *Life*, 108.

[40] Morris, *Troubles*, II, 408. John Cornelius was a secular priest who (although without authorisation) pronounced vows as a Jesuit just before his execution at Dorchester in July 1594. I am grateful for this point to Thomas McCoog.

[41] PRO, SP 12/188/37, fo. 118r.

[42] *Ibid*. Gower was among those named on the arrest warrants issued to Surrey JPs on 24 June 1593 after the death of the first viscount. See below in this chapter; *APC 1592–3*, 328–9.

[43] Morris, *Troubles*, II, 408.   [44] Challoner, *Memoirs*, 201.

[45] *HMCS* IV, 432; Hatfield House, Cecil MS 170, fo. 21r (Sir Michael Blount to Sir Robert Cecil, 7 December 1593).

1570 Anthony Garnett was paying out expenses to workmen for installing glass in Francis Browne's chamber at Cowdray, so he was certainly welcome there at that time. In November 1573 Montague was planning to travel up to London via Henley Park, Francis's residence.[46]

By the beginning of the 1580s the capital was seething with Catholic activity, with priests such as Edward Osborne and William Dean celebrating Masses for a variety of Catholic patrons at several different venues.[47] It was undoubtedly much easier for Montague's friends and relatives in London to circumvent any policy of excluding certain sorts of Catholic from his residences which he may have successfully enforced at Cowdray and Battle. Montague House seems to have been a place where a variety of Catholics could stay or pass through, or perhaps even maintain some kind of smaller establishment of their own in the muddle of tenements around the core of the viscount's official residence. As we have seen, Robert Persons and George Blackwell had, when they were touring round London collecting material and references to refute Alban Langdale's manuscript treatise which justified occasional conformity, actually gained admittance to Montague House in order to root around in Langdale's library which was shelved there.[48]

It is remarkable that nothing (much) was done about people such as the first viscount's brother, Francis Browne. One can only assume that this was in part because the viscount, though he may not actively have endorsed and encouraged his more daring and radical relatives, was, even if indirectly, affording them a measure of protection. Though Francis was arrested in 1581 with Charles Bassett,[49] and his house, Henley Park (which one of Walsingham's informants reported in July 1586 was never without three or four priests),[50] was searched after the Babington plot broke, one of the searchers was the viscount's Surrey friend and confidant Sir William More. Browne remained under house arrest with Sir William for over two years. But Sir William received a note of gratitude from the viscount himself for making Loseley available for this purpose, so his brother's ordeal cannot have been all that unbearable.[51]

The first viscount's second son, George, was basically a conformist. (He refused to take the oath of supremacy but was not indicted as a recusant.) As early as 1584, however, we find him entertaining a seminary priest called Samuel Twyford, a man who was busily reconciling Catholics in the

---

[46] BL, Additional MS 33508, fo. 55r; SHC, LM 6729/8/51. In June 1571 Montague took his brother's part in a land dispute between Francis and Lord Mountjoy, PRO, SP 46/29, fo. 54r.
[47] PRO, SP 12/152/54, fo. 97r.   [48] See ch. 5, p. 162 above.   [49] CRS 2, 183.
[50] PRO, SP 12/191/23.
[51] Loseley MSS, 642, 645, 664; SHC, LM 6729/8/118. In April 1584 Montague had written to Sir William More on behalf of one of his brothers, probably Francis, who had been summoned to appear before More, SHC, LM 6729/8/94.

Oxfordshire region at exactly that time.[52] Montague's chaplain Robert Gray alleged that Sir George was an acquaintance of the Sussex Jesuit John Curry. Gray described in August 1593 how, three years before, when he was staying at Cowdray, 'Sir George Browne took him to speak with a learned man, Father Curry, the Jesuit', at George Dennis's house at Todham.[53] The topic for discussion was the hand of Constance Cuffauld, a lady-in-waiting at Cowdray. She was pledged to one of Montague's servants, Richard Lambe, but Sir George fancied her himself.[54]

Curry was resident generally, Gray said, with Anthony Browne, the first viscount's eldest son.[55] In fact, like Fennell, Curry had *entrées* at a number of places, for example with the Gages, the Darells and the Lane family of Fishbourne, as well as with Robert Barnes at Mapledurham.[56] He was a friend of the Jesuit Jasper Heywood, William Weston's predecessor as Jesuit superior in England. Heywood used him as a courier between himself and Robert Persons (whom Heywood hated) concerning the divisive issue of fasting. He had also been a distributor of Campion's books.[57] Curry was noted in the 1590s to be consorting with the priest John Cornelius. This friendship gave him access to the Arundells' residence at Chideock.[58] According to the appellant priest William Watson, Curry held extreme political opinions. Watson claimed that William Allen's *Admonition to the People and Nobility of England* of 1588, which denounced Elizabeth as a heretic and a bastard, was endorsed by Curry who, 'speaking in a faint bravado of that booke', said that it would 'bite' in time to come.[59]

We might imagine that this clustering of seminarists and Jesuits around some of the younger Catholic members of the Browne family was merely a function of the dying off of the now rather small pool of Marian priests.

[52] Anstr. I, 365; Foley VI, 723. Sir Anthony Hungerford of Black Bourton, co. Oxford, noted that, aged twenty, he was 'addicted to the Roman religion' and, when his father forced him 'to goe to church', via a physician called George Etheridge 'then living in Oxford' (once a fellow of Corpus Christi and regius professor of Greek) he 'was brought to one Twiford a priest or Jesuit' by whom he 'was reconciled to the Roman Church', Anthony Hungerford, *The Advise of a Sonne* (Oxford, 1616), 47; Davidson, RC, 542, 646–8. (Etheridge served as physician for several years to Archbishop Nicholas Heath, Montague's friend and political ally, *ibid.*, 648.)

[53] For the second Viscount Montague's friendship with the Dennis family, see PRO, C 2/James I/K6/35, mm. 1a, 2a, 6a. Richard Knowles brought a chancery action in May 1607 against Montague and George Dennis. He claimed that Montague, as lord of the manor of Cocking, had, at Dennis's persuasion, granted Dennis a lease of property in the manor which was, alleged Knowles, governed by an arrangement with the former lord of the manor, the twelfth earl of Arundel, whereby all the manor's copyholders had surrendered their estates in return for leases for three lives.

[54] *CSPD 1591–4*, 380; Mott, HR, 152. Constance Cuffauld's mother Mary was the daughter of Sir Geoffrey Pole of Lordington, a nephew of Cardinal Reginald Pole.

[55] *CSPD 1591–4*, 380.

[56] Foley I, 382, 396–7; PRO, SP 12/168/33, fo. 78r; BL, Lansdowne MS 72, no. 67, fo. 184r; TD III, cciii.

[57] Foley I, 396–7; McCoog, *Society*, 168.   [58] Foley I, 397.   [59] Watson, *Decacordon*, 239.

Second-generation post-Reformation Catholics, children of the original opponents of the Elizabethan settlement of religion, would naturally turn to the new clergy for the celebration of the sacraments and all the functions required from a (Catholic) household chaplain. But we might want to pause before describing the transfer from a Marian clerical Catholic culture to a predominantly seminarist one as, even if in some sense inevitable, an automatic or politically value-free, seamless and painless transition.

The State certainly did not see the seminarists as mere replacements for the Marians who had separated or semi-separated from the Church of England after 1559. The penal legislation of the Elizabethan period made that increasingly plain. Marians and seminarists may, as Patrick McGrath argued, have shared central Catholic theological beliefs;[60] but, as John Bossy makes crystal clear, the Elizabethan seminarists tended to commit themselves to ideological positions and ecclesiastical practices which were a radical challenge to the *status quo* and to the don't-ask-don't-tell arrangement which had previously governed the relationship between the regime and most of the queen's Catholic subjects.[61] This would have been as obvious to the first viscount as to other contemporaries. And it makes it all the more remarkable that Montague, knowing full well that such people were starting to accumulate around him, did nothing (very much) to put a stop to it.

Slightly surprisingly, there is no evidence that Montague made any real attempt to exploit the ecclesiastical heritage of rights of presentation which the Brownes had accumulated as part of their estate. (The first viscount had a truly staggering number of advowsons in his gift at one time or another.[62]) As Timothy McCann shows, there was a considerable residuum of conservative clergy left in the diocese of Chichester even after the ravages of visitation and deprivation. Many were shoved out of, or simply resigned, their livings but many also bit their lips and stayed in post, waiting for better times. Surely it would have made sense for someone such as Montague to appeal to and foster this fund of conservative clerical culture through the exercise of his own patronage? Of course, there was no necessary correspondence between the views of the patron and the views of a benefice's incumbent.

---

[60] P. McGrath, 'Elizabethan Catholicism: A Reconsideration', *JEH* 35 (1984), 414–28.

[61] Bossy, 'Character'.

[62] As Jeremy Goring notes, Montague possessed 'no fewer than 16 of the 42 advowsons in the deaneries of Hastings and Dallington' alone, J. Goring, 'The Reformation of the Ministry in Elizabethan Sussex', *JEH* 34 (1983), 345–66, at p. 353. For church livings held and controlled at some point in this period in Sussex by the Brownes, see *VCH Sussex* IV, 42 (Bepton parish in Easebourne Hundred), 57 (Fernhurst chapel), 78 (Midhurst and Easbourne), 84 (Stedham), 93 (Compton), VII, 212 (Poynings), IX, 26 (All Saints, Hastings), 85 (Hollington), 111 (Battle), 114 (Whatlington), 147 (Beckley), 156 (Peasemarsh), 160 (Iden), 162 (Playden), 232 (Brede), 264 (Brightling), 264 (Bodiam), 268 (Ewhurst), 276 (Northiam). Among the Surrey clerical livings to which the first Viscount Montague had rights of presentation were Horsley, West Horsley, Send and Wanborough, BL, Harleian MS 595, no. 11, fo. 213v.

The crypto-Catholic Henry Shales had been presented to Hangleton by the staunchly Protestant Richard Bellingham.[63] But Montague would have been an obvious person for people such as Shales to approach. There is apparently little evidence that they, with the exception of Montague's household chaplains (who had lost their own benefices), ever did.[64]

If, therefore, Montague was neither fighting a desperate rearguard action to maintain the conservative/Catholic culture of local parishes, nor was he positively advancing the cause of seminarist clericalism, we might well ask how far his household was a properly Catholicised space.

Notoriously, one of the primary concerns of Jesuits such as John Gerard, once they had invested the necessary time and effort in recruiting a particular gentleman to their cause, was to Catholicise the gentleman's household. This could go as far as getting rid of all the service personnel who did not measure up.[65] John Gee claimed that the Catholic clergy did not stop with the household but tried to Catholicise the tenantry as well.[66]

This was something which did not happen at Cowdray during the first viscount's lifetime. Montague made a point of declaring that many of his household servants were not recusants at all, and that, in any case, he never tried to influence them towards Catholicism. In 1592 he claimed that

I seeke to drawe no man to that religeon, neather chylde nor servant, but let them doo theyr conscyences therein as God shall putt in theyre myndes. My servantes are well knowen syx of the cheefest of them that I putt in trust for my busynes to be of religeon contrarye to my self. I meddell not with them therein, but leave them to God and themselves.

And he further stressed that

---

[63] McCann, 'Clergy'; Peckham, 'Institutions'; Manning, *Religion*, 267; PRO, PROB 11/80, fos. 360r–361r.

[64] Perhaps many Catholic patrons saw advowsons simply as a source of revenue. During the row over the ultra-Catholic Thomas, Baron Arundell's estate after his death in 1639, it was alleged that 'his lordship in his lyfe tyme had receyved many great summes of money for presentacions to Church lyvings', AAW, A XXIV, no. 29, p. 102. The complete lack of interest shown by the Brownes in controlling who was appointed to these benefices was, however, one of the key mechanisms by which puritan clergy were infiltrated into the county, particularly in East Sussex. As Goring shows, Montague was 'normally prepared to lease his patronage rights to anyone willing to pay for them', and it was 'through Montague's grants of next presentation that some of the most militant Protestants gained preferment in the Church of England'. Goring speculates that Bishop Curteys may have made funds available for the purchase of such grants, Goring, 'The Reformation of the Ministry', 353. Towards the end of the sixteenth century, many of the rights of presentation which had been inherited by Montague's widow, Lady Magdalen, were assigned to her son Sir George Browne. Perhaps this was a conscience issue for her, but Sir George, a conformist (at least during Elizabeth's reign), seems to have been unfussy as to who was admitted to serve these parishes.

[65] Bossy, *ECC*, 169–70.

[66] T. Harmsen (ed.), *John Gee's Foot out of the Snare (1624)* (Nijmegen, 1992), 142.

I let no servant I have, nor any other from commynge to churche, neather doo I wyll them to goo to churche, but leave them as I sayd before to theyre owne conscyenses to doo as theye thinke good. And theare ys no man that when he cometh to me to serve me I doo aske what religeon he ys of.

The first viscount absolutely denied that he had ever 'advyzed' any of his household 'to forbeare goinge to the churche'.[67]

It is true that for long periods of time after 1559 we cannot detect anything particularly or overtly Catholic happening at either Cowdray or Battle, though we can safely assume that Montague and his immediate family received the sacraments from their Marian Catholic chaplains.[68] It would appear that, in his household, religion was, as far as possible, kept separate from political issues. This is definitely the impression which the first viscount, in his grandiloquent farewell speech to his friends and neighbours at West Horsley in early 1592, tried to give.[69]

But was Montague protesting too much when he claimed that he regarded religion as a merely private, indeed almost incidental, matter? We may suspect that life within the household at Cowdray and Battle was rather more Catholic than Montague cared to admit. For example, secular and clerical roles were not kept entirely separate. As we have just observed, the Marian cleric and former Oxford don Anthony Garnett worked as Montague's steward for many years. In March 1567 we find him arranging for domestic repairs at Cowdray by borrowing one of Montague's carpenters back from William More at Loseley.[70] In August 1575 we see him trying to

---

[67] SHC, LM 1856; Questier, LF, 251–3. There is a distinct contrast between Montague's administration of this aspect of his household and, say, Lord Burghley's fussy micromanagement of his servants' attendance at household prayers, P. Croft, 'The New English Church in One Family: William, Mildred and Robert Cecil', in S. Platten (ed.), *Anglicanism and the Western Tradition* (Norwich, 2003), 65–89, at p. 77. For the extent to which Montague's administration of this aspect of his household could be seen as merely traditional, within the context of what was required by other lords of the period, see Mertes, *The English Noble Household 1250–1600*, 146, 148–9. While the practice of a particular style of piety could work to unify a household, and compulsory attendance at services could be used to inculcate hierarchical values into the lord's retinue, it is possible that it would not have been regarded as unusual for only the closest members of the family and most trusted servants to have attended the lord's devotions.

[68] In 1628 the second Viscount Montague recalled that he had been 'christened Anthonie by good Doctor Langdall', the first viscount's senior chaplain, AAW, A XXII, no. 66, p. 378.

[69] Questier, LF, 246–53. On this occasion Montague claimed that 'this Christmas tyme last', the earl of Cumberland 'my wyves good kynsman and his good ladye, beinge here' at West Horsley 'with me', 'used at theyre pleasure in this my house excersyse of preaching, and prayer' at the hands of Richard Joshua. Joshua had come to the benefice in September 1588, appointed there by Montague's stepmother, Elizabeth, dowager countess of Lincoln. Montague said that 'dyverse of my servantes dyd repayre to here' Joshua, 'to the number of seven and fortye of them at the leaste: which I never fownde fawlte with in anye of them', *ibid.*, 251–2. Joshua, it appears, had no sympathy for Catholic nonconformists, FSL, L.b. 213.

[70] Loseley MSS, 619; SHC, LM 6729/8/20.

speed up Montague's building programme at River Park, which was behind schedule for want of stone masons.[71] He was responsible for the employment and salaries of various labourers on the demesne of Montague's estate, particularly in the 'hop garden', and even went to some trouble to ensure there was a competent gardener to trim Cowdray's hedges.[72] He also acted as Montague's secretary and diary organiser,[73] and he ensured that Montague's servants looked the part. In March 1570 one Henry Palmer informed Garnett that Thomas Phillips and he had dealt for Montague's 'liveries' and they had provided his lordship with very good 'cloths'.[74] He was in charge, too, of purchasing both essential and luxury comestibles for his master;[75] he frequently witnessed land transaction deeds on the first viscount's behalf, and occasionally he stood as a trustee, with fellow Browne retainers such as Thomas Churchar,[76] a lawyer of the Middle Temple, and Roger Brinkborne, for sections of Montague's estate.[77]

It seems likely that if the household was being presided over by officials such as Garnett, who was an ordained Marian priest and had separated from the Church of England over the Elizabethan settlement of religion, this must have inflected the household's religious and ideological tone.

---

[71] Loseley MSS, 628; SHC, LM 6729/8/56.   [72] BL, Additional MS 33508, fos. 47r, 17r.

[73] For example we come across him, on 11 October 1571, writing to More from Cowdray enquiring whether Loseley House was free from 'mesles or small pockes' and whether More would be at home on 18 October, because Montague purposed to visit him on that day as he was making the journey back from London, Loseley MSS, 624.

[74] BL, Additional MS 33508, fo. 2r. In 1583 Garnett can be found reluctantly instructing one of Montague's servants to refrain from wearing Montague's badge until Montague was permitted to increase the number of his retainers, HEH, BA 56/1552. For the second Viscount Montague's instructions about wearing of livery by his servants, see Breight, 'Caressing', 165 n. 41.

[75] See e.g. BL, Additional MS 33508, fos. 3r, 11r, 12r, 13r, 13v, 19r, 20r, 44r. See also Mertes, *The English Noble Household 1250–1600*, 46.

[76] At the end of the first viscount's will, Thomas Churchar, one of the executors, is named as one of the viscount's servants, WSRO, SAS/BA 67. In March 1590 Montague informed Sir William More that in the present dispute between himself and the bishop of Winchester, 'I doo nothinge, butt advised by my counsell learned', and 'will cause Chercher to attend upon you shortly', SHC, LM 6729/8/111.

[77] In November 1569 Churchar and Brinkborne were parties to a deed which settled part of the estate on Anthony Browne, Montague's son and heir, and on Montague's other children, WSRO, SAS/BA 41. Garnett and Churchar were also joined in a deed of covenant of 1 April 1584 by which Montague settled the same and other property in a different format on his heir Anthony and Anthony's son, Anthony Maria, WSRO, SAS/BA 54. With Brinkborne and Robert Dormer (Montague's son-in-law), Garnett witnessed the deed of purchase of the manor of Cocking by Montague from Lord Lumley in February 1584, SRS 19, 107. Brinkborne may well have been a relative of the Kentish priest Christopher Dryland, who used the alias of Brinkborne and who was being harboured in 1584 in the household of the Shelleys at Mapledurham in Hampshire, PRO, SP 12/168/34, fo. 82v; cf. Anstr. I, 105–6. When Thomas and John Shelley fell foul of Richard Topcliffe just after the first viscount's death, it was Brinkborne who was required by the privy council to guarantee their custody, from which they were released only when they conformed, APC 1592, 368.

It may be that those who caused trouble within the household were irritated by its Catholic character. It is possible that the future betrayer of Edmund Campion, George Eliot, who is known to have held the office of a steward in the Roper household (and later in the Petre establishment at Ingatestone) came to the Ropers from the Brownes. The Brownes were kin to the Ropers through the marriage of Lucy Browne and Thomas Roper.[78] In early August 1564 Montague wrote a letter of apology to William More at Loseley because he had discharged a gentleman, one George Eliot, a kinsman of More, from his service. Montague claimed that he had got rid of him because he was insolent rather than because of any specific ideological clash of opinions between them. Montague had recently reproved him for his loose manner of life. But 'I assure yow att one of the clocke after mydneightt he raysed my wiff and me' and was unbelievably rude. Montague lost his temper but, in the 'mydell of my anger and displeasaunt speache, he moved to me a sute to recomende him for mariage'. 'Finally the same day he commeth to me smylinge'; Eliot proceeded to inform Montague that he had been shooting his deer.

He had strykenid a bucke in my parke here with a gonne which he sayd being a yonge mans parte he trusted I wolde take well. I assure yow Mr Moore I was vexid att the hert, nott with the thinge which is a meere trifill and the deare liveth, but with his dishonest nature to steal from his master, who not yett xx dayes past gave him a bucke.[79]

This does sound rather like the bloody-mindedness of the 'traitor' Eliot who procured Campion's arrest, and who, when he offered further information to the regime in August 1581, included details about the principal Catholic households on the Sussex/Hampshire border. He named in particular Viscount Montague's and that of his son-in-law the earl of Southampton.[80]

And, as we have seen, there were some people in the viscount's service, even in the early years of Elizabeth's reign, who did not quite measure up to the loyalist image which Montague so carefully cultivated. We have already come across his servants John Hall and George Chamberlain who were

---

[78] E. E. Reynolds, *Campion and Persons* (1980), 117–18.

[79] Eliot would have killed more of Montague's deer if he had been able to suborn a recently sacked household servant who was a better shot than Eliot. But 'all this', said Montague, 'offendid nott me so moche as his insufferable pride', SHC, LM 6729/8/13.

[80] Eliot also denounced Lady Paulet, daughter of William, Baron Windsor. She was married first to Henry Sandys of the Vyne at Sherborne St John in Hampshire, and then to Sir George Paulet. She was thus related by marriage to Mabel, Sir Walter Sandys's wife, who was herself the daughter of the first earl of Southampton and sister-in-law of Montague's daughter, the second earl's countess. Eliot named also the old countess of Pembroke, who, as we have seen above, was linked in with the Browne entourage via the services of the Marian priest called Wilson, BL, Lansdowne MS 33, no. 60, fo. 146r; Mott, HR, 291–3, 351.

called into question over the Ridolfi plot.[81] Later on, the Catholic tendencies of some of the first viscount's attendants were even more noticeable. Among the gentlemen-servants waiting on Montague in the mid-1580s who were regarded as suspect was a younger member of the Wyborne family of Pembury,[82] perhaps Edward Wyborne, the younger brother of the recusant William Wyborne.[83]

Other people within the household were clearly and ideologically Catholic in a way that the first viscount himself could never be. As we have already seen, some of Montague's servants were known to be associating with seminarists such as John Owen.[84] One can only assume that William Fitzherbert and his son Thomas (the future Jesuit) were both drawn to the viscount's service because of what they perceived as the prevailing Catholic ideological tone of the household. By the late 1570s the Fitzherbert family was regarded as extremely dangerous and disruptive by the critics of the Derbyshire Catholic community. (They became a particular target for Richard Topcliffe who effectively dispossessed them of Padley Hall.[85]) Fitzherbert was drawn into the Society of Jesus by his friendship with Campion and Persons.[86]

Another servant of the family who had strong Catholic inclinations, perhaps even of a radical kind, was the steward William Spencer. In later years he was remembered as the man who had introduced Guy Fawkes into Montague's household.[87] He had witnessed Montague's will of 19 July 1592 and also the marriage settlement, dated 20 January 1592, between Montague and Lord Buckhurst, for Buckhurst's daughter and Montague's grandson.[88]

[81] See ch. 4, pp. 146–7 above.   [82] PRO, SP 12/195/107, fo. 184r.

[83] We find William Wyborne sitting in the Tower in November 1586 charged with harbouring seminarist clergy and financially assisting some of those who were imprisoned, PRO, SP 12/195/32, fo. 49r. William and Edward were sons of John Wyborne who was, like Montague, a Sussex ironmaster, and who had purchased a manor from Sir Anthony Browne, PRO, C 142/340/183. In April 1606 a 'Mrs Wyborne', possibly Edward's wife, was said to have a lodging in Montague House in Southwark, PRO, SP 14/20/20, fo. 40r. The individual called Wyborne who served in the Browne houschold was identified for arrest and interrogation by Richard Topcliffe in mid-1593. See below in this chapter; APC 1592–3, 328–9.

[84] See ch. 5, pp. 168–9 above.   [85] Hasler, *HC*, III, 515, II, 125–6.

[86] After Campion had written the inflammatory *Rationes Decem*, Robert Persons gave it to Thomas Fitzherbert in manuscript and told him 'that it was Father Campions to be printed, and therefore recommended yt to me not only to read but also to examine the places of [the] Fathers alleadged therein (because I might have more free recourse to publick libraryes in London than priests or religious could have) besides that after yt was printed Father Campion himself gave me one of the first printed coppyes as his owne worke', AAW, A II, no. 38, pp. 185–6. Fitzherbert became a correspondent and supporter of Mary Stuart. See AAW, A IV, no. 5, p. 41 (c. 1586), a copy of a note from Mary Stuart to Thomas Fitzherbert, mentioning his good disposition towards her.

[87] Guy Fawkes was one of the witnesses of Spencer's will of 11 December 1593, PRO, PROB 11/84, fo. 235r–v.

[88] WSRO, SAS/BA 67, 66.

Figure 21.   Wall brass to William Spencer (d. 1594) in the parish church
(All Hallows) at Tillington, West Sussex. Spencer, a steward of the
Browne family, briefly secured Guy Fawkes's admission into the second
Viscount Montague's service.

Spencer did not long survive the first viscount's death. A brass plaque in
the parish church at Tillington records Spencer's death in February 1594.
(See Figure 21.) It describes him as a 'gentleman of great wisdome, learning, pietye and discretion, sometymes steward of [the] houshold to the right
honourable Antonye Viscount Mountague'.[89] Two undated letters from
Montague's steward Anthony Garnett to Sir William More had made
enquiries concerning the character of one 'Mr Spenser', presumably the same
man. One of these letters says that Spencer came from Oxenford, one of
Montague's Surrey manors, and that Spencer was 'desirous' to wear Lord
Montague's livery. Garnett said he himself 'was very willinge he should so
doe, both because I esteme the gentleman honest, wise and sufficiente, and
able sondrye wayes to stand my lord in steade, both here, and in those parts

[89] This plaque was noticed in 1835 by Thomas Horsfield on the floor of the south aisle of
Lurgashall parish church, i.e. where Spencer, his mother and his wife (who 'dyed godly')
appear to have been buried, T. W. Horsfield, *The History . . . of Sussex* (2 vols., 1835), II,
181.

especyally northward, wher his lyvinge doth lye, as also in that he was some tyme under my tutell'. Garnett mentioned, however, that Spencer had been reported to More as a harbourer of opinions which were offensive to the State.[90]

Thus, in the midst of the outwardly conformist establishment which the first Viscount Montague maintained, there lurked some people who might have been reckoned not quite so conformable and reliable as their master. Indeed, it appears that the regime did not accept at face value the viscount's guarantees that all his friends, followers and servants were dependable and loyal. Very soon after Montague's death we get an immediate sense of the latent hostility towards and suspicion of his household which were harboured by some people. Topcliffe and others descended like a ton of bricks on the Brownes' establishment. A privy council letter of 24 June 1593, directed to the Surrey JPs William Morgan, Sir William More, Lawrence Stoughton (Morgan and Stoughton had been present at the valedictory dinner party given by Montague at West Horsley in January 1592)[91] and Topcliffe himself, informed them that 'there hathe [been] discouvered unto us that at this presente there are remayning in certaine places within the countie of Surrey divers dangerous persons charged to have ben privie to some practises against the queene's Majestie and her estate, of whome sondrie are supposed to be residing in the howse or howses of the old Lady Montague'. They were '[Robert] Gray, an old priest Danby, [Francis] Gower, Wyborne, Anthony Fletcher, Thownesende alias Thomson, and Francisce [Rydell], a prest, all which persons and their severall offences are best knowen to you, Mr Topcliffe'. The JPs, with Topcliffe, were instructed to 'enter . . . into the howse or howses of the said Lady Montague within any parte of the countie of Surrey' and make appropriate searches, seizing 'letters, papers and writinges' belonging to these people, and then to arrest them and interrogate them, although the searching should be carried out 'with reguarde to the quallitie of the ladie'.[92]

Francis Rydell served also as one of the first viscount's stewards (and would have been known to the Surrey JPs who would have recently seen him attending Montague at West Horsley). Topcliffe described him as a 'rebel and traitorous priest'. Rydell was also one of the executors of the first viscount's will.[93] (The Marian priest Danby may be the same as the William Danby who served the young second Viscount Montague as 'gentleman of his horse'.[94]) In fact, as the Montague network came under severe pressure from Topcliffe's

---

[90] SHC, LM 6729/8/125, 126.   [91] Questier, *LF*, 247.
[92] *APC 1592–3*, 328–9.
[93] WSRO, SAS/BA 67. He is the 'Father Frauncis' identified in privy council letters of July 1593, *APC 1592–3*, 400, 406.
[94] See ch. 8, p. 235 below.

obsessional pursuit of the Jesuit Robert Southwell, Rydell had absconded. His desperate attempts to escape arrest revealed the existence of the routes of linkage and sympathy which ran between various Catholic houses across several counties. On 19 September 1593 Topcliffe listed for Lord Burghley's benefit what he had discovered about Rydell. He was 'late steward to the old Lord Montague and Lady Montague'. He had held property 'worth 1000^l, which was near Woking, Surrey, upon land belonging to Lord Montague'. Rydell had gone to see the Staffordshire gentleman William Bassett at Longford in Derbyshire, where he also had 'conference' with Nicholas Langford 'the papist, and Bassett's cousin germain'. Then he rushed off to Buxton 'where he met Sir Robert Dormer and his wife', Montague's daughter, accompanied by her seminary priest William Harris (and, among others, Sir Henry Constable of Burton Constable in Holderness, with his wife Margaret (Dormer) and her 'traitorous priest' Cuthbert Johnson, and Sir Thomas Lee of Stoneley and his wife).[95] Topcliffe tracked Rydell's flight – 'from Buxton' Rydell 'went to a tower of Lord Windsor', in Derbyshire, 'let on lease to Edward Bentley'. Bentley had been 'lately condemned for treason', i.e. over the Mary Stuart business, but he was now at liberty. His wife was a Roper, and, in fact, one of Montague's nieces. There Rydell was 'harboured and relieved' by Lord Windsor's tenants and servants. Then news came that the recently deceased viscount's other Marian chaplains, Robert Gray and Anthony Garnett, had been taken. And so Rydell, said Topcliffe, 'fled northward'.[96]

William Bassett, Rydell's friend, was believed to have recently made some very disloyal speeches. He had prophesied a violent end to the Tudor regime and expatiated on how he hoped to profit from its demise.[97] Bassett was related to the Fitzherbert family (whose ruin Richard Topcliffe had tried so hard to procure)[98] and had come into conflict with Thomas Fitzherbert, the renegade nephew of Sir Thomas Fitzherbert. Bassett had tried to prevent the nephew's election as an MP.[99] Sir Thomas was a stubborn recusant. (Bassett had been brought up in his house.)[100] According to Thomas, the

---

[95] *CSPD 1591–4*, 372.

[96] *CSPD 1591–4*, 372. For Edward Bentley, see A. Loomie, 'A Grandniece of Thomas More: Catherine Bentley *ca.* 1565–*ca.* 1625', *Moreana* 29 (1971), 13–15.

[97] In April 1593 Topcliffe published his suspicions of Bassett during the passage in parliament of the legislation against Catholic separatists. Robert Gray was told about it by Lady Dormer and Lord Wharton when they were at the house of Sir George Browne, Hasler, *HC*, III, 515; *CSPD 1591–4*, 380.

[98] BL, Harleian MS 7042, fos. 225v–226v; Hasler, *HC*, II, 125–6, I, 404.

[99] Thomas had betrayed his father, John Fitzherbert, following the unravelling of the Babington conspiracy. Thomas's arrangement with Topcliffe was that, for a fee, Topcliffe should help him to acquire his childless uncle Sir Thomas's estate after his death, although Sir Thomas had disinherited him in 1591.

[100] BL, Harleian MS 7042, fo. 225v.

traitor-nephew, at the time that Lord Paget fled through Sussex out of the country, assisted by some of the Sussex Catholic gentry, Bassett procured a man to go to Derbyshire quickly and destroy incriminating correspondence at his residences of Blore and Langley Meynell. Allegedly also, Bassett was so worried about the evidence that Lord Paget's priest Robert Sutton might be compelled to give against him (Bassett) that he actually hastened Sutton's execution in July 1588. (Sutton was one of the circle of clergy betrayed by Ralph Betham who, as we saw, was familiar with the Dormer family.) But, in the case of others who were about to be arrested, Bassett managed to warn them in advance. It was said that Bassett kept in touch with the future priest Thomas Fitzherbert, 'his dearest darling and Spanish trator'.[101] All these people were on the fringes of the entourage of the earl of Shrewsbury, an entourage where it seems some of the Babington plot had been concocted.[102]

The first viscount's partially conformist priest Robert Gray, also on the arrest warrants of mid-1593, was equally badly tainted by his association with these same doubtful and suspect people. (He had taught Bassett in the Fitzherbert household many years earlier.[103]) Gray also fled northwards, trying to escape Topcliffe. And he went along a route marked out by many of the same residences that Rydell visited, from the Dormers at Wing in Buckinghamshire all the way up to the Constable family of Burton Constable. Gray resorted to Nicholas Langford, also formerly his pupil, in Derbyshire. It was reported that 'the Scottish queen had written to Mr Langforde, that he shulde sticke to his religion, and she wolde make him a duke, and make Robert Gray archbishop of Canterbury'.[104] Gray confessed that he had talked with William Bassett about whether Elizabeth might be considered illegitimate.[105]

One can see how the suspicious Topcliffeian mind might think that there was a propensity among some of the Brownes' servants, even the ones who

---

[101] *Ibid.*; Anstr. I, 343. Anthony Fitzherbert, Thomas's brother, was only with much effort persuaded into conformity in 1591, M. Questier, *Conversion, Politics and Religion in England, 1580–1625* (Cambridge, 1996), 130; PRO, SP 46/47, fo. 135r.

[102] One of the sixth earl of Shrewsbury's stewards, Nicholas Williamson, administered what remained of the attainted estates of the traitor Anthony Babington and corresponded with many of these people, especially Anthony Fitzherbert, William Bassett and Nicholas Langford, the polymath Thomas Allen at Gloucester Hall in Oxford and Edmund Rainolds (the Catholic brother of the puritan John Rainolds) who came close to disaster for possessing a copy of 'Leicester's Commonwealth'. See PRO, SP 46/47–9; M. Foster, 'Thomas Allen of Gloucester Hall, Oxford (1540–1632)', *Oxoniensia* 46 (1981), 99–128; *APC 1592–3*, 205, 209, 351, 352.

[103] BL, Harleian MS 7042, fo. 225v; *CSPD 1591–4*, 379–81.

[104] A. Clifford (ed.), *The State Papers and Letters of Sir Ralph Sadler* (2 vols., Edinburgh, 1809), II, 521.

[105] *CSPD 1591–4*, 379–80.

wore an occasionally conformist mask, to break out and move into full separation, and transgress other aspects of the penal law against particular forms of Catholic activity. The future martyr George Napper, who was a relative of the Ropers and hence of Montague himself (in whose household Napper had served), had been released from imprisonment in the Wood Street Counter in London in July 1589 after taking a form of oath which declared limitations on papal authority. He, however, went off to the seminary at Douai in 1594 and was ordained in 1596.[106] Anthony Fletcher, another Montague retainer who was, as we saw, identified and marked down for arrest in 1593, also eventually went to the seminary (after the death of his wife).[107] (Fletcher's son, godson to the second of the Jacobean archpriests, George Birkhead, followed him shortly thereafter.[108]) One of Montague's servants who fell under suspicion in the mid-1580s, William Coningsby, was a fervent proselytiser. In the mid-1590s we find him, now a member of the second viscount's household, persuading another servant, Henry Lanman, to Catholicism.[109]

Another servant of the Brownes who was, on the surface, a conformist, but had relatives who were more aggressively Catholic, was John Arden. In 1594 the second viscount admitted that among the recusant servants in his household, whom he had inherited from his grandfather, was 'John Arderne the keeper of his parke', but Arden 'now comethe to the church'.[110] In general, the Ardens trod a delicate line between recusancy and conformity, sometimes being convicted of recusant nonconformity but then evincing a

---

[106] Anstr. I, 243.

[107] *Ibid.*, II, 113. It appears that he may, in the 1590s, have become a servant to Mary (Dormer), wife of Anthony Browne, the first viscount's eldest son. A privy council letter of 20 June 1596, directed to her at River Park in Tillington parish, informed her that, following the arrest of 'sundrie popishe priestes and . . . their adherents . . . in and about Sussex', the council had evidence against other people, including 'one Anthonie Fletcher who at the tyme served your selfe in place of creditt and so doth now'; and now he must be 'spoken withall', *APC 1596*, 481. Fletcher was interviewed by the council on 27 June, but no further action appears to have been taken against him, *ibid.*, 500.

[108] *NAGB*, 93, 194; Anstr. II, 113, 114.

[109] Henry Lanman's father, a servant of Sir Christopher Hatton, in whose household Henry spent one year, initially placed him with a clerk in the Petty Bag office. Then, after the deaths of both Hatton and the clerk, he gravitated to the Brownes' household where he served the second viscount for a total of six years. Lanman said he was converted from 'schism' to Catholicism when he was aged twenty-two, i.e. in 1595, through 'discussion with William Coningsby, one of the many Catholics whom he met in the family of Lord Montague'. Lanman 'read many books lent to him by this man', especially those written by John Rastell and Thomas Harding against Bishop John Jewel. Initially Lanman hesitated over whether to become a recusant but was introduced by Coningsby to the priest Richard Davies who induced him to break entirely with the established Church and reconciled him to the Church of Rome 'on the Saturday within the Octave of Corpus Christi 1596', CRS 54, 87–8; Anstr. I, 98.

[110] BL, Harleian MS 7042, fo. 143r.

willingness to conform. William Arden of Midhurst, for example, was a conformist.[111] But we know, from other sources, that the Arden family which resided mainly in Chichester was often regarded as offensively Catholic. One of them, Robert Arden, was a Jesuit who became a close associate of Cardinal William Allen.[112]

Even comparatively humble individuals in the household seem to have been dealt with once the protecting hand of their master, the first viscount, was removed. One of his kitchen staff, Robert Goldsmith, was arrested by Richard Young in January 1593, only a few months after Montague's death. Goldsmith was a recusant separatist and refused to discuss the issue of religion with Church-of-England preachers. He admitted that he had received sacramental absolution from a priest, though he would not say which one.[113]

---

[111] William Arden was a son-in-law of William Coldham, whose family, as we saw, maintained close links, tenurial and service-based, with the Brownes during this period, Berry, *Sussex*, 2; see above in this chapter. For William Arden's recusancy and his statute conformity in front of Bishop Samuel Harsnett at Aldingbourne manor chapel, see PRO, E 368/539, mem. 147d, E 368/544, mem. 139a. John Arden appears to have used the alias of Butcher, and was dead by 1596, PRO, E 368/488, mem. 113a, E 368/528 mem. 167a; CRS 61, 235. His father seems to have been the John Arden who was convicted of recusancy at the Sussex assizes in June 1597, described as being resident at Easebourne, Cockburn, *Sussex Assizes: Elizabeth*, no. 1720; WSRO, Ep. I/23/7, fos. 11r–v, 38v. See PRO, E 368/491, mem. 137a, for the marriage settlement for William Arden and Eleanor Coldham (arranged by John Arden of Easebourne, PRO, E 368/528, mem. 167a) of property 'voc. Chilnershe in paroch de Lurgashall', by a deed dated 1 October 1591, with remainder to John Arden alias Butcher, presumably William's brother.

[112] See CRS 74, 106. In December 1590 John Arden, Robert's brother (they were both sons of Lawrence Arden who sat as MP for Chichester in 1558), was quizzed 'conserninge any daungerous attempt against the French kinge his person or estate', and about his own dealings with English fugitives, PRO, SP 12/234/66, fo. 107r. He confessed that he was involved in a correspondence with Henry Jarves (or Gervase), probably a brother of the priest George Gervase of Bosham. Henry was a Sussex man who was now serving in the regiment of Sir William Stanley in Flanders. See also Bindoff, *HC*, I, 330. He was dispatched, after the Armada came to grief, to observe the disposition of the English fleet and to ascertain the opinions of the Catholic peers about the 1588 debacle. He said that he was told that, if he failed in his mission, his brother Robert's credit would suffer as a result. See *CSPF 1590–1*, 298–9; *APC 1591*, 52. In October 1595, however, John Arden wrote to Sir Robert Cecil from the Marshalsea prison in Southwark, professing his loyalty and offering his services, *CSPD 1595–7*, 118, 159; E. Duffy, 'William, Cardinal Allen, 1532–1594', *RH* 22 (1995), 265–90, at p. 287. For this John Arden's career as a double-agent, or as a go-between for moderate Catholics and the regime, see also CRS 58, 229, 230, 231, 235, 240; Hammer, *Polarisation*, 192. In September 1613 Anthony Champney wrote to Thomas More about possible candidates for places in the newly established secular clergy house of studies in Paris, the Collège d'Arras, and named 'one [Robert] Arden whoe was amongst the Jesuites a longe . . . tyme whoe ys verie learned in the [H]ebrewe and Greeke', AAW, A XII, no. 173, p. 384. In June 1615 George Arden of Chichester (brother of Robert and John) was involved in a star chamber case over his alleged papist sympathies and his use of local government machinery to deal with Chichester puritans who gadded to sermons in North Mundham (a redoubt of the puritan Bowyer family), PRO, STAC 8/22/12, mem. 6a.

[113] CRS 60, 50.

But the first viscount's household official who drew most attention to the volatile and overtly Catholic character of parts of the Montague entourage was Robert Barnes. He and John Shelley of Mapledurham, even during the first viscount's time, worked to provide a seminarist clergy for the Hampshire/Sussex border region,[114] though Barnes does not appear to have become fully and stubbornly recusant until the Jacobean period.[115] Robert Gray's account of the meeting between Sir George Browne, the Jesuit John Curry and Constance Cuffauld at George Dennis's house at Todham noted that Barnes had been there as well. Barnes, said Gray, had a landed estate in Cambridgeshire;[116] Gray had seen Curry at Barnes's house.[117] Benjamin Beard claimed that Barnes had been overseas with the Babington plot suspect John Butler but had returned 'without taking orders'. Apparently Barnes must have considered becoming a priest.[118] He was then caught up in Topcliffe's purge of the Jesuit Robert Southwell's associates, including the Bellamy family (tainted already by the Babington conspiracy). Anne Bellamy, the betrayer of Southwell, named Barnes as one of the patrons

---

[114] See above in this chapter. A privy council letter to the lords lieutenant, ordering the prevention of the transport of Catholics' children out of the country, named Mary Shelley, the widow of Henry Shelley of Mapledurham (who was brother to John Shelley, Viscount Montague's servant). In *c.* 1586 (seven years before) she 'went beyond seas accompanied with her youngest sonn and daughter' and two servants, 'having mainteynance out of Mapledurham', as was deposed by Michael Thompson and also by Joan Boies, 'servant to Robert Barnes alias Strange that kepe[s] the house', BL, Harleian MS 7042, fo. 166r; Mott, HR, 378. Lord Keeper Puckering noted, on the basis of Benjamin Beard's reports, that Shelley 'lyeth at Barnes farme (or Bailes farme) as it were in an old parke payled and locked [so] that none can come yn without a kea', PRO, SP 12/248/116, fo. 250r. (The farm was, apparently, part of Montague's estate, PRO, PROB 11/81, fo. 163v; ESRO, BA 67.) Shelley's 'consorts' included 'Strange [i.e. Barnes] . . . that was towardes my Lord Mountague and kept a collidge of preests (as yt weare) at Maplederham', PRO, SP 12/248/116, fo. 250r. Barnes was also an associate of Swithin Wells who assisted him and Shelley with the placement of seminary clergy arriving from the Continent, *CSPD 1591–4*, 510; Mott, HR, 22.

[115] A 'Ricardus Straunge alias Barnes de Buriton', having been fined for nine months recusancy, was marked down in the 1592–3 recusant roll for sequestration by exchequer commission, but I can find no evidence of further proceedings against him in Elizabeth's reign, CRS 18, 288. Only in 1609 was Barnes finally stung by an exchequer inquisition into his property (in Surrey), at a hearing presided over by Sir Thomas Bishop at Midhurst, although the potential proceeds of his recusancy, along with those of a Cowdray man called John Gittons, had already been made the subject of a royal grant in mid-1608, PRO, E 368/537, mem. 74a; *CSPD 1603–10*, 442; PRO, SO 3/4; cf. *HMCS* XX, 199. In November 1613 we find him witnessing, in the company of other Browne servants (John Bennett and John Cape), a deed drawn up between the second viscount and various local men from Easebourne and Woolbeding, WSRO, SAS/BA 73.

[116] This may identify Montague's steward with the Robert Barnes of Harlton, co. Cambridge, who sold his estate in Harlton to Dr Thomas Friar, a prominent Catholic physician, PRO, C 2/James I/F6/58, mem. 2a; FSL, L.b. 223; W. Munk, *The Roll of the Royal College of Physicians of London* (3 vols., 1878), I, 73.

[117] *CSPD 1591–4*, 381.   [118] PRO, SP 12/248/105, fo. 232r.

of George Birkhead, the future archpriest of the English secular clergy, who would come to reside at Cowdray early in the seventeenth century.[119]

John Shelley, Barnes's friend and associate, had conformist moments in the 1580s and 1590s but he eventually went into exile.[120] He was a relative, through his wife Elizabeth, of the Jesuit Thomas Owen.[121] Rather similar to Barnes and Shelley was Richard Lambe, the northerner who came to Midhurst to serve the first viscount.[122] (We find him witnessing a deed on the viscount's behalf in 1584, along with Shelley himself and Francis Gower.[123]) He was a blood relative of the archpriest George Birkhead. We may conjecture that Birkhead came to Cowdray in the early seventeenth century in part through the agency of his kinsman who was now ensconced in the household of the second viscount. (Lambe also played host to the secular priest Benjamin Norton who was, like Shelley, a relative of Thomas Owen SJ.[124]) Lambe married one of the gentlewomen-servants in the Browne household, Constance Cuffauld, despite, as we noted above, the attentions paid to her by Sir George, the first viscount's son. The Lambes had property both at River Park in Tillington (one of the Browne family's estates),[125] and at Midhurst.[126]

What we have here, then, seems to be a significant number of the first Viscount Montague's servants becoming involved in the Catholic seminarist and political project in the second half of Elizabeth's reign in a way which was somewhat out of step with their master's own much-trumpeted conformist ecclesiastical credentials. Within his outwardly conformist household we can actually see an important fraction of the Catholic community becoming more clericalised, even separatist, in its inclinations. We may even speculate, though we cannot prove it, that this was something which the first viscount

[119] Mott, HR, 22; ch. 8, p. 235 below.
[120] Even if his occasional conformity was simply a cover for the assistance which he rendered to seminarists, his conformity at the direction of the privy council in late 1592, and his 'frequenting the church and hearing of divine service and sermons', drove him into such feelings of guilt that he felt compelled to purge his 'schismatic' state when he went to France in 1596, Mott, HR, 378–9.
[121] For Shelley's service with Montague, see Mott, HR, 377–8.
[122] See ch. 3, p. 96 above.   [123] WSRO, SAS/BA 58.
[124] NAGB, 232. Norton was a leading member of the clerical entourage around the second Viscount Montague in the early seventeenth century.
[125] WSRO, Ep. I/17/11, fo. 37r.
[126] Anstr. II, 78. An exchequer commission at Lewes in October 1610, headed by Sir Walter Covert, noted that Richard Lambe had goods at Midhurst worth twenty shillings, PRO, E 368/539, mem. 147d. Richard's son, Anthony, became a Jesuit even though, according to Norton, the family chaplain, his brother William's education at the Society of Jesus's college at St Omer had been unsatisfactory, NAGB, 93. Richard Lambe's daughter Anne married Richard Mico, whose brother Walter became a Catholic in 1614 and entered the Society, Anstr. II, 221; CRS 54, 294.

at least foresaw and, while he did not actively promote it, he certainly did nothing positively to prevent it.

We will now go on to see what happened to this fraction of the community, and in particular to see how far it was caught up in the well-known factional battles which racked English Catholicism from within during the late Elizabethan period and for most of the early seventeenth century. If, as is generally accepted, the apparently often petty and inconsequential in-fighting of the appellant controversy grew out of a much larger and more significant series of concerns within the Catholic community, and indeed out of the changing relationship in the 1590s between Catholicism and the State, as Catholics, among others, waited for the accession of James Stuart and anticipated a fundamental alteration in their position vis-à-vis the crown, then it is clearly worth looking again at the lay patronage networks (including the Brownes') which underwrote and supported the clerical mouthpieces which claimed to be giving voice to the community's concerns and aspirations.

7

A period of transition

The end for the ageing first Viscount Montague came, relatively suddenly as
it turned out, in October 1592. His will, of 19 July 1592, directed that he was
to be buried either at Midhurst or at Battle – in the event it was Midhurst.
The funeral expenses were not to exceed 1,000 marks. His executors were
instructed 'to erect a seemly tombe with three great images of himself and
his two wyves and all their armes placed about it'.[1]

Montague was an enthusiast for monuments. In Titchfield parish church
there is a huge tomb constructed, from alabaster and marble, for the first
earl and countess of Southampton and for the second earl (Montague's son-
in-law) (see Figure 22). The second earl's will had ordered his executors
to build two monuments, one for his parents and one for himself. But this
composite and magnificent tomb was built instead.[2] The craftsman who
was hired to execute it was Gerard Johnson, a Flemish refugee resident in
Montague Close in St Saviour's parish in Southwark.[3] He also designed and
built the funeral monument for the first viscount and his two wives, as well as
the table-tomb and brass of 1595 constructed for Montague's cousin John
Gage in the parish church of West Firle, and the monument in All Saints
parish church at Wing to Sir William Dormer (d. 1575), whose son married
Montague's daughter Elizabeth. Montague's monument was architecturally
almost identical to the Wriothesley tomb. Montague may himself have laid
down the basic specifications for both of them.[4]

---

[1] WSRO, SAS/BA 67.

[2] A deed relating to the construction of this monument is dated 6 May 1594, so it seems reasonable to assume that it was completed, at the earliest, in the mid-1590s, HRO, 5M53/262.

[3] Gerard Johnson's name appears regularly in the Southwark sacramental token books for this
period, LMA, P92/SAV/184–200.

[4] Mott, HR, 545–6; N. Pevsner and D. Lloyd, *The Buildings of England: Hampshire and
the Isle of Wight* (1967), 624–5; *The Parish Church of St. Peter Titchfield, Fareham* (n.p.,
n.d.), 9; B. W. Greenfield, 'The Wriothesley Tomb in Titchfield, Hants: Its Effigial Statues

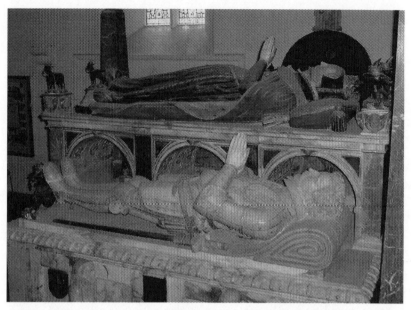

Figure 22.   Funeral monument of the Wriothesley family, in Titchfield parish church (St Peter). On the top of the monument lies an effigy of Jane, countess of Southampton, widow of Sir Thomas Wriothesley, first earl of Southampton, whose effigy is located on the far side of the monument. On the near side lies the effigy of Henry Wriothesley, second earl of Southampton (d. 1581).

The first viscount's will placed quite a weight of expectations on his young heir – his grandson. He was to inherit his grandfather's 'choller of golde of the order and all Georges, chaines, garters and roabes of the order of estate and parliament', as well as all the family portraits, which, as we saw, recorded the great moments in the Brownes' history of service to the crown.[5] In making provision for the younger children and other family members, the estate was partitioned. But the young heir to the title would still be immensely wealthy.

In the early years, however, the views of the new but young head of the family were something of an enigma. He had been deprived of paternal guidance in June 1592, when his father predeceased his grandfather. He

and Heraldry', *Proceedings of the Hampshire Field Club* (1889), 65–82, at pp. 66–70; Hope, *Cowdray*, 110; 'The Gage Monuments, Firle', *Sussex Notes and Queries* 2 (1929), 175–7; ESRO, ACC 5312; K. A. Esdaile, *English Monumental Sculpture since the Renaissance* (New York, 1927), 16, 117–18; R. Gem, *All Saints Church, Wing* (2002). The design of the Dormer monument is a virtual duplicate of the one built by Gerard Johnson for the fourth earl of Rutland at Bottesford, Esdaile, *English Monumental Sculpture*, plate 1.
[5] WSRO, SAS/BA 67; ch. 1, pp. 26–7, 29, ch. 3, p. 69 above.

became decidedly Catholic, and, as we shall see, he was soon in trouble for his Catholic opinions. But it may be that the key to determining the ideological tenor of the Brownes' family and other connections from the early 1590s onwards lies principally with the dowager viscountess, Lady Magdalen, and her own entourage.

Lady Magdalen had remained remarkably silent during her husband's life. Indeed we know very little about her except what is contained in the posthumous account published by her chaplain Richard Smith in 1609.[6] (Smith's *Life of the Most Honorable and Vertuous Lady the La. Magdalen Viscountesse Montague* was, as we remarked above, based on the funeral sermon which he preached for her 'before a great audience' with 'her familiar acquaintance there present'.[7]) Probably her opinions were influenced by and subsumed under those of her husband while he lived. She seems to have been very close to him. Smith described how her famed piety lent itself to domestic bliss. For, 'being of her own nature and education addicted unto piety, by the further inducements of her husband's example [she] more speedily ran the course of virtue', and 'they lived together in great love and amity thirty-six years'. Smith claimed that, as he was composing his account of his deceased patroness, he 'lighted by chance on a letter of Dr [Alban] Langdale', who was 'for many years their confessor, wherein, in testimony of their love and piety, he thus speaketh unto them: "Fare ye well most loving couple, of one mind, of one love, and (which is rare in this world) of one piety"'.[8] Now, of course, Smith was hagiographising the woman and idealising the Brownes' domestic establishment. He was, therefore, hardly going to say that they had rows, even if they did. On the other hand, Smith's account was published almost immediately after her death and was therefore unlikely to have been a complete fiction.

So, what kind of Catholic was Lady Magdalen? According to Roger Manning, she simply followed her husband's lead in political matters and, as a matter of course, took over, after her husband's death, his role as the protector of Sussex Catholics. Montague's 'unique position as the most important Catholic in Sussex' was 'derived from his unquestioned loyalty to the queen and his scrupulous moderation in religious matters'. Lady Magdalen was, suggests Manning, of the same mind. They both

drew a careful distinction between what they considered to be legitimate means of preserving their faith and what could only be construed as treason. This distinction was not based upon what could be done safely and what might bring ruin; it arose from an attempt to draw a line between what was God's and what was rightfully the queen's.

[6] See Southern, *ERH*. For a portrait of Smith, executed when he was in exile in France, see Figure 23.
[7] Southern, *ERH*, 3–4; ch. 3, p. 74 above.   [8] Southern, *ERH*, 21.

Figure 23.   Portrait of Richard Smith (d. 1655), bishop of Chalcedon.

Manning notes that 'Lady Montague twice offered' to let Richard Smith 'set up a printing press in her household, yet she consistently refused to be drawn into any plots'.[9]

But, of course, this was precisely the issue. There was a rather large middle ground between saying the rosary and, say, fomenting a *coup d'état*. Possession and use of a private printing press was not always regarded as the first sign of an obedient and loyal-hearted subject. One of Edmund Campion's and Robert Persons's most potent weapons had been the secret printing press, which was disassembled, moved and reassembled as occasion required and allowed them and their confederates an *entrée* into the public consciousness which the mid-Elizabethan regime had wished to deny them.

As we have just seen, while Richard Topcliffe was on the rampage in 1593, some of the central Catholic members of the first viscount's household fled to Lady Magdalen for protection rather than to the second viscount, her grandson.[10] But the viscountess may herself have already started sailing close to the wind. Smith, in so many words, seems to say precisely this. Having praised to the skies the Catholic orthodoxy of the first viscount (even while admitting that he had conformed for most of his life and claiming that he had had to be corrected towards the end of his days by a household chaplain), he then says that Lady Magdalen, in her married state, 'was constrained to think, as the Apostle saith, how . . . to please her husband'. But when 'that band' was dissolved, she acquired 'a more settled freedom of exercising her virtue' and 'applied herself more attentively to the service of God'.[11]

This could be taken to mean simply that she became absorbed in the round of pious observance which Smith describes. It could also mean that she started to exploit her new freedom in order to do things which would not have been possible for her while her husband was alive. Sharon Kettering has demonstrated how, in early modern France, the influence of noblewomen during this period, excluded from 'male-dominated institutions' of government 'to which women could not belong', might well prove quite considerable. For, she argues, 'the patron–client ties and networks dominating noble society were informal, fluid, non-institutional and well suited to the exercise of indirect power through personal relationships by women'. These ties 'often began as kinship or marriage ties', and could be significant in determining the advancement of clients of such families. Widowhood would usually confer an extra degree of authority here.[12]

---

[9] Manning, *Religion*, 160–1. For Lady Magdalen's protection of Catholics, see *ibid.*, 132; W. C. Renshaw (ed.), 'Ecclesiastical Returns for 81 Parishes in East Sussex Made in 1603', *SRS* 4 (1905), 3–17, at p. 7.

[10] *APC 1592–3*, 399; ch. 6, pp. 199–200 above. [11] Southern, *ERH*, 23.

[12] S. Kettering, 'The Patronage Power of Early Modern French Noblewomen', *HJ* 32 (1989), 817–41, at p. 818; B. Harris, 'Women and Politics in Early Tudor England', *HJ* 33 (1990), 259–81, at p. 269.

One crucial feature of the viscountess's clerical patronage in the years after her husband's death was that she took as household chaplains, *inter alia*, Richard Smith himself and Thomas More, two of the leading figures in the movement among the Catholic seminarist clergy which sought to reform the way in which Catholicism, particularly clerical Catholicism, in England was promoted, sustained and governed.

Smith was a firebrand who, as we shall see, brought not peace but a sword to the early seventeenth-century English Catholic community. Despite a marked tendency towards self-pity and morbid depression, Smith's ambitions grew larger in the 1610s as he accessed a stream of patronage directly from the French Court in the form of the friendship of Armand-Jean du Plessis, bishop of Luçon, the future cardinal-duc de Richelieu. Thomas More was a great-grandson of his namesake the famous lord chancellor and was, of course, kin to the Brownes through the Roper marriage made by the first viscount's sister Lucy. He had been on the fringes of the appellant dispute but had not seriously blotted his copybook by exhibiting too extreme oppositional tendencies, though George Blackwell, in a letter to the priest William Bishop, complained that More had 'violated the order' given in Blackwell's 'common letter' to his opponents, had been disobedient in 'defendinge by writinge the tumultuous proceedinges of the discontented' and was in Blackwell's opinion 'without satisfaction made to me . . . unworthie to come to Gods alter'. His 'headdie and rash ignorant writings' were 'in prejudicium fidei et contemptum ecclesiasticae disciplinae'.[13]

Then, towards the end of her life, and as her grandson, the second viscount, started to pose and posture as a leader within the Catholic community, Lady Magdalen's clerical entourage transferred to him.[14] Here

---

[13] Inner Temple, Petyt MS 47, fo. 223r (transcript at ABSJ). On 14 March previously, More had been among those priests who were warned by Blackwell against publishing their objections to his government, *ibid.*, fos. 74r–3r (*sic*). Smith mentioned that Lady Magdalen kept a third priest at Battle, 'M. Thomas Smith, Bachelor of Divinity, a man no less venerable for his learning, worthy piety, and unwearied endeavour in helping his country, than for his gravity of years', about whom, however, relatively little is known, Southern, *ERH*, 43; Anstr. I, 323. We know that Lady Magdalen had other priests as well, for example the individual whose name was heard by the informer who reported it in *c.* March/April 1603 as 'Santon' who 'lyeth at the Ladie Mountegues house in St Mary Overis', PRO, SP 14/1/7, fo. 18v. This may be the same man as the 'Mr Sampton' named by an informer in *c.* April 1605 as having an *entrée* at Montague House, AAW, B 48, no. 42, fo. 111r. But nothing else seems to be known about him.

[14] Smith noted that there was no animosity, and perhaps even a real affection, between Lady Magdalen and her stepson and stepgrandson. She 'tenderly loved her children and, what she could without injury to others, carefully aimed at their preferment', but she refrained from trying to supplant Anthony Browne, the first viscount's son by his first wife, Jane Radcliffe, and had 'so solicitous a care of his health as if he had been her own child'. In fact, 'the present most honourable [second] Viscount Montague . . . imputeth the benefit of his own and his father's life to the rare piety of this mother-in-law'. Even when some unspecified incident occurred which would have allowed her to have 'raised the fortunes of her own children'

we have a path being described, as it were, from the post-Reformation conservatism of the first viscount, through a transitional phase in which the Catholicism of the Brownes was, in some sense, radicalised, or at least refined and concentrated, under the influence of the dowager viscountess. The clerical members of the entourage would stake a claim to a real measure of influence within the English Catholic community during the Jacobean period. They would also intrude, from time to time, into larger political issues, and they would do this in a manner which many Protestants found difficult to tolerate.

John Bossy has seen Lady Magdalen's household at Battle as a throwback to the pre-missionary era – a place distinguished by 'solidarity' in religion, a 'solidarity' which took its character from the religion of the master. The master was responsible for the behaviour of the rest of his 'family'. There was therefore an unspoken compact between the State and the great men who typically controlled such establishments. The great man would guarantee the behaviour of those under his charge and would then, as a *quid pro quo*, be allowed to do more or less as he pleased within doors, and to entertain and employ whom he liked. As Bossy says, 'it seems at least to have been fairly usual, during the early decades of the mission, for a distinction to be drawn between senior and more intimate servants, who would be Catholics, and the rest, who would not'.[15] This certainly appears to have been the case in the first Viscount Montague's household before 1592. As we have seen, the first viscount publicly adverted to the fact that many of his servants were fully conformist, and that he made no demands of them even that they should profess his own religion.[16]

By contrast, Richard Smith's account of Lady Magdalen's household staff insisted that they nearly all were Catholic. Presumably all, or almost all, of her servants attended Mass at Battle Abbey, or 'Little Rome' as the locals contemptuously called it. But they did not individually tend to fall under suspicion because of that. So Bossy makes a distinction between the large-scale but highly untypical household of people such as Lady Magdalen and the markedly smaller households of (still prominent) gentry where this kind of solidarity was much more difficult to achieve. In consequence, in these smaller domestic units, there was lay–clerical discord. The gentry sometimes sent their servants to church to appease the State, and their seminarist chaplains got hot under the collar about this and demanded that the servants and retainers should be fully Catholic (both for reasons of security and of godliness).[17]

at Anthony Browne's expense, 'she was so far from making use thereof, to the injury of her son-in-law [i.e. stepson] . . . that she pacified her husband and reduced him into favour', Southern, *ERH*, 22.
[15] Bossy, *ECC*, 168–9. [16] Questier, *LF*, 252; ch. 6, pp. 193–4 above.
[17] Bossy, *ECC*, 169.

Smith's account of Lady Magdalen's religion describes her and it in largely uncomplicated terms. Grounded in the piety of Mary Tudor's Court, her religious sensibilities were in some sense merely normal, though her spiritual enthusiasms made her unusual. Her faith was shown forth in her liberality and generosity rather than through political gesture or any kind of studied or systematic polemical position taken in the face of the Elizabethan settlement of religion. Smith says that 'she maintained a great family, which consisted of eighty persons and sometimes more, and almost all Catholics, and these she maintained, not only for her honour (as is the manner of noble persons), but also to support them in the Catholic religion'. She also showed an actual as opposed to a merely public concern for the poor, and

when she desisted from her prayers, she accustomed to spend much time in sewing shirts or smocks for poor men and women, in which exercise she seemed to take much pleasure; sometimes also, when she had leisure, she visited the poor in their own houses and sent them either medicines or meat or wood or money, as she perceived their need, and when she could not perform this herself she sent her waiting women.[18]

The Catholicism of her retainers was, according to Smith, a natural out-crop or product of the brand of social justice which she herself dispensed in making sure that they were properly treated and protected from the spite of the malicious. To her household she 'allowed not only plentiful food and competent wages, but (which is much more to be esteemed) afforded them the same benefit of the word of God and the sacraments that she herself enjoyed, and, as far as she could, secured them from vexations and perse-cution of heretics'. Smith believed that this 'kind of liberality' was 'far to be preferred before even the distribution of very great sums of money in alms'. Her 'pious liberality' created and conserved 'a visible church or company of Catholics'.[19]

Her Catholicism was 'evident, not by one act, but by the whole progress of her life'.

For in those times, so turbulent and so exceeding subject to mutation under the kings Henry VIII and Edward VI and Queen Elizabeth, she remained most constant in her faith. And if in the beginning of the reign of Queen Elizabeth, she went sometimes to heretical churches, that may rather be imputed to the defect of instruction than want of zeal. For when she understood it to be unlawful she did most constantly abhor it.

Smith does not say at exactly what point she began to abhor it, though he effectively concedes that there were no recusancy proceedings against her during Elizabeth's reign. They started only after James's accession. Perhaps

[18] Southern, *ERH*, 39, 40. For evidence of her alms-giving, see ESRO, RAF 3/4, *passim*.
[19] Southern, *ERH*, 39.

her conformity lasted longer than he implies.[20] Or maybe her husband's conformity shielded her increasingly separatist tendencies, although he died over ten years before James came to the throne. Smith notes that 'under Queen Elizabeth she endured no other persecution for matter of religion than that she was once accused to the pretended bishop of Canterbury, her house twice searched, and her priest once taken and imprisoned', evidently a reference to the misfortunes of Robert Gray.[21]

Smith describes in lavish detail the arrangements made at Battle for the expression of Lady Magdalen's Catholicism. Famously

she built a chapel in her house (which in such a persecution was to be admired) and there placed a very fair altar of stone, whereto she made an ascent with steps and enclosed it with rails, and, to have everything conformable, she built a choir for singers and set up a pulpit for the priests, which perhaps is not to be seen in all England besides. Here almost every week was a sermon made, and on solemn feasts the sacrifice of the Mass was celebrated with singing and musical instruments, and sometimes also with deacon and subdeacon. And such was the concourse and resort of Catholics, that sometimes there were 120 together, and 60 communicants at a time had the benefit of the Blessed Sacrament. And such was the number of Catholics resident in her house and the multitude and note of such as repaired thither, that even the heretics, to the eternal glory of the name of the Lady Magdalen, gave it the title of *Little Rome*.[22]

Her household evidently enjoyed a substantial measure of protection from high up in the regime. Perhaps we should not be surprised by this. Lady Magdalen's stepgrandson had, after all, married the daughter of Lord Buckhurst, the future earl of Dorset, and she herself was godmother to the rising star Sir Julius Caesar who became chancellor of the exchequer during James's reign.[23]

---

[20] Among the inhabitants of Montague Close who received sacramental tokens in *c*. 1593 is listed 'Ladye Mountekew', though of course this may indicate not the dowager viscountess but the second viscount's wife Jane, the daughter of Lord Buckhurst, LMA, P92/SAV/187, p. 19.

[21] Southern, *ERH*, 41–2; BL, Lansdowne MS 82, no. 49, fo. 103r; see below in this chapter.

[22] Southern, *ERH*, 43. The exact position of this chapel at Battle is uncertain, but it may have been in what was formerly the 'novices' chamber' located at the south end of the east range of Battle Abbey (see Figure 24). I am very grateful to Richard Clark for his assistance with this point. For the organisation and significance of the chapel in noble households during this period, see K. Mertes, *The English Noble Household 1250–1600* (Oxford, 1988), ch. 5. Mertes comments that 'nearly every aristocratic household, large or small, had the means for creating a religious community', but 'a great deal depended on' the individual lord's or lady's 'own sense of piety'. Such piety could work 'to bond the household into a spiritual unit', *ibid.*, 146. This was something which clearly happened at Battle.

[23] In Elizabeth's reign, Lady Magdalen occasionally petitioned Sir Julius Caesar in his official capacity as a master of the court of requests, BL, Additional MS 12506, fo. 73r. See also *CSPD 1601–3*, 147; BL, Additional MS 12506, fos. 161r, 173r; L. M. Hill, *Bench and Bureaucracy* (1988), 2, 3.

Figure 24.   A view of the interior of the 'novices' chamber' at the south end of the east range of Battle Abbey. This is one possible location, suggested by local historians, for the celebration of Mass at the direction of Lady Magdalen Browne, Viscountess Montague.

This, however, did not mean, of itself, that the Catholics at Battle were seen as entirely unobjectionable. There were some intensely hostile reports during the 1590s about what the dowager viscountess was up to. Her critics believed that she was having a cataclysmically evil effect on religious and political culture in East Sussex.

Reading between the lines of Smith's biography, sometimes merely reading the lines themselves, we are often inclined to wonder how 'normal' and uncontentious Lady Magdalen's supposedly everyday charitable impulses were. Smith adds that 'her alms, distributed every second day at her gates unto the poor, were plentiful and such as some of the richer Protestants did calumniate that they augmented the number of beggars and nourished their idleness'.[24] In late 1597 one of those who was doing the distributing of these alms was, it seems, the wife of a local recusant Edward Goldwyer who would be repeatedly fined and sequestrated in James's reign. In Lady Magdalen's accounts we find listed John Cape's 'allowance of money by him delivered to the hands of Mistris Goldwier at Battle this 8 November 1597 to be by her distributed to certen pore people there by her ladyships appoyntment at her departure from thence', as she and her household moved off to London. Even though the sum involved was only twelve shillings it is possible that to a censurer of the Browne household and establishment at Battle this might look like a Catholic exercise in attracting the popular acclaim of the ignorant and unwashed, and therefore might be justifiably regarded as socially and politically undesirable.[25]

Smith sweetly hit the nail directly on the head when he noted both that the locals called Battle Abbey 'Little Rome' and that 'the very name of Rome is to most so odious that they use all their industry and utmost endeavour to extinguish it'. Smith's hagiography does rather imply that Lady Magdalen did not merely practise her religion but positively flaunted it.

She did serve God publicly in the sight of all, that by her example she might encourage all; and, when she walked abroad, by her beads or cross which she used to wear about her neck she professed herself to be a Catholic, even to whatsoever heretical beholders; and so manifest was her religion that scarce any in England had heard her name who knew her not also to be a Catholic.[26]

As we have already remarked, Smith said that Lady Magdalen suggested he should set up his own printing press in her house. (Presumably this was in some way connected with the composition of his polemical book against the much-hated renegade priest Thomas Bell, which Smith published in 1605,

---

[24] Southern, *ERH*, 40.
[25] ESRO, RAF 3/4, fo. 26r. For Edward Goldwyer, see *NAGB*, 95, 104, 168.
[26] Southern, *ERH*, 44.

although the book was eventually printed at Douai.[27]) Smith glossed this as simply an aspect of her piety and zeal. 'Yea, so far stretched the fortitude of this blessed woman in propagating the Catholic faith that she twice offered me leave to set up a press to print Catholic books in her house, which had been done but that it was most difficult and almost impossible in such an ample family to conceal such a matter from heretics.' Smith was not joking. The search for secret presses early in James's reign was a regular obsession and employment of spies and informers such as William Udall.[28]

In these circumstances, it was not surprising that Lady Magdalen excited a certain amount of local hostility. There is an acerbic report about her and her entourage which bears reciting in some detail. Written at some point in or shortly after late September 1597,[29] it claimed that 'since the Lady Montagues coming to dwel at Battle', by which the writer presumably meant to dwell permanently, i.e. after the death of her husband, 'religion in that countrey, and especially in that towne, is greatly decayed; as may appear by these fewe poyntes'. Among the 'poyntes' were the fact that

D. Withens, deane of Battle, where the Lady Montague lyeth, is suspected to be very backward in religion. For this 2 yeares and more he nether ministreth the communion, nor receaveth it. But commonly if there be a communion he getteth some other to doe it and ether getteth himselfe out of the towne or keepeth his house. His wife cometh scarse twise a year to church.

She and her children refused to receive communion.[30] The writer continued that Withens was so flagrant in his brand of Catholicism that the 'company which he keepeth is most with recusantes, especially one D. Gray',

---

[27] Richard Smith, *An Answer to Thomas Bels Late Challeng* (Douai, 1605). Conceivably the offer of the press may have been for the printing of Smith's address to James I written in 1603–4. The only surviving copies are from the second edition: Richard Smith, *Epistola Historica de Mutuis Officiis inter Sedem Apostolicam & Magnae Britanniae Reges Christianos, Anglice olim Scripta, ad Seren. M. Britanniae Regem Iacobum* (Cologne [imprint false, printed at Paris], 1637; ARCR I, no. 1094); AAW, A XXVIII, no. 171, p. 557 (Smith to John Southcot, 7/17 October 1636, mentioning that almost all the copies of the original edition had been burnt).

[28] Harris, 'Reports', *passim*.

[29] BL, Lansdowne MS 82, no. 49, fo. 103r–v. The report's reference to Francis Dacre's servant John Johnson fixes the date after 24 September 1597.

[30] Withens was appointed dean of Battle in March 1572 and took the rectory of Northiam in May 1576 (the previous rector having been appointed by the first Viscount Montague), Peckham, 'Institutions'. He resigned on 2 November 1583 when Richard Frewen instituted John Frewen there in his place. In Lady Magdalen's account book for 1597 Withens is mentioned as in receipt of the 'pencion' to which the dean of the exempt jurisdiction of Battle was entitled in the original grant of Battle Abbey to Sir Anthony Browne, ESRO, RAF 3/4, fo. 22v; *VCH Sussex* IX, 106. Withens had been vice-chancellor of Oxford university. His funeral brass (see Figure 25) is in St Mary's parish church, Battle, Mosse, *ME*, 24. For his will of 28 September 1614, see PRO, PROB 11/125, fo. 479v.

Figure 25.   Funeral brass of John Withens, dean of Battle (d. 1614) in Battle
parish church (St Mary), East Sussex.

presumably the Marian priest Robert Gray;[31] and also one 'M. [Edward] Terry'.[32] Terry 'was a scholmayster in Battle and had the bringing up of most of the gentlemen in that countrey. He likewise was committed . . . by Sir Francis Walsingham and hath continued in prison till Lent last, and then came to Battle, wher he now dwelleth, a recusant, and is suspected to doe much harme.' He and Withens were 'great companions'.[33] The writer knew quite a lot about Robert Gray. He was a 'priest, whom Sir Francys Walsingham [had once] committed [to prison], and about a year agoe he was confined' again; but now he had been released and 'liveth in my ladyes house, being suspected to doe much harme both with the deane and other theraboutes', quite a tribute to the aged and quivering wreck who had confessed everything to Topcliffe in 1593.[34] He also 'of late . . . hath found out an holy wel in Battle parke, whither many, especially women, resort, like a . . . pilgrimage; and called it D. Grayes wel'. There had 'bene above a score together there at evening prayer tyme on a Sunday'.

Evidently this hostile critic of Lady Magdalen's household did not regard all this as a proper part of the natural economy of gentry and aristocratic religion, or of any 'live-and-let-live' arrangement with the State. He noted that 'the jurisdiction of the place is in the deane; wholly exempt from the byshops visitation; and is altogether neglected by him; so that they doe what the[y] list'. As we saw, Bishop Curteys had enquired about this matter in 1570 and had been persuaded to leave the issue alone.[35] In Battle there were many 'that never receave the communion; and come very seldome at church'. This was the bad side of partial conformity, a slap in the face for the regime rather than an acceptable compromise. Undoubtedly, had Withens been asked to answer these charges, he would have said that he was a good conformist and helped to ensure conformity as best he could. In October 1593, as Timothy McCann has ascertained, Withens and the churchwardens of Battle were admonishing Alice Terry, the schoolmaster's wife, that 'she shoulde resorte

---

[31] Gray died in 1597, i.e. at around the time that this hostile account of Lady Magdalen was written, and was buried in the church of St Saviour, Southwark, F. T. Dollman, *The Priory of St. Mary Overie, Southwark* (1881), 29.

[32] T. J. McCann, 'Catholic Schoolmasters in Sussex, 1558–1603: Addenda and Corrigenda to Beales's Catholic Schoolmasters', *RH* 12 (1973–4), 235–7, at pp. 236–7. See ch. 2, p. 32 above. Bishop Curteys's list (of 26 October 1577) of recusants in Chichester diocese includes 'Tarry, late of Battle, schoolmaster', PRO, SP 12/117/15, fo. 36r.

[33] In 1597, aged about seventy-four, Terry was still in receipt of a pension from Lady Magdalen, ESRO, RAF 3/4, fo. 21v. In mid-April 1593 he had been interrogated, at about the same time that other Browne retainers were being arrested and interrogated, although Terry had been in prison in London for a year already. He had been detained on a privy council warrant by Richard Young. 'The cause of his comitting was for recusancy', but he was 'not indicted to his knowledge'. He had been a recusant for twelve years, and intended to stay that way. He claimed to have had no dealings with seminarists, but would not swear to that effect, McCann, 'Catholic Schoolmasters', 236.

[34] See ch. 6, p. 201 above.   [35] See ch. 2, pp. 32–3 above.

and come to the church', though 'she saythe yt ys againste her conscience to goe unto the churche nowe', 'but yf she can bee persuaded in her minde she will doe yt'.[36] We may suspect that critics of Withens and of other hangers-on in Lady Magdalen's entourage and circle would not have regarded this kind of 'enforcement' of conformity as particularly stringent, in fact hardly an enforcement at all.

The noncommunicants and partial conformists in the region were, however, not just ageing schoolmasters and superannuated Church-of-England clergymen. 'On the other side of Battle parke', at Catsfield, 'dwelleth Mr Edmond Pelham, the chiefest justice of peace in that rape, and ruleth most; who is very backward in religion himselfe, cometh to church but slakly' and 'hath not this twelvemonth and more receaved the communion'. His wife, Eleanor, 'was a profest recusant both when the[y] dwelt at Battle and wher they now dwel'. At this time Eleanor's family, the Darells, were starting to suffer serious harassment. Their residence at Scotney Castle would be turned upside down more than once as the local Protestant justices searched in vain for the Jesuit Richard Blount.[37] Perhaps this increasing pressure was what caused Eleanor to lapse into partial conformity. Lady Magdalen's critic noted that, 'since the last parlament', Eleanor 'hath bene at church; and now useth it twise or thrise a yeare; but she never receaveth the communion'. Pelham himself 'hath two daughters maryed, who never received the communion, and come to church as the mother doth'. Anyway, Pelham was 'chiefe of my Lady Montagues counsel'. And he was 'a great man with the deane of Battle', i.e. John Withens.[38]

The anonymous critic alleged that the Darell household had a destabilising effect on the county, and that Pelham was not prepared to do anything about it. 'A litle before the siege of Calis', which began when Spanish soldiers arrived outside the town in March 1596,[39] 'one Mr Dorrel of Scotney, a notorious recusant', presumably Pelham's brother-in-law Henry Darell, 'lay there hovering about toward the sea coast'. And, 'at the poynt that our men wer to be shipped from Rye and Dover to Calis', one of the Darell household's servants 'mounted upon a gelding worth 20 markes and wel appoynted, having a case of pistols, rid thorow Sussex and a great part'

---

[36] McCann, 'Catholic Schoolmasters', 236–7.

[37] See ch. 2, p. 44 above. Pelham had in 1587 been noted in a survey of the justices as a 'cold' professor in religion, Hasler, *HC*, III, 192–3; H. Ellis (ed.), 'Certificate concerning the Justices of the Peace in Sussex in 1587', *SAC* 2 (1849), 58–60, at p. 58. Allegedly Eleanor Pelham had been reconciled to Rome in her brother Henry Darell's house, BL, Lansdowne MS 72, no. 67, fo. 184r.

[38] In Lady Magdalen's 1597 accounts, money had been disbursed 'to Mr Pelham and to Mr Forster for counsell 20ˢ and for drawinge and ingrossinge of an answere returned into the chancery', ESRO, RAF 3/4, fo. 22v.

[39] W. MacCaffrey, *Elizabeth I: War and Politics 1588–1603* (Princeton, 1992), 202.

of the Kentish weald, 'with an alarum that the Spaniardes were landed at 3 places in Sussex, had burned Borne and Pemsey . . . and could not be stayed'. But he 'left his cloke in a cunstables hand; and, being pursued, forsooke his horse and ran two miles a foote, till he was taken and brought to Rye'.

The justice in front of whom he was brought was none other than Pelham. In the company of other JPs, Pelham merely 'rebuked him and committed him to the towne house', though 'many gentlemen there were of opinion that he should be sent' to appear in front of the privy council.

Pelham would probably have argued that Darell's servant was nothing but a crackpot. According to our hostile critic, however, 'upon that false alarum there was the greatest hurly burly [and] wofullest outcryes of people . . . that ever was in mans memory. The soldiers at Rye [were] ready to march out of the towne toward Borne; and the service [was] greatly hindred by that meanes.' At this point 'my Lady Montagues people, seeing the towne of Battle in that uprore and miserable state, rejoyced and shewed signes of joy; insomuch that the people fel to great exclamations and cursinges of them openly in the streates'. Further, 'when newes was brought that Calis was won, they gave out thes speeches: God be thanked, we shall have better neyghboures'.[40]

It is possible that Lady Magdalen experienced similar censures in her parish of St Saviour in Southwark. The parish vestry minute book of St Saviour's shows, in 1593, that 'a new dore should be made in our church wall entringe into my L. Mountacutes howse in place of the old dore stopped up of late by some one of the church wardens withowt consent of the rest'.[41] This entry suggests that the blocking up of the door may have occurred, if only briefly, after the death of the first viscount. Perhaps there was, even if among only a minority of the parish, a certain unwillingness that one of the leading receptacles of papists in London, now no longer under the eye of the deceased conformist first viscount, should admit of direct access to the local parish church. Certainly the puritan lecturers whom Paul Seaver has discovered at St Saviour's during Lady Magdalen's time would have been less than impressed with her religious stance.[42]

Smith's account of Lady Magdalen's life insisted, as we saw, that she had banished all the passions of the mind induced by the ruin of the Dacre family.[43] But, of course, in the 1590s, her brother, Francis Dacre, who had suffered a good deal more ruin than she had, and who seriously resented it, was still running around Europe, offering his services to anyone he thought

---

[40] BL, Lansdowne MS 82, no. 49, fo. 103r.
[41] LMA, P92/SAV/450, p. 284; Dollman, *The Priory of St. Mary Overie, Southwark*, 29.
[42] See P. Seaver, *The Puritan Lectureships* (1975), 106, 150, 214, 217, 224, 234, 236.
[43] See ch. 3, pp. 73–4 above.

might restore him to what he considered to be his rightful estate. His servant John Whitfield confessed, under interrogation in November 1593, that 'Fraunces Dacres went into Scotlande the xviith daie of September now fowre yeeres past, being moved thereunto by discontentement, because he received not such favour at her Majest[i]e's handes as he expected.'[44] He took his son and heir with him. The lad was to be educated in the French and Latin tongues at Douai. The intention was that he should eventually go to serve at the Spanish Court. While in Scotland, Francis 'conversed with . . . the Earl Bothwell for the most parte untill the erle was imprisoned', and then with leading Scottish Catholic peers. And 'he was called the Lord Dacres amongest all the lordes and gentry in Scotland'. Prior to his departure from James VI's realm in autumn 1591 he 'receved letters from Bruxelles' from various people. Among them was the brother-in-law of the martyr Margaret Clitherow, William, who had been an associate of, and secretary to, the first Viscount Montague's chaplain Alban Langdale. He also obtained commendatory letters from Sir John Seton to several Spanish notables to admit him 'into the fronter townes in Spaine', and in particular a letter to Sir William Semple in Spain who was already infamous because he 'did yeelde the towne' of Lierre 'in the Low Countries to the Spaniardes'. Once Dacre was in Spain he conferred with Semple on many occasions.[45]

Whitfield claimed that Dacre had been in contact with the duchess of Feria, and also with 'Sir Francis Englefild and Father [Robert] Personnes', in order 'to further him in his sutes to the king'. Englefield and Persons referred him to Don Juan de Idiaquez and to the Scottish Jesuit William Creighton. In Madrid, Dacre finally met Creighton, Englefield and the duchess. Persons had supplied him with a spiel to present to Philip II, though it was 'in some thinges' altered by Creighton. 'The effect was to make yt knowne to the king' how Dacre's

---

[44] Whitfield's examination of 15 November 1593 was taken by Lord Keeper Puckering and was signed also by Sir Thomas Heneage, who was kin to the second Viscount Montague, and the overseer of the first viscount's will, WSRO, SAS/BA 67. Heneage had married the second viscount's aunt, the widow of the earl of Southampton. The viscount's parliamentary patronage at Midhurst was made available to Heneage, some of whose nominees held this seat, including e.g. in 1589 Samuel, the son of the martyrologist John Foxe, Hasler, *HC*, II, 155–6. Some Catholics reported that Heneage himself had Catholics in his entourage, PRO, SP 12/248/99, fo. 221r.

[45] CRS 60, 91–2; CRS 2, 180. Whitfield confessed also that 'in the Lent before Mr Dacre went out of Scotland he sent me with a letter out of Scotland . . . to his daughter', Frances Dacre, 'at Sir Robert Dormers hous in Buckingham shire'. Dacre wanted Frances to journey north into Scotland and then they would depart for Spain 'ther to be with the duches of Feria', although Lady Dormer (Montague's daughter, and the duchess's sister-in-law) refused to release her. But she nevertheless 'delivered by his daughter unto me thre messadges sent as tokens from Mistris Dormer to the duches of Feria in the behalf of Francis Dacre that she would be a help unto hym in his buusines [*sic*]', CRS 5, 227.

brethren had dyed in his service, and that the cause of their bannishment was in respect of conscience; and that, after the death of both his brethren, he made title to the lande and was barred from the common lawe of the realme and justice; and was well thought of nether by the quene nor the counsell because he was Catholikely affected; that he thought himself happie to be dryven into a Catholique countrie, where he might live in the service of God untill yt should please God to sende a Catholique prince in[to] his countrie who, he hoped, would restore him to all the lyving which was his auncestors.

Creighton evidently wanted Dacre to go back to Scotland and exert his influence there; Persons presumably did not. (Creighton and Persons would soon be engaged in a bitter quarrel about how far Catholics should unequivocally support James VI.[46]) Dacre 'was perswaded by Father Creighton that the king would have graunted him his pencion to have ben paid in Scotland, because he was most able to doe the king service in Scotland, as he informed the king'.

According to Whitfield, Dacre, 'after his coming into Spaine, was lett to understande that those Englishmen that offered service to the king, and desired entertaynement of him, must sett downe howe and wherein they could doe the king service'. So he worked out a project for an incursion across England's northern border. He came to the conclusion that 'the best waie to invade Englande was to lande forces in Scotlande at Kirkowbre, neere to Dumfrise, and not farr from Carlyle, and so to passe into England uppon the west borders'. This was the area where Dacre was 'borne and best knowne and befrended; and there was the place that he could doe the king best service'. One of Sir William Stanley's men, Francis Jackson, told Dacre that Persons 'was of an other opinion, and thought the best waie for invasion of England was neere unto London; and therefore', if Dacre 'did take that course, Father Personnes would geve him no furtheraunce'.[47]

Although Dacre obtained a pension from Philip of eighty crowns a month, he was clearly not going to supplant Persons in the Spaniards' confidence and conferences. Disillusioned, 'he departed from Madrid towardes Rome before the king had signed his warraunt for the same pencion', though it was paid to him afterwards by Creighton's means.[48]

---

[46] See T. M. McCoog, 'Harmony Disrupted: Robert Parsons, S.J., William Crichton, S.J., and the Question of Elizabeth's Successor, 1581–1603', *Archivum Historicum Societatis Iesu* 73 (2004), 149–220.

[47] CRS 60, 92–4; ch. 3, p. 74 above.

[48] CRS 60, 94; A. J. Loomie, *The Spanish Elizabethans* (New York, 1963), 105–6. Francis Dacre's supposed enmity with the Jesuits was widely written up and reported in the course of the appellant dispute. In William Watson's preface to Thomas Bluet's *Important Considerations* (1601), sig. **4v, it is alleged that Robert Persons victimised anyone among the exiles who did not wholeheartedly endorse the infanta's right to succeed Elizabeth, and 'this disfavouring, disgusting, and utterly refusing to applaude to Parsons Spanified title, was the originall, chiefe and only cause of the high disgrace which sundrie of our nation lived in

What all this amounted to was that someone quite close to the centre of the Browne family, reckoned by many to be a political loose cannon, was parading about all over the Continent, trying to inflect James VI's dynastic ambitions with a pro-Catholic gloss. Dacre had been in contact with the English priest at the top of the 'most wanted' list in the northern province, John Boste, whom the regime also knew had once been a servant in the first viscount's household. In November 1593 Edward Pemberton told the customs official Anthony Atkinson that at Douai the recent arrest of Boste 'was talked over . . . and how he was a bishop, and God be thanked of his long reign for he had done much good'. Also, 'the Lord Dacres' had been 'at Doway a month past', and the king of Spain had allowed him '40 crowns a month, and he had a pension of the pope', and it was rumoured that he would try to get back into England in a few months' time.[49] Whitfield confessed that in the summer before Dacre fled Scotland for Spain he sought Boste's 'counsell' about 'what was best for hym to doe as touching his going into Spain or into Flanders first, and also he desiered his company to have gone with him'.[50]

Not surprisingly, Dacre was attainted at the end of 1593.[51] Whitfield volunteered the information that

a messadg came to Francis Dacre when he was in Scotland that he should haisten hymself out of Scotland for ther was no goodnesse meant hym by her Majestie nor her counsell but delay of tyme. He knewe not from whence the messadg came . . . but it came from one who was of creditt both with her Majestie and with the councell, and as he thought it came from my Lord Mountague or some frindes of his in the South.

The fact that Dacre and many other Catholic exiles had finally realised that there was going to be no successful Spanish military descent on Elizabeth's realm, and now sought to make their peace with the regime, did not, in

beyond the seas, ever since that faction began to waxe hote; but especially it was the cause of the Lord Dacre his departure out of Spaine, and all other of the Spanish dominions, suffering many gusts, calamities, and dishonorable calumnies, as slaundered by the Jesuiticall Spanish faction to be a spie for England, to have intended to have set the Spanishe fleete on fire . . . and that his lordship came but into Scotland to colour his vices, as being (say they most injuriously and falsly) a libertine, an atheist, of no religion. And all this because true Camillus-like he stoode on the behalfe of his soveraigne, the kingdome, and the crowne of England, against the Spanish infantaes surmised title to the same.' See also Watson, *Decacordon*, 38, 113, 147–8, 176–7; cf. Robert Persons, *A Manifestation of the Great Folly and Bad Spirit of Certayne in England Calling Themselves Secular Priestes* (Antwerp, 1602), fos. 50r, 109r–v [sig. Eer–v], refuting Watson's claims.

[49] *HMCS* XIII, 497.

[50] Apparently Boste said that 'if he had knowen Francis Dacres purpose before he had gone forth of England, he could have gotten him passadg from Newcastell or theraboutes in a ship that had commed laitly out of Flanders to Flanders again before his going out of England', CRS 5, 226–7.

[51] CRS 60, 96.

many Protestants' eyes, make up for these exiles' earlier lapses of political judgment. In fact, the prospect of the wild geese coming home was probably more offensive than the fact of their flight from the realm in the first place. In a letter of December 1595, Dacre wrote from Liège to his eldest daughter Eleanor asking her 'to deal with their friends to employ their credit so that, by some honourable means procured from her Majesty, their house may be restored to its ancient state, and pardon and licence obtained for him and his son to return to their country's service'. She was to allege in support of his petition that 'he and his son' had left the king of Spain's dominions and service. Dacre mentioned that his dearest friends included his sister Lady Magdalen and his nephew Francis Clifford.[52]

Other reports, in September/October 1596, insisted that Dacre was still among the number of the English Catholics who were being relied upon to publicise James's claim to succeed Elizabeth and to draw James to favour the Catholic cause.[53] Of course, there is nothing here which suggests that Lady Magdalen had ever been in sympathy with Dacre's politics. In fact, when John Johnson, one of Dacre's servants, turned up in Battle in autumn 1597, she facilitated his arrest and made sure that he was taken up to London.[54] The JP Henry Apsley reported to Lord Buckhurst on 25 September that 'this last night . . . came one John Jonson to Batell, born at Antwerp (as he says) and now serves Mr Francis Dacres, who is at Paris, whom he left about the 25th of September (French style) with letters for Mistress Elinor Dacres his daughter, which were delivered to Mistress Elizabeth Dacres her sister, Mistress Elinor not being well'. This spurred Lady Magdalen into action. She caused Johnson to be apprehended. He was bundled off to Apsley 'with that letter and others addressed to the earl of Essex or Lady Warwick'.[55] Dacre's letters protested loyalty to Elizabeth and claimed that he was no longer inclined to remain in the service of the king of Spain. On the same day Lady Magdalen herself reported the arrest to Lord Burghley, remarking particularly upon the packet of correspondence to the earl of Essex. She said that

in regard to my duty to her Majesty I presently sent my servant and a constable to take the messenger and his letters to Mr Apsley, the next justice to me; still I could not hold myself satisfied without writing to you, not doubting that, if upon examination the matter fall out to be no way undutiful or against his allegiance, I shall have your favour for his suit. I have also sent up my niece to testify to the manner and matter, if necessary.[56]

But our critical writer did not view Lady Magdalen's vaunted 'loyalty' so favourably. He noted that 'there was apprehended at Battle a welaged

[52] *HMCS* XIII, 547.   [53] See e.g. *CSP Scotland 1595–7*, 320–1.
[54] See Manning, *Religion*, 161.   [55] *HMCS* VII, 396.   [56] *Ibid.*, 401.

man', i.e. John Johnson.[57] Johnson 'confessed that he was servaunt to one
Mr Dacres brother to the Lady Montague' and that 'he then came from
his sayd mayster with letters and messages to his maysters daughters being
then with the sayd lady. The constable threatned to send him away unles he
could find suretyes. Wherupon he sent into my ladyships house, and some
of her gentlemen becam suertyes for him.' The writer was far from sure that
Johnson had not in fact received a covert welcome from this supposedly loyal
Catholic household.[58] (In the margin of Lady Magdalen's critic's narrative
was added the note that 'when Calis was taken, ther was much speech at
Battle of the great services that the sayd Dacres' had performed there.)

   And, the critic fumed, had anything very strenuous or rigorous in fact been
done about all this? No, it had not. For 'the next day M. Henry Apsley came
to the towne' and 'the constable desired him to examine the man . . . and . . . to
cary him to' Lady Magdalen's friend 'Mr Edmund Pelham'. On the next
morning Pelham turned up, 'tooke the man from the officer, thanked the
constable for his good service, and sayd he would send him up to the lord
treasurer'. However, the constable and 'other honest men' suspected that 'it
was not soe done'. They had been fobbed off 'to stop their further com-
playnt'. Indeed, Lord Buckhurst was intensely embarrassed and refused to
deal any further in the matter, on the grounds of his kinship to the Brownes,
even though he had received a packet of Dacre's 'letters . . . sent . . . by
the old Lady Montague'.[59] To a suspicious mind, such as our critic's or the
constable's, it would not have helped to know that Lady Magdalen had only
recently been lobbying her godson, Sir Julius Caesar, on Dacre's behalf.[60]

   The great hoo-ha in which Edmund Pelham turned up to collar the miscre-
ant looked like a charade to dupe local public opinion. And indeed, though
Johnson was sent up to London, he was accompanied by Lady Magdalen's
trusted servant, James Gildridge, the bailiff of Battle, who himself had well-
known recusant relatives.[61] (Lady Magdalen's accounts for 1597 record that

---

[57] Our writer dated this incident 'a litle before the siege of Calis', although Johnson was arrested
   in Battle on 24 September 1597, i.e. at least eighteen months later.
[58] See also *HMCS* XIV, 57.
[59] BL, Lansdowne MS 82, no. 49, fo. 103r–v; *HMCS* VII, 402; Hatfield House, Cecil MS 55,
   fo. 72r.
[60] On 26 July 1597 Lady Magdalen had informed Caesar that 'althoughe your extraordinary
   and freendely care . . . hathe not as yet taken that effect with hir Majesty as wee hoped',
   yet the queen was apparently still extending her 'grace and bounty bothe toward my neeces
   and my self', and so Lady Magdalen had directed Dacre's daughter Eleanor to keep trying to
   make friends at Court, even though the queen was less than impressed by Dacre's 'undutyfull
   regarde of suche meanes as have beene offered him for his retourne', BL, Lansdowne MS
   158, fo. 10r.
[61] James Gildridge was 'baylief of Battell and collector of the rentes of Battell, Agmerhurst and
   the colledg of Hastings', ESRO, RAF 3/4, fo. 1r. The Gildridge family was one of the leading
   Catholic clans in the east of the county. The main recusant branch of the family was based

Gildridge claimed an allowance of forty-two shillings and four pence for 'the charges of him self and of John Johnson servaunte unto Mr Frauncis [Dacre] stayenge in London and attendinge at the Court concerninge certen lettres sent from the said Mr Dacres unto the lordes of the counsell'.[62]) We may suspect that Lady Magdalen wanted as favourable a gloss put upon Johnson's arrival as was possible in the circumstances.

Other dubious persons, not native to the district, were also hanging about Battle. There were real doubts whether the local security service was any use, and it was 'an easy matter for any seminarie priestes or seditious persons to be landed there'. It was known that at Pevensey there was 'one Martin', a 'sercher', whose wife had become 'a professed Catholique and recusant' three or four years before. He lived 'in a lone house, hard by the haven syde, and keepeth a great inne'. There were others dwelling in the same area, recusant separatists such as Henry Norton, whose movements were suspicious. In fine, 'the number of recusantes dayly increaseth in the countrey; and religion sensibly goeth backward'.[63]

In November 1600 a candidate for the seminary programme in Rome, one John Browne (no relation to the family at Cowdray), related that he had decided to go abroad after converting to Catholicism, and was, in early 1600, 'captured while waiting on the shore, and was placed for 3 or 4 days in a prison of lethal squalor'. He was carried up to London and was interrogated by Lord Cobham, lord warden of the Cinque Ports, who suspected both that he was a priest and that he was carrying letters to France from Lady Magdalen or, possibly, from her brother-in-law Sir Alexander Culpeper.[64] Browne was then sent (by Lord Buckhurst) to the Marshalsea where he met William Singleton and Francis Barnaby.[65] Barnaby was shortly to become a chaplain to the deceased first viscount's sister Mabel, countess of Kildare. Singleton advised him not to be formally received into the Church of Rome before he was released because, 'having been captured at a dangerous time, and being a former guest of Lady Montague and Sir Alexander Culpeper, both Catholics, he would certainly be hanged if he was discovered to be a Catholic'.[66]

Some of the local justices tried, shortly after James's accession, to break up Lady Magdalen's household, though, according to Richard Smith, they were restrained by order of the council. Smith narrated that 'some few years

at Beddingham, next door to the Gages at West Firle. For James Gildridge's will (of 1 April 1625), in which he bequeaths his soul to the Blessed Trinity, see PRO, PROB 11/145, fo. 303r.
[62] ESRO, RAF 3/4, fo. 4v.
[63] BL, Lansdowne MS 82, no. 49, fo. 103v. For Henry Norton, see ch. 6, p. 187 above.
[64] Culpeper had died in January 1600.
[65] Barnaby was in the Marshalsea from 13 June 1599 to October 1601, Anstr. I, 22–3.
[66] CRS 54, 98.

Figure 26.   The gatehouse of Battle Abbey, East Sussex.

before her death certain Protestants, in hatred of her religion', unsuccessfully 'sought the destruction of her and all her family'. Their leader was the Protestant JP Sir Thomas May who ordered the arrest of her servants. But he was himself shortly afterwards 'ignominiously convented before public authority and cast into prison for debt, where he lay long, and at the setting forth of this work was shamefully dismissed of the commission of the peace'.[67] There were others too, notably one Nicholas Cobbe of Battle, who entertained a pathological hatred of her. But he got his just deserts. For 'a little after he began to seek the ruin of the Lady Magdalen', he had 'a knife thrust into his belly by his own wife'. And 'being for some heinous fact apprehended by officers, and even by heretics pursued to punishment', he 'at length by letters' was compelled to 'beg pardon of the Lady Magdalen'. And there was another man called Benet who, frustrated beyond measure that his plans to bring about her downfall had not taken effect, took to standing outside the gatehouse at Battle (see Figure 26) and screaming abuse at her. But he took

---

[67] Southern, *ERH*, 53. May is listed in the Southwark sacramental token books as dwelling in 1605 in Montague Close. The alleged incident may well have taken place in Southwark rather than in Sussex, Southern, *ERH*, 83; LMA, P92/SAV/197, p. 22.

his own life, presumably driven thereto by his own malice and the will of God.[68]

Even Richard Smith admits that her 'courageous constancy' 'bred her great envy in her heretical neighbours', though apparently not until after she had been in Sussex for a good many years. These neighbours 'presented her name and the names of almost all her family to the judges in public assizes for not observing the law of coming to church every month . . . upon which law the Lady Magdalen was the first of the nobility that ever in England was accused in public judgment'.[69] Smith claimed that she responded to the news of these measures against her with complete equanimity, a 'pleasing countenance' and a protestation of loyalty to King James.[70] But her emergence into overt recusancy, made by Smith to look so gradual and so easily explicable, was clearly not perceived with charity or equanimity by some of her neighbours.[71]

After all, most of what we know about Lady Magdalen's circle comes from inside it. The surviving record of this family, as indeed with so much Catholicism during the period, is a self-image. When set against this self-image, the carping of anti-popish commentators looks, to modern eyes, decidedly weird. For there is no evidence that Lady Magdalen and her friends were ever involved in political conspiracies, or even seriously tried to challenge the power and authority of the local State.

But the perception of these Catholics by hostile Protestant observers was, one suspects, a reaction to more intangible and less easily defined characteristics and attitudes – the kind which do not generally find their way into the archival records on which historians tend to rely. After her death, Catholic clergy reported searches and sequestrations of some intensity in East Sussex, particularly around the Battle area in *c.* 1610–12, though they tended to gloss it as simply part of a wider unfocused persecution which, they claimed, was the same in all places at all times.[72] Among those who were noted by the priest Benjamin Norton as subject to the predatory attentions of the 'knaves' was David Lomer, who held property at Battle and was probably

---

[68] Southern, *ERH*, 53–4.   [69] *Ibid.*, 46.   [70] *Ibid.*, 45.

[71] Admittedly, she continued to enjoy official protection. After the Gunpowder plot she secured an order from the privy council that the imminent search of her house, presumably Montague House rather than Battle Abbey, should be carried out by four JPs of her own choice. A search in 1606 to arrest one of her priests quasi-miraculously came to no effect. The priest left London for Battle unobserved. Another attempt (by her enemy Nicholas Cobbe) to arrest the same priest as he left Battle Abbey also failed, Southern, *ERH*, 55–6. When, in 1607, the issue of her non-attendance at church was raised, 'she was so far from incurring any detriment thereby as that it wrought her more security than before'. The privy council via a letter of 19 April 1607 to the attorney-general 'commanded that no sentence should proceed against her', on the grounds of her status, age and former fidelity to Queen Elizabeth, Southern, *ERH*, 54. In the Cecil papers there is a letter of 16 April 1607 from the earl of Shrewsbury, her kinsman, to the earl of Salisbury petitioning on her behalf, *HMCS XIX*, 97.

[72] *NAGB*, 104, 168.

in the Browne family's service.[73] Similarly prosecuted was the former clerk of Lady Magdalen's kitchen, John Cape.[74] And so was Edward Wyborne, a relative by marriage of Benjamin Norton. (As we have seen, one of the Wybornes had been resident at Cowdray with the first viscount, and was then named by Topcliffe as being with Lady Magdalen after the viscount's death.[75]) He was regularly dealt with for his religion and recusancy during the Jacobean period.[76]

By no stretch of the imagination, therefore, can Lady Magdalen's household at Battle in the late sixteenth and early seventeenth centuries be seen as ideologically vacant, a reflection of how things were in pre-seminarist times, or an example of what happened when Catholicism allegedly withdrew from political reality and the wider world into the gentrified atmosphere of the country house.

Of course, by mid-1608 Lady Magdalen was dead.[77] But her demise actually seems to have given her clergy the opportunity to engage in the intra-Catholic factional quarrels of this period in a way that they had not previously done. The seeds of their future activism had, in effect, been nurtured in her household during her lifetime. Certainly the clergy who looked directly to the Brownes did not underestimate the force of her contribution to their cause. In 1609, Richard Smith related that his own boss, 'the most reverend archpriest of England, M. George Birkhead, in his letters directed to me, lamented her death, as it were, said he, of a great mother in Israel, and the priests in England did everywhere extol her as the worthy patroness of the holy faith and the singular ornament of the Catholic religion in England'.[78] Smith also remembered her as a guarantor of the Catholicism of the Browne family, impliedly a far more effective one than her husband had been. For 'whereas she left living above thirty of her children, nephews and nieces,

---

[73] *Ibid.*, 104. Sir George Browne's son had a servant called Edward Lomer (presumably a relative of David Lomer) who was one of the beneficiaries mentioned in Sir George Browne's will of 21 November 1614, PRO, PROB 11/125, fo. 488r–v.

[74] *NAGB*, 104; ESRO, RAF 3/4, fos. 8r, 25r. The Cape family were retainers of the Brownes, A. F. Allison, 'Franciscan Books in English, 1559–1640', *RH* 3 (1955), 16–65, at pp. 48–9. John Cape, who served Lady Magdalen, was a relative, perhaps the father, of William Cape who in 1610 was a factor for Richard Smith when Smith was trying to sell his books in England, ESRO, RAF 3/4, fo. 10r; *NAGB*, 75.

[75] See ch. 6, p. 197 above.

[76] See PRO, SO 3/4 (January 1608); PRO SO 3/5 (March 1610); PRO, E 368/549, mem. 192e; *HMCS* XVIII, 359–60; *NAGB*, 92. Wyborne seems to have married Susanna, daughter of Richard Warnford of Sevenhampton, Wiltshire, who, it appears, was the priest Benjamin Norton's half-sister. (Norton's mother is referred to in 1580s' documents as 'Mrs Warnford'; Norton in his letters always refers to Wyborne's wife with affection, BL, Additional MS 37140; *NAGB, passim*; Mott, HR, 283.)

[77] She died on 8 April 1608, after suffering a stroke in January of the same year, PRO, C 142/304/31; GEC IX, 99.

[78] Southern, *ERH*, 65.

she left them all constant professors of the Catholic faith'. And the constant profession which she inculcated was no cultural formality. 'Albeit she most tenderly affected her children, yet she so much preferred faith before nature that she would often say she should exceedingly rejoice to see any of them to die for the Catholic faith. Neither do I doubt but, if Almighty God had tried her, we should have seen in her the courage of the mother of the Machabees.'[79]

[79] *Ibid.*, 46. When it came to the law of God, one thing that the said matriarchal figure in II Machabees 7 was not known for was compromise.

8

The 1590s to the Gunpowder plot

THE SECOND VISCOUNT MONTAGUE STARTS TO LOOK ABOUT HIMSELF

Lady Magdalen, the dowager Viscountess Montague, was clearly a powerful focus for Catholics in the late sixteenth and early seventeenth centuries in both Sussex and Southwark. She attracted seminarist chaplains who had an agenda which was, as we shall see, extremely ambitious. After her death they used her reputation for zealous Catholicism and undoubted piety to advance their cause. They chose to turn her into a saint: hence Richard Smith's famous encomium of her.

But, after she was gone, would her priests and friends be able to rely on the holder of the family's title – her stepgrandson, Anthony Maria Browne, the second Viscount Montague? After all, he and the Lady Magdalen had hit it off very well. Why should he not be sympathetic to their courses? Perhaps he already was? The second viscount's father, Anthony Browne, had himself been of a Catholic temperament. Indeed, in the early 1590s (before his premature death) he may have been attracting Catholic interest, in part because it must have been expected that he would fairly soon inherit his father's estates and mantle. The informer Robert Hammond denounced him for associating with Catholic undesirables.[1] According to Robert Gray, the Jesuit John Curry had been at River Park, Anthony Browne's residence.[2] Thomas Simpson, who was ordained as a priest in the early 1580s by the cardinal of Guise and who conformed in spring 1593,[3] had, it seems, some sort of *entrée* at River Park. Richard Young, who was involved with Richard Topcliffe in the sweep against south-coast Catholicism at this point, reported to Lord Keeper Puckering on 25 February 1593 that he had arrested Simpson (who practised 'to withdrawe hir Majesties subjectes in reconsilinge them to

---

[1] See ch. 5, p. 176 above.   [2] *CSPD 1591–4*, 380.   [3] Anstr. I, 318.

the pope of Roome from their due obedience to hir Majestie'). Simpson had preached Anthony Browne's funeral sermon in 1592.[4]

Anthony, however, may well have deliberately imitated his conformist father, the first viscount. Perhaps, for that very reason, Simpson's delicate straddling of the line between separatist clericalism and statute conformity was acceptable to him. Simpson's conformity, like Robert Gray's and Anthony Garnett's, was undoubtedly part of a more general response among the Browne entourage to Topcliffe's sudden onslaught after their protector the first viscount and his son had died.[5]

One important formative influence on the second viscount was his marriage on 3 February 1592 to Lord Buckhurst's daughter.[6] A matrimonial alliance with the clan of one of the still-rising stars of the late Elizabethan regime was of momentous significance for the Browne family,[7] though we might wonder why Buckhurst should have decided to match his daughter with the first Viscount Montague's grandson, soon to become the head of a family which already had strong Catholic inclinations. The informer Robert Hammond positively grieved to see the 'Lord Buckhursts daughter' Jane Sackville 'whollie committed to the discrecion of Mr Antonie Brownes sonne for matters of conscience'.[8] Perhaps Buckhurst thought the Brownes were sufficiently conformist to take the edge off what, on some readings, might have been regarded as a rather politically dangerous union.

In June 1593 the second viscount's first child, a boy, was born. The child's baptism was intended to be an important social event. The godparents were to be the queen, Lord Burghley and the earl of Sussex.[9]

---

[4] Young noted the Catholics with whom Simpson had been, including Lancelot Gildridge at Beddingham and Henry Darell at Scotney. He had been 'at Mr Taylers, whoe married Mr Forteskewes widdow and is sonne in lawe' to Richard Lewkenor 'the lawyer'. (Simpson performed the wedding service.) Simpson had also visited Edward Gage's house at Bentley in Framfield, and William Shelley's at Michelgrove, and had been with Lady Frances Paulet of Borley in Essex, and 'with Mr [John] Southcote whoe married hir daughter' Magdalene, PRO, SP 12/244/48, fo. 101r; P. R. Knell, 'Lady Elizabeth Paulet – Recusant or Church Papist?', *ER* 8 (1966), 1–10, at p. 9. The priest John Southcot (son of the above John Southcot) subsequently became a trusted associate of the seminary clergy who relied on the Brownes' patronage. See chs. 13 and 14 below.

[5] Simpson was never an enthusiastic professor of his new-found Protestantism. Rewarded with a benefice at Kelvedon in Essex, he was later found to be preaching allegedly popish doctrine and was deprived, Anstr. I, 318.

[6] Berry, *Sussex*, 354.

[7] For the marriage settlement of 20 January 1592, see WSRO, SAS/BA 65, 66.

[8] BL, Lansdowne MS 99, no. 60, fo. 163r.

[9] The earl of Sussex, on 28 June, asked Sir William More to represent him as proxy godparent at the christening, because, the earl explained, he was too ill to travel, Loseley MSS, 651; SHC, LM 6729/10/87, LM 6729/9/34.

Here it looks as if the young peer was being successfully incorporated and absorbed into the culture of the Court.[10] We can assume that Anthony Maria had been present at the Cowdray entertainments laid on for the queen in August 1591. Perhaps the establishment was trying to keep him on side. But everything went wrong. For the child died on the very day appointed for the baptism. To see a male heir perish so early may have had a bad effect on the young man. He may, as he later intimated, have started looking about for an explanation for the tragedy. Was this a providential judgment on him for his dalliance with the established Church?

On his own account, he decided not to take such a risk with his second child, male or female. No dalliance with conformity would be allowed to prejudice its chances of survival. On 22 May 1594 we find the second viscount being given the third degree by Archbishop Whitgift and Lord Keeper Puckering.[11] They wanted to know why he had not resorted to the established Church to baptise his newborn daughter, Mary. He confessed that he had himself christened the girl, but denied that he had a dispensation from Rome to do this, 'or to come to church, or for anything els'. The reason he had done this, he said, was because previously he had consented to the christening of his son, 'after the manner now used, and the child dieing the daye appointed for the christning, and was upon the sodaine christened by a woman, it did after troble his conscyens'. In an agony of grief, perplexity and resentment he fell to talking with Robert Barnes, 'dwelling nere to' Cowdray, and some of his other attendants, including 'Robert Gage, his gentleman usher', William Danby 'the gentleman of his horse', Christopher Whitehair, receiver of some of his rents, John Webb, one of his 'chamber' and a man called Rigby who belonged to his 'wardrobe'. These people were all solidly Catholic. (Barnes was arrested shortly afterwards, on 5 June.[12]) Barnes, said Montague, came to tell him of 'his sonnes death'. Montague confided to Barnes that he thought it was God's punishment 'to take away his sonne' because he had 'consentyd to have it christnyd after the manner now used. And therupon', he said, 'if ever God sent hym any more children, he wold take another cours for yt'. Montague tried to protect Barnes, however, by saying that Barnes was absent when he christened the child.

---

[10] Two months earlier, on 5 March 1593, the young man had been present to witness the 1593 parliament in session, although the Lords' journal describes him as 'infra aetatem', *LJ* II, 173.

[11] BL, Harleian MS 7042, fo. 153r.

[12] TD III, ccii. Barnes alleged in court in July 1598 that 'the original' of all his troubles was Anne Bellamy's confession concerning the harbouring of the Jesuit Robert Southwell at Uxendon manor (near Wembley), where Barnes had been with Southwell and George Birkhead, the future archpriest and senior chaplain of the second Viscount Montague, TD III, cxcvii, cxcix, cc.

The second viscount performed this do-it-yourself baptism at the house of his father-in-law Lord Buckhurst in London, where Jane, the mother, was recovering. Buckhurst 'movyd him to think' of suitable godparents 'for the christning'. Montague 'answeryd that the manner of christning trobled his conscyens', and asked Buckhurst to be content if he made alternative arrangements. This allegedly sent Buckhurst into a frenzy. The enraged father-in-law had said that he 'wold withstand yt', though Montague promised that the baptism would be done in such a way (by 'some that he wold privilie bryng thither') that Buckhurst 'shold not know yt'. Buckhurst fumed in reply that 'he wold then looke better to hym, and he wold make sure ther shold no such acte be done ther, and if any came thither to do any such thing (putting his fist to his mouth) he very ernestly sayd he wold pull them in peces with his teeth'.

The second viscount was understandably taken aback by this display of in-law-ish bad temper. He ditched his plan of getting a Catholic cleric, perhaps even a seminary priest, to perform the baptism. Instead he did it himself. He was persuaded that a man might lawfully do so in case of necessity, and this was just such a case. He waited until the attention of the crowd of attendants around his wife was temporarily distracted. Taking up his wife's 'little sylver box, wherin sugar was comonlye put', he tipped the sugar out, filled the box with water and concealed the box under his hat. Then he approached the nearby cradle and 'tooke as much water as he could in his hands, putting it on the childs face, making therwith a crosse saying, I baptise thee Marye in the name of the Father and of the Sonne and of the Holy Ghost'.

The christening was entirely his own idea, he confessed, though he had once heard Lady Magdalen tell Dr Alban Langdale that, in the case of 'one child that was latelye before borne in her house and dyed, she had christnyd yt before yt dyed, and asked the doctor yf she had done well, and he sayd yt was well done'. 'And upon this and upon some bokes that this examinant had red callyd Navarre,[13] part of [Cardinal] Bellarmine, and some other cases of consciens touching matrimony and baptisme', and having listened with interest to various friends and acquaintances arguing about it, the young viscount was persuaded that this was the correct and godly thing to do.

So, it seems that until shortly after he succeeded to the family title and estates Anthony Maria had been outwardly conformist. He told Whitgift and Puckering that he had 'no chaplen in his house, nor any service ther sayd'. Rather, he recited 'his private prayers in Latyn, at which [Robert] Barnes hath most commonly bene with hym (and no other at any tyme) onles

---

[13] This is a reference to the work of the Spanish casuist Martin de Azpilcueta, perhaps his *Enchiridion sive Manuale Confessariorum et Poenitentiorum* (Antwerp, 1581), ch. 22, pp. 473–4, where the issue of lay baptism is dealt with.

some of his chamber came by chance'. (These prayers were from 'the Ladie Matins of the Romish breviarye'.) In other words, he was using Catholic prayer forms but he was not availing himself of the regular ministrations of seminarist clergymen. He may even have conformed to the extent that he attended the liturgy of the established Church. Certainly no suspicion of recusancy had attached itself to him before this christening incident. Being demanded by whom he had been instructed in religion, 'he sayth' that it was

only by the sayd Dr Langdale in his grandfathers house (albeit there were also then 3 other preests viz. [Anthony] Garnet, [Robert] Gray and Francis Ryther [Rydell], 2 of them at one tyme, the other 2 at another tyme), but he was never instructyd by any of them but Dr Langdale onely, saving some tymes he conferryd with Mr Gray.

But he had then evidently changed his mind about such things. Montague endeavoured to excuse himself to Whitgift and Puckering by saying that, apart from those he had mentioned, there were only three other recusants in his household, namely 'Harry Jhonson and his wyfe (who was this exam-inants nurse) and John Arderne the keper of his parke', who, in any case, 'now comethe to the church as this examinant is enformyd'.[14] However, this separatist segment of his entourage was not recruited by him, for 'these before namyd recusants he had not taken into his service'. Rather, they had been 'servants to his grandfather at [the] tyme of his death and were well favouryd by hym and by this examinants father'.[15]

But it could hardly not have been noticed that the disastrous private christening incident occurred not long after the regime's agents, principally Richard Topcliffe, started to round up the known Catholic remnants of the first viscount's circle, principally Garnett, Gray and Rydell.[16] These arrests, of men that the young viscount probably knew well, may well have conspired to alienate the young lord from the political and religious establishment.[17] Perhaps the two things – the death of the unfortunate child, for whom the Church-of-England baptism had been planned, and the regime's hostility – became linked together in his mind. Certainly, the young man was now start-ing to exhibit the kind of intense interest in Catholicism which he would later demonstrate in his writings and in his distribution of clerical patronage. We might even speculate that the performance of the baptism of his daughter shows that Montague himself wanted, at some level, to be a priest. What is absolutely clear, however, is that the government became exceedingly con-cerned that, in the battle for hearts and minds, the heart and mind of this

[14] For Arden, see ch. 6, p. 202 above.
[15] BL, Harleian MS 7042, fos. 153r–154r.   [16] See ch. 6, pp. 199–200 above.
[17] It is perhaps worth noting also that Sir Michael Blount claimed in late 1593 that the servants of 'the yong Vicounte Mountague' were involved in a plot to spring the seminary priest John Boste from prison, Hatfield House, Cecil MS 170, fo. 21r. Boste had, it appears, once served the first viscount. See ch. 6, p. 184 above.

potential new leader of the English Catholic community were developing independent tendencies. As we know from perusing parish registers, many Catholic families, even those with recusant tendencies who were noticed, at least from time to time, for their absences from divine service, were prepared to have their children christened in the local parish church. To recoil from even this most basic contact with the established Church, in a sacrament which was necessarily acknowledged by Catholics as valid even when performed under Church-of-England auspices, was pretty radical. No wonder that the privy councillors interrogated him so fiercely.

And, though Montague made all the conventional protestations of sorrow for having offended the queen, he did not get off particularly lightly. It appears that he was kept under restraint for some time, though his confinement seems to have taken the comparatively easy and lenient form of house arrest with Lord Buckhurst. On 31 July 1594 we find Montague writing to Lord Keeper Puckering from Sackville House, asking to speak with two of his 'late servants', namely Christopher Whitehair ('who had greate doeinges for me', and was still not entirely discharged of them) and William Danby ('who may . . . yealde up his charge of the stable').[18]

With a degree of rhetorical exaggeration, Henry Lanman, who, as we saw, was converted to Catholicism in Montague's household by William Coningsby, declared that 'for the interval of one year or thereabouts' Montague was 'kept most inhumanly in strict custody because of his constant confession of the Catholic faith'. House arrest at Sackville House was hardly likely to have been inhumane, or even particularly arduous. But Lanman claimed that 'during this time' the young viscount 'was unable to keep any Catholic servants, not even myself' (which may explain why Montague referred to Whitehair and Danby as his 'late' employees).[19] There is evidence from another source that the viscount's local prestige and position were badly threatened by his fall from political grace at this time. Roger Manning has shown how the luckless viscount's four deer parks which were situated within the Cowdray estates were ravaged by poachers who saw their chance when 'the said viscount . . . was under restraint and prison[er] at and by' the queen's 'commandment'.[20]

---

[18] Lord Buckhurst was amenable to all this, though Puckering was 'not well satisfied' because not all the suspects in this affair, particularly Robert Gage whom Montague had 'sent . . . into Walles', had come forward. See BL, Harleian MS 6996, fos. 192r, 194r.

[19] CRS 54, 87; ch. 6, p. 202 above. Lanman said that when Montague's 'imprisonment was somewhat relaxed, he recalled me from my father's house, where I had been living in the meantime. He kept me with him until he obtained full liberty (or as much as he desired), when he went to his house in the country', at which point Lanman, 'in the full enjoyment of his favour and generosity', decided to enrol at the English College in Rome, *ibid.*, 87–8.

[20] R. B. Manning, *Hunters and Poachers* (Oxford, 1993), 223.

All in all, then, this episode looks like a rather unsuccessful attempt by the regime to prevent a Catholic entourage coalescing around this impressionable young peer. Had he once been of anything like the same mind as his conformist grandfather, now, it seems, he was not. Indeed, in Sir John Harington's famous *Metamorphosis of Ajax*, there is an obscure reference to the second viscount, the new master of Cowdray: 'the young lord I heare doth *patrisare*', i.e. he takes after his father, 'or rather I should say *avisare*', in other words, takes after his grandfather. And Harington adds 'that is a good word, if he will marke it', implying that the new viscount was not, in fact, quite emulating the first viscount, though in what way Harington does not exactly specify.[21]

In January 1595 another rebuff followed. Montague's suit to be accorded precedence above the younger son of a duke, namely Thomas Howard, the attainted fourth duke of Norfolk's second son, was rejected by a commission composed of Lord Burghley, Lord Howard of Effingham and Lord Hunsdon.[22]

By mid-1595, however, things had returned to at least a semblance of calm and normality. The viscount received on 7 May a grant during the queen's pleasure of the office of steward of the manor and hundred of Godalming.[23] In 1596 he was named, in Harington's *Metamorphosis*, as a supporter of the earl of Essex.[24] By July 1597, he was running messages to and from the earl.[25] Essex attracted a number of Catholic supporters. Notoriously, these included some of the future Gunpowder plotters, people who believed that Essex was sufficiently flexible in his opinions to accommodate them, and that one day his political ambitions might coincide with an overturning of the Elizabethan settlement of religion.[26]

The second Viscount Montague, of course, was not one of Essex's swordsmen. But his opinions about religion were now hardening into the zealous certainty that he would display publicly in the early Jacobean period. In *c.* 1597 he wrote a manuscript tract,[27] which was intended as an advice to

---

[21] E. S. Donno (ed.), *Sir John Harington's A New Discourse of a Stale Subject, Called the Metamorphosis of Ajax* (1962), 224.

[22] BL, Stowe MS 1047, fo. 264v.   [23] Loseley MSS, 654.

[24] P. Hammer, *The Polarisation of Elizabethan Politics* (Cambridge, 1999), 287; J. Scott-Warren, *Sir John Harington and the Book as Gift* (Oxford, 2001), 87, 90. The setting for the *Metamorphosis* was Wardour Castle in Wiltshire, the home of the Arundells, where Montague's cousins the earl of Southampton and his sister, the wife of Sir Thomas Arundell, were present, Donno, *Metamorphosis*, 18.

[25] HMCS VII, 329.   [26] Hammer, *Polarisation*, 174–8.

[27] The title page of Montague's 'Instruction to my daughter Marie Browne in the principall groundes, and moste necessarie pointes of the Catholique faithe' (Gillow Library MS, on microfilm at WSRO) dates the tract to 1597. However, at the end of the manuscript it is stated to have been completed on 15 August 1598. It bears the approbation of the archpriest George Blackwell, *ibid.*, 150.

his daughter, urging her to embrace and practise the true religion. The tract is quite outspoken about the problem of religious division. Montague warns against compromise with Protestants who might tell her that the Church of England and the Church of Rome have things in common. *Au contraire*, he protested, they did not. These Protestants will insist that salvation may be had in the Church of Rome and also among them in the Church of England. Montague argues that the two faiths are utterly different. The communion of saints is limited to those in communion with the Catholic Church. It excludes, therefore, 'all infidells, heretiques and scismatiques'. The Catholic Church must be defined by reference to true faith, the essential constituent of which is to believe that God through Christ, and Christ through his apostles, 'and amonge them by his blessed Apostle St Peter (as cheife of them) to whome also he gave the supreame charge of his Church and flocke, hath delivered, and by his successors the bishoppes of the See of Rome contynued, that holie Catholique and apostolique Church' which cannot err in any matter of faith.[28]

If he had been a conformist at one time, he now rejected any such compliance. He refutes the commonplace strands of argument which many Protestant polemicists used to persuade Catholics that conformity was not only a legal requirement but licit, even praiseworthy, even for those who did not enthuse about the prevailing ecclesiastical and theological tenor of the English Church. Though not explicitly phrasing his advice in the context of church attendance, Montague nevertheless instructed his daughter that 'if they whoe shall have the wretched and (to themselves noe less than unto you) unfortunate mynde to thrust this suggestion into your weake and tender judgment, shall see themselves . . . to be frustrated of their wicked . . . hope', in other words their intention to persuade her to adopt their opinions,

they will (I knowe) not soe give over their endevour to corrupte you, but will finde out a newe meane, and much more perilous snare, wherein . . . cunningly to intrappe you; and that by seeking to make you beleeve that you looke not uprightlie and indifferently into the cause; for that they (as it is like they will saie) are of the same beleefe whereof you are, as namely they beleeve in the same God that you beleeve in, and other thinges more they will likewise saie, that themselves doe beleeve equallie

---

[28] 'Instruction', 5, 16. Montague urged the possibility of pursuing perfection in religion, and recommended various volumes on the topic. He mentioned that 'one of later tyme, written first in Spanish by the excellent learned man Diego di Stella, I my selfe have seene translated into our tongue, by a reverende and vertuous preiste who will as I hope in tyme to comme publishe it to the good of many', *ibid.*, 73–4. Montague's neighbour at Warblington, the recusant George Cotton, had already translated and published Diego de Estella's tract *Libro de vanidad del mundo* as *The Contempte of the World* (Rouen, 1584). See ARCR II, no. 160. Another edition (ARCR II, no. 161) of the same translation was produced in 1604 and copies of it were among the books which were seized at the Venetian ambassador's residence in London in 1609. The embassy chaplain, William Law, who had been hoarding these books, was on the fringes of Montague's entourage, *NAGB*, 61.

with you; and, amonge other their guilfull pretences, somme of the more learned and craftie sorte of heretiques perhappes will tell you that they are sclaundered in that they are reported to denie diverse pointes of necessarie beleife, which they to you will seeme to holde, as the doctrine of good workes, for one, which they will proteste (though untruly) that they doe not denie.[29]

The second viscount seems to be talking from bitter personal experience. Here, it seems, are echoes of arguments which he must have recently had with Protestant divines. The pro-conformity discourses which he recites and condemns are certainly not the same as the Catholic ones which he might in his youth have heard from such conformity theorists as Cowdray's household chaplain Alban Langdale. It appears that, during the period after Montague was called into question over the private christening incident, he may have been subjected to some kind of official attempt to get him to change his mind about religion, and that this proselytising effort was based on exactly this sort of 'moderate' reasoning about how much the two Churches had in common, and why, therefore, a Catholic might with a safe conscience conform to the Church of England. Perhaps this is what lies behind the undeniably bitter tone of Montague's tirade against the heretics who will allow of anything you ask, even the true substantial body of Christ in the sacrament, 'and all this they will . . . speake keeping a secrette glasse in their mynde'; and claim also that the Church of England allows auricular confession, 'which if you enter considerately and deepley into, you shall then finde it to bee but a verie trifle of their owne frameing and deviseinge' (because the Protestants' understanding of repentance is itself irredeemably corrupt). Montague claimed that if you ask them why they must be separate from the Church of Rome they say that 'although the first breache of unitie was on their parte from the Church of Roome', and they do not 'commende' the act of separation in itself, nor 'would [they] for their owne parte have wished' it, they believe 'that they have nowe a newe union (which God knowes they have not) made amonge themselves'.[30]

All of this does sound very like the product of arguments which the young viscount may have had with moderate Church-of-England divines, though we do not know who they were. It is not unreasonable to speculate that this private 'instruction' written for his daughter, as yet still only a very young child, and unlikely to read it for many years, was a reaction to the treatment he had received from the government in the mid-1590s. It also suggests that the Elizabethan regime had gone out of its way to keep him on side through moderation and accommodation rather than through outright

---

[29] 'Instruction', 81. cf. for example, John Dove, *A Perswasion to the English Recusants to Reconcile Themselves to the Church of England* (1602), 17–18; Francis Bunny, *An Answere to a Popish Libell* (Oxford, 1607), 96.

[30] 'Instruction', 82–3, 85–6.

Figure 27. *The Three Brothers Browne* (1598) by Isaac Oliver. (Gouache and watercolour on vellum on card.) Represented are Anthony Maria Browne, second Viscount Montague, flanked by his younger brothers (John, on the left, and William, on the right). The fourth figure is evidently a gentleman servant of the family.

coercion. But Montague had evidently started to reinterpret the thrust of his family's Catholicism and to invest it with a harder edge. He claimed that his grandfather, the first viscount, had sorrowed to see his countrymen run into error and perdition and had sought to prevent the same in his children. The first viscount, announced Anthony Maria proudly, had written a 'booke' for his grandson and heir concerning the abomination of heresy and the excellence of Catholic truth. Anthony Maria says he wants his daughter Mary[31] to read what the first viscount had written on this subject.[32]

---

[31] He sometimes refers to her in the 'Instruction' as 'Margaret'.   [32] 'Instruction', 130–2.

In 1598 someone, presumably the second viscount, commissioned Isaac Oliver to paint himself and his brothers John and William[33] (see Figure 27). Karen Hearn has shown that this portrait consciously mimics Marc Duval's 1579 depiction of the Coligny brothers, while Mary Trull argues that the intention was to show that the Browne brothers were, like the Coligny family, adherents of 'an embattled religious cause' and that 'the portrait signifies communal loyalty and singleness of purpose'. But whereas the Coligny brothers are depicted bearing weapons, the Brownes are not, or at least wear daggers rather than swords. The observer of the painting may have been intended to conclude that the Brownes did not pose a military threat to the State in the way that some French Huguenots had recently done. The second viscount was evidently not a soldier-type. The portrait, however, could also be taken to represent and celebrate a unity of Catholic religious identity and purpose within the Browne family, and perhaps also among the family's servants, since a gentleman-servant is depicted at the far right of the painting.[34]

As late as April 1600 it seems that Montague was again under some form of restraint; for what, it is not exactly clear. Writing from Sackville House in the middle of that month, he proudly informed Sir Robert Cecil that he was

> emboldened to make my suit unto you that, whereas I am by her Majesty's favour now shortly to appear before you and the council for my further enlargement, I may by your favour be graced with such equal and upright conditions as may be offered to a subject who giveth place to no man living in obedience to his prince, nor holdeth any other religion than by which I am taught to prefer her Majesty to all other potentates.[35]

Perhaps Montague was trying to distinguish himself from others in his family circle (notably his great-uncle, Francis Dacre) who were still regarded with considerable suspicion. In the later 1590s Dacre had returned to Scotland and was now consorting with Scottish Catholic Hispanophiles such as George Ker who, in turn, were using him to curry favour with James VI. John Udall, a prolific tale-teller about the activities of papists, warned the earl of Essex in March 1599 that Dacre was welcomed in Scotland with Essex's 'good applause, and that your lordship mediateth his peace'.[36] Thomas

---

[33] Karen Hearn suggests that 'the architecture in the background' in the painting 'is possibly a true representation of one of the two long galleries at Cowdray', K. Hearn, *Dynasties* (1995), 134.

[34] *Ibid.*, 134; M. Trull, 'Constructing Privacy: The Montague Family and the Performance of Household Affect' (forthcoming). I am very grateful to Dr Trull for allowing me to see this paper and to draw on its conclusions. She discusses at some length the problem of the identity of the fourth character (the 'servant') in the painting. It is tempting to identify the servant with the, at this date, still-imprisoned Robert Barnes.

[35] *HMCS* X, 109.   [36] *Ibid.*, VIII, 88, 114–15, 129.

Wenman alerted the earl in the following August that James was pledging himself to all and sundry in order to secure the English crown for himself, and that the Scots were greedily dividing up their imagined share of the spoils of office in England in anticipation of Elizabeth's death. Wenman also said that James intended to rely on 'the Catholic faction, to whom he promises great favours, and the Lord Francis Dacres is the means to intimate the king's good affection toward them, by his private letters, which he does daily'. There were 'certain books now in printing' which tended 'to that end, wherein shall be declared the king's right to the crown, as also what he mindeth to do touching the repealing of certain cruel statutes (so he terms them) now in force'. Wenman reminded Essex that 'not long since, you wrote a letter as from her Majesty to the said Dacres, wherein you offered him 200ˡ by the year so he lived anywhere but in that suspected place'. These words had been taken by James 'in very ill part'. In a fit of pique 'he gave Dacres a protection under the great seal, making it felony for whosoever should assault or by any mean molest the said Lord Dacres'. 'This Dacres', urged Wenman, 'is a most spiteful and dangerous man, and one [who] will do much hurt when he shall have ability to put his mischievous resolutions in practice.'[37]

Dacre himself put it about that a pension from the queen would stimulate even further his natural obedience to her.[38] But it seems fairly clear that he was trying to worm his way into the Scottish establishment in anticipation of the favour he might receive when James set off southwards to claim his own.

THE ENTOURAGE STRIKES AN OBLIQUE BLOW FOR TOLERANCE

Now, admittedly, the second Viscount Montague, like his stepgrandmother, could consistently and credibly claim that he had nothing to do with the schemes of the busiest of the Catholic schemer-exiles. However, others within his immediate entourage did not stay so quiet. And, unlike Francis Dacre, they did not flee abroad but stayed at home to needle and discomfort the regime. One such was Robert Barnes. Barnes had, as we saw, been arrested, shortly after his master, in 1594. According to Barnes's own account, which may be somewhat embroidered, he was then subjected to Richard Topcliffe's malicious and sadistic attempts to secure evidence that he was a patron and

---

[37] *Ibid.*, IX, 307–9.

[38] *Ibid.*, X, 61. Dacre approached his sister, Lady Magdalen, in March 1600, admitting that he was still in bad odour in England for his 'going about to mach my self and my sonne here . . . and . . . in sekinge to gett my doughter Besse from you to mach her here'. Dacre insisted that he had come to Scotland from Spain only to be that much nearer to his prince, Elizabeth, and to his native country, *ibid.*, X, 71; Hatfield House, Cecil MS 77, fo. 49r–v. See also *HMCS* X, 291.

sustainer of Catholic clergymen. Eventually Barnes was brought to trial in 1598, charged with harbouring the Franciscan priest John Jones. Jones was dragged to execution on 12 July 1598 (and his head was stuck on a pole in Southwark, a dreadful warning to some of his Catholic friends there).[39] Barnes was also found guilty. But the trial was not the mere formality which such occasions were meant to be, at least not as far as Barnes was concerned (if his own account is to be believed). Barnes's extremely detailed narrative of the proceedings deals mainly with his own defiant indictment of Topcliffe's malpractice in harassing various Catholic families. Montague was nowhere named in these proceedings. But the fact remains that one of Montague's principal gentleman-servants was one of the first to question, ridicule and subvert, publicly and with some measure of official allowance, the canons of anti-popery as they were represented and expounded by the Elizabethan regime's factotum Topcliffe.

Much of the contemporary Catholic complaint literature seethed with hatred for Topcliffe. In Barnes's narrative, Topcliffe's rampant sexuality is paralleled only by his phenomenal greed and his capacity for mindless cruelty.[40] As Christopher Devlin reconstructs it, in 1592, Topcliffe, the 'obscene favourite', already flustered by the priest Thomas Pormort's scaffold revelations (that Topcliffe used to boast of his sexual familiarity with the queen)[41] was seriously embarrassed by the public knowledge of his treatment of Anne Bellamy. The queen seems genuinely to have disapproved of what he did to the girl. Robbery, extortion, perjury, even murder she might countenance in her favourites, says Devlin, but against rape she set her face sternly. It appears that this Catholic maiden had indeed been deflowered by the ageing Topcliffe, and it became impossible to conceal this fact when Anne Bellamy became disconcertingly and visibly pregnant. A scheme had to be concocted for restoring him into the queen's good graces. That scheme was the arrest of the saintly Jesuit Robert Southwell. By a complicated trade-off, the originator of the scheme, one Nicholas Jones,[42] would marry the Bellamy girl (to hide her shame), thus netting him a fortune, while she would have to provide the Jesuit's head on a plate, so to speak.[43]

---

[39] Challoner, *Memoirs*, 234–5. Jane Wiseman was also condemned for receiving and maintaining John Jones, P. Caraman (ed.), *John Gerard* (1951), 52.

[40] For Topcliffe as an anti-papist, see J. Bossy, *Under the Molehill* (2001), 146.

[41] Devlin, *Life*, 274–5; Challoner, *Memoirs*, 186. Topcliffe may have served in the young Elizabeth's household, Bossy, *Under the Molehill*, 146.

[42] Nicholas Jones is described by Barnes as a servant of the keeper of the Gatehouse prison, TD III, cxcviii.

[43] Devlin, *Life*, 275–6. It has to be said, though, that since Anne Bellamy finally gave birth at Christmas 1592 and had provided the evidence against Southwell in *c*. May 1592, and her 'rapid' wedding to Topcliffe's accomplice had taken place in July, it is not clear how far her pregnancy affected this sequence of events, TD III, cxcviii–cxcix. (She was also aged twenty-nine rather than being the innocent and defenceless child of the standard Catholic narrative.)

Barnes was embroiled in all this disgusting sleaze because the Shelleys of Mapledurham, with whom he was associated as an organiser of the Catholic clerical infrastructure in Hampshire and Sussex, were second cousins to Southwell. According to Topcliffe, Southwell had been at Cowdray in the summer of 1590.[44]

There are signs even before Barnes's trial that Topcliffe was not as adept at public relations as he might once have been. According to the Society of Jesus's own accounts of the trial of Southwell, the severely weakened Jesuit had dramatically accused Topcliffe of inhuman tortures. In a furious exchange between them, Southwell caught his antagonist entirely off guard, even luring him into a seeming admission that his proceedings against the Catholics were generated by mere malice ('Thou art a bad man', 'I would blow you all to dust, if I could', 'What, all?', 'Ey, all', 'What, soule and body too?').[45] Southwell's treatment had caused Topcliffe's temporary disgrace at Court.[46]

Now a privy council letter to the keeper of the Gatehouse prison, where Barnes was incarcerated, noted that 'notwithstanding commaundment given you that one Robert Barnes showld have the libertie of the prizon, yet by Mr Topclifs direccion he is kept close prizoner, whereat wee do not a little marvel'. The keeper was ordered to permit Barnes the liberty of the prison and to attend on the council to explain himself.[47]

In March 1596, Barnes's servant for the last eighteen years, one John Harrison, a Shropshire man, was still being questioned by Topcliffe in the Bridewell in order to get him to confess that Barnes had been consorting with various priests (including George Birkhead and George Jetter).[48] Apparently Topcliffe also had another go at the Marian priest Robert Gray. He threatened to maltreat him if he would not sign a confession implicating Barnes. Under duress Gray signed, but afterwards retracted.[49] Among other Catholics whom Topcliffe had tried to bully was one Doctor Thomas Friar. Topcliffe accused him that 'he kneeled and asked Mr [John] Jones's blessing'. He also charged the recusant Thomas Peacock that he 'had relieved the said Jones, and had one hundred Masses said in his houses'. Friar (who was a well-known physician and intimate of some of the Catholic secular clergy) and Peacock were both cleared.[50]

---

[44] Devlin, *Life*, 219. See ch. 6, p. 184 above.
[45] CRS 5, 335; Devlin, *Life*, 309–10, 311.   [46] Hasler, *HC*, III, 514.
[47] *APC 1595–6*, 237, cf. p. 254. According to Barnes, eventually the privy council agreed that his long and inhumane detention was against justice, though Topcliffe, who was finding difficulty getting witnesses to testify that Barnes had harboured the Franciscan John Jones, managed to have him reincarcerated, TD III, ccx, ccxi.
[48] PRO, SP 12/256/71, fo. 167r; TD III, ccvi–ccvii. Harrison denied all Topcliffe's charges but died from the brutal treatment inflicted on him, TD III, cvii.
[49] TD III, ccvi.   [50] TD III, ccxii. For Dr Thomas Friar, see ch. 6, p. 204 above.

Barnes's trial, in mid-1598,[51] was a disaster – for Topcliffe, even though Barnes himself was convicted.[52] Looked at from a different perspective from the one adopted by Devlin, namely the perspective of a regime now in two minds about how far to press forward with a severe policy against leading members of the Catholic community, Topcliffe looks less like the savage architect of a mindless and insane persecution and more like the ditched activist whose enthusiasms were no longer either officially palatable or necessary. As Bossy points out, even in the crisis years of the early 1580s, Elizabeth was 'extremely loath to be known to her subjects, to foreign princes, and to Christendom at large, as a torturer'.[53]

Taking into account, however, that Barnes was one of the second Viscount Montague's closest confidants, and had been involved with the Catholic clerical organisation in the Hampshire/Sussex border region for a long time, harbouring and associating with seminary clergy who would come to settle in the patronage structure now becoming available via the second viscount and his kin, the whole thing looks also rather like the Brownes' revenge against Topcliffe for the round-up of their clergy in 1593. Here was the opportunity to launch a public relations *coup* against an attack dog, or rather an attack dinosaur, of an ageing, in fact dying, regime, using the evil-counsellor style of rhetoric which had inflected so many of the Catholic critiques of the queen and her government during recent years.

Barnes's narrative attested that he and Jane Wiseman were indicted in King's Bench on 30 June 1598 'for hearing sundry Masses', and for 'relieving and harbouring' two priests, George Hethersall and John Jones. Even at this stage of the proceedings, according to Barnes, he managed to get a stab in at Topcliffe by informing the judge that 'my adversary, Topcliffe, had oftentimes threatened me to pick out a jury that should condemn me'. Barnes said he would prefer to be judged not by a jury but by 'my lord chief justice, Mr Attorney-General, Mr Solicitor, Mr Bacon, and Mr Recorder of London, before whom my cause hath been often discussed, and I cleared by them, many times, of all Mr Topcliffe's inventions against me', though this was not permitted. Barnes was arraigned on the 'Monday following', when he rehearsed the same claims about Topcliffe's plans to subvert due process of law.

There was only one crown witness against Barnes, one Nicholas Blackwell (Jane Wiseman's servant). Blackwell alleged that he had 'brought . . . [John] Jones, alias Buckly, to the new Gatehouse, where . . . Jones did lie two nights with me, and said two Masses', at which various people were present – 'Mrs

[51] See TD III, appendix 37 (the arraignment and speech of Robert Barnes of 3 July 1598). For the original manuscript, see Stonyhurst, MS Anglia A II, no. 41. See also *CSPD 1598–1601*, 144.
[52] PRO, E 178/487.   [53] Bossy, *Under the Molehill*, 87.

Wiseman, Mrs Bellamy, two of Mrs Bellamy's daughters, Stannardine Passy', and Barnes himself, who served Jones at the altar. Blackwell said that Barnes paid Jones for his services. A witness statement by Stannardine Passy, who refused to appear, was read out. Barnes alleged that Passy had been forced to sign an affidavit which was none of his composing, and had denied the matter before the attorney-general who, unfortunately, was not present in court.[54] Blackwell also averred that he was the one who conducted the priest Hethersall to the Gatehouse prison in order for him to celebrate Mass there.

Barnes cross-questioned Blackwell, and to his own satisfaction proved Blackwell's testimony to be a perjured tissue of lies. Topcliffe stated that Hethersall had been put into the Bridewell for possessing a copy of the inflammatory tract entitled *A Conference about the Next Succession to the Crown of England*, but Barnes denied that he personally had ever seen the book. At this point Barnes 'desired . . . leave to declare' his 'innocency'. He proceeded to reveal to the court his list of Topcliffe's crimes. He narrated the story of Anne Bellamy, who 'about the twenty-sixth day of January' 1592 'was committed to the Gatehouse'. There the unfortunate impregnation occurred. She then betrayed Robert Southwell (who was arrested at Uxendon on 25 June 1592), and she was spirited off to Lincolnshire, by now married to the loathsome Nicholas Jones. When the Bellamy family refused to play ball in handing over one of their more lucrative manors, Topcliffe persuaded her to make accusations against others. Among those she accused was Barnes himself, because he 'found [i.e. maintained] one Birket', i.e. George Birkhead, the future archpriest and central figure in the Brownes' clerical patronage structure. She claimed, too, that Barnes had dispatched the Jesuits Robert Persons and Jasper Heywood, and also Richard Bristow ('that notorious traitor') to her house from Barnes's 'house in Barbican'. Topcliffe swore she could prove that Barnes had 'harboured fifty-six priests'.[55]

Topcliffe had browbeaten Mrs Bellamy into backing up her daughter's accusations. But the mother then retracted everything and died in prison. Topcliffe's next ploy to batten on Barnes's Hampshire property was the arrest of the former clerical servant of the first Viscount Montague, Anthony Garnett and also 'James Atkinson, a kinsman of his and his servant', whom

---

[54] Barnes alleged that Topcliffe had tried to blackmail Passy into testifying by threatening to indict him for hearing Mass in Newgate. For George Hethersall, see T. F. Knox (ed.), *The First and Second Diaries of the English College, Douay* (1878), 206, 232, 234. For Passy, see CRS 53, 158.

[55] Barnes elaborated that 'the cause whereof she accused me was that I should pay for the board of one Hall, alias Birket, a seminary priest, at her father's house, about twenty years since', TD III, cc.

Nicholas Jones allegedly suborned to give evidence against Barnes.[56] When Atkinson tried to double-cross Jones and Topcliffe by getting a warning out about their plans, Topcliffe laid 'paper and ink before him' and ordered him to 'write what he could say concerning priests resorting' to Barnes's house at Mapledurham in Hampshire. When he refused, Jones vowed that 'unless he told another tale, he would dash out his brains with his sword; and Mr Topcliffe' swore that if Atkinson 'would not accuse me [Barnes], he [Topcliffe] would chop off his legs with his sword that lay there'. If he still refused to comply, Topcliffe claimed that he would 'break his thighs, send him to a place where the plague should devour him (being, at that time, in the city of London), or else where the rats should eat the flesh from his bones'. After this, Atkinson considered that indiscretion was the better part of valour, and 'was compelled to set down whatsoever they two would have him to set down, or dictated unto him; which he did with such trembling' that Jones politely enquired whether he was afflicted 'with a quaking ague'.[57] Barnes larded all this with magnificent protestations of his own loyalty to the queen.[58]

We have only Barnes's word that the proceedings in court took the form that he related. But this whole episode was, by any standard, an extraordinary indictment of a formerly trusted servant of the regime. Barnes's account of the trial admits that other evidence which he tried to bring into court was disallowed. Still, the overall effect was to represent the treatment of Southwell and a string of other Catholics as utterly indefensible. Southwell's trial had been provoked, so the traditional Jesuit line goes, by the linking of Southwell's name with the bandying about of the doctrine of equivocation. As

---

[56] On 24 December 1594 Archbishop Whitgift was ordered by the council finally to release, from the Gatehouse and the Marshalsea, Anthony Garnett and Robert Gray, both described as over seventy-two years of age. Whitgift was also told to try to secure their conformity in religion. (See also *APC 1592–3*, 475, 487, for letters to Topcliffe, the dean of Windsor and others to the same effect.) They are both described as having been imprisoned for a long time, though the arrest warrants for Garnett and Gray had gone out only on 24 June and again on 16 and 19 July 1593 when it was known that they were taking refuge 'in the howse of the Ladie Mountagew', LPL, MS 3470, fo. 150r; *APC 1592–3*, 328, 399–400, 406; ch. 6, pp. 199–200 above. In February 1597, at the Southwark assizes, 'Anthony Garnett, clerk' was indicted for recusancy, Cockburn, *Surrey Assizes: Elizabeth*, no. 2713.

[57] The gist of Atkinson's forced confession was that he had persuaded the future Jesuit Thomas Stanney, 'at my house of Mapledurham', that he 'should be a mean to make an atonement between one Mr Grey' (Robert Gray, formerly the first Viscount Montague's chaplain) and Anthony Garnett. Atkinson also said that he saw Barnes associating with George Jetter, who later served as a chaplain to the Cottons at Warblington, and with the Jesuit John Curry. All this, Barnes denied. Atkinson then retracted his evidence before various law officers on 8 October 1594. He died in Bridewell early the following year, TD III, cciii–cciv.

[58] On 23 July 1598 Barnes followed up his protestations in court by writing to Sir Robert Cecil admitting that he had copied out the well-known book of exorcisms issuing out of the Jesuit William Weston's sessions of demon expulsion in the mid-1580s. But he swore he had not harboured John Jones. He stated that he had shown 'manifest good signs' of his loyalty in 1588, perhaps in the company of the first Viscount Montague, which was 'well known to many captains and gentlemen in the country', *HMCS* VIII, 273–4.

Peter Marshall has demonstrated, the public teaching of mental reservation on grounds of conscience was death to the early modern system of criminal law and interrogation based on oath.[59] Now Barnes's trial was turning on precisely the issue which had led to Southwell's downfall – namely reservation in conscience of information demanded by sovereign authority. The Southwell issue was in a sense being rehearsed all over again. And compared with Southwell's comparatively weak performance, Barnes was (though we are, of course, reliant on his own account of what he said) far more belligerent and militant in the face of his accusers. In particular he brought up the torture issue. Southwell had merely said 'I have been tortured ten times. I had rather have endured ten executions.' Now Barnes alleged, apparently without being interrupted, 'Mr Topcliffe, seeing that I would not voluntarily confess it, caused Stannardine Passy to take me away, and to lay irons upon me, wherein I lay ten days and nights: after, he sent for me, and threatened to pick out a jury that should condemn me, and that he would hang me up at Mapledurham gates.' Topcliffe told Barnes plainly that he would send him 'to the Tower, there to be racked, to Bridewell to be tormented; and, going with him from Mr Attorney's' to the house of Topcliffe's cousin Thomas, Lord Burgh,[60] in front of Burgh's dwelling 'he threatened to hang me as high as the trees growing there, so as he would make my head and feet to meet together, but he would enforce me to confess it'.[61] The most the bench was prepared to do to intervene was to tell Barnes that he was not entirely helping his own case by concentrating merely on blackening Topcliffe's character.[62]

THE APPELLANT DISPUTE (1598–1602) AND THE EMERGENCE OF THE SECOND VISCOUNT MONTAGUE AS A CATHOLIC LEADER

The second Viscount Montague's late twenties coincided with the time of the appellant dispute. This spat is remembered by historians primarily as an exercise and showcase for the polemical talents of the more active and acrimonious of the Catholic clergy. (For short-hand purposes the principal factions among those clergy are frequently referred to, by historians, as the 'Jesuits' and the 'seculars'.) Montague is, in fact, barely cited in the polemical texts and in the general wrangling between the warring Catholic factions. But it can hardly not have been noticed that Lady Magdalen's entourage was not aligned with the Society of Jesus. Thomas More, who, as we saw, clashed with the pro-Jesuit archpriest George Blackwell,[63] was already her chaplain.

---

[59] P. Marshall, 'Papist as Heretic: The Burning of John Forest, 1538', *HJ* 41 (1998), 351–74.
[60] Topcliffe was a grandson of Thomas, third Baron Burgh, Hasler, *HC*, III, 513.
[61] Devlin, *Life*, 309; TD III, cciii.   [62] TD III, ccvii.   [63] See ch. 7, p. 212 above.

Richard Smith developed a lethal hatred for the Jesuit Robert Persons and, by association, for the rest of the order, a hatred which was entirely reciprocated.

It may be worth re-capping some aspects of this late Elizabethan intra-Catholic faction fight in order to construe the second Viscount Montague's politico-ecclesial position at the end of the queen's reign and to set the scene for the structure, opinions and aspirations of the Brownes' entire entourage, though particularly its clerical wing, during the early seventeenth century.

This dispute was, on the surface, a series of arguments about the patterns and institutions of clerical authority via which English Catholics were governed from Rome – arguments which were often characterised by the heights of supreme bitchiness of the kind to which only middle-aged clerics can generally aspire. The appointment in 1598 of George Blackwell as archpriest over the English secular clergy was taken by many Catholic secular clergymen and their friends to be a Jesuit *coup*, since Blackwell was believed to be not just a friend but also a creature of the Society of Jesus.

At its most basic, the dispute was about the nature of clerical authority in the fledgling English Catholic Church. There had already been rancorous arguments over this issue during the notorious 'stirs' in Wisbech Castle where leading Catholic clerics were imprisoned; and also during the quarrels at the English College in Rome. Some of the secular priests then evolved a scheme for setting up a clerical 'association' to establish proper subordination among the clergy, a scheme which the Jesuits regarded with profound hostility since it looked to them like an effort to dominate and subjugate the religious orders. The pious aspirations of this project, for example to abolish pluralism (among priests in gentry residences and chaplaincies) and to institute proper regulation of the funds made available by lay patrons seemed (to the Jesuits and their friends) distinctly threatening – a grab for power by one Catholic faction (albeit a large one) at the expense of other Catholics. Here, in embryo, was a system of clerical discipline which could be turned on those who were deemed, by the system's controllers, not to have measured up.

The papacy, of course, was extremely cautious in its creation of the English archpresbyterate (the action which triggered the controversy). The archpriest had some measure of disciplinary authority over the secular clergy, but none over the regulars or the laity. He did not, in other words, have episcopal power. Also, it was decided not to set up the archpriest by means of a papal breve but via the 'constitutive letters' of the cardinal protector of the English nation, Henry Cajetan. This gave Blackwell's critics the opportunity to question his authority.[64]

[64] For an account of the appellant dispute, see J. H. Pollen, *The Institution of the Archpriest Blackwell* (1920), 23. For the Wisbech stirs and the disputes at the English College in Rome, see CRS 51; P. Lake with M. Questier, *The Antichrist's Lewd Hat* (2002), ch. 8. See also TD III, 45; John Colleton, *A Iust Defence of the Slandered Priestes* (1602); John Bennett, *The Hope of Peace* (1601), 19; AAW, A VI, nos. 77, 78.

Although the appellants, in their first appeal to Rome in 1598–9, got a very rough ride in the Holy City, thanks mainly to the machinations of Robert Persons, they regrouped and, with French diplomatic assistance for their second appeal, started to achieve a substantial section of their programme, although Blackwell was not forced to step down at this time.[65] (By this stage the appellants also enjoyed the patronage of key figures in the Elizabethan regime, notably Bishop Richard Bancroft.)

Judgment came finally in August 1602. The commission of cardinals which had been set up to decide the issue reprimanded Blackwell for his failings as well as the appellants for theirs. The accusation of 'schism' which had been levelled by Blackwell against his enemies was dismissed. But in the matter of the errors detected by the Jesuits in the appellants' writings (specifically that they denied the papal deposing power), and the appellants' counter-charge that Jesuit politicking had provoked the wrath of the State, there was something of a stalemate. The appellants in Rome renounced the more passionate publications in their cause, notably William Watson's work. Silence was imposed by papal fiat. The clause in Blackwell's breve which had commanded him to communicate, in the exercise of his authority, with the Jesuits in England was withdrawn. This seemed to be a victory for the appellants, even though the archpriest regime was not dismantled.[66] After further representations during the last two weeks of August and the first two weeks of September 1602, Blackwell was also commanded to appoint the next three of his assistants[67] (as vacancies occurred in their ranks) out of the number of his opponents. On 12 October the papal breve summarising the various judgments made in these issues was distributed to the protagonists in Rome, and off it went to England.[68]

Traditionally, these quarrels among English Catholics have been treated entirely in a vacuum. There is a tacit assumption that they are of interest only to Catholic historians (or historians of late sixteenth- and early seventeenth-century Catholicism, in that those two categories of scholar are distinct), and have nothing to say to us other than to confirm that the English Catholic

---

[65] Pollen, *Institution*; J. Bossy, 'Henri IV, the Appellants and the Jesuits', *RH* 8 (1965), 80–112.

[66] Pollen, *Institution*, 90–1.

[67] The archpriest's assistants exercised limited authority under his direction in the various geographical districts of the rudimentary Catholic clerical system of ecclesiastical administration. The cardinal protector nominated six of the twelve assistants, with the archpriest appointing the other six, Guilday, *ECR*, 104. When Edward Bennett was appointed as an assistant to George Birkhead in 1609 he was charged to 'have a charitable care to helpe, advise and direct all our brethren who live within the sayd circuite or frequent the same. If any controversy or difference (which God forbyd) should happen to fale owt amongest your selfes, or with others; or any of them carry them selfes otherwise than the dignity of there vocation doth require, then doe I give you autority to call them, or hym, before you, and as you in your discretion find cause soe to proceed with them', AAW, B 24, no. 54.

[68] Pollen, *Institution*, 94.

community in *c.* 1600 was weak, divided and self-obsessed – cut off from the mainstream of politics and indeed from almost everything else.

Such a view is, however, deeply misleading. The reason that the controversy attracted so much contemporary attention, and so much published material was generated by and during it, was because the participants were involved in a high-stakes game both with each other and with the late Elizabethan regime. The right to speak for the Catholic constituency or community, or at least the ability to be able to claim to do so, was itself a political issue of some considerable moment. Significantly, the issues which were rehearsed during the appellant controversy were often remarkably similar to those topics which were debated among Church-of-England divines in the course of the presbyterian agitation: Church government, ecclesiastical discipline, access to and control over Church patronage and so on. The appellant dispute was a testing ground also for some of the contemporary theses about how far the laity, and particularly the great lay patrons of the clergy, and their entourages, had 'triumphed' over the clergy in the post-Reformation Church. Here the attitudes and general disposition of those entourages would be crucial to the structure of the community once the dust had settled. In fact, the recovery of those patronage networks, the (at least) nine-tenths of the Catholic community which was not usually in plain view, and what they were doing, is an essential though generally overlooked key for interpreting the wider ramifications and significance of the quarrel.

On some very real level, this was also a debate about how Catholics should position themselves politically as they lined up to greet James Stuart. It was far from clear what sort and style of government, under the Scottish king, would replace Elizabeth's. It was possible, even likely, that the law governing ecclesiastical conformity might be radically amended. As it became virtually certain that the plum would fall to James, the brand of uncompromising resistance to royal authority which had characterised some of the Catholic political thought of the Elizabethan period, particularly that which had been associated with the Jesuits, began to look very *passé*. Those, such as Robert Persons, who had generated it started to back-pedal furiously on their previous statements about the rights of other candidates to succeed Elizabeth, and of the rights of the commonwealth to determine who should take the crown.[69]

The appellants, however, insisted that it was too late for such regrets. They pointed to themselves as the deserving recipients of royal favour. In order to garner support from other Catholics, and to impress and please the regime, they insisted that the Jesuits' meddling had itself caused the Elizabethan

---

[69] See e.g. Robert Persons, *A Briefe Apologie, or Defence of the Catholike Ecclesiastical Hierarchie* (Antwerp, 1601), fos. 187v–188v.

persecution. The logic of what they were saying was that, in the new Stuart era, when the stumbling block of the succession was finally sorted out, the new regime should take no umbrage at the admittedly separatist but nevertheless thoroughly politically loyal (and, be it noted, mostly secular and not regular) clergy of the Catholic community who would simply get on with performing their proper, merely religious and godly, function. Such people would, in fact, be potentially useful to a government which would inevitably be faced with all sorts of opposition and criticism from unquiet (puritan) spirits within the Church of England, spirits which good Catholics had always opposed. When William Watson, a leading opponent of the archpriest Blackwell, poured scorn on the new archpresbyteral mode of governing English Catholics he made great play with the words (arch)priest and (arch)presbyter (as opposed, of course, to bishop). 'The very word archpresbiter is anomalum abolendum quite oute of use in Gods Churche at this day, ergo an innovation, never like to be allowed of by the pope yf he knew it.'[70] In his notorious *Decacordon*, the raciest and rudest of all the appellants' tracts, Watson insisted that the Jesuits sought to 'overthrow the ecclesiasticall dignity'.[71] Watson and others were keenly aware that it made sense to equate, for Richard Bancroft's benefit and delectation, the Jesuits with presbyterian-type conspiracy of the kind that Bancroft was so adept at uncovering. Watson noted that 'it is just agreing withe the puritanes to have this kind of arch-presbitery, and Dolemans private rules of government tende to noe lesse in morall matters'.[72] Since the unfortunate earl of Essex had had notoriously mixed religious tastes when it came to patronage, the appellants, conscious that the regime had blackened his name with stories that his conspiracy and rebellion had contained papistical elements, played up the decapitated earl's alleged puritan links. Anthony Copley bemoaned the 'great puritan-partie' and 'great pittie it was' that 'so noble a subject as the earle of Essex, and with him so manie worthie gentlemen' were 'made use of by it in his discontents to the end wee saw. Such spirit have puritanes, and so unfortunate was that poore earle.' And 'so unfortunate' too were 'those few Catholickes that of ignorance (I dare sweare) of his project stucke to him in those suds'.[73] Also, the more explicit appellant accusations against the Jesuits of corrupting faith, as opposed to order and discipline, are not dissimilar to conformist denunciations of puritans and separatists for making the same errors. Watson more or less unambiguously accused the Jesuits of perfectionist heresy.[74]

---

[70] Law, *AC*, I, 97.   [71] Watson, *Decacordon*, 15.

[72] Law, *AC*, I, 97–8. 'Doleman' is a reference to the pseudonym under which *The Conference about the Next Succession to the Crown of England* (Antwerp, 1594) was written.

[73] Anthony Copley, *An Answere to a Letter of a Iesuited Gentleman* (1601), 69.

[74] Watson, *Decacordon*, 213–20.

This analysis inevitably drew the scorn of the Jesuits, principally from the acid pen of Robert Persons. He probably spoke for many when he refuted the appellants' rehearsal of recent political history, and of the regime's harshness toward Catholics. Here we have a part-private/part-public debate about the status and role of Catholicism in a non-Catholic State, a debate which further politicised the Catholic community.

A great deal of the debate took the form of publicly aired petitions for toleration, combined with arguments about which of the English Catholics had most truly suffered for the faith. Persons, on behalf of the Jesuit wing of the Catholic movement, claimed that the Church was built up by the example and witness of holy martyrs (whose holy martyrdom was itself proof that their motivation was purely religious). Persons believed that it was 'an intolerable calumny' to say, as the appellants did, that his own political activities had 'resulted in lamentable tragedies for Catholics'. If, by tragedies, his critics were thinking of those who had been executed for their 'confession of our holy faith', then they should reflect that 'in the space of more than twenty years during which Fr Persons has been negotiating in the cause of Catholics there will not be found even one individual who through his fault has suffered in any way'. The only Catholics who were guilty of exacerbating the government's wrath were the Jesuits', indeed all true Catholics', opponents, for example those misled and deeply despicable people who had brought about the doom of the tragic Scottish queen.[75] This itself should give the Jesuits' critics pause to think about which Catholics had really supported the cause and the rights of the Stuarts.

In a memorial written for Pope Clement VIII in 1602 concerning the secular priests' proposals for a toleration in England, and their *quid pro quo* that the Jesuits should be expelled from the realm, Persons claimed that some of the secular clergy were pandering to 'the malice and enmity of the heretics'. He utterly condemned 'the artifices they use to calumniate Catholics and to palliate and cover up the persecution with the pretext and cloak of religion and in the interests of the State, so as to render the Catholics odious in the eyes of the people, and thus dim the glory that is due to their martyrdoms'. Persons then rehearsed the Jesuit line about the true faith of Edmund Campion and subsequent martyrs, and that 'among all the fathers of the Society and seminary priests who have been imprisoned, tortured or martyred since the beginning of the persecution there has not been found so much as one on whom could be fastened the charge of treason or in whose case necessities of State could be alleged'. The only exception was John Ballard, the Babington conspirator. Ballard was employed 'in the days of the queen of Scots of blessed memory' by the 'enemies of Cardinal Allen . . . Fr Persons and of

---

[75] AAW, A VI, no. 20 (transcript and translation at ABSJ).

the whole Society'. He had been aligned with the devious Thomas Morgan and Charles Paget. So the Jesuits were happy to admit that he was a traitor – indeed the only Elizabethan priest who had truly fallen into treason during the queen's reign. But, as for the other priests who had been executed for treason (whom the appellants were now claiming had perished because of the unwise political engagements of the Jesuits), they had died only for their religion. Indeed, the regime had conceded as much by offering them their lives if only they would recant.

Here Persons was reversing the polarities of the anti-popish canon, into which canon he believed some of his own Catholic enemies had deliberately tapped in order to attack the Society of Jesus. He alleged that they, in fact, were the ones whose willingness to immerse themselves in the filth and mire of politics had jeopardised the Catholic movement. Toleration at any price was a toleration not worth having – especially if it meant expulsion from the realm of those who had done most to preserve the purity of the faith, for example by setting up, as the Jesuits had done, the seminaries to which the State so unreasonably objected. The spiteful appellants wanted, said Persons, to do a deal with the State to guarantee themselves a lazy security. The price which they were prepared to pay was the cutting off of English Catholicism's life-blood. This was the wicked motive for their objection to the archpriest regime (which the appellants had claimed was merely a cover for the Jesuits' domination of the English Catholic body to its own detriment). But, Persons explained to the pope, 'in the course of forty years of persecution the Catholics have increased to such an extent that from the handful they were at first they have now grown to be a very large and strong body under the archpriest as head and directly subordinate to your Holiness', and so the queen 'takes the view that, as long as the seminaries are in existence and this subordination persists, along with the activity and zeal of the fathers of the Society, this body is going to grow larger every day, and the authority of your Holiness' will be 'maintained there'; and this 'seems to her to be incompatible with her own authority'.[76]

Most of the toleration petitions spawned by both sides in this quarrel resemble, at first glance, appeals merely to be left in peace. Whether you believe them or not, they seem to take the form of a promise that in return for the State not enforcing the penal statute law against Catholics, the Catholic clergy will hide themselves away in their gentry patrons' residences and do what all simple Catholic parish clergy the world over should do – celebrate the Mass, hear confessions, baptise and so on. And this is probably not an entirely false reading. We should not imagine that the toleration literature

[76] ARSJ, Anglia MS 36/i, fo. 101r (transcript and translation at ABSJ).

was merely a Trojan horse, designed to deflect attention from Catholic plans to launch a *coup d'état* at the first convenient opportunity.

But it takes only the briefest of comparisons with the puritan petitioning which anticipated and accompanied the Stuart succession, mirroring and shadowing the Catholic printed tracts and manuscript supplications and entreaties to the new king, and using very similar tactics and rhetoric, to see that the Catholics who lobbied both the late Elizabethan regime and the new regime of James Stuart were not really predicting their own retirement from the political fray to quiet idyllic rural backwaters, filled only with the sound of clattering rosary beads. Rather, what we see in the appellant controversy's polemic and in its tolerationist agenda, both before and after the accession, is a struggle between factions for power and dominion within the Catholic community, factions which simultaneously kept an eye on their Protestant opponents, and tried to refute some of the rhetoric of Protestant reform by sporting and spouting their own brand of reform rhetoric. This, after all, was what the appellant controversy was about, i.e. what kind of disciplinary structures were necessary to govern the allegedly burgeoning number of English Catholics. Each side wanted to convince a number of different audiences – the crown, the Roman curia, other English Catholics (particularly the clergy's lay patrons) and perhaps a wider public at large – that their reforming solutions to the problems of Catholics within the English Church (though they were not members of the Church of England) were good and godly, and should serve as a means of reintegrating a sizeable percentage of Catholics (each Catholic faction claimed that they represented the vast majority of English Catholics) into the social mainstream, where they could be relied on by the crown as a loyalist constituency and a bulwark against the perils of puritan enthusiasm.

These quarrels were also structurally related to the changing balance of contemporary European power politics. The adherents of the archpriest, several of whom were either Jesuits or supporters of the Society, tended to look to the Spaniards for emotional and diplomatic sustenance at the Court of Rome. The archpriest's opponents were inclined to look to the French. It is possible, therefore, to interpret the final phase of the appellant quarrel as one of the later acts in the political watershed represented by the collapse in the 1590s of the Holy League and the defeat of Philip II's intervention in France. John Bossy's entire thesis concerning English Catholicism in this period hinges on the change in attitude among the English Catholic clergy's patrons in France, as the rhetoric and ideology of resistance were now necessarily abandoned. The new consensus in France about political order and obedience to the monarchical will was appropriated by those secular clergymen who opposed the Jesuits, and they used it to construe their relationship with the English government to which they professed loyalty and from which they looked for toleration. They stressed the widespread hostility in France to the Jesuits; and they played up the virtues of 'Gallican' political views.[77] These divisions within the Catholic community were then further politicised by the need to gain and retain the goodwill of James VI.

Although the papacy tried to impose closure on the whole incident, via the mechanism of a papal breve, the disputes and factional confrontations which had become so public during the appellant business bubbled vigorously away for many years to come. And these confrontations started to widen out in their scope and significance. Or rather, the relatively narrow questions which were rehearsed during the appellant controversy were taken and applied more generally to the English Catholic community.

Even though the technical issue of the dispute was whether the arch-priest Blackwell's appointment had been valid or not, John Colleton stated that among the appellants' reasons for not accepting the 'constitutive letters' appointing Blackwell were 'aswell several truths concealed, as falsities related'. Among these truths concealed 'was our designe at that time and readiest purpose to make sute by supplication to his Holinesse for creating of bishoppes in our Church'. This pro-episcopal lobby among the clergy wanted 'to reduce (as much as in us lay) the broken state of our Church to an uniformitie of ecclesiasticall hierarchie, and customarie regiment with all Christendome'. They were driven by

a most sensible feeling of those manifest damages we dayly sustaine, and which day by day more increase upon us, for lacke of such spirituall comforts as accompanie that divine and sacred kind of government: to wit, the ministring of the sacrament of confirmation, the consecrating of holy oyles, with many mo[r]e. The first whereof [is] a comfort so many waies necessary for increase of strength and true courage in these our no weak combats, as not anything (the infinite number of our lay Catholickes considered, who never received the benefite of this sacrament) can lightly appeare to be of greater or equall necessitie.

Indeed Colleton could describe the history of the (Catholic) English Church since the Reformation almost exclusively by reference to the absence of episcopacy:

it is now more than 40 yeares past since we had a Catholike bishop at libertie in place to exercise his function; and for these latter twenty yeares, and somewhat more, our countrey hath not had a Catholicke English bishop either in prison or out of prison; albeit Ireland, an iland subject to her Majestie, in travelling in like diversitie of religions as England doth, was never in all this while destitute of one, two, or more, made successively by the favour and appointment of the Sea Apostolicke.

---

[77] J. Bossy, 'English Catholicism and the Link with France' (Ph.D., Cambridge, 1961); Bossy, *ECC*, 54.

Should 'our brethren and the Catholikes of our realme' consider even for a moment how many graces flow from this sacrament of confirmation they 'would also most willingly joyne in one supplication with us to his Holines, that it would please him either to appoint suffragans, or give episcopall authoritie to some such as should live and converse among us'. For, asked Colleton,

to what other thing can we more impute the grievous defection and fall of so many from the Church, in the time of their triall, than to the want of the sacrament of confirmation, in which the fulnesse, strength and speciall protection of the Holy Ghost, both firmely to beleeve, and constantly to professe our faith, are given in such measure

and through which 'the grace of baptisme, according to the doctrine of divines, is . . . perfected?' Colleton even cited a work written by the pope, Clement VIII, to the effect that grace could find fulfilment only through reception of confirmation.[78]

THE VISCOUNT AND THE APPELLANTS

Although we have virtually no direct testimony of what Anthony Maria Browne, second Viscount Montague thought about all this, there are signs that he was moving towards some kind of empathy with the appellant position, perhaps as the weight of opinion within his entourage shifted in that direction.

We know that some of his servants, such as Robert Barnes, were probably inclined towards the Society of Jesus. But some of his other retainers and acquaintances were not. In 1596 Montague's great-uncle Charles, the illegitimate son of Sir Anthony Browne, had refused to sign a petition which was being hawked around Flanders in favour of the Society.[79] There were other relatives and friends, or friends of friends, who could also be seen

---

[78] Colleton, *Iust Defence*, 15–17.

[79] See AAW, A V, nos. 96, 97; Knox, *The First and Second Diaries*, 408. See also AAW, A V, no. 57 (a petition of 28 May 1595 against Hugh Owen, signed by Charles Browne); CRS 52, 220. Charles Browne was usually regarded as belonging to the Spanish faction among the English exiles in Flanders, PRO, SP 12/203/30, fo. 47r; Knox, *The First and Second Diaries*, 403. He petitioned for the Spanish pension lists to be reformed in order to exclude the critics of Spanish policy, A. J. Loomie, 'Spain and the English Catholic Exiles' (Ph.D., London, 1957), 199–200. But although Browne was not always on good terms with Charles Paget (*CSPD 1595–7*, 37), Christopher Bagshaw recalled, for example, that Browne had expressed criticism of the Jesuits after news broke of the 'Hesketh' plot in 1594, Christopher Bagshaw, *A Sparing Discoverie of our English Iesuits* (1601), 60. The appellants' courier, Robert Fisher, later claimed that among those who gave him encouragement in Flanders were Charles Browne and Alban Langdale's former secretary William Clitherow, CRS 51, 249. In 1604–5 Browne was living in Montague Close, probably in Montague House itself, LMA, P92/SAV/196, p. 16, P92/SAV/197, p. 22.

as fautors of the broader political position which the appellants claimed
to represent. Francis Dacre, Lady Magdalen's brother, was, as we noted
in the previous chapter, an enemy of Robert Persons and was lauded as a
sound man by the appellants. Lewis Lewkenor, the future master of ceremonies at the Jacobean Court, had returned to England in the 1590s fed
up with his lot in Flanders and full of bile against the Spaniards. He was
returned to parliament for Montague's borough of Midhurst in 1597.[80]
A couple of years before, he had published an anti-Spanish invective entitled *A Discours of the Usage of the English Fugitives by the Spaniard*.[81]
Lewkenor condemned the Spaniards for their tyranny, their plotting, their
factions and their hatred of good Englishmen, and their duping of English
Catholics into believing that they, the Spaniards, had their best interests at
heart in their policy. He identified Dacre as one of the unfortunate English
victims of Spanish ingratitude. Here Lewkenor poses as a kind of *politique*, denying that one should change political allegiance for the sake of
religion.

Lewkenor's public posturing as a reformed Hispanophile is remarkably
similar to the line and tone taken by another Sussex Catholic, Anthony
Copley, who at this time dedicated one of his literary works (*A Fig for For-
tune*)[82] to the second Viscount Montague, his kinsman (indirectly, through
their joint relationship with the Gage and Shelley families). In one of his anti-
Jesuit appellant tracts, entitled *Another Letter of M*ʳ*. A. C. to his Dis-Iesuited
Kinseman*, Copley asked, rhetorically, 'what may we probably expect at
Spaines hands, were it [England] under her aw', than 'tyrannie in octavo'.
Famously, he observed that Spanish rule in England would mean nothing less
than 'the rape of your daughter, the buggerie of your sonne or the sodomizing
of your sow'.[83] The stories which he had originally told to the regime in the
early 1590s about Spanish brutality now found their way into his own published polemic. He claimed that the Spaniards, even in 1588, had despised the
English exiles in Flanders who had enlisted under Spanish colours. They 'little
pretended the cause of religion or any good to it, as our Inglishe Catholikes
allwais supposed'. The brave earl of Westmorland was insulted by them to
his face.[84]

[80] Hasler, *HC*, II, 473.
[81] Later editions of Lewkenor's book were entitled *The Estate of English Fugitives*. See CRS
52, 219–21.
[82] T. J. McCann, '"The Known Style of a Dedication is Flattery": Anthony Browne, 2nd
Viscount Montague of Cowdray and his Sussex Flatterers', *RH* 19 (1989), 396–410, at
pp. 401–2; A. Shell, *Catholicism, Controversy, and the English Literary Imagination
1558–1660* (Cambridge, 1999), 134–7.
[83] Anthony Copley, *Another Letter of M*ʳ*. A. C. to his Dis-Iesuited Kinseman, concerning the
Appeale, State, Iesuites* (1602), 15.
[84] BL, Lansdowne MS 64, no. 9, fos. 34v–35r; Copley, *An Answere*, 62.

As Timothy McCann remarks, 'there is no evidence to suggest' that the second Viscount Montague and Anthony Copley were actually friends. Montague 'does not seem to have been solicited for help when Copley was imprisoned, and does not seem to have sheltered Copley on his estates when in trouble with the civil and ecclesiastical authorities'. Nor was Copley seeking advancement from Montague.[85] Yet, as Alison Shell's in-depth reading of Copley's *Fig for Fortune* shows, the protestations of loyalty to the sovereign expressed therein are not wholly directed to the Protestant reader but are clearly also a reproach to the Jesuits.[86] It must be significant that this brand of literary loyalism, with an anti-Jesuit twist, should have been dedicated to the second viscount. It seems highly likely that Copley was calling on him to show himself as a true-hearted Catholic Englishman, in the sense of lending his patronage to those who were trying to incorporate themselves into the regime's good books by demonising the assumed political preferences and radicalism of the Catholics who belonged to or were associated with the Society of Jesus. Perhaps, also, Copley was encouraging the young lord to assume the loyalist mantle of his grandfather, the first viscount.

Copley argued that the Jesuits' programme for a national conversion to the faith was a political nightmare, akin, indeed directly related, to the appalling threat represented by Spain:

> it is . . . at a word the whole state of our countrey which the Jesuits labour (whether in zeale to their founder who was a Spaniard, or in gratitude to Spaines benefits, and generally of the house of Austrich to their Societie) to subject to Spaine; and in such faction, and in such hope, have under pretence of Catholicke religion alreadie wonne unto the Spaniard much ground in our countrey; which (now that the plot is growne to a head in the arch-priest) they stronglie maintaine, and daily gaine more and more in the hearts of Englishmen.

Copley thought that it was 'a shame that either religion should be so profaned, or English nature so stained'. Grace should never be used to 'prevaricate nature, but to accomplish it'. Instead, 'why not let England continue English, and worke it selfe Catholicke againe (if it please God) in English manner?' 'Are they so much of God Almighties counsaile as to know whether is more to his honour the . . . practise of the seminaries (as hitherto) for the good of his Church and our countrie or the Spanish sword?'[87]

The fact that Montague was looked to by the likes of Copley does not necessarily mean that he sympathised with everything that the appellants said.

[85] McCann, 'The Known Style', 402.

[86] Shell, *Catholicism, Controversy, and the English Literary Imagination*, 114, 134–7, 195.

[87] Copley, *An Answere*, 39, 54–5. Copley also claimed that other Sussex Catholics, his own kin, were loyalists like himself, for example John Thatcher, the heir to the Thatcher family's estates in Westham, M. J. Urquhart, 'A Sussex Recusant Family', *Dublin Review* 512 (1967), 162–70, at p. 168; cf. *CSPD 1598–1601*, 380.

Catholicism and Community in Early Modern England

We certainly have no evidence that Montague was hostile to the archpriest Blackwell. Indeed, Blackwell was resident with Montague for a time, or was at the very least harboured by some of Montague's servants.[88]

Even if Montague was still making up his mind about how to position himself on the issues raised by the appellant dispute, the government was already sifting evidence and reports which implied that he and his friends were going to start posing as overtly Catholic figures. There was a search of Montague House in August 1599, although Lady Montague had managed to secure that sympathetic JPs should take charge of it.[89] By August 1601 the informer John Bird was supplying information about the saying of Masses in Southwark. He was sure that they were being said in 'the liberty of the Lord Mountacute' by the strongly anti-Jesuit priests Anthony Rouse, Robert Barwise and William Clarke.[90] In September 1601 Montague received a privy council letter telling him not to turn up to the forthcoming parliament 'forasmuche as there is cause . . . that your lordship's apparance should be forborne' in the queen's sight 'and in this assemblie', though since the other peers who were similarly told to absent themselves included Rutland, Bedford and Mountjoy, it may be that this was because Montague was likewise tainted by support for the recently executed earl of Essex.[91] In February 1602, narrated the Jesuit Richard Blount, a Scottish 'puritan' was convicted in star chamber 'for some bold speeches uttered against some of the lords of the council', for he had 'written a letter to some friend, wherein he taxed' Lord Treasurer Buckhurst and Sir Robert Cecil 'of papistry', as also Sir John Fortescue, Archbishop John Whitgift and Bishop Richard Bancroft, 'saying that all of them made way for papistry; that good laws were enacted against them but none executed, and a good proclamation lately set forth against

---

[88] Contemporary references to Blackwell's residences are somewhat confusing. A witness of a conversation between London priests in c. March/April 1603 claimed both that 'Mr Blackwell lyeth in the next house to the Blacke Bull in St Johns streete' and also 'that it is thought that the archprest lyeth much at Mr Hares house neare the Spitle', PRO, SP 14/1/7, fo. 18v. In July 1603 an informer told Lord Chief Justice Popham that William Wright SJ had said 'that the archpriest, when he will speak with anybody, meets them at some appointed place, but else he keeps a house and lives at it', HMCS XV, 217. However, a letter from another informer, also tentatively dated to July 1603, declared that 'this very day I have been in company with the archpriest at Mountague House', though Blackwell had lodgings elsewhere, ibid., 219. On 30 June 1604, a correspondent of Sir Thomas Chaloner wrote that Blackwell was 'better knowne' to Montague 'than I to yow and hath oftner dyned at his table and lyve[d] in his howse than the king of England hath done in his owne realme', PRO, SP 14/8/83, fo. 167r. Later, towards the end of 1605, Blackwell was said to be with the 'Lord Montagues steward', John Loane, at 'Montacute Howse', as well as with 'the Lady Arundell and Mrs Mayney', PRO, SP 14/19/111, fo. 198r; HMCS XVII, 500–1; The Lives of Philip Howard, Earl of Arundel, and of Anne Dacres his Wife (1857), 216–17.
[89] Southern, ERH, 81–2; CSPD 1598–1601, 288.   [90] HMCS XI, 362.
[91] APC 1601–4, 221, 220, 218. Montague gave his proxy for the session to Lord Buckhurst, LJ II, 226.

priests, but it proved ridiculous, for that, by my lord of London', Bishop Bancroft, 'especially, and others, they were still countenanced'. This bold puritan also stated that 'my Lady Buckhurst nursed papistry in her lap' and that 'she heard Mass with my Lord Montacute in Salisbury Court'. (For this presumption the puritan was condemned 'to stand upon the pillory, and to have one ear cut off in Cheapside and the other in Oxford'.)[92]

Another anti-papist who was punished for his effrontery in voicing doubts about the soundness of the regime's principal men (and notably about Lord Buckhurst, Montague's father-in-law) was the customs official Anthony Atkinson.[93] Atkinson had also gleaned information about what was going on at Montague House: 'Montague lodgings doth harbour Blackwell ... and a number of Jesuits and seminaries, and none dare meddle or speak of any sanctuary that belongs [to] him, the lord treasurer or his.'[94]

One John Ellis, of Broadmayne in Dorset, also passed on disturbing information about the second viscount. Ellis had once been among the Catholics' number and was persuaded that their religion was true. But, seeing that 'they were so dangerously disposed towards the State (as he conceived by the speeches of those that were inward with them)', he was 'moved ... to grow into dislike of their courses, and upon conference to reform himself'.[95] Ellis said that, led by the 'better sort', of whom Montague was one, the papists were planning an apocalyptic day of rebellion, and intended thereby to alter the succession. On 30 August 1602, Lord Chief Justice Popham informed Sir Robert Cecil of what Ellis had told him – 'that there should be a plot or combination set down amongst the papists of England, which is distributed or divided into eight parts of this realm, for a party to be made ... when opportunity may serve them'. Ellis 'had heard it spoken amongst such as were so given, that it was a duke's wife whom they seemed to depend upon; whereof you can make use and easily gather the sense, and what work the priests have in hand'. Popham and Ellis clearly understood this to refer to the prominent exile, Jane Dormer, duchess of Feria, who was kin, of course, to Montague.[96]

Ellis's minders instructed him not to discover himself to his former co-religionists but to continue posing as a Catholic and to keep dishing the dirt on them. On 11 September, Ellis claimed that

---

[92] Foley I, 18–19. William Wright SJ was reported by an informer to have said that 'the Lord Treasurer Buckhurst is but an indifferent statesman, for ... I am sure ... he was sworn to the Catholic religion in Rome, and reconciled there', *HMCS* XV, 217.

[93] Atkinson retailed stories about Buckhurst's immediate family: 'his son [Robert], daughter [Anne Glemham] and servants are odious to the most part of the kingdom that are Protestants', and Buckhurst, his son-in-law, Sir Henry Glemham 'and others their friends will set up popery and bring in the infant[a]'. They were calling Atkinson a 'bloodsucker' for arresting priests, *HMCS* XII, 565–7.

[94] *Ibid.*, 565–7.   [95] *Ibid.*, 332, 366.   [96] *Ibid.*, 332–3.

as the common report is amongst them, they have in several parts of the realm a plot, which they call a card or map, in which their practices do consist, and there is set down what they be that have conspired against her Majesty's person and the State, how many priests have come into this realm, what particular persons have been converted by them, whereby they that have done most service that way may be best rewarded when their time serveth. In which card is set down also what wellwillers they have to join with them when their time doth come, for so they term it, and how they are then to divide themselves.

In this 'card' it was, said Ellis, 'set down that their strengths are to be divided into eight parts of the realm', and 'this card is in every country of this realm where any store of recusants are'. According to Ellis, 'the general map for all England remaineth, they say, in Lord Montague's hands, upon whom they all principally depend of any great person'.

Now, clearly a lot of what Ellis was saying, especially his claim that there were 700 priests named in the 'card', was plain bunkum. But he may have been picking up, within the Catholic community, the sort of private comments which were really not supposed to be aired in public, or at least aired outside privileged circles of Catholic insiders. Conceivably this might have included (as Ellis claimed 'principal recusants' were telling 'the poorer sort') that it was advisable to 'hold patience until the good day cometh, and then all will be well', and that 'it will not be long before the good day will come'.[97]

What is significant here is that the second Viscount Montague was being talked about as a leader within the Catholic community. It seems to have been expected by some that his entourage would be a focus for Catholic political activity after the accession of Elizabeth's successor. It is worth noting that it was in January 1603, just before Elizabeth's death and James's accession, that Richard Smith insisted on leaving Douai and returning to England. Here he entered the household of Lady Magdalen, where his friend Thomas More had been for nearly ten years. Almost immediately Smith would join the toleration campaign to bend James I's ear,[98] and he would begin to agitate against Jesuit influence within the community.[99]

Was Montague starting to think, at this time, that he might establish some manner of precedence for himself among the English Catholics? A papal breve was issued to Montague by Clement VIII on 5 February 1603 stating that the pope had learned from a servant whom Montague had sent to him how much Montague had suffered for the Catholic faith even from his youth. The pope praised his zeal therefore and bade him labour for the maintenance

---

[97] *Ibid.*, 366–7.
[98] See Richard Smith, *Epistola Historica de Mutuis Officiis inter Sedem Apostolicam & Magnae Britanniae Reges Christianos, Anglice olim Scripta, ad Seren. M. Britanniae Regem Iacobum* (Cologne [imprint false, printed at Paris], 1637; ARCR I, no. 1094).
[99] Anstr. I, 322.

of unity and peace among his fellow Catholics. A second breve of 13 February, at Montague's request, granted a plenary indulgence to all the faithful who after confession and communion should visit his chapel and pray for the usual intentions on the festival of Corpus Christi and all the feasts of the Blessed Virgin Mary and their octaves.[100]

THE ACCESSION OF JAMES STUART

As Elizabeth's death approached, suspect Catholic gentry, particularly in Sussex and Hampshire, were placed under restraint to avoid any local confusion or agitation as the transition of power was effected.[101] On 16 March the Hampshire JPs informed the council that, 'according to your letters of February 22, we at several places have tasted the affection of the country by opening to them the imminent dangers unto the whole estate by those devoted enemies, Spain and the archduke'.[102]

There was evidently a swirl of political rumour and speculation in Sussex (as indeed there was in other counties). In July 1603 various Sussex men were had up for their recent treasonable or suspect speeches. One Lewis Bennett had said, apparently in a state of some confusion about contemporary ecclesio-political terminology, 'that if our newe kinge should alter the religion that now is, that it would bee as good or better and that the Catholickes weare the trewe Protestantes and that the puritantes [sic] and Brownistes weare but dissemblers'. (Bennett also believed that 'images weare more avaylable for playne ignorant unlearned menn' than 'sermons weare, for that sermons went in at one eare and out at another eare but images would bee better kept in mynde'.)[103] But such comments, however garbled, could be taken to mean that some local Catholics had been thinking and saying that they were the new regime's truest supporters.

The second Viscount Montague, like Sir Robert Dormer and several other Catholics, had made sure to send up to London fulsome assurances of absolute loyalty and reliability. He wrote from Cowdray on 22 March 1603 that he was grieved by news of the queen's illness and that he would 'always be ready to concur with your lordships in whatsoever may tend to the best peace and benefit of our country'.[104]

But Montague did not simply sit and twiddle his thumbs. A toleration tract published under the name of John Lacey but, according to John Bossy, probably written by Sir Thomas Tresham, informed its readers that there

---

[100] AAW, A VII, nos. 80, 81. A papal grant of 7/17 April 1625 noted that the second Viscount Montague had 'erected in' his 'own house and fittingly adorned a private chapel in honour of the Blessed Sacrament and of the Blessed Virgin Mary', Foley VI, 537.
[101] *HMCS* XII, 676.   [102] *Ibid.*, 676.
[103] PRO, SP 14/2/96, fo. 238r.   [104] *HMCS* XII, 699.

was 'general joy and applause' at James's accession, and good offices were performed towards him by Catholics 'with such alacrity in most places of the realme', in particular by 'the Viscount Montigue largly casting money among the people', as well as by other Catholic peers such as Baron Windsor and Baron Mordaunt.[105]

Clearly it was advisable for prominent Catholics to declare their loyalty to the new king. But such declarations were, to some, politically troubling. In Sandeep Kaushik's excellent account of Sir Thomas Tresham's public displays of loyalism, Sir Thomas's 'loyal' statements had a biting polemical edge. In such statements Tresham was also claiming that he should be allowed back into the fold of political favour, particularly in county government. This was highly offensive to those who still looked disdainfully at him and his Catholicism.[106] After Elizabeth's death, Tresham noisily proclaimed James's title in Northampton and Kettering. He seems to have wrong-footed some of his opponents into seeming less loyal to the new king than he was. (At Kettering he provoked a godly preacher to mutter that James should be acknowledged only if he proved 'sound in religion'. This allowed Tresham to exploit arguments more usually used against English Catholics. Tresham lectured his audience there on their duty to acknowledge a lawful sovereign whether he was of the same religion as them or not.)[107]

Other Catholics put on similar performances of political loyalism. Baron Arundell of Wardour, Montague's cousin, reminded the earl of Salisbury in 1606 that he had 'caused King James to be proclaimed in Shaftesbury on a market day, eight days before any neighbour town durst do the like'.[108] When the archpriest George Blackwell was being interrogated in mid-1607 he asserted that 'upon the late queenes death, when his Majestie was proclaimed king, he [Blackwell] was very joyfull' and that he 'sent wine to a bonfire' not far from where he was living.[109]

Here notable Catholics, with Montague among their number, were acting out the fantasies of the appellant tracts, establishing a stake in the new

---

[105] John Lacey, *A Petition Apologeticall, Presented to the Kinges Most Excellent Maiesty, by the Lay Catholikes of England, in Iuly Last* (Douai, 1604), 8–9; Bossy, *ECC*, 37–9. John Gerard noted that, at James's accession, 'Catholic noblemen at London cast store of money about the streets in sign of their universal joy', J. Morris (ed.), *The Condition of Catholics under James I: Father Gerard's Narrative of the Gunpowder Plot* (1871), 25.

[106] S. Kaushik, 'Resistance, Loyalty and Recusant Politics: Sir Thomas Tresham and the Elizabethan State', *Midland History* 21 (1996), 37–72, at pp. 60–1.

[107] *Ibid.*

[108] *HMCS* XVIII, 376. Cf. D. Lunn, 'Chaplains to the English Regiment in Spanish Flanders, 1605–06', *RH* 11 (1971–2), 133–55, at p. 138, citing William Camden's statement that Arundell was, just before Elizabeth's death, committed 'to a gentleman's house for speeches' made by 'turbulent spirits as concerning him', or because 'he had lately made some provision of armour'.

[109] AAW, OB I/i, no. 14 fo. 34r.

political order, demonstrating politically their right to say and do things which would have been looked at askance, or even punished, at most points in the previous twenty years.[110] This was also a means for some Catholics to steal a march on their own Catholic opponents by implying that those opponents lacked a true understanding of the loyalty due to the new sovereign.

One of the martyrological tracts published at this time, first in 1602 and then again in 1603, which appears to have come from within the Sussex/Hampshire Catholic community, was the short pamphlet dealing with the death of Edmund Gennings and the conversion of his brother John.[111] Gennings was a priest, ordained in 1590, who had been arrested and executed in late 1591. He had, the pamphlet said, contacted his brother John before his arrest, but his brother was not in sympathy with him, and, according to his own account, felt a great sense of relief when he knew that Edmund had been strung up and disembowelled. (Subsequently, however, he experienced terrible pangs of conscience, converted to the Church of Rome, entered the English College in Rome in 1598 and eventually joined the Franciscan order.)[112]

John Gennings's story, as it is set out in this short pamphlet, may be nothing more than the simple truth. But there was a significant polemical subtext throughout the narrative of his brother Edmund's life and death. For the taking of Edmund Gennings had been one of Richard Topcliffe's great triumphs. Edmund had been arrested at the London residence of the well-known Hampshire recusant Swithin Wells. (Wells was executed on the same day as the priest for feloniously harbouring him.) Wells was, as we saw, part of the following of the second earl of Southampton, and Edmund had been used at one time as a go-between from his own master Richard Sherwood, who subsequently became a priest, to the gentleman-martyr James Leyburn, a relative by marriage of the earl of Southampton. Leyburn publicly expressed a deep hatred of Elizabeth, and he was executed in 1583.[113] (The pamphlet also has an appendix justifying the layman Wells.[114])

The pamphlet may not, in fact, have been written by John Gennings himself,[115] but the circle in which he moved clearly expected to derive

[110] An undated informer's report, which can be assigned on internal evidence to late 1602 or early 1603, implies that there was a plan to use Montague House as part of an attempt to take advantage of the imminent accession of James, AAW, B 48, no. 42, fo. 111r.

[111] *The Life and Death of Mr. Edmund Geninges priest* (St Omer, 1614). See ARCR II, no. 338.

[112] CRS 5, 207.

[113] *Ibid.*, 205–6; J. H. Pollen, *Acts of English Martyrs* (1891), 216, 220; J. S. Cockburn, *A History of English Assizes 1558–1714* (Cambridge, 1972), 209.

[114] John Gennings, *The Life and Death of Mʳ Edmund Geninges* (St Omer, 1614), 103–10.

[115] ARCR II, p. 250.

considerable propaganda value from it. (We have already seen how the second viscount's gentleman-retainer Robert Barnes had helped to destroy Topcliffe's reputation.) In all probability the little book's publication was timed to exploit James's accession. Although it was printed on the Jesuit St Omer College press, the approbation for the tract was given by John Redman who was reckoned to be one of the secular clergy's supporters, and was a friend of Richard Smith.[116]

Very shortly after James's accession the new regime discovered and exposed the Main and Bye plots. Embarrassingly, for the secular clergy, the Bye conspiracy had been concocted by two of the appellants, William Watson and William Clarke. But what might have been an opportunity simply for a rush of anti-popish propaganda became the occasion for a flood of loyalist outpourings, outpourings which came from both wings of the Catholic movement. The archpriest Blackwell and the gentleman John Gage (nephew and heir of the leading Sussex recusant John Gage who had died in 1598) had been among the first to insist on denouncing the Bye plot to the regime. They were both within Montague's entourage, and Gage was kin to Montague. (Gage served as a go-between for Blackwell to Sir Robert Cecil.) Anthony Copley betrayed the plot to Blackwell, and then it was simply a race between people from both main Catholic factions to see who could tell the government first.[117] Blackwell had written some sort of *ad clerum* letter warning Catholic priests to be vigilant about a possible conspiracy against the crown by discontented Catholics. The letter, by accident or design, came to the eyes of the government.[118]

It must have seemed to the Brownes that the new regime was displaying a thoroughly un-Elizabethan inclusivity and openness. It was being said for example that the second viscount's uncle, Sir George Browne, was about to be integrated into the Court (even though an informer had reported around March 1603 that 'a Jesuet lyeth . . . in Sir George Brownes house'). No such appointment occurred, but only, it was alleged, because Sir George refused to take the oath of supremacy. James Gildridge, Lady Magdalen's

---

[116] Anstr. I, 128–9, 287; Questier, PM, 494.

[117] Richard Bancroft reported to Sir Robert Cecil on 9 August 1603 that the appellant Francis Barnaby 'was upon Sunday at the Court with the Lord Abbot of Kinlosse', armed with more details about both the Bye plot and the Main plot. Bancroft thought that Barnaby had not been entirely straight with the authorities, and only revealed all when he 'supposed that Mr Blackwell had laid a bait to have catched him, and that the other priests assured him that if he went not to me they would themselves disclose what he had told them', HMCS XV, 227.

[118] See M. Nicholls, 'Treasons Reward: The Punishment of Conspirators in the Bye Plot of 1603', *HJ* 38 (1995), 821–42, at pp. 830–4; PRO, SP 14/2/51, fo. 129r ('The free and voluntarie declaration of mee Anthony Copley . . .', 14 July 1603); PRO, SP 14/3/7. i; Hamilton, *Chronicle*, I, 90; HMCS XV, 153–4; AAW, A VII, no. 91, p. 453 (Blackwell to Gage, 26 June 1603, justifying the letter which warned against the conspiracy).

servant, was told by two of her other retainers, Richard Heighes and Thomas Middlemore, 'that Sir George Broune was one of the kinge's men, and was sworne one of the esquiers of the body. "What"', said Gildridge, '"is he sworne to the supremmasie?"' Heighes and Middlemore 'said no, nether would [he] be'. Gildridge 'semed to marvell at it. Then they replied that he was also a justice of peace.' And, with Gildridge 'marvelinge' just as 'mutch at this, they said that there would not be so mutch curyous loking for the oth of the supremasie as there had bin, for divers other were left unsworne as well as Sir George Broune'.[119]

But the Bye plot, in which people close-ish to the Brownes, such as the appellant priest William Watson and his friend Anthony Copley, were involved, conclusively showed how much political tension and frustration were still seething just below the surface of the early Jacobean Catholic community. The plot demonstrated how difficult it was going to be to hold the community together. And, indeed, not all Catholics, or even crypto-Catholics, were going to be able to bask in the favour of the new sovereign. Henry Howard had at last commenced his irresistible rise to true greatness. But others, for example Sir John Fortescue, the head of a large and essen-tially Catholic nexus which stretched into Sussex and Hampshire, found that the new sovereign's favour did not extend to him. It was no secret that he was hostile to Scots in general – 'I have always carried a suspicious mind of the whole nation' – and had believed that conditions should be imposed on James before his entrance into the kingdom. It was hardly a surprise that he was soon dismissed from the chancellorship of the exchequer.[120]

Even those who had postured vigorously as loyalists before the accession were not necessarily going to reap their expected reward. It emerged that Francis Dacre, Lady Magdalen's brother, was a lot less welcome to James after the accession than before it. Although one overly optimistic Catholic commentator rejoiced that 'Lord Dakers ys restored', on 19 November 1604 the earl of Worcester informed Sir Robert Cecil (now Viscount Cranborne) that 'this day the king being a hunting by chance cast his eye upon Fran-cis Dakers'. When they got back home, James intimated that he was not particularly happy that people such as Dacre were hanging about the royal presence. Had there not been, James asked, 'some proceeding against him by the council for his abuse'? Worcester prevaricated and said 'I was sure I set my hand to a letter for him, but belike he could not be found, or else was

[119] PRO, SP 14/1/7, fo. 18v; VA, Borghese III 124, g. 1°. 84; CRS 60, 145.
[120] L. L. Peck, 'Goodwin *v.* Fortescue: The Local Context of Parliamentary Controversy', *Parliamentary History* 3 (1984), 33–56, at pp. 48–50; Hasler, *HC*, II, 151; T. Birch (ed.), *Memoirs of the Reign of Queen Elizabeth* (2 vols., 1754), I, 464. Fortescue's son Sir Francis married into the Manners family, and Sir Francis's wife, Grace (Manners), was converted by John Gerard, Caraman, *John Gerard*, 161–2, 244.

committed and after discharged.' Worcester's report is somewhat opaque, but James was apparently now a good deal less enthusiastic about seeing some of his former Catholic friends.[121]

In fact, the Catholics' struggle to represent themselves to the Jacobean regime as loyal and dependable was only just beginning. It was going to be a struggle in which the influence and courage of leading men in the Catholic community were going to be crucial in making the Catholic case to a wider public. There are notes in the State papers of a conversation in *c*. April 1603, shortly before the Bye plot broke, between an unnamed man and various Catholic clerics in the London prison chamber of the appellant priest Thomas Bluet. They were talking about the prospect of compelling the new king to grant some form of toleration. One said, 'we are stronge in England and we may force the kinge to graunte a tolleracion if that all Catholics wold joyne together and be constant for that we shold fight upon a good cause and dobtelesse God would prosper them'. Anthony Rouse asked rhetorically 'what will not any prince doe to gaine a kingedome?', and he remarked that although James was 'a Protestant in shewe yet is he a Catholic in hart and mynde'. Francis Barnaby, who would soon go off to serve Montague's great-aunt, the countess of Kildare, opined that if the Catholics 'had a head they might doe some good but they have non and withall the cheifest of them are worse than hereticks without any reason or conscience and if any such matter were attempted they shold suddenlie be discovered'. Another priest, Richard Griffin, had apparently confronted Richard Bancroft and had shown him 'what danger the king did alwaies stand in if he would not graunte libertie of conscience and with all what badd seedes and members the Jesuets and the puritaine[s] are for that as longe' as any of them 'doe rage in England the land will never be in quiet but full in mutenie the one for the king of Spain the other for such as the king hath banished out of Scotland'.

One of those present then ventured to say 'that if any greate noble man of England would have bene the heade of [the] Catholics, as the earle of Worcester, Northumberland or such, then might they well have compelled the king to graunte libertie of conscience'. The assembled clergy could, however, very well think of a suitable and theologically orthodox nobleman – the second Viscount Montague. Indeed they believed that he was the 'one noble man Catholic in England', 'a man well noted and knowne'. The only drawback was that he was 'never brought up in martiall affaires but only to his studie'. The 'comynaltie' would not follow or respond to the bookish

---

[121] LPL, Fairhurst MSS 2006, fos. 177r–178v (transcript at ABSJ); *HMCS* XVI, 358. See also *HMCS* XX, 294, XXI, 177.

Montague in the way that they would greet peers such as the earl of Worcester or the earl of Northumberland.[122]

Significantly, though, Montague here seems to get the vote of the appellant or anti-Jesuit faction in the Catholic community. Some of them genuinely believed that he had leadership potential. In the days immediately after the Gunpowder conspiracy was detected, the informer John Bird rushed to denounce the Browne entourage (the group of Catholics with which he was most familiar) and declared that, 'as the viscount is of the Romish Church in England held for their grand captain and firm pillar, so are his houses receptacles for all such dangerous guests at their arrivals from Rome and foreign countries'.[123]

Montague may, therefore, even while labouring under considerable disadvantages (relative youth, no political track record and no obvious means of exerting actual authority over Catholics outside his own entourage), have been starting to agitate for a substantial share of the leadership of the Catholic community. And this agitation soon led him into open defiance of the regime.

Most of the language in which James had talked about toleration of dissent and about his own irenical attitude towards divisions between the Churches was, as one might expect, remarkably flexible. It allowed for a sharp about-turn if necessary. The about-turn came less than a year after his accession. In February 1604 James suddenly reversed his previous position and now presented a hostile face towards papists. One of the Westminster Cathedral archive manuscripts which summarises the main parts of a speech by the king, dated to 1604, may represent his mind. Here James subtly glosses most of the recent language which he had been using about Catholics so as to change radically the meaning of the relevant terms. As is well known, one of the bees in James's theological bonnet was the idea of summoning a general council of the Church to resolve the differences in Western Christendom and reduce Europe to religious peace and order. In this forthright discourse, however, James seemed to be envisaging a general council not so much as a means of resolving differences among Christians in order to initiate a period of universal harmony but, instead, as a defence against the unjust usurpations of the papacy which, James said, threatened all Christian princes, not just himself. He referred to parliamentary bills which 'might be prepared as should prevent hereafter the like daungers and mischiefes'.[124] James's point

---

[122] PRO, SP 14/1/7, fos. 18r–19r. About eighteen months later, just after the Gunpowder plot, one George Southwick from Paris informed Levinus Munck that 'I must justifie the great packett I saw directed to my Lord Montecute and the conference had amongst the preistes about his weaknes', PRO, SP 14/16/44, fo. 84r.
[123] *HMCS* XVII, 475–6.   [124] AAW, A VII, no. 102, pp. 497–500.

was expressed in a proclamation of 22 February 1604, the tone of which was uncompromising:

when wee consider and observe the course and claime of that Sea, wee have no reason to imagine that princes of our religion and profession can expect any assurance long to continue, unlesse it might be assented by mediation of other princes Christian that some good course might be taken (by a generall councell free and lawfully called) to plucke up those roots of dangers and jealousies which arise for cause of religion as well betweene princes and princes, as betweene them and their subjects, and to make it manifest that no State or potentate either hath or can challenge power to dispose of earthly kingdomes or monarchies, or to dispense with subjects obedience to their naturall soveraignes.[125]

As the king started to renege on the various promises which his Catholic subjects took him to have made to them, and as the difference between royal and Catholic interpretations of tolerance became clear, Montague stepped forward to add his voice to those of the crown's Catholic critics. In an extraordinarily risky and high-profile manoeuvre he decided to denounce, in the House of Lords on 25 June 1604, the new anti-recusant legislation brought before it, legislation which would pass into law as 'An Acte for the due Execution of the Statutes against Jesuits, Seminary Preistes, Recusants etc'.[126]

He had been present, on and off, in the Lords up to June; and it seems that he aspired to be an active working peer. On 27 March, he sat on a committee to consider the restitution in blood of the exile Charles Paget. On 7 May he was on a committee with, among others, his cousin the third earl of Southampton in order to consider a bill for the naturalisation of their Sussex kinsmen William and Thomas Copley. (The committee was 'appointed to meet upon Thursday morning, the 10th of May, by seven of the clock, at the Little Chamber', and 'the bill [was] delivered to my Lord Viscount Mountagu'.) He sat on several other committees concerned with issues as diverse as legal process in the exchequer and the Elizabethan statute of 1563 governing labourers.[127]

Quite astonishingly, in view of his subsequent speech against the 1604 recusancy bill, we can see from the Lords' journal that he was, again with his cousin Southampton and with the Catholic peers Monteagle and Windsor, appointed on 19 June to the committee which considered the revised bill 'for the execution of the statutes against Jesuits, seminary priests, recusants etc.'.[128]

---

[125] Larkin and Hughes, *SRP*, I, 73.
[126] For the provisions of the statute, see *SR* IV, 1020–1.   [127] *LJ* II, 267, 291, 293, 298.
[128] *Ibid.*, 324. On 16 June the bill had been 'returned to the House by the lord chancellor . . . with certain amendments, which amendments being many, insomuch that they could not well be inserted in the bill', the lord chancellor 'signified' that it was better to 'offer a new bill to the House, agreeing in substance with the former bill, adding the said amendments', *ibid.*, 322.

Perhaps Montague believed that he could exploit the difficulties which the bill was apparently now in. For even the version which came before the Lords on 23 June 'was . . . found to be so imperfect as the said committees thought fit to frame a third bill . . . which was presented to the House by the lord chancellor'.[129] We may assume that Montague had voiced his concerns in the committee which considered the bill. Either way, he did little to disguise his disapproval of the measure. And he decided to attack it at virtually the last possible stage – its third reading in the Lords.

As he rose to speak, he undoubtedly had in his mind the example of his grandfather, the first viscount, a man of conscience, moderate and in no way disloyal to his sovereign.[130] Like his grandfather, he felt compelled to speak out against a statute which he believed to be both politically unwise and utterly unjustifiable. There had already been a lot of Catholic agitation before parliament met. Parliament was now the focus of the Catholic petitioning campaign which was being traduced by Protestant conformist writers and a few puritans, such as Francis Bunny, who produced immediate and scathing replies to the Catholics' demands.[131] The recent royal proclamation of 22 February provoked the appellant priest John Colleton's retort, his *Supplication*, which should, Colleton said, be 'read and pondered by the lords, knights and burgesses of the present parliament'.[132] Richard Broughton, another of the secular priests who, during the Jacobean period, would be a stalwart of the Brownes' clerical entourage, produced a massive manuscript, likewise aimed at the members of the 1604 parliament; it was entitled 'A playne and manifest Confutation of the Englishe Protestant religion in particular as yt was sett forthe and continued by the late Queene Elizabeth'.[133]

But the political circumstances of the second viscount's toleration speech in 1604 and his grandfather's speech of 1559 were quite different. The first viscount had argued for a conservative settlement of religion in the wake of the

---

[129] *Ibid.*, 326.

[130] The Catholic who, up to and around 1608, compiled two manuscript volumes which now rest in the Bodleian Library (Bodl., MS Eng. Th. b1 and b2), and whose work is our source for the speech in parliament delivered by the first viscount in March 1559 and the speech there by the second viscount in June 1604, placed them next to each other in his text, *ibid.*, fos. 839v–847r.

[131] See Milward II, 72–6.

[132] A. J. Loomie, *Toleration and Diplomacy* (Philadelphia, 1963), 28; John Colleton, *A Supplication to the Kings Most Excellent Maiestie* (n.p. [printed secretly in England], 1604), sig. Ar.

[133] Broughton's work contains forty-five chapters with two prefaces, the first dated 31 December 1603. The second of these prefaces, dedicated to the nobility and gentry in the 1604 parliament, is an extensive toleration petition, and complains of the many malicious Protestant and puritan pamphlets against Catholic religion since the accession of James, Bodl., MS Add. A 125, fo. 11r. Though the manuscript is dated 2 February 1604, it also bears Blackwell's approbation of 14 June 1604.

utter failure and indeed dissolution of the Marian Catholic regime and establishment. The obstacles which the first viscount and other conservatives in parliament placed in the government's way were really no more than pyrrhic victories. In 1604, the second viscount used, on the face of it, similar terms and sentiments to those which his grandfather had employed. But, by calling for toleration, he was performing a fundamentally different operation. Here, the recently dissolved, if not exactly failed, Elizabethan regime had been both a thoroughly Protestant one and a regime of a peculiarly conformist cast of mind. It was expected that James's accession would be accompanied by some significant changes in the way that the law which governed the Church was codified and administered. The political instabilities created by the change of regime and dynasty were already being manipulated by both puritans and Catholics. Among those Catholics was the second Viscount Montague.

After the third reading of the new bill, on 25 June, Montague stood up to speak. (He had already pronounced, more briefly, against the bill two days before, when it received its first and second readings and was engrossed.) As his grandfather had done in his oration in 1559, the second viscount obscured his initial path of attack with mealy-mouthed expressions of unwillingness to speak, professions of inadequacy and fear of offence. He would address the matter only 'according as yt doth dyrectly concerne the poynt of religion; (for to speake uppon theis same poynts of pollicie and such like thinges I confesse I have no knowledg, nor understanding of them . . .)'. He was

full of feare, the which, if I should goe about to conceale, my very countenaunce and gesture woulde bewraye. I doo therfore acknowledge my owne pusillanimytie and want of contrarye proceeding partly owt of the reverence of my harte and mynde towards your lordships whom I am most fearefull and loathe to offende as having no manner of wyll to speake any thinge out of any spirite of opposition or lesse regardfull respect towards your lordships but out of the necessarye discharge of my conscience in this most important cause,

and partly also because he was aware that he went against 'the whole swaye and streame of the tyme'. Having rehearsed a ridiculous story about a Henrician friar who, having planned to preach an anti-Dissolution sermon and seeing 'some of the greatest persons of estate' suddenly appear among the auditory, quickly improvised a catatonic trance and spirit possession to get himself off the hook ('I come to delyver an ambassage, not from man, but from God him self'), Montague recited some offensive scriptural verses about the virtues of free and unrestrained speech in the face of the oppressor. He then launched into his tirade. 'Nowe therfore to speake of this bill in generall and fynding yt to bee in every parte full of severitie', he deduced that the bill was intended for one of the two following reasons (neither of which was valid or praiseworthy): either the bill had been got up 'in regarde of our dissonance from your lordships in matter of religion', and therefore your lordships be . . . desyrous to punishe us without any suche respecte, resting pleased even in this that punishment be used uppon us, as uppon persons that for our religion you like not, or els that your lordships, being desyrous to bring us to be in religion as yourselves are, do conceive likelyhoode by this severitie to worke this effect.

Such a mode of proceeding against Catholics was unreasonable. Catholics would not change their religion. Unreasonable it was also since 'our Churche and faithe is . . . approved by authoritie of the holie Scriptures which, thoughe yt be no point to be nowe disputed, yet I my lords am able to make good against any man in England that is not better than my self'.

Next he rehearsed the standard contemporary Catholic polemical line that the Roman Catholic faith of their own time was identical to the religion of the early Church. He referred by implication to the line taken in, for example, the recently published *Treatise of Three Conversions* by the Jesuit Robert Persons. Persons's tract insisted that the true faith was planted in England while England was in communion with Rome and was under Rome's jurisdiction.[134] By Roman Catholics, 'Christianitie yt self hath bene planted and established amongst us', in other words by men such as 'Fugatius and Damianus' and 'St Augustine and his associates from St Gregorie'. 'Otherwise than by meanes of this our religion we have no knowledg of Christianitie at all.' He denied that, 'in contynuance of tyme, errour or impurytie . . . by surreption entred into our religion'. Even if it were true, Catholics would be mad to 'be drawne unto that religion which is now professed here in England', since this would be to admit that God's providence had failed. God did not make mistakes when supervising the propagation of the gospel. And

if yt were necessarie to alter and reforme, and that any thinge might have beene amisse after theis mens labours, yet what manner of men they, out of whom the religion nowe used in England hath beene collected, Luther and Calvyn . . . and the rest of that company were for such a purpose, alas my lords I leave it to your selves to judge.

He emphasised that it was 'impossible' to make Catholics leave their religion 'for yt hath never beene that the Churche hath bene suppressed by persecution, but hath beene therby encreased'.

Montague recalled 'certeyne wordes that were uppon Saterday last spoken in this place by a nobleman uppon occasion of my speeche then offred unto your lordships against the ingrossing of this bill'. He noted that the peer had 'vehemently urged that the bill was fytt to passe for sundry respects, and among others for the precise order taken therin against the bringing upp of youthe in our religion, which is nowe by wante of such former provision (as

---

[134] Robert Persons, *A Treatise of Three Conversions* (3 vols., St Omer, 1603–4).

his lordship reported) greatly through out this lande augmented'.[135] Montague argued, however, that the common perception of an increase in the number of people professing Catholic belief since James's accession could hardly be attributed to children being educated as Catholics. It was the conscious decision instead of 'persons of ripe yeares'. Their lordships 'maye be pleased to observe that there must needs bee some extraordinarye matter in our religion that draweth awaye so great numbers from that wherin thay have beene brought upp from their infancies'. Only the plain and self-evident truth of Catholicism could have persuaded these people. For 'with us they cann expecte no honnour, no promocion, no offices, nor matters either of proffitt or reputacion', but 'they must looke for disgrace, for losse of their goodes and estates, for ymprisonment and afflictions yea and for deathe, so that, by that provision, I see no likelyhoode of that effect to ensewe which that lord so much desired'.

This could hardly have been taken as anything other than a veiled threat. Montague was alleging that out on the streets there was a great sea-change in progress. People were deserting the established Church in droves. Nor was this necessarily mere empty rhetoric. The regime was becoming aware that the number of Catholic conformists who were lapsing into separatism had significantly increased since the partial relaxation of the recusancy statutes in 1603.[136]

In a peroration, Montague assumed a mood of what must have seemed to many of his hearers supercilious and hypocritical humility (considering the breathtaking nature of what he was saying). He harped on about 'the dutie which I owe unto all my [Catholic] brethren'. He closed by disclaiming the Bye plot and the practices of William Watson and William Clarke, though many of his hearers would probably have taken little comfort from that.[137]

Montague's speech caused outrage. Such outrage would have been sharpened by the fact that he was the son-in-law of Lord Buckhurst (recently created earl of Dorset), about whose personal religious opinions, as we saw, rumours had been circulating for some time. (Juan de Tassis, sitting in Brussels in anticipation of the Anglo-Spanish negotiations which led to the Treaty of London, wrote that Buckhurst was broadly in favour of some measure of tolerance for Catholics.[138]) The House of Lords' journal records that Montague

---

[135] The 1604 recusancy bill dealt in some detail with the placement of children at foreign Catholic educational institutions, *SR* IV, 1021.

[136] See e.g. CRS 53, 147–8; J. A. Hilton, 'Catholic Recusancy in County Durham, 1559–1625' (M. Phil., Leeds, 1974), 147, 148, 153.

[137] Bodl., MS Eng. Th. b2, fos. 845r–847r. I am very grateful to Margaret Sena for supplying me with a copy of this speech.

[138] Manning, *Religion*, 233; Loomie, *Toleration*, 16.

did not only declare his open and earnest dissent from the bill but undertook (as it were by way of apology for all the sorts of recusants) the defence of their religion, and to inveigh against the whole state of religion now established in this realm; pretending the great antiquity of theirs and the novelty of this; saying, that we had been misled to forsake the religion of our fathers and to follow some light persons, of late time sprung up, that were of unsound doctrine and evil life, or to such effect.[139]

The bishops of Bath and Wells, of London, of Winchester and of St David's 'answered in all points'. Then the lord chancellor Sir Thomas Egerton 'interposed a motion, declaring to the lords that he doubted whether it might stand with the good order of the House, and with his duty, that such a speech should be suffered in the House as the Lord Viscount Mountague used', and that Montague should presume '(by pretence of speaking to a bill) to inveigh and speak generally against the whole state of religion established, and to speak directly in maintaining of the popish religion, so much derogating as it doth from the king's Majesty's royal and supreme authority and government'. Egerton 'signified that it was to be considered whether the suffering of such a speech might stand with their duty and allegiance unto his Majesty'. Various peers delivered their opinions unanimously that 'it was a very offensive speech', and that it should not be 'suffered to pass without some censure, animadversion and punishment'. Only Thomas, Lord Burghley gave it as his opinion that 'the best and fittest punishment would be to let him pass unregarded and unpunished; because he supposed that the Lord Viscount Mountague did affect a glory therein, and would be glad to get the more reputation among the papists, both at home and abroad, if he should be censured or punished in any sort for their cause'. The Lords' journal noted that 'in conclusion it was thought meet that some order should be taken for the censuring of the said lord for his presumptuous speech, but the determination thereof was deferred and respited until the next sitting of the Lords; and the bill, being put to the question, was passed by far the greater part of the House'.[140]

The following day 'the matter was renewed, and brought in question again, touching the Lord Viscount Mountagu', and it was resolved that Montague had 'given great cause of scandal and offence to the said House' and that he 'deserved to be severely censured and punished for the same'. It was ordered that he should be 'committed to the prison of the Fleet, and there remain until further order shall be taken concerning him; and thereupon the warden of the Fleet was sent for, and required to take the said Lord Viscount Mountagu into his custody, and so to detain him untill he should receive order from their lordships to the contrary'. After making a retraction of his views he was released on 30 June, with condition that he should come to

---

[139] *LJ* II, 328.   [140] *Ibid.*

the Lords on 2 July and 'make known, by his own speech, his mislike of his said former offence, and give satisfaction unto the House for the same'. He duly delivered an apology. He 'did signify unto all the lords, how far it was, and ever should be, from him, to do any thing out of any ill disposition, or meaning to offend them', and protested his 'most humble and dutiful zeal towards His Majesty'.[141]

Despite the apology, Montague's speech clearly caused a stir within the Catholic community. Sir Thomas Chaloner was informed on 30 June that

> for my Lord Mountegues commyttment yt is muche lamented amonge our trayterous papistes whoe affirme that he is worthye to be prayde for to the worldes end and that he shalbe enrolled for yt: I meane the spech he used as they say, viz: my honor, landes and lyfe are deere but my sowle deerer and I will never yelde to this bill (quothe he) meaninge againstes [*sic*] papistes wyves to be payde for by a penall statute aswell as the husbande.[142]

To illustrate how potentially damaging Montague's oral challenge to the regime was (damaging, that is, to the precarious balancing act to which James's desire for limited tolerance had committed his government), we need only to look at the manuscript and verbal gauntlets thrown down by Montague's own kinsman Thomas Pounde, the long-term prisoner for religion under Elizabeth. Pounde challenged the regime's proceedings in autumn 1604 against the Catholic layman Laurence Baily. Baily had been executed at Lancaster for helping an apprehended priest to escape.[143] Pounde presented a petition to the king lamenting the cruelties which he alleged were inflicted on Catholics. In particular he protested against the 'two justices of Lancashire circuit', Sir Edward Phelips and Sir John Savile, 'in many points concerning their last circuit in summer in Lancashire at Manchester assizes'.[144] He also made 'inference of scandalous imputation against justices of peace and jurors'; and he defamed 'the time past (Queen Elizabeth's government) and time present' and referred to 'God's vengeance in time to come'.[145] Pounde was dragged before the star chamber on 29 November 1604 for a set-piece exposition of the government's case against Catholic nonconformity.[146] The attorney-general Sir Edward Coke browbeat the defendant. Coke made a long oration about how mistaken the Catholics were if they believed that there was likely to be any change in the law. He expatiated on the 'necessity of

---

[141] *Ibid.*, 329, 334, 336; BL, Lansdowne MS 512, fos. 139r–142r.

[142] PRO, SP 14/8/83, fo. 167r.

[143] Challoner, *Memoirs*, 280. There is some doubt about the exact date of the execution.

[144] It was noted by an informant against northern Catholics in *c*. 1604–5 that 'the recusantes in the North doe sett theyr rest upon it to procure Baron Savyle and Sir Edward Phillips to be removed owt of that circuit, bicause they finde them so resolute in the discharging of theyr dutyes against recusants', AAW, B 48, no. 42, fo. 110r.

[145] *HMC, Report on Manuscripts in Various Collections* III (1904), 140.   [146] Foley III, 603.

his Majesty's confirming' the Elizabethan penal code against Catholics. Next Coke stressed 'how profitable to these realms it would be to have the same laws put in speedy, due and exact execution' and also 'how inconvenient' it would be 'to have any toleration of religion or connivance of permitting favour to the Catholics in matter of religion'.[147]

Pounde's trial served as a public justification of the new courses being taken against recusant Catholicism. Coke 'seriously protested that there were above fifteen hundred recusants converted and become communicants upon the execution' of the unfortunate layman Laurence Baily and of another Catholic called Rawson, who, he insisted, had both 'died Protestants'. Furthermore he claimed that the justice dispensed to Pounde was a great official *coup* against the Catholic cause (even though the court had spent some time ridiculing Pounde's claim to be a 'prolocutor' for the realm's Catholics, and Sir Robert Cecil had said that he was no more than 'a weak and feeble-witted old man'). For 'where in the course of his whole narration and charge' Coke 'severed Mr Pownde's proceeding from matter or nature of religion, yet afterwards in sounding the day's victory he gloried in triumphant wise, saying that this day the Protestant religion had gained the greatest victory against the Catholics that at any time erst they had'.[148]

Three more Catholics were executed in the North in August and September 1605.[149] As part of this exercise in instilling some discipline into northern Catholics, Pounde was dragged round the assizes at York and Lancaster to make public submission for his fault. It was subsequently claimed that many of the recusants indicted at Lancaster had submitted.[150] And similar reports were received from other counties and dioceses where Protestant officialdom reckoned that it had dealt out sharp and well-deserved punishment to Catholics.[151]

THE GUNPOWDER PLOT

This, then, was one of the contexts for the Gunpowder conspiracy which was detected in November 1605. Modern historians have never fully agreed upon the exact nature of its origins. But the project appears to have originated among a small group of wealthy Catholic gentry who tended to look for spiritual guidance to an almost exclusively Jesuit clerical cadre – including the Jesuit superior in England, Henry Garnet.

Considering that the second Viscount Montague may, at this time, have been gravitating towards the Catholic clergymen who were hostile to Jesuit

[147] ARSJ, Anglia MS 37, fo. 116r–v [new foliation]; *HMC, Various Collections* III, 140–1.
[148] *HMC, Various Collections* III, 144, 145. [149] Challoner, *Memoirs*, 280–1.
[150] Foley III, 136–8. [151] See e.g. *HMCS* XVII, 157, 360, 427.

assertions of leadership within the Catholic community, one might have expected that he would neither have been involved in nor been blamed for this debacle, and perhaps might even have tried to profit from it in order to demonstrate his loyalty.

But it turned out differently. For he was known to be a friend of the conspirator Robert Catesby, his relative by marriage.[152] Indeed Montague had to confess that he had been talking with Catesby 'the Tuesday fortnight before All Saints' Day' when Montague had gone to see his aunt, Mary (the dowager countess of Southampton), at the Savoy.[153] And Guy Fawkes, 'the miserable fellow . . . that should have been the bloody executioner of this woful tragedy', had for a short time performed the function of a footman in the first Viscount Montague's household, and 'should seem to have been . . . [a] servant' to the future second viscount 'for some four months about the time of . . . [his] marriage' in February 1592, though he had been dismissed by the viscount 'upon some dislike he had of him'. In *c.* April 1593 Fawkes returned, 'coming to' William Spencer, 'that was, as it were, my steward and his kinsman'. Spencer 'entreated me, that for that instant (being some few days)' Fawkes 'might wait at my table, which he did, and departed'; but 'from that time I never had to do with him, nor scarcely thought of him'.[154]

But Montague had been out of London on 5 November. He was one of the papist peers who would not have been present had the bomb gone off. Fawkes was forced to confess that Catesby had personally counselled Montague not to come to the parliament because he would do no good there, though Montague denied that any specific warning had been given him to absent himself.[155] The viscount admitted that he had indeed met Catesby on 15 October in the Savoy. Catesby asked him whether he intended to take his seat in the parliament. Montague replied that he would attend the House of Lords unless the king allowed him to be absent. Catesby suggested that Montague would definitely do better not to go, and Montague agreed (though probably for a different reason from the one which Catesby had in mind).[156] Montague's official excuse was, as Thomas Phelippes reported to

---

[152] The second Viscount Montague's uncle, Sir Henry Browne, took as his first wife Anne, the sister of Robert Catesby.

[153] Godfrey Goodman, ed. J. S. Brewer, *The Court of King James the First* (2 vols., 1839), II, 122. For Montague's efforts to explain away his recent contacts with Catesby, see PRO, SP 14/216/48A, 74, 86, cited in M. Nicholls, *Investigating Gunpowder Plot* (Manchester, 1991), 30.

[154] *CSPD 1603–10*, 255; PRO, SP 14/215/86; Goodman, *Court of King James*, II, 123–4. For Spencer, see ch. 6, pp. 197–9 above.

[155] *CSPD 1603–10*, 258; PRO, SP 14/215/100; *CSPD 1603–10*, 251; PRO, SP 14/215/74, though cf. PRO, SP 14/215/86.

[156] *CSPD 1603–10*, 251; Goodman, *Court of King James*, I, 120–2.

Hugh Owen, that 'havinge had experience the laste sittinge' in 1604 'how evill hit was taken which he spake in behalfe of the Catholiques, beinge therfore committed, he had greate reason now to avoyde the comminge thither'. He understood that 'more violente courses' were 'nowe intended' against Catholics 'which he could not with his conscience passe over with silence'. Thus he would inevitably 'incurre . . . displeasure' if and when he shot his mouth off in the upper House again.[157]

Montague was temporarily imprisoned,[158] but he was never brought to book in the way that e.g. the earl of Northumberland, another more-than-likely innocent man, was. Presumably this was, as Phelippes said, because of the benign influence of Montague's father-in-law, the earl of Dorset. Dorset would 'helpe to gett him out of the bryars'.[159]

As the proceedings against Northumberland were meant to demonstrate to the world, the conspiracy was intended by the regime to be understood as a kind of baronial revolt, even though the conspirators who engaged with the government's forces in the Midlands were manifestly not retainers in a Catholic nobleman's private army. On 2 December 1605 Salisbury instructed Sir Thomas Edmondes in Flanders that, whenever the topic of the plot should come up in conversation, 'because divers noblemen are committed, as the Viscount Montague, Lord Mordant and Lord Sturton', Edmondes was to say it was 'taken in hand for the cause of religion, and that in all the traitors' consultations they were very careful to preserve such noblemen as were Catholics from the blow'. Northumberland was justly suspected, wrote Salisbury, because of his dealings with Thomas Percy and because he had postured as an advocate for the Catholics. He had 'upon the death of the queen and after . . . declared often to the king that the Catholics had offered themselves to depend upon him in all their courses so far'.[160]

The regime was certainly not convinced that Montague's entourage was clear from guilt, though Montague's uncle Sir Henry, Robert Catesby's brother-in-law, publicly conformed in 1607 at the Sussex assizes (a quite unprecedented thing for the son of a peer to do).[161] Particularly in London the family was kept under surveillance. The informer John Bird had, as we have already seen, assured the regime just after the plot broke that funny things were going on in Montague House, especially in Lady Magdalen's

---

[157] PRO SP 14/17/62, fo. 85r.   [158] Goodman, *Court of King James*, II, 113, 117.

[159] PRO, SP 14/17/62, fo. 85r. For Montague's self-exculpatory letters to Dorset, see Goodman, *Court of King James*, II, 118–24.

[160] HMCS XVII, 535.

[161] Cockburn, *Sussex Assizes: James I*, nos. 90, 91. Robert Warren, one of the plotter Ambrose Rookwood's servants, confessed that he went to Rushton 'for Sir Henrie Browne's child', his daughter Margaret, and 'another of Mr Catesbies and brought them to Ashbie Ledgers and left them with my Ladie Catesbie', PRO, SP 14/216/77, fo. 124r.

part of the property.[162] It looks as if some of the staff at Montague House did maintain contacts with the Jesuits in London. The doorman and keeper of the house, David Ringsteed, was said to be very intimate with Richard Fulwood, Henry Garnet's friend.[163]

Richard Smith's account of Lady Magdalen's life claimed, as we have noted in the previous chapter, that her house was turned upside down in the wake of the conspiracy. Although at first she ensured that 'none besides four, by herself nominated, should search her house', Smith had to admit that

whiles she lay in London in the yeare 1606, a Protestant, seeing one go into her house whom he suspected (but falsely) to be one of those whom the king had proclaimed guilty of the powder-treason, declared the same to the king's council, who instantly authorized officers, that most watchfully beset both hers and the adjoyning houses from Wednesday at two of the clock in the morning till Saturday noon following.[164]

Smith is referring to the raid on Montague Close authorised and carried out very early in the morning on 9 April 1606, evidently because the authorities thought that the Jesuit Henry Garnet's friends were there. Sir John Popham narrated it for Salisbury's benefit. It was conducted by some of the Surrey justices of the peace. It relied on the use of 'a watch[man] in the tower of St Mary Overyes' (i.e. the tower of the parish church of St Saviour), a kind of stationary precursor of the modern helicopter 'eye-in-the-sky' search unit, in order to detect any attempt by those living within the Close to break cover. They also searched Montague House itself. Before the JPs 'entred the howse' they came to 'the gate', but David Ringsteed, 'the keeper of the howse, wold not suffer them to enter', and so they were held up for 'quarter of an hower untyll they sawe' someone trying to flee, but they still 'cold not gett in' and as a result 'were driven to send for sledgys to breke open the gate'. During the delay 'they in the tower sawe one other rune over a court into the lodgyng of a servant of one Mrs Wyborne bare legged and but with a cloke cast over hyme'. Another man was pursued but also evaded arrest. When the searchers burst into the lodgings occupied by Mrs Wyborne they found that there had been other occupants there until very recently, and they discovered that 'yesternyght Sir George Browne with thre[e] strangers supped or were very late together' there. This was confirmed by the discovery of spare apparel and weapons – 'thre[e] rapyrs, the owners not knowne'.[165]

---

[162] *HMCS* XVII, 475–6; see above in this chapter.

[163] PRO, SP 14/20/20, fo. 40v. Ringsteed was a recusant, though one entry in the Southwark sacramental token books in 1602 suggests that he may have briefly conformed in that year, Cockburn, *Surrey Assizes: Elizabeth*, nos. 1832, 2599, 3114; *idem, Surrey Assizes: James I*, no. 89; LMA, P92/SAV/195, p. 33.

[164] Southern, *ERH*, 55–6.

[165] PRO SP 14/20/20, fo. 40r. The search also picked up Richard Carey, apparently in an adjoining property. Carey was a financial agent for the Catholic clergy, *ibid.*, fos. 40v–41r, SP 14/20/21, fo. 42r; *NAGB*, 42.

Dudley Carleton (who himself was touched by the plot, since he served the unfortunate earl of Northumberland)[166] informed John Chamberlain on 17 April that, 'since the search at Montague House, it is remembered by some country people that they saw a man cross the marketplace with a cloak only over his shirt and slip shoes'.[167]

Richard Smith recalled that 'Lady Magdalen's priest', presumably a reference to himself, 'was then absent' because he was on the road towards Battle Abbey. But the priest 'understanding that two of her family were fallen grievously sick, instantly taking horse, returned to London the same day that the search began'. Smith's account then rejoices at his/the priest's escape from danger. He says that 'Almighty God so protected the Lady Magdalen that at the very instant when the priest, suspecting no danger, entered into the house, the watchmen for a quarter of an hour were gone aside'. And

even two days after, when it was esteemed most dangerous for him to remain there any longer, he went again out of the house in the midst of the watch, not one of them apprehending him, albeit amongst them there were three that knew him well to be a priest and did speak of him to each other and with their fingers pointed at him.[168]

Smith is probably being disingenuous here. The reader is being persuaded to believe that God in some way prevented the guard from arresting Smith. But we know that the regime was looking for specific suspects – those who were implicated in the plot. They were unlikely to have had any interest in Smith.[169]

Evidence of links between the plotters and the Sussex and Hampshire gentry who were allied to Montague came to light subsequently. The priest George Gervase (a relative of the Shelleys and Lewkenors) was arrested in February and executed in the following April; he was suspected of complicity in the conspiracy.[170] On 20 November 1605 Edmondes had reported to

---

[166] Nicholls, *Investigating Gunpowder Plot*, 174.
[167] M. Lee (ed.), *Dudley Carleton to John Chamberlain 1603–1624: Jacobean Letters* (New Brunswick, 1972), 77.
[168] Southern, *ERH*, 55–6.
[169] In July 1612 Smith complained to Thomas More that their enemies in Paris were slandering the secular priests, including Smith, telling the French bishops 'that we were Jesuitted men and I in particuler a powder traiter', which was a 'senseles and unchristian calumnie', *NAGB*, 180.
[170] Anstr. II, 128–9; PRO, SP 14/19/2; *HMCS* XX, 153, 203. Gervase came from Bosham. His mother was a Shelley. Agnes Mott argues that she was the daughter of Thomas Shelley of Mapledurham, and thus she was the sister of Montague's servant John Shelley, Mott, HR, pedigree B of Shelley family. (Anstruther reconstructs the family's genealogy differently, Anstr. II, 290–1.) Among those who were listed in the late 1590s as members of Sir William Stanley's regiment was a 'quarter maister' called 'Jarvis a Sussex man coosen [to] Sergeant Leutner, sergeant of the lawe', i.e. Sir Richard Lewkenor, the friend of, and legal adviser to, the first Viscount Montague. This was probably a reference to Henry Gervase, George's military brother, PRO, SP 78/42, fo. 265v (for which reference I am grateful to Dr Paul Hammer); Challoner, *Memoirs*, 295; *HMCS* IV, 328.

Salisbury that Guy Fawkes 'was a long time accompanied with a kinsman of his called Harrington' (probably the Franciscan friar Martin Harrington) 'that was born in the North, served here as a soldier, afterwards turned priest and went into England more than a year since and, it is said, still remains there. Harrington's elder brother serves the old Lady of Southampton', Montague's aunt, whom Montague had been visiting just before the plot was discovered.[171]

One of the people who was tarred by association with the earl of Northumberland was the earl's servant Robert Newport.[172] It is possible that this man was a brother of Richard Newport the priest, from Welton in Northamptonshire, a future martyr, and former travelling companion of the priest George Gervase.[173] Newport was kin to the Northamptonshire Ishams, a branch of which family regularly corresponded with the priests at the centre of Montague's entourage in the mid-Jacobean period.[174] (The priest Charles Newport, another brother, conveyed accounts of recent Catholic martyrdoms across the Channel to the English secular clergy in Paris.[175])

One can see here how the government, even if it had no interest in arresting Richard Smith, might come to regard some of the clergy in Montague's entourage with deep suspicion. In 1612 Montague turned up to Richard Newport's execution in a public display of support for somebody whom he may have regarded as one of his followers. The Catholic secular priests believed that Newport's treatment, and particularly his brutal execution, could be attributed to his rebuke to the trial judge over the question of whether Catholics or Protestants were truer subjects of the king. Richard Broughton, a close friend of the second viscount's chaplains, and himself a frequenter of the palace at Cowdray, reported that Newport got some retaliation in before he went to his gruesome death. 'Some say that Mr Newport suffred the more evell death because . . . when the judge told him that papists were the first traytors to the king he replyed' (with a pointed reference to the threat made by Ker of Fawdonside to the life of Mary Stuart and her unborn son, as her secretary David Rizzio was murdered almost in front of her) 'no, it was the Protestants for that they had killed him in his mothers wombe if the pistoll could have bene discharged'.[176] What

[171] *HMCS* XVII, 509; *NAGB*, 229.   [172] *CSPD 1603–10*, 257.

[173] *Visitation of Northamptonshire 1618–1619*, 119; Foley V, 581; AAW, A VIII, no. 52, p. 287.

[174] *NAGB*, 65, 89, 119, 163, 164, 197, 198, 200.

[175] AAW, A XV, no. 81, p. 217. Both Charles and Richard had been with the Gunpowder plot suspect Lord Mordaunt at Drayton House in Northamptonshire in 1606, Anstr. I, 248.

[176] AAW, A XI, no. 103, p. 289; Challoner, *Memoirs*, 327; J. Guy, '*My Heart is my Own': The Life of Mary Queen of Scots* (2004), 315. John Hawkins has pointed out to me that the Newports of Welton were related to the recusant Hobson family of Ningwood on the Isle of Wight. Thus Richard and Charles Newport would have had familial connections with the south-coast region near Cowdray.

was made, in the Catholic martyrological narrative of Newport's death, to sound like loyal sentiments and affection for the king was undoubtedly also intended to be polemically provocative.

In the course of the tracking and arrest of the Jesuit Thomas Garnet (nephew to the executed Jesuit superior Henry Garnet), the renegade Catholic priest William Atkinson reported that one John Browne had told him that 'theire was noe true religion in England, nether was theire any true and lawfull clergie', and that

yf the Gonpowder treason had taken effect many thousand would have rejoyced, who nowe semed to speake against it. And that it was the most wittiest project that ever was invented for that this land should nott have beene able to have beene furnished with so many politique men to maintaine a false religion at least in twoe hundred yeares.

Atkinson said that he protested 'that it was a most barbarous practize', but Browne answered that 'many lerned men and religious priests would then never have interprized such a matter'. Browne also expressed support for the traitor earl of Tyrone, and said it was wrong that 'ii or thre base borne lords shall have any such a worthye mans heade in their power'. Atkinson retorted that this was a matter for the king. Browne answered 'that the king mentt well butt did nothing butt comitted the whole rule of his kyngdomes' to the earls of Salisbury and Northampton and to Sir Thomas Egerton. Modesty forbade Atkinson to repeat how basely Browne spoke of Salisbury and Egerton, but apparently not, with the same degree of spite, of the conformist Catholic earl of Northampton. (The identity of John Browne cannot be established with certainty from Atkinson's report but it is possible that he was the recusant John Browne of Chichester, the second Viscount Montague's brother.)[177]

Montague, however, wriggled out of the web which had temporarily threatened to trap him. On 20 August 1606 Dudley Carleton noted that 'my Lord Montague crept out of the Tower two days since to his father-in-law's house upon composition of £200' with the lieutenant of the Tower 'which is all his fine and ransom'.[178] Unlike Mordaunt and Stourton, and of course the thoroughly ill-fated Northumberland, Montague escaped the ordeal of a trial.[179] We do not really know how far Montague had to make

---

[177] AAW, A VIII, no. 85, pp. 431–2. It is not clear whether this John Browne is the same as the 'gentleman' called Browne who was the subject of a further set of informations (of 23 October 1607) by Atkinson contained in the Cecil papers. Browne is said to have averred 'that all the Irish nobility have taken a secret oath of allegiance to the pope, and vowed they would never draw sword in defence of King James', and that the debt-ridden James was parasitising the English State and nation and was generally unpopular. Browne also 'affirmed it was most expedient that the pope should be supreme king over all other kings', *HMCS XIX*, 295–6.

[178] Lee, *Dudley Carleton to John Chamberlain 1603–1624*, 90.

[179] Nicholls, *Investigating Gunpowder Plot*, 74.

concessions to get out of trouble. The vestry minute book of his Southwark parish, St Saviour's, recorded on 17 September 1606 that the churchwardens were ordered to 'laye open and make a newe dore for my Lord Mountague and his familye to comme to church' and for 'the same dore to be made where such a dore was before'.[180] But we have no evidence that the viscount gave any signs of conformity at this time (or subsequently), even though some of his 'familye' living in Montague House tended to conform.[181]

CONCLUSION

Scholars have argued endlessly about the origins of the Gunpowder plot – how far it was brought on by the earl of Salisbury once its existence was known, and to what extent the interrogations and trial proceedings were manipulated to make it seem far more clericalised than it actually was, in other words to implicate the Jesuits in England. But one undoubted effect that it did have, intended or otherwise, was completely to erase any chance for political action or enterprise that a recusant peer such as the second Viscount Montague might have had while James remained king, at least in the sense of having a public role or pursuing a public career in the way that the conformist earl of Northampton did. Montague did not appear in the House of Lords again until 1621.

However, this is not the same as saying that Catholicism's political potential was itself erased by the plot. John Bossy famously opined that the conspiracy was the 'last fling of the Elizabethan tradition of a politically engaged Catholicism', and 'in its own grotesque way it figured the end of an epoch; it helped to precipitate a withdrawal of Catholics from the general concerns of the commonwealth'.[182] Clearly there is a lot of truth in this, certainly in the sense that, after November 1605, Elizabethan Catholic political ideas about resistance to monarchy were more or less irrelevant. But this did not mean that Catholics were thereby excluded from the political process. Even those, such as Montague, whose outspokenness seemed to consign them to the outer darkness, were never completely marginalised. For all the snide remarks about his pretensions exceeding his capacity and even his physical appearance – the secular clergy chaplains of the Brownes (adverting to his

---

[180] LMA, P92/SAV/450, p. 401. For the doorway from Montague House into the church, see ch. 7, p. 222 above.
[181] Considering that there had been a number of bitter disputes in the preceding years between the viscount and the churchwardens over tithes owed to the church, disputes which apparently were not resolved, it is perhaps unlikely that he would have used such a door. See LMA, P92/SAV/450, pp. 343, 351, 361, 369, 390.
[182] J. Bossy, 'The English Catholic Community 1603–1625', in A. G. R. Smith (ed.), *The Reign of James VI and I* (1973), 91–105, at pp. 95, 96.

shortness of stature)[183] occasionally referred to him as the 'litle lord'[184] – his Catholicism itself remained a political statement, a constant reminder of the alternatives open to the regime if its 'Protestant' policy lines started to fail; a standing counterfactual option if James's much-vaunted middle-way stance on everything from foreign policy to the government of the Church of England began to break down.

Of course, in the years after the plot, the second viscount remains often obscured from view and apparently inactive. In order to detect what he may have been doing we need to look now into the principal ideological developments within the entourage of this leading Catholic peer, to work out whom he had around him at particular times and what *they* were doing, and then estimate how far his agenda (as far as we can establish it) coincided or conflicted with the agenda of his clients and friends, especially the clerical ones. Professor Bossy demonstrated how much there was to be said about what went on inside the Catholic community, and in particular how the internal dynamics of the community, and the often conflicting interests of laymen and clerics within it, were crucial for contemporary Catholicism. We can see many of these conflicts being worked out under the eye of the second viscount as his household, already a repository for some of the leading Catholic clerical figures of the period, became a centre for some of the most overt factional activity within contemporary English Catholicism. It seems to have become a vehicle for the ambitions of some of those who aimed to dominate and reform the English Catholic community from the inside and work some significant political changes in Catholicism's status on the outside, notably in the community's relationship with the regime and State.

The second Viscount Montague's entourage, therefore, continued to act as a forum for debates about the future of the Catholic community in England. In the next two chapters I propose to take time out, as it were, to look first at why the Catholic clerical issues of the period were politically so significant; and then to try to establish who wielded what kinds of influence within the second viscount's entourage, before proceeding to see how his entourage became embroiled in some of the stormier conflictual politics of the 1610s, 1620s and 1630s.

---

[183] Isaac Oliver's portrait of the Browne brothers (see Figure 27) indicates that the second viscount was noticeably shorter than John Browne and William Browne.
[184] See e.g. *NAGB*, 113.

9

Catholic politics and clerical culture after the accession of James Stuart

Let us pause at this point to consider the question of why we should be bothered about what the second Viscount Montague's, or any contemporary English Catholic patron's, chaplains did. They have certainly been off the radar screens of most historians of the period. There were never that many of them. Of their number, many, as far as we know, never did anything very earth-shattering. (The biographical accounts of them in, for example, Godfrey Anstruther's *Seminary Priests* often run to no more than a few lines.)[1] Even those who were caught up in the 'persecution', and about whom we know a bit more simply for that reason, frequently remain two-dimensional figures. Indeed, the martyrological memoirs compiled by contemporary Catholics appear slight when compared with the ponderous *œuvre* of John Foxe on the Marian martyrs.

Furthermore, there is always a suspicion that because, in the context of the English Church, these Catholic priests were entirely separatist, they were therefore untypical. It is notable how, in Christopher Marsh's recent overview of popular religion in the sixteenth century, the ageing revisionist account of the Catholic seminarist clergy is accepted more or less uncritically because it fits Marsh's larger interpretive frame, where the religious activists of the period are regarded as unrepresentative. In other words, the form of religion followed by most Englishmen during the period was unaffected by the particular concerns, and perhaps delusions, of the self-appointed gurus of supposedly 'true' religion.[2] The overall effect is to play down the capacity of religious division, articulated at an intellectual level which was so far above the humble piety of the piously humble, to affect what people actually thought and did. If this is true for the puritans, it must be the case also for the Catholics. Catholic missioner clergy experienced religious proscription, could not publish and sell books openly, had no benefices in the English

---

[1] In part this is because of the low survival rate of Catholic archives. For the destruction of Catholic clerical archives, see e.g. Guilday, *ECR*, 74–5.

[2] C. Marsh, *Popular Religion in Sixteenth-Century England* (1998).

Church and were restricted to the houses of a minority of the gentry; and, in sum, since few Englishmen ever saw a seminary priest, the history of the English Catholic clergy in this period must be that of declining influence and, at times, virtual irrelevance.

This, however, is a potentially false perspective. As I hope to show, the clerical entourages which clustered around notable lay Catholics in this period, both aristocrats and gentry, constituted essential sounding-boards for their patrons, and also discussion groups for debate about key aspects of Catholic political and religious theory. They also had access to, indeed sometimes they constituted, intelligence networks which were relied upon by a series of interested parties, particularly foreign ambassadors in London and statesmen abroad. This gave them an influence quite out of proportion to their numbers and even to the material resources of their patrons. And their claim to represent the whole community, both clerical and lay, meant that their own intellectual differences and polemical quarrels could become struggles for the heart of the Catholic community itself.

A significant number of the seminary clergy were, of course, drawn from the ranks of the gentry. It is hardly surprising that these clergymen should rely for patronage on their immediate social circles and kin in England. (The patronage and resources which a separated English Catholic Church-in-embryo required could really not be supplied, in England, by anyone else.) The Jesuits deliberately sought the goodwill of the socially and politically powerful. A cipher list from 1609 reveals the codes by which specific Jesuit 'churches' were known. These 'churches', as Thomas McCoog shows, were defined 'not geographically but according to families'. In all probability the Jesuit who ministered to each 'church' resided with the family whose name was 'entered at the head of the list and placed apart' from the subsequent names of the gentry families in the same 'church'. The church designated by the letters A.B. was in the charge of Robert Jones, in which church we find, for example, Lord Herbert, heir to the fourth earl of Worcester, and the powerful gentry family of Morgan. The letters A.P. designated the church in the care of John Percy (a church which included, among others, Lord Vaux). Michael Walpole's church (C.D.) included Lord Mordaunt, Baron Arundell's son Thomas, and Thomas Sackville, the fourth son of the earl of Dorset. Anthony Hoskins's church (H.A.) incorporated Lord Petre's heir, while Thomas Abercrombie's church (G.V.) embraced Lord Lumley, and Richard Blount's church (N.O.) had the earl of Arundel, his mother, Lord William Howard, the countess of Worcester and Lady Windsor. William Wright's church (W.G.) included the countess of Rutland and the earl of Rutland's sister.[3]

[3] T. M. McCoog, 'The Society of Jesus in England, 1623–1688: An Institutional Study' (Ph.D., Warwick, 1984), 194.

But Thomas McCoog points out how complex the Society's policy here actually was. It was certainly more than merely a contemplation of where a Jesuit missioner could accommodate himself most comfortably. The Jesuits' *Constitutions* envisaged that the Jesuit missioner priest would seek out the resorts and residences of the powerful and influential in order to spread as widely as possible the spiritual aid given, in the first instance, to such people, i.e. because it would be 'mediated to others under their guidance and control'. Of course, in a country where the State and the established Church regarded organised Catholicism as a threat, it was not clear how far such a policy would be successful.[4] Yet the experience of post-Reformation Catholicism in England modulated between periods of (relative) persecution and (relative) toleration. Opportunities might well present themselves, at certain times, to extend the Society's spiritual and pastoral ministrations far beyond the confines of its patrons' residences. McCoog comments also that 'as long as the influential were able to exercise their position in order to implement what they had received from the Society, Ignatius's paradigm' could work.[5]

However, in the recent historiography of the English Reformation, scraps of evidence about the background, education and careers of the more-often-than-not gentrified clergy have been welded on to a grossly overschematised equivalent of the well-known, supposedly adversarial, relationship between Protestantism and 'the people'. Seminarist Catholicism takes on, if not the theology, then all the elitist and anti-populist characteristics of Reformed religion. For Christopher Haigh, the Protestant Reformation was a failure, at least as an evangelical exercise. But part of the State's reforming purpose was achieved, even if indirectly, by a social separation within the Catholic community between the new seminary priests (who should have held the sacred flame aloft) and the mass of the people who looked to them to take the place of the gradually expiring cadre of Marian priests who had separated or semi-separated from the Church of England in or after 1559. Whereas the puritans at least briefly, if unproductively, visited the dark corners of the land, the seminarists were, for the most part, not interested in approaching those people whom the puritans tried but failed to convert. The height of their ambition was a gentry house where they could be entertained in a style to which they were accustomed and where they could discourse with those who enjoyed a similar standard of education and had similar intellectual interests.[6] Says Dr Haigh, 'it is clear that, as a Capuchin visitor observed in 1632,

[4] *Ibid.*, 186–7.   [5] *Ibid.*, 186.
[6] C. Haigh, 'The Fall of a Church or the Rise of a Sect? Post-Reformation Catholicism in England', *HJ* 21 (1978), 182–6; *idem*, 'The Continuity of Catholicism in the English Reformation', *Past and Present* 93 (1981), 37–69; *idem*, 'From Monopoly to Minority: Catholicism in Early Modern England', *TRHS*, 5th series, 31 (1981), 129–47; *idem*, 'The Church of England, the Catholics and the People', in *idem* (ed.), *The Reign of Elizabeth I* (1984), 195–219.

the missioners preferred comfort and security in the houses of the gentry to risking poverty and arrest by working in the open'.[7] Popular Catholicism became, in consequence, a *deraciné* conservatism, cut adrift when the seminarists' cultural elitism distorted the true relationship between Catholic, Protestant and popular forces in the English Church.

The revisionist 'seigneurialisation' thesis draws heavily on the loyalist propaganda of the late sixteenth century put about by those priests (the appellants) who set themselves up in opposition to a Jesuit-dominated English Catholicism and claimed that the State should tolerate them since they, the anti-Jesuit priests, were simply the natural successors to the pre-Reformation clergy of England. They should, therefore, be distinguished from all Jesuits, puritans, practisers and politicians. Against them the State could have no quarrel because their religion was one of private devotion and ministration to the faithful, not a public challenge to any kind of temporal authority, and hardly any, even, to the official religion of the State Church. Offensive Catholic politicking was, of course, something rather un-English. And, typically, it was conducted largely from abroad by priests who had sold themselves to foreign powers.[8]

In particular it was a canting Jesuited style of religion which was at the root of the conflict between Catholics and the State. The leading anti-Jesuits consistently identified the Society as the main political fly in the religious ointment. In a manuscript of 1635 (which was filed in the papers of the English secular clergy's agent at Rome) the same line, even at a time of relative peace for English Catholics, was still being trotted out: 'by experience and by common report the Jesuitts are generally reputed by the Catholicks of England, that are not partiall, to have bin the cheefe causes of all troubles and discords which have molested this Church any time these forty yeares more or lesse'. They had brought misery to Catholics through 'contumelious bookes' and 'unquiett attempts'. All would be immediately set to rights if they were to be evicted from the realm.[9] The argument here was that if the seminarist clergy (or at least the overwhelming majority of them, who were, impliedly, not Jesuited) were left to serve their patrons in peace they themselves would prove no trouble to the State or to the established Church.

Of course, the revisionist thesis about the gentry's monopolisation of the seminarist clergy does contain a (microscopic) grain of truth. The seminarists by and large did not seek to revive a pre-Reformation Catholic culture, or minister to whole parishes in the way that, undoubtedly, in the 1560s, many conservative and Catholic-minded Church-of-England clergymen were able to do. But Haigh goes further and argues that seminarist chaplains, including those who eventually clustered around leading patrons such as the second

[7] Haigh, 'Continuity', 59.   [8] *Ibid.*, 38, 55.   [9] AAW, B 48, no. 27.

Viscount Montague, had effectively withdrawn from the post-Reformation battle for hearts and minds.

This, however, stems largely from seeing the seminarists as something that they were not – namely simple pastors – parochial replacements for the Marian clergy who stayed on in the parishes after the Elizabethan restoration of Protestant religion. For Haigh, 'the missionaries were unable to sustain and strengthen existing Catholic loyalties' in particular areas and among particular social groups, partly through 'geographical maldistribution' and 'social selectivity'.[10]

This is not to say that some contemporaries may not themselves have made such observations. But, as with a large number of things which were said about ecclesiastical matters in this period, contemporaries' comments on this issue tended to be polemically coloured and glossed, generated for specific polemical and political purposes and occasions, and it is arguably unwise to take them at face value.[11]

What we are seeing here, in the arguments about clerical function, is another version of the debates first explicitly aired in the appellant dispute (described in the previous chapter) about the nature and prospects of Catholicism in England. The antagonistic Catholic factions, fighting it out for influence in Rome and for tolerance from the Stuart regime, claimed that their own prescriptions for the 'mission' were the best means for increasing the number of English Catholics (the 'conversion of England' in contemporary Catholic parlance) and that their own Catholic opponents' devices and attitudes would lead the whole English Catholic movement and Church to their doom. They also claimed that their own vision of how the clergy should be regulated and governed (for many of the seculars, this meant through a reinstituted episcopate; for many religious, it meant anything but that) would make the Catholic clergy acceptable to the State, even to the extent of being a recognised support and bulwark of good social and political order, a boon to, not a bane of, the 'commonwealth'. The sheer intensity of the power politics which informed these intra-Catholic disputes, every bit as bitter and intense as, say, the conformist–presbyterian debates of the 1580s and 1590s, means that such quarrels cannot be read merely as a commentary on the state of the clerical ministry available to those in England who still regarded themselves as Catholics. Whatever else they were, the seminary clergy were not a replacement for ageing Marian clerics (many of whom, we know, did not conduct a perambulant ministry to the rural poor either).[12]

---

[10] C. Haigh, 'Revisionism, the Reformation and the History of English Catholicism', *JEH* 36 (1985), 394–405 at p. 403.

[11] See e.g. *Ibid.*, 404, citing AAW, A XXVIII, no. 62, pp. 239–42 (now printed in *NCC*, 269–72).

[12] Many of those Marian clerics, in fact, seem to have behaved more like Haigh's typical 'snobbish' seminarist, or at least not like his archetypal 'good cheer' Catholic. As we have

THE ROLE OF THE CLERGY

We are still left, though, with the problem of how to analyse the clergy's pastoral and other roles. The sum total of Patrick McGrath's response to Haigh was that Haigh ignored and devalued the contribution which the seminarist clergy made to the lives of Catholics in England.[13] This may well have been true. Haigh paid little attention to what seminary priests actually did. On the other hand, McGrath and others have told us little about the political and socio-cultural impact of having a fully separatist seminarist clergy let loose on the English scene.

A totally different approach to the problem of how to interpret the relationship between the seminarists and other Catholics, principally their gentry patrons, was taken by John Bossy. Bossy described post-Reformation Catholicism by using a sociological model of the gentry's and the priests' conflicting interests. Almost immediately after the 1559 settlement the Catholic gentry came to an accommodation with the Elizabethan regime about how their Catholicism might be expressed – namely that, within the household, religious practice was a gentleman's own business. Outside the household, it was the queen's business. This was something which 'the government, at least provisionally, accepted'.

It was this arrangement which the seminary priests upset: 'when conflict came, it came as a struggle between two notions of social obligation, and was fought in the debatable land between the order of the household and the order of government'. For Bossy, the seminarist experiment of the mid-Elizabethan period contained an activism which disrupted this previous 'natural economy' of religion between clergy and gentry. Between 'the outlook of the gentry and that of the clerks, coexistence was in the long run impossible'. The carefully planned and executed mission of Edmund Campion was part of this new spiritual and political activism. But while, temporarily, the 'dynamism' of the clerks carried the gentry along, there was bound to be a reaction in the end.

So, for Bossy, the Catholic seminarist clergymen of the middle of Elizabeth's reign were '"alienated intellectuals"', 'agents of transcendental

seen, Alban Langdale frequented the household of the first Viscount Montague, a thoroughly aristocratic setting for his long retirement, as did the priest and former master of Balliol, Anthony Garnett, who acted as Montague's steward. The Marian priest John Felton, arrested by the bishop of Worcester in late 1582, was noted to have served many leading local gentry families, including the Throckmortons, Pakingtons, Middlemores and Talbots, PRO, SP 12/156/29. i. Some Marian priests, such as Anthony Atkinson, acted as tutors in noble households, J. C. H. Aveling, *Northern Catholics* (1966), 35. The Marian priest Alban Dolman was, as we saw, described as having the port and style of a gentleman, *HMCS* III, 89; ch. 6, p. 186 above.
[13] P. McGrath, 'A Reply to Dr. Haigh', *JEH* 36 (1985), 405–6.

alteration battering at the foundations of tradition, including their own'.[14] Bossy's account of Catholic Counter-Reformation clericalism as a modernising force seems right, and can be given an even more explicit political twist. For in the 1580s the Catholic clergy in England were, if not exactly agents of a foreign power, nevertheless hand-in-glove with some foreign powers and ideological causes which looked as though they might well be the forces of the future, notably a rampant Spain and the Holy League in France (a cause which did in some sense win in the end – with the conversion of Henry IV). And if England did subscribe from time to time to the pan-European 'Protestant cause', that cause often did not look particularly healthy. Bossy demonstrated, in his doctoral thesis, how the politics of the English Catholic clergy who sought patronage among the French, especially among the League, followed ideological developments (in, for example, resistance theory) in France.

But after the collapse of the League and the *ralliement* to Henry IV, and when it became certain that James VI would succeed Elizabeth, the radical underpinnings for seminarist clerical activism were redundant. The gentry, ideologically, regained the upper hand. They reimposed control over their priests in return for being left largely in peace by the State.[15]

Many patrons were less than enthusiastic about their priests engaging in popular evangelisation or taking upon them any kind of public role or responsibility. The archpriest George Birkhead complained in January 1614 that a priest in Staffordshire whom he wished to become one of his twelve 'assistants' claimed that he could not accept Birkhead's nomination of him to this post, 'though willinge of him selfe', 'because his patrone threatneth him to putt him out of the doores'.[16]

When Bossy's scheme of Catholicism was duly dumbed down into textbook-style summaries, his well-known dictum that Catholicism had proceeded from 'inertia to inertia' in three generations was all too often taken simply as a statement that Catholicism, which had temporarily tried to

---

[14] J. Bossy, 'Unthinking the Sixteenth-Century Wars of Religion', in T. Kselman (ed.), *Belief in History* (1991), 267–85, at pp. 273–4. In this essay Bossy appears to say that he has rejected crucial planks of his own position on these matters, but his case appears to be a good deal more complex than a public retraction, and his other work on the European Counter-Reformation still heavily subscribes to the idea of Counter–Reforming religion as an agent of modernisation.

[15] Bossy, 'Character', *passim*.

[16] *NAGB*, 270. The victory of the Elizabethan Catholic gentry over their priests, who were forced into a social compact (described so well by Professor Bossy) in which the gentleman was the dominant partner and the priest the subservient one, is encapsulated in that famous vignette where a gentry patroness quarrelled with and apparently ejected her seminarist chaplain (John Radford) after he had kicked her little dog down the stairs. See Anstr. I, 284.

challenge the Elizabethan State, retreated into private and became politically inactive at some point late during Elizabeth's reign.[17]

But this did less than justice to the complexities and nuances of Bossy's argument. His description of Elizabethan Catholicism as a sociological battle between gentry and clerks, while both cerebrally smart and intellectually compelling, is also empirically justifiable at a number of levels. His account of the Jesuits regarding England as a mission territory, more like the New World than a European Christian State, also works well, and can be read off from the mounds of evidence about the Society's difficulties with their more 'traditional' Catholic critics who simply could not accept distinctively Jesuit clerical models and strategies. I do not see how anything very much can be added to Bossy's work on this score.

However, Bossy achieved part of his intended effect by making a conscious separation between the history of Catholicism inside the English Catholic community and Catholicism's history outside it. This was part of an argument that English Catholicism's progress was dictated primarily by what went on within the community; it was not an argument that the community's relationship with the State and with Protestant Englishmen did not matter. So it seems not entirely unreasonable to take up the issue again of where and how clerical Catholicism engendered political conflict outside as well as inside the Catholic community, and, indeed, how the priests' battles with each other, particularly as they fought to win the approbation and patronage of leading lay Catholics, had significant political ramifications outside the community.

In large part this was because each faction and each party to these quarrels claimed that if the State were to recognise the justice of their cause and allow them a measure of tolerance (and, by implication, deny it to their opponents) this would bring about good and transformative effects within the wider commonwealth. For example, as we have noted in some of the appellants' discourses, and as we shall see below in some detail, one of the principal modes of justification advanced by Catholics for the (State-tolerated) reinstitution of episcopacy within the English Catholic community was a polemical critique of an explicitly or implicitly anti-hierarchical indiscipline inside their own Church. The often-rehearsed arguments of some secular clergymen that a Catholic episcopate in England would help to curb political extremism among Catholics (should any such extremism be detected), and to promote the true worship of God, were self-evidently analogous to

---

[17] See e.g. J.C.H. Aveling, *The Handle and the Axe* (1976), 72. One can see how Haigh's misreading of Bossy would account for subsequent readers of Bossy and Haigh misreading Bossy as well. See e.g. Marsh, *Popular Religion*, 181–2, though Marsh has clearly understood that there is something wrong with Haigh's opposite case.

the 'avant-garde conformist' (as some historians call it) rhetoric of hierarchalist elements within the Church of England, elements which were anxious
and determined to do something about puritanism. The puritan threat, so
the Protestant avant-garde conformists argued, was not only corrosive of all
good order in the Church but was, in addition, anti-monarchical and repub-
lican in its rejection of aspects of the crown's stewardship over the Church,
in its Calvinist leanings generally and in its sympathy for the Dutch.

This is, to some extent, to jump ahead of ourselves, and to anticipate events
and developments in the late 1610s and during the 1620s and 1630s. But the
point remains that the 'internal' history of the English Catholic community
and its clergy was not, during this period, sealed off from the outside world.
The 'public' nature of these intra-Catholic disputes can be perceived also
in the way that Protestant anti-popery polemic picked up on and popularised
the already circulating personalised accusatory material which was generated
within the community by internal tensions and rifts. The English 'Protestant'
anti-Jesuit tradition was in part created by the spilling out into the public
domain of these tensions and rifts. William Watson's *Decacordon* is a regular
source of anti-Jesuit stories. The renegade priest Thomas Bell wrote a tract
in 1603 which rehearsed the divisions between the Catholic factions in the
appellant dispute. John Gee, Henry Yaxley and James Wadsworth, among
others, cited various books, published during the course of the appellant
controversy, to garnish their accounts of the dangers of popery.[18] When,
in the mid-1620s, Wadsworth denounced his own Catholic past, a good
deal of his denunciation of his former Catholic friends relied for its effect
on public knowledge of the disputes among English Catholics about the
alleged ambitions and hypocrisy of many of the Catholic religious orders,
and particularly of the Jesuits. Wadsworth's tone and style were deliberately
reminiscent of the appellant dispute. His revelations would have coincided
with the effusion into the public domain of the struggles between the recently
instituted Catholic episcopal hierarchy (presided over by the newly consecrated Bishop Richard Smith) and its Catholic opponents and critics in the
mid- to late 1620s. Wadsworth described 'the severall professions of the
Jesuites': 'the first and chiefe of them are machiavillians, who doe nothing
but imploy themselves in matters of State', and

these are they that observe these ten commandements which follow. 1. To seeke riches
and wealth. 2. To governe the world. 3. To reform the clergy. 4. To be still jocund
and merry. 5. To drink white and red wine. 6. To correct texts of Scripture. 7. To
receive all tithes. 8. To make a slave of their ghostly child. 9. To keepe their owne,
and live on another mans purse. 10. To govern their neighbours wife.

---

[18] See e.g. Thomas Bell, *The Anatomie of Popish Tyrannie* (1603); Henry Yaxley, *Morbus et
Antidotus* (1630), 3–4 and *passim*; T. Harmsen (ed.), *John Gee's Foot out of the Snare (1624)*
(Nijmegen, 1992); James Wadsworth, *The English Spanish Pilgrime* (1629).

And 'these ten commandments they divide into two parts, All for me; and Nothing for thee'.[19]

Bossy's account of the internal history of contemporary Catholicism in England as part of the 'nonconforming' tradition[20] makes clear how 'missionary' Catholicism would almost inevitably pose problems and challenges which, of their own nature, were likely to become public. The formation of the continental seminaries had effects which were not clearly foreseen, at least not by their founders. The spearhead of the new clergy, men such as Edmund Campion and Robert Persons, had the 'missionary' spirit. This was a spirit which they could not discern in the Church of England at all. And this was what they criticised the English Church for, rather than simply because it was not Catholic. In consequence, they were utterly at odds with the conservative religion of the parishes which is seen by both Haigh and McGrath as the focus of 'Catholic' resistance to the Protestant Reformation.[21]

But there was, initially, no obvious English venue or arena in which to exercise their view of the supremacy of the spiritual realm and the high calling of the clergy. The Marian Church had not been a suitable place for it. Exile in Louvain was equally unpromising. (As Bossy remarks, initially Poland seemed a better bet for the early English Jesuits, and Persons wanted to go to 'the Indies'.)[22] What about the seminaries? Perhaps they were the new vehicle for the mission. The founder of the seminary movement was, after all, William Allen, an activist and political firebrand.[23] And yet, as Bossy states, Allen was very much governed by a pre-Reformation mentality, and only dimly saw his way towards the mission. In other words, the sudden combination of spiritual and political vigour which for Bossy is the hallmark of mid-Elizabethan Catholicism, a bout of intense activism spearheaded by seminarists, was not an automatic result simply of setting up seminaries. For although Allen did indeed call on the Society of Jesus for the seminaries' administration and spiritual ethos, it was far from clear that all that the seminaries were designed to do was to support the pattern of missionary activity in England which some English members of the Society took to be the ideal and, indeed, natural activity for a Counter-Reformation priest. That pattern (established in the autobiographical accounts written by e.g. the Jesuits John Gerard and William Weston), consisting of heroic evangelisation in the face of the severest organisational difficulties, imprisonment and the

---

[19] Wadsworth, *The English Spanish Pilgrime*, 28–9. See also P. Lake, 'Anti-popery: The Structure of a Prejudice', in R. Cust and A. Hughes (eds.), *Conflict in Early Stuart England* (1989), 72–106.

[20] Bossy, *ECC*, 5–6.   [21] *Ibid.*, 16–17.   [22] *Ibid.*

[23] For the history of the seminary movement, see e.g. M. E. Williams, *The Venerable English College, Rome* (1979); A. C. F. Beales, *Education under Penalty* (1963).

threat of death, and imbued with an intense sense not just of the hostility between Catholicism and Protestantism, but also between the spirit and the world (or rather, the world, the flesh and the devil), was, we might think, from many of the Catholic narratives of the period, simply the norm. As Bossy has pointed out, it made sense for the Jesuits, faced with the hostility of the State, to rationalise their position in England by talking about England as 'a Protestant country where their skills were specially needed and the restrictions on their activity in Catholic countries did not apply'.[24] It was a blank slate where they could create the Church anew, in an evangelical rather than in an institutional sense.

The apparently chance 'survival' of missionary autobiographies, such as John Gerard's, should, therefore, be seen for what they are – not the reveries of retired missioners, merely recording what life had been like while they were in England, but, instead, deeply polemical accounts of how the Catholic Church in England should function.[25]

The sheer hatred which many English Catholics felt for Jesuits such as Gerard shows that the sunny and uplifting Jesuit accounts of the 'mission' are much more complex and elaborate than they look at first glance. These Jesuit narratives describe a godly community which was allegedly so well constructed and so zealous that its own evangelistic impulses in effect supplied all its necessary regulation and underpinning. The networks of gentry houses and patronage created and secured by missioners such as Gerard were the groundwork of a new and purer Church, a miniature commonwealth almost. But the Jesuits' enemies, both Catholic and Protestant, redescribed the Society's gentry patronage networks as a form of exploitation in which the Jesuits' professed spirituality became a means of extracting money out of gullible 'ghostly children' and wellwillers, damaging and destroying the wider ecclesiastical commonwealth of which their own organisation was merely a grotesque parody.[26]

---

[24] Bossy, *ECC*, 24.

[25] Cf. Haigh's rather unsubtle comment, in his review of Bossy, *ECC*, that 'Dr Bossy's selection of evidence has seriously skewed his perspective on the structure and spirituality of the community: how different the book would have been if Gerard's autobiography . . . had not survived!', Haigh, 'Fall of a Church', 183. In fact, it is really the other way round. How different would Bossy's book have to have been if its author knew that Gerard had *not* written such an account!

[26] Such critiques were very different from the censures which English Jesuits received from other Jesuits who disapproved of the special arrangements made for the independent English mission – i.e. which rendered it distinct from other Jesuit missions (which were organised into provinces). The English arrangement seemed to introduce divisions, based on national identity, into an order the spiritual unity of which was thought by some to be jeopardised by such a provision. Claudio Acquaviva had protected the English members of the Society from such attacks until his death in 1615. The problem was solved only by elevating the English mission into a vice-province in 1619 (and a full province in 1623), CRS 74, 17.

'THE CONVERSION OF ENGLAND'

In other words, almost from its inception, the Catholic mission created controversies even within the community about what its missionary function was supposed to be. Was the first natural flush of enthusiasm, characterised by the Campion–Persons challenge to the mid-Elizabethan regime, necessarily the best way to continue the Catholic clergy's presence in England? The buzz word of the age concerning the state of the clergy was reform. One of the claims made by Allen for the seminaries was that they were a purifying force for good in this respect. But, in England, how were such standards to be maintained? How were the clergy to be managed and governed? And what about the traditional forms of clerical authority over the laity? And, if the seminaries were still supposed to serve as spearheads of the Catholic assault on heretical error, what sort of priests should they be turning out? How should such priests be educated? How should they divide their time between combating heresy and serving the liturgical and sacramental needs of Catholic patrons? And, crucially, what model of clerical formation and ministry would lead to the 'conversion of England' (whatever that was)?

The early seventeenth century saw increasing disagreement among Catholics about what the seminarist clergy were actually for. Some Catholics started to claim that the clergy's original purpose had been conceived in circumstances which no longer pertained. The state of religion in England was not now going to be subject to a sudden change. The clergy could no longer maintain the fiction that they were the agents who would re-Catholicise the realm in one fell politically underwritten swoop. In fact, their role was now going to be much more like that of the clergy of the established Church. They needed, some Catholics argued therefore, to publish learned books, to have higher degrees and to be governed by an established episcopal hierarchy. Otherwise the Catholic laity, especially the gentry, would not accept them.

There was not a great deal of room for compromise here. The warring factions painted their opposites as entirely malign forces for evil, putting their own interests before those of the wider community.

Consider, for example, Thomas Fitzherbert's *Defence of the Catholyke Cause* of 1602. The tract was in large part a rejection of the accusations levelled against the Society of Jesus during the investigation of the Squire plot. But Fitzherbert wrote more generally about the function and purposes of the Society. Just as God had raised up, he said, in every age, a 'remedy' for every 'disease', 'for every poyson an antidote', such as Augustine against Pelagius, 'against the heretyks called Albigenses, a Dominik and his holy order of the fryer preachers', so lastly in this our age, against a Martyn Luther and his cursed crue of vitious apostates, he raysed an Ignatius de Loyola with his blessed company, of vertuous and apostolical priests, commonly called Jesuites, whom though the Devil and all his instruments . . . have no lesse impugned than the Catholike Churche it selfe, which they defend, yet neverthelesse theyr holy Societie is through the providence of God propagated and spred throughout the Christian world from one pole to the other; and therby the wrackes and ruynes of Christendome repayred, infidels converted, heretyks confounded, youth instructed, the weake edifyed, no lesse to the glory of God than to the confusion of his enimyes and theirs.[27]

These were breathtaking claims in the English context, for so much negative comment had recently attached itself to the Society there. Fitzherbert simply rejected all the accusations of political conspiracy which had been made against the Jesuits. Moreover his tract could hardly, even though it was formally directed against a series of named Protestant tracts,[28] be considered in isolation from the appellant controversy in which the Jesuits and their friends had been accused, by other Catholics, of unwise political activities. Rather than simply assert that they were no more than humble Christians, Fitzherbert went on to glory in the role assumed by the Jesuits in other countries, roles which were evidently far from merely pastoral. In effect, he argued that the conversion of England could be accomplished only along Jesuit lines, or at least at the Jesuits' direction.

Against Jesuit claims that the Society's enemies, out of mere jealousy, tried (though without success) to emulate their spiritual prowess, and ended up betraying Catholicism when (almost inevitably) they sold out to the regime, William Watson replied that only the secular clergy (by which he meant those among them who opposed the Society) sought a proper spiritual conversion of their native land, or at least more soundly than any Jesuit, 'for that the seculars take the very direct course that our savior Christ left . . . to all his apostles to imitate', namely

first, to seeke the conversion of soules by preaching and teaching and good example giving by word and action. Secondly, by doing all things gratis, taking onely things necessary for their maintenance and relieving of their present wants. Thirdly, not fishing after unlawfull gaines to inrich themselves . . . Fiftly, to make no exceptions of persons in bestowing of Gods graces upon them, but as ready to goe barefoot to save a poore beggars soule as in a coche of gold to reconcile a king.[29]

Anthony Copley rejoiced at 'this likelihood wee have of Catholike religion yet once againe in our countrie by our owne, not forraine, neither yet warlike but peacefull and even voluntarie, meanes'. Even at the present time, 'manie convertites come in daylie, and out of question infinite more would,

---

[27] Thomas Fitzherbert, *A Defence of the Catholyke Cause* (Antwerp, 1602), fos. 46v–47r.
[28] See Milward I, nos. 514–28, for the tractate controversy to which Fitzherbert's work was a contribution.
[29] Watson, *Decacordon*, 184.

were it not that *Leo est in via* (*viz*) the penall lawes of the land'.[30] In other words, cease to annoy the prince, and toleration will follow, and with it, *en masse*, those conversions which the Jesuits tended to claim were their own special province. But the conversions which *were* sponsored by the Jesuits were glossed and inflected, by writers such as Copley, as both intolerable to the State and of doubtful authenticity, since the Society's motives were themselves bad. Instead the anti-Jesuits' more acceptable understanding of conversion, not bound up with ungodly doctrines of political resistance to sovereign authority, would be a way to attract those to Catholicism who might otherwise be repelled.

But, in turn, writers such as Robert Persons reversed the polemical trans-formers in order to roast opponents such as Watson and Copley. All the intra-Catholic strife in England was reinterpreted by Persons and his friends in order to claim that the Society had, out of mere humility and goodwill, done its best to prevent trouble and had even looked after the best inter-ests of its Catholic detractors. Even the appointment of George Blackwell as archpriest had been necessary only because of the divisions among the clergy in England. When a real spirit of humility and charity prevailed, there would be no need for a superior of this kind at all. Blackwell was appointed merely in order to protect the Society from calumniation over the matter of 'governing secular priests'.[31]

Persons dwelt at length on difference of spirits, a central Ignatian topic. As for the 'passionate disordered brethren, broken out from us . . . by intemper-ate heate of emulation and contention, the best direction that we can give for Catholike mens behaviour and carriage towards them is, as towards brethren and frends in a frenzie or traunce, as men rather possessed with violent and raging spirits', to beware them. 'To the end we may know and consider with what spirits they are possessed or ruled by', Persons insisted that Catholics should note, as he did, that 'the difference of spirit betweene man and man is the greatest and most important difference that in moral matters can be observed'. For Persons it was self-evident that Watson could not pretend to any sound spiritual sense or vocation. 'The first and most notorious point of his wicked spirit (contrary to that of Christ and all good Christians and Catholike men synce that tyme) is against religious men and their profes-sion.' And Watson committed a virtual heresy by affirming a proposition long since condemned by theologians such as Thomas Aquinas 'that the lyfe and state of secular priests is more perfit than the state of religious men'.[32]

---

[30] Anthony Copley, *An Answere to a Letter of a Iesuited Gentleman* (1601), 68.

[31] Robert Persons, *A Briefe Apologie, or Defence of the Catholike Ecclesiastical Hierarchie* (Antwerp, 1601), fos. 98v–100r.

[32] Robert Persons, *A Manifestation of the Great Folly and Bad Spirit of Certayne in England Calling Themselves Secular Priestes* (Antwerp, 1602), fos. 102v–103r, 104v.

Here a version of the perfectionist trains of thought which Watson had perceived and condemned among the Jesuits was being enlisted to turn his accusations back on himself. Here it was possible to interpret the appellant controversy, itself technically an argument about various kinds of ecclesiastical jurisdiction, as part of the battle between true and false religion in England. Said Persons, 'this fellow and his compagnions do delight themselves . . . with secularity and apostasy, and divers yea the most of the cheefest heads of this faction are notoriously knowen to have slydden back eyther from the habit or vocation of religious lyfe to [a] secular' life. And 'it is probably suspected that a notorious apostata or two have had their hands also in the compiling' of Watson's scandalous writings. Who, therefore, could doubt that the whole appellant project was characterised by the spirit of apostasy?[33]

Persons insisted that 'it is a soare sentence of the Apostle concerning some that runne of wilfulnes: *tradidit illos Deus in reprobum sensum.* God hath delivered them over to a reprobate sense, not to consider what they do'. These reprobates were the men who had

done iniquity in the land of the saynts; which whether England may now be called or no, where so much suffering is, so much bloud shed, so many prisons filled with confessors; whether the seminaryes also may be called the land of the saynts, wherin so many innocent lambes are brought up in all vertue, fervour and devotion to be sacrifices unto Christ, in their due tyme; and whether the seditions and troubles mooved in the one and the other land by these men (both in the seminaryes we meane and in England) may be called iniquity, we leave to other men to consider; and therby also to ponder where and upon whom the dreadful consequence of this threat of almighty God may light if the cause be not remooved.[34]

No reader could be in any doubt that Persons was saying that the appellants were on the road to abandoning their Catholic priestly orders altogether and conforming to the Church of England. Their 'conversion' of England would inevitably be a farce and a chaos.

But others, such as Anthony Copley, replied that they expected Catholicism to grow and flourish in England through an ordered course – of building up the true Catholic Church in England institutionally, by regularising its structures, procedures and discipline, and by preventing quarrels and squabbles which, it could be argued, occurred precisely because of a lack of hierarchy and clear lines of jurisdiction. The relationship between Catholic clergy and laity, between patron and chaplain, needed to be overseen and regulated. Only by doing this would the evils of faction be prevented from becoming embedded in the social fabric of the community.

---

[33] Persons, *Manifestation*, fo. 107v.   [34] Persons, *Briefe Apologie*, fo. 206r–v.

Copley described how he perceived the Society of Jesus's presence in England to impede the growth of Catholicism: 'it is now above twentie yeeres since this Societie' came 'first into our countrie', and all that time

it hath laine . . . like a tub, heavie upon the grasse-plot both of it and our Church, whereby manie an uglie toade, evet, sow-worme, and other like venom-vermin have bred under it, the grasse being cleane withered away. High time therefore it is, that it be removed hence to her out-landish place againe, wherby both those vermin may either flie with it, or die here; and fresh floures grow up in the plot, such as before time did.

In this horticultural image Copley describes the increase of true religion as a natural process which should not be impeded by unnaturally blocking out the sun, the light of grace which nurtures and furthers the growth of the Church.[35]

Of course, it would be wrong to see the history of the English Catholic clergy of the period as simply a story of absolute and irreconcilable division between two clearly defined parties which, after quarrels and hostilities, broke completely apart, with no subsequent contact, as they pursued their own separate visions of what Catholicism in England should be like. In theory this was what should have happened after the appellant controversy was resolved by papal decree, a decree which ordered that the administration of the Jesuits and of the secular clergy in England should be kept separate. But we know that all the way through the period there were many among the secular clergy who sympathised with and even joined the Society and other religious orders.[36] Conversely, some members of the other religious orders, who were establishing themselves in England, sometimes joined with the seculars in opposing the Jesuit line on certain issues (notably when some Benedictines took the same line as some of the secular priests on the issue of the Jacobean oath of allegiance).

In other words there was, in practice, no complete institutional severance of personnel, no complete separation between proponents and practitioners of different styles of clerical ministry. It was not the case that all Jesuits were always at enmity with all other Catholic clerical groups (as many Protestants and Catholics liked to think) or that those Catholics who criticised them were irreconcilably estranged from them at all times and in all places.

In short there was always the potential for slippage between the theoretically clear and mutually self-exclusive positions constructed by the protagonists on either side. The outrage expressed by some of the secular clergy at what they claimed was the religious orders', particularly the Jesuits', clerical

[35] Copley, *An Answere*, 115.
[36] J. Bossy, 'The English Catholic Community 1603–1625', in A. G. R. Smith (ed.), *The Reign of James VI and I* (1973), 91–105, at p. 98.

and spiritual one-upmanship was not shared by all secular priests. Although, increasingly, professed English Jesuits tended to have done or completed their training within Jesuit novitiates, there were still requests to join the Society from those who had done the seminary course and had been ordained as secular priests.

It was, therefore, far from clear that the grand claims made by the Jesuits' most vocal enemies among the seculars that they truly represented the secular clergy, and that all the seculars shared the same opinions about the role of the religious, were actually true. John Bavant, an eminent and well-respected man among the Jacobean secular clergy, deliberately undermined the process of gathering support for the appointment of a bishop from among the ranks of the secular clergy. In a long missive to Robert Persons, written in March 1610, he declared that the archpriest George Birkhead's agents

do not directly ask whether the priests wish to vote in favour of bishops, as Mr [John] Mush had openly asked last year and received very many denials; but (in order to multiply the number of suffrages and increase the body of opinion) they proceed to some questions of a more general kind, viz. whether we are willing to obey superiors, and what persons we think most worthy of the episcopal dignity, so that they may elicit something in our answers whence it may appear that we have given some sort of consent, however indirect, in this matter of bishops.[37]

Bavant was suggesting that there were many secular priests who were not wholly in sympathy with the position of the new archpriest and his leading secular clergy supporters.

Bavant, formerly a friend of the Jesuit Edmund Campion, did not conceal the fact that he thought some of his secular priest friends were going about things the wrong way. He had written a seemingly moderate but in fact rather sharp letter to Birkhead in November 1608 about the activities of those who opposed the Jesuits. In particular 'they name them selfes, and some others with them, the body of the clergie of England', which claim Bavant thought to be misleading. They could not justifiably pose as representatives of all the clergy. They were deeply suspect in their dealings with the regime. They held doubtful opinions about the new oath of allegiance which Rome had condemned. And, moreover,

yf by theyr bisshopes at home and theyr agentes at Rome theyr meaning nowe be correspondent to theyr former purposes, viz: to establish so perfect a government amoungst them selfes as they imagine they shall, that the Jesuites shalbe secluded from intermedling with us in this our harvest worke . . . first they shall in so doeing manifestly shewe them selfes to joyne with our greatest adversaries to affect [sic] that which they have many wayes sought and wrought for these many ye[a]rs. For they knowe well and we ought to knowe better that without the helpe of the Jesuites our government would prove but a weake government. They knowe allso and we must acknowledge (yf we be not to[o] ungratfull) that in maner all [the] helpes we

[37] CRS 41, 99.

have to doe our countrey good maye justly be attributed to them. Most of us have had our learning and many allso theyr aeducation under them. And they have bene eyther the beginners or the great furtherors of the colleges we have any where for the contynewall supplie of learned men for tyme to come.

Bavant also implied that the patronage networks which supported the clergy had been largely constructed by the efforts of the Jesuits. 'We have litle creadit or frendshipe in any countrye but by theyr procurement.'[38]

Another priest, Ralph Stamford, who was, like Bavant, one of the arch-priest's assistants, had similar reservations.[39] In a letter to Birkhead, of 9 June 1610, he said that he did not think Birkhead's agent in Rome, Richard Smith, was representing properly and accurately the views of all the clergy. Stamford referred tetchily to the fact that he had once been a fellow of an Oxford College (Oriel) and was accustomed to the privilege of free suf-frage. He was definitely not happy about Smith being given licence to do 'what he pleaseth in our names' in Rome. Stamford did not approve of the proposals being presented by Smith to the papal curia for the reform (i.e. de-Jesuitification) of the seminaries. He said that when in the past he had had disagreements with Birkhead's predecessor George Blackwell, the suppos-edly dictatorial Blackwell had in fact been far more amenable than Birkhead now was. Stamford wanted the project of appointing a bishop to be dropped. He strongly objected to Thomas More (Birkhead's and Smith's friend) being allowed to rampage around the country collecting signatures and consents: 'if mens consentes be agayne required therto in particular, I could wishe the matter were more sincerily handled than of late it hath bin. For one tolde me his name was set therto without being asked, agaynst his will.'[40]

Like many others, including even some Jesuits, Bavant had no objection *per se* to the return of Catholic episcopal authority to England, or indeed to any of the secular clergy leadership's proposals, though he evidently doubted the motives of the more outspoken members of the anti-Jesuit lobby, and feared what they would do if they got their hands on the authority which they were seeking from Rome.[41] Bavant also denied, in his letter of March 1610 to Robert Persons, many of the premises on which the most ideologically

---

[38] *Ibid.*, 83–4.
[39] Ralph Stamford had been an assistant to the archpriest George Blackwell, and he had once, in 1586, been arrested near the Brownes' establishment at Battle, Anstr. I, 331.
[40] AAW, B 24, no. 65.
[41] CRS 41, 100. Robert Persons himself made much of the fact that he had been a proponent of an early scheme to create two bishops for English Catholics in the later 1590s (though, clearly, he did not envisage that episcopal authority should be granted to his opponents), VA, Lat. 6227, fo. 184r (transcript and translation at ABSJ); Persons, *Briefe Apologie*, fos. 101v–102r. In Persons's famous memorandum concerning the reforming measures which should be implemented if England ever returned to the Catholic faith, there are extensive passages on the role of episcopacy in accomplishing these reforms. See Robert Persons, ed. E. Gee, *The Jesuit's Memorial for the Intended Reformation of England* (1690), esp. pp. 119–34.

zealous of the secular priests based their own claims to represent a continuation of the Church which had existed in England before the Reformation. Bavant was furious that Thomas More, who returned to England in late 1609, went about saying, in order to intimidate the opponents of the episcopacy project, that 'there is a certain cardinal, intimate with the pope . . . who expressed great surprise that we did not retain the succession of bishops in England throughout this time of persecution'.[42] Bavant contested the, as it were, 'avant-garde' conformist attitude to episcopal authority expressed by some of the secular clergy. In his letter to Birkhead (cited above) of November 1608 he deliberately (as did others) poured cold water on the claims that episcopacy would have a beneficial effect on English Catholicism. On the contrary, it would animate the Catholics' enemies to come down even harder on them than they had done previously. Inevitably they would be punished for this flagrant challenge to the royal supremacy. He also exploited the seculars' own claims that such a bishop would not behave like a lordly prelate: 'such a bisshoppe differing neyther in personable presence, habite, nor porte, from any other poor priste, should rather blemishe that dignitie than honor yt: and, being barred (as he must be) from all open use of his function and faculties, should hardly performe those offices which some expecte'.[43]

Further, in his letter to Persons, Bavant questioned whether that bishop's function was really necessary: for 'what important service can' the bishop 'perform which is not in the power of other priests, except indeed to confer Holy Orders (which it seems more suitable to have done in the places abroad where we have seminaries for study)', to 'consecrate the holy oils' and to 'confirm those who here amongst us can have this sacrament only in desire'? All of these tasks and functions could, said Bavant, be provided for in other ways.[44]

Now, most of these objections to episcopacy were simply what one would expect from the most committed opponents of the pro-episcopal lobby among the secular clergy. We might therefore see Bavant as a stooge for the Jesuit enemies of the appellant priests. But Bavant was, it appears, not just a mouthpiece for the Society. He had occasionally been quite critical of the Jesuits. So here we have an analogy of the way in which some entirely conformist clergy in the Church of England were reluctant to see full conformity enforced on or extorted from ministers whose tender consciences prevented them from making the full and uncompromising compliance which 'avant-garde' conformists believed was essential. In the Church of England, those who argued against the imposition of strict conformity (which they themselves did not see as a test of true religion or as a necessary component of a

[42] CRS 41, 99.   [43] *Ibid.*, 76.   [44] *Ibid.*, 98.

true Church) claimed that such an imposition would cause division where it ought not to exist – and that Protestants should instead make common cause against other dangers, notably the Church of Rome.[45] There was, it seems, a similar sense and sentiment (after changing the relevant labels) among many Catholics who doubted the wisdom of forcing the episcopacy issue in the way that some of the English secular clergy clearly wanted.

What the anti-Jesuit priests feared most, however, was the presence within their own ranks of those whom they called 'votive brethren' (i.e. those sec-ular clergymen who had secretly vowed to enter the Society). Such people would undermine and corrupt all the anti-Jesuits' efforts to straighten out the structures of authority in England and the lines of communication between English Catholics and Rome. It was known, for example, that Thomas Wor-thington, the secular priest who was president of the English College at Douai, had bound himself by vow to the fathers of the Society (in fact, directly to his mentor, Robert Persons).[46] George Birkhead complained in April 1610 that Worthington 'will admitt none' from England into the col-lege 'but commended by them', i.e. the Jesuits.[47]

The seculars were delighted when Thomas Fitzherbert finally showed him-self in his true colours by actually joining the Society in July 1614. (As early as August 1606, he had made a private vow to enter the Society.[48]) Robert Pett, one of the second Viscount Montague's chaplains, remarked with bit-ing sarcasm that 'it is never to[o] late to make change of the best way to perfection'.[49]

In about 1626, just before the notorious 'approbation' controversy broke,[50] a manuscript account of the causes of disagreement between Jesuits and seculars specifically included 'votive' brethren. It alleged that, when the Jesuits were prevented from recruiting directly from the seminaries into the Society, the Jesuit administrators of those Society-controlled seminaries made students vow that they would enter the Society in England when their Jesuit friends should call for them. As the memorandum pointed out, these secret vowed Jesuits 'made the broyles' in England 'to seeme to be among' the secular priests alone. The Society could thus pose as unified and har-monious, the best and truest representative of the entire English Catholic community, and could accuse the secular clergy of being factionalised and incapable therefore of bearing the responsibility of episcopal government which they claimed was their special privilege and right.[51]

[45] See esp. P. Lake, *Anglicans and Puritans?* (1987); K. C. Fincham, 'Clerical Conformity from Whitgift to Laud', in P. Lake and M. Questier (eds.), *Conformity and Orthodoxy in the English Church, c. 1560–1660* (2000), 125–58.
[46] TD V, iv–v; P. Lake with M. Questier, *The Antichrist's Lewd Hat* (2002), 298.
[47] AAW, A IX, no. 31, p. 77.   [48] CRS 74, 170; Anstr. I, 117.
[49] AAW, A XIII, no. 185, p. 465.   [50] See ch. 13 below.
[51] AAW, A XX, no. 38, p. 139.

Throughout the 1620s and 1630s, even when the division between secular and regular clergy seemed to be at its most bitter and starkly defined, we find whispers and rumours about secular clergymen who were believed to be wholly 'Jesuited'.[52]

CATHOLICISM AND THE ISSUE OF HIERARCHY

Clearly there were similarities between the concerns aired among both Protestants and Catholics about how far the augmentation of episcopal authority would (or would not) edify and strengthen the Church. It is not entirely fanciful to argue that the 'approbation' controversy of the later 1620s, in which the religious orders balked at submitting to the authority of the recently consecrated Bishop Richard Smith (who insisted that they must apply to him to ratify their sacramental ministry expressed in the hearing of confessions), was caused by a kind of Catholic 'subscription campaign'. As with Whitgift's crusade in the early 1580s, what looked on one level like a rather technical administrative issue, a sort of clerical validation exercise, turned into a battle royal of opposing ideologies which touched on a good deal more than the mechanics of subscription or 'approbation'.

The debates among English Catholics over the best forms of government within the Church, and over the reconciling of duty and obedience towards spiritual and temporal sources of authority (debates which raged all during James's reign), were still raging when dissentient voices within the Church of England, such as Richard Montagu's, started asking difficult questions about the limits of conformity and the boundaries of orthodoxy, and the relationship of the English Church to other Churches.

Let us look briefly in a bit more detail at Catholic attitudes to the question of hierarchy as a 'conformist' issue. As we shall see in chapter 14, contemporaries' perceptions of the similarities between 'Laudianism' / 'Arminianism' and Roman Catholicism were informed not merely by apparent likenesses between Catholic and Arminian attitudes to the theology of grace. Probably rather more significant would have been the obvious analogies between Laudian ideals of conformity and hierarchy and the discourses within English Catholic polemic which attacked opponents of hierarchical regulation in really much the same terms that Laudians used in order to

---

[52] See, for example, the cases of John Wakeman (Anstr. II, 331), Edward Haughton (Anstr. II, 151; AAW, A XXVI, no. 86, p. 235), and Edward Manning (AAW, A XXVII, no. 7, p. 17; AAW, B 48, no. 4). Equally there were others, for example George Hesketh, who had left the religious orders, and who might therefore have been expected to sympathise no longer with the regulars, and yet, or so it seemed to the regular clergy's opponents, still followed the religious orders' line, PRO, SP 16/133/12, fo. 17r–v; Anstr. II, 155. For the case of Edward Morgan, see Anstr. II, 224; PRO, SP 16/99/19, fo. 189r–v; CRS 75, 245.

excoriate their 'puritan' opponents. The Catholic 'conformist' case stated that it was not just desirable but essential, for the health and well-being of English Catholics, that they should enjoy again the institutional and hierarchical structures which were the norm in episcopal Christian Churches.

This idea was expressed volubly by leading secular priests, and especially by those who formed the mainstay of the clerical wing of the Browne family's entourage. This entourage included, at one time or another, many of those people who would campaign most vigorously for one of the secular clergy to be invested with ordinary episcopal jurisdiction in order to bring the Catholic Church in England to its right state again.

It did not take a genius to see that once the pro-episcopal lobbyists had got their hands on jurisdictional authority of this kind they would prob-ably use it to do horrible things to their Catholic critics and opponents, many of whom were located among the religious orders. They would almost certainly use the weapons of episcopal justice against lay patrons of the reli-gious. And there was also, it seems, an attempt by the pro-episcopal lobby to align itself with the conformist ideologues in the Church of England. Even as James's reign began, there were readily apparent opportunities for certain Catholics to exploit aspects of Bancroftian conformist thought and pose as, in some sense, supporters of the royal will in the more general struggle against the evil of clerical nonconformity, from whatever source it came.

Of course, at the beginning of James's reign, the regime still refused to grant Catholics the toleration for which they pleaded. Nevertheless, the logic of the appellants' rhetoric and programme was clearly to make their Catholicism acceptable to the new king, and also to foment confusion in the supposedly dominant and coherent contemporary master-division between Protestantism and Catholicism. Bancroft himself was forced to secure a cast-iron guarantee from the privy council that his dealings with the appellants would be regarded as above board. Some of his Protestant critics said that he tended towards papistry. He was, at best, falling prey to, and at worst actu-ally facilitating, a clever plot to advance the Catholic cause. Some papists were pretending that there was a false dichotomy between moderate and 'Jesuited' Catholicism so as to inveigle themselves (posing as moderates) into the regime's good graces.[53] In April 1602, the Jesuit Richard Holtby noticed a 'puritane pamphlett very lately wrytten' which accused Bancroft of 'highe treason for lycensinge and favoringe the appellants and there appeale'. In the pamphlet Bancroft was 'very unmannerly dealt withall in the style and phrase of wrytinge . . . where in steede of "lordship", the "l" beinge turned

[53] Foley I, 12, 18–19.

into a "t" (of purpose as it is supposed) it smoothly runneth his "tordship", which beinge generally observed here hath caused his lordship to make diligent search after the booke and author therof'.[54]

In June 1604 the imprisoned minister Henoch Clapham, in a petition to Prince Henry, denounced Bancroft. 'By the permission (if not by the maintenance) of the present bishop of London', William Watson's appellant tract, his *Decacordon*, was published, and in 'Pauls Churchyard' it was more 'vendible to all sorts of people than the blessed Bible, whereby it came to passe that papists bragged of their day, and Protestants generally feared the erection (at least the fre permission) of popery in her Majesties tyme'. And 'som others, more deeply looking into the matter, did feare that it tended to the castinge up of a trenche betwene the English crowne and your royall father his righte'. Clapham claimed that 'forthwith [he] did in publique sermons daly oppose . . . Watsons Quodlibets and the fre permission thereof as against writings directly trayterous; and against the abettors thereof, as against accessories to treason'. Bancroft heard about it, sent for Clapham and said it 'appeared' by 'my medling in State-matters, that I was a mad-man and no minister; reviling me with unsavorie nick-names, threatninge to coole me in prison', where Bancroft duly sent him (though he was released almost immediately by the bishop's order).[55]

Now, obviously, the appellants were not simply Bancroftians in disguise. But in the peculiar circumstances of the late Elizabethan/early Jacobean period, they necessarily had to represent their cause and ideals as supportive, not subversive, of the crown, just as much as they had to posture, in order to retain the favour of the Roman curia, as champions of the prerogatives of the papacy. (In turn, the appellants' Catholic critics simply accused them of meddling in politics and provoking the regime to cause dissension within the English Catholic community.)

So a significant part of the struggle over the reinstitution of a hierarchy in England involved a series of negotiations with both the Roman curia and the English State, a State which might rightly be very suspicious of the deeper implications of the supposedly limited reforming aims of the Catholic hierarchalists. The supporters of such a reinstitution would have to work quite hard to prove that the order and discipline which a separate Catholic hierarchy would foster and enforce would benefit the State, not damage it. The pro-episcopal lobby's enemies, a loose coalition of Jesuits, other sympathetic clergy and lay patrons, would try to prove exactly the opposite – that this would be a State within a State which no Catholic, who was truly loyal to the crown, could possibly endorse or support.

---

[54] AAW, A VII, no. 36, pp. 213–14.   [55] BL, Royal MS 18 A XIX, fos. 2r, 3r–v.

THE POLITICS OF CLERICAL RESIDENCE

One of the key components of the 'seigneurialisation' thesis which describes how Catholicism became, after the Reformation, a religion primarily of the gentry, is the claim that the Catholic seminarist clergy were transformed, in essence, into mere servants of the gentry and aristocratic families with which they resided. Yet it is clear that the factional struggles over forms of clerical government and associated issues actually and inevitably dragged in the priests' patrons. Indeed the patronage which they dispensed was itself a central topic of those struggles. And their own Catholicism was in part defined by the type of clergy they employed and the kind of spiritual and political advice and counsel which they received from them. Robert Catesby's decision to annihilate, if he could, the political establishment assembled in parliament in November 1605 was justified, in his own mind, by the advice which he had received from Jesuit priests, particularly Thomas Stevenson who wrote a tract for him on the topic of political resistance.[56] Henry Garnet SJ claimed that he persuaded Catesby against whatever it was he was planning. But evidently Garnet did not do it very vigorously. Indeed Garnet's justification of himself would only have demonstrated to his accusers exactly how powerful and influential a priest's role was likely to be in these circumstances, and how likely a priest and patron were to think in concert, with the lead coming, on certain issues, from the priest.[57]

For all the inevitable material reliance and even dependence of a priest-chaplain on his patron-employer, the gentry were still to some extent bound or at least likely to listen to and take advice from their clerical clients. Indeed the famous, artless, almost naive account written by John Gerard SJ of how he went around various gentry houses, exploiting the extant marital and kinship structures of the families which he visited, was interpreted by his Catholic critics as a cynical and factional exercise in recruitment (although they would probably have tried to do exactly the same thing themselves). William Watson's *Decacordon*, in a brilliant exposition and parody of the missioner Jesuit's technique, describes how, 'when the Jesuits find one fit for their turne, they insinuate themselves into him' and 'keepe him company'. They use their doctrine of callings to work their way into their victims' confidence, 'shewing how necessary it is for every man to understand and know . . . which [calling] particularly belongeth to himselfe'. 'Then after they have layd these grounds, no marvell if the party so cunningly and kindly caried on, do fall into their traps.'

One of these 'traps' was the recruitment of gentry into the Jesuits' own ranks, allegedly so that the Society could get its hands on their money.

[56] *NAGB*, 120.   [57] *HMCS* XVIII, 95–6.

Meditations from the Spiritual Exercises were used to induce the exerci-
tant to consider which religious order he would like to join (if he were so
minded). And, if his choice was not the Society, his Jesuit mentor 'beginneth
to cast many doubts . . . and . . . adviseth him to consider with himselfe
better of his choise'.

Watson gives examples of people with whom he claims this kind of decep-
tion has been practised. He says he would give many more but he will
'enlarge . . . [him] selfe' only 'with a few goolden threedes of Father John
Gerrards web'. Gerard 'was the man that caused Henrie Drurie to entere into
ther exercise; and thereby got him to sell the mannor of Lozell in Suffolke,
and other lands to the value of 3500 pounds, and got all the mony himselfe;
the said Drurie having chosen to be a lay brother'. Among others who were
persuaded to part with huge cash sums was the future renegade Anthony
Rouse. There was also 'Maister Thomas Everard, of whom' Gerard 'had
many good bookes and other things'. Gerard gave the Spiritual Exercises to
Edward Walpole 'whome he caused to sell the mannor of Tuddenham, and
had of him about 1000 markes'. He got £400 from James Linacre, a prisoner
in the Clink, and then 'under pretence of the said exercise he cousined Sir
Edmond Huddlestones sonne and heire by sundry sleights of above 1000
pounds'. He got Thomas Wiseman's land from him by the same means. Walter Hastings and William Wiseman had been similarly impoverished. And so
the list goes on. It includes quite a few women who had been carried off to
be nuns. In this way the Jesuits mulct their gentry victims, completely overturning the true relationship between patron and client, 'in somuch as some
in jest would say: "such a one is Gilberted"' (referring to George Gilbert,
Robert Persons's friend) '"and such a one is Druried"'. Gerard's creation of
his missionary circuit was thus redescribed by Watson as a parasitic colonis-
ing of these allegedly unsuspecting and gullible gentry.[58]

Putting William Watson's diatribes against the Jesuits alongside Gerard's
account of his own dealings with various Catholic patrons, we can see how
there was at least the semblance of a fit between the Jesuits' own version
of their dealings, their Catholic enemies' narrative of the same and also, of
course, the Protestant anti-popish account of the Jesuit world conspiracy, a
conspiracy which replicated Gerard's activities on a much grander scale.

There seems to have been, therefore, a running battle between different
clerical factions to appropriate and retain the patronage which came to
them via the gentry and aristocracy, and also to influence the ideological
composition and preferences of the entourages of leading Catholic laymen.
Richard Smith claimed that the Jesuits and their supporters did their best to

---

[58] Watson, *Decacordon*, 86–7, 88, 89–91. For Rouse, see P. Caraman (ed.), *John Gerard* (1951),
25, 220–1, 236.

filch patrons from those clergy who were not sympathetic to them. They did this by spreading rumours among the gentry that those clergy could not be trusted not to reveal Catholics' secrets to the State. Smith said that 'the first cause of the miseries of the secular priests in England, beyond the external afflictions occasioned by the heretics, is the calumny, repeated over and over again by certain Catholics, by which even the chief of the clergy, and even some of the assistants themselves, are falsely accused of dealing directly or indirectly with the heretics'. Smith said that

rumours are often spread around that some large number or other of the priests (no names being given) have lapsed and betrayed the interests of Catholics to the heretics. Hence it happens that many of the Catholic laity fear that under the guise of a priest they may find a traitor, and consequently refuse to give hospitality to any priest who is not well known to them. Consequently those who are not so well known suffer the greatest distress; they are unable to work for the salvation of our country; they are forced to live in public inns amongst persons of most dissolute life, with peril both to soul and body; and thus the whole body of the clergy falls into the gravest disrepute.[59]

As late as April 1632 we find Thomas Longueville writing to tell Peter Biddulph, the secular clergy's agent in Rome, about

the miserable state in which such as I doe stand . . . by reason of the opposition of the Jesuits: whithersoever I ame sent by my superiour, that is to what place soever, according to the custom of our living here, the Jesuits doe endeavour to hinder my entrance thither by diffaming me, telling the people that I was thrust out of the English College in Douai for sedition.

Longueville added that

the ladies and woemen, with whome they dwel, are to that end by them emploied to prefer others in our places and to take exceptions against us; as a great ladie of theirs did, where Mr Wigmore lives; to settle one in my place taking exceptions against seditious priests; and how false this imputation laid against me is you knoe far wel.

Also 'they persecute me in an other manner for they have aimed to buye me out of the places where I have been resident'.

Mr Wigmore . . . did offer to the gentlewoman, with whome I did live, to mentaine her one of his Jesuits in her house, to pay for his dyet, to provide for his horsemeate, so that she should be at no charges neither for horse nor man; and I to keepe my self in was forst for this reason to release al allowance and tel her that I would have nothing of her but my diet, although I knew not where to have other helpe; but my adversaries with their wealth . . . have prevailed

so that 'I am forced to be gone'.[60]

---

[59] CRS 41, 144.   [60] AAW, B 47, no. 149.

CONCLUSION

The conflict over patronage resources was not, therefore, just over how much money, or 'alms', would be forthcoming from the aristocratic and gentry families who sponsored the mission, though that was unquestionably an important issue. It was also about the ecclesiastical preferences and loyalties within those families and within the wider entourages around those families. In the case of a major aristocratic Catholic family, such as the Brownes, the alignment of the whole entourage, or most of the entourage, behind a particular clerical faction or cause could make a crucial difference to that faction's or cause's prospects, and could fundamentally alter the balance of power and influence within the community.

With these thoughts in mind let us turn to examine the composition of the second Viscount Montague's household in order to see how these ideas about the politics of the English Catholic community worked in practice, i.e. within a specific aristocratic entourage. I also want to try to explain why the activities of some of Montague's clients and followers not only contribute material for the narrative of Roman Catholicism in England during the early Stuart period but, on some level, are also the story of an attempted *coup* for control of the English Catholic community. As we shall see, it is far from clear that this attempt to assert dominance over the community ever really succeeded. But it had important transformative effects within that community and significantly changed the relationship between Catholicism and the regime and State in England.

10

The household and circle of the second Viscount Montague

There had evidently been a radical change of clerical culture in the household of the head of the Browne family by the beginning of the seventeenth century. We have already seen that several of Anthony Maria Browne, second Viscount Montague's servants were convinced Catholics, notably Richard Lambe,[1] William Coningsby and Robert Barnes.[2] Montague's experiences as a young man in the 1590s probably served to push him towards more overt expressions of Catholicism than he had made (or been allowed to make) in his childhood and adolescence.[3] There was clearly something of a Catholicising process going on around him now in a way that was not the case when the first viscount was alive. We have noted how, in the 1590s, Henry Lanman, Montague's servant, was persuaded towards Catholicism by the arguments of his fellow servant William Coningsby.[4] (Lanman was actually reconciled to the Church of Rome by the priest Richard Davies who, we know, was a friend of the first viscount's brother, Francis Browne.[5]) There was even more of this explicit household Catholicism in evidence after 1605. Some of the family's servants enrolled at the seminaries on the Continent. Richard Lambe's son Anthony, who had been one of the second viscount's pages, entered the English College in Rome.[6] Anthony Fletcher, one of Montague's stewards, when he lost his wife, travelled to Rome and enlisted at the English College in 1609. He was ordained shortly

---

[1] See WSRO, SAS/BA 58.   [2] See ch. 6, pp. 202, 204, 205 above.
[3] See ch. 8, pp. 234–43 above.   [4] See ch. 6, p. 202, and ch. 8, p. 238 above.
[5] Davies had also been at the house of Dorothy White in Winchester, and with the Bellamies at Harrow-on-the-Hill (where Montague's future chaplain George Birkhead also resided). In December 1586 he was noted as the man who had 'conducted Campion . . . [and] Persons . . . through England', Anstr. I, 98; CRS 2, 274. Davies, who wrote up the martyrologies of, among other priests, Nicholas Woodfen, noted that after Woodfen had arrived in London, 'by the help of Mr Francis Brown, the old Lord Montague's brother, I got him apparel, and furnished him in such sort as he took a chamber in Fleet Street', Challoner, *Memoirs*, 112.
[6] See ch. 6, p. 205 above; Anstr. II, 181–2; CRS 54, 252; PRO, SP 14/12/26. On 22 March/1 April 1615 Robert Pett reported from Brussels to Thomas More in Rome that another son, Francis Lambe, had, as he had been told by William Cape, 'come over' and had 'gone to Lovayne with a Benedictine moncke', AAW, A XIV, no. 75, p. 253.

afterwards (on 18 December 1610). He used the alias of Blackwell. This suggests that there may have been a link between him and the former and now disgraced archpriest George Blackwell.[7] Fletcher's son Thomas, whose godfather was the archpriest George Birkhead,[8] also entered the English College, in November 1610. Another seminarist from the Montague stable was Anthony Whitehair.[9] His father Christopher was a stalwart Browne retainer, named, as we saw, in 1594 by Montague as his servant and the receiver of some of his rents.[10] Montague paid Anthony's education expenses at the college at St Omer. Anthony entered the seminary at Valladolid in 1613.[11]

The second viscount's household was, it seems, becoming more narrowly Catholic in its general focus, with even the more minor domestic staff now being known to be Catholics. For example, David Ringsteed, the doorkeeper at Montague House in Southwark, who fell under suspicion after the Gunpowder plot, seems to have been from the Hampshire recusant family of that name. Another Catholic domestic servant, Matthew Woodward, employed by the viscount in Southwark, seems to have been the man of that name at Lodsworth in Sussex whose wife was detected and excommunicated for her recusant nonconformity in January 1601.[12] In August 1611 Thomas Heath, a Winchester Catholic and close associate of Montague's chaplains, was sent to live in London, probably in Montague House or in the surrounding Close. He was used by the archpriest Birkhead to deal with the senior

---

[7] Anstr. II, 113; ch. 6, p. 202 above.   [8] *NAGB*, 93.   [9] Anstr. II, 354–5.

[10] BL, Harleian MS 7042, fo. 153r, MS 6996, fo. 192r; ch. 8, p. 235 above.

[11] As we saw in chapter 8, Henry Lanman said that Montague was forced in 1594 to dismiss all his Catholic servants. As a way of paying off Whitehair, Montague made him a grant, 'in consideration that the said Christopher had theretofore in the tender years of the same viscount taken great care, pains and travell for him (and had therein and since that time faithfully and truly served him the said viscount and was ready to do so), of the rectory and parsonage of Easborne . . . together with the parsonage barn situate within the park of Cowdrey and all the glebe lands, tithes etc. belonging' to it, WSRO, SAS/BA 69. In 1605, Whitehair was living in Montague Close, and was apparently a conformist, LMA, P92/SAV/197, p. 22. But Benjamin Norton reported to Thomas More in early July 1613 that 'heere is alreadye a poore man one Mr Christopher Whitheere sent for to appeare beefor his grace of Canterburye', AAW, A XII, no. 126, p. 279. A 'M^{ris} Whitheare' was listed as holding property in the 'Close of St Mary Ovaries' in Southwark at around this time, SHC, LM 882.

[12] CRS 60, 117. On 11 October 1609 George Birkhead advised Richard Smith to 'direct' his 'letters to Mathew Woodward at S. Marie Overies', AAW, A VIII, no. 161, p. 643. A chancery case concerning the leasing arrangements of Montague House and the Close in Southwark described Woodward as 'bailiffe' to the second Viscount Montague for the property, PRO, C 3/394/40. See also SHC, LM 882; LMA, P92/SAV/196, p. 16, P92/SAV/197, p. 23, P92/SAV/198, p. 30. Up to 1609 he appears to have been a conformist, but in that year and in 1610 the Southwark sacramental token books describe him as a recusant and show that he refused to receive communion in St Saviour's, LMA, P92/SAV/199, p. 31, P92/SAV/200, p. 31; see also PRO, E 377/21. By 1612 he was conforming again, LMA, P92/SAV/201, p. 30.

secular clergy's correspondence as it shuttled backwards and forwards between London, Paris and Rome.[13]

It is clear that, as the household seems to have become more overtly Catholic in its inclinations, some of the servants employed there became increasingly central to some of the Brownes' projects. For example, William Cape helped to arrange the distribution of polemical books published by the family's chaplain Richard Smith.[14] One of Montague's stewards, John Loane, who appears to have been a brother of the leading Kentish recusant Samuel Loane of Sevenoaks, was described by hostile sources as a close friend of the viscount, and heavily involved in the liturgical activity in Montague House.[15]

CHAPLAINS

As we have already seen, a cadre of Catholic clerics started to accumulate around the Brownes in the late 1590s and early 1600s, initially in the shape of the secular priests Thomas More (from 1594) and Richard Smith (from 1603) who were chaplains to Lady Magdalen.

The question we have to ask, however, is – does the gathering of seminary priests around a group of intermarrying and kin-related Catholic families signify anything more than the economics of clerical supply and aristocratic and gentry demand? How far were patterns of clerical service in the households of Catholic notables constructed by accident? It will be suggested in the course of this chapter that the employment within the immediate entourage

---

[13] We can guess at Heath's whereabouts from his report which describes the administration of the 1606 oath of allegiance in Southwark, AAW, A X, no. 108, p. 317.

[14] AAW, B 47, no. 174. William Cape was an uncompromising Catholic, and well known to the authorities. In June 1614, as he returned to England, he was arrested at Dover and, 'notwithstanding my passe I was tendred the oath, after refusall wherof I was sifted and searched and my lettres sent to the lord warden, and consequently to the bishop of Canterbury, and my selfe detained prisoner there till answeare was retourned to send me back againe', AAW, A XIII, no. 157, p. 403. Robert Pett reported in September 1615 that Cape was in Newgate prison, AAW, A XIV, no. 159, p. 495. In late 1622 Cape was entrusted with conveying over to the Continent the heir to the Montague title, Francis Browne, AAW, A XVI, no. 173, p. 669. In October 1624, as the Catholic newsletter network was humming with political reports about the proposed French match for Prince Charles, William Cape was one of the writers keeping the English secular clergy in Paris supplied with information, AAW, B 27, no. 31.

[15] See *HMCS* XVII, 475–6; John Philpott, ed. J. J. Howard, *The Visitation of Kent . . . 1619* (1898), 139; PRO, SP 12/193/9, fo. 14r–v; PRO, C 2/James I/L3/16. He may have been the same man as the recusant John Loane (or John Love in some documents) who was often described as being resident and/or having property at Balcombe and at Eastergate, PRO, E 368/541, mem. 114a; *CSPD 1603–10*, 383; PRO, SO 3/3; WSRO, Ep. II/9/12, fo. 8v; PRO, E 368/528, mem. 231a, E 368/541, mem. 114a; *NAGB*, 222. An exchequer enquiry into his property in 1611, conducted by Sir Barnard Whetstones, found that Loane had goods at Barnhorne 'in paroch de Bexhill', which was a manor belonging to Viscount Montague, PRO, E 368/541, mem. 124b.

of the second Viscount Montague, and among his leading gentry and aristocratic relatives, of a series of quite prominent and intellectually proficient
chaplains helped to transform the kind of Catholicism which served in this
period to identify the viscount, his entourage and kin. Naturally, this was
not a completely uniform and self-sealing process. The viscount was never
entirely the slave of one particular line of thought among his clerical servants,
and at times seems even to have been at variance with some of them. But, by
trying in this chapter to piece together what are, it has to be admitted, often
rather obscure pieces of evidence about how far his and his wider family's
clerical needs were met, we may be able to see how his entourage was confessionally politicised and itself became capable of disseminating ideas on a
range of politico-ecclesiastical topics.

Both Smith and More were at the forefront of the campaign, launched
by their superior, the archpriest Birkhead, to reform aspects of the English
Catholic community and its clergy. Smith was probably the most ambitious
of the priests who served the Brownes and their kin. In 1624 he was appointed
as a bishop (of the titular see of Chalcedon in Asia Minor) to govern the
English Catholics. But his colleague Thomas More was also an influential
figure. As we saw, he had been briefly caught up in the appellants' quarrel
with Birkhead's predecessor Blackwell.[16] According to Birkhead, who used
More to drum up support for Birkhead's own proposals for clerical reorgan-
isation and reform, More was 'an honest man, full of charitie and exceeding
laborious to helpe our cause'. Curiously, Birkhead quibbled, 'he lacketh a
shew of gravitie'. This caused the second Viscount Montague, Birkhead's
'patron', to be 'somewhat averse from his preferment in that respect, though
he otherwise liketh him well enough'.[17] But nobody else ever voiced doubts
about More's capacity or gravity. After his death he was remembered by
his brother Cresacre as the 'chiefe pillar of our family'.[18] The second viscount's son and heir Francis 'and his famelye [of] 5 or 6' were among the
mourners at More's funeral in Rome in 1625.[19] Smith's biography of Lady
Magdalen stressed that his friend More was

great grandchild and direct heir of that famous Sir Thomas More, sometime lord
chancellor of England and a most worthy martyr; who, seeking to participate rather
of the virtues than of the lands of his great grandfather, having resigned unto his
younger brother a most ample patrimony, and, being adorned with learning and
virtues and made priest, devoted himself wholly to the conversion of his country, in
which industry he hath laudably employed himself these twenty years.[20]

[16] See ch. 7, p. 212 above.   [17] AAW, A VIII, no. 191, pp. 713–14.
[18] D. Shanahan, 'The Family of St. Thomas More in Essex, 1581–1640', *ER* 7 (1966), 105–14,
at p. 112.
[19] D. Shanahan, 'The Death of Thomas More, Secular Priest, Great-Grandson of St Thomas
More', *RH* 7 (1963–4), 23–33, at p. 26.
[20] Southern, *ERH*, 43.

Smith and More moved from the Battle Abbey establishment of Lady Magdalen to the second Viscount Montague's own household after their beloved patroness died in 1608. And we can detect several other secular priests who at this time were living either at Cowdray or with families which were connected with the Brownes in some way, in effect all part of a kin-based network of patrons. A letter from Thomas Wilson to the earl of Salisbury written on 20 November 1605, shortly after the Gunpowder plot, identified as many of the priests' residences as Wilson knew of. Apart from the arch-priest Blackwell, Wilson listed Cuthbert Johnson 'amongst the Tirwitts in Lincolnshire'.[21] George Birkhead was 'with the Lord Montague', a position which may, as we saw, have been obtained for him because of Birkhead's kin relationship to Montague's gentleman-servant Richard Lambe.[22] Henry Shaw, one of Blackwell's assistants, was 'with Sir Francis Lacon', the first viscount's son-in-law, 'in Lancashire or Yorkshire'; Lacon was 'about to levy a regiment for the archduke' in Flanders.[23]

It is worth trying to discuss in a bit more detail the second Viscount Montague's clerical entourage in order to determine (or at least guess) what he wanted from his priests and what they wanted from him. The most prominent cleric that Montague would have known directly within his own entourage in his early years was, ironically, the archpriest Blackwell. We have already seen that it is far from clear what Blackwell's living arrangements in London were. He seems to have had lodgings of his own, yet informers repeatedly insisted that he had access to Montague House, and associated, if not with the viscount personally, then at least with some of his followers, particularly the steward John Loane.[24] Blackwell was one of the sons of Margaret Blackwell. She had estates at North Chapel in Sussex and was involved in the Sussex iron industry. She was also a cousin of Bishop Thomas Thirlby, who had been the first Viscount Montague's colleague in diplomatic missions abroad on behalf of Mary Tudor.[25]

---

[21] The second Viscount Montague later arranged a marriage into the Tirwhit family for his daughter Catherine. See ch. 3, p. 97 above.

[22] See ch. 6, p. 205 above.

[23] *HMCS* XVII, 500–1. See also PRO, SP 14/19/111.   [24] See ch. 8, p. 262 above.

[25] A. Jessopp, *One Generation of a Norfolk House* (1879), 118, 125–7; ch. 4, pp. 113–16 above. The Blackwells were retainers and clients of the earls of Northumberland rather than the Brownes. A letter written by the seventh earl of Northumberland in *c.* 1569–70 said that Thomas Blackwell was 'my learned steward, my receiver, and a dealer for my things' at Petworth, *HMCS* XIII, 109–10. A February 1574 list of ironmasters in Sussex (PRO, SP 12/95/21, fo. 51r) notes that the late earl of Northumberland had one forge and one furnace 'in Petworthe greate parke . . . in the handes of Mr [William] Blackwell', C. S. Cattell, 'The 1574 Lists of Wealden Ironworks', *SAC* 117 (1979), 161–71, at p. 165. In January 1584 one of the imprisoned eighth earl's footmen stated that he had been sent by the 'clerk of the kitchen to the brewer to lay in xii barrells of beere' in Mrs Blackwell's house in London (in the parish of St Andrew by the Wardrobe) where the countess of Northumberland was appointed to stay when she came to the city, PRO, SP 12/167/13, fo. 24v.

George Blackwell was, as we saw in the previous chapter, reliably reputed to be pro-Jesuit. He was believed to have acted as the Society's stooge during the appellant controversy. At least this was what his opponents said when they sought an explanation for his high-handed behaviour towards them. The Blackwells were relatives of the Jesuit Edmund Campion and of the Walpole family, one of whom, the Jesuit Henry Walpole, had been martyred in 1595.[26]

How close Blackwell was to the second Viscount Montague, therefore, we do not really know.[27] If Montague was sympathetic towards the appellants during the archpriest controversy, in the same way that he later posed, from time to time, as a patron of the anti-Jesuit secular clergy, then it would seem odd that Blackwell should have continued to hover around Montague House.[28] There is certainly no clear evidence that he was at any stage, before his arrest in 1607 and his loss of his archpresbyteral dignity and authority in 1608, ejected by Montague from his circle.

Of course, it may be that the young viscount had not yet decided definitely to plump for one or other side in the intra-Catholic factional divisions of the time. Alternatively, he may have been trying to sustain as wide and inclusive a patronage circle as possible, one that could incorporate individuals as diverse as Blackwell and Anthony Copley (who cordially loathed each other).[29] Even George Birkhead, who would, as Blackwell's successor, lead the struggle against Jesuit influence over the affairs of the secular clergy, had been thought at one time to be basically friendly to the Jesuits. Some of the anti-Jesuit priests, such as Christopher Bagshaw, distrusted him for precisely this reason.[30] In late 1628 Montague himself recalled that William Bishop, the virulent anti-Jesuit leader of the first appeal to Rome, had been one of

---

[26] Margaret Blackwell's father was Thomas Campion. See L. Campion, *The Family of Edmund Campion* (1975), 20–3; Jessopp, *One Generation*, 119. After Bishop Thirlby's imprisonment, his ward William Walpole, relative of the several future Jesuits of that name, was entrusted to the Blackwells, and married Blackwell's youngest daughter. While resident at Fittleworth, Walpole became a manager of Margaret Blackwell's Sussex ironworks, *ibid.*, 117–20.

[27] In early 1600 there were two recusants at Fernhurst (very close to Cowdray), named William and Thomas Blackwell, who may have been George Blackwell's brothers, Jessopp, *One Generation*, 125. William Blackwell was assessed for his recusancy on moveable goods at Fernhurst on 6 October 1610, PRO, E 368/539, mem. 147d. Thomas Blackwell conformed in 1611 in front of Bishop Harsnett at Aldingbourne, PRO, E 368/541, mem. 110a.

[28] Henry Lanman, Montague's servant who was converted to Catholicism and was drawn, in early 1600, to enter the Society of Jesus by the Jesuit Joseph (or Joshua) Pullen, says he took this step with the assistance of both Blackwell and the Jesuit superior Henry Garnet, CRS 54, 88–9; CRS 75, 273.

[29] Copley intimated in print that Blackwell had preached a sermon in which he criticised a noblewoman present, whereupon she turned Protestant. Copley also accused Blackwell of being a schismatic (because he had thwarted the appellant priests' justified appeal), Anthony Copley, *An Answere to a Letter of a Iesuited Gentleman* (1601), 21.

[30] *NAGB*, 48. See ch. 11, p. 347 below.

'the three, who by my helpe procured Mr George Brickhead [*sic*], the late archpreist, to alter his manner of dealinge by [i.e. with] the Societie'.[31]

However, clerics such as Bagshaw, Copley and Blackwell were, even by 1605, really yesterday's men. They had been damaged in the appellant debates over the issues of political allegiance and loyalty to the regime. Within this particular section of the Catholic community, the future belonged to a tightly knit group of other Catholic clerics, not necessarily 'new' or even younger, but ideologically more focused and adept. They would try to use the second viscount as a patron to further their clerical aims and agenda. This is not to say that Montague deliberately surrounded himself with self-proclaimed moderates, devotees of the 'middle way' who were determined not to offend anyone. In fact, as we shall see, he found himself in political difficulties at various points in James's reign precisely because of those clergy with whom he associated. However, the principal clergymen who acted as his chaplains at this time, such as Birkhead, Smith and even More (who had, admittedly, fallen foul of Blackwell), had kept more or less clear of the main appellant disputes, even though most of them were or became opponents of the Jesuits. And even those clergy within Montague's wider entourage, such as Edward Bennett, and perhaps also William Bishop, who had been directly involved in the appellant project, recovered their reputation within the English Catholic community and at Rome.

A snapshot of the main clerical members in the Montague entourage is provided by a manuscript list of priests compiled in 1610. It is a register of those who were prepared to go on the record to demand the appointment of a bishop to rule over English Catholics. (The list was drawn up by Thomas More, now chaplain to the second viscount, and by the secular priest John Colleton.)[32] In the Sussex names on the list (organised into three separate columns) we have evidence of how strongly intertwined with the Montague circle much of the early seventeenth-century reform-of-the-clergy campaign within the English Catholic community actually was. About some of those cited in the first column we know little. But, for example, we have here Richard Davies, the priest who reconciled Montague's servant Henry Lanman to the Church of Rome.[33] Also present here are Thomas Manger, who is mentioned in the correspondence of the viscount's chaplains,[34] George Tias, whose family had been tenants of the priest Thomas More's family at Barnburgh in Yorkshire, and followed the Mores southwards in the early 1580s,[35] Edmund Tindall (son of the recusant Thomas Tindall of Arlington in East Sussex),[36] William Harrison (Birkhead's successor as archpriest),

---

[31] AA, 312–13.
[32] AAW, OB I/i, no. 26, fo. 53r. The list contains names of priests from several counties.
[33] See above in this chapter.   [34] *NAGB*, 172.   [35] *Ibid.*, 37.   [36] Anstr. II, 322.

John Gennings (brother of the famous martyr Edmund Gennings),[37] Richard Newport (the future martyr and relative of several of these priests)[38] and Benjamin Norton (the indefatigable, though permanently morose, priest resident at Midhurst, principally with the viscount's gentleman-servant Richard Lambe).[39]

A second, much briefer, column lists the names of clergymen who were based primarily at Cowdray. Here we have the 'archepriest' (George Birkhead), Richard Smith, More himself and Edward Weston (who was soon, in fact, to become alienated from the Montague entourage and make his way to the ideologically ambivalent household of Edward Gage at Bentley in the East Sussex parish of Framfield).[40] Last in this column we find Robert Pett. He was shortly to be sent to reside in Brussels in order to work as an agent for the transmission of the correspondence and memoranda which were to be dispatched from Montague's household to the curia in Rome, bombarding the cardinals there with what was planned to look like a mass campaign by the majority of English secular clergy for the reform of their Church.[41] While in Brussels, Pett dealt with quite large sums of money which were being invested (apparently) in the business of supplying the Spanish troops in Flanders. It is not exactly clear where this money was coming from, but it could well have been provided by Montague himself, with Pett acting as his agent.[42]

Pett was also a dealer and agent for Sir William Roper, whose family became heavily involved in the secular clergy's affairs. Two of Roper's sons were part of Thomas More's circle of friends at Rome.[43] Pett claimed that the Jesuits in Brussels knew what his function there was, and they hated him for it. On 9/19 September 1615 he wrote to More that Thomas Sackville, the deceased first earl of Dorset's youngest son, was in Brussels for the profession of 'two religious in the English monasterie' at which were present 'almost all the English in this towne' except Pett, from which 'yow may sea that I

---

[37] *NAGB*, 108, 111. John Gennings became a Franciscan but was always counted as a friend of this faction among the secular clergy. In the disputes of the mid-1620s between Richard Smith and the regulars, Gennings was prepared to compel members of his order to obey Smith, AAW, A XX, no. 67, p. 241.

[38] See ch. 8, pp. 284–5 above.   [39] *NAGB, passim.*

[40] *Ibid.*, 111, 196. See below in this chapter.

[41] There was a recusant and unlicensed schoolteacher at Midhurst in 1602 called Thomas Pett who may have been a relative of the priest, T. J. McCann, 'Catholic Schoolmasters in Sussex, 1558–1603: Addenda and Corrigenda to Beales's Catholic Schoolmasters', *RH* 12 (1973–4), 235–7, at p. 236.

[42] *NAGB, passim.* For an explanation of this business set-up, involving Gabriel Colford and William Cawley, see *HMCD* III, 185.

[43] Questier, *PM*, 492–3. Sir William Roper was one of a number of prominent English gentlemen whose activities on the Continent infuriated the mid-Jacobean regime, AAW, A XIV, no. 113, p. 356. See ch. 2, p. 58 above.

remayne still an excommunicated person wher our English Fathers [Jesuits] have any power or priviledge'.[44]

Finally, in our 1610 Sussex clergy list, a third column (written in the hand of John Colleton, the future dean of the secular clergy's episcopal chapter) includes Colleton himself, John Jackson (a very blunt Yorkshireman, and future chaplain to Montague's relatives, the Arundell family of Wardour Castle in Wiltshire),[45] Thomas Somers (a martyr whose cause, like Richard Newport's, was heavily promoted by these priests),[46] John Lockwood (a future intimate of the secular clergy leadership)[47] and William Clitherow (the stepson of the celebrated York martyr Margaret Clitherow, whose chaplain John Mush became one of the archpriest Birkhead's assistants, and whose relative, of the same name, had been Alban Langdale's secretary at Cowdray),[48] Henry Mayler (who became a professor of theology at Douai)[49] and George Fairburn.[50]

To this quite extensive network of priests we can add others who, though not based in Sussex, were central to the projects and self-image of the second Viscount Montague's family, for example the two Bennett brothers, Edward and John. Edward Bennett was usually resident with 'old' Lady Dormer, the first Viscount Montague's daughter Elizabeth. In early August 1624, the papal nuncio in Paris, Bernardino Spada, remarked of Bennett (a potential successor at this point to William Bishop as titular bishop of Chalcedon) that he was 'active and ardent', though very anti-Jesuit, and that he ruled 'one might say, with a rod of iron – the house of Lady Dormer', 'in whose house . . . justice itself has no authority, and therefore he is safe from surprises and sudden searches'.[51]

The Bennetts' nephew Joseph Haynes also joined the second viscount's clerical entourage.[52] Matthew Kellison at Douai wrote to More on 24

---

[44] AAW, A XIV, no. 173, p. 535.

[45] Jackson was described by a French Capuchin in July 1622 as 'l'ausmonier du Baron d'Arondel Catholique', AAW, A XVI, no. 122, p. 496. It is clear from Jackson's correspondence that he had an *entrée* at Court in the early 1610s, perhaps via Blanche Arundell (who was also mentioned by the Brownes' friend Benjamin Norton in his correspondence as a close friend of Norton's own patroness Katherine Pole). See *NAGB*, *passim*, for Jackson, and *ibid.*, p. 210, for Blanche Arundell.

[46] *NAGB*, 20, 96, 98. For Richard Newport, see ch. 8, pp. 284–5 above.   [47] Anstr. I, 211.

[48] *Ibid.*, II, 64; ch. 7, p. 223 above. Though John Mush was, it seems, never really an inner-circle member of the second viscount's entourage, one letter of the viscount to him in 1608 addresses him as 'cousin'. Mush's alias was 'Ratcliffe', and there may indeed have been some familial connection between the two (since Montague's grandmother, the first viscount's first wife, was a Radcliffe, daughter of the earl of Sussex), Questier, *PM*, 500. For the significance of the term 'cousin' in early modern kinship networks, see S. Kettering, 'Patronage and Kinship in Early Modern France', *French Historical Studies* 16 (1989), 408–35, at p. 418.

[49] Anstr. I, 223–4.   [50] *Ibid.*, II, 98.   [51] Allison, RS, 175.

[52] Together with his uncle John Bennett, Haynes had been arrested down in the West Country at some point before December 1610. They were both imprisoned in the Clink (near Montague

October/3 November 1614 that he had 'dealt with the nuncio' in Flanders 'to have one or two grateful men here about me' such as 'Mr Haynes, who now is with my Lord Montague'.[53] (In October 1622 we find Haynes reporting that he heard 'daly new complaints of poore Catholiques', and that 'divers [Catholics] in Sussex about Midhurst', i.e. near Montague's palace of Cowdray, 'keepe ther howses and dare not walke out for feare'.[54]) As we shall see, Haynes became a key negotiator on behalf of the secular clergy during the period of the attempted Anglo-Spanish dynastic treaty of the early 1620s. He had been a friend of John Williams at Cambridge, and this opened up a crucial line of communication with the regime, since Williams, the lord keeper, was a central member of the group in government which was trying to secure the success of the Spanish match.[55]

Montague included among his clergy clients the Somersetshire man Edward Kenion. In 1599 Kenion had been imprisoned in Winchester, and had escaped the usually fatal experience of a treason trial by a few hours when he was sprung from gaol by a gang of Hampshire recusants. Subsequently he became a chaplain at Cowdray.[56] A regular purveyor of news and comment within the entourage was Richard Broughton who, after 1601, became a much-published polemicist. He tells us himself that he was tied into a number of Catholic families, including the Stonors in Oxfordshire. This made him a kinsman of the Brownes.[57] It appears that he was also a relative of the Leyburns. A letter from the priest George Leyburn, written in September 1631, describes him affectionately as 'my cousin Broughton'.[58] John Leyburn, George Leyburn's nephew, spent 1640–5 as a travelling tutor to the eldest son of the third Viscount Montague.[59] Broughton was present at George Birkhead's bedside when the archpriest died in April 1614.[60]

House). Richard Broughton recorded that when Archbishop George Abbot was trying (in September 1612) to get some of the Catholic clergy to promise, in exchange for being allowed into exile, that they would never return into the realm, Haynes 'told Canterbury that he had rather go to hanging than to banishment, for that was never his seeking', though he did in fact go, in October 1612, AAW, A XI, no. 190, p. 551; BL, Lansdowne MS 92, no. 107, fo. 190r; Anstr. II, 153; TD V, 92.

[53] TD V, cc. Haynes had returned to England from exile in February 1614.

[54] AAW, A XVI, no. 162, p. 619.   [55] See ch. 12, p. 400 below.

[56] Anstr. I, 196–7.   [57] AAW, A XV, no. 195, p. 514.

[58] CRS 22, 177. George Leyburn was a relative of the martyr James Leyburn (executed in 1583) who was a first cousin of the first Viscount Montague's sister-in-law Anne Dacre (wife of Philip Howard, earl of Arundel), J. H. Pollen, *Acts of English Martyrs* (1891), 212. George Leyburn was also a cousin of the prominent Paris-based priest Henry Holden whose mother, Eleanor, was a daughter of the well-known recusant Miles Gerard of Ince (uncle of Edward Kenion), AAW, A XXVIII, no. 211, p. 656; Anstr. II, 158. This also made Leyburn a relative of Richard Lascelles who was a close friend of Richard Smith, as indeed was Leyburn, Anstr. II, 184.

[59] In the early 1650s John Leyburn was secretary to Bishop Smith. After the Restoration he had an annuity paid to him by the third viscount, Anstr. II, 196.

[60] AAW, A XIII, no. 71, p. 175.

One of the clergymen whose newsletters throw a vivid light on the gentry culture in which this brand of Catholicism was grounded was Benjamin Norton. He was never actually stationed at Cowdray, though the whining tone of many of his gossipy missives to Thomas More in Rome make it clear that he would have much preferred to be ensconced in Montague's palace. He was, as we have seen, principally resident with the Lambe family in Midhurst, though he spent time also with Edward Wyborne and his wife (Norton's half-sister), and formed a very close personal attachment to Katherine Pole.[61] Norton was a supporter of the reform programme associated with the secular clergy led by the archpriests Birkhead and Harrison, and then, later, by the successive bishops of Chalcedon, William Bishop and Richard Smith. Norton himself had come out of the Shelley family network in Sussex. He was the nephew of Edward Shelley of Warminghurst who was hanged in August 1588 for harbouring the seminarist William Dean.[62] Norton had been taught by one of the early Hampshire opponents of the Elizabethan Reformation, John Bodey, who was executed in November 1583.[63] As Norton noted in 1626 he was instructed by Bodey in 'Mr Archdeacon [William] Shelley his fathers howse', i.e. the household of Richard Shelley of Warminghurst. Richard Shelley, the martyr Edward's brother, had been the front man for the ill-fated 1585 toleration petition, which, as we saw in chapter 3, he had put directly into the queen's hands before being dragged away and imprisoned.

Crucial also to the second viscount's clergy patronage network was the Pole family of Lordington (though in this period none of them was ordained). Although in 1558 the collapse of the Marian regime and the death of Cardinal Pole had seemed to point the way towards political obscurity for this family, it retained memories of its Plantagenet and Yorkist past and inheritance (a political tradition to which, as we have seen, the Brownes reckoned they also belonged).[64] Arthur Pole, one of the cardinal's nephews, had, we noted above, fallen under suspicion in the early 1560s for talking too openly about his Yorkist credentials.[65] In October 1584 Ralph Miller, the Hampshire Catholic activist, confessed that among the exiles in Rouen with whom he had consorted was 'Mr Jeffrey Poole who is thought there to bee one that will make clayme to the crowne'.[66] In mid-1586, the generally well-informed Malivery Catilyn noted that Geoffrey Pole 'pretendeth hym self to be duke of Suffolk and swearith he shall lyve to be possessed of the same'.[67] In February 1605 a report about goings-on in Spain noted that Philip III had recently 'sent to divers of the nobility of Rome the habits and honours of

---

[61] *NAGB*, 209–10, 221, 229–30, 235.   [62] CRS 5, 395; Mott, HR, 284–5.
[63] CRS 5, 39–44. For the public impact made by the executions of John Bodey and his fellow martyr John Slade, see e.g. FSL, L.b. 198.
[64] See ch. 3, p. 69 above.   [65] See ch. 4, p. 128 above.
[66] PRO, SP 12/173/64, fo. 100r.   [67] PRO, SP 12/190/62, fo. 130v.

the cavaliers of the Toison or Santiago; and that amongst the rest' Arthur Pole, Geoffrey's son, 'is honoured with one of those orders and with 1000 crowns yearly; and the king designs to make his brother, Geoffrey Poole, a cardinal'.[68] A month earlier Sir Robert Cecil had been informed from France that 'here is advertisement from Rome' that Philip III had sent to the Holy City 'to dyvers of the nobilitie the dignitye and ornament of his ordre, where emonge the rest, he is pleased to grace Mr Arthur Poole'. It was being said in Rome that Arthur 'laboureth to advance his younger brother to a cardynalls hatt'.[69]

In Rome the Poles had inserted themselves into the household of Cardinal Edward Farnese, who became cardinal protector of the English nation. (In 1590, as we learn from a list of English rebels, 'Jeffrey Pooles sonne' was at Piacenza 'in the duke of Parma his pallace there'.[70] Presumably the Poles were handed on, as clients, from the duke, Alexander Farnese, to the cardinal, his son Edward.) The observer of the Pole brothers' progress in February 1605 noted that 'concerning Arthur Poole I think the beginning of his favour came from the late stir in the Cardinal Farnese, his master's house'. Although the exact circumstances of the 'stir' are lost, Pole apparently 'was the first that began it', and 'wounded the officer of justice and afterwards banded himself very bravely with the Spanish ambassador in the cardinal's behalf against the pope and the rest'. The writer clearly thought the Poles were ridiculous. He called the younger Geoffrey Pole 'a raw dissolute young man, whom I left at the Court of Spain at my departure, more likely to follow a coach than to be a cardinal'. Furthermore, 'both these brothers let not to give out amongst their friends what pretensions they have in England by their great blood, and therefore I know not how this should be taken here that Spain should do them these favours at this time'.[71]

Ridiculous or not, somebody took the trouble to murder Arthur Pole in Rome in 1605. The English ambassador at Venice, Sir Henry Wotton, noted on 8 July 1605 that Pole, a 'fruit of the Roman Court', was, 'on St John Baptist eve', 'found dead in the street of three wounds, on his finger a jewel of great value, in his purse fourteen Spanish doubles' and 'about his neck a clock of artificial workmanship' (so the motive was probably something other than robbery). The following day he was 'buried at the Jesuits' college by the Cardenal Farnese very solemnly in the Farnesian tombe'.[72] The younger Geoffrey Pole remained in Farnese's entourage and favour (as Sir Thomas Edmondes noted in August 1607). During 1606 he was observed travelling about the

[68] *HMCS* XVII, 67. Arthur and the younger Geoffrey were brothers of Benjamin Norton's friend and patroness Katherine Pole.
[69] BL, Cotton MS Caligula E XI, fo. 108r.   [70] BL, Lansdowne MS 68, no. 70, fo. 159v.
[71] *HMCS* XVII, 67.   [72] Smith, *Life*, I, 330.

Continent and consorting with the exile Sir Robert Bassett.[73] The Poles' association with Farnese was crucial to the clergy reform programme pursued by
the priests in Montague's household because it gave them access to the ear
of the cardinal protector, i.e. Farnese himself. Geoffrey was furiously anti-
Jesuit, and the Jesuits were not too keen on him. Robert Persons remarked in
March 1596 that, in the battle to appropriate the deceased Cardinal Allen's
influence, the anti-Jesuit faction had 'had the temerity to urge through their
friends in Rome that some Englishman be made a cardinal', and they had
'proposed to his Holiness the names of Poole . . . and other similar young
men who' were 'quite incapable and unfitted for the dignity of that office'.[74]
Pole had entered the English College in Rome in February 1592, though he
was never ordained.[75] The factional divisions within the college over various political issues helped to give rise to some very lurid accusations by the
pro-Jesuits there that Pole was involved with seminarists who were actively
homosexual. This elicited counter-accusations that Pole and others had been
sexually abused by some of the Jesuit administrators of the college.[76] Whatever the truth of these stories, Pole was happy to join the clerical cadre,
within Montague's entourage, who were campaigning to root out the influence of the Society of Jesus among English Catholics, and particularly in the
seminaries.[77]

Even on the fringes of the Brownes' circle of clerical friends and
acquaintances, it appears that pre-existing kin networks were of some real
consequence in the evolution of the clerical wing of Montague's entourage.
Obviously not all priests who held high office among the secular clergy were
relatives of the Brownes and their friends. But it is extraordinary just how
many were. One who was absorbed into the second viscount's entourage on
the basis, it seems, of familial connections, was John Southcot. He was related
to the Ropers as well as to the Stonors[78] and to the prominent Catholic Herefordshire family of Seaborne, which had its own marital links with the Wells
family in Hampshire.[79] Southcot also addressed the leading secular priest

[73] *HMCS* XIX, 221. On 24 April/4 May 1606 an informant noted from Paris that 'there
arrived here yesternight Sir Robert Basset and Mr Geffrey Pole, lately come *ab urbe*', *HMCS*
XVIII, 120. See also *HMCS* XVIII, 132; Questier, *PM*, 486–7. Pole's friend Bassett was a
relative of the More family and was the probable author one of the principal sixteenth-
century biographies of Sir Thomas More, 'The Lyfe of Syr Thomas More . . . by Ro. Ba.',
H. Trevor-Roper, *Catholics, Anglicans and Puritans* (1987), 21, 285.
[74] English College, Valladolid, legajo 34 (Robert Persons to Don Juan de Idiaquez, 16/26 March
1596, transcript and translation at ABSJ).
[75] CRS 37, 86.
[76] P. Lake with M. Questier, *The Antichrist's Lewd Hat* (2002), 290–1.
[77] *NAGB, passim.*   [78] AAW, A XIII, no. 127, p. 323.
[79] W. C. Metcalfe (ed.), *The Visitations of Essex* (2 vols., Harleian Society 13–14, 1878–9), I,
491. The prospective seminarist Andrew Wigmore noted in 1628 that he was related to the
Ropers, the Southcots and the Seabornes, 'omnes Catholici', CRS 55, 403.

Edward Bennett, chaplain to the Dormers at Wing, as 'deere cosen'.[80] He became a figure of influence and authority in the secular clergy's affairs. We find him coming to England in 1621 in the company of the Spanish ambassador Carlos Coloma when it looked as if the dynastic match between Prince Charles and the infanta Doña Maria might really go ahead.[81] (He was secretary to the secular clergy's episcopal chapter for a short time in 1632.[82]) Southcot, like the Bennett brothers, had an *entrée* at the Dormers' residence at Wing in Buckinghamshire. The Dormer family, in particular Lady Elizabeth Dormer, the first Viscount Montague's daughter, was active in trying to organise Catholic support for the Stuart regime's proposals to wed Prince Charles to the Spanish princess. In 1625, Southcot's journal notes that 'he fell dangerously sick in his way to Wing at the end of August in the plague yeare'.[83] It is possible that the priest William Clifford, who moved in the same circles as these clergy and was well regarded by them, was their friend in part because of his relationship to the family of the earl of Cumberland, which itself had a kin relationship with the Brownes. (The heir to the Cumberland title had been brought up with the Brownes in Sussex before the 1569 rebellion.[84]) William's brother Henry was an agent for the secular clergy in Antwerp, and married into the well-known Catholic family of Tempest.[85]

In other cases, we are inclined to suspect, even if we cannot necessarily prove it, that it was the kinship between particular priests which brought them into the centre of the Brownes' clerical network. For example, the priest Edward Maddison's mother was the sister of the Kentish cleric John Bosvile, himself an assistant to the archpriests Birkhead and Harrison, and the secular clergy's agent in Rome from 1629 to 1631.[86] Maddison was sent to Madrid in November 1619 as agent for Douai, the secular priests' flagship college. Bosvile was himself a cousin of the

---

[80] AAW, A XXVIII, no. 148, p. 493. Southcot's grandfather (a member of the judiciary) and father were noted for their Catholic proclivities. In 1584 the informer Thomas Dodwell reported that at Southampton House in Holborn there were present at Mass, among others, Judge Southcot's son and heir, i.e. John Southcot of Witham in Essex, the father of the future priest, Foley VI, 721. See also Hyland, *CP*, 318–19; FSL, L.b. 232.

[81] Anstr. II, 305; CRS 1, 97.   [82] Anstr. II, 305.   [83] CRS 1, 98.

[84] See ch. 3, pp. 97–8 above; Hamilton, *Chronicle*, II, 134–5, I, 127–8, 128–9; Anstr. II, 62–3. In September 1655 William Clifford was reckoned by George Leyburn to be a suitable candidate to replace the deceased Richard Smith as bishop of Chalcedon, *ibid.*, 63.

[85] Henry Clifford married Catherine Tempest, daughter of Thomas Tempest, and granddaughter of Robert Tempest of Holmeside, co. Durham, Hamilton, *Chronicle*, II, 134. Her will of August 1649 mentioned her relatives Augustine and Anthony Belson, William Roper, and Henry East, all from families within the kin circle of the Brownes, *ibid.*, 134–5.

[86] Anstr. II, 207. In autumn 1614 William Bishop described John Bosvile as 'one of the surest friends we have in England', AAW, A XIII, no. 214, p. 543. For Bosvile's appointment as clergy agent, see Anstr. I, 45; AAW, A XXII, no. 83. For Bosvile family deeds in the Battle Abbey archive, see e.g. HEH, BA 57/1582, BA 58/1093, 1646.

Worcestershire recusant Thomas Middlemore who had moved from his own county into Sussex.[87] Middlemore was a close friend of the priest Benjamin Norton.[88]

To see how closely even a little-known and apparently minor member of the entourage could be networked into the nexus of social, marital and religious relationships which underpinned that entourage, we can consider the priest Richard Wright. His last will and testament gives us an account of those he knew and valued during his clerical career. 'In primis' he announced proudly, 'I doe give unto the reverende Richard lord bishoppe of Calcedon one breviary in 2 volumes in 4° bounden in vellam which the Vicounte Montague deceased gave unto me.' Wright's other bequests went primarily to local Catholic families such as the Brittaines and the Cuffaulds in Hampshire (relatives of the Poles and the Lambes).[89]

There does seem to be a remarkable profusion of kinship and other linkages here. Taken together they suggest that the clerical servants of the second viscount and his relatives were not appointed simply on a first-come-first-served basis. They were not recruited by their patrons merely because a certain number of chaplains were required to supply gentry and aristocratic Catholics' sacramental needs, or at least not just for that reason. Rather, what we seem to have in this brief reconstruction of who knew and was related to whom among this group of families is a snapshot of the concentration of a particular style of Catholicism in a powerful and widespread social unit. It is difficult to escape the conclusion that the second viscount's kin and patronage network was the groundwork for the construction of one of the principal Catholic clerical factions of the period, the heirs of the appellants in effect, whose rhetoric about the possibility, and indeed necessity, of the reform of the English Catholic community from within supplies us with one of the principal Catholic narratives of that community during the late sixteenth and early seventeenth centuries.[90]

It was one of the axioms of John Bossy's account of the English Catholic community of the period that the grandiose programme and ambitions of the Catholic secular clergy ran into the brick wall of gentry opposition while the Jesuits, a self-consciously missionary clergy primarily serving gentry

---

[87] In March 1600 Thomas Middlemore was mentioned as being in the service of Robert Sackville, the Catholic future second earl of Dorset, *CSPD 1598–1601*, 411. Middlemore was one of the recusants around Battle who were indicted for recusancy at the assizes in July 1605, *NAGB*, 95.

[88] See W. P. W. Phillimore with W. F. Carter, *Some Account of the Family of Middlemore of Warwickshire and Worcestershire* (1901), 180–2. In September 1613 Norton informed More that the pursuivants 'were with . . . Mr Middlemore in Waterdowne Forreste and other poore Catholiques in the easte of Sussex', AAW, A XII, no. 164, p. 365.

[89] AAW, A XXVI, no. 50, p. 151.

[90] For one version of this narrative, see Hughes, *RCR*, section III.

chaplaincies, had an easier ride. In the sense that Montague's chaplains' schemes for reinstituting Catholic episcopacy in England were extremely unpopular with some noblemen and gentry (and foundered in part for that reason) this is undoubtedly true. At the same time, the fact that this pro-episcopal lobby relied on aristocratic and gentry patrons tells us that the political battles between different sections of the community were not the product of a struggle between the gentry/laity on the one hand and clergy-men on the other. What we have here is a series of conflicts in which patrons and clients, on different sides, fought each other. As we remarked in the two previous chapters, this was a period during which many contemporaries perceived the likelihood of a far-reaching change of religious culture in the English Church. To those Catholics who were struggling to assert an ideo-logical dominance over others within the Jacobean Catholic community, it appeared that one change which was genuinely likely was some form of royal tolerance of Catholicism. This would be a fulfilment of the prospect which had been briefly grasped during the appellant controversy but was then lost shortly after James's accession. If there should come a new and more toler-ant era, those Catholics who had won these intra-Catholic patron-sponsored battles for ideological supremacy would be the ones best placed to benefit from any new spirit of moderation in the early Stuart polity. There was, indeed, all to play for.

DIVISIONS WITHIN THE ENTOURAGE

It is one thing to say that Anthony Maria Browne, second Viscount Mon-tague, was the patron of a significant number of clergy. It is quite another, however, to say what that patronage actually entailed. Was he a benign local bigwig who collected chaplains as if they were fashion accessories but did not need them anything like as much as they needed him? Was he mentally vacant, a space to be filled by whatever they told him? Was he just a noble cushion, bearing the imprint of whoever last sat on him? Or did he have ideas of his own? If he did, how far did those ideas natu-rally coincide with the ambitions of his clerical staff? Did he supply them with leadership? Did he in some sense dictate what his clergy thought and did?

It has to be said that there are no particularly easy answers to these ques-tions. If Montague's main function was simply to serve as a cash dispenser for the clergy, it is difficult to explain why his chaplains, when they were promoting their suits and petitions at Rome, frequently complained about being short of money. Montague was very wealthy. Had he wanted to keep his priests in the style to which they evidently would have liked to become accustomed, he could easily have done that. They would not then have been reduced to griping, as they did, even about the cost of postage for their letters to and from Rome and other European capitals.

It is fairly clear, however, that Montague was a thinking man's patron. His manuscript treatise, entitled 'An Apologeticall Answere', a 701-page defence of Bishop Richard Smith, composed (as the perfectly appalling prose style of the tract proves) by himself and not for him merely to sign, shows that he took an active interest in the internal politics of the Catholic community, and entertained clear, if not always clearly expressed, ideas about it. At crucial points in the struggles between the various Catholic factions during the early seventeenth century he intervened at Rome by writing letters in support of this or that position or course of action. Nevertheless, he did not consistently support the same faction and the same set of ideological positions. For while, at times, as we shall see, he allowed his influence to be used by the secular clergy leaders who wanted to reduce the power of the religious orders in England, he was not an enemy of the religious in the way that some of his secular clergy chaplains were.[91] After *c.* 1615, he started recruiting Benedictines into his service. He appointed a Benedictine tutor, one Edward Smith, for his son Francis.[92] Not all of the secular clergy were particularly happy that Montague consorted so closely with such people. In May 1626 Benjamin Norton protested to Richard Smith about the Benedictine Edward Ashe, Montague's chaplain, and 'those of Mr Ashe his companye'. 'I must complayne to your good lordship and trulye tell you thatt theye ar verry bolde, unmannerlye and boysterouse.'[93]

Montague also offered his patronage to the Franciscans, for whom he had a high regard. He described William Stanney OFM as 'a religious man of great estimacion'.[94] In his will, Montague desired to be buried in a Capuchin friar's habit. He bequeathed to his son Francis 'the crosse of gould which I usually were about my necke, having in it a piece of the holy cross', the authenticity of which had been guaranteed by 'Father James Browne a Scottish man of the order of St. Francis of Paula'; Browne had seen 'the same cut off from a famous piece of the holy cross of great bigness in France'.[95] Montague translated and in 1610 published *The Life of the Holie Father*

---

[91] See ch. 13, *passim* below.
[92] AAW, A XVI, no. 173, p. 669; ch. 12, p. 392 below. According to James Wadsworth, this monk, who accompanied Francis Browne to Madrid in late 1622, was labouring to persuade him to become a Benedictine, and 'made him every day to meditate upon death, and the danger of living in the world, thinking thereby to draw him' to their order, or 'at least to be well affected thereunto', James Wadsworth, *The English Spanish Pilgrime* (1629), 49.
[93] CRS 5, 392.   [94] AAW, A XXII, no. 66, p. 374.
[95] WSRO, SAS/BA 74. (Montague's will was never presented for probate, M. Fitch (ed.), *Index to Administrations in the Prerogative Court of Canterbury 1631–1648* (British Record Society, 1986), 287; PRO, C 2/Charles I/T28/59, mm. 1a, 2a.) Thomas Sackville, Montague's brother-in-law, was also noted as a patron of the Capuchins, *NAGB*, 198.

S. Francis Written by Saint Bonaventure.[96] Montague's first cousin Margaret Powell was a patroness of the Franciscan civil-war martyr Thomas Bullaker.[97] Montague's sister Jane, who married Sir Francis Englefield (d. 1631), was similarly looked to as a patron by the Franciscans.[98] One of the historians of the Capuchin order suggests that the success of Capuchin evangelists at Court in James's reign caused Montague in 1617 to try to secure that more Capuchins should be sent to serve the English Catholics.[99]

Montague even planned to send some of his daughters into religion. Peter Beauvoir reported to William Trumbull on 7 January 1608 that 'from hence have been conveyed of late two daughters of the Lord Montagu towards some religious house'.[100] The manuscript advice composed by the second viscount

[96] ARCR II, no. 92. Antony Allison discovered that a manuscript of the translation with Montague's own dedicatory epistle to his fellow countrymen was prepared by him for the press and dated 25 March 1604, shortly before his famous intervention in the 1604 parliament. (The manuscript book is bound with another translation by Montague, 'of the greater Psalter of the Blessed Virgin formerly thought to be by St Bonaventure'.) The 1610 version, edited by Edward Hughes (for whom see A. F. Allison, 'Franciscan Books in English, 1559–1640', *RH* 3 (1955), 16–65, at pp. 37–40), omits this dedicatory epistle and prints one of Hughes's own. The 1635 edition, published after Montague's death (in 1629), has Montague's preface put back. It also contains an approbation by the Franciscan John Gennings, *ibid.*, 40.

[97] John Bullaker, the martyr's father, dedicated his book *An English Expositor* (1616) to the second viscount's wife, Jane, from whom he had 'former experiences of your ladyship['s] favour towards me'. He hoped it would become available to ladies and gentlewomen in part through her patronage, Davidson, RC, 95–6; T. J. McCann, ' "The Known Style of a Dedication is Flattery": Anthony Browne, 2nd Viscount Montague of Cowdray and his Sussex Flatterers', *RH* 19 (1989), 396–410, at pp. 405–6.

[98] The Franciscan text entitled *The Historie of S. Elizabeth* (Brussels, 1633) has a dedicatory epistle to 'the Lady Englefield the elder' signed with the initials of George Perrot, who was the Franciscan titular guardian of Reading from 1630. Perrot's dedication to her states that she was a Franciscan tertiary. The 1635 edition of Montague's translation of St Bonaventure's life of St Francis is dedicated to Winefrid Englefield, Montague's nephew's wife, Allison, 'Franciscan Books', 40.

[99] Father Cuthbert, *The Capuchins* (2 vols., 1928), II, 338. Montague may also, in the early 1620s, have offered to provide money for the foundation of a novitiate for the Discalced Carmelites. This may have had something to do with the Carmelite Thomas Dawson (Simon Stock) who was a client and chaplain of the Roper family, Montague's relatives, Codignola, *CHL*, 74, 88, 173, 180. See ch. 11, p. 381 below.

[100] *HMCD* II, 460. The Spanish noblewoman Luisa de Carvajal understood that Montague had sent 'two daughters to Flanders to beg for a bishop for England', *Epistolario de Luisa de Carvajal y Mendoza* (digital edition, Alicante, 1999), letter 100. (I am very grateful to Glyn Redworth for bringing this source to my attention.) Robert Persons believed that Montague's early resentment of the Jesuits had been stirred up by some English members of the Society in Flanders 'crossing his wishes in connection with a convent of "Clarissas" that he was supporting', CRS 41, 6. A letter from Jane Dormer, duchess of Feria, to Montague in July 1610 referred to 'the joy and comfort I receaved' from a letter from 'my deere neece your blessed and beloved daughter, Sister Marie, sent me from St Omers', AAW, A IX, no. 69, p. 233. (In February 1612 Robert Pett recorded that Montague's 'little daughter' was with 'the Poore Clares of St Omers', AAW, A XI, no. 16, p. 43.) The duchess also referred to 'my good neeces your lordships daughters in Lesborne', AAW, A IX, no. 69, p. 234.

in 1597, his 'Instruction to my daughter [Mary]', urged the girl towards the religious ideal of perfection, traditionally associated by Catholics with entry into a religious order.[101] Correspondence from 1616 indicates that one of his daughters, sent over to Flanders to try her vocation, then joined Mary Ward's institute, a foundation which subsequently attracted vitriolic condemnation from most of Montague's secular clergy chaplains.[102]

The Society of Jesus was, in the later 1610s and during the 1620s, itself not excluded from Montague's good graces, even though Montague had strongly disapproved of Robert Persons and, up to *c.* 1614, had championed his chaplains' efforts to reduce the Jesuits' influence over English Catholics. Montague regarded the Jesuit Sylvester Norris as his 'good freind'.[103] As we shall see in chapter 13, a list of London clergy in the late 1620s noted three Jesuits who were 'at the Lord Montaigues', one of whom was John Huddleston, the son of Henry Huddleston and Dorothy, daughter of Lord Robert and Lady Elizabeth Dormer, the first Viscount Montague's son-in-law and daughter.[104] Montague's 1628 tractate defence of Richard Smith implies that the Jesuit Lawrence Anderton at one time had occupied a room in Montague's house in Drury Lane.[105]

So it is possible that, from time to time, there really was a divergence between the second viscount and some of his secular clergy chaplains about how far they were there to serve his interests, and how far he was there to facilitate their projects. Montague's brother-in-law, Thomas Sackville, seems to have been of a similarly wide swallow in his patronage of the Catholic clergy. Sackville, a passionate Catholic, an ascetic and an aspirant vegetarian,[106] drove some of the secular priests to despair as he scattered his largesse far and wide, completely disregarding their sniffs and scoffs that some, among the clergy, were in fact more deserving than others. Sackville had, for example, put up a considerable sum of money in order to found an institution in Paris (the Collège d'Arras) where leading members of the

Ann and Lucy Browne had been sent to Portugal. In 1628 Montague wrote that he had formerly engaged himself 'to pay 2000^{li} or more to the monastery of Sion in Lisbone for my two daughters there', AA, 105; AAW, A XXII, no. 66, p. 374. (For the payment of the money, see AA, 107, and for the Lisbon Bridgettine community, see Bellenger, *EWP*, 12.) In 1615 a report on children of English Catholics who were abroad noted that two of Lord Montague's daughters were living with 'the French nunns' at St Omer, and a daughter of Sir George Browne was there too, PRO, SP 14/80/57, fo. 84r.

[101] 'Instruction to my daughter Marie Browne, in the principall groundes, and moste necessarie pointes of the Catholique faithe' (Gillow Library MS, on microfilm at WSRO), 73–4.

[102] AAW, A XV, no. 102, pp. 271–2, no. 148, p. 395; Henriette Peters, *Mary Ward* (Leominster, 1994), 255. See also *APC 1616–17*, 254. A daughter (Joanna or Jane) of Sir George Browne also joined Ward's foundation, Davidson, RC, 91.

[103] AA, 148. Admittedly, Norris had formerly been on the appellant wing of the secular clergy before he joined the Society.

[104] PRO, SP 16/529/94, fo. 146v; Anstr. II, 162–3.

[105] AA, 468. See ch. 13, p. 445 below.   [106] AAW, A XV, no. 96, p. 253, no. 104, pp. 279–80.

English secular clergy could live and study. The trouble was that, though he seemed to get on well enough with the secular clergymen who came to reside there, he was also friendly with the Jesuits. He was a patron of the Jesuit scholasticate at Liège; and later he was a supporter of the Institute of Mary Ward. And in mid-1616 he became involved in the Benedictines' negotiations for union between the order's two congregations in England.[107] Secular clergymen such as Robert Pett could hardly believe how indiscriminate he was in his affections. On 22 May/1 April 1615 Pett was irritated to observe Sackville (who had recently been sent into exile after one of his servants, Edward Worsley, went berserk and tried to attack Archbishop Abbot)[108] coming through Brussels on the way to Louvain, accompanied by 'Mr [Thomas] Keale' and two Jesuits.[109]

Pett still claimed to think that Sackville was 'a gentilman of greater worth than the world can esteme him at',[110] and even that he still fervently desired to assist the secular clergy.[111] The real problem was that he was not prepared meekly to endorse the secular clergy leadership's line about what form of ecclesiastical government was the best for the English Catholic community.

Sackville may have been articulating views shared by his brother-in-law the second viscount. While at times they both appeared to commend what the secular clergy were doing, at other times they did not. On 26 March/5 April 1616 Anthony Champney wrote to Thomas More that he was amazed that Sackville should 'deny' Champney's thesis, namely that the divisions among the Catholics, especially among the clergy, were the greatest disaster ever to befall our 'countrie'. Champney asked sarcastically whether Sackville 'understandeth more of oure countries estate than all other men'.[112] Sackville's irenicism was leading him, therefore, to question the secular clergy leaders' programme for reforming the Church, a programme which, as we shall see in subsequent chapters, was intended to establish an episcopal authority over the religious orders which some of the religious, especially among the Jesuits and the Benedictines, simply would not accept. According to More, Sackville 'litle respecteth ordinarie jurisdiction and would have the laitie and others at libertie to choose them selves leaders and directors'.[113]

---

[107] *NAGB*, 85–6; Peters, *Mary Ward*, 221–2, 225, 226–36, 241–5, 258–9. For the negotiations with the Benedictines, see AAW, A XV, no. 96, p. 253. In June 1617 the Jesuit general wrote a letter to Sackville expressing gratitude for his friendship, ARSJ, Anglia MS 1/i, 148. In November 1619 the general wrote to Sackville again, glad that he approved of the conversion of the Jesuit mission in England into a vice-province, *ibid.*, fo. 116v.

[108] See AAW, A XIII, no. 261, p. 681, no. 264, p. 687; *HMCD* V, 37, 42, 78; *CSPD Addenda 1580–1625*, 597; T. Birch (ed.), *The Court and Times of James the First* (2 vols., 1848), II, 198–9; AAW, A XIV, no. 19, p. 55, no. 22, p. 63, no. 35, p. 102.

[109] AAW, A XIV, no. 75, p. 254. Keel was professed as a Jesuit in November 1617, CRS 75, 219.

[110] AAW, A XIV, no. 81, p. 271.

[111] *Ibid.*, no. 93, p. 303.   [112] *Ibid.*, A XV, no. 58, p. 151.   [113] *Ibid.*, no. 73, p. 195.

In this articulation of clergy discontents we can see the potential for conflict between lay patrons and clerical clients. Such conflict might occur among and between those patrons and clients who believed that they were acting in each other's best interests. However much respect they might have for each other, clerical and lay interests and perceptions were often fundamentally opposed. To a lay patron the superiority which some of the clergy seemed to be aiming at might be subversive of all good order, just as to the clergy it seemed subversive to give too much sway to the laity.

Now, in some ways, all this simply confirms John Bossy's conclusion that the secular clergy leaders aimed too high in this period and found they could not overtop the gentry who were not prepared to put up with their schemes for world domination. It seems certain that Montague believed in the necessity of maintaining the superiority and independence of the great lay patron within the Catholic community.[114]

Here, however, we also have an indication of how serious and far-reaching the consequences might be if a patron did decide to back unequivocally one particular ideological line or viewpoint among his clients and friends. And, indeed, under certain circumstances, patrons such as Montague would come down off the fence and effectively endorse the line and programme of one particular lobby. At crucial points, as in 1608–9, when George Birkhead launched his campaign at Rome to reform the English Catholic community from the inside (principally by weeding out the Jesuits' influence), and again in the early 1620s when the newly consecrated William Bishop arrived in the country, and in the later 1620s when some of the regulars and their lay patrons launched their own campaign to eject Bishop Richard Smith from the community, the second Viscount Montague was to be found firmly supporting the reforming rhetoric of the leading secular clergymen within his entourage.[115]

This throwing of the patron's weight behind a particular option or policy could, of course, cause real polarisation within his household and entourage. Montague's unequivocal support for Birkhead in the mid-Jacobean period certainly seems to have alienated Anthony Fletcher, one of Montague's household servants. The widowed Fletcher, as we saw, had gone off to the English College in Rome in 1609, and was ordained a year later.[116] On 17 March 1611 Birkhead sent his congratulations to Fletcher via Thomas More in Rome, and said he hoped that Fletcher and his son (who had entered the college in November 1610) would both make good priests.[117] In August 1611 Birkhead sent a note to Fletcher that he should 'praie for a Barbara the youngest of seven', i.e. Montague's recently born daughter.[118] Fletcher was

---

[114] See ch. 13, *passim* below.   [115] See chs. 11, 12 and 13 below.
[116] Anstr. II, 113; ch. 6, p. 202 above.   [117] AAW, A X, no. 24, p. 58.
[118] *Ibid.*, no. 97, p. 274.

dispatched to England in September 1612. He, however, in late 1612/early 1613 entered the Society.[119] What induced Fletcher to do this is not clear. But it appears that his new ecclesiastical affiliation may have been informed by real doubts about what some of his former confrères at Cowdray and their master were now doing. His affection for, and determination to enter, the Society did little for his credit at Cowdray. Birkhead wrote to Thomas More in November 1612 that 'I am sorie Mr Fletcher is' on his way 'home'. 'He will fynd great difficultie heare of a place. I could wishe he [had] provided [for] himselfe in the Low Countrie[s] for a tyme.' As he came, Fletcher carried with him a demand direct from Pope Paul V that the seculars must settle their quarrels with the religious. Champney reported to More on 30 March/9 April 1613 that 'Mr Anthonie Fletcher ys arrived' in England 'but dothe not profess him self Jesuite. He presented to his owld lorde', Viscount Montague, 'a crucifix from his Holiness and would gladdly have hadd entrance and entertaynment but was refused'.[120]

The senior secular priest and polemical writer Edward Weston provides us with another instance of the polarising process at work in the Montague entourage. He had been at Cowdray during this period,[121] but he was gradually being frozen out. We do not quite know why, but it was probably to do with his attitudes on the vexed question of the proper Catholic response to the 1606 oath of allegiance. He was more pro-active in condemning it than some of Montague's priests, even though technically all of them subscribed to the papal breves which said that it could not be taken by Catholics. Even his defence of Richard Smith's polemical tract against the renegade Thomas Bell, a tract which contained some rather liberal passages on the topic of papal political power, looked suspiciously like praising Smith with faint damns.[122] Weston later wrote a scathing tractate critique of the ideological position of the monk Thomas Preston who defended the regime's stance on the question of the oath. Several other clergy around Montague evidently deemed Weston's tract to be impolitic.[123] By this time Weston had already decamped to the household of Edward Gage at Bentley where (until Gage's death in 1614) there was more ideological leeway for those who sympathised with

---

[119] Anstr. II, 113; CRS 74, 171.

[120] AAW, A XII, no. 72, p. 154; *NAGB*, 194. In the early 1620s we find Fletcher, clearly by now a trusted figure in the Society's affairs in England, in correspondence with the Jesuit general and agitating for Richard Blount SJ to be brought back to England, ARSJ, Anglia MS 1/i, fo. 150r.

[121] Weston became one of George Birkhead's advisers when Birkhead became archpriest, and thus gained admittance to Cowdray. In 1609 he signed a petition for a bishop to be granted to the English clergy, A. F. Allison, 'The Later Life and Writings of Joseph Creswell, S. J. (1556–1623)', *RH* 15 (1979), 79–144, at p. 110.

[122] *Ibid.*, 110, 111.

[123] *Ibid.*, 111. Weston's tract caused a search to be made for him in Sussex, *NAGB*, 172, 177, 182.

what was regarded as a Jesuit line on such dangerous and difficult issues.[124]
Weston's tract against Preston was intended for the eyes of Lord Vaux, and
was meant to strengthen Vaux's opposition to the oath. Vaux was a leading
patron of the Society of Jesus.[125] When Weston left the country in 1612 he
went immediately to Douai. There, with other pro-Jesuit staff, he caused
general dissension in the college. He was an opponent of Matthew Kellison,
who took over the presidency of the college in late 1613.[126] Weston was, by
now, very critical of what he saw as the ideological errors of his former colleagues. He was even censuring his former patron. According to Robert Pett,
on 20/30 September 1612, 'D. Weston . . . speaketh much in dispraise of my
lord [Montague] and findeth faulte with all proceadings of our clergie.'[127]

Lewd stories about his period of residence at Cowdray were then allowed,
evidently by Catholics, to circulate. They were eventually picked up by a
much-gratified Archbishop Abbot. On 9 September 1613 Abbot informed
William Trumbull that Weston was 'a loose man of life, as I find by my
examination of a pretty boy who remained in the house in England where
the doctor resided, and for the foulness whereof he was willed by the master
of the house', Viscount Montague, 'to be gone'.[128] Abbot had also claimed
that, 'a little before Queen Elizabeth's death', Weston 'published *De Triplici
Hominis Officio* containing virulent matter against the State, but remaining
at Douai he was presently blown away, being accused in the English College
there of fornication with his laundress'.[129] These same stories were used
against the now allegedly bi-sexual Weston when the contrary faction at
Douai, led by the new president, Kellison, was trying to get rid of him.[130]

If the tendency was for all of the entourage or following of a great lay
patron such as Montague to follow the lead given by the master, we might
well think that the decision by individuals such as Fletcher and Weston
to vacate the master's service would lead to greater harmony and quietness within the Catholic community. For there would then be at least
the semblance of ideological uniformity and unity within each household
and, perhaps, an agreement to differ between individual entourages and
patrons. However, even the briefest surveys of Montague's wider kin network
show how wide of the mark such a judgment would be. Indeed, the lack of
consensus which we perceive there shows us exactly how important the

---

[124] *NAGB*, 182.   [125] Allison, 'Later Life', 111–12.   [126] *Ibid.*, 112; *NAGB, passim.*
[127] AAW, A XI, no. 174, p. 511.   [128] *HMCD* IV, 194.   [129] *Ibid.*, 114.
[130] Allison, 'Later Life', 115–16. This rift between Weston and Montague may have later healed.
As Allison notes, while Weston was resident in Bruges in the 1620s, one of the people
who consulted him about various matters 'of conscience . . . was Viscount Montague of
Cowdray', *ibid.*, 117. Nevertheless, in December 1627, Weston was still opposing Richard
Smith, who was, now with Montague's support, pressing his campaign to assert his episcopal
authority over the religious, AAW, A XXI, no. 1, p. 1.

338   *Catholicism and Community in Early Modern England*

factional battles of the clergy must have been. The disunity and differences of opinion within the Brownes' network made it an arena for conflict over the key questions which affected Catholics in the early seventeenth century. While the second Viscount Montague may for much of the time have been relatively even-handed in his patronage, and, at other times, have tended strongly towards the leading secular priests who were in his service, his ageing great-uncle Francis was, by contrast, a well-known supporter of the Society. The viscount's uncle Sir George was rumoured to incline the same way, and his sister Dorothy's brother-in-law, Roger Lee, was a Jesuit.[131] Though Montague's aunt, Lady Elizabeth Dormer, made quite a strong ideological statement by deciding to employ Edward and John Bennett as chaplains, Dorothy Dormer married Henry Huddlestone, and their household became one of the premier Jesuit residences, celebrated in the account of the Jesuit mission written by John Gerard.[132] Even the Arundell family of Wardour, Montague's relatives, who generally supported the secular clergy leadership in its projects, had ideological fractures among its members. Montague's son-in-law William Arundell was noted in the later 1620s to be harbouring the Benedictine superior, Benedict Jones. Jones was an extremely bitter critic of Richard Smith.[133]

Most flagrantly of all, William Browne, the second Viscount Montague's brother, actually became a lay Jesuit in October 1612.[134] According to the Society's annals he led a life of exemplary and humble piety. He assisted in purchasing the property for the Society's new college at Liège in 1614.[135] The entry into the Society of this younger member of the second viscount's generation was clearly not as uncontroversial as Jesuit accounts of his simple and godly life make out. The scandalous exposé by the renegade James Wadsworth of the Catholic religious orders and educational institutions on the Continent included in its general gossip the claim that the Jesuits had extracted a huge sum, 'no lesse than 10000 pound sterling', from Montague's brother. He had then been made the 'porter of the colledge at St Omers'.[136] Here Wadsworth may be picking up on and repeating the rude remarks of Catholics who claimed that the Society subverted the established social order

---

[131] Foley I, 456–65.
[132] See M. Hodgetts, *Secret Hiding Places* (Dublin, 1989), 57–8, 167–8; P. Caraman (ed.), *John Gerard* (1951), 33; Foley V, 583. The Huddlestones' son Sir Robert married, first, Bridget, daughter of Lord Teynham (d. February 1641), head of the ennobled branch of the Roper family, very pro-Jesuit in their inclinations; and, secondly, Mary Tufton, daughter of the earl of Thanet. His second son, John, became a Jesuit. Henry Huddlestone seems not to have been on good terms with his mother-in-law, Lady Dormer, *HMCS* XIV, 110.
[133] PRO, SP 16/529/94, fo. 146r.
[134] CRS 74, 129. William Browne's forfeiture for recusancy was granted to Edward Carpenter in May 1609, *CSPD 1603–10*, 511; PRO, SO 3/4 (May 1609).
[135] Foley II, 428ff, 439. See CRS 74, 15; Allison, 'Later Life', 84–9.
[136] Wadsworth, *The English Spanish Pilgrime*, 30.

by treating the children of socially exalted Catholics in a demeaning way. But the Jesuits positively celebrated the poverty of life and praiseworthy humility of this patron, a jewel of their order. The Annual Letter produced at the college at Liège in 1637 took particular care to record that 'he most studiously sought out and tenderly loved the lowest offices in our colleges'. Specifically, 'for fourteen years he spent almost two hours daily in the kitchen in washing the dishes' and other menial tasks from which he derived spiritual pleasure and enlightenment. This 'showed itself outwardly in his countenance, and was a sign of heavenly light whereby he penetrated into the hidden treasures of these employments, which are not revealed except to such as are truly little'. At the time that the gardens were being laid out he worked as a 'common hodman', and

with a sack or hodman's basket on his back, which he so fastened by a double cord over his breast as to leave his hands at liberty, in which he held his *Imitation of Christ* by Thomas a Kempis, he would carry rubbish backwards and forwards; and whilst they were filling his hod with earth or stones . . . he would sit for a little upon the trunk of a tree and draw something from the book wherewith in the meantime to feed his soul; nor did any dilatoriness show itself in his countenance or gait.

The Jesuits admitted, however, that this did not seem seemly to his family at all. 'These things were so public that from the first they became known by report to his sisters and mother . . . who, from mistaken ideas, interpreting them in a wrong light, were indignant, and reprobated these exercises of humility as stains upon the honour of the noble family.' But he rebuked them, telling them that they had 'delights, whilst I in the meantime, of the divine bounty, overflow with heavenly joys'. He eventually died nursing plague victims.[137]

CONCLUSION

On one level, this account of extended Catholic families and their chaplains can be read as no more than the story of early modern ecclesiastical consumer choice. Families with different preferences employed different clergymen or, rather, looked to a range of clergymen for different styles of clerical service. This practice meshed nicely in many cases with the structure of these families

[137] Foley II, 428ff (quotations at pp. 434, 435). Wadsworth also claimed that the Jesuits had ensnared and abused Stanislaus Browne, 'sonne and heire to Mr Anthony Browne, brother to the Vicount Montague'. Stanislaus (a son, in fact, of the second viscount's brother John) 'after two yeeres abode' at St Omer, 'wearied by their tyranicall discipline, and desirous to get his necke from their yoake, counterfeited a letter from his father to the rector of the . . . colledge', a letter which summoned him home. But the ruse was discovered, and the rector gave it as his opinion that 'if ever' Stanislaus 'should bee in England' again 'hee would turne Protestant', Wadsworth, *The English Spanish Pilgrime*, 26–7.

since these clergy were often kin to their patrons. In some ways this actually underpinned and strengthened the English Catholic community.

On the other hand, not everyone within this network of families was entirely happy with live-and-let-live arrangements of this kind. Some believed that this was a recipe for chaos and disorder, a chaos and disorder which had been all too publicly displayed during the appellant controversy, and which ought to be rectified. As we have already seen, some Catholics argued that the way to reform the community was to make the English Catholic Church (such as it was) more like Churches in other European States which were themselves Catholic, in particular to reinstitute the episcopal mechanisms of government which were so significantly absent amongst English Catholics.

However, as Rome's dithering over the appellant dispute had demonstrated, the Holy Father and his curial officials were unlikely to rush to intervene or force the issue. They would, as they had done in the appellant business, continue to receive conflicting advice from different sections of the community. In the face of this, their tendency would generally be to do little or nothing.

For those who wanted to bring about sweeping reforms within the community, the only way to proceed was to recruit support from leading Catholic families. Inevitably this meant destabilising the uneasy but at least relatively even balance between different clerical factions and their patrons. It would inevitably involve an attempt by the reformers to assert ideological dominance over those who opposed them. It was easy to see how much additional conflict and trouble this would cause, though many of the Catholic clergy, notably many of the people whom we have been looking at in this chapter, thought that such conflict was a price worth paying.

As we have also remarked, there are distinct echoes here of several scholars' accounts of the ructions caused by the 'avant-garde' conformist mentality and programme in the early Stuart Church. There seems to be at least a family likeness between the two attempts, Protestant and Catholic, to change crucial aspects of the clerical and ecclesiastical culture within their respective communions in England. Much of the rest of this book will attempt, within the confines of its topic of the aristocratic entourage, to determine how far this is true.

11

'Grand captain' or 'little lord': the second Viscount Montague as Catholic leader

We have already witnessed how, at the time of James Stuart's accession, the second Viscount Montague tried to make a pitch for public attention and for some measure of influence among his fellow Catholics. And in the 1604 parliament he had made a noisy though disastrous bid to set himself up as a leading representative of the Catholic community in its opposition to the new recusancy legislation. His involvement in the Gunpowder debacle, we might imagine, would have persuaded him that it would be better to retire gracefully from view and not to meddle in such matters again.[1]

But this he evidently did not do. The year after his public reverse in the House of Lords we find him lobbying the papacy in support of the secular clergy who were asking that Rome should intervene in order to reform the state of English Catholicism. A letter from Montague to Pope Paul V, dated 15 August 1605, summarised the conditions under which Catholics lived in England, and put the case for the reinstitution of Catholic episcopal government within the realm.[2]

In incredibly florid Latin, Montague set out many of the key issues which figure repeatedly in most of the secular clergy's protestations and petitions to the curia during the Jacobean period. The persecution was getting worse ('persecutio magis magisque quotidie innovatur'). Rumours were spreading to foreign princes, however, that this had nothing to do with religion. Catholics, it was said, were punished only for disobedience to the law and for plots against the king ('sparsis ad exteros principes undequaque rumoribus, nihil in nos omnino acerbitatis ob fidem, sed tum ob inobedientiam contra leges regias, tum ob pessimas in regem regnumque machinationes, aliquando

---

[1] See ch. 8, pp. 266, 272–8, 279–85 above.
[2] The letter, or a copy of it, is in the Westminster Cathedral archives (AAW, B 24, no. 16). As Leo Hicks speculated, this letter may have been connected with the abortive journey in May 1606 of John Cecil and Anthony Champney to petition Paul V to grant the secular clergy's suit for a bishop, TD V, 10; CRS 41, 5. A list of reasons for such an appointment, contained in the Westminster Cathedral archives, and dated to 29 October 1605, may have been the burden of whatever Cecil and Champney presented to the curial authorities, AAW, B 24, no. 18.

et non nisi ex mera necessitate satis moderate exerceri'). Montague protested that Catholics were not disobedient to the temporal power, except in the sense of obeying God rather than man. The Catholics adhered to their supreme pastor with absolute affection of the heart, and they relied on him to instruct them how to distinguish between their duty to God and their duty to Caesar. Not all Catholics were equally virtuous, however. Some were purchasing immunity from the law with money; but Montague could not commend this since it was not for the common good. English Catholics looked, nevertheless, to the pope to promote good and godly discipline and order among them.

Then Montague turned to the principal issue. The powers of the archpriest were too limited; he should be invested with the authority of a bishop. This, Montague implied, would be an extension of the pope's own authority and power, since he was the bishop of bishops. A new bishop in England would administer the sacrament of confirmation, a means of strengthening Catholics' faith. There was no danger of such a bishop making the persecution any worse. The laws were already as severe as they could be against mere priests. In any case, such a man would never be so imprudent as to provoke the State.[3]

The regime continued to regard Montague with suspicion. In April 1608 the Spanish noblewoman resident in London, Luisa de Carvajal, described Montague as 'outstanding in his zeal for the Catholic religion'.[4] And in 1611 Montague crossed some sort of personal Rubicon by refusing the new oath of allegiance.[5] This was quite a radical step for someone whose personal rhetoric was pegged so heavily to the virtues of moderation, and whose own Catholic chaplains had made so much of their rejection of 'Jesuit' political extremism.

Yet his very public aristocratic snub to the regime was, it seems, a quite carefully calculated effort to assert his place as a leader among contemporary Catholics. And he did this at exactly the same time that some of his chaplains were making their bid for ideological dominance within the Catholic community.

As is well known, the oath of allegiance, promulgated in statute during the parliamentary session of 1606, was an attempt by the crown to define what political loyalty should mean for James's Catholic subjects. James announced in his published defence of the oath that it was set forth so that his subjects

---

[3] AAW, B 24, no. 16. I am grateful to Thomas McCoog for providing a translation of this letter. For an account of the limitations of the archpriest's powers, see Hughes, *RCR*, 296–7.

[4] *Epistolario de Luisa de Carvajal y Mendoza* (digital edition, Alicante, 1999), letter 93. I am very grateful to Glyn Redworth for this point.

[5] See below in this chapter.

'should make cleare profession' of their resolution 'faithfully to persist in his Majesties obedience according to their naturall allegiance', and thus

> his Majestie might make a separation, not onely betweene all his good subjects in generall, and unfaithfull traitors that intended to withdraw themselves from his Majesties obedience; but specially to make a separation betweene so many of his Majesties subjects, who, although they were otherwise popishly affected, yet retained in their hearts the print of their naturall duetie to their soveraigne; and those who, being caried away with the like fanaticall zeale that the powder traitors were, could not conteine themselves within the bounds of their naturall allegiance.[6]

Historians disagree about exactly what the ideological import of the oath was. Some more or less accept James's own line that it was no more than a simple loyalty test and was intended only to make a clear division between his Catholic subjects who wanted to kill him and the ones who did not. And, indeed, it is possible to make a strong case that the oath sought to exploit a European consensus about the relationship between spiritual and temporal power, a consensus shared by many Catholics as well as by many Protestants. Others see it as a veiled version of the oath of supremacy, a radical invasion of an area of conscience with which Catholics, who themselves would have no truck with violent resistance to James's regime, would inevitably have almost insuperable difficulties, and therefore could not take the oath as it stood.[7]

Of course, during the Jacobean period, there was a wide range of opinion among Catholics on how far it was possible to go, and particularly about what forms of words might be employed, in order to placate the regime's demands for public displays of loyalty. Many lay Catholics took the oath, or publicly gave out signals that they condoned it. Probably the vast majority of the Catholic community had in some sense supported the right of the Stuarts to succeed Elizabeth. The last thing they wanted was to refuse a loyalty oath to a king who was the son of Mary, queen of Scots.

But it proved virtually impossible, or at least very difficult, to maintain one's standing at the centre of the Catholic community if one defended the oath. The most intellectually respectable supporter of the regime's position on loyalty, the Benedictine monk Thomas Preston, was forced to write under a pseudonym. Robert Drury and Roger Cadwallader, two of the priests who had offered the Protestation of Allegiance to Elizabeth in January 1603, refused the 1606 oath and were executed.[8] The near impossibility, at least

[6] K. Fincham and P. Lake, 'The Ecclesiastical Policy of King James I', *JBS* 24 (1985), 170–207, at p. 184; James I, *Triplici Nodo, Triplex Cuneus. Or an Apologie for the Oath of Allegiance* (1607), 3.
[7] J.V. Gifford, 'The Controversy over the Oath of Allegiance of 1606' (D. Phil., Oxford, 1971), 48.
[8] Bossy, *ECC*, 41.

for the Catholic clergy, of approving the oath was demonstrated by the fate of the archpriest George Blackwell. After his arrest in 1607 he was subjected to an intensive grilling by royal commissioners who questioned him closely about his opinion of the oath. In fact, his natural inclination had always been to accept the oath, but papal condemnation of it, via two breves, had made it impossible for him to lobby in favour of the regime on this issue. Now, however, he allowed his name to be put to a long printed account of how he had accepted the regime's case that current Catholic attempts to distinguish between their duty to the king and their obedience to Rome were not acceptable.[9]

Blackwell was deposed and replaced by none other than Montague's senior chaplain George Birkhead. Birkhead was, in many ways, an unlikely Catholic leader. Increasingly ill at this time, and afflicted with a tendency to complain about almost everything, he seems a surprising choice as the spearhead of the English Catholic secular clergy's wing of the Counter-Reformation. Nevertheless, Birkhead was resident at the centre of one of the most extensive Catholic aristocratic entourages in early seventeenth-century England. Several of the most active and ambitious secular clergymen, notably Richard Smith and Thomas More, were already in that same entourage. With a patron who was from time to time sympathetic to many of these men's intended courses, the stage was set for some potentially explosive interventions in the politics of the Catholic community.

THE PRO-EPISCOPAL LOBBY MAKES ITS MOVE

Soon after the death of Lady Magdalen in April 1608 plans were being laid to launch a series of petitions or suits at Rome for a radical shake-up in the governance and structure of key aspects of the English Catholic community.[10] Birkhead now commissioned Smith and More to head his new agency in Rome. They were instructed to urge the curia to think seriously about the issues affecting English Catholics.

It was no coincidence that, almost immediately, Smith's Latin account of Lady Magdalen's life, with its flattering comments about her, her relatives and her clergy, which we have already reviewed in some detail,[11] was printed abroad and flagged in Rome as an attention-gaining device to attract the approbation of the curial authorities responsible for English affairs. It was

---

[9] *A Large Examination taken at Lambeth According to his Maiesties Direction, Point by Point, of Mr. George Blakwell, Made Archpriest of England, by Pope Clement 8* (1607).

[10] As we have already seen, Montague was believed to have sent two of his daughters, in April 1608, to Flanders in order to lobby for the appointment of a bishop, ch. 10, p. 332 above; *Epistolario de Luisa de Carvajal y Mendoza*, letter 100.

[11] See ch. 7, pp. 209, 211–16, 217–18, 222, 228–32 above.

dedicated to Edward Farnese, cardinal protector of the English nation, who, as we have seen, acted as a patron to the Pole family, the Brownes' near neighbours in Sussex.[12]

Smith's agenda in his account of his patroness was clear. He was saying that this noble family, the Brownes, were worthy benefactors and champions of the secular clergy, priests who were quite unlike the dangerous Jesuits whose ghostly children had so wickedly tried to destroy the king and parliament with gunpowder and had risked a terrible retribution against all English Catholics. Though these moderate priests and their moderate patrons were still harassed by the Protestants and were still in some very real sense suffering for the faith, the nastiest expressions of contemporary anti-Catholicism came now not directly from the centre of the regime but from Protestant fanatics, from whom the regime had actually protected Lady Magdalen, at least when her plight was brought to its attention. Also, Lady Magdalen's household was a model of what an alternative and Catholic Church in England could look like if the authorities in Rome would care to make adequate provision for it. It was made plain, however, in Smith's text that the practical toleration which Lady Magdalen had enjoyed had not been bought by compromising with Protestant heresy.

The significance of the ecclesiological messages embedded in Smith's little book was not lost on other Catholics. On 12/22 July 1610 Smith received a commendatory note from 'Brother Gabriel de S. Maria', i.e. William Gifford OSB, who lived at the Benedictine foundation at Dieulouard. Gifford had been close to the epicentre of the original opposition to the English Jesuits' extension of their influence over the Catholic mission in the Elizabethan period. He acknowledged his 'obligation' to Smith 'in particular for the religious token you sent me, I meane the life and deathe of that woorthie ladie which trulie I red over verbatim not without teares, and thanke you for your gratefull labour therein'.[13] It appears that King James himself was aware of the hagiography's implications. Smith wrote to More on 27 November/7 December 1610 that 'the king I heare is greatly offended with my litle booke of my ladies life which the Venice embassador is said to have presented unto him'.[14]

This was the ideological platform, then, on which the secular clergy's pitch to Rome would be made. Birkhead had tried, briefly, to get results by working through the deposed archpriest Blackwell's agent, Thomas Fitzherbert (formerly an employee at Cowdray), and also by trying to be nice to Robert

[12] Richard Smith, *Vita Illustrissime, ac Piissimae Dominae Magdalenae Montis-acuti in Anglia Vicecomitissae* (Rome, 1609). An English translation of the work appeared in 1627. See ARCR I, no. 1098; ARCR II, no. 707; Southern, *ERH*; ch. 10, pp. 326–7 above.
[13] AAW, A IX, no. 54, p. 151. For Gifford, see Anstr. I, 132–3.
[14] AAW, A IX, no. 103, p. 337.

Persons. But it soon became clear that, on its own, this would not have the desired effect. (Niceness was not a quality which Persons ever rated very highly.)[15] So it was decided to send Smith and More to Rome instead. Smith was to become Birkhead's agent, joined in commission with Fitzherbert.

In Rome, Smith, assisted by More, would present an entire programme to set things straight within the English Catholic community, to reform it, and thus purge away its ills and corruptions. This reform would be achieved principally by improving the standard of the clergy educated at the seminaries, and by introducing an episcopal form of authority among and over all the clergy and the laity as well. (Inevitably, this was phrased by reference to a critique of the evil effects which the religious orders, and notably the Society of Jesus, might be reckoned to have had on the Catholic Church in England.)[16]

Birkhead informed Edward Bennett, the Dormers' chaplain, on 21 February 1609 that 'my factor', Smith, 'is not yet gon nor his companion' (More). 'He hath not as yet his passe, nor his bill of exchaunge. But I thinke he will make haist, for the time draweth on.' Although there was an attempt to maintain a cloak of secrecy over this mission, Birkhead admitted that 'it is given out at London that fastinge and prainge is published for the good success of some that are departed to make suit for bishops'.[17] On 8 March Birkhead wrote to Bennett that 'our freind my factor', Smith, 'departed with his compagnion Mr More out of this land upon the 26 of February at two of the clock in the morninge', though they did not dare take all the relevant documentation with them which they would need in Rome. Smith's 'writinges were left behind for another to carie after him'.[18]

In fact the second viscount himself had to obtain the privy council passes necessary for Smith and More to travel abroad. It seems highly unlikely that it was not known what the passes were really for (even though, ironically, they included the customary clause that their recipients should not go to Rome!). The passes were signed by, among other councillors, Archbishop Richard Bancroft who had shown such an interest during the appellant controversy when the appellants' representatives were dispatched to the Holy City. (In May 1609, Richard Holtby SJ alerted his confrere Robert Persons that Bancroft 'looketh dailie for newes' of Smith's 'negotiations'.)[19]

---

[15] See *NAGB*, introduction; cf. CRS 41.
[16] For a summary of what the reform programme consisted of, see *NAGB*, 4–6.
[17] AAW, B 24, no. 48.   [18] *Ibid.*, no. 49.
[19] *NAGB*, introduction, esp. pp. 6–8; AAW, A VIII, nos. 92, 94, 105, p. 498. Smith complained to the Inquisition that Holtby was spreading rumours against him, including the story that Bancroft had an interest in the outcome of Smith and More's mission, Archivio della Congregazione per la Dottrina della Fede, St. St. Ss1-b, 'Anglicana', pars 1^a, fo. 312r (cited in G. Crosignani, 'Strokes of Censure between Richard Smith and Robert Parsons, SJ: A Denunciation at the Holy Office of *The Iudgement of a Catholicke English-Man* (1608)' (forthcoming)).

There was a faint (though not very long-lived) hope that the Jesuits might be brought to cooperate. Birkhead had not been one of the appellants. To the end of his life he always referred to Persons as his 'old friend'. If Persons's friendship with the new archpriest could be cultivated, perhaps the ageing Jesuit's predictable tendency to try to liquidate anyone who confronted him might be assuaged and deflected. In his letter to Edward Bennett (of 8 March) Birkhead rejoiced that 'I have also received now of late [a letter] from my old frend out of the farre countrie, who signifieth that the greatest hath had notice from Paris of my doinges for peace, and thinketh well thereof.' Persons had heard spiteful rumours that some of his own 'companie' were not likely to cooperate but he assured Birkhead that, in fact, 'they are and wilbe as forward as any men els'. Birkhead concluded optimistically that Smith would be welcome in Rome 'and shall fynd very good interteinment, and have also good successe, yf he use the matter with confidence and trust, yet tempered with prudence and discretion, as I trust he will'.[20]

But inevitably it was going to be difficult to maintain the peace. Not only were 'prudence' and 'discretion' not Richard Smith's main attributes. There were also old-guard appellants around, including the eminently certifiable enemy of Persons, Christopher Bagshaw, who believed that Birkhead was far too easygoing towards the irascible Jesuit, and therefore was himself not to be trusted.[21] Bagshaw and others would certainly try to hinder any step which Birkhead took towards reconciliation. The problem was that they could at least claim to have been the people who had won the secular clergy's victory (of sorts) in the appellant controversy when the papacy ruled that Jesuit and secular modes and mechanisms of administration and government should be kept separate. Birkhead could not ignore such sentiments. And, without support from the anti-Jesuit wing of the community, there was little point in Birkhead's dispatch of his agents in the first place. But immoderate railing and streams of ruderies would alarm the papal curia and completely undermine Birkhead's claim that the time was right and that things were calm and settled enough to install a species of local episcopal authority over English Catholics. As he warned Edward Bennett,

because I perceive it to be ill taken that those of the Societie [of Jesus] are rumored to be backward in our concord, I wish that in any case no such surmises should passe from any of us, nor also any other exasperatinge wordes; for they do our cause no good. Diverse compleintes are often brought unto me of sundrie speeches uttered by some of myne, of which they inferre that we meane not the peace which we pretend.[22]

For all Birkhead's outward optimism, it was plain enough that the linchpin of the seculars' reform proposals, the restoration of episcopacy, was going to

[20] AAW, B 24, no. 49.   [21] NAGB, 48.   [22] AAW, B 24, no. 49.

be extremely divisive. Those who proposed it had no intention that episcopal jurisdiction and authority should be conferred on anyone who was not in the tight little group around the archpriest. And once they had got hold of it they would inevitably start to use their newly acquired power in order to discipline the clergy (and their lay patrons) who did not see things in the same light as they did.[23]

The Jesuits played up for all they were worth the potential risks and dangers of appointing a bishop. But, as we shall see in subsequent chapters, events proved how prescient the critics of the pro-episcopal lobby were. The first bishop appointed in the 1620s was the old appellant warhorse William Bishop and the second was, with strong French backing, Richard Smith himself. Priests such as Bishop and Smith had whole files of information and material on the moral and liturgical failings of the regulars and their patrons. It was not hard to see what would happen once these episcopal appointees got around to exercising their disciplinary powers and reforming agenda. The religious who had been most at enmity with the pro-episcopal lobby rightly feared that attempts would be made to eject them from their gentry residences and that episcopal authority would be used to start collaring the sources of patronage which came to the clergy from the Catholic laity.[24]

The setting out of a reform programme such as the one which Birkhead proposed also had large ideological ramifications, however much its proposers spoke the language of moderation and peace. For, if one took such proposals to their logical ends, here was a Catholic version of the 'conformist' programme of reform which certain Church-of-England clerics, particularly Richard Bancroft, had been ramming through against those whom they regarded as tainted with puritan nonconformity. Within the Church of England, conformity meant, in practice, mainly ceremonial conformity, adherence to the prayer book and its rubrics, and so on. Among the Catholics, ceremonial conformity was not an issue. What conformity meant here (though Catholics did not as readily use the word) was the obedience and subjection of all the clergy to one system of Church government. However, the rhetoric used by Church-of-England and Catholic proponents of the benefits of conformist thought, and of hierarchalist order, decency and discipline, was remarkably similar, while the counter-arguments that such 'reforms' would cripple and undermine the spreading of the Word of God by damaging the ministry, in particular by disciplining the most vigorous and evangelical of churchmen, were also very alike.

Initially, in Rome, things seemed to go quite well for Birkhead's agents. The first audience with Pope Paul V, on 14/24 May 1609, brought a swift confirmation that Clement VIII had meant what he said when he pronounced

---

[23] See also ch. 9, p. 309 above.   [24] *NAGB*, 5–6; chs. 12 and 13 below.

that there should be a practical separation between the government of the seculars and of the Jesuits, in other words between the Jesuit superior and the archpriest's regime.

But the rest of Smith's proposals for reform[25] soon ran into opposition, and suffered the general delay and slow death in committee which were the fate of many controversial proposals aired before the Roman curia. Before the arrival of the archpriest's representatives, the pope had pronounced that the *status quo* in England was not to be changed without a general agreement among all the English clergy that such a change was desirable and acceptable.[26]

The papacy had good reason to worry that Birkhead's claim that the vast majority of the secular clergy in England were supporters of the proposed reforms was not strictly true. Some priests started muttering that they were not sure whether Birkhead's proposals were sensible. How far was the Society of Jesus a threat to Catholicism in England? Was this the right time to try to introduce episcopacy? Would this not simply antagonise the regime against Catholics more than it was antagonised already?

In an effort to drum up support for the proposals which Smith had laid out at Rome, Thomas More returned to England in late 1609 to go on a kind of quasi-episcopal visitation. In theory the visitation's purpose was to take soundings, but it was in practice meant (also) to obtain the blessing of, and, it was hoped, signatures from, all the secular clergy to prove to the Roman curia that there was massive and overwhelming, in fact virtually unanimous, support among the English clergy for what Birkhead was proposing. The regime seems to have known that More was coming back into the country for precisely this purpose, but he was not stopped.[27] He had trouble, though, with people such as the archpriest's assistant John Bavant. Bavant was the ageing but influential cleric who had been called in as an arbitrator in the 'Wisbech Stirs' back in the mid-1590s. As we saw in chapter 9, he let it be known that he was not entirely in favour of what was being done in all the clergy's names. He believed that More was extorting signatures from people who were, like himself, unwilling to give them.[28]

One can sense the concealed fury in More's early 1610 report to Smith about his lobbying of the clergy. 'I have bene visiting the cowntrie abroad, especiallie D. Bavan[t]s circuit, wher I find him' and others 'stif against bishops or the manteining of an agent' in Rome. More believed that Bavant had

[25] See *NAGB*, 7.

[26] Permission was granted eventually for a modification of the rules governing the award of higher degrees to the clergy, and, later, for a collegiate foundation in Paris, *NAGB*, 7–8.

[27] *NAGB*, 8. Benjamin Norton had recently been sent to visit all the archpriest's assistants to sound out their opinions, *ibid*.

[28] *NAGB*, 13, 55, 60, 68, 70, 115; ch. 9, pp. 304–6 above.

support even from the influential secular priest Richard Broughton, as well as, less surprisingly, from priests, such as William Hanse, who were resident with families which were known to be favourers of the Jesuits.[29] Bavant was 'not to be drawn from anie opinion he holdeth as is apparent by his conceipt of the kings Majestie whom in noe case he wil have thought to persecute us otherwise than in pollicie, as minding in time to doe us good a[n]d set up Catholic religion we know not how soone'. More suspected that this was merely an excuse to oppose the archpriest's reform programme. 'This is soe settled in his head that al the art one can use is not able to dispossesse his brains therof. I fear much that he is egged forward by some that wold not have unitie amongst us, and work what may be, underhand, to hinder our archpriests proceedings in his clergies behalf.' Bavant was also militating in favour of Thomas Worthington, the current president of Douai College, who was known to be an ardent supporter of the Society. Worthington was 'casting beyond the moon as if whatsoever were intended the upshot wold be the expelling' of the Jesuits 'out of England'.[30]

Geoffrey Pole now turned up in Rome, deeply desirous, we may imagine, to cause as much grief to the archpriest's enemies as he could. He had left the country on 7 March with Thomas More, intending that they should be back in Rome before the canonisation of Cardinal Charles Borromeo.[31] This in itself was a high-profile event and of immense significance for the wing of the secular clergy aligned against the Jesuits. Borromeo could be seen as an ideal type of Counter-Reformation bishop. He had instilled order and discipline in the diocese under his charge – Milan – in a manner similar to the one which it was hoped a bishop in England might use to quell the 'chaos Anglicanum'. Borromeo was regarded by some as having been opposed to the pretensions of the Society.[32]

Smith was not, however, the right man for the delicate task of prolonged negotiation. Soon he was on bad terms with Persons and Fitzherbert. Fitzherbert was dismissed by Birkhead as his co-agent. Then Persons (or somebody else, but almost certainly Persons) decided that Smith's polemical tract of 1605 written against the renegade Thomas Bell, with its notable failure properly to denounce Bell's refutation of the papal deposing power, was too offensive to leave unnoticed by the Holy Office. Smith soon found himself being investigated for an alleged lapse in doctrinal judgment, even perhaps the sin of heterodox belief, on this important question. Persons wanted to call Smith's and the seculars' bluff on the loyalism issue. Such people were

[29] Anstr. I, 147–8.   [30] *NAGB*, 68.   [31] AAW, A IX, no. 27.

[32] Borromeo had also been the patron of the Welsh priest Owen Lewis, whom he had appointed in 1579 as his vicar-general. Lewis had been looked to by many of the English clergy as Cardinal Allen's natural successor, and as a necessary counterweight to the influence of Robert Persons, Anstr. I, 209–10.

posturing as loyal and moderate, and they were publicly lambasting the Jesuits for their alleged political extremism. But how did they think that a godly Catholic should respond when the prerogatives of the Holy See were challenged by a regime such as King James's?[33]

Persons's fury caused Smith to have a nervous breakdown. Word went around that Smith had been seen weeping, from either frustration or fear, outside the Inquisition's offices in Rome.[34] By September 1610 he had clearly had enough. He resigned his agency and departed for Paris, leaving More as agent in his place to continue the struggle. When Smith arrived in Paris he was, for a time, in a bad and 'melancholie' state.[35] The whole incident was remembered with bitterness for years afterwards.[36]

[33] See *NAGB*, 8, 140; CRS 41, 122–3. Ginevra Crosignani has unearthed a manuscript in the records of the Inquisition entitled 'Ragioni perche non si deve ammettere la nuova accusa del libro del P. Personi scritti [*sic*] contra il giuramento di lealta' (Archivio della Congregazione per la Dottrina della Fede, Indice, protocolli S, fos. 453r–454v). This document defends Persons (and his book *The Iudgment of a Catholicke English-man* (St Omer, 1608)) against the attacks of Smith, More and William Alabaster, after Alabaster, in late summer 1609, backed up by Smith and More, retaliated against Persons (claiming that Persons's own book was heterodox on the question of the papal deposing power). It denies that Persons had denounced Smith to the Inquisition, although there is, in the Stonyhurst archive, a 'censura brevis', written by Persons, of Smith's book, CRS 41, 123. I am very grateful to Dr Crosignani for this information. (During 1608, Alabaster had been the subject of Inquisition proceedings against him for his doctrinal errors, and he had formally abjured them on 17/27 January 1609, Crosignani, 'Strokes of Censure'.) The accusations against Persons were resubmitted by More to the pope and the Inquisition in July 1611, but without success, *ibid.*; *NAGB*, 128–9.

[34] Ginevra Crosignani has established that there were, however, no formal proceedings against Smith by the Inquisition. But on 13/23 December 1609 a memorandum by Smith, presented by More, was dealt with by the Inquisition. The memorandum petitioned that, since there had been no formal delation of his book against Thomas Bell, he should be exonerated from the imputations currently being made against it, Archivio della Congregazione per la Dottrina della Fede, St. St. Ss1-b, 'Anglicana', pars 1ª, fo. 312r (cited in Crosignani, 'Strokes of Censure'). However, at the end of December, the pope personally overruled a decision by the Inquisition cardinals to grant Smith the attestation of immunity which he desired, *ibid.* The Jesuits claimed, probably correctly, that the decision to refrain from formal censure of Smith was taken only to avoid further controversy. The pope was certainly not convinced of Smith's innocence, *ibid.*

[35] *NAGB*, 9.

[36] In September 1614 Champney wrote to More that Paul Green had 'passed this way this last week out of Spayn for Ingland', and Thomas Rant, the Oratorian priest, had 'expostulated with him the matter of giveinge' Smith's 'booke against Bell to the Inquisitione which before us all he professeth upon his preisthood he never did', AAW, A XIII, no. 194, p. 490; Anstr. I, 137. In November 1624 Smith wrote to More from Paris that More should remind their friends in the French embassy in Rome that 'Father Fitzherbert was one of the accusers of my booke against Bel to the Inquisition', AAW, B 27, no. 40. In his 'Apologeticall Answere' of late 1628, Viscount Montague himself notes that 'my now lord bishop (whome God longe preserve)' was 'of longe tyme by them [the Jesuits] not favoured, in so much as his booke against Bell was by one or mo[r]e of them put into the Inquisition', but 'it was returned with a verie honorable testimonie of that profound devine and excellent ornament of these tymes, the most illustrious and most reverend Cardinall Bellarmine of famous memorie', AA, 313.

What was the second Viscount Montague's role in all this? He had, as we saw, been the author of a long letter of 15 August 1605 to the pope demanding reform. This was the first time that Montague publicly entered the lists in the Catholic ecclesiastical reform debate. When Montague's letter arrived in Rome, Persons had used his influence to make sure that it was not presented. Persons later explained, in a self-justificatory missive to Birkhead of 25 June/5 July 1608, that he was moved only by solicitude for the viscount's safety. The leaking out of the existence of such a letter would, claimed Persons, have imperilled Montague. Thomas Fitzherbert made a similar excuse to Birkhead in letters of May and August 1608. Fitzherbert also mentioned that Montague had insisted that the letter be returned to him.[37]

The English Jesuits and their friends moved very quickly to stymie the appointment of a bishop. In the Jesuit archives in Rome there is, from this period, a list of reasons for and against, but mainly against, an episcopal appointment. (These reasons would be expounded and amplified up until the point when William Bishop was consecrated as bishop of Chalcedon in 1623.) In reply to the sort of arguments which Montague and others were articulating, it was alleged that confirmation was not a necessary rite; and in any case a mere priest could consecrate the holy oils and confer the sacrament. Under a heavy persecution it would be folly to appoint a bishop since he would not in practice have adequate disciplinary authority ('ullam jurisdictionem fori externi qua disciplinam inter sacerdotes et Catholicos laicos observandam'). The writer added that, if there were to be more than one bishop, problems would arise about the extent of their individual jurisdictions.[38]

On 27 November 1608, not long before Smith and More set out, Montague had penned an extended missive to Edward Bennett, Montague's aunt's

A draft of February 1628 for a section of Montague's book, entitled 'A Moderate Replie, written by a Friend of the Secular Clergie in Answere to A.B. the Reverend Priests disgracefull letter of the 29 [i.e. 25] November 1627', said that 'an encomium or commendacion of the booke . . . was given by Cardinal Bellarmine himselfe, one of the judges of that bench in these wordes: est bonus et doctus liber', AAW, A XXII, no. 32, p. 178. Ginevra Crosignani, who has located a Jesuit account (ARSJ, Anglia MS 36/ii, fo. 231r–v) of the incident which admits that Bellarmine came down in Smith's favour, explains that Bellarmine's opinion would have been delivered in December 1609 when the Inquisition cardinals decided to grant Smith the certificate of immunity which he sought, i.e. before the pope intervened and overruled them, Crosignani, 'Strokes of Censure'.

37 CRS 41, 5–7. In mid-1610 the viscount decided that the letter should be sent back to Rome again. In early 1612 we find Birkhead writing to More to say 'I hope the great packet', i.e. the lists of names attached to the petition for the appointment of a bishop, 'is with yow by this, and when yow exhibit those things, yow must also deliver the thick letter of my host', i.e. Montague, AAW, A XI, no. 10, p. 23. On 26 January/5 February 1612 Smith instructed More not to forget to present 'my lords old letter', AAW, A XI, no. 14, p. 39.

38 ARSJ, Anglia MS 31/i, fos. 451r–453v.

chaplain. The missive was evidently intended as a kind of official statement
of his position. It is his most explicit account of his sympathy with what
his chaplains were now doing. The letter fulminates against perceived Jesuit
opposition to Smith's agency which was currently in preparation.[39] Montague wrote, 'my good and . . . loving frind, I am sory it is my fortune to
write you so crosse nues'. These bad tidings caused him 'daily . . . to think
wee have falsehoode in fellowshipp'. So angry was he with those whom he
believed to be 'theyr aucthors' that he confessed 'I knowe not how to keepe
my selfe in temper.' Montague hoped that God would give himself and his
friends 'all patience and the spiritte of wisdomme and fortitude whereby,
like zealouse champions of our Catholique commonwealthe', they would be
able to defend themselves 'against Father Parsons, Mr Fitzherbert and theyr
adhearing oppressors'. Montague did not despair of 'our Christian liberty',
which 'no ecclesiasticall hierarchie ever denied too the humble children of
our holy Mother the Church'. Montague mentioned that Thomas Fitzherbert
had 'most resulutely written' to Birkhead that the pope had commanded that
'no procurators shall comme to Roome' and now Smith 'dareth not to goe'.
Indeed Montague himself 'coulde wish the jurney to be respited for a time
till both the cleargy and layty had too eache other beemoned our selfes of
that wofull misery whereto wee may not neede too doubte but the fathers of
the Society have broughte us, raising theyr lofty towers with our unfortunate
ruines'.

Montague complained, referring here to his own suppressed letter of
August 1605 to Paul V, 'alas what hath eyther the cleargie or wee of the
laity demerited too bee debarred of accesse eyther by person or by letter
too the Sea Apostolique'. It was, after all, for the sake of the pope's 'eminent prerogative [that] we loose our lives and livelihoodes, while Father
Parsons flourisheth (if he tiranize not) at Roome; and his brethren heere
commonly skape all reall daunger. You see I wander in passion, but with
too great reason.' Montague commended his chaplain Birkhead's diligence.
The angry viscount also wished Bennett's 'presence heere, desiring for mine
owne parte . . . if any service may bee in mee too doe too so good a cause,
not to pretermitt the performance, though with losse of my life and what I
am worth'. In a postscript Montague added that Smith was 'divers waies dis-
couradged and much lamenteth our common misery', and that 'it were good
that suddenly through divers partes of Ingland coppies of letters directed to
the colledg[e] of the Inquisition, with request to meediate with his Holinesse
for procurators with convenient circumstances, were sent too the priestes,
that, beeing by them subscribed, they mighte bee safely sent awaie'.[40]

---

[39] AAW, B 47, no. 145; TD V, lii. The letter is endorsed 'all my Lord Montagues owne hand
cujus memoria in beneditia'.
[40] AAW, B 47, no. 145.

Once Smith and More got to Rome, Montague wrote words of encouragement to them as well.[41] A letter from Montague to Smith survives, dated 6 July 1609.[42] The letter urges him on, and sends greetings from Montague's son Francis 'et sororibus suis'. Another letter, of 4 August 1609, reminisces about the recently deceased Lady Magdalen, dowager Viscountess Montague, and expresses Montague's hostility to Thomas Fitzherbert for impeding the archpriest's purposes. Montague mentioned that he had received two letters from Smith, and that he personally had written to and received letters from the cardinal vice-protector, Lorenzo Bianchetti.[43] Montague was showing so much commitment to the cause that on 4 October Birkhead lamented that 'my patrons over earnest invectives' had offended an unnamed gentleman and his sister and had 'rebated' their 'zealous affection to us'.[44]

Perhaps we are seeing merely the vehemence of a still young-ish peer, itching to get his ideological teeth into something, indeed anything, after failing so dismally on the national political stage when he was ritually humiliated in the House of Lords in 1604. Perhaps he perceived that his and other lay patrons' interests were served in some way by keeping control of the proposed reform programme and the appointment of a priest to hold and exercise episcopal authority in England. If that man were to be one of Montague's own entourage, his own evident ambition to lead a significant section of the Catholic movement could be more effectually realised.

It seems clear that Montague was trying to construct a public position for himself as the focus of and guarantee for any significant ecclesiastical reforms of the English Catholic scene. Among the supposedly 'personal' but in fact highly public and much copied letters which we find circulating in manuscript at this time was a missive of 23 June/3 July 1610 to Montague from his cousin Jane Dormer, duchess of Feria.[45] The motive behind the letter was, it seems, to pour a certain amount of cold water on the cordial surface irenicism of another circulating manuscript letter, namely Robert Persons's heart-warming and pious deathbed oration of April 1610. In the form of an epistle, this had been addressed to Birkhead. It expressed a great yearning that all English Catholics should live in peace and unity. The duchess said that she was 'moved uppon a letter come to me which Father Parsons in his death bedd wrote to the archpriest, the coppie wherof I send to your lordship'. Her 'harty desire' was 'to see the intent effected, which is peace and unitye amongst our Catholikes, and the wished increase and happie proceedinges of God his service in our countrie. The matter yt self is a motive sufficient to stur any to do their best endeavours for the sweet and

[41] See AAW, A XI, no. 10, p. 33.   [42] AAW, A VIII, no. 126, p. 547.
[43] *Ibid.*, no. 135, p. 567.   [44] *Ibid.*, no. 159, p. 635.
[45] A copy of the letter made its way to Rome, AAW, A IX, no. 69.

peaceable furtherance of soe commendable and charitable a worke.' She claimed to think that it was only 'a discontented jelocie of some particuler persons' that 'hath made the oppinion of the quarrell generall, takinge occasion uppon any sleight matter that hath not concurred to their humor to feed the passion of this contradiction'. Sweet reason would soon sort it out. Montague might wonder why she wrote to 'intreat your helpe to amend yt and to put in your assistance and authoritie to perswade a finall end of these idle and harmfull contraversies'. The answer was, she claimed, that she had come to an agreement with some of the English Jesuits at Madrid that 'peacable union' was possible and 'they and all of the Societie that remayne in England shall yeeld and incline to all that I shall thinke good and is fitt for Christians'. Montague, she suggested, should 'labour to doe the same with the other syde'.

Between the two of them, the duchess of Feria and Viscount Montague (acting as self-proclaimed honest brokers), the whole English controversy could be peacefully ended, and, some might well suspect, the English clerical scene thoroughly stitched up. In case anyone perusing the letter should misunderstand how eminently suitable Montague was as a settler of quarrels, she added 'I have bine bould to choose out your lordship, in this Christian and meritorious action, as hee whose wisdome and zeale desarvethe and desyreth all good meanes to the perfectinge of any worke wherin God may be glorified, and his Church advaunced.'[46] It looks as if this was a propaganda exercise to disabuse anyone who thought that the Jesuits and Jesuit opinion were the key to resolving these disputes, or that the Society had some prior right to instruct other Catholics how to live in peace and charity.

MONTAGUE CONFRONTS THE REGIME

The second viscount's loan of his reputation to, and his support for, the archpresbyteral reform project coincided in 1610–11 with another bout of sharp hostility between the regime and the king's Catholic subjects. In Montague's case, as we briefly mentioned at the start of this chapter, this culminated in his refusal to take the oath of allegiance. Although the oath had passed into law in 1606, tendering of the oath really began with a proclamation of 2 June 1610 and an accompanying act, 7 & 8 James I, c. 6 ('An Acte for administringe the Oath of Allegiance and Reformacion of Married Women

---

[46] *Ibid.*, no. 69, pp. 233–4. At the same time Birkhead penned a letter (dated 9 September 1610), thoroughly retaliatory in its general sweetness of tone, to Robert Jones, the Jesuit superior in England, evidently designed to parallel Persons's, saying that he too wanted the dissensions to end, *ibid.*, no. 69, pp. 234–5.

Recusantes').[47] In mid-1610 Birkhead reported to Smith that, following the new proclamation, 'the prisons are filled againe' and the oath 'is more exacted than ever'. Every fortnight 'the justices are to offer the oath'.[48]

What is significant here is that, although stringent tendering and enforcement of the oath were clearly triggered by the assassination of the French king Henry IV in May 1610 and by James's worries about how this event would affect people's understanding of the authority of his God-given office, Montague's troubles were not the result simply of being caught up in a sudden round of indiscriminate oath-tendering which affected all Catholics equally.

The irony is that, while Richard Bancroft seems to have had a hand in stirring up the Catholic community's discontents and appears to have known about the agency to Rome in 1609,[49] James was getting very irritated with Catholic attempts to bolster the political power and influence of the clergy within the Catholic community. Montague House was subject to repeated searches in this period. Catholic newsletters make it clear that these searches were connected with off-the-cuff comments by the king that he was fed up to the back teeth with those Catholic nobles who harboured seminary priests. The harassment of Montague and his immediate family, who were clearly not fanatical would-be regicides, is otherwise hard to explain.

On 22 March 1609 Birkhead wrote to Smith, already on his journey to Rome, that 'our adversaries continue their spoilinge courses'. A Hampshire Catholic called Richard Carey had been arrested in Southwark. They 'found a stranger with him, whom they have putt in the Gate House for suspicion of [being] a preist, because he shuffled of[f] the oath. They say it is the foote man', one Marshall, one of Montague's servants, 'that yow saw amongst us not long since.' The authorities were trying to find the large sums of money which it was known that lay Catholics were raising for the maintenance of their clergy.[50] On 16 May Birkhead reported that various renegade clergy, including William Atkinson, Anthony Rouse and Thomas Finch, were making their inside knowledge of the Catholic community available to the agents of the high commission. 'No man can peepe out of the dores, but is caught.' The priest John Varder 'was apprehended of late by Atkinson in East Smithfield'. First Atkinson 'cried, traitour traitour' but 'no man wold sturre to helpe him'. Then 'he maliciously cried out, a powder traitour, and . . . everie man laid handes uppon' the unfortunate Varder. 'And so the poore innocent man was taken, ledd to the Tower, and from thence to Newgate.'[51]

---

[47] The 1610 statute directed that wide classes of people (courtiers, officials, lawyers, university men and so on) should have the oath tendered to them. It made no exceptions in favour of peers as the 1606 statute had done, *SR* IV, 1162–4.

[48] AAW, A IX, no. 42, p. 115, no. 54, p. 149.   [49] *NAGB*, 7.

[50] AAW, A VIII, no. 96, p. 471.   [51] *Ibid.*, no. 110, p. 507.

In September 1609 the searchers rampaged through Montague House again, and, though they apparently did not find the man for whom they were looking, William Udall reported that one William Kinsman, a servant of Thomas Habington, was arrested in the course of the search. Kinsman confessed that he had been a dealer in the Catholic book trade.[52] There was another raid, employing twelve constables, of Montague's Southwark home at Easter 1610.[53]

For a short time, things were quiet. But on 16/26 October 1610 Richard Smith, who had just arrived back in Paris from Rome, encountered Thomas Sackville, Montague's brother-in-law. Sackville gave him the 'heavie news that my Lord Montacute had dissolved his house and that the king every daie spake against him for mainteining soe many Catholiks, for sending to Rome about bishops and the like'. (Sackville referred here to the dispatch back to Rome of Montague's intercepted letter of August 1605.) Sackville added that Montague was 'like to fall into troble and that him self desireth to get leave to travel'.[54]

The second viscount engaged in a desperate bout of damage limitation. He wrote from Cowdray to the earl of Salisbury on 2 November 1610 thanking him for his favour and asking that if the king, to whom he professed all loyalty, had taken displeasure against him for his religion only, 'whereuppon dependeth the wellfare of my soule', then he would be grateful if the earl would 'bee pleased to stand my good lord'.[55] On 16/26 November, Robert Pett in Brussels was picking up the news of the proceedings against Montague. A priest called Francis Tichborne had just arrived in Brussels with the news that Montague was saying that 'he did daylye expect a commissione from the counsell'. Birkhead had fled Cowdray, and Montague's 'ladye and daughters were gon to London'. Montague 'had intelligence that a Scotishe jentilman' had 'beged the halfe of his livinge'.[56]

On 18 November there was yet another raid on Montague House. In a letter to Geoffrey Pole of 22 November, Benjamin Norton regretted that 'the book which you sent was like to have bene taken on Sunday last in a search at London wher ther were six preistes taken in secret places in . . . Montague House, and . . . it is . . . feared that the Lord Montacute wil be called

---

[52] In December 1610 Edward Kinsman, William's brother, was indicted for refusing the oath, Harris, 'Reports', 256, 258.

[53] This raid soon became the subject of a star chamber action against the allegedly corrupt proceedings of the high commission pursuivants, particularly Humphrey Cross, who directed it, PRO, STAC 8/15/8, mem. 2a.

[54] AAW, A IX, no. 83, p. 279. Smith informed More on 30 October/9 November 1610 that 'the most heavie news wherof I wrote in my last of my Lord Montacutes trobles and the dispersion of his house proveth too true. And the cause therof is said to be a letter of his to the pope which is comen to the kings hands', ibid., no. 87, p. 291.

[55] Hatfield House, Cecil MS 128, fo. 163r.

[56] AAW, A IX, no. 97, p. 321. For Tichborne, see Anstr. II, 320.

in question'. Richard Lambe, Pole's cousin, was arrested 'at Mathew Wood-wards that morning, and payed sweetlie for it'. Woodward and his wife were imprisoned.[57]

Perhaps almost inevitably, Montague was now faced with the oath. Leo Hicks argues that, because Smith reported to More in December 1610 that Montague was still at liberty and his household had not been dispersed, the tendering of the oath to him was quite separate from Montague's earlier brushes with authority during that year.[58] However, the likelihood is that the two things were directly connected. Richard Broughton recorded on 14 April 1611 that James had recently spoken sharply to the bishops and to privy councillors about noblemen and ladies harbouring priests who might try to kill him.[59] (At this time Montague was making provision for his children out of his estates, probably anticipating the financial disaster, through forfeiture, which he rightly feared might befall him.[60])

Montague continued to ingratiate himself with Salisbury.[61] But the death of his father-in-law the earl of Dorset in 1608 had removed his principal protector on the council. On 29 May, William Bishop noted that 'there have been pursivants' at Easebourne Priory, near Cowdray, 'and at one other house thereby to seek after a priest by name, but the[y] found nothing. Some say that one of the impudent knaves went to the parke of Cowd[r]ey to demand after the same person by name, but having a nescio hominem, departed with a fly in his eare.'[62] This was probably not the best way to keep in the authorities' good books. Birkhead reported on 30 May that 'this bishop of Canterbury', the recently appointed George Abbot,

is most hote in pursuinge us; it is said that, by his means, the Lord Montague was of late commanded to appeare before the counsell. Yf he had gon no dowbt most probable it is that they wold have ministred the oath unto him, which for certen, all men think, he wold have refused, albeit as redie as any man to sweare unto all points whatsoever belonge[s] to temporall allegiaunce.

But God had providentially prevented it, for 'even at the same time (as it is said) that the pursuivant was addressed unto him, he fell into a tertian fever', a recurrent malaria-type infection, 'which shrewdly handled him for eyght or nyne fitts as they say. Which beinge advertised to the counsell, they advised him to stay till he was amended.' This gave 'some of his industrious

---

[57] *NAGB*, 96.   [58] CRS 41, 6.   [59] AAW, A X, no. 36, p. 91.

[60] In the surviving Browne family papers there is a deed poll of appointment of 14 July 1611 whereby, under power reserved in a deed between Montague, Sir Robert Dormer, Sir John Dormer and Sir Francis Englefield of 24 April 1611, payments as marriage portions (or, if unmarried, then at the age of thirty years) should be made to his daughters Mary, Catherine, Anne, Lucy, and his youngest daughter Mary (who eventually married Robert, Baron Petre), and a payment of £2,000 should be made to his son Francis, WSRO, SAS/BA 72.

[61] *CSPD 1611–18*, 32.   [62] AAW, A X, no. 48, p. 119.

frends' a breathing space to lobby on his behalf so that now 'he remaineth at home, with no small hope of some ease by way of composition, which yow may be sure will cost him well'.[63]

As Richard Smith, in Paris, later described it, Montague's opportune illness, his 'tertian ague', struck him on the 'very daie that the warrant was made for his coming up before the councel'. This gave Henry Howard, earl of Northampton the opportunity to fix a compromise whereby the full praemunire penalty would not be inflicted. 'My Lord Henry delt that his premunire should be changed into a fine first of four thousand and after of six.'[64] By 30 May/9 June 1611 Smith had learned that his master had gone up to London to try to compound on favourable terms, but he had been imprisoned in the Fleet. The composition for the statutory penalty of total forfeiture for refusal of the oath was a hefty enough loss even for the wealthy viscount.[65] (A series of property dispositions was made in order to cover the fine. The sum of £6,000 was raised by selling the manor of Wanborough in Surrey. Further cash was procured at this time by granting tenancies in Montague House and by leasing out property in the surrounding Close.[66])

---

[63] *Ibid.*, no. 51, p. 125.

[64] *Ibid.*, no. 126, p. 363. For references to the levy of £4,000 rather than £6,000, see *CSPD 1611–18*, 60, 120.

[65] AAW, A X, no. 66, p. 177. Robert Pett described how 'our freands in Sussex are not onlye terrified as yow write but alsoe touched even to the quicke. My Lord Montague hath by a messenger ben sent for before the counsell, wher makinge his appearance the oath was tendered unto him which he refusinge was demissed for that night unto Dorset house . . . and the next day the clarke of the counsell was sent unto him to conducte him to the Fleet', *ibid.*, no. 87, p. 240.

[66] Smith stated on 16/26 September 1611 that Montague 'hath paied one thousand alreadie and must paie twoe more this next terme, and the other foure [*sic*] after one year, and withal hath spent about this busines one other thousande. Yet hath he gotten his libertie to goe whither he will and pardon for all that is past and promise to be ofered the oathe no more', AAW, A X, no. 126, p. 363. See also PRO, SP 46/70, fo. 1r; PRO, E 401/2419 (for which reference I am grateful to Simon Healy); BL, Harleian MS 6847, no. 4, fos. 20v–21r (a bill 'for the sellinge of certaine mannours and lands of the right honorable Antonie Viscount Mountag[u]e towards payment of his debts and raising his daughters portions'). This bill recites, *inter alia*, that by an indenture of July 1611, 'inrolled in chancery', Montague 'bargayned and sould the manor of Wanborough and the . . . capitall messuage . . . called Mountague House and divers other howses adjoyninge scituate in the parish of St Saviors', and also 'other houses, to the said bargaynees' (Sir Francis Englefield, Sir John Dormer and Sir Robert Dormer) and 'their heires . . . upon trust and confidence for raysing £6000 by sale thereof to satisfie so much due to his Majestie'. And 'for raysing the said £6000 due to his Majestie the said bargaynees with the consent of the said viscount soulde the manor of Wandeborrowe for £6000 while the capitall messuage and other the howses in St Saviours' were left 'unsould'. A chancery case brought in November 1624 by Thomas Gayer and his wife against Montague's former housekeeper in Southwark, Matthew Woodward, stated that Woodward had taken a lease 'for certeine yeres then enduringe of one capitall messuage called Montague House and of certeine other houses, closes and tenementes thereunto belonging within the Close of St Maryoveryes [*sic*] in that parishe of St Savyours', though Woodward had since (on 25 May 1616) assigned his interest to one William Ashby, PRO, C 2/James

But whether this disaster had been anticipated or not, the clergy in Montague's entourage soon moved to exploit it to good effect. For them, the second viscount was a martyr in the making – living proof of the willingness of good Catholics to suffer in defence of papal prerogatives. This was refutation enough of all the defamatory rumours spread about by their enemies (mainly the Jesuits) that such Catholics were weak on the issue of the oath and, like the appellants, were too willing to compromise with the regime for their own ease and benefit. Montague's clerical entourage was determined, therefore, that his suffering should not be in vain.

Enclosed in the letter of 14 June 1611 which Birkhead transmitted to Thomas More in Rome for the eyes of the secular clergy's friend Cardinal Edward Farnese, the archpriest sent a grandiloquent Latin narrative of Montague's afflictions and his unswerving loyalty to the Holy See and the true Catholic religion, and how, even though his friends had interceded for him, he was still prepared to suffer great loss rather than give way on the matter of the oath. It described how Montague was suffering for the sake of the Catholic religion alone. He was prepared to sacrifice all, even his patrimony, to sustain the pope's authority in England. Scottish courtier-cormorants were picking over his estate.[67] But he would stand firm.[68]

Birkhead, sitting in Montague House, had received the substance of his narrative from an unnamed friend, 'one [who] writeth of him [Montague] unto me in this sort'. Birkhead advised More 'yow may read this inclosed, and seale yt uppe and deliver yt at your leisure'. Birkhead further informed his friend that Montague was 'in the Fleet for denyinge the oath, but [was] well used', and 'God be thanked he is merie and hath made confessionem gloriosam. He was brought into the councell chamber' by 'my lord of Northampton'. Henry Howard had been, as we saw, working behind the

---

I/G11/31, mem. 1a, C 2/James I/G3/13. (Woodward had since died intestate.) Woodward had obtained the lease (at least of Montague House) from one Thomas Willmer of Lincoln's Inn by a transaction of 1 August 1608, Willmer having obtained the property by an indenture, from Montague himself, of 8 July 1608, PRO, C 2/James I/G3/13, mem. 1a; PRO, C 3/394/40. For a description of the extent of the property which passed to Ashby, and which he passed by lease to Christopher Goodlake and Matthias Fowle in February 1622, see PRO, C 2/James I/G10/39, mem. 1a. For other litigation concerning the property, see PRO, C 2/James I/A1/5. After the second viscount's death it was claimed in chancery that he had died heavily in debt, PRO, C 2/Charles I/T28/59, mem. 2a. For the tenants who moved into Montague House in 1611–12, see LMA, P92/SAV/201, pp. 30–1.

[67] For the greedy Scotsmen to whom the king granted Montague's forfeiture (Sir David Murray and Esmé Stuart, Lord D'Aubigny), see *CSPD 1611–18*, 60, 120. Robert Ker, Viscount Rochester, however, informed the earl of Northampton on 8 October 1612 that he had refused a grant of Montague's forfeiture, *ibid.*, 151. See N. Cuddy, 'The Conflicting Loyalties of a "Vulger Counselor": The Third Earl of Southampton, 1597–1624', in J. Morrill, P. Slack and D. Woolf (eds.), *Public Duty and Private Conscience in Seventeenth-Century England* (Oxford, 1993), 121–50, at pp. 140–1.

[68] AAW, A X, no. 72, p. 191.

scenes to secure the deal whereby Montague would escape total forfeiture. Montague 'at the first protested his fidelitie to his Majestie in most effectuall wordes and manner but desyred to be excused touching the oath quia multa continet contra fidem'. Northampton now 'spake in his behalfe how loial he had shewed himself, adding that perhaps in tyme more might be obteined of him'. Stressing Montague's absolute refusal to compromise, so different from the example set by the other Catholic lords, Birkhead rejoiced that Montague 'replied that by Gods grace he wold ever be the same man that now he is, and requested them to have no other conceit of him'. When the highly unsympathetic Lord Zouch asked him point-blank 'whether he had refused the oath', Montague 'with a loude voice said, yes my lord I do refuse it'. Birkhead lamented that 'it is feared that not many of his worth will follow his example'. But in many ways that was all to the good. It would be an object lesson to those in Rome that anybody who doubted the true worth of this Catholic peer and his circle should revise their opinions. (Anyway, breezed Birkhead airily, all he had to do was find the money and he would be let out.)[69]

Montague's stubbornness also gave these clergy the opportunity to take a principled stand on the issue of the oath. Even if they did not want to lay the blame for their troubles directly at the door of the regime, it was crucial for their case at Rome to prove that Jacobean anti-Catholicism, while not on the same savage scale as the Elizabethan variety, was still a serious persecutory initiative against those who out of mere conscience maintained the Catholic faith. Montague's example was ideal for this purpose. It enabled his secular clergy friends and chaplains to posture as the principal supporters of the pope's spiritual prerogatives. Edward Bennett noted the appearance of the proclamation of 31 May 1611 ('whereby it is commanded, that the oath of allegeance be administred according to the lawes'),[70] and remarked that 'the oath most be offered to every body: the litle lord', Montague, 'hath refused it', and 'he payeth 6000^{li}'. 'I thinck hereafter there is no dainger of taking the oath with interpretation' (i.e. in a qualified form), for the regime 'will have it taken secundum litteram'.[71]

In other words, the fate of the second viscount showed that the regime was not prepared to compromise over the issue of the oath; and Montague's bravery had shown the Catholic community what the proper, dignified and godly response to the regime's demands herein should be. Bennett gloried that Montague had moved to prevent the regime picking off the leading lay Catholics who, after Montague's courageous example, would have to display the same heroism if they wanted to retain their integrity and reputation.

[69] *Ibid.*, no. 73, p. 193.
[70] Larkin and Hughes, *SRP*, I, no. 118.   [71] *NAGB*, 113.

And, for Montague's entourage, it seemed that their patron's courage truly set him apart from other leading Catholic laymen. Smith claimed that no one, really, except Montague 'and his people' denied the oath.[72] The regime, said Bennett, 'supposing it will not be taken as it lieth . . . will put every man to it, and they that deny it fall into the praemuniry and soe must either lose all or mak a hard composition as the litle lord did'.[73]

On 30 June Montague obtained his pardon for refusal of the oath and also, significantly, for the offence of recusancy (though we have no evidence that he had yet been prosecuted under the recusancy statutes for separatism), and for harbouring seminary priests and for sending his children abroad contrary to statute.[74] On 6 July Birkhead noted that Montague was still incarcerated and indeed had been in the Fleet for over a month now. Five days later Birkhead set about making sure that Paul V recognised the full extent of Montague's sacrifice.[75] Birkhead penned yet another account for the eyes of the pope. He described how far Montague had risked all for the sake of upholding the papal prerogative. Birkhead stressed how Montague had also been warned not to keep Catholic clergy in his household. In other words the valiant nobleman was suffering for the sake of the sacramental practice of the Catholic faith. Birkhead drew the lesson from it all that, unless the pope granted that episcopal rule should be established among the English Catholics, the faith in England was likely to be destroyed. As it was, it was being sustained only by the rare example and bravery of men such as Montague. And how many could be expected to follow his example? 'Vides jam Beatissime Pater quomodo affligimur, digneris tuis nos auxillis consolari.'[76]

Richard Smith had been in England (for a brief visit) while all this was going on. He had delayed his return to France until after the christening of Montague's daughter Barbara.[77] When he got back to Paris he added his voice to those which were constructing Montague's reputation as a virtual martyr. He wrote a strong letter to More in Rome (larded also with several stories about opponents of bishops coming to sticky providential ends). He insisted that what More had heard of Montague 'is I am sure far under the

---

[72] AAW, A X, no. 117, p. 339.   [73] *NAGB*, 113–14.

[74] *CSPD 1611–18*, 51; AAW, A XI, no. 14, p. 39; *Epistolario de Luisa de Carvajal y Mendoza*, letter 130. See ch. 10, p. 332 above (and see above in this chapter) for Montague's sending his daughters abroad which, as we saw, was linked with the campaign for the appointment of a bishop.

[75] AAW, A X, no. 84, p. 233. As soon as an account of Montague's treatment was communicated to Robert Pett in Brussels by Montague's servant William Cape, who was at St Omer, 'in a letter dated the 26th of June', Pett immediately 'communicated [it] unto' the papal nuncio 'who seamed to be much agreved at the newes', *ibid.*, no. 87, p. 240.

[76] *Ibid.*, no. 88, p. 241. This letter is printed in TD V, cxlii–cxliii.

[77] *NAGB*, 103, 115.

truthe and his deserts, wherof I was a[n] eye witnes of all. For he, being content to let' William Bishop

goe away for a time because he was a publik person, wold, notwithstanding that he expected every daie to have his house searched (for which end were three warrants granted), wold I saie nevertheles have me and an other staie with him. And knowing what a great combate he was to endure did both by general confession and other religious means provide him and strengthen him self most religiously and that with such comfort of mynd as he seemed some times to be overjoyed when he thought he should

lose all 'for so good a cause'. 'And indeed, knowing no other, tooke as good order as he could for his twoe eldest daughters who also like children of such a father endeavoured to animate him in his heroical course.' Jane, his wife, was far less convinced, said Smith, about the necessity of suffering for the cause quite so much.[78] She bewailed 'her case through his undoing'. But Montague 'bad her be . . . contented saying that if the walls of his house were of silver, the tiles and lead of gold, and the stuffing of jewells and pretious stones, yet he wold think it too litle' to lose 'for this cause'. Smith mentioned the composition which, as we have just seen, was brokered by the earl of Northampton. But the heroic viscount was in fact 'more willing' to forfeit 'all than paie that fine, saying that his example wold have encouraged others'. Indeed, he would have done so 'had not his litle boye', his heir Francis, 'bene so young and therby in danger to have bene in his absence infected with heresie'. When Montague appeared before the council and the oath was put to him, 'he resolutely refused it protesting withal his hartie alleigance to the king in most effectual words'. The earl of Northampton, said Smith, expressed the hope that 'in time' Montague might be 'perswaded to take the oathe'. The viscount then 'kneled downe . . . and besought them not to be so conceited of him but that by Gods grace he wold die in the same faith and religion which he now professed'.[79]

Montague's clergy insisted that his refusal of the oath in no way detracted from the natural loyalty which he owed to his sovereign. Birkhead described how, when the 'councell in a sort offered him the oth . . . he refused it absolutely, yet protested that all things belonginge to his alledgiance he wold sware unto, so they were sett a part from the said oth. Because the oth as it lieth' contained 'so many thinges' against faith, 'he durst not presume

---

[78] Jane Browne's religion remains somewhat obscure. Edward Topsell stated that she did not share her husband's faith, T. J. McCann, '"The Known Style of a Dedication is Flattery": Anthony Browne, 2nd Viscount Montague of Cowdray and his Sussex Flatterers', *RH* 19 (1989), 396–410, at p. 403. But she made a substantial financial contribution towards the founding of the Catholic secular clergy's institute in Paris (the Collège d'Arras), see below in this chapter.

[79] AAW, A X, no. 126, p. 363.

to decide by his oth a point of so great moment; for which stout profession many, even both Catholics and Protestants, commend him', though Birkhead feared (or perhaps was secretly pleased) that 'few will follow him'.[80]

The easy and florid quasi-martyrological terms in which Montague's refusal was couched and described by his chaplains disguised the fact that what Montague had done was seriously contentious. Admittedly, the papacy had condemned the oath and had said that there were many things in it against faith (even if it was never made clear, in the curial breves which condemned it, what these things were).[81] On the other hand, the oath was deliberately phrased in such a way that European Catholic opinion was likely to be divided over its interpretation, and about whether it offended against the Catholic faith.[82] No one else of such high standing among the English Catholic laity was yet taking such a hard line, though the Jesuited Lord Vaux would soon also refuse the oath. Other Catholics, such as Lord William Howard, were saying that nobody of any sense would refuse it.[83]

Notables such as Howard could resort to Catholic clergy who, even if not prepared to say directly that all Catholics should take the oath, nevertheless used a series of philosophical, if not sophistical, arguments to come down on the side of the regime, and in effect justify those Catholics who believed that they were not morally required to go out on a limb for the papacy over this issue. Thomas Preston, the Benedictine monk who became an apologist for the regime on the question of the oath, was clearly part of the Howard entourage.[84] In the Clink prison Preston was soon joined by other Catholic clergymen who either approved the general principles expressed in the oath or were actually prepared to take it.

Of course, a number of lay Catholics did refuse the oath. Some of them, such as the Kentish recusant Sir Henry James, suffered the penalties of the law for their obstinacy.[85] But such people were relatively few and far between. Catholics such as Montague's kinsman the Yorkshireman Richard Cholmeley, who was himself an unyielding recusant nonconformist, still took the oath.[86]

---

[80] *Ibid.*, no. 84, p. 233.
[81] A. F. Allison, 'An English Gallican: Henry Holden, (1596/7–1662)', *RH* 22 (1995), 319–49, at p. 339.
[82] M. C. Questier, 'Loyalty, Religion and State Power in Early Modern England: English Romanism and the Jacobean Oath of Allegiance', *HJ* 40 (1997), 311–29, at pp. 320–1.
[83] *NAGB*, 117.
[84] A. M. C. Forster, 'The Real Roger Widdrington', *RH* 11 (1971–2), 196–205.
[85] H. Bowler, 'Sir Henry James of Smarden, Kent, and Clerkenwell, Recusant (*c.* 1559–1625)', in A. E. J. Hollaender and W. Kellaway (eds.), *Studies in London History* (1969), 289–313, at pp. 307–8; AAW, A XII, no. 235, p. 524; PRO, SO 3/6 (March 1614, November 1615).
[86] *The Memorandum Book of Richard Cholmeley of Brandsby 1602–1623* (North Yorkshire County Record Office Publications no. 44, 1988), 44, 59.

There were in fact several attempts to work out a casuistical compromise whereby the oath could be taken with a prior declaration that the taker took it only so far as it affected his temporal allegiance. Technically neither the regime nor most leading Catholic clerics would countenance such a practice. But several priests within the wider Montague network, such as John Mush, evidently thought that it was possible to reach some such compromise tolerable to both Catholics and the State. Mush framed what he thought was a perfectly acceptable formula for taking the oath (and went so far as to dispatch it for perusal to Rome). In no way, he claimed, was this counter to Catholic orthodoxy on the question of papal prerogatives and authority.[87]

Birkhead intimated to More, however, that to many Catholics the second viscount must have looked like an extremist. In a letter of 3 August 1611, Birkhead mentioned that 'some of our good frends have said that the Lord Montague will sacrifice Cowdrie to the pope', though, Birkhead added with unctuous piety, 'surely yf I had as much to loose, it shold all be sacrificed in that quarrell'.[88] In September, Smith admitted baldly that, in spite of Montague's heroic labours for the faith, 'we hear of none of worth that followeth his example'. 'His backfreinds' and others 'both in England and Flanders crie out against him for admitting such a great fine' (though, said Smith, it was the king's 'pleasure to take what he list') while, on the other hand, 'some wold have him undone and stick not to saie that his libertie doth more hurt than good to the Catholic cause'.[89]

By November, even more painful rumours were circulating about Montague. While some were not content with tapping their foreheads and scorning his great sacrifice as needless heroism, others were going in the opposite direction and sniffily questioning whether he had been particularly heroic at all. There was more than a hint here that the Society of Jesus and its allies were behind these aspersions. Birkhead warned More,

be yow assured that all is false which yow have h[e]ard of the Lord Montague. He is condemned to pay 6000[li] and is not yet in securitie as many do think. His confession was exemplar[i]e, as nombers can witnesse. Many in deed have indevoured to diminishe the commendacion which he deserved, but it cannot be. He was never questioned about preists, and therfor [it is] not likely he wold discover his secretts, beinge no wise pressed there unto.

[87] Mush's attempt at a compromise left him open to the attacks of critics such as the carping Jesuit Richard Holtby who said that Mush was displaying the same kind of weakness which had been shown by full-blown Catholic apologists for the oath. Birkhead and his colleagues had to berate Mush until he backed down and withdrew his opinion, *NAGB*, 98, 119, 120–4, 129.

[88] AAW, A X, no. 97, p. 273. Birkhead reiterated 'sith the Lord Montague hath adventured his estate, I see no cause why we should be afferd to adventure ours', *ibid*.

[89] *Ibid*. no. 126, p. 363.

So, it was being rumoured that Montague had escaped the full severity of the law by squealing on some of the Catholic clergy. But Birkhead insisted 'beleve me, all such reports are false'.[90]

Thus Montague's flagrant rejection of what was probably the majority lay Catholic position, a moderated acceptance of the oath, was nothing like as normal, especially for a self-proclaimed loyalist, as his chaplains tried to make out. Nor was it simply acclaimed by all English Catholics. As with his controversial and disastrous speech in the 1604 parliament it was, again, in some sense, a bid for leadership of the Catholic community by setting a striking example which was intended to gain maximum attention at home and abroad.

We should note, however, that the secular clergy's publicising of Montague's tremendous demonstration of resolve and of loyalty to the papacy coincided with and was intended to underpin Birkhead's and his colleagues' launch of their suit to the curia to appoint one of the English Catholic secular clergy to exercise episcopal authority in England. Birkhead's letter of 17 July which described for More how 'the Lord Montague is now returned from prison to his house againe, with six thowsand pound sett upon his head for his redemption from the penaltie of the law for deniall of the oath', informed More also that Birkhead and Smith 'have sent yow above an 100 voices for bishops' and also the candidates 'whome everie man nameth'.[91]

The whole episcopal project relied on Montague and his followers being able to pose convincingly as the epitome of good order and doctrinal ortho-doxy, and to persuade the world that his chaplains stood at the head of a large and united body of secular clergy, while the religious orders were disordered, divided and ill-disciplined.

But, embarrassingly, at exactly this time, Montague's entourage itself started showing signs of indiscipline and disorder. (We have already seen how the Cowdray priest Edward Weston refused to cooperate with Birk-head's projects.) Then, rather worse, was the business, which we have already

---

[90] *Ibid.*, no. 142, p. 403. See also *ibid.*, no. 167. Other priests, such as John Jackson, stressed that Montague remained subject to harassment. For example, wrote Jackson on 26 January 1612, 'the circumcellions wear never soe outragious and in such flocks as now they be. Noe man can stur for them.' William Atkinson 'and an other wear soe bold as to take one of the Lord Mountague his men', John Bennett, 'owt of his company as he was riding and attending' on 'his lordship up to London within thease 3 dayes', AAW, A XI, no. 7, p. 17, no. 13, p. 36. For Bennett, see WSRO, SAS/BA 73 (a deed of November 1613, witnessed by Bennett, Robert Barnes and John Cape). On 3 February 1612 Birkhead reported to More that though Montague was now being forced to fork out the composition for his forfeiture, 'it protecteth him nothinge for receyving of preists', AAW, A XI, no. 13, p. 35. On 20/30 September 1612 Robert Pett relayed to More the information he had from Edward Weston (who had recently fled the country) that the occupants of Cowdray were so worried by recent events that they had, under cover of darkness, moved all the Catholic liturgical paraphernalia in the house up to London, *ibid.*, no. 174, p. 511.

[91] AAW, A X, no. 93, p. 263.

briefly mentioned,[92] of the apostasy of John Copley, a member of one of the group of Sussex families on which the second viscount really should have been able to rely as the bedrock of his local support. Copley had moved to Cowdray to serve as a chaplain there, and he had acted as Birkhead's secretary in the copying out of the material supporting the suit to Rome for a grant of episcopal jurisdiction. On 31 March 1612, Birkhead notified More that when William Bishop had recently been interrogated by Archbishop Abbot, Abbot had shown him 'a particuler of all them that had given voices to be bishops'. 'Mr Copley belike' commented Birkhead 'was privie to that matter' and this 'was true indeed for he was trusted to range them in order'.[93]

Not only, therefore, had one of Montague's chaplains betrayed the entire pro-episcopal lobby's plans to the State. He had also committed the ultimate sin of renouncing the true religion. His motive for doing this was not, it was suspected, primarily theological, though he wrote an entire book of polemical religious reasons for his change of religion. Rather it was just good old-fashioned lust. He had, it was alleged, been seduced by a floozy of a maidservant in Montague's household (one Rebecca Moon). He then married her, an event which provoked comment from newsletter writers such as John Chamberlain.[94] Birkhead moaned to More that 'yow know that in other places many scandals have fallen out, but now the lik judgments are fallen upon this poore companie. Mr John Copley hath forsaken us and upon the sudden conformed him selfe to the tyme.' What a strange thing it was that he had been 'borne, baptised and brought up amongest Catholiques', and 'was of civil conversation and welbeloved of a great number, and well able to manteyne him selfe'? But 'passion or some diabolical suggestion' had 'altered his good course and brought him to plaine apostasie, as we evidently see by a letter of his hand to a frend of myne, whome he earnestly persuadeth to do the like and to conforme him selfe to the religion professed heare and to reject the implicite faith of the sea of Rome'. 'O tempora, O mores', lamented Birkhead. 'Yf out of our owne bosomes be cast forth so great a stinch, what shall we expect at the hands of others who have not halfe the means to preserve them selves that we have?'[95]

---

[92] See ch. 3, p. 107 above.   [93] *NAGB*, 150.

[94] John Chamberlain noted on 29 January 1612 that Copley, 'falling in love with an auncient Catholike maide . . . that attended the children, they have both left theyre profession and fallen to mariage', McClure, *Letters*, I, 331. According to Birkhead, 'the woman that seduced Mr Copley was comended' by one 'Mr Byrd to the place where she was to be interteyned, and, by the Jesuit which reconciled her, to Mr Copley him selfe, who by her allurementes is become an heretique', *NAGB*, 137.

[95] AAW, A XI, no. 10, p. 23. It was some comfort for Birkhead that although 'Mr Copley is desperate in his apostasie . . . I am enformed he will do no harme against us, though the pursivantes much urge him therunto', *ibid.*, no. 84, p. 239. Nevertheless Edward Bennett

Cowdray was evidently not quite the kind of well-ordered and well-governed commonwealth which the pro-episcopal lobby proclaimed as the ideal model for a reformed English Catholic community. (It was little use to pretend, as did Birkhead and others, that this was simply what happened when you did not have all the normal mechanisms of ecclesiastical government to regulate and discipline the clergy and laity.) One of the vital issues in the appellant debate had been the question of which bloc or tendency among the English Catholics was more likely to see its adherents remain faithful to the see of Rome and which was more likely to turn traitor and apostatise. One of the principal appellant sound-bites was that, pound for pound, there were fewer apostates among the secular clergy. So Copley's defection really did not help. The Jesuits could, and undoubtedly would, use it to demonstrate that it was the seculars who fell out of charity with other Catholic clergy, particularly those in the missionary religious orders. It was, said the Jesuits, the often ill-trained secular clergy who were the ones who were most likely to kick over the traces and join the Church of England.

There were other embarrassing points of weakness too. William Bishop, the ageing appellant who was a central figure in the pro-episcopal group, was generally known to be wobbly on the question of the papal deposing power. His arguments against the oath of allegiance could be comprehended by some as virtual endorsements of it. Matthew Kellison, though no Gallican, was also regarded by these secular priests' enemies as a ripe target for the same kind of accusations.[96] John Jackson (who was vehemently critical of the tardiness with which Rome responded to the secular clergy's suits) was believed to be of basically the same opinion as Thomas Preston (even though Jackson technically rejected Preston's position).[97]

---

heard quite to the contrary – 'they say Mr Copley beginneth to play his parte'; he had not only 'written a book' but also 'thretneth the archpriest', *ibid.* no. 122, p. 332; John Copley, *Doctrinall and Morall Observations* (1612).

[96] In a letter to More of 8/18 October 1614 Robert Pett mentioned that Kellison, on a visit to Brussels, had told him that he, Kellison, was accused to be 'a favorer of those which mainteyne the opinion agaynst the popes authority in temporalibus or at the least a favorer of the same opinion'; and he was now struggling to clear his name, AAW, A XIII, no. 230, p. 589.

[97] TD IV, clvii–clix. The papal breve of 12/22 January 1608 which appointed Birkhead ordered him to deprive Blackwell and those clerics who supported him of their priestly faculties if they did not conform themselves to the pope's injunctions against the oath. These priests were, as named by Birkhead on 16 August 1611, William Warmington, Richard Sheldon, Anthony Hebburn and Edward Collier, *ibid.*, clxxvi. To this list Thomas Preston added John Jackson when he mentioned this issue in his *Theologicall Disputation* (1613), 253–4. Undoubtedly Bishop and Jackson were quasi-Gallican in some of their opinions. Jackson certainly gave signs of being underwhelmed with the papacy. In a letter to More of 5 January 1615 he launched into a diatribe against Paul V for turning a 'deaf ear' to all their just requests, and for favouring their enemies. Jackson recalled that when Robert Charnock, one of the original appellants, 'came from Rome being' forbidden by Paul V and Cardinal Henry Cajetan from

At this point, the Jesuits retaliated in kind. They acquired their own quasi-martyr, Lord Vaux. In February 1612 he also refused to take the oath. He penned a letter, evidently intended for circulation, about how he would bear his suffering with magnificent fortitude. This was the kind of distressed and afflicted aristocrat who might threaten the second Viscount Montague's pre-eminent position in the suffering peer stakes.[98]

This unstated but very real antagonism between the two Catholic entourages may have been reflected and played out in the conflict between the Wyborne family and Ambrose Vaux, which all came out first in a punch-up at the Globe theatre in Southwark (down the road from Montague House) and then in a star chamber action in April 1613. Ambrose Vaux, a much indebted man, had married Elizabeth, the widow of the recently deceased William Wyborne, the Kentish recusant who, as we saw, was on the fringes of the Montague entourage. (His brother Edward, brother-in-law to the priest Benjamin Norton, may have been at Cowdray in the 1580s.)[99] But there had been a separation, and she was now being protected by her brother-in-law Edward Wyborne, Dudley Norton (kin to the Wybornes) and Sir Richard Blount.[100] Vaux claimed that Blount, Norton and Edward Wyborne had then persuaded the newly wed Elizabeth to separate from Vaux, telling her that her own property would serve for her maintenance. During the previous August, Vaux had learned that his absent wife had gone to a play at the Globe in Southwark. He went to the theatre himself and tried to persuade her to return to a life of married bliss, but Norton *et al.* knocked him about and

returning to 'his owne country, he sayd to the pope . . . when he tooke his leave that if ever he had occasion agayne he wold never sue to Rome but to our Lord Jesus for from Rome he expected noe help'. Jackson believed it was 'not the worst speech that ever he spake, for we find . . . litle helpe' from Rome. He had heard that a book had been published 'to shew that the Court of Rome was the cause of continuance of all our miseries', and he wished that he had 'kept a copie to have sent to the pope himselfe', AAW, A XIV, no. 6, p. 16.

[98] See ARSJ, Anglia MS 31/i, fo. 462r ('Aviso segreto del Barono Vaux', dated 2 June and 17 June 1612). Vaux professed to believe that it was not the prison which brought contentment to him so much as the goodness of God to a man who finds himself in such a place. (I am grateful to Thomas McCoog for assistance with translating this letter.)

[99] See ch. 6, p. 197 above.

[100] PRO, STAC 8/289/3. Vaux alleged that Blount and Norton fraudulently caused a deed of gift to be drawn up after the date of the marriage contract whereby Elizabeth Wyborne's personal property was made over to them, *ibid.*, mem. 3a (bill of complaint, dated 7 April 1613), and it was sealed after the marriage took place. In 1603 the regime had granted a lease of the forfeited two-thirds of the estate of William Wyborne to Sir Richard Blount. See also *CSPD 1627–8*, 496. Dudley Norton stated that William Wyborne had made Norton and Blount his executors, PRO, STAC 8/289/3, mem. 3a. See also PRO, E 134/13 James I/Easter 16, a case which apparently shows Norton protecting Wyborne property in Kent. (The documents for this exchequer case are currently misplaced in, or missing from, the Public Record Office.) William Wyborne had died on 31 January 1612, PRO, E 368/545, mem. 122a. (Vaux's case was probably not helped by his inability to remember on which day he had married Wyborne's widow, even though the marriage had taken place only a few months before; he believed the ceremony had been on either 3 April or 5 April 1612.)

took Elizabeth away with them. The defendants, as we might expect, told an entirely different story. Blount and Norton stressed their duty as executors to William Wyborne and said that the alleged property transactions were directed towards paying off his debts. Norton claimed that Vaux was the one who had offered violence at the Globe.[101]

As the second Viscount Montague came under scrutiny from the privy council and the king, so those who were known to be within his own social and religious circle came under pressure from the State's lesser officials and enforcers. From the newsletters sent to Rome during this period by Benjamin Norton we learn that leading Sussex recusants, most of whom either had or still served the Brownes in some capacity, or were their tenants, were being dealt with by exchequer commissions and were being generally bothered and molested.[102] On 10 September 1613 he noted that two of the regular high commission pursuivants, Tarbox and Wragge, had been ravaging the area. 'By the firste or seconde of September' they came 'to Midhurste and searched one Mrs Elizabethe Arden her howse and one Christopher Frankes his howse and tooke crucifixes from folks necks'.[103]

Among those whom the second viscount's chaplains reckoned were included in this bout of persecution were the priestly martyrs of 1610. The four victims of that year were Roger Cadwallader, George Napper, John Roberts and Thomas Somers. Roberts was a Benedictine but was regarded as a friend by the secular clergy who recorded in great detail the double execution (of Roberts and Somers) which took place on 10 December. Roberts had been a notable opponent of the Jesuits, as at one time had been Cadwallader, though there were doubts about whether Cadwallader, shortly before his execution, had changed his opinion about the Society.[104] Napper had, as we have already noted, once been at Cowdray. Even though there is no proof that he had recently been in direct contact with the second viscount's entourage, there was a kin relationship between him and Thomas More. More collated the accounts of his martyrdom.[105] Napper was commemorated not just for his courage but also because, allegedly, his final wish had

---

[101] Blount's reply in star chamber mentioned that the transfer of Elizabeth Wyborne's property had been entirely legal, the deed in question being sealed on 2 April 1612, and that he had set all this out in his defence in chancery to Vaux's action against him there, PRO, STAC 8/289/3, mem. 1a.

[102] See *NAGB, passim*, esp. letters 14, 29, 30, 42, 44.

[103] AAW, A XII, no. 164, p. 365. Elizabeth Arden was probably a relative of the Arden family which had been in service with the first Viscount Montague. The Frankes family had moved from Yorkshire to live in Midhurst, near to the Brownes, *NAGB*, 181; ch. 3, p. 96 above.

[104] See *NAGB*, 108.

[105] Joan Napper, George's sister, married Thomas Greenwood, and their eldest son married Thomas More's sister, Grace, with whom More remained in contact while he was in Rome, Davidson, RC, 200.

been to see a bishop appointed to govern the English Catholics.[106] The leading secular clergy also insisted that these four priests had died principally for their refusal to take the oath of allegiance. Here was yet more proof that the Jesuits' mutterings that they alone were the true defenders of papal prerogatives were slanders and slurs on the character of the secular priests. In rather gruesome fashion, bits of these mid-Jacobean martyrs were packaged up and sent through the post to Rome, particularly for their friend Cardinal Farnese to see.[107] Edward Bennett noted in June 1611 that 'ther hath been much adoe to get Mr Cadwalladers head, who most constantly died only because he refused the oath'. Bennett wished the pope 'had it in his hand'.[108]

In 1612 there was another batch of executions. The victims were the Benedictine William Scot, and the secular priests Richard Newport and John Almond, and a layman, John Mawson. As we have already seen, Newport was tied into the Browne entourage at the fringes. He was kin to the Isham family, who were particular friends of the second viscount's chaplain Robert Pett.[109] William Scot had, as Anthony Champney commented, 'beene ... banished ... verie lately to witt with Mr Kenione by the Savoyen embassadour his sute'. (Edward Kenion was, as we saw, one of the Montague entourage and a future chaplain to the family.)[110] Dramatically, Montague, who had recently and very publicly been punished for his refusal of the oath of allegiance, turned up to watch the executions of Scot and Newport on 30 May, even though they were put to death at an unreasonably early hour of the day. (It was noticed by the Spanish ambassador Alonso de Velasco that 'at five in the morning ... they dragged them away from prison on the sled, although they are accustomed to do it at eight'.[111]) The priests had refused the same oath which Montague had himself declined.[112]

The second viscount's priests commemorated Newport's and Scot's executions by collecting providentialist stories about them. Benjamin Norton, always an enthusiast for such tales, recorded that 'the very day that

---

[106] *NAGB*, 20, 30, 32, 86, 96, 98, 99. One of the narratives of the Napper martyrdom was written up by Anthony Tuchiner, *ibid.*, 86; Mott, HR, 445; PRO, SP 12/160/25, fo. 57r. In the Elizabethan period Tuchiner's links were with the Caryll and Cotton families, generally regarded as friends of the Jesuits; but by 1610 Tuchiner was regarded as a friend of the seculars. He eventually became a member of the seculars' episcopal chapter, Anstr. I, 364. Like the priest Benjamin Norton he had been educated by the schoolmaster-martyr John Bodey, Mott, HR, 445.

[107] *NAGB*, 96.

[108] *Ibid.*, 112. In December 1624 Thomas Roper wrote to Thomas Rant that he might now 'dispose of that relique which you have in your custody', namely Cadwallader's head, 'and if you shall so like of it you may leave it' to the secular clergy's Collège d'Arras 'after your decease'. Roper added 'I take it to be of Mr Cadwallader and not of Mr Napper', though he was 'not alltogeather certayne thereof', AAW, B 27, no. 86.

[109] See ch. 8, p. 284 above. For John Mawson, see CRS 22, 187–93.

[110] AAW, A XI, no. 113, p. 311. See ch. 10, p. 324 above.

[111] CRS 64, 196.　[112] McClure, *Letters*, I, 355; ch. 8, p. 284 above.

Mr Newport and Mr Scott were executed, which was upon Whitson eve, in the west part abowt Plimowth for 3 miles the sea appeared as red as blood'. The local people were dumbstruck, and 'they took of the water in tubs, wherin standinge but a whil it congeald lik putrified blood'. The putrifying liquid 'cast such a stenche that no man cowld abyde the smell'. All this made 'many to wonder, and feare alsoe that it is a signe of some hevy plague to fall upon us'.[113] Narratives of the deaths of Newport and Scot started to travel around Europe. Champney in Paris noted on 23 June/3 July, just over three weeks afterwards, that 'we have the certayne relatione' of their executions. 'They dyed with great constancie and muche edificatione to all.' The news was making an impact on foreigners as well, for 'there ys a Frenche gentleman, who hath writt largely of the maner of theyre arreyngment and deathe, whose letter ys comen' to the hands of the papal nuncio in Paris. The nuncio was 'muche contented therewith and no doubt will signify yt thither'.[114]

At the same time, however, as the secular clergy did battle with their clerical enemies in England, they tried, with their lay patrons' backing, to shore up and increase their reputation for erudition. One of the crucial weapons in the war between the Jesuits and their secular clergy opponents was academic lustre or, rather, a reputation for the kind of learning which could be used to refute Protestant heresy and represent the Catholic case on a range of issues to best advantage in front of lay audiences. A central plank of the archpriest's reform programme was the revamping of the educational system whereby seminarists were prepared for ordination. But the archpriest's men felt that the seculars were seriously disadvantaged by having no institute for higher studies – no college where their leading lights could apply their intellectual talents to a defence of the Catholic cause and, at the same time, promote their own reputations.

Inherent in the missionary enterprise there had always been deep ambiguities about how the faith in England was to be restored. The whole seminary project implied an intellectual confrontation with Protestantism which necessitated the publishing and dissemination of measured, grave and reasoned polemical responses to leading Protestant figures. This was not something which could easily be done in the seclusion of a gentry residence. Large libraries and adequate leisure were essential, but they were not generally available in England. The religious orders, with their own novitiates, did have these facilities. Moreover their postulants, not trained in the seminaries, did not have to abide by the mission oath which bound the seminarist in

---

[113] *NAGB*, 177.
[114] AAW, A XI, no. 113, p. 311. The propaganda potential of the event was noticed and exploited by the Spaniards; they recorded the presence at the execution of the earl of Arundel and his young son, but not Montague, CRS 64, 196.

conscience to return to England and labour in the English vineyard. The critics of the regulars argued that the regulars extracted the best wits from among the total pool of potential clergy. Thus they parasitised the Catholic clerical system for their own benefit while the wider body of English Catholicism suffered in consequence. The cause of the 'English clergy' was being damaged by intellectual starvation. The Jesuits' administration of e.g. the English College in Rome, and their indirect influence even at Douai, through their hateful creature and president of the college Thomas Worthington, were designed to siphon off the most promising seminarians into the Jesuit order. This left the dross in the seminaries where they were treated as dunces by their Jesuit masters. This was a plot, in effect, to diminish the reputation of the seculars as a body, thus elevating the influence and authority of the religious, particularly the Jesuits. If no remedy were forthcoming, this two-tier travesty would ruin the prospects for renascent Counter-Reformation Catholicism in England.

This issue had, in fact, been raised during the appellant controversy. The Jesuits' alleged scorn for the other members of the clergy had been characterised by William Watson with hilarious immediacy:

when they come to play the flirts and parasits with the secular priests, then imagine that you see so many puppets dancing the anticke, with sundry ptishes, face-makings, shaking of their heads, and diverse verie disdainful exclamations as 'ah hah hah: a seminary, an old Queene Mary priest, a secular, ah ah ah ah: alas poore men: you shall see them all leape at a crust ere it be long'.[115]

Watson claimed that the Jesuits

make it a booke of commonplaces for ordinary discoursers, at all assemblies, in all companies, and, with a stagean countenance, as actors in the pageant of a play upon these matters, do come out with a prologue, for the advancement of the Jesuits in this manner, viz: 'O rare and admirable persons; the wonders of the world; glory of these, renowne of former, fame of future dayes; the most learned, the most prudent, the most brave, the most politike, the most worthy, the most renowned, the most orderly, discrete, and of best governement, for education, example of life and instruction; the most vertuous, holy, sainctly, angelicall, the most devout, the most perfect, the most religious, the most what not of worthy regard or reckning' . . . For it is inough to make knowne (forsooth) 'he is a Jesuit': ergo 'silence': ergo 'yeeld', ergo 'stoope in his presence' etc. And then must come forth sundry famous acts, of this and that Jesuit, 'for their learned bookes, their profound doctrine, their wholesome counsell, their good examples given, even their very lookes, jesture and conversation, being able to win any creature'.[116]

In reply, the Jesuits alleged that if the missionary vocation were watered down, the cause of the English Catholics would suffer, as those who trained for the mission went off to become fat and lazy as quasi-academics in potty

[115] Watson, *Decacordon*, 16.   [116] *Ibid.*, 15–16.

little foreign colleges. In an exact inversion of their enemies' case, the Jesuits also said that, if their critics succeeded in seizing control of the seminaries, the standards there would inevitably be lowered. The quality-conscious Catholic gentry patrons in England would start to reject the priests sent to them from the seminaries because they were of an inadequate standard. Here the Jesuits' educational purposes were being represented as essential to the continuation of the English mission in its entirety.

One of the Jesuits' principal claims to fame and respect was their alleged capacity to engage successfully in debate with leading Protestant polemicists and preachers, thus confronting heresy and winning converts to the faith. This was the boast made in, for example, John Gerard's famous manuscript autobiography.[117] (Edmund Campion was the role model and acknowledged hero in this respect.) In the period of *de facto* toleration in the early 1620s during the Spanish match negotiations, leading English Jesuits issued forth in order to dispute, before rowdy and mixed audiences, with Protestants such as Archbishop George Abbot's chaplain Daniel Featley.[118]

Whether the Jesuits were temperamentally more suited to this style of confrontation or not (and some claimed that they were), the seculars had no wish to let the contest go by default. They argued, however, that the Jesuits' sometimes extremely confrontational methods (in tandem with their reputation for political radicalism) were potentially very offensive to the regime from which Catholics hoped one day to merit toleration. A more staid and respectable mode of disputation was called for. Catholic clergy should concentrate on producing learned tomes of polemical theology, scholastic and measured, more obviously 'religious' than 'political'.

At about the same time that the second Viscount Montague was under the gun in England, the secular clergy secured the establishment of a writers' institute in Paris. The second viscount's brother-in-law, Thomas Sackville, was, as we saw above, in effect the patronal founder.[119] It was a place that he clearly liked since he came and stayed there. He exercised a real influence over how it was regulated.[120] His sister, Jane (Montague's wife), gave a substantial amount to the college, apparently the same sum as he himself did.[121] The technical aim of the institute, known as the Collège d'Arras, was to serve as a place for senior clergy to live and write polemical works to persuade heretics to the true faith. Suitable conditions, it was alleged, did not exist for

---

[117] P. Caraman (ed.), *John Gerard* (1951).   [118] Milward II, 216–27.

[119] For his original endowment of the college, see *NAGB*, 86.

[120] A letter of September 1620 from the archpriest William Harrison to Sackville refers to the rules which had been drawn up with the privity, and possibly at the direction, of Sackville, AAW, A XVI, no. 43. See also AAW, B 27, no. 35; AAW, B 26, no. 139.

[121] See R. Belvederi (ed.), *Guido Bentivoglio Diplomatico* (2 vols., n.p., 1947), II, 215, for a 'cifra' added to a letter from Brussels of 7/17 September 1611, indicating that Montague's wife Jane has made a donation to the Collège d'Arras of '6 mill. scudi'.

this sort of thing at the seminary at Douai, certainly not while the Jesuited Thomas Worthington was running it.[122] The college's founding members were leading lights among the pro-episcopal clergy: Richard Smith and his cousin William Rayner, William Bishop (who had recently been allowed into exile) and Anthony Champney (the future dean of the secular clergy's episcopal chapter).

The new college and its facilities would therefore give the seculars the opportunity to disprove the rumours that the secular clergy were all thick, mentally incapable, the dregs of the seminaries and not suitable to serve as chaplains to the gentry, gentry who, allegedly, were sometimes better edu- cated than their secular clergy chaplains. It would be primarily a house of writers where the best brains among the secular priests would read and study and then turn out polemical books to rival those of the best wits among the Protestant polemicists of the age. This would vindicate the seculars' claim to be leading the battle against Protestant heresy in England, through respectable and entirely 'religious' means, without the taint of unwise polit- ical engagements.

But the college, noted subsequently for the sedentary existence of most of those priests who acquired a billet there,[123] had, at its inception, another and arguably more ambitious purpose. It was also intended to instigate an intellectual and organisational revolution among the secular clergy.[124] In particular, the college would serve to augment 'the exercise of preaching which for want of use is greatlie decayed amongst us'. In this fashion it would ensure 'that every mans merittes may be known, and not leaft as now they are to the slanderous tongs of such as by our disgrace seeke to prefer them selves and to devide us'. Such a college would also function as an arm of clerical government and regulation, in the absence of those normal and formal structures which Rome, in its infinite wisdom, was temporarily withholding from the English mission. It would enable 'his Holinesse . . . [to] be enformed by the secular cleargie touching the affairs of the secular cleargie, and not onlie by others, who perhaps do emulate them'. And 'wheras we hope in tyme his Holinesse will contynew the succession of our Church in England by ordinary bishopps, one or manie, we may by this collegiate life know our

---

[122] For the foundation of the college, see *NAGB*, 8, 10, 50, 86, 118, 149.

[123] The literary output of the members of the college can be followed up in ARCR I and II. One of the books produced there by Anthony Champney, his *Treatise of the Vocation of Bishops* (1616), was a manifesto for the secular clergy who were trying to secure the appointment of a bishop. It was a reply to Francis Mason's *Of the Consecration of Bishops in the Church of England* (1613), a book which had been commissioned by George Abbot.

[124] Originally it was hoped that the college of writers would reside at Douai, i.e. with the seminary, but in the end it was founded at Paris, in part through the generosity of a French Benedictine monastery (the abbey of St Vaast at Arras) which provided the building.

men most fit to be presented'. It was to be a training ground therefore for
the future leaders of the Catholic community in England.

Paris was an ideal place for these clerics to operate. It gave them contact
with the Sorbonne, where Anthony Champney had picked up a divinity
degree. The Sorbonne, when it was asked its opinion on King James's formula
about the relationship between royal and papal authority, came out publicly
against the Jacobean oath of allegiance. The Jesuits were not popular there,
and this was all to the good. While Montague had broadcast to all Europe his
orthodox faith by refusing the oath, the secular clergy leadership still wanted
to be seen as good subjects of King James. Hence some of the college members
turned out books tingéd with loyalist sentiment. This led, inevitably, to the
denunciation of some of the college's members, especially William Bishop,
for allegedly harbouring Prestonian opinions.[125]

We can see, in the first flush of enthusiasm which these secular clergymen experienced in the founding of their new institute, a desire to ape and
equal their Jesuit opponents. It was a flush in which some of the Sussex lay
Catholics became involved. In 1612, according to a polemical tract published much later (in 1635), there was a disputation in Paris between Daniel
Featley (currently serving as chaplain to the English ambassador, Sir Thomas
Edmondes) and Richard Smith. It is clear from the names of the Catholics
in the audience that the disputation was sponsored by members of the Sussex Catholic community who had social connections with and within Montague's immediate entourage.

For the secular clergy at the Collège d'Arras, this was evidently an inaugu-
ral display of their new institute's members' prowess. It was to be a demonstration by the seculars that they were equally adept at and enthusiastic for
the polemical vehicle of the staged disputation, something which undoubtedly many English Catholics thought was the Jesuits' special preserve.

> Master Daniel Featlie being in France, chaplaine to the embassadour of our late
> soveraigne, there came to Paris one M. Knevet, halfe-brother to M. John Foord, an
> honest and vertuous gentleman the[n] living in that cittie. This M. Knevet, being,
> upon his arrivall there, put in mind that he was mistaken in the matter of religion,
> which is the thing a man should principallie attend unto, and that before Luther al
> knowne Churches did beleeve that which he saw there in Fraunce openlie professed,
> tould his brother (M. Foord) he would see one of ours defend it before M. Featlie,
> whom he did esteeme a greate scholler. Withall he acquainted . . . M. Featlie with the
> busines, and with the point he meant should be discussed.

Featley believed that he himself was 'alone hard enough' for the 'whole
Church of Rome', and rose to the challenge. 'To performe it with the more
applause' he made intensive preparations for the encounter. 'At leingth, upon

[125] AAW, A XIV, no. 152, p. 476.

the third of September, word was sent to . . . [Richard] Smith (who being then in towne was entreated to undertake the cause) that he should provide himself for the morrow.'[126] And the, in the end rather inconsequential, disputation took place on the following day, with various observers in attendance, including John Pory, the playwright Ben Jonson and the poet Henry Constable.[127]

The college, therefore, was intended both to boost the secular clergy's reputation and also, one suspects, to set an example to other Catholic clergymen. It would establish a standard of learning to which those trained in the seminaries should aspire. As the priest Thomas Martin commented in 1611, 'our cuntry now needeth not a number of preists, but she wanteth only lerned preists who may be able to daunt the enemy, grace the cause and honor the profession which we undertake'. There were too many young and badly educated priests. Martin recalled with horror that he had 'seene a Catholick gentilwoman (cum rubore loquor) by her very judgment to determyne an ordinary doubt in lerning, when a preist notably forgott himself and unjustly persisted in his error'.[128]

Many of the issues with which the Catholic clergy (and their gentry patrons) were faced could be discussed only by reference to complex philosophical principles and argument. This inevitably meant that it was possible for demonstrably better educated clerics to posture as, in some very real sense, more powerful exponents of Catholic truth in the face of Protestant opponents and the State than seminarists whose training was perfunctory and shallow. On the vexed topics, for example, of political loyalty and allegiance, or of conformity, Catholics faced a veritable minefield of difficulties. These issues could be hammered out and resolved only via a reasoned casuistical approach, in which the finely trained mind and capacity for argument of the resident chaplain might be essential. An expert in casuistry who could

---

[126] The third son of John Ford (d. 21 November 1583) and his wife, Magdalen, of Harting and of Wenham in Rogate is the John Ford mentioned here. Magdalen Ford remarried Henry Knevett of Warwick, and this accounts for the relationship to the 'M. Knevet' cited in the tract. See Berry, *Sussex*, 182.

[127] W. Powell, *John Pory 1572–1636* (Chapel Hill, 1977), 39–41; L. I., *The Relection of a Conference Touching the Reall Presence. Or a Bachelours Censure, of a Masters Apologie for Doctour Featlie* (Douai, 1635), 4–7. This work contains an edition of Edmund Lechmere's *The Conference Mentioned by Doctour Featly in the End of his Sacrilege* (Douai, 1632). See ARCR II, nos. 461, 489. As William Powell notes, Daniel Featley published in 1630 his own account of the conference, presumably to help put the knife into Smith who was at that point being harassed both by the fury of his regular clergy opponents and by the State, Powell, *John Pory*, 41; Daniel Featley, *The Grand Sacrilege of the Church of Rome* (1630). In Featley's tract there is a separate account of the incident by Pory and Jonson, or, rather, by Pory with Jonson's certification of its accuracy, *The Summe and Substance of a Disputation* (1630).

[128] AAW, A X, no. 68, pp. 181–2.

deal with issues such as the oath of allegiance was going to command a great deal of respect.

It is possible that many of the complaints aired by the pro-episcopal lobby that the Jesuits advised Catholics to take the oath and that the secular priests were blamed by all sides for upholding papal prerogatives simply reflect the lobby's difficulties in holding their own against the religious when dealing with this thorny casuistical matter. But there was also an unresolved issue here over what exactly was meant by learning. As David Lunn points out, 'the quality that a patron looked for most in a priest was', indeed, '"learning"'. But this was not 'the learning of an *érudit* but that of a *savant*, wisdom rather than bibliolatry'.[129] And it was not clear that, for example, the activity of the Collège d'Arras was going to produce *savants*. With their reputation for giving spiritual counsel, it was the religious who were perhaps more likely to be turned to than some of the seculars, particularly in the confessional.[130]

Richard Smith, formerly resident at Cowdray with the second Viscount Montague, was on most tests the leading intellectual light at the Collège d'Arras. It soon became clear, however, that his allegiance to his patron in England was weakening. The second viscount in fact wanted Smith to return home and to perform his duties as a household chaplain. Smith, however, had no intention of doing any such thing. For he had a new and (soon-to-become) phenomenally powerful patron, Armand-Jean du Plessis, bishop of Luçon, the future Cardinal Richelieu.[131] Smith wrote to More on 18/28 August 1612 that 'I am at this present somewhat perplexed for my lord is very earnest to have me home, I having now bene here his allotted time, and there being none to preach' or to take George Birkhead's place 'if God shold call him'. Edward Kenion, now in exile, and himself moving into the bishop of Luçon's network, had written to Smith urging him to 'come to Poitou', to live with the bishop. Kenion insisted that Smith's 'presence wil be to [the] exceding good of our countrie', even though the priests at the Collège d'Arras

---

[129] Lunn, *EB*, 159.

[130] Cf. however the debate between Eamon Duffy and John Bossy over the quality of the seminarist clergy in the seventeenth century, E. Duffy, 'The English Secular Clergy and the Counter-Reformation', *JEH* 34 (1983), 214–30. Duffy argues that the English secular clergy were imbued with the high ideals of their pastoral functions, ideals which were, according to the Council of Trent's thought and stipulations, properly the preserve of the seculars and not the religious. That they were so enthused is undoubtedly the case. The disagreement, such as it is, between Bossy and Duffy stems from their looking at the same thing from different perspectives. Duffy discerns the aspirations; Bossy puts them in the context of the political realities of a situation in which the ideals of the secular clergy's hierarchalism, and its associated educational programme, were virtually unrealisable.

[131] For Smith's relationship with Richelieu, see Allison, RS, 168–9. In the 1620s Richelieu was willing to maintain Smith financially in a manner which Montague clearly always refused or was unable to do, AAW, A XXVII, no. 87, cf. AAW, A XXVIII, no. 104, AAW A XXIX, nos. 3, 5, 15.

were 'loath' to let Smith 'departe hence'. Smith did not want to dump his
patron in England. But he intimated that he had a higher loyalty, namely
to the good of the cause. There would soon be quite enough scholars in the
Collège d'Arras and so 'I see no such need of my abode here'. Smith added,
obediently but untruthfully, that if Montague would 'be content, and others
desire it, I wil not spare to prejudice my self yet more'.[132] By the end of
September, it was clear that Smith had had a bellyful of the college, for, said
his cousin William Rayner, 'he hath been much disgusted with . . . [William]
Bishops proceedings'. Smith had nobly said that if Montague should 'send
for him (and so he hath alwayes sayd) he will goe unto him'. 'Yet he told me
he had written' to Montague 'to forbear him a while'.[133] On 5/15 October,
Smith again wrote to More and admitted that Montague, who believed that
his chaplains' first loyalty should be to him, 'was inexorable' over the issue
of whether Smith should 'staie any longer at Paris'. Smith conceded that
it was 'not for the good of our cause' to loose Montague's goodwill 'and
that my abode at Paris can not so much profite our cause over my abode
in England as the losse of my lords favour may do us harme, and therfor I
think it not best to offend one who hath so well deserved of us all already
and will herafter, for so small advantage'.[134]

But whatever the second viscount wanted, it was clear that Smith had
made up his mind. And with 'his' bishop he decided to remain. By January
1613, Montague had bowed to Smith's will, an odd thing in a patron–client
relationship (except that Smith now had more than one patron). Smith wrote
to More that he was 'like to be emploied here' with the bishop of Luçon
'yet longer, because my lord having consented to my longer staie on this
side of [the] seas, at the request of my brethren at Paris, my bishop hath
begged their interest and they have graunted it. And surely if God afford
occasion I hope nether they nor our countrie shall' lose out 'by my staie
here'. The opportunity was just too good to miss.[135] Perhaps it was obvious
to the clergy now that a foreign patron might be able to give them the
things, particularly lots of cash and the capacity to interfere in the counsels
of European regimes, and especially in the curia in Rome, in a way that
no domestic patron ever could. The 1620s were to prove Smith absolutely
right. It appears that Montague may even have accepted this reality, for
in November 1616 Smith wrote to More that while Montague was still
'desirous of my returne', nevertheless he 'continueth stil his ancient favour
towardes me as lately Mr Kenion hath written from thence'.[136]

Despite his irritation with Smith, Montague did not desert his senior chaplain, the ailing Birkhead, or withdraw his support from the secular clergy's

[132] AAW, A XI, no. 140, p. 389.   [133] Ibid., no. 173, p. 509.
[134] Ibid., no. 181, p. 527.   [135] AAW, A XII no. 30, p. 69.   [136] AAW, A XV, no. 168,
p. 449.

projects, at least while Birkhead lived. In April 1613 John Jackson informed More that he had 'acquainted that worthy noble man [Montague] with your desire to have leave in his name to signifie to his Holines the nature of his greaf and the triall that his litle regard of our suites doth put him and others unto'. Montague had 'answered . . . that he was very willing that you shold not only signifie soe much in his name but also, if yow please, write that or what els yow shold think good as from him'. For that purpose Montague had in fact given More 'his seall, which mee thinks yow might make much good use of'.[137] In July 1613 Birkhead testified with gratitude how much Montague was still going out on a limb for his priests. The viscount had again been called in question about the secular clergy's affairs. Archbishop Abbot interrogated him. 'My greatest frend', as Birkhead called Montague, 'was called of late' in front of Abbot who 'used him courteously, and onely asked whether he knew the archpriest by the name of . . . Birkhead, which he did not much denie'. But 'it was before his Majesties pardon', so Montague presumably felt on safe ground here. Abbot 'dismissed him in most gentle manner', but, added Birkhead in a postscript, not before Montague had had 'much talke with the lord of Canturbury' about whether Catholics in England should have the privilege of local episcopal jurisdiction, and see it exercised over them by a Catholic clergyman. Montague 'proved evidently' the 'necessity' of all this, and 'how advantagiouse yt might be to the State, and furthermore he assured him that there cold not be a more quiet archpriest or lesse offensive to the estat than he that now is'.[138]

Exactly what Abbot thought of Montague's musings we can only speculate. It may have confirmed in Abbot's mind the need for Francis Mason's tract on the Church-of-England episcopate, a tract which was published in that same year. It is hard to believe that the archbishop could have stayed particularly calm while Montague explained to him that his own senior chaplain, Birkhead, should be granted episcopal authority throughout King James's English and Scottish realms.[139] On the other hand, what we are seeing here is the pro-episcopal lobby's principal patron putting forward the arguments which remained central to these clerics' public case, namely that English Catholicism would cause the regime a lot fewer political problems if it were brought under an overarching Catholic authority within the realm.

Even as the secular clergy's suit for episcopal jurisdiction proceeded at Rome, Birkhead's days were clearly numbered. For some time he had been racked by ill health, and he died, early in the morning, on 6 April 1614. Richard Broughton, who came to Birkhead's bedside, penned a moving

---

[137] AAW, A XII, no. 79, p. 169.   [138] *Ibid.*, no. 132, p. 293.

[139] For subsequent (superficially cordial) contact in 1619 between Montague and the archbishop, apparently concerning the prospective settlement of Montague's estates by means of a private act of parliament, see SHC, LM 6729/10/125, 132; ch. 12, p. 410 below.

account of how Birkhead left money to the Jesuits as well as to the Benedictines and Franciscans, and to the seminary at Douai, a bequest which would be overseen and administered by Montague himself.[140]

While Birkhead was dying, 'callinge and invocatinge our Blessed Saviour . . . [and] his glorious mother', there were practical issues to be addressed. It was essential to find a replacement quickly from the clergy within the same group. At Birkhead's bedside, Broughton put the archpriest in mind 'to have care in what he could' of his priests' 'hereafter good'. Broughton reminded him to 'assigne some to execute his office till another were constituted', and John Colleton was appointed in front of witnesses. Birkhead had also 'written two letters on his death bed'. One was 'to the superior of the Jesuits to desire ther charitable concurrence and correspondence with the poore [secular] clargie'. This was a kind of revenge, one assumes, for the asphyxiating goodwill of Robert Persons's last missive to Birkhead. And there was also one to 'his lovinge brethren to intreat charitie and unitie amongest themselves', i.e. a command not to step out of line as their new superior was being lobbied for and chosen. Copies were dispatched to Rome for circulation there. The dying archpriest also signed a letter to the cardinal protector desiring that his successor should be chosen from among his twelve assistants.[141]

No one, however, knew whom Rome would appoint. The election of William Harrison as the third of the archpriests came as a total surprise.[142] Not that he was unwelcome to them, certainly not a disaster in the way that, say, Thomas Worthington would have been.[143] Though it was rumoured that some of the regular clergy had been involved in the canvassing prior to his election, one of the regulars who was consulted about Harrison's election was the Carmelite friar Thomas Dawson. Dawson was, in fact, a Roper family chaplain, and his influence and opinions should have been quite acceptable to the main body of the pro-episcopal lobby.[144]

But Anthony Champney expressed his displeasure on 29 January/8 February 1616 in a letter to More. Champney said that the clergy in Paris had heard from Jackson that Harrison was now installed at Cowdray. But his election 'was not in such sort as you and Mr More seem to understand'. For Dawson 'bare the sway' during the consultations about it. He had secretly

---

[140] AAW, A XIII, no. 141, p. 363.

[141] *Ibid.*, no. 71, p. 175. Anthony Champney kept More informed of the talks held with the Paris nuncio about the election, *ibid.*, no. 161, pp. 411–12.

[142] For the papal breve of 1/11 July 1615 appointing Harrison, see TD V, clxxx. Harrison had been vice-president at Douai, Anstr. I, 152; TD V, 67.

[143] John Cecil speculated that Harrison would be more favourably inclined to the Jesuits than Birkhead had been, AAW, A XV, no. 65, p. 173.

[144] Guilday, *ECR*, 349; TD V, 65; Hibbard, *CI*, 257.

received a message from 'the nuncio of Brussels, and, I think, some cardinal from Rome . . . that [the man] whom he sent them word of as liked by the rest, the same should be chosen; as though they more credited him than all the ancient priests'. Champney intimated that certain people had dealt behind the scenes to suggest to the nuncio that 'you there and I know not who else are unfit for the office' because they were rumoured to impugn papal authority and to approve of the books written by the monk Thomas Preston.[145]

This was exactly the sort of thing that the leading secular priests had been fighting against for years. And it had all happened with the oversight if not the positive approval of some of their lay patrons. It seems that Harrison was picked in part because some members of the Browne family circle, particularly the Ropers and the Dormers, thought that he should succeed Birkhead.[146] Of course, we have evidence, though from much later on, that Montague was distinctly unimpressed with Harrison.[147] But the Dormers had already been influential in raising Harrison to an assistantship. At the time of Harrison's nomination, Birkhead recalled that Geoffrey Pole had advised against appointing Harrison to such an office, but John Mush had commended him to 'his friend', Montague's aunt Lady Dormer, 'and she, with other friends, hath made great insinuation that he might succeed in his office'. 'Considering her merits I have yielded', wrote Birkhead. 'I know the man is but soft, yet honest, and sincere, and emulated of none, and, I hope, will help to conserve our peace.'[148] (Harrison's election may also have been influenced by his relationship to the Bentley family, kin to the Ropers.[149])

However, whether Harrison was thought acceptable or not, the appointment of another archpriest was regarded by most of this clerical faction as merely a stop-gap measure. What was needed was a bishop. The suit for one had failed when presented at Rome by Thomas More, Birkhead's agent. But one day soon, they hoped, the opportunity would come to try again.

THE COURT, MID-JACOBEAN POLITICS AND THE BROWNES

The mid-Jacobean regime was, in several ways, politically schizophrenic. As Simon Adams has shown, James tried to balance his commitment to the European 'Protestant cause' with a determination to wed the Stuart heir to

---

[145] AAW, A XV, no. 25, p. 63, printed in TD V, clxxix–clxxx. John Jackson agreed with Champney that Rome's consultation process was a scandal, AAW, A XV, no. 13, p. 33.

[146] Harrison was closely associated with the Dormer family. His will of 10 May 1621 makes bequests to Lady Dormer, and leaves his corporal to the altar in the chapel at Wing, AAW, A XVI, no. 59.

[147] See ch. 13, p. 445 below.   [148] TD V, 67.

[149] Questier, PM, 494. Harrison's will made a bequest to his cousin Frederick Bentley, AAW, A XVI, no. 59.

one of the major Catholic royal families of Europe. Inevitably this caused dislocations at the heart of the Stuart regime, as different factions, frequently identified with one or other of these foreign policy modes, struggled for influence.[150] Catholics necessarily had to negotiate their way around these conflicting policy lines. In order to show up their Protestant enemies, and taint them with the mark of political disloyalty to the crown, it was necessary for Catholics to prove to the regime that, by contrast, James's Catholic subjects were supporters of the king's whole dynastic policy and his plans for the succession (even though they were continually looking to support and exploit those of James's initiatives which implied closer ties with Catholic powers, particularly the Habsburgs and the Bourbons).

Following the near disaster of the second Viscount Montague's refusal of the oath of allegiance, the Brownes did, it seems, study hard to appear supportive of the regime. Sir George Browne, although temporarily resident abroad, made a showy demonstration of mourning for the death of Prince Henry in late 1612.[151] Then, in 1613, the viscount laid out a small fortune on sartorial display to celebrate the wedding of James's daughter. John Chamberlain noted on 18 February 1613 that, on the occasion of the marriage of Frederick V, elector palatine and Princess Elizabeth, 'the Lord Montague (that hath paide reasonablie well for recusancie) bestowed fifteen hundred pound in apparell for his two daughters'.[152]

This was, for the Brownes, undoubtedly a major public political statement as well as an expensive social occasion. There were rumours doing the rounds before the Palatine match that the Catholics were opposed to it, and even had plans to rise in rebellion. Indeed, the recent disarming of Catholics, directed by the privy council, had been sparked by just such rumours of Catholics' disloyalty.[153] It was all the more remarkable because the elector palatine was the leading Protestant prince in mainland Europe. We may speculate that the Browne family was trying to show the king and the Court that they were supporting royal dynastic and foreign policy whatever its religious connotations and inflections. And the appearance of Montague's children at the marriage was clearly intended to prove that his loyalty, if it had ever been in doubt, was now beyond question.

Of course, we know relatively little about what Montague and his friends were doing during the mid- to late 1610s. But we may be sure that they were still asserting their Catholic identity. For example, Montague was at this time arranging for his daughters to marry into known and prominent Catholic families. On 19/29 September 1613 Robert Pett recorded that Montague's retainer William Cape 'writeth unto me that my Lord Montague his second

---

[150] Adams, 'Protestant Cause', chs. 6–9.   [151] NAGB, 223.
[152] McClure, Letters, I, 425.   [153] NAGB, 211.

daughter Mrs Katherine is maried' to William Tirwhit, 'a gentilman of good livinge and revenewes, and that Mrs Marie may marie' William Paulet 'the Lord Sainte Jones, sone and heyer to the lord marques [of Winchester], wherto my lord doth much incline'.[154] Lord St John was the son of the eldest daughter of Thomas Cecil, earl of Exeter. She had been the first earl of Salisbury's favourite niece. Montague may have deliberately been trying to introduce his daughter into this branch of the Cecil family.[155]

The Brownes may also have started to become involved, even if tangentially, in the ecclesio-political squabbles of the Church of England. Benjamin Carier, the notorious royal chaplain and 'Arminian *avant la lettre*', seems to have converted to Rome with the assistance of Catholics who were within the wider entourage of Viscount Montague. Carier was certainly on good terms with the Cowdray priest Robert Pett in Brussels. (Anthony Champney remarked in May 1614 that, when Carier came to the Collège d'Arras at Paris to dine with the clergy there, he 'confesseth to be behowldinge to Mr Pett for his love and good offices'.[156]) Indeed, it looked as if Carier could be added to the staff of the Collège d'Arras. He had been a founding member of the Church-of-England equivalent institution, Chelsea College, which enjoyed a royal financial subsidy. This would have been rather a neat transfer from the one academy to its competitor; a real feather in the cap of the rival Catholic college across the Channel. The poet Henry Constable, one of the secular clergy's lay associates, was instructed to recruit him for the Paris writers' institute.[157]

---

[154] Neither daughter was particularly happy about the matches arranged for them. Cape said that Mary Browne had 'noe inclination therunto haveinge settled her affection on Sir Thomas Sommerset, second sonne to the erle of Worcester, who in revenewes hath not above five hundred pounds by the yeare' though otherwise 'he be a very worthy and proper gentilman', AAW, A XII, no. 177, p. 391. For the marriage settlement and portion (various manors in Sussex, Hampshire and Surrey to be held for twenty-one years as 'security for £10,000 for the marriage portion of Lady Mary St John', transferred to trustees by Montague on 23 November 1613), see WSRO, SAS/BA 75. Edward Bennett observed on 14 February 1614 that both Montague's daughters were 'unhappily macht'. This 'matter disquieteth' the Browne circle 'not a litle and not without great cause given by those two unquiett husbands', AAW, A XIII, no. 28, p. 67. Three days later, John Chamberlain was reporting exactly the same gossip about Mary Browne, McClure, *Letters*, I, 512. Members of the entourage put the best gloss they could on the matter, and in fact Mary learned to live with Paulet (though he survived only until 1621). Francis Hore claimed on 19/29 March 1615 that 'all differences' were settled between Montague's 'noble virtuous daughter and sonn in law my Lord St John: they are att Basing and [are] good frinds', AAW, A XIV, no. 71, p. 239. However, on 21 December 1616, John Chamberlain reported a rumour that Mary was likely to replace Jane Drummond as Anne of Denmark's principal lady of the bedchamber, 'the rather for that she is now turning from poperie and procuring a nullitie of her mariage, by reason of her husbands impotencie, so she may have backe the 10000[li] she brought, wherupon they are almost at a point', McClure, *Letters*, II, 45.

[155] I am very grateful for this point to Pauline Croft.   [156] AAW, A XIII, no. 103, p. 263.

[157] G. Wickes, 'Henry Constable, Poet and Courtier, 1562–1613', *BS* 2 (1953–4), 272–300, at p. 293.

Obviously, Carier had his own agenda. Some of the seculars, such as Matthew Kellison, found it difficult to understand how, as a recent convert, Carier 'seemed to make so litle difference betwixt the religion of Ingland established by the State and ours'. But he displayed an unmitigated contempt for Calvinists and puritans. And so Kellison remarked that 'he is a rare man, and to be honored and loved'.[158] He was a walking exemplar of many of the polemical points and positions which Catholics such as Kellison had made central to their bid for leadership of the community. His conversion seemed to prove many of the leading secular priests' key claims about the nature of the Church of England and the disposition of the crown towards the religious factions within it. Champney noted that Carier was being 'recalled into England with great promises'. This could be taken as evidence that a moderate kind of Catholicism, at least as regards issues such as the oath of allegiance (which Carier seemed not to condemn), combined with outright hostility towards 'the puritans', might be acceptable to the king. James, in other words, could be held to account over his repeated statements that he excoriated extremists from either side but would show favour to those who were 'moderates'. There seemed to be a pool of potentially influential moderate Church-of-England men, some of whom Champney claimed had been Carier's friends. Perhaps there was really going to be a sea change in the balance of opinion within the established Church concerning Roman Catholicism?[159]

But, however moderate an image the second viscount's entourage constructed for itself, the fact remains that this section of the Catholic community was not simply being assimilated into mainstream political culture or the life of the Court. They were, it seems, not really in the same boat as some of the great Catholic courtier families, for example the Somersets. And the extent to which they still could not rely on official protection or the regime's good will was demonstrated by the appalling treatment of Montague's uncle, Sir George Browne, at the hands of the rampantly anti-popish Archbishop Abbot. On 5 January 1615 John Jackson reported to Thomas More that 'Sir George Brown died on New Year eve', and 'his body was buryed in St Mary Overyes [St Saviour's] church in the chancell, as I take it with his ancestors'. But

4 dayes after, the archbishop of Canterbury caused the coffin to be taken up and opened that the churchwardens might assure him that the bodye was there, for he would not trust to the oaths of his servants upon an information that forsooth his body was to be caried beyond sea and a logg buried in steed therof. And being enformed his bodie was there, he commaunded that it shold neyther be buried in church nor church yeard.

[158] AAW, A XIII, no. 104, p. 265.
[159] *NAGB*, 27–8; AAW, A XII, no. 190, p. 421; M. Questier, 'Crypto-Papism, Anti-Calvinism and Conversion: The Enigma of Benjamin Carier', *JEH* 47 (1996), 45–64.

Furthermore, Abbot ordered that the body should be buried beside the high-way, 'and that the greatest lord, earle or other person . . . shold not intreat him to the contrary' unless the king himself commanded it.[160]

This was pretty unpleasant, considering that the impeccably loyal Sir George had been decently laid to rest in the Southwark parish church of his own family. A week later Benjamin Norton also related the shocking news to More: 'as I made an end of my letter I . . . . [heard] that Syr George Brown' died 'at Stepney where they refused to burye hime. And soe he was caried by his frendes and buried at St Mary Overies, where he had not rested three dayes but the bushop of Canterbury caused his body to be taken up and soe lieth above grown[d] where the saxton laieth his spades and shoveles.'[161] (Abbot's spite would not have been lessened by the confronta-tion, two weeks before, between him and Edward Worsley, the mad, or at least extremely embittered, Catholic servant of Montague's brother-in-law Thomas Sackville. Worsley managed to get into Abbot's rooms in Lambeth Palace and spent some time verbally abusing the archbishop until he was dragged away by Abbot's attendants.[162])

The Brownes were evidently still viewed by some in the establishment as deeply suspect. In March 1615 the deputy lieutenants of Sussex were to be found writing to their superiors about the recent command to compile accurate lists of Catholic separatists: they wanted official backing in order to deal with the second viscount's household 'where wee heare are verie manie recusantes'.[163] Undoubtedly, knowledge of how potentially destabil-ising and damaging the Brownes' clergy's episcopal ambitions might prove •
to the exercise of the royal supremacy could not but have ensured that the Brownes and their kin would continue to be regarded with a suspicious eye by many in authority. The record of the second viscount's entourage in the later Jacobean period, as we shall see, did not necessarily assuage such fears.

---

[160] AAW, A XIV, no. 5, p. 11.
[161] *Ibid.*, no. 11, p. 29. For the account of this incident by Benjamin Norton, see *ibid.*, no. 12. Edmund Bolton, a friend of Thomas More, said that 'they would not let him bee enterred although (as is said) an hundred pound[s]' was 'proferd for it', *ibid.*, no. 41, p. 117. Sir George Browne's old-style Catholic will of 21 November 1614 bequeathed his soul to God 'and to the most blessed virgin Marie', and to all the holy company of heaven, PRO, PROB 11/125, fo. 488r–v.
[162] See ch. 10, p. 334 above.   [163] ESRO, XA 63, fo. 27r.

12

The later Jacobean and early Caroline period

It is almost axiomatic among historians that the later years of James's reign were a time of relative peace and quiet for Catholics. In fact, the extant narratives of the later Jacobean period do not mention English Catholics much, even while James's projects for a Catholic marriage for Prince Charles were causing all sorts of political difficulties for the crown. These difficulties became exponentially worse after James's son-in-law, the elector palatine, had been deprived of his recently acquired crown in Bohemia and had been ejected from his own principality, the Palatinate of the Rhine. However, the process which led finally to Prince Charles being married to a foreign Catholic bride was one in which most contemporaries assumed that English Catholics had a vested interest and one which they would manipulate for their own advantage, and use in order to make common cause with foreigners for their mutual benefit.

The second Viscount Montague was not himself, it seems, at the forefront of Catholic attempts to muscle in on the political process during the late 1610s and early 1620s. He never attempted to repeat his interventionist tactics in the parliament of 1604, or his challenge to the regime in 1611 over the issue of allegiance. But he was not entirely absent from the stage. And it is certainly possible to detect members of his family circle and entourage who heavily engaged themselves in the political arena.

Let us look briefly, via the snapshot provided by the surviving evidence of the second viscount's kin circle, friends, chaplains and servants, at the Catholic political scene in this period, and try to understand why Catholics should often have been viewed, locally and nationally, with such hostility, and why the Catholic community should have been believed to entertain vaulting political ambitions which threatened the settlement of religion in the Church of England.

The second Viscount Montague was present at the start of the 1621 parliament. He voted in a division of 8 February, and was mentioned in the impeachment proceedings against Bacon.[1] He did not turn up while the lord chancellor was actually under attack. But the seventeenth of the charges laid against Bacon (as recorded in the Lords' journal) stated that, 'in the Lord Mountague's cause', i.e. the legal process to deal with Montague's debts, Bacon 'received from the Lord Mountague six or seven hundred pounds; and more was paid at the ending of the cause'.[2] While there were protests against individual members in the parliament who were reckoned to be Catholic, such as the MPs returned for Gatton by the Copleys (Sir Henry Brittaine and John Holles, whose elections were overturned),[3] and, later on in the parliament, the notorious Sir Henry Spiller,[4] Montague was not directly touched by such sentiments. The Lords dealt with a bill for settling his pressing debt problems, the same issue as had come before Bacon in chancery, and in particular for sorting out a defaulting trustee, his brother-in-law Sir Francis Englefield who had failed in his duty to administer the dispositions of the estate which had been made in the 1610s.[5]

At this time, Montague's daughter Mary, Lady St John, remarried William Arundell, son of Thomas, Baron Arundell of Wardour. On 19 December

---

[1] F. H. Relf (ed.), *Notes of the Debates in the House of Lords . . . A.D. 1621, 1625, 1628* (Camden Society, 42, 1929), 2; S. R. Gardiner (ed.), *Notes of the Debates in the House of Lords . . . A.D. 1621* (2 vols., Camden Society, 103, new series 24, 1870–9), I, 9; S. R. Gardiner, *Prince Charles and the Spanish Marriage* (2 vols., 1869), I, 464.

[2] *LJ* III, 85–6, 99. Montague appears to have dealt with Bacon about his debts and his estate as far back as November 1615, SHC, LM 6729/10/124.

[3] Hamilton, *Chronicle*, I, 88.

[4] Spiller, an exchequer official with Howard patronage, sat for Arundel in the parliaments of 1614, 1621, 1624 and 1625, and for Thetford in 1628. He sat for Midhurst in 1626, and was on good terms with leading recusant families, including some which were resident in, or had links with, Sussex. In 1610 Thomas Felton had accused Spiller of procuring 'letters from the lords of the councell to the justices of assize at Newgate . . . to spare the indictment of Robert Tirwhite esq., a greate recusant, and had for it £500 besides a yearely pencion', PRO, SP 14/56/27A, fo. 55v. The Tirwhits had property in Sussex (see ch. 2, p. 40 and ch. 3, p. 97 above), and, as we saw, William Tirwhit married the second Viscount Montague's daughter Catherine. In June 1612 Edward Gage of Bentley, Montague's cousin, wrote from Liège to Spiller, his 'very good frend', trying to arrange that, if he returned to England, he should not be required to take the oath of allegiance, BL, Lansdowne MS 153, fo. 83r. In 1624 Spiller's brother, Robert, a steward of the dowager countess of Arundel, was party to a property settlement by Montague in 1613 on the marquis of Winchester, Sir Richard Weston, Sir Richard Fermour and Sir Anthony Mayne, WSRO, SAS/BA 75; BL, Additional MS 16967, fo. 23r.

[5] *LJ* III, 136 (first reading, 28 May 1621), 139 (second reading, 29 May 1621). At second-reading stage, it was committed, *inter alia*, to Montague's cousin the third earl of Dorset and also to Robert Petre who had recently married Montague's daughter. The bill got a third reading on 30 May, and 'was put to the question, and assented unto', *LJ* III, 142, but did not pass in this almost legislation-free session. For the bill, see BL, Harleian MS 6847, no. 4, fos. 20v–21r; ch. 11, p. 359 above; Gardiner, *Prince Charles and the Spanish Marriage*,

1621 Edward Bennett reported to his brother John in Rome that 'my Lady St John' had married Arundell 'by whom I have been very kindly interteyned', and that Joseph Haynes, the Bennetts' nephew, 'liketh hyme well'.[6]

Among the members of Montague's kin circle who were trying to insert themselves directly into the crown's negotiations with the Spaniards was Baron Arundell himself. Arundell got involved in the diplomacy for implementing the toleration for Catholic recusants brokered by the Spaniards. Sir George Calvert observed on 12 August 1623 that 'the Spanish ambassadors, finding no lawyer in town whom they could advise with about the pardon for the recusants, have sent for Lord Arundel[l] of Wardour, now in the country'. Calvert was reluctant to help them contact him but dared not offend the Spanish diplomats, so fearful were he and the match-promoting Court party that they might foul up the negotiations.[7] Catholics eagerly conjectured as to the amount of influence that they would enjoy if the Spanish match were to go ahead. A correspondent of the priest William Bishop speculated about the changes which would inevitably take place at the Court. There would be a Catholic clerical entourage around the infanta if she were finally to wed Prince Charles. The king would also have to admit prominent Catholics to high political office. Bishop's friend made a 'things-to-do' list in the wake of the expected happy event: in particular, 'two noblemen at the least' should be 'made 2 of the kings privy councell, that they may there deale for the Catholikes'. Among the 'fittest men' that Bishop's friend could imagine were 'the Lord William Howard, the Lord Arundell of Wardor, the Lord Harbert, the Lord Ewers, Sir Thomas Savage' and possibly the earl of Clanrickard; and the two best qualified were Howard and Arundell, being 'the wisest, the gravest and fittest of them'.[8]

On 18 August Calvert reported to Sir Edward Conway that Arundell was 'very sorry he did not receive the king's command before coming from the country, but will endeavour to excuse himself from the employment to the ambassadors, without letting them know that he does so by command'.[9] But the publicity generated by Arundell's interference could not be controlled so easily. John Chamberlain observed twelve days later that 'our papists are verie busie and earnest (by the Spanish ambassadors meanes) to have a publike toleration'. James was trying to avoid conceding a full legal toleration but was 'pleased to graunt them pardon for what is past, with a dispensation for exercise of their religion in their owne houses under the broad seale for five and twenty shillings or fowr nobles a peece'. The height of the Catholics'

I, 464. In the 1624 parliament, the problem of Montague's property and debts was addressed again, PRO, C 89/11/76; 21 James I, c. 48; see below in this chapter.
[6] AAW, A XVI, no. 75, p. 254. On 4 August 1621, following the recent death of Lord St John, John Chamberlain was already aware that his widow planned to wed Arundell, McClure, *Letters*, II, 396.
[7] *CSPD 1623–5*, 53.   [8] AAW, B 25, no. 82.   [9] *CSPD 1623–5*, 58.

ambition, thought Chamberlain, was shown by their grumpy ungratefulness even for this massive concession; they were saying that this would merely 'discover their number and qualitie'. Even James lost patience. Chamberlain noted that 'the Lord Arundell of Warder is saide to be committed to his house for . . . entermedling too much in these matters'. James suspected that 'our papists (for their owne ends) are the greatest hinderance of the speedie dispatching the match, and sayes he will make them repent yt, yf he find they continue to crosse him'.[10]

This, however, did not dampen Arundell's ardour. As Christmas approached, Montague's zealous cousin, described by Chamberlain as a notorious 'busie bodie', 'made meanes to the king that he might be' the Catholics' 'agent in Court', as the Huguenots 'have theirs in Fraunce'.[11]

But now a crucial development pointed to a potentially dramatic extension of Montague's entourage's influence. While the Spanish match negotiations continued, the secular clergy who still looked to him as one of their major patrons became heavily involved in the diplomatic commerce between the Stuart regime, the Spaniards and the Roman curia. As Charles Dodd remarked, the 'negotiation for the Spanish match', as well as 'the accession of a new pontiff', Gregory XV, 'offered a favourable opportunity' to steal in, comparatively unexpectedly, and cajole the curia into investing one of the secular clergy, inevitably one of the pro-episcopal lobby, with episcopal authority.[12]

The diplomatic logic was not hard to detect. The Catholic pro-episcopal lobby would vigorously lend its voice in support of the marriage negotiations if the papacy were to grant these priests what they wanted, namely some form of episcopal hierarchy in England. The Stuart regime would understand the significance of the deal, and would take care not to react with the sort of hostility which would normally greet such papist presumption. A State-tolerated Roman Catholic episcopal hierarchy would itself be a sign that the relationship between the Stuart regime and the Catholics was becoming more harmonious, one of the essential criteria without evidence of which the papal curia would not grant the necessary dispensation for the match. The Spaniards also claimed that they could not proceed without a papal recognition that the match was licit (though increasingly the English negotiators suspected that the Spaniards' much-trumpeted scruples were being used as an excuse to prevaricate on the issue and to ensure that the Palatinate question would be settled by military force in favour of the Habsburgs). James, however, continued to believe, in the face of much of the evidence, that the Spaniards would proceed with the marriage, and more or less on his own

[10] McClure, *Letters*, II, 513.   [11] *Ibid.*, II, 535.   [12] TD V, 82.

terms. He badly needed, therefore, the English Catholics to keep sending the right messages to Rome.

The Catholics could, in fact, be set to work here in the royal service. In the meantime, the Catholic pro-episcopal lobby could use this diplomatic juncture to beat the living ideological daylights out of their own Catholic opponents. They could claim that their Catholic (mainly Jesuit) opponents' resistance to an episcopal appointment in England not only aligned them with the Church of England's own opponents of episcopal authority but was tantamount to an attempt to stop the marriage altogether. Their machinations threatened to destroy the possibility of toleration for Catholics in England and, perhaps, even the reabsorption of the realm into communion with Rome. The negotiations for the dispensation coincided nicely, therefore, with the pro-episcopal lobby's own suit for one of their number to be granted episcopal authority in England. For if one of the conditions for a restored hierarchy was some proof that a bishop would be able to carry out his episcopal functions effectively in a still technically schismatic but now essentially tolerant State, a match between the Stuart heir and a Spanish princess was prima facie pretty good evidence of exactly that.

John Bennett, the Dormers' chaplain, was selected to go to Rome as clergy agent to replace Montague's chaplain Thomas More. But Bennett's function there would clearly include the performance of any necessary diplomatic cajolery to facilitate the marriage.[13] The archpriest William Harrison died suddenly in 1621, just as Bennett was about to depart. Bennett's instructions were swiftly redrawn. He was ordered to ask for a replacement for Harrison, preferably one who would enjoy the rank and status of a bishop. (At first Bennett was told to request that the man appointed should be Diego de Lafuente, the chaplain of the Spanish ambassador Gondomar. But the aim was, of course, for one of the secular clergy's number to get it in the end.)[14] Bennett's pass to travel, dated 12 September 1621, was obtained from the secretary of State, Sir George Calvert. It specifically declared that 'this bearer John Bennett, gentleman, is upon spetiall occasion concerning his Majesties service to make his repaire into forraigne partes'.[15] One Spanish narrator of the marriage negotiations noted the terms of Bennett's licence. He observed that although 'publicly it was given out that' Bennett 'had come in the name of the English clergy to assist in soliciting the dispensation', this was itself

---

[13] Thomas More departed for Spain to recover some of the arrears of the pension owed to the college at Douai by the Spanish crown.

[14] TD V, 83. Lafuente was involved in the shuttle diplomacy which took place at this time in order to secure the required dispensation from Rome, *CSPV 1619–21*, 276, 450, 458; S. R. Gardiner (ed.), *Narrative of the Spanish Marriage Treaty* (Camden Society, 101, 1869), 161–2. See also *CSPV 1621–3*, 403.

[15] AAW, A XVI, no. 63, p. 221.

a 'pretext', for Bennett was in fact acting as a personal envoy from James. Once at Rome, Bennett claimed that 'the king was well inclined towards the Mass, which was news which had much influence upon all who heard it'.[16]

By October, Gondomar was corresponding with Bennett from London, and William Bishop was soon in touch with Lafuente in Rome. (Lafuente had been sent by Gondomar back to Spain, and had then been dispatched to Rome by Philip III to obtain the dispensation.[17]) Before Gondomar left London for Spain in mid-1622, he was approached by the patrons of the secular clergy, especially Lady Dormer (Montague's aunt). She 'came to London expressly to take leave of the count of Gondomar and to be acquaynted with his successour'. She had promised that 'shee would commend unto him ernestly the case of the clergie'.[18] Undoubtedly the second viscount was involved at some level in the discussions which Gondomar had with English Catholics. In May 1622 the earl of Leicester noted that Gondomar was visiting either Cowdray 'or Mr Cotton at Warblington'. But Cowdray was the more likely place.[19] Gondomar was always reckoned by the secular clergy in Montague's circle to have been a good friend to them, unlike his successor as Spanish ambassador in London, Carlos Coloma, who leaned towards the Society of Jesus. (By August 1622 the Jesuit general, Muzio Vitelleschi, was fuming that the secular priests in England were trying to alienate Gondomar from the Society.[20]) In November 1622 William Harewell informed John Bennett that Montague and his son (who was now being packed off to Spain) 'had been at Wing', i.e. with the Dormers, during 'the latter end of this summer. For now their is great league betwixt both those houses.'[21]

It is interesting to speculate as to why Francis Browne should have been sent out of the country in late 1622 (a grant to travel for three years was issued to him at this time).[22] It could have been merely a matter of going on the grand tour. But it does appear that the family was trying to position

[16] Gardiner, *Narrative*, 168–9. In a letter of November 1621 the Jesuit general Muzio Vitelleschi promised Richard Blount SJ that he would ensure that Bennett's embassy in Rome did not hurt Catholics in England, i.e. the Jesuits and their patrons. In December the general asked Blount to pray for divine aid to counter Bennett's mischief-making, ARSJ, Anglia MS 1/i, fo. 148r–v.

[17] TD V, 120; AAW, A XVI, no. 91; *CSPV 1621–3*, 158; CRS 68, 144. For the setting up of the papal commission to study the dispensation issue, see *CSPV 1621–3*, 158. In January 1622 Joseph Haynes intimated that the seculars had already sent Lafuente a request to help them in their suit for episcopal authority, though Lafuente had politely declined, AAW, A XVI, no. 94, p. 405.

[18] AAW, A XVI, no. 112, p. 463.   [19] *CSPD 1619–23*, 394.

[20] ARSJ, Anglia MS 1/i, fo. 161v.   [21] AAW, A XVI, no. 173, p. 669.

[22] *CSPD 1619–23*, 449. On 2 November 1622 William Cape was at Dover procuring a place on a ship for Francis Browne to go abroad. On the same day Francis arrived in Dover with his tutor, a Benedictine monk, Edward Smith. Francis was *en route* for Spain, reported William Harewell, 'there to spend some time, and a great deale of money', AAW, A XVI, no. 173, p. 669; Lunn, *EB*, 229; PRO, SP 16/178/43; Anstr. II, 299.

itself to take advantage of the match if the Anglo-Spanish treaty was success-fully concluded. The embittered James Wadsworth described how in early 1623 he had arrived in Madrid where his father was teaching English to the infanta. The younger Wadsworth proceeded to make friends with Francis Browne and his cousin Anthony Englefield. It seems that they were both placed initially in the household of the English ambassador, Sir John Digby, earl of Bristol, though their Benedictine tutors, alleged Wadsworth, soon drew them to reside elsewhere in the city.[23] Almost certainly, the second viscount was anticipating that a large measure of influence and authority, both within the Catholic community and perhaps outside it as well, would accrue to his family if the great diplomatic *coup* which was being planned by Gondomar and James (and which, in mid-1623, would be thrust forward by the impetuous journey to Madrid undertaken by Prince Charles and his travelling companion George Villiers, duke of Buckingham) came off.

Montague's aunt, 'old Lady Dormer', was especially vehement in sup-porting the clergy's various projects. Of Lady Dormer's patronage, Edward Bennett exclaimed, in a letter of September 1622 to his brother John, 'God blesse her . . . We would not have stood without her.'[24] The new Baron Dormer was equally supportive. (In November 1621 John Bennett had remarked that 'the Jesuits here are making catalogues of lay people's names, who forsooth would have no bishops; and this, as a great weapon, they pur-pose to use', and they add 'that never a Catholic in England desireth bishops but my Lord Dormer'.)[25]

In Paris, on 1/11 May 1622, Anthony Champney was speculating in a letter to John Bennett in Rome about which one of their circle could be infiltrated closest to the infanta. 'If the match goe forward it would be con-venient we hadd some honest freind nere the queene.' They had thought about it at Paris, and their choice fell on 'Mr Clifford of Antwerpe who, as you knowe, by you and your freinds meanes, was preferred to the duches of

---

[23] James Wadsworth, *The English Spanish Pilgrime* (1629), 48–9. On 8 October 1624 Thomas Roper wrote to Thomas More that Montague had 'received a warrante from the coun-cell . . . to recaule his sonne from Spayne', and Montague certified the council on 21 October that he had instructed Francis to return home, AAW, B 27, no. 10.

[24] AAW, A XVI, no. 140, p. 550. Later, in November 1624, we find her writing to Sir Robert Cotton, asking to borrow books for unnamed 'well-willers to antiquitie' who were 'desirous to publish' the lives of some 'memorable men . . . especially of our owne nation', and thus 'give light to manie partes of our historie'. In particular she wanted 'the life and miracles of St Alban in prose and verse, and a very old copie of saints-lives, writt, as it is thought, before the Conquest', BL, Cotton MS Julius C III, fo. 155r. St Alban figured in Richard Broughton's *Ecclesiasticall Historie of Great Britaine* (Douai, 1633), 426, 433–6, an account which cited a number of manuscript narratives of the saint's life including a 'Manuscr. Antiq. Vitae S. Albani' (p. 426). Cotton's manuscripts may have been borrowed for Broughton's benefit. For Lady Dormer's borrowing of books from Cotton, see K. Sharpe, *Sir Robert Cotton 1586–1631: History and Politics in Early Modern England* (Oxford, 1979), 61, 74.

[25] TD V, ccxxxii.

Feria and quitt himselfe well'. Clifford was a distant blood relative of Montague, though, as Champney points out here, he was essentially a Dormer contact. Champney added, 'I wrote hereof to your brother', Edward Bennett, Lady Dormer's chaplain, 'and he liketh verie well both of the thing and of the man'.[26] The seculars had other well-placed people around the Spanish diplomats. William Harewell observed, in a letter of 16/26 October 1622 to John Bennett, that another member of their circle, William Law, who 'was quondam my schoolefellowe heere', was now serving as 'capellano to the Spanish embassador in England' and could be relied on for transmission of news.[27]

Another patron to whom the seculars sued for assistance was the archdeacon of Cambrai, Francisco de Carondolet. He was in England for a time, attending on the ambassador Coloma, and in mid-August 1623 he was angling to be made almoner to the infanta.[28] He was a consistent supporter of the secular clergy leadership's line. He had come to Matthew Kellison's defence when Kellison was lambasted for his recent book *The Right and Iurisdiction of the Prelate and the Prince*.[29]

Having established his lines of communication with the seculars' various representatives, agents, correspondents, friends and newsletter writers in London, Paris, Douai, Antwerp and other places, John Bennett now engaged in a battle royal with the Catholics who (the leading secular priests alleged) opposed a re-established hierarchy in England. Here the Catholic pro-episcopal lobby's struggles with their Catholic enemies would be fought out on essentially the same terrain which James and his political opponents battled over as the king fought to secure the treaty with Spain.

Some sense of the impact of these Catholic factions' attempts to represent themselves in the best possible light to the regime and the public can be glimpsed from the theological polemic which they produced. During the early 1620s they enjoyed, from time to time, something close to complete tolerance from the regime. Evangelical activists such as the Jesuit John Percy (better

---

[26] AAW, A XVI, no. 108, p. 450. The duke of Feria also thought it was a good idea. The duke of Feria's mother was Jane Dormer (d. 1612).

[27] AAW, A XVI, no. 171, p. 663. For William Law, see *NAGB*, 61.

[28] *CSPD 1623–5*, 58.

[29] AAW, A XVII, no. 6, p. 21. Carondolet was prepared to guarantee Cardinal Millini that James would not take offence if the clergy were granted a bishop, *ibid*. In March 1623 he presented 'a fair guilt cuppe with [a] cover' to the seminary at Douai, *ibid*., no. 10, p. 33. He was allegedly perceived as an opponent by the Jesuits and their friends. In July 1624 William Newman in Lisbon claimed to know of a conspiracy, in which the Jesuits' front man Sir Tobie Mathew was involved, to 'remove' Carondolet (apparently from his archdeaconry), AAW, B 47, no. 166. In February 1623 William Harewell, who had accompanied John Bennett to Rome, made a trip from Douai to Brussels to consult with Carondolet, and Carondolet made a return visit to Douai. His subsequent visit to England was used to defuse royal opposition to the appointment of a Catholic bishop in England, CRS 10, 400.

known by his alias of Fisher) roamed around London looking for Protestants to confront and confute in semi-public debates about key issues of doctrine. Also, in May 1622, Percy (brought out from his prison accommodation to the Court) confronted a battery of Church-of-England divines and the king himself, in a supposedly private disputation which was intended to resolve the religious doubts of the countess of Buckingham, mother of the royal favourite. Those who gathered there on the first day (24 May) included the duke of Buckingham, the countess, Buckingham's wife Katherine (Manners) who was on the verge of converting to Rome (and soon did), and Lord Keeper Williams, and (it seems) the king as well. On the following day, James himself did most of the arguing. On 26 May the principal disputant to enter the lists against Percy was William Laud. Here the topic for discussion was the compatibility of the Roman and English Churches.[30] News of the debates soon started to leak out. And the event was clearly intended by Percy as a great propaganda *coup*, just as at the Court the use of divines such as Laud, rather than e.g. George Abbot and his friends, pointed to the rise of a new strain of churchmanship, a strain which could be relied on not to criticise royal foreign policy. By late August the Jesuit general knew that Percy and another Jesuit, John Floyd, were preparing an answer 'ad capita . . . a rege scripta tradita'. In early October the general was eagerly asking for more news about the debate between Percy and the king, and in mid-December he was insisting that Percy had not been worsted in the polemical contest.[31]

Obviously there was nothing in all this which was explicitly aimed at the Jesuits' English Catholic opponents. But it was so different a model of Catholic activism from the clerical and ecclesiastical ideals held up by the pro-episcopal lobby as the right and proper mode for restoring the Church in England (for achieving, as they termed it, the 'conversion' of their country) that it could hardly not be taken as a critique of the strategies of the hierarchalists among the English Catholic secular clergy.

Certainly many secular priests were exceedingly sniffy about the polemical achievements of Percy and other Jesuits. One of Percy's best-known exploits was his confrontation with Archbishop Abbot's chaplain Daniel Featley over the spiritual health of one Edward Buggs, an ageing cousin

---

[30] T. H. Wadkins, 'King James I meets John Percy, S.J. (25 May, 1622): An Unpublished Manuscript from the Religious Controversies Surrounding the Countess of Buckingham's Conversion', *RH* 19 (1988), 146–54; William Laud, *An Answere to Mr Fishers Relation of a Third Conference betwene a Certaine B. (as He Stiles Him) and Himselfe* (1624).

[31] ARSJ, Anglia MS 1/i, fos. 161v, 163r, 166r. The general was glad that Lord Keeper Williams had forbidden Percy from publishing his account of the dispute, but by February 1623 the general had evidently seen a draft of Percy's reply to what James had said (a reply which was finally published in 1625), *ibid.*, fos. 166r, 168r; John Percy, *The Answere unto the Nine Points of Controversy, Proposed by our Late Soveraygne* (St Omer, 1625).

of the very Protestant Sir Humphrey Linde. Buggs was resident in Drury Lane. According to contemporary accounts of the disputation, he had been persuaded to Catholicism by some Catholics 'then about him'.[32] This is almost certainly a reference to Percy. Percy served as confessor-chaplain to the recusant Sir Anthony Buggs who himself lived in Drury Lane. Sir Anthony was a relative, probably the brother, of Edward Buggs.[33] An informer's report written at some point before March 1627 listed Catholics who were resident there: Sir Anthony Buggs himself, Sir Lewis Lewkenor and Sir Edmund Lenthall (among others). Their houses were all, allegedly, linked by a gallery. The gallery provided a means 'to conveye' 'suspect persons away thorow stables into the felldes'. At Sir Lewis Lewkenor's house 'lyeth Father Foster the Jeseuit', presumably Robert Forster, who was a nephew of the Gunpowder plotter Ambrose Rookwood.[34]

But it is also possible that the Catholics who first persuaded Edward Buggs to Catholicism included people in the second Viscount Montague's household. At this point, Montague's London residence was in Drury Lane, and, later, in June 1627, an informer, Alexander Couler, noted 'on[e] Cape . . . the Lord Montacutes man dwelling in Drury Lane at the house which was Sir Lewis Lewkenors', purchased 'by the said lord for such persons'.[35] It is likely that the Jesuit Percy's proselytising was perceived by other Catholics in Drury Lane as, in some sense, a challenge or threat to them. Certainly these

[32] Daniel Featley, *The Fisher Catched in his Owne Net* (1623), 1–5.

[33] PRO, SP 16/229/132, fo. 258r; W. R. Powell (ed.), *A History of the County of Essex* (Victoria County History, Oxford, 1983), VIII, 137.

[34] PRO, SP 16/229/132, fo. 258r; CRS 74, 154–5; CRS 54, 178. Forster was confessor to Lady Lewkenor. Sir Lewis Lewkenor died in March 1627. Another Drury Lane house, identified as a Jesuit residence, was raided in mid-March 1628, at around the same time as the search of the Clerkenwell Jesuit novitiate (see ch. 13, pp. 440–2 below), on notification that 'there was a daungerous Jesuite, one Bastell', there, PRO, SP 16/98/109, fo. 266r.

[35] PRO, SP 16/68/8, fo. 12r. An undated informer's report, probably from *c.* 1625–7, noted that 'ther is one Ceape a pretended servant to the Lord Mounttegeu of Coudarie wich is convictted', i.e. of recusancy, and 'haieth taken a house in Druarie Lane in the Lord Mounttegues name, but my lord never cam[e] at this house yett', and, because 'it is said to bee the Lord Mounttegues house', the informer and others could not enter it without a special warrant, PRO, SP 16/229/133, fo. 259r. During a Commons debate in June 1628, Laurence Whitaker, MP for Peterborough, complained, referring to Drury Lane, that 'I can show you now a little Rome or a little Douai' in London. 'There is among them nobility, gentry, clergy, lawyers; there is 3 papists to one Protestant', so that 'more go to Mass than to the church', C. Russell, *Parliaments and English Politics 1621–1629* (Oxford, 1979), 381; R. C. Johnson, M. F. Keeler, M. J. Cole and W. B. Bidwell (eds.), *Commons Debates 1628* (6 vols., 1977–83), IV, 151, 156, 163, 166, 173. On 18 July 1629 Secretary Coke recorded that Richard Smith would soon be in town and would be at Montague's house in Drury Lane, where the housekeeper, Cape, was in charge of three bags, one of which was marked 'A for agent', presumably the post being sent out to the clergy agent in Rome. Another was marked 'C', and was the common purse for clergy funds, PRO, SP 16/147/12, fo. 22r. See also PRO, SP 16/229/131, fos. 254v–255r.

antagonistic wings or factions of the London Catholic scene were sometimes in extremely close geographical proximity to each other.[36]

John Bennett was, of course, not the only Catholic clergyman in Rome during this period with Stuart royal accreditation. George Gage, a friend of Sir Tobie Mathew, was also being deployed by the regime as a roving ambassador between London and the papal Court.[37] The regime may have sensed that it had more chance of getting Rome's agreement to grant a dispensation for the proposed marriage between Charles and the infanta if it called on both the major clerical factions of the English Catholic community for their help. It may also have believed that it would achieve its objective while they, in turn, would to some extent cancel each other out. Certainly each was inclined to accuse the other of being a hindrance to the planned Anglo-Spanish alliance. Each said that the other's selfish ambitions threatened to disrupt the smooth course of the diplomacy which was necessary to see the match completed. By December 1621 Edward Bennett, John Bennett's brother, was sending messages to Rome that the Jesuits had now effectively sold out to the Stuart regime over the match. He implied that they had given up trying to win concessions for English Catholics. They were, he said, also using the current diplomatic to-ing and fro-ing to oppose the secular clergy's suit for the appointment of a bishop to rule directly over the Catholics in England. Allegedly the Jesuits were putting it about that the required dispensation had already been granted and that Gage had made representations to Gregory XV against an episcopal appointment.[38]

John Bennett, however, managed to secure an official revocation of the previous decision against the nomination of a bishop. The issue was referred again to the Inquisition. Bennett recited all the stock reasons why episcopal government should be re-established over English Catholics. He emphasised

---

[36] A note in the State Papers records the names of those found on 18 December 1625 in the house of one Mr Bradshaw in Drury Lane. Among them was the wife of Sir Thomas Gerard, the second viscount's relative by marriage. (Montague's mother had taken as her third husband this Sir Thomas Gerard's father, who had died in February 1621.) There was also a Captain John Langworth there. He appears to have been from the Kentish Catholic family which, as we have seen, had links with the Ropers, who were also Montague's relatives, PRO, SP 16/12/8, fo. 18r; Questier, *PM*, 486. In January 1626 Sir Edward Conway noted that Langworth had been 'taken for a priest', *CSPD 1625–6*, 213.

[37] Gage was ordained, together with Tobie Mathew, by Cardinal Bellarmine in Rome in May 1614. He was twice dispatched to Rome by the king to facilitate the marriage treaty with Spain, Anstr. II, 120.

[38] AAW, A XVI, no. 75, p. 253. Gage had arrived in Rome in June 1621 to seek the necessary dispensation. He found the pope dismayed at the news of the 1621 parliament's hostility to Catholics. The pope insisted that James should 'do many things', i.e. to ensure toleration, 'which are not evident at the present', CRS 68, 150. For Gage's two audiences with the pope (on 6/16 June and 28 June/8 July), with the pope's strictures being delivered at the latter meeting, see Gardiner, *Narrative*, 164. For Gage's departure for England in July 1622, see *CSPV 1621–3*, 376.

the need for order, unity and discipline. Ignoring the dissenting voices of Gage and Thomas Fitzherbert (rector of the English College), Bennett claimed that there was now virtual unanimity for such an appointment among the English Catholics. His line was supported by curial officials such as Ottavio Bandini, the most senior of the Inquisition cardinals, and by the cardinal protector Luigi Ludovisi, and the French cardinal Louis de Nogaret de La Valette.[39] The secretary of the Congregation for the Propagation of the Faith (De Propaganda Fide), Francesco Ingoli,[40] was likewise a friend to the seculars, as was Cardinal François Sourdis, though in mid-1622 Sourdis returned to his archbishopric of Bourdeaux.[41] The man allegedly responsible for obtaining Richelieu's cardinal's hat, Sébastien Bouthillier, bishop of Aire, similarly proved himself to be one of their supporters.[42] Cardinal Giovanni Millini's arguments against the appointment of a bishop for England no longer held sway as they had done in the 1610s.[43]

At John Bennett's first audience with Gregory XV the topic of the dispensation was raised. A committee of cardinals was appointed to deal with the issue. The basic premise was that a dispensation could be granted only for the good of the Church. Since the rhetoric of the clergy's episcopalian suit rested on a nearly identical premise, it was easy to see how the thinking behind the two issues or suits could start to bleed into each other.[44] It was decided in June 1621 that an episcopal appointment should be made for England and Scotland. It remained only to secure nominations for the post.[45]

In other words, the highly contentious determination of the Stuart regime to press ahead with the Spanish match project suddenly catapulted a section of the English Catholic clergy into a position of formerly undreamed of influence and authority (a section which was roughly coterminous, in

---

[39] TD V, 84–5; Allison, RS, 159–60.

[40] AAW, B 25, no. 55. Ingoli consistently supported, from within his power base of the Congregation for the Propagation of the Faith (established by Gregory XV in 1622), the English Catholic pro-episcopal lobby, Hughes, *RCR*, 341, 342, 363–5, 385, 387, 389, 397, 400, 402–6.

[41] AAW, B 25, no. 58.

[42] AAW, A XVI, no. 180, p. 685. Bouthillier died in January 1625.

[43] Thomas Rant noted, among the jottings he made in late 1623, that 'in Gregory 15 tyme, Milino was in such disgrace, that his breade and wyne (bouck de Court) was taken from him'. And while Millini was 'thus low, and the Jesuits wrought by him, and . . . Bandino ruled all under Gregory 15, this was a fitt tyme for Mr Bennet to labore in', AAW, B 25, no. 102. For Millini's lack of sympathy for the English secular clergy leadership's episcopal ambitions, see *NAGB*, 158; Allison, RS, 159–60.

[44] TD V, 120.

[45] *Ibid.*, 87. For the nomination process, see *ibid.*, 87ff. On 13/23 July the Venetian ambassador in Rome, Ranier Zen, had heard only about the proposal for an appointment, and noted that 'the Jesuits oppose this vigorously, saying that it will not be proper . . . without the king's participation and consent', *CSPV 1621–3*, 376.

its leadership, with the group which looked to peers such as the second Viscount Montague and his kin, particularly the Dormers and the Arundells, for patronage). The proposed marriage enabled clerics such as John Bennett to put the case to the regime that a Catholic bishop, as long as he was one of the anti-Jesuit secular clergymen, would be a source of political support, an authority who, the Stuarts could be sure, would underwrite their Spanish policy. These secular priests would also undertake manfully to prevent any kind of Catholic political activism which threatened the regime. This activism, it was alleged, was most likely to come from the Jesuitical firebrands who, through their plotting and their ambition, had always jeopardised the Catholics' relationship with the State.

Any moves the regime made to grant some kind of tolerance to Catholics would then be represented as the fruit of moderate Catholics' dealings with the crown, and of the essential wisdom of the uniting of English Catholic opinion behind a newly appointed bishop with authority over the whole community. On 30 September/10 October 1622, John Bennett wrote to his brother Edward that he had translated into Latin and communicated to the Roman curia the famous letter of Lord Keeper Williams 'which they were well pleased with'. The letter transmitted to all the relevant authorities the royal command that prosecutions under the anti-recusancy statutes should cease. The secular priests' Catholic adversaries were livid and 'would fain have made the matter doubtful; for they would not that this Court should conceive well of his Majesty; but it availeth not'. These same adversaries had tried to undermine the suit for a bishop, and now they 'fly to his Majesty of England for help, and here give out that his Majesty is offended with the motion'. This gave John Bennett the opportunity to posture as a loyal supporter of the king and his causes. 'There is no means to assure his Majesty' against those Catholics who cavilled at his policy 'but to bring in bishops, whom his Holiness will charge so to govern his people that it be without offence to his Majesty; and, if bishops had governed heretofore, his Majesty had not been troubled with such plots as have been discovered, to the hazard of his Majesty and ignominy of Catholic religion'. Edward Bennett, who attended on Lady Dormer, and had direct access to the Court through Gondomar, was instructed to explain for the benefit of the king how limited the secular clergy's aims actually were. He was ordered

to satisfy his Majesty [that] 1°. We seek but one bishop; 2°. Titular *in partibus infidelium*, not in England, so as there will be no cause of emulation with them at home; 3°. His jurisdiction will not be larger than that of the archpriest; 4°. It will be limited and known; 5°. It will serve to keep our opposites in order; 6°. It will oblige the superior to account of his own and his subjects' actions, and consequently preserve his Majesty and estate from all trouble that way.

Edward Bennett was to 'make means that his Majesty may understand these things' in order that the opponents of such an appointment 'do not prevail'.

Significantly, John Bennett's solicitude for the service of his king was not unconditional. It had a sting in the tail. Indirectly, messages were being sent back to the Court that the king should appropriately reward his Catholic supporters or he would most certainly rue the day that he did not.

> But particularly his Majesty must be informed that, if he should be against ordinary jurisdiction, without which Catholic religion cannot stand, they here [in Rome] presently will take heed thereof; and bring his Holiness into jealousy that his Majesty meaneth not well towards Catholics, and that all is but a shew; and so make him doubtful to proceed in the matter of dispensation,

especially since James suffered 'so many bishops in Ireland . . . without inconvenience'. Edward was instructed to work through his diplomatic contacts to ascertain what James's attitude was to a reinstituted Catholic hierarchy in England: 'you shall do well to press the ambassador [Gondomar] to know whether he thinketh that his Majesty is so averted from bishops that rather than [that] he will admit them . . . he will break peace, marriage and all'.[46]

The Bennetts used their nephew Joseph Haynes to run messages to his acquaintance, Williams, the lord keeper, and to assure him that the secular clergy leadership had no intention of setting up a hierarchy which would rival the establishment one. Haynes's good standing with the ambassadors in London meant that he could also be used to disparage the pro-episcopal lobby's Jesuited enemies.[47]

THE CONSECRATION OF WILLIAM BISHOP AS BISHOP OF CHALCEDON

As we know, the proposed Anglo-Spanish treaty started to fall apart during the second half of 1623. But just as the negotiations began to go sour, the breakthrough came over the question of an episcopal appointment in England. William Bishop, the former representative in Rome of the appellants back in 1598, was the man chosen to receive the episcopal dignity and authority that Rome now decided to confer on an English clergyman.[48] Six people had been recommended by the secular clergy. (Another six names of people basically unacceptable to the secular clergy leadership had also been passed to Rome.)[49] Bishop, however, was the one to whom the plum

---

[46] TD V, cclii–ccliii.   [47] TD V, ccxxxii–ccxxxiii.

[48] The breve of appointment dispatched from Gregory XV to William Bishop is dated 13/23 March 1623, TD IV, cclxxiii.

[49] AAW, A XVI, no. 166, p. 27.

fell.[50] He was consecrated at Paris on 25 May/4 June 1623. On 18/28 July he started his journey for England, and he landed at Dover.[51]

Bishop had never been, as far as we know, an insider in the Montague entourage in quite the same way as some other leading secular priests, though, as we saw in the previous chapter, while Montague awaited his summons in 1611 to take the oath of allegiance, he instructed Bishop to 'goe away for a time' and thus escape the impending descent by the regime's agents on Montague's followers.[52] There had been a tiff between Bishop and Richard Smith in the secular clergy's writers' institute in Paris, the Collège d'Arras, over certain aspects of the college's organisation, particularly over whether Smith's cousin William Rayner was an acceptable man to have on the foundation.[53] But Bishop was, evidently, ideologically on the same wavelength as many other members of the Montague entourage. And although Bishop had been out of the country for some time (since his exile in 1611 in fact), he was soon surrounded by many of the leading men in Montague's circle. William Harewell later recalled that Edward Bennett 'was most about my lord the time he was heere, and cheefest of his counsell', and that 'it pleased my lord also to make use of my service the best part of his time amongst us so that I was no lesse privie to all his proceedinges, from the first to the last, than another'.[54]

We can see why Bishop's appointment was potentially such an important *coup* for those who had sponsored his candidacy. The point was that Bishop represented the usefully disreputable end of the secular clergy spectrum. For while it was tempting for the former appellants to distance themselves as far as possible from the archpriest controversy, in many ways a thoroughly unsavoury episode which had done no one much credit, the fact remained that Bishop was one of the few people left within the pale of acceptability to Rome who was known to have been an uncompromising opponent of the Jesuits, and to be a partisan (even if a tacit one) of the Stuart regime's line on what constituted proper and acceptable political loyalty to the king. Archbishop Abbot had said that Bishop's reasons *against* the oath of allegiance were the best he had ever heard. Bishop had, in fact, got about as close to approving the regime's thinking behind the oath as it was possible for a Catholic to do without being formally censured by Rome.[55] He was one of the few credible candidates for the new episcopal post who would be more or less *persona grata* to the regime.

---

[50] Cardinal Millini had been against the appointment until nearly the end. Even in October 1622 he was still writing around for nominations for another archpriest, *ibid.*, no. 158, p. 611.
[51] Anstr. I, 37.   [52] AAW, A X, no. 126, p. 363; ch. 11, p. 363 above.
[53] *NAGB*, 178, 180, 181, 231.   [54] AAW, B 26, no. 82.   [55] *NAGB*, 111, 149.

A great deal of what we know about Bishop's term of office has to be culled from the encomium penned by Edward Bennett about his master after Bishop's death in April 1624. It was sent to Rome in order to persuade the curia that Bishop had been a great success, had unified the English Catholics and had not offended the State, and that another bishop should be appointed as soon as possible in order to carry on the good work.

Bishop, said Bennett, had shown great vigour and resolve. Returning into his native land, he disembarked at Dover, and 'comming to land, about twelve of the clocke att night, presently went twelve . . . miles a foote', though he was 'a man of threescore and tenn yeares of age', to 'avoyd the danger of spies and serchers'. He was guided to 'the house of a Catholick gentleman', namely Montague's cousin Sir William Roper. Bishop then made straight for London in order 'to prevent the rumor of his coming, and in soe large a citty with greate facility [to] lye hiden if any trouble should arise'. He took up residence with Lady Dormer, Montague's aunt and Bennett's own patroness who was 'most . . . ready to further the encrease of Catholike religion and mayntayne Christs preists'. Bishop immediately summoned the leading secular clergymen around him. Montague had, meanwhile, heard of his arrival, and on 1 August 1623 sent Bishop a letter 'of great curteisy and devotion'.[56] Montague then 'sent . . . a coache with honorable attendance to convey' Bishop 'into the country', i.e. to Cowdray. 'The entreaty was soe earnest, there was noe place left for refusall.'

Whether he felt like declining or not, the visit to Cowdray was the opportunity for a massive demonstration of episcopal power and of the whole ideological programme of this fraction of the English Catholic community. And so, 'taking with him some ecclesiasticall persons of prime note, hee departed the citty and, in some fewe dayes of his aboad' with Montague, 'hee gave the holy sacrament of confirmation to him and some foure hundred besides more or lesse'. Bennett played up the political significance of Bishop's mass confirmation rally. 'We should say something of the alacrity of the faythfull people compassing about or desiring to see their newe pastour soe long sought for.' Bennett says he can hardly find the words to describe the enthusiasm of those who revelled in 'the very hope of seeing a bishop'.[57] Joseph Haynes rejoiced to Thomas Rant, on Christmas Day 1623, that 'you can not ymagine with what joy and welcome he [Bishop] is received by al sortes of welmeaninge good Catholiques. I send you hereinclosed a letter [which] was written unto him by my Lord Mountague at his first comminge. You may make use of it as you see cause.' Montague 'sent for him afterwards to his house where 500 were confirmed with wonderfull joyfull harts

---

[56] The letter was carried to Bishop by a Sussex priest called Thomas Young. See Anstr. I, 391.
[57] AAW, B 26, no. 32; CRS 10, 401–3; AAW, B 25, no. 92; AAW, A XVII, no. 29 (a notarial copy of the same letter).

to have' a Catholic bishop 'amongest them and most certaine it is [that] nothinge doth strenthen and healpe forward Catholique religion here in our country more than to have reverend bishops amongest us which have ever bin in much more esteeme with us than in other parts'.[58]

Here the episcopally conferred sacrament of confirmation was not merely a liturgico-sacramental procedure. It had a heavy intra-Catholic polemical implication as well. The performance of the rite of confirmation was a crucial practical demonstration of one of the main planks of the episcopal party's claims to authority over and against its Catholic critics.[59]

Bishop then rushed back to London to start creating and instituting all the necessary structures of episcopal government. He 'instituted twenty archdea-cons throughe the severall parts of England, adjoyning to every one their rurall deanes and notaries'. Five vicar-generals (four in 1623 and another subsequently) were then appointed out of the pool of archdeacons.[60] The function of these officials was to exercise authority in the bishop's name in a specific area: the five areas were – the North, South, East, West and Midlands.[61] Bishop erected his own episcopal chapter by letters patent of 10 September 1623. The chapter had nineteen canons, one of whom was the dean (John Colleton). Exercising the powers of a cathedral chapter, it would assist in the work of ecclesiastical government. It would, when neces-sary, elect Bishop's successor. After all of which pre-emptive system-building, Bishop dutifully certified what he had done to 'the Sea Apostolike, humbly beseeching our Holy Father's blessing and approbation'.[62]

Bishop's action was, however, highly controversial. He was operating on the assumption that he 'should assume that forme of jurisdiction which was knowne to have been in use in our country according to holy canons before this unhappy schisme', in other words, that he had been granted full ordinary jurisdiction.[63] But many other Catholics, and indeed Rome itself, disagreed.

The papacy in fact never ratified Bishop's actions in this respect.[64] Cardinal Francesco Albizzi, writing thirty years later, summarised the curial position. William Bishop had rashly asserted his 'ordinary' status, 'though he held his powers at the pope's good pleasure and subject to the higher authority of the papal nuncio in France acting as ordinary for England'. The 'cardinals were amazed at the novelty of the proceedings, so opposed to the sacred canons, alien to the custom of the Church, without the slightest precedent in antiquity, and injurious to the prerogatives of the Apostolic See'. Rome

---

[58] AAW, A XVII, no. 59, p. 191.
[59] See M. Questier, 'The Politics of Episcopacy in the Later Jacobean and Early Caroline Catholic Community: The Approbation Controversy in Context' (forthcoming).
[60] CRS 10, 403; TD IV, cclxxiii–cclxxiv.
[61] In 1624 a vicar-general was appointed for the South-West, and in 1625 Richard Smith created a north-eastern vicar-general as well. See AAW, A XIX, nos. 59, 116; Allison, QJ, 140.
[62] CRS 10, 402–3.   [63] *Ibid.*, 403.   [64] Allison, RS, 150–1.

'judged that' it 'ought by no means to give approval to' Bishop's assertion of ordinary jurisdiction and his creation of the chapter.[65]

The secular clergy's representatives in Rome, notably Thomas Rant, made considerable efforts to persuade curial officials and the pope himself that Bishop was proving a great success, and that his appointment was not jeopardising the current Anglo-Spanish negotiations.[66]

But Bishop's appointment and episcopate were open to hostile sniping from a number of critics. John Gee, the famous-for-a-day renegade Catholic of 1624, pointed with sarcastic anti-popish merriment to 'old M. Bishop, sometimes prisoner in the Gatehouse, now perking up and flanting with the vain, aeriall, fantastick bubble of an episcopall title, far-fetcht and yet lightly given'. Bishop had 'rambled up and down Staffordshire, Buckinghamshire and other places, under the name of the bishop of Chalcedon; catching the ignorant, vulgar and devoted Romanists with the pomp of his pontificall attire and that empty name of a bishoprick; whereunto he hath as much right as he hath lands there'. His trumpeting of the special virtue of his episcopal conferral of the sacrament of confirmation was equally ridiculous, thought Gee: 'the confirmation of our children by our English bishops' was quite good enough, 'but, if an Eutopian, Chalcedonian, new-nothing, puffe-paste titulado come with faculties in his budget from Rome, where he was miraculously created ex nihilo, then what gadding, what gazing, what prostration, to receive but one drop of that sacred deaw'.[67] One suspects that a number of Jesuits (who were also targets of Gee's pen) would have smiled wryly at this account of the new bishop, even if they could not openly endorse such sentiments.[68]

The portrait painted of William Bishop immediately after the conferment of his episcopal title shows a man of vigour, sitting proudly, dressed in the apparel of a missionary bishop, surrounded by the emblems of his office, his mitre and crozier. By his elbow there is a pile of substantial printed works, presumably his own, and he casually holds one in his left hand.[69] (See Figure 28.) Though he reigned for less than a year, he was not a lameduck bishop. Even the sarcastic Gee had to admit that he doubted not but

---

[65] *Ibid.*, 163–4.

[66] AAW, B 25, nos. 102, 103. The members of the curia, notably Cardinal Bandini, who accepted the seculars' line about the re-establishment of Catholic episcopacy in England had a real interest in the policy being seen to work, AAW, B 25, no. 103.

[67] T. Harmsen (ed.), *John Gee's Foot out of the Snare (1624)* (Nijmegen, 1992), 122. See also K. Fincham, *Prelate as Pastor* (Oxford, 1990), 123–9.

[68] Even as Bishop arrived in England, the Jesuit general was agreeing with the English Jesuit provincial Richard Blount that Bishop would divide the English Catholic community (as if it was not divided enough already), ARSJ, Anglia MS 1/i, fo. 179r.

[69] The portrait hangs in the upper library in Clergy House at Westminster Cathedral. It was an important propaganda statement about the quality of the secular clergy, whose ranks contained such eminent people, and from whom such a bishop could be safely chosen.

Figure 28.   Portrait of William Bishop, bishop of Chalcedon.

that the Catholics would now just as easily 'presume to the same liberty
heer in England which they have used of late in Ireland', a liberty which
included intruding bishops 'to supplant the Church-government there in
force'.[70] And, as Gee noted, Bishop had indeed been exercising his episcopal
functions, whatever the difficulties thrust in his way. One of those functions
was to bring the sacrament of confirmation to the English people so long
deprived of that channel of grace. In a letter which Bishop sent to Rant he
certified that he had visited some counties to give confirmation to the faithful
and had been very well received everywhere, even by families where the
Jesuits were traditionally in residence. Everyone rejoiced in the restoration
of the episcopal dignity, though a few malign spirits murmured secretly that
it would be the cause of dissension among Catholics. The king evidently
connived, thought Bishop, at his presence in the realm.[71] It was only the
obstructive George Abbot who was anxious to arrest him and to use him as
a pretext for breaking off the Spanish match.[72]

Bishop's conferment of the sacrament of confirmation on thousands of his
admirers and well-wishers was a practical demonstration of the seculars' case
that the clergy's new bishop would be a spiritual man first and foremost and
would not lay claim to any of the jurisdictional functions of the holders of the
country's established sees. But it was also a way of bringing large numbers
of Catholics into direct contact with the new bishop. Indeed, the bestowal
of the sacrament by the new bishop served in some sense to consolidate and
bind together those who participated in this ritual. In addition, we can be
sure, it was a way for the second Viscount Montague (standing at the head of
those waiting to be confirmed by the bishop) and other lay patrons to assert
their centrality within the new clerical structures which William Bishop and
his friends were creating.

In the short and highly polemically charged manuscript encomium which,
we noted, was written by Bishop's chief lieutenant, Edward Bennett, soon
after Bishop's death, it was narrated that, having arrived in July and established himself in London, the year being 'farre spent' already, he was anxious
to dispense as widely as possible the sacrament of confirmation 'before the

[70] Harmsen, *John Gee's Foot out of the Snare (1624)*, 122.
[71] AAW, A XVII, no. 55, p. 181. In 1629 Matthew Kellison insisted that James not only 'did
not oppose' Bishop's 'entrance' into the kingdom but, 'after he knew that he was entred and
was in London, he would not commaund him to be apprehended', Matthew Kellison, *A
Treatise of the Hierarchie and Divers Orders of the Church against the Anarchie of Calvin*
(Douai, 1629), 391.
[72] AAW, A XVII, no. 55, p. 181. Extraordinarily, considering that this letter was dated
5 December 1623, Bishop thought that the match with Spain would still go ahead. He
reported that Prince Charles had been at a banquet given by the duke of Buckingham where
Charles referred to the infanta as 'amata sua', while James was said to have wished that all
the opponents of the match were hanged.

depthe of winter'. Therefore he began his 'pious progresse' and spent 'some two monthes or there aboutes in that holy worke'. He succeeded in giving 'Christes badge and cognisance to two thousand more or lesse', and he was 'received with great joy and concourse of the faythfull people which way soever hee went, as much as the tymes would permitt' before he returned to London 'a little before the beginning of winter'. It was extraordinary, said Bennett, 'with what great ardour of mind not only the vulgar sort of Catholiques, but allso persons of worthe and quality, and many of the prime ranke of nobilitie flocked' to him, 'seeking the holy sacrament of confirmation'. Nor did 'this heate grow cold whilst the [1624] Parliament was raginge, but flamed upp soe much more ardently soe that his lordshipp was forced to withdraw himselfe a little, lest overmuch concourse should happ to stirre upp the magistrate'.

In Bennett's analysis, what might well be represented by others as half-heartedness or even cowardice on William Bishop's part became prudence and restraint. English Catholics could be certain that their bishop would always refrain from unnecessarily provoking the State against them. And although Bishop 'thought fitt to yeild somewhat to the times, yett would hee in noe wise bee wholy wantinge to the desires of pious people, but takinge occasion by turnes repayred even to the poorer sorte, desirous to comfort all of what quality soever, withe the dispensation of Gods word and heavenly grace'. No one should fall into the error of thinking that Bishop kept a low profile while the supposedly more courageous religious orders such as the Jesuits underwent imprisonment and risked openly confronting the Church of England's heretical ministers. In fact, he had received a curt message from 'a principall man of State who feared much the fury of the raging puritanes assembled in parliament and therefore wished him to departe the kingdome for a tyme, appointinge some substitute in his place'. But Bishop replied, employing the rhetoric of the expectant and eager martyr, that this was no way for a Catholic bishop to behave and 'hee feared not the threatts of the parliament'. 'Twice had hee suffered imprisonment for Christs sake', but he was 'now ready to returne thither agayne or, if they pleased to practise upon him some severer decree, hee was willing to indure it'. For 'hee came not into England with resolution to turne his backe upon the first sight of the wolfe but to loose his life for the good of his sheepe'.[73]

It was claimed also that 'some hundreds after his entrance into the kingdome imbraced the Catholike fayth', and many more Catholics were 'forwards' because of the means offered to receive confirmation. This was the crucial proof which was needed to show that the Catholic hierarchalists had been right all along. To restore the faith in England implied, in fact

[73] AAW, B 26, no. 32.

required, a putting back of the ecclesiastical structures which had been lacking ever since the Elizabethan restoration of Protestantism. Here also was a tacit indictment of the strategy of the religious orders, at least as a method for bringing about the 'conversion of England'. Their approach had plainly not worked. Their 'missionary' style neglected the setting up of the permanent institutional forms and procedures which were required to safeguard and foster the flame of the faith.[74]

At the same time, Bishop did his best to make the world believe that he was offering friendship and reconciliation to his Catholic critics. On his arrival, he and his supporters hurried to spread it about that his was a unifying influence which would override the factious divisions which had split the Catholic movement in England.[75] He proclaimed his determination to make a peace with as many of the religious as he could. He wrote to Thomas Rant on 18 December 1623 that 'I am entered into covenant with the Benedictins of the English congregation to hold good correspondence one with another, the Carmelites and Cappucins do promise the like, and the Jesuites a farr of[f] have made some meanes for the same.'[76] Of course, making peace with the Carmelites and the Capuchins was a far different matter from dealing with the often rather irritable English Jesuits. But Bishop was trying to show here that he felt able to make peace with all the religious orders. This itself partially concealed a claim or assertion that those few who still opposed him were selfishly insisting on their rights and privileges. Such opposition was the mere malice and self-aggrandisement of a small minority of the religious.

Bennett recounted that Bishop had 'framed certain canons or rules by which all occasions of contention might bee partly cutt off, partly debated with rule and order', and thus 'might bee quietly ended'. He proposed these canons to the Benedictines first, who accepted them. Then they were broached by one of his vicars-general to the Jesuit provincial Richard Blount who, caught on the hop by the unexpected and highly unwelcome hand of friendship, said that he could not enter into an agreement without first informing the Jesuit general, after which he would assent, though clearly the Jesuits had as little intention of assenting as the seculars had of making a genuine peace (at least with the Jesuits).[77]

---

[74] *Ibid.*
[75] See e.g. AAW, A XVII, no. 38 (a letter of 10 September 1623 from William Bishop to Cardinal Millini certifying that he is well received in England by everyone, as far as he knows).
[76] *Ibid.*, no. 58, p. 189.
[77] AAW, B 26, no. 32. In August 1623 and then again in January 1624 the Jesuit general, Vitelleschi, congratulated Richard Blount for refusing to talk to William Bishop. A subsequent letter, in mid-February 1624, point-blank instructed Blount to tell Bishop, should he demand obedience from the Jesuits, that he had no jurisdiction over regulars, ARSJ, Anglia MS 1/i, fo. 181r, Anglia MS 1/ii, fos. 190v, 191v. In August 1624 the general ticked off Blount for meeting with Edward Bennett in April to discuss this issue, *ibid.*, fo. 202r.

THE 1624 PARLIAMENT, THE FRENCH MATCH AND THE DEATH OF WILLIAM BISHOP

In the wake of the collapse of the projected Spanish alliance, the 1624 parliament was particularly hostile to Catholics and Catholicism. The failure of the match opened the floodgates to waves of anti-popery sermons and tracts. Thomas More, who had briefly returned to London, retailed the news that the speaker Sir Thomas Crew, 'in his oration after his acceptance by his Majestie . . . made a bitter and sharp invective against Catholicks' and wished an exact and severe execution of the penal law against them, with the banishment of all priests and religious. Another MP said that all Catholics should be ejected from the realm. Two bishops in the Lords spoke against the bishop of Chalcedon (who had now gone deep under cover) and also against Matthew Kellison, the president of the English College at Douai, who was known to be temporarily in England on financial business. Kellison's friends told him that it was time for him to go back to Douai.[78] (At the opening of Convocation, on 21 February, Joseph Hall had delivered a strongly anti-Catholic sermon.[79])

The Venetian ambassador Alvise Valaresso recorded that the Monday following parliament's assembly was 'spent in confirming the election of some of the members and in giving to all the oath which excludes the pope's sovereignty'. Valaresso said that 'six Catholic lords' refused to take it and were shut out. Marco Antonio Moresini, the Venetian ambassador in the Netherlands, named four of the excluded peers – Windsor, Morley, Vaux and the second Viscount Montague himself. All four, according to Moresini, 'lean to the Spaniards, from what they say'. However, by 5/15 March, Valaresso

According to William Harewell in January 1625 the canons in question were evidence 'of that eager pursute of peace and friendly correspondence which our cleargie desires to hould with all religious bodies labouring in this harvest; a point so cleere that it needes no other proofs (besides these canons) to overthrowe that prodigious maxime of our adversaries, so frequently buzzed into the eares of superiores, that episcopal authoritie in England will serve but for a firebrand to raise more factions and combustions in this Church than ever were before', AAW, B 47, no. 89. For the articles of the peace made between Bishop and the Benedictines, see ARSJ, Anglia MS 31/i, fo. 423r ('Capita praecipua articulorum inter Reverendum D. Episcopum Calcedonensem, et venerabilem ordinem Sancti Benedicti', signed by William Bishop and three leading Benedictines). See also AAW, A XIX, no. 54 ('Canones ecclesiastici ad pacem et disciplinam inter clerum secularem et monachos Benedictinos conservandas a Reverendissimo in Christo Patre et Domino Gulielmo episcopo Chalcedonensis propositi'), cited and discussed in Hughes, *RCR*, 326–8. For Bishop's peace-making strategy, see Lunn, 'Opposition', 2–3. See also AAW, A XIX, no. 84 (a paper of September 1625, concerning the Jesuits' objections to the articles or canons of discipline and concord between the secular clergy and the Benedictines).

78 AAW, B 26, no. 14. For Crew's speech, which was sharp against Catholics although tactfully discreet about the Spanish match, see R. E. Ruigh, *The Parliament of 1624* (Harvard, 1971), 158–9.

79 T. Cogswell, *The Blessed Revolution* (Cambridge, 1989), 169.

understood that 'the six Catholic peers have re-entered parliament, as they have changed their minds and taken the oath which they previously refused'. Valaresso said that it was 'not known whether the change was due to their consciences' or the result of 'the absolution of their confessors'.[80] This story seems inherently unlikely in Montague's case, and indeed in Vaux's as well. It would have been ludicrous for them, after they had so publicly pinned their colours to the mast of refusal (in the controversy over the oath of allegiance), to have caved in now and to have complied as the Venetian ambassador described.

Considering how high a public profile William Bishop now had, it is slightly surprising that Montague, as a known Catholic patron, and indeed the other lay members of his circle, for example the Dormers, should not have attracted more opprobrium in parliament.[81] He was present in the Lords very briefly – at the start of the session and then on 8 and 9 March, just before a recusancy bill was introduced there. He was there again on 17 March and after that he vanished, although in mid-May the House intervened to protect his parliamentary privileges by punishing those who had arrested one of his servants.[82] The only real contribution which Montague seems to have made to the 1624 session was the private bill introduced to sort out and enforce the dispositions of his property which he had made in the early 1610s.[83] As Conrad Russell comments, 'this act is . . . an interesting example of double thinking about recusancy, for Viscount Montagu was a recusant. The use in which he was protected by this act was precisely one of those uses made by recusants to avoid forfeiture which were prohibited by another bill which passed

---

[80] *CSPV 1623–5*, 232, 247, 242. See also Gardiner, *Narrative*, 277.

[81] Sir Thomas Gerard, son of Montague's recently deceased stepfather, was expelled from the Commons. He had been elected even though he failed to take the necessary oaths and refused to receive the communion. He fled to take refuge with the Spanish ambassador, AAW, A XVII, no. 104, p. 339. For Gerard, see Ruigh, *Parliament of 1624*, 89, 259–60.

[82] *LJ* III, 249, 251, 264, 372, 402. This servant, one Bennett, may have been the family retainer John Bennett who, as we saw, was arrested by William Atkinson back in 1613. See ch. 11, p. 366 above.

[83] The 1624 act which dealt with Montague's property was based on the unsuccessful bill of 1621. The committee which considered it included three of Montague's relatives, namely the earl of Southampton, the earl of Dorset and Lord St John of Basing, and also George Abbot who reported on 17 March 1624 that the bill was 'fit to pass, but with many amendments'. The committee heard the 'allegations' of Sir Francis Englefield, which 'proved but vain', *LJ* III, 266. Abbot had corresponded with Montague, it seems, about the settlement of his estates as far back as 1619. In the autumn of that year Montague had been making plans to visit Abbot, apparently to discuss this business, SHC, LM 6729/10/125. In December 1619 Montague told Sir George More how much he regretted that, owing to a misunderstanding, Abbot had concluded that Montague 'had no confidence in him' and 'did distrust him'. Montague declared that 'I well knowe howe farre I am from distrust of him, and the contynuall evidences of his well wishinge to mee have made mee to contynue . . . more confident of him than is fitt to expresse', SHC, LM 6729/10/132.

both Houses and was vetoed the same Parliament'.[84] Russell is certainly right here, although at this point Montague was not actually a convicted recusant, and therefore was not subject to the forfeitures which struck those who were indicted and condemned under the extant parliamentary legislation against Catholic separatism. But Russell could have made even more of the oddness of this parliamentary schizophrenia (especially considering that George Abbot was a supporter of the bill). Montague was also, after all, one of the sponsors of a potential revolution in English ecclesiastical affairs, a revolution of which many members must have been aware, and which, for many, must have constituted an utter scandal, the deliberate manipulation by a popish aristocratic faction of the regime's current foreign policy problems.

The collapse of the negotiations with the Spaniards undoubtedly looked like, and indeed was viewed by many Protestants as, a kick in the teeth for rampantly optimistic Catholic activists. As John Chamberlain noted with unconcealed joy on 20 December 1623, 'the papists' were 'hanging downe their heads, that were so brag of late'. Lord Kensington had recently departed for France, clearly in order to settle the preliminaries for a match between Prince Charles and the House of Bourbon.[85]

And then there followed another, though not exactly unpredictable, calamity. In April, William Bishop died. John Colleton lamented, in a letter of mid-June 1624 to Pope Urban VIII, how everything had immediately started to fall apart after Bishop's death. With the chapter's authority unconfirmed by Rome, no one could assume interim authority as a vicar capitular (the normal process in a valid episcopal chapter) while they waited for a new bishop to be chosen. Colleton also reminded Cardinal Francesco Barberini (the papal secretary of State) that the Jesuits would strongly oppose a new appointment. The chapter then set about nominating candidates to be put

---

[84] Russell, *Parliaments and English Politics*, 195–6, citing 21 James I, c. 48; PRO, C 89/11/76 (endorsed 18 October 1624). For the passage of the bill, see also *LJ* III, 248, 254. Following an order on 14 May that Sir Francis Englefield should answer for his 'slanderous brief' in chancery against William Arundell and his wife, Englefield was 'called to the bar' on 27 May 'to answer the complaint made to the House touching the scandalous brief of the said Sir Francis Englefieldes bill exhibited to the House of Commons'; and he was 'admonished to attend the earl marshal and the earl of Southampton, to be reconciled unto Mr Arundell', *LJ* III, 413.

The statute provided that the earls of Southampton and Dorset and Baron Petre should hold all the property which had not already been sold towards the performance of the trust; and Lady St John should receive, as well as £1,000 in damages, £600 p.a. out of the profits for her maintenance until her portion with damages was paid, the residue of which it was for the trustees to raise, and there should be allotted 'the sum of £1,000' to 'Frances Browne of her fathers free and voluntary bounty and gifte, above the portion of £2,000' which she had already been granted. The Dormer family was to be discharged of its trusteeship, and Englefield was ordered to 'make a just, true and perfect accompt of the profittes of the land and monyes by him received', PRO, C 89/11/76, mm. 3a–4a.

[85] McClure, *Letters*, II, 535.

forward for Rome's scrutiny. A secret ballot was held and the result was dispatched to Thomas Rant, the new clergy agent in Rome.[86]

There was indeed opposition from those Catholic factions which were uneasy about the process to replace William Bishop. As late as May 1624 we find the English Jesuits trying, through the rector of the English College in Rome, Thomas Fitzherbert, to make representations to the curia about what were alleged to be the ill effects of the appointment of Bishop and the danger to be feared from a successor to him, a successor chosen from within his own party. The writer of an advice paper on the topic claimed that, since there was a continuing and sharp persecution in England at this time, no bishop could properly perform his duties there. To have a bishop who could not function properly would be to 'encourage a spirit of pride and emulation among the clergy'. Some people were saying that more than one bishop was needed, but this would enrage the State and cause more suffering to Catholics. The writer argued that sustaining a bishop would be a further needless financial imposition on the already impoverished laity who were suffering under the crushing weight of recusancy fines. He also urged that if another bishop were appointed he should not be allowed to dictate which priests should reside with which patrons. Nor should the bishop interfere 'in the affairs of those who have other superiors, for this causes great confusion and discord'.[87] Here each side was trying to show that the good of the Church would be best served by their own view of what was both necessary and possible for the government of English Catholics.

It became known that Rome was consulting quite widely on who should replace Bishop. Among those contacted were leading lay Catholics (many of whom tended to side with the regulars). As the process of replacing Bishop was dragged out by seemingly interminable delay, some of the secular clergy were driven into paroxysms of fury by rumours not just that their enemies were being consulted on the choice of the new bishop but even that the new bishop would be a member of one of the religious orders. All the conspiracy-theory traumas of the appellant controversy were revived. William Harewell wrote in fury to Rant on 24 April/4 May 1624 that the thing 'which hath at this present [time] given me most occasion to putt pen to paper is a letter which a Catholique of speciall note and qualitie in this land is certainly reported to have writt unto his Holines uppon the death' of Bishop. This Catholic informed the pope 'that it were expedient for our

[86] Allison, RS, 152–3.

[87] *Ibid.*, 156–7. The tension in Rome between these representatives of rival parties was overt. Thomas Rant recorded that Thomas Fitzherbert had told John Bennett, the clergy agent, that 'hee woulde gett him putt out of Rome'; Bennett retorted, 'yow are a cokscombe', AAW, B 25, no. 102.

countrie to have religious men to [be] our bishops, and thereuppon makes humble suite to his Holiness so to appoint it'.[88]

But it was not just the awful prospect of the appointment of one of the hostile religious, or of one of their stooges, which most concerned Harewell. The real problem, he alleged, was the basic structural defect in the Church caused by the laity's (or at least a certain section of the laity's) patronage and their consequent authority over their priests. The power of such people over all the clergy was so vast precisely because they made common cause with and operated through members of the religious orders. Harewell asked,

if way should be given to such motions, and conceipts of particular persons and those lay people too, what effect will it produce, but that shortely we shall have the Church governed not by ecclesiasticall prelates or clergie men but by the laytie? Withall as one moves for one religious order, so will another move and sue for another order, and a third person for a third order etc., and the [secular] clergie, which is the maine pillar and the very bodie of Gods Church, shall be cast aside as a needelesse part of the house of God.

The election of 'ecclesiasticall prelates' should proceed canonically, not through 'lay mens privat plottes and projects'. And, he said,

that you may the better understand whither these particular affections of lay people tend, there is a knight, whome I knowe well, who out of a certaine disgust he tooke unto my lord bishop deceased, because he would not at his sute and instance make the priest that lived with him (a yong man, and no waies fitt for that dignitie) an archdeacon in his Lucianical spiritt (for I cannot in conscience stile it otherwise), spoke both dishonorably of my lord before his death and, since, gives out very bouldely and peremptoriely there shall be no more bishops heere.[89]

Meanwhile Harewell stressed that William Bishop's incumbency had been a rip-roaring success. The majority of the English Catholics wanted more of the same. 'What flocking there was to the bishop and what inquirie after him by all sortes of Catholiques for the benefitt of the sacrament and for composing of controversies betwixt partie and partie, whilst he was amongst us, is almost incredible.' Even as he lay dying 'there were divers of good qualitie come up to London from severall partes thereabout', expressly in order to be confirmed by him. So extraordinary had the charismatic Bishop been that more than one bishop would now be needed to fill the void.[90]

At the end of October 1624, George Fisher wrote a long exhortatory letter to Thomas More in the Holy City, a letter which was clearly intended for translation and for waving under the noses of the relevant curial officials as they consulted about making the new episcopal appointment. Fisher said that he was distressed that 'our body should be so neglected and that the

[88] AAW, B 26, no. 50.   [89] *Ibid.*   [90] *Ibid.*

suggestions of our adversaries should have more credit than our informations'. It was a common theme among the leading seculars that the regulars
were wholly at the direction of their lay patrons, patrons who also interfered
in the appointment of ecclesiastical officials. In Fisher's 'simple judgement',
'you should doe well . . . to speake plainly to his Holines and to let him
understand how distastfully it is taken of the clergy here that they may not
freely make choice of ther owne head'. The pope should be urged to consider
'what a confusion' this would cause 'in the Church if other countries should
be at the directions of religious men and should have no other superiors but
such as they apoint. What is this but to subvert the goverment apointed by
Christ and to submit the clergy to the religious to the utter subversion of that
monarchicall regimen wich Christ instituted?' It would be a good thing 'to
let his Holines understand what a shame it is to give credit to on[e] or tow
lay men or tow or three externe priests against the whole clergy. What is this
but to obscure and disgrace the clergy and to subject them to the censure
of lay men and to governe them at ther pleasure who know not well how
to governe themselves.' The normally taciturn Fisher declared that he was
'allmost angry' to 'thinke that the [Roman] Court should be carried away
with such informations'.[91]

THE PRIESTS AND THE DIPLOMATS

The second Viscount Montague's secular clergy chaplains, who were mostly
Francophiles, had nevertheless thoroughly approved of the Spanish match.
As we have observed, Montague's family and its clergy clients were on good
terms with Gondomar. The French frequently voiced their suspicions of the
English Catholics and accused them of being Hispanomaniacs, as Anthony
Champney noted with fury in January 1625.[92] But the English Catholic community's attitudes were more complex than this. Even those who might more
often than not look to the Spaniards for assistance could be persuaded, under
the right circumstances, to switch their allegiances to the representatives of
the Bourbon dynasty.

When the whole bruising episcopal selection process started again, in order
to replace William Bishop, it was conducted with an eye to how the new
appointee would respond to the forthcoming dynastic treaty with France.
Among those who were lobbied for support by Viscount Montague's friends
were the French allies and patrons of the secular clergy. As the project for
a French dynastic alliance proceeded, it was likely that the French would

[91] AAW, B 47, no. 156.
[92] *Ibid.*, no. 45. This was also the view of the Venetian ambassador Girolamo Lando in
September 1622, *CSPV 1621–3*, 446.

enlist sympathetic strands of English Catholicism as a source of support for the treaty. Because of the time lag between, on the one hand, the regime's final acceptance that James's preferred option of a Spanish bride for Prince Charles and a negotiated settlement over the Palatinate were both as good as dead and, on the other, the hammering out of the details of Charles's and Buckingham's new preferred option (of a French match and a war against the Habsburgs), the secular clergy leaders were left just enough time to move laterally, crab-like, from attendance and dependence on the Spaniards to reliance on the French.

In return for the English Catholics' application of a certain amount of oil to the wheels of diplomacy in Rome, it was expected that the French would interfere to push forward the cause of Catholic toleration and to achieve at least the same concessions that the Spaniards had sought. As Thomas Roper wrote in November 1624, when the French diplomats were known to be griping that English Catholics were too pro-Spanish, 'if we might from France receave the like ease we did from Spayne we should as soone be Frenche as Spaniardes'.[93] After the proposed Spanish match was finally dashed, the Spanish ambassador Carlos Coloma lamented that now his chapel was deserted. All the English Catholics were with the French. It was, complained Coloma, reckoned to be a crime to go anywhere near the Spanish embassy (at Exeter House).[94]

On 13/23 July 1624 Richard Smith had optimistically written to Thomas Rant in Rome that, concerning 'the mach with France', James had 'agreed to all the articles which the French proposed. The summe for Catholikes is that they shal not be persecuted for practise of their religion in privat.' But 'more the duke [of Buckingham] wold not agree unto lest he shold offend the puritans of whome he hath made him self head. But, if the Catholikes carie them selves moderatly, more in time wilbe granted.'[95] On 4/14 August, Matthew Kellison noted that he had heard from Champney in Paris that the French match was concluded and that Pierre de Bérulle had gone to Rome to seek the dispensation. Bérulle arrived there in late September.[96]

It was time for the Catholic clergy to bring some pressure to bear on their new friends, the French diplomats in London. On 21 August, the Arundell family's chaplain John Jackson made his entrance at the French embassy to see the ambassador, the marquis d'Effiat. Jackson explained to him that

---

[93] AAW, B 27, no. 58.
[94] CRS 68, 168; Cogswell, *Blessed Revolution*, 127.   [95] AAW, B 26, no. 90.
[96] *Ibid.*, no. 100; R. E. Schreiber, *The First Carlisle* (Philadelphia, 1984), 81–2. Pierre de Bérulle was the head of the Oratory, in which institution Thomas Rant was one of the six English members. For Bérulle's theology and ecclesiastical thought, see P. A. Klevgard, 'Society and Politics in Counter-Reformation France: A Study of Bérulle, Vincent de Paul, Olier and Bossuet' (Ph.D., Northwestern, 1971), ch. 2.

he was 'comme in the behalfe of the dean and cleargy 1. to present our respects' and '2. to signifie the causes why he heard not of us sooner'. Having recited the secular clergy's rather weak and pathetic excuses for not resorting to him sooner, Jackson 'desired that he wold take the cleargy also into his favour and protection and if we cold serve him in any thing he shold finde us ready'. To this Effiat 'curteously replyed', though, unfortunately, he seemed completely oblivious of the existence of the episcopal chapter instituted by William Bishop. Jackson said he knew that Bérulle 'was sent from the king of France' to Rome to get the necessary papal dispensation. If Effiat thought it helpful, Jackson would arrange for the secular clergy's agent in Rome to be ordered 'to concurr with him therin'. Effiat 'seemed to take the offer in extraordinarie kinde maner and promised me severall tymes he wold write to his maister of it and of us and that now he did see we were not Spaniards'.[97]

Jackson took the opportunity to mention how the Spanish ambassador Coloma had, in a moment of panic and misled by the Jesuits, temporarily fouled up the seculars' suit for an episcopal appointment in 1623. (Coloma had believed that such an appointment would stymie the negotiations for the Anglo-Spanish treaty and so dashed off a letter to Rome to try to frustrate Bishop's elevation.) Jackson added how grateful the seculars had been that 'the king of France his lettres came about the same tyme commaunding his imbassador at Rome to deall with his Holiness effectually about bishops which did us a great pleasure and we desired his Majestie shold know our thankfulnes'.

Once again it was somewhat distressing that the slightly *distrait* Effiat did not really seem to know what Jackson was talking about. But still the Frenchman 'gave willing ear to all and promised much kindness and caused a writing to be shewed unto me concerning the good of Catholics which he purposed to procure the king to subscribe to being the next day to goe towards Woodstock to meet him'.[98] Jackson said also that when Effiat came back from Woodstock he would 'labor that . . . others may also goe unto him'. It looked as if the French willingness to play the 'toleration' card would have some effect. Someone had told Jackson that 'when it was perceaved that France stood upon condicions for Catholics' James angrily turned to Prince Charles and exclaimed 'yow see to what pass yow have brought this business'.[99]

The pro-episcopal lobby was not, however, the only Catholic pressure group with which Effiat had conversed. For the Jesuits, particularly the Jesuit provincial Richard Blount, had been with him. Patrick Anderson SJ was actually resident in the French embassy, and had acted as Effiat's chaplain

[97] AAW, B 26, no. 109.   [98] *Ibid.*   [99] *Ibid.*; Schreiber, *The First Carlisle*, 63.

when Effiat had attended James on progress.[100] It was difficult not to suspect that Blount's overtures to the French were connected with the known project of the Jesuits to secure that one of their number, or at least one of their friends, should be invested with episcopal authority in England.

RICHARD SMITH SUCCEEDS WILLIAM BISHOP

The complex story of the nomination of Richard Smith, formerly the second Viscount Montague's domestic chaplain, and since *c.* 1613 a follower of Richelieu, has already been told in definitive detail by Antony Allison.[101] The crucial point to make here is that the selection of Smith, who showed himself even more aggressive in his determination to change the prevailing structure and ethos of large sections of the English Catholic community than his predecessor William Bishop had been, came not just at the recommendation but at the very insistence of the French as part of the diplomacy over the match. (Smith, it was reckoned, would deliver English Catholic support for the treaty.) Despite the distinctly rocky patches in his relationship with the second viscount (who, as we shall see in the next chapter, did in the end support him vigorously against his Catholic enemies during the later 1620s), Smith had always been greatly respected by the clergy in the entourage around Montague. Admittedly, the new supremo over the English clerical establishment was in many ways quite unsuitable for the task. Smith's capacity for bearing grievances was almost legendary. He would not, it seems, even have been the definite first choice of the other leading secular clergymen if the matter had been left entirely to them.[102] But the combination of English Catholic lay patronage and the French regime's support created an unstoppable momentum which resulted in his election.

Moreover, the deal made with Smith meant that this particular clerical faction had, at one stroke, catapulted itself on to the threshold of hitherto

---

[100] For Anderson, see W. Forbes-Leith, *Narratives of Scottish Catholics under Mary Stuart and James VI* (1889), 291, 317–47.

[101] Allison, RS.

[102] Antony Allison has shown that Smith was not the preferred candidate of the English secular clergy. The French intervened virtually to force his election as part of their diplomatic strategy to secure the marriage between Charles and Henrietta Maria. In a list of reasons drawn up by Rant for Smith's appointment over the heads of the others who had been recommended, it was argued that he was less aged, more vigorous, better known in England, better acquainted with the Court of Rome and, finally, the king of France demanded him, AAW, A XVIII, no. 57, p. 345. In the end Urban VIII appointed the French Cardinal La Valette to oversee the process in the Inquisition. This ensured that Smith would be appointed. Some of the secular clergy were less than happy that the appointment process had effectively been hijacked by the French, for their credit would suffer 'with the princes of the contrarie faction', Allison, RS, 182–7. As Allison shows, someone put up, at Rome, an 'alternative list of candidates' to the one sent by the members of the deceased William Bishop's episcopal chapter, Allison, RS, 158–9.

undreamed-of power and influence both at the royal Court in London and at the papal Court in Rome. Smith was ideally placed (because of his friendship with Richelieu) to exploit both the French need for English Catholic friends and the French willingness to interfere at Rome on the pro-episcopal lobby's behalf. On 23 May/2 June 1624 Smith wrote to Rant in Rome that he had approached Richelieu about the appointment of another bishop as well as 'to obtaine as good conditions for Catholiks' as the Spaniards had obtained. Richelieu told Smith that 'he had before my coming procured that his king had written to his embassadour in Rome for to deale earnestly with his Holines for to give us an other bishop; and that he wold doe what he cold for the other [matter]'.[103] One of the key qualifications for a new authority-figure within the Catholic community would be the capacity to deliver a *modus vivendi* with the State. And Smith had good hopes of doing this. On 13/23 July, Smith reported that King James 'hath agreed to all the articles which the French proposed. The summe for Catholikes is that they shal not be persecuted for practise of their religion in privat.'[104]

The pro-episcopal lobby was aware that, whichever one of their number was elected, he would inevitably meet opposition. Smith insisted even in early June 1624 that 'the Jesuites' had 'dealt with' the Spanish ambassador, the marquis de Inojosa, 'for to oppose against bishops'. If Inojosa had cooperated with the Jesuits, then Rant must 'certifie his Holines' that Inojosa was 'no freind to the [secular] clergie, and that he . . . shamfully reviled our good bishop when he first came to visite him'. The pope should be urged 'rather [to] give eare to the other embassadors'.[105] At the end of July, Edward Bennett wrote to Rome that 'it is heer reported' that the rector of the English College in Rome, Thomas Fitzherbert, 'opposeth hym self to bushops, and that he giveth owt' that 'my lord of Chalcedon' favoured the oath of allegiance.[106] In the first week of August, John Jackson noted that the Jesuits' friends were saying that there would not be another bishop. For 'some give out in France that if' William Bishop 'had lived there wold have been a schisme in Ingland'.[107]

Part of the whispering campaign against the renewed bid for authority by the pro-episcopal lobby rehearsed quasi-puritan critiques of the worldly aspects of episcopal status and display. Some people had been putting it about that the pro-episcopal lobby's prelatical pretensions would force English Catholics to shell out in order to allow the new bishop to live in episcopal clover. The rumour had spread that 'the laitie would have no bishop because of the charge of mainetayning him', and that Smith 'ment to taxe all the Catholics of this kingdom for that purpose', a most 'tedious' and 'ungratfull'

[103] AAW, B 26, no. 64.   [104] *Ibid.*, no. 90.
[105] *Ibid.*, no. 64.   [106] *Ibid.*, no. 94.   [107] *Ibid.*, no. 98.

burden. But this was an 'imposture of our adversaries', a 'calumnie' designed to make Smith 'odious'. In retaliation, William Harewell testified in October 1624 that he had been witness to Smith's predecessor's almost parsimonious personal habits 'during his pastorall charge heere'. William Bishop had never 'urged any to the least contribution'. But

finding divers gentlemen of worth readie of their owne accord to allow somewhat yeerely by way of contribution towards his mainetenance, and the defraying of those common charges whereunto his office was subject, he kindely thanked them and gave them to understand he would not refuse any charitie or benevolence which should come freely from any man of abilitie. But to oblige any one thereunto he would not, howsoever de jure he might.

However, the Jesuit Francis Walsingham told Harewell that 'he doubted not but there might be collected 1000^li a yeere through the realme for my lords mainetenance which (he sayed) he thought would be a competent meanes'. Harewell had retorted 'yes', but

if the charitie of the gentrie should extend it selfe so far as to make it more, though it were 10000^li, he knew how to employ it to Gods honor and glorie. For his owne person, a litle would suffice (insomuch that I have heard my lord say for himselfe he would not be a penny charge (for mainetenance) to any, God having sufficiently provided him of his owne for that).

But the bishop would necessarily have 'his agents abroad in severall places', and 'officers and others about him'. He would also have 'extraordinarie occasions of employing men from place to place'. 'Poore priestes, and many distressed Catholicks . . . would expect reliefe from him.' There were also the 'seminaries abroad' to be provided for. And it was 'his office to see none in want'. Walsingham then took it upon himself to breeze it about that Harewell had said that 'a bishop would not heere be mainetained under 10000^li a yeere', which, said Harewell, was 'both slanderous and scandalous'.[108] The same rumours were spread about in Rome by Thomas Fitzherbert.[109]

Here we see a recycling of instantly recognisable contemporary arguments about the connection between patronal funds and the clerical estate. These arguments had bulked large in the appellant dispute, and were not dissimilar to those aired in the Elizabethan presbyterian controversies, especially in the Marprelate tracts and the conformists' counterblasts.[110] In the appellant polemics, the Jesuits were accused of siphoning funds out of the

---

[108] AAW, B 27, no. 9. This issue of the financial maintenance of a Catholic bishop in England was raised by Rudesind Barlow's *Epistola R. Adm. P. Praesidis Generalis et Regiminis totius Congregationis Angliae Ord. S. Benedicti ad RR. Provinciales et ad Definitores eiusdem Congregationis in Apostolica Missione laborantes* (known as Barlow's *Mandatum*), (question 8). See AA, 291.

[109] Allison, RS, 157.

[110] See P. Lake with M. Questier, *The Antichrist's Lewd Hat* (2002), section IV.

country for their own use. They parasitically drained away, so it was said, the money which would otherwise have been available to sustain Catholicism in England. Harewell said that 'I have for certaine heard that the Jesuites have from hence made over 10000[li] in one yeere to theirs in the Low Countries.' And, fumed Harewell, if anyone wanted proof of 'what large gubbs they have carried away', it was necessary only to look at 'their stately buildinges and foundations in Flanders and Liege, and the decayed estates of many gentlemen with whome they have lived heere'.[111]

The campaign to discredit Smith had been in full swing for some time before he arrived in England. His past was being dredged up, in particular the claim that had formerly been made by Persons and Fitzherbert that he was wobbly on the issue of the papal deposing power.[112] It was also said that he had, in effect, denied that a member of the religious orders could be invested with ordinary jurisdiction by the pope. Richelieu had commiserated with Smith because Smith's opponents made him out to be 'an heretik'.[113]

Smith and his friends, however, were calculating that the complex inter-play of political forces at work in the Anglo-French treaty negotiations would decisively benefit them and their cause in the end. On 2/12 September 1624, Smith reported to More that on the vigil of Our Lady's Nativity the match with France was concluded. It was signed by both parties with good conditions for Catholics 'and in some pointes better than thos of Spayne'. Therefore, urged Smith, More should join earnestly with the founder of the Oratory, Pierre de Bérulle, who was at this point in Rome, and should strive to secure the necessary papal dispensation. This was the diplomatic support from the English Catholic community which Richelieu's friendship with Smith was supposed to deliver, though it could be delivered only if it appeared that the French were going to make real efforts to secure some prac-tical form of toleration for Catholics in England. Smith guaranteed More that Richelieu had commended the suit for a bishop to Bérulle and to the nuncio in Paris. The pay-off for Smith and his friends would be that the renewed episcopal jurisdiction would be conferred on them, not on one of their 'opposites'.[114]

In the end, French backing for Smith's candidacy did prove conclusive. On 2/12 January 1625 Smith was consecrated by the Paris nuncio Bernardino Spada, with Richelieu and the bishop of Bayonne present to assist him. By virtue of a papal breve issued to Smith on 4 January, he succeeded William Bishop as bishop over the clergy and laity of England and Scotland. (The terms of this breve, which he received in early March, nevertheless infuriated him. He had not been created an ordinary. Instead his powers were held

---

[111] AAW, B 27, no. 9.   [112] See ch. 11, pp. 350–1 above.
[113] AAW, B 27, no. 40.   [114] AAW, B 26, no. 122.

during the pope's pleasure and were subordinate to the authority of the papal nuncio in Paris, just as Bishop's had been.[115] Here was the stuff of future controversy.)

Now, however, the real concern was to get the new bishop into England before the arrival of Charles's bride, Henrietta Maria, and to start infiltrating the bishop's friends into the Court where they could cluster loyally and optimistically around her. For, Smith's supporters feared, once the treaty was concluded, it would be all too easy for both the Bourbon and Stuart regimes to forget their promises to the Catholics. Smith's partisans also shuddered at the prospect that clergy from other entourages and factions who were out of sympathy with the new bishop would themselves start to take up positions of influence within the Court. On 25 November/5 December, Smith relayed the news to his friend More (who was still in Rome, but now had not long to live) that a good bishop would become almoner to Henrietta Maria, and 'divers English preists' might be 'her chaplens, amongst whome I have named you if you please to accept of it when you returne'. This was necessary in order to beat off the competition, for the Jesuits 'give out that they shal have the place of the confessor, but that is not certaine' and, thank God, 'some report that our English embassador says they shall pass over their bellies before that be'.[116]

In the diplomatic to-ing and fro-ing here, one can see how the second Viscount Montague's family and entourage were involved in underwriting the leading secular priests' attempts to exploit as far as possible the opportunities presented by the Anglo-French treaty, even while Montague himself appeared to stay largely in the background. During the negotiations Smith kept in contact with his English friends via Montague's servants and kin. The information which they could send to him was crucial for Smith if he was to interfere effectively in the diplomatic process. He needed to know how far to badger Richelieu and the French negotiators for the match about conditions for English Catholics. He also needed proof that the French were intervening effectively on behalf of English Catholic recusants if he wanted credibly to represent his faction as able to deliver toleration to the Catholic community. On 16/26 September 1624 he had informed More that as soon as King James agreed the articles for the treaty, the secretary of State, Henri-Auguste de Loménie, seigneur de Villeauxclercs, would 'goe into England to take his oathe'. One of the Cape family, who served Montague,

[115] AAW, B 47, nos. 12, 13, 21; Allison, RS, 189–90; Allison, QJ, *passim*. For the papal breve appointing Smith, see AAW, A XVII, no. 18.
[116] AAW, B 27, no. 70. The Jesuit general, Vitelleschi, in August 1625 noted John Percy's and other Jesuits' hopes that they might be able to influence the composition of the queen's entourage, ARSJ, Anglia MS 1/ii, fo. 222v.

writeth to me from London of the 24 of their August that the persecution for enditing, presenting, convictions and informing was never worse and yet our king had promised the French embassador that there should be no more persecution after the 5 of their August. Yet Catholiks goe to the embassadours chappells as befor and I heare not of anie searches of houses.[117]

On 14/24 October Smith reported that more encouraging news had come to him from England 'very lately' via 'Mr Warner, governor to my Lord Peters sonnes'. Warner

assureth me that the French embassador befor his comming had obtained a letter of the king to the chancelour of the exchequer to cease al writts against Catholiks and that the chancelor had sent writtes into al shires for to stay the persecution of goodes, and that the embassador had procured the goodes of 60 or 80 Catholiks to be restored to them.

Since the ambassador's arrival, 'we have certaine newes that the parlament is proroged till the 2 of February'. This was very welcome since 'a litle befor, Catholiks had bene much trobled as we understood by letters and perhaps yet are in the north partes more remote from London'.[118]

Smith, in other words, needed to evince an irrepressible optimism in order to demonstrate to the community that the secular clergy leadership's strategy was working. But in order to extract the best possible terms from both regimes he needed to be able to show that, where 'persecution' persisted, it was both cruel and unacceptable. For this purpose Smith solicited stories from, among others, his own circle of friends and relations in the Midlands that leading anti-popish JPs were still harassing Catholics. (For example, Smith received a copy of a circular order, dated 15 September 1624, for the delation of the names of recusants, by parish churchwardens, to 'the next generall sessions of the peace to be holden at Spittle' in Lincolnshire.[119])

But it was also crucial to point to and play up to best effect whatever signs of tolerance could be attributed directly to the regime in London. For otherwise the risk was that Smith and his faction would be seen to have failed. (Undoubtedly that was exactly the impression which the Jesuits' reports and stories of 'persecution' tried to create at this time.) It was vital for Smith and his supporters to show that the French match would benefit the English Catholic community.

---

[117] AAW, B 26, no. 142.

[118] AAW, B 27, no. 29. Robert Petre had recently married Montague's daughter Mary.

[119] AAW, A XVIII, no. 58, p. 347 (a document sent to Smith in a letter of 19 October by an unnamed individual who described himself as one 'who married your cousin Fayth', *ibid.*, no. 75, p. 395). See also AAW, A XIX, no. 4 ('Complaintes of extremities and wronges done unto the Catholickes in the parishe of Botsworthe in the county of Lincolne by the churche wardens of the sayed parishe by vertue of Sir Nicholas Sanderson his warrantes by worde and writinge').

The delay of Smith's arrival in England was caused by the French, not the English, regime. The French did not want his appearance in England to disrupt the finalisation of the treaty. Richelieu refused to give him leave to travel until it was all sewn up. As Smith complained in Paris on 3/13 March 1625, 'I wold gladly be gone hence, but my cardinal doth not yet find it fit, and the nonce seemeth not foreward becaus, as he saieth, he hath not yet anie instructions for me, so that I think it wilbe Easter befor I departe hence.'[120] His faculties had come, he told More twelve days later, in 'the last poste but one, and I wold gladly be gone hence', but, said a clearly unconvinced Smith, 'my cardinal wisheth me to stay yet a litle, and I doubt not but it is both for my owne and the common good, though he tell me not wherin'.[121]

In May 1625, however, Smith was able airily to record that he had arrived 'safely' in 'England . . . and found matters in good termes for Catholiks'. Clearly he wanted to link directly his own arrival with a lifting of the law's penalties against recusant nonconformity and the appearance, at least, of a true and durable toleration. 'Monsieur de Fiat, soone after my coming, obtained of the king letters to the treasurer, chancelor and archbishops for to surcease al persecution of Catholiks and to set at libertie al prisoners.' There were orders dispatched to 'restore al moneys taken since Trinitie terme last'. Assurances were given to the French that all promises on religious liberty would be honoured. It was only because, 'as yet, the warrants are not published' that 'yesterday some Catholiks were arrested for the 20^l a moneth and some others cited to appeare before' the high commission, 'but this I hope wil not continew'.[122]

In fact, on 1 May, the new king, Charles, had notified Lord Keeper Williams that, 'in contemplation of his marriage', Williams should 'give warrant and direction to all judges and other officers to forbear all manner of proceedings against his Majesty's Roman Catholic subjects'.[123] Almost immediately pardons started to go out to specific recusants and priests.[124]

Naturally, this did not stop individual officers enforcing what they, correctly, believed the law still to be. Sir John Hippisley wrote from Dover on 8 June that he had arrested and locked up seven people who had landed at the port and refused to take the oath of allegiance.[125] All through the summer, recusancy prosecutions would go on. These arraignments would bite the Catholic great and good as well as the more ordinary recusant nonconformists. For example, at the summer assizes in Kent, the earl of Clanrickard was indicted, though Charles immediately ordered this

---

[120] AAW, B 47, no. 15.   [121] *Ibid.*, no. 17.   [122] *Ibid.*, no. 20.
[123] CSPD 1625–6, 16.   [124] *Ibid.*, 19.   [125] *Ibid.*, 40.

particular prosecution to cease.[126] A great deal was going to depend on what happened when parliament was finally recalled.[127]

It was soon clear that parliament would militate against any general relaxation of penalties for recusancy. In the House of Lords on 4 July, George Carleton, bishop of Chichester, reminded peers that in his diocese 'there was a bishop of the Roman Church', the recently arrived Smith, who 'did acte the partes of a bishop in a noblemans howse', i.e. Viscount Montague's household, 'and I thought it my duty to enfourme the howse'. The Commons' petition against recusants was then read. And measures were considered for restricting the Catholic impact that Henrietta Maria would have.[128]

So Smith's much-vaunted optimism was less a prediction of what, in some objective sense, would or even might happen. Rather it was a gloss on how the jumble of stories about the conditions enjoyed or suffered by Catholics in England should be interpreted. The law against Catholic separation was, of course, never enforced uniformly at all times in all places. Just as the implementation of the anti-Catholic statutes varied in its efficiency from locality to locality, so it was unlikely that any single government attempt to rein in the execution of the recusancy statutes would completely hinder their enforcement, even if the regime intended such a thing to happen (which, in any case, it did not). What was really going to count, as far as Catholics were concerned, was how the reports and stories of tolerance or mistreatment of Catholics would be received and interpreted by a number of different audiences and interest groups, Catholic and Protestant, foreign and English.

In fact, there was quite a lot of evidence around that after the temporary tolerations of 1622, 1623 and 1624, things were getting back to normal or, actually, rather worse than normal. For example, in March 1625 at the Southwark assizes, in what had once been Montague's backyard, a crackdown was launched against Surrey recusants. Though we do not have the records of ecclesiastical court proceedings for this period for the relevant archdeaconry, the assizes' proceedings against recusant nonconformists here had been notable for their rarity. Only a handful of recusants had been prosecuted in this area during James's reign (and relatively few in Surrey as

---

[126] *Ibid.*, 62, 63; J. S. Cockburn (ed.), *Calendar of Assize Records: Kent Indictments: James I* (1980), no. 993.

[127] AAW, B 47, no. 131.

[128] Relf, *Notes of the Debates in the House of Lords . . . 1621, 1625, 1628*, 58. Montague was absent from the whole of the 1625 session of parliament except the opening day (18 June), *LJ* III, 435; M. Jansson and W. B. Bidwell (eds.), *Proceedings in Parliament 1625* (New Haven, 1987), 45. Other Catholics with leave of absence included Baron Arundell of Wardour, the earls of Rutland, Bristol and Shrewsbury, the marquis of Winchester, Baron Petre and Lord St John of Basing, *CSPD 1625–6*, 537, 540–2; Jansson and Bidwell, *Proceedings in Parliament 1625*, 45, 47.

a whole). Now eighty-one Surrey recusants were arraigned for a notional period of recusancy of three months between 1 August and 1 November 1624. Twenty-five were from the three Southwark parishes of St George (nine), Montague's former haunt of St Saviour (nine) and St Olave (seven).[129] Back in Montague's home county of Sussex, large numbers of recusants were indicted and convicted, both for being separatists and for harbouring others who refused to conform.[130]

RICHARD SMITH ENTERS UPON HIS DOMAIN

Even as Smith made his journey across the Channel, however, things seemed to presage the future tempest which he would provoke in England as he began to insist on his episcopal authority and dignity. On 4/14 May 1625 Anthony Champney reported to Rome that 'my lord is at last gone for Ingland. God speed him well.' Nevertheless, since his departure, rumours had reached the ears of Effiat that Smith had 'done him verie ill offices in Paris'. Effiat was now 'highly displeased with him'. 'These be the good offices of some back freinds', stormed Champney, 'which I doubt not will light upon their owne heades'.[131] In May, Thomas Rant, on the verge of leaving Rome, noted 'a secret mutteringe theere is amonge our good freinds that the bishop of Chalcedon is symoniack with the cardinal that made him, since to attaine that dignetye hee was faine to surrender a pension of 200 crownes per annum which the cardinal payde him'.[132]

Perhaps partly in response to these slights on his character and honesty, Smith tried to assert visibly as much of his episcopal dignity as he could. He took an almost childish delight in his new episcopal apparel. Towards the end of his letter to More of 3/13 March 1625 he noted, 'after I had written thus far, I receaved my episcopal ornaments, which I had caused to be made, which cost me above 80[li] sterling'.[133] He had genuine pretensions to grandeur. On 15/25 March he remarked, clearly with pleasure, that in the last letter which More had penned to him, 'you wrote to me as archbishop of Chalcedon and so did some to my predecessor, and indeed Chalcedon was made a metropolitan see by the general counsel held there, and it were for the honor of our clergie and countrie that I were such'. But, wrote Smith, emerging at last from his reverie, 'in my bul I am named . . . [only a] bishop'.[134]

Eight days after Smith arrived in England, he formally asserted his rights over his province. On 6 May the ceremony of the publication of his breves

[129] Cockburn, *Surrey Assizes: James I*, no. 1749. In St Mary Magdalen, Bermondsey, to the East, and in Lambeth to the West, there were four apiece.
[130] Cockburn, *Sussex Assizes: James I*, nos. 802–9.   [131] AAW, B 47, no. 52.
[132] AAW, A XIX, no. 32, p. 105.   [133] AAW, B 47, no. 15.   [134] *Ibid.*, no. 17.

was held in the Buckinghamshire residence of Lord Dormer. In front of two clergymen who were notaries apostolic, he produced the two documents which attested his status (a letter from the Paris nuncio, concerning his consecration, and the papal breve of 25 December 1624/4 January 1625 which granted his faculties). Central members of William Bishop's episcopal regime and of the wider Montague clerical entourage were in attendance, notably Edward Bennett and John Jackson.[135] (A 'Relazione' of the state of religion which the Italian priest Gregorio Panzani compiled in the mid-1630s, in collaboration with the secular clergy leadership, remembered that Smith, after his arrival, 'many times . . . said solemn High Mass with deacons and subdeacons, with organs and music in the large chapel which Viscount Montague has in his villa'. Like Bishop, he 'gave the sacrament of confirmation to many'.[136])

An account of Smith's perambulant episcopate, which lies among Sir John Coke's papers on recusant affairs, describes the circuit which he customarily travelled and how he moved between Catholic aristocratic houses. He toured in style – by coach, attended usually by nine or ten priests. Coke's memorandum noted that Smith 'liveth ordinarily in the howse of the Ladie Mordant, widow, mother to the Lord Mordant and sister to the president of Wales' at Turvey in Bedfordshire. The report observed that one of Lord Montague's daughters (presumably Frances, who married John Blomer of Hatherop, Gloucestershire, in May 1628) 'is browght up with the Ladie Mordant, whom Dr Smith sanctified with holy water and sweet oyle'.[137]

From Turvey, Smith's circuit took him to 'the Ladie Dormers in Buckingham shire at Wing' or at a house called Chanders in a wood near Aylesbury, or to her son Anthony's house near Missenden. From there he would proceed to the palace at Cowdray and attend on his old master, Montague. Then he would go to perhaps his most outspoken aristocratic supporter, Baron Arundell, at Wardour, and 'thence to Grafton to the lord of Shrewsburie', near Bromsgrove. After Grafton the next port of call was Sir Basil Brooke's house near Shrewsbury. Then off he would go into Lancashire. Visiting London was less to his fancy, and he left the administration of that part of his province mainly to John Colleton, who was dean of the chapter (and resident with Sir William Roper), and to Colleton's coadjutor George Fisher. Though the report is slightly garbled, making Fisher and his alias of 'Musket' out to be two different people, it notes that Fisher (for the 'most part at the Ladie Dormers', perhaps meaning at her house in the Savoy) was

135 Allison, RS, 193–4; AA, 392–3.
136 VA, Barberini MS LVI, 156 (transcript and translation at ABSJ).
137 For the Blomer family, see CRS 11, 513.

also resident at Lord Stourton's in Clerkenwell, at Sir Henry Guildford's at Maidenhead and also in Montague's house in Drury Lane.[138]

The fact that Smith kept himself away from the capital was not necessarily of much comfort to Coke. In Coke's papers there is a memorandum (of uncertain date)[139] which describes how the aristocratic Catholic entourages in the capital were a significant cause of London's reputation as a hotbed of popery. 'All sorts and degrees of papists doe daily resort to and about London out of all parts of the realme, to free and shelter themselfes from the lawes, remaining here privately or unknowne shifting monthly or weekly from howse to howse, from parish to parish, haveing all their servantes papists about them.' Just in case they should get fingered by the law, 'for their better protection, every of them have some perticuler relacion or frend to some noble man or woeman whoe upon every occasion petitions privately for them either to the king, queen, duke or his master'.

Our informant here listed the principal peers who were responsible – peers who had 'howses in and about London which be receptacles and, in a sort, secure colleges for preists and others'. Baron Stourton, the earl of Shrewsbury and, apparently, Baron Roper all made their Clerkenwell establishments available to the Jesuits, and, in Stourton's case, to the Benedictines as well. (It is a little difficult to believe that, in Stourton's household, both the Jesuits and Smith's official, Fisher, were made equally welcome. On the other hand, as we shall see, Viscount Montague's own patronage broadened out in the late 1610s and during the 1620s, and this may have been typical of several peers.)

Also listed was Montague's establishment at Drury Lane, where the earl of Ormond resided as well. Montague's aunt, Lady Dormer, was performing the same patronage function in the Savoy,[140] and Baron Arundell did the same in Holborn. Baron Petre's house in Aldersgate Street was open to the Jesuits. The 'old countess of Arundel' had establishments in the Strand, in Highgate and at Greenwich. The countess of Kildare had a house for the same patronal purpose at Westminster.

There were also, the writer alleged, 'divers private lodgeings taken by noble men, for preists and Jesuites security only, [such] as the Lord Ewers, the Lord Vaux and the Lord Abergavenny with many others'.[141] The informer was presumably thinking here of, *inter alia*, the house owned and run for

---

[138] For this account, written in March 1628, see PRO, SP 16/99/19, fo. 189r (printed in *Camden Miscellany* 2 (1853), 59–60); Foley I, 138; PRO, SP 16/229/133, fo. 259r. A later report placed Colleton, when in town, at Lord Arundell's London establishment, PRO, SP 16/529/94, fo. 146r.

[139] It is conjecturally assigned in *CSPD* to March 1628.

[140] For Lady Dormer's residence in the Savoy, see PRO, SP 16/98/122, fo. 300r.

[141] PRO, SP 16/98/122, fos. 299r–300r.

Montague by his servant Cape in Drury Lane. Another informer noted that various clergy resided there, including 'Mosket', i.e. George Fisher, 'the popes archdeceon for London'.[142] In other words, Montague and his kin were, like other peers, known to provide a secure London base for their priests' ministries, ministries which were viewed, by the Catholics' critics, as anything but private and pastoral.

THE END OF THE HONEYMOON PERIOD

Unfortunately for the English Catholic community, the period of cooperation and religious *détente* between Henrietta Maria's Catholic entourage and her husband the king did not last very long. Complaints about the overtness of the queen's Catholicism led to the repatriation of most of her Oratorian priests. Only one Scot and one Frenchman among them were permitted to remain behind.[143] (Charles ordered Buckingham in the first week of August 1626 to throw them all out, though Charles may have been inveigled into doing this by Buckingham himself and the earl of Carlisle.[144]) The conduct of Henrietta's French attendants, who seem to have used the occasions of Catholic religious festivals as a way of separating her from Charles, i.e. by enjoining sexual abstinence before particular saints' days, contributed to these difficulties.[145]

The regime now moved to remedy the perceived laxity of its policy towards Catholics. A proclamation of 14 August 1625 ordered Englishmen at the seminaries to return into the realm, and it instructed that the penal laws should be enforced against the Catholic clergy.[146] The judges were directed to make sure that, on their circuits, the appropriate sanctions were inflicted on Catholics.[147] Simultaneously, stories flooded in from the provinces that the papists were angrily combining and swarming, determined to resist the will of the crown and its officials. Among these reports were rumours that this sort of thing was going on even in aristocratic households.[148] There was another round of disarming in order to pre-empt any civil disorder, perhaps even rebellion, by Catholics. One order, of 30 October 1625, was specifically directed at the Catholic peerage (including the second Viscount Montague). Although the searches for weapons turned up very little, the inspection of Elizabeth Vaux's house turned nasty. Lord Vaux vigorously set

---

[142] PRO, SP 16/229/133, fo. 259r.
[143] C. Hibbard, 'Henrietta Maria and the Transition from Princess to Queen', *The Court Historian* 5 (2000), 15–28, at p. 26.
[144] TD V, 161–2; Schreiber, *The First Carlisle*, 96, 98.
[145] Hibbard, 'Henrietta Maria', 24; *CSPV 1625–6*, 107.
[146] Larkin, *SRP*, II, 52.   [147] AAW, A XIX, no. 89; *CSPD 1625–6*, 142.
[148] PRO, SP 16/6/68, 68. i, ii, iii; PRO, SP 16/6/104.

about one of the searchers with a blunt instrument. In Montague's case, the search carried out by Bishop Carleton of Chichester (who, as we saw, had obliquely attacked Montague in parliament by complaining about Bishop Smith's activities in Chichester diocese) was something of a ritual humiliation. Carleton 'receaved of the Lord Vicount Mowntague the 7 of December 1625 . . . 31 pikes known as arming pikes; 13 lances or horsemens staves; 16 brown bills; 3 partisans, 7 pairs of gauntlets; 1 broken pike and 2 broken lances'. (The pikes, it had to be admitted, were mostly 'worme eaten' and the other equipment was 'very old'.)[149] In February 1626 Montague's name appeared on a list of 161 recusants indicted at the Newgate gaol delivery.[150]

Soon there was an attempted purge of those Catholics who were reckoned to have infiltrated themselves into local government offices. There had already been one parliamentary enquiry in 1624 into this scandal.[151] Now in June 1626 there was another. The Commons petitioned the king to remove not just recusants but also those who were suspected in religion. One of those named was Montague himself, who served as a commissioner of sewers in Sussex.[152]

On 7 January 1626 Secretary Conway issued an arrest warrant for George Fisher, Thomas Worthington and Richard Smith himself.[153] At the same time that Smith was starting to gallivant around the home counties, conducting visitations and trying to establish his authority over English Catholics, the regime picked up a Scottish priest called John Trumbull who claimed to have similar authority to perform the same functions in Scotland and Ireland as Smith performed in England, and who was trying to make contact with Smith's officials.[154] To the regime this may have resembled a sinister strategy, sponsored by Smith, to extend the tentacles of his power further into Charles's dominions.

Some of the secular clergy's patrons and friends tried to use their influence with the regime to get special consideration for specific clergymen. For example, Edmund Bolton had petitioned Secretary Conway in late December

---

[149] PRO, SP 16/11/39, 39. i; Anstruther, *Vaux*, 441–3; PRO, SP 16/9/18. See also T. Cogswell, *Home Divisions* (Manchester, 1996), 98.

[150] PRO, SP 16/21/23, fo. 33r.

[151] *LJ* III, 289–90, 291, 297–8, 304, 316, 394–6.

[152] Among other Catholic office-holders listed for Sussex and Surrey were Sir John Shelley, John Finch, Sir John Gage, Sir John Caryll, Sir Henry Guildford, Sir Henry Compton, Sir Edward Francis, Sir Garret Kempe, Edward Gage, Thomas Middlemore, James Rootes, William Scott, Robert Spiller and John Thatcher, BL, Harleian MS 160, no. 15, fo. 95r; W. B. Bidwell and M. Jansson (eds.), *Proceedings in Parliament 1626* (4 vols., 1991–6), IV, 212, 214.

[153] *CSPD 1625–6*, 215.

[154] AAW, A XX, no. 22, pp. 83–4; *CSPD 1625–6*, 320. See also *ibid.*, 261, 392, 436, 458; PRO, SP 16/44/84, SP 16/529/93, fo. 144r–v; AAW, A XX, no. 28, p. 101. See also *CSPD 1627–8*, 367.

1625, reminding him that the recently deceased king had 'suffered him with his wife and family to live in peace to the conscience in which he was bred' and had also granted him a similar grace 'for any three or four priests, but he only named John Colleton, a man of about fourscore years of age, and of so great integrity that he had leave to live free abroad under Queen Elizabeth and King James'. An accompanying petition from Colleton reminded the regime that in April 1622 he had been granted a personal protection from proceedings against him.[155]

The irony, however, was that, even with the regime now increasingly under attack from its Protestant critics in parliament, the king evidently did not intend to do anything very draconian about Catholics.[156] To those who really worried about the insidious and creeping effects of popery, it looked as if the regime was being remarkably feeble about the Catholic issue.

We can certainly detect some members of the pro-episcopal patronage network inveigling themselves into the Caroline regime's good graces, or at least trying to. In late 1626 we find Baron Arundell sending advice papers to the regime in which he generously offered to share his ideas about revenue gathering. In particular he drew attention to his (unnamed) 'lesser project' which would be 'less displeasing to the realme, more honest and just' and 'of greater valew than the loane that is now labored for'.[157] Here we have a reversal of the scenario where anti-Catholic promoters and projectors advised the crown how it could extract more revenue from its subjects, in part by mulcting recusant separatists more severely than usual.[158] Arundell's offers of service in this field of government activity prefigured the involvement, which Richard Cust has expertly traced, of Catholic peers such as Viscount Dunbar, Baron Eure, Baron Petre, Baron Tufton and Lord St John in the collection of the Forced Loan.[159]

It was not long before a combination of factors steered the regime towards a compounding policy for dealing with recusants, a policy in which the 'give-and-take' arrangements which had characterised a good deal of the State's proceedings against Catholics during the Jacobean period were now put on an official basis. The new system was that, in return for steady and

---

[155] *CSPD 1625–6*, 191. For Bolton's Catholicism, see BL, Cotton MS Julius C III, fo. 28r; Edmund Bolton, *Hypercritica* (Oxford, 1722), section II, 232.

[156] Cf. Hughes, *RCR*, 333–4.

[157] All that Arundell asked in return was that he should be 'secured from conviction for recusancie and from all other penalties of the lawe whereunto Catholickes are subject more than others', be granted a one fifth rake-off of the crown's profits from the project and be given some legal assistance in his current battle with his relatives about the disposition of his own property, PRO, SP 16/38/95, fo. 128r–v, SP 16/38/96, fo. 130r.

[158] See M. Questier, 'Sir Henry Spiller, Recusancy and the Efficiency of the Jacobean Exchequer', *HR* 66 (1993), 251–66, esp. p. 264.

[159] R. Cust, *The Forced Loan and English Politics 1626–1628* (Oxford, 1987), 248–9.

sometimes quite substantial payments to the recusancy commissioners, the recusant could, in effect, purchase immunity from the petty harassments and bullying of all the other agencies which had been charged with or had taken upon themselves the enforcement of the recusancy statutes.

But this scheme did not actually bite until the 1630s.[160] In the later 1620s, there were still several members of the regime who were far from tolerant towards Catholics. In early January 1627 the two secretaries of State, Conway and Coke, ordered again the apprehension of Richard Smith and George Fisher.[161] It is possible that there was no real intention of arresting Smith. But Fisher was actively hunted down. As Godfrey Anstruther points out, a number of raids were mounted to find him, with rival pursuivants writing scathing reports about each other's incompetence. Thomas Mayo was described in May 1627 as 'sharking up and down from house to house in city and count[r]y with an open mouth for the bishop' and for Fisher.[162] Fisher was lodged in the Gatehouse prison by December 1627.[163]

CONCLUSION

In spite of the rather precarious position of the English Catholics who hoped most to profit from the Anglo-French treaty, the diplomatic manoeuvring which proceeded within the Catholic community in synchronisation with the negotiations for the marriage alliance was no side-issue. It was possible for Protestant contemporaries to interpret the Catholics' renewal of the hierarchical experiment within their community as a distinctly unpleasant mutation of the Catholic threat, an insidious, inveigling, two-faced attempt to worm their way into the establishment.

Furthermore, the debacle of the later 1620s' parliamentary sessions radically changed the regime's, and particularly Charles's, mind about who was the real enemy within. This is not to say that Charles simply became some kind of crypto- or closet Catholic. But the political impasse over revenue and foreign policy, as well as over the regulation and governance of the Church of England, meant that Catholicism inevitably moved into a rather different relationship with the king and the State. Or rather, the conflictual aspects of Charles's encounters with 'Protestant' public opinion opened up a series of gambits which Catholics could exploit (in much the same way that they had exploited such opportunities during the political crisis caused by the Spanish match). Now, in many ways, this led only to a reopening of discussions and issues with which we are already very familiar – the question of loyalty, the

[160] See ch. 14, pp. 486–9 below.
[161] Anstr. II, 104; *CSPD 1627–8*, 7.   [162] Anstr. II, 105.
[163] *CSPD 1627–8*, 480. For the regime's measures against Smith and his officials in the later 1620s, see ch. 13, pp. 464–7 below.

possibility of tolerance/toleration and so on. But the crucial point here is that what we might term the 'radical' phase of Bishop Richard Smith's attempt to rule the world, or at least the English Catholic bits of it which were within range of him and his archdeacons and other officers, coincided almost exactly with the political meltdown in parliament in 1628–9. Thus the review (in the next chapter) of the otherwise reasonably well-known, although somewhat 'in-house', story of the struggle between, on the one hand, supporters of Catholic episcopal jurisdiction in England and, on the other, their Catholic critics (principally the Jesuits, some Benedictines and their lay patrons) is also a retelling of the series of political engagements between the crown and the Catholic community which started now in earnest and continued up to (and beyond) the civil war. In these struggles the part played by Catholic clerics' patrons was, as we shall see, a pivotal one. Often unseen, or mentioned only in passing in the clergy's accounts of their increasingly internecine struggles, it is clear that patronal support was eagerly sought and relied on, and in many ways it was what allowed these clergy to seek to establish superiority over their own Catholic enemies and critics. Certainly, the second Viscount Montague was quite heavily engaged in the clerical controversies of the later 1620s.

At the same time, these struggles were not limited to the ranks of the Catholic clergy and their patrons. Just as in earlier episodes which sparked Catholic–Protestant conflict (for example, the appellant dispute, the 1603 succession, the early Jacobean Catholic toleration campaigns and the 1620s' dynastic treaty negotiations), there was a several-cornered contest between different Catholic and Protestant groups, listening to and, by turns, both excoriating and trying to play off each other to their own best advantage. For example, Secretary Coke had an informer, one John Cleare, who infiltrated Richard Smith's entourage and was trusted by Smith. Cleare had instructions to report on Smith's struggles against his Catholic enemies.[164] In 1628 we find a Benedictine tract against Smith, Rudesind Barlow's *Mandatum*, being presented to George Abbot.[165] At least one piece of correspondence written by Smith (addressed to a Benedictine superior, Joseph Prater) concerning a sermon preached against the religious, exists in the State Papers in a copy made by Bishop William Laud.[166] While we may be sure that the anti-popish Archbishop Abbot did not in any real sense sympathise with the Benedictines, nor Laud with Smith, the logic of these Catholic adversaries' positions could not but engage the interest and attention of leading men in the Church of England.

[164] *CSPD 1627–8*, 543.   [165] See ch. 13, p. 464 below.   [166] PRO, SP 16/59/80.

13

The second Viscount Montague, his entourage and the approbation controversy

It was almost inevitable that once Richard Smith had returned, armed with his new episcopal status and authority, to the bosom of those aristocratic families which traditionally rendered support to him and his friends, he would take the opportunity to try to realise what had previously been just hierarchalist hallucinations. Of course, he and his circle would claim that his rule over the Catholic community in England was purely benign and, indeed, fruitful, just as William Bishop's had been. Faction and discontent arose, Smith claimed, merely because of the emulous bitterness of his enemies. When he started to insist that Catholic clergymen in England should turn to him for 'approbation', i.e. the (theoretically automatic) licensing of missionary priests to hear the confessions of their ghostly children, his critics maliciously (said Smith) seized on this instance of his dutiful attention to his flock's spiritual welfare in order to attack him.

Smith's claims about the peacefulness and benignity of his rule were, however, in their essentials, severely economical with the truth. As David Lunn has shown from the archives of the Congregation for the Propagation of the Faith (De Propaganda Fide), in autumn 1626 Smith launched a visitation of the entire country and, though virtually no formal records of it survive, he occupied himself at this time by transmitting rude messages to Rome about his critics in the religious orders. In his September 1626 report to the cardinal protector, he noted that 'certain regulars', some of whom had 'fled their order' and others having been simply 'expelled', had 'made their way into this vineyard'. 'After the fashion of the other priests sent here by authority of the Holy See', they were 'administering the sacraments, not having received (so far as my knowledge goes) any faculties nor approbation lawfully had'. He requested that the congregation should suspend the Jesuit sodality of the Immaculate Conception on the grounds that it was divisive and factious. Smith alleged also that the Jesuits opposed his visitation.[1] At the same time,

---

[1] Lunn, 'Opposition', 6; Hughes, *RCR*, 337–40, 349. In mid-February 1626 the Jesuit general, Muzio Vitelleschi, had written to the Jesuit provincial in England, Richard Blount, approving

he and his officers began to gather (one assumes for publication) records and narratives of Catholic martyrdom. Their aim was clearly to compile an authoritative Catholic martyrological tradition, one of the distinguishing features of which would be that the religious orders, and notably the Jesuits, would be, if not quite excluded from it, undeniably a good deal less prominent than they would have liked.[2]

The approbation controversy was, in its formal arguments, a dispute of only slightly less tedium than the appellant business of nearly thirty years before, though of approximately equal vitriol. However, in order to indicate what was at stake, it will be necessary, briefly, to outline how the question of approbation turned into a much larger debate on the nature of episcopal authority. And I want to show that it was inevitable, given the attitudes of Bishop Smith and his patrons and supporters, that something of the kind would take place, that it would be a crucial issue in Catholic circles and that it would have a transformative effect on the English Catholic community.

Naturally, in many ways, this bout of in-fighting was extremely embarrassing for English Catholics who had almost all, at some stage, subscribed to a rhetoric of unity in the face of the persecuting Protestant State. Therefore, instead of admitting that the conflict took place between two powerful and ideologically coherent factions, the explanatory mode adopted (by both sides) was, just as it had been in the appellant dispute, that the quarrel was the product of the malice of a few individuals who might be presumed to be acting exclusively out of self-interest and who had no vision for Catholicism outside the selfish preoccupations of their own faction or group. But merely to reproduce such accounts of this dispute is a positive bar to any kind of understanding of how and why the quarrel was structured in the way that it was, and in particular why certain patrons (such as the second Viscount Montague and his relatives) should have supported some clergy rather than others; and whether their support was always unconditional; and generally what all this meant for patron–client and clergy–laity relationships and the politics of the Catholic community in this period.[3]

These issues were, in themselves, hardly novel. Ever since the installation of the archpriest George Blackwell there had been disputes and quarrels about how far missionary clergy were conforming to godly patterns and ideals desirable and suitable for men of their profession. What was different

his decision to withdraw Jesuits from houses where Smith might try to enforce his visitation, ARSJ, Anglia MS 1/ii, fo. 228r. In January 1628 the Congregation for the Propagation of the Faith agreed to suppress the English Jesuit missioners' lay confraternities, AAW, B 48, no. 51.

[2] AAW, A XX, no. 102, p. 355; CRS 5, 393.

[3] See, for example, Hughes, *RCR*, book III, ch. 3, which narrates Richard Smith's troubled episcopate almost completely in the terms used by Smith and his supporters in order to describe it.

now was that one particular faction had the trappings and instruments of episcopal authority and was able, in theory, to start enforcing one version of what those godly patterns were, to the possible (and some people thought certain) exclusion of other versions.

Crucially, as I have already argued,[4] this was happening at almost exactly the same time that various avant-garde conformist elements were, on one reading, making almost precisely the same kind of bid to enforce novel patterns of godly behaviour in the Church of England, and were using not dissimilar weapons to do it. In both cases, Church of England and Catholic, the agencies making the bid claimed to be moderate and mainstream, restoring and not revolutionising the Church, and acting entirely in harmony with the traditions which all members of their Churches could be sure that they had inherited from the time of their inception. Significantly, also, we may conclude that the bid by English Catholic avant-garde conformists failed (at least in its immediate ambitions) while, temporarily, the bid by avant-garde conformist elements in the Church of England succeeded. This was in large part because of structural differences between the two. The English Catholic conformist impulse was reliant on resources which were much more limited than those available to the Laudians. In the end, however, we might infer that a lot of English Catholics (i.e. Smith's opponents) knew something which William Laud and King Charles did not, or at least that there was some kind of conscious decision by a significant number of Catholics not to go down the route which was being espoused by leading men in the Church of England. But certain Catholic patronage networks and nexuses (including a significant section of the Browne family and its entourage) were going to have an exceedingly good try before they conceded defeat on this issue.

EPISCOPAL GOVERNMENT AND A RHETORIC OF ORDER

However petty and artificial some of the approbation debates were, a rhetoric of order and discipline was a key component of the manifesto of anyone who aspired to an overarching authority within the English Catholic community. And, as we shall see, virtually all of the polemic bandied about in the approbation controversy dealt almost exclusively with order and discipline: how far would a bishop restore the godly state of English Catholics? Or would his presence create more troubles than it settled? As the secular clergy's Roman agent was advised in July 1627 (though such advice could have been drawn from most of the hierarchalist Catholic memoranda and polemical tracts over the past twenty or so years),

---

[4] See ch. 10, p. 340 above.

the necessity of having this authority here well established and continued is apparent to any indifferent judge, both for the comfort of the good and for the correction of the bad. For, without this authority, the wisest men that understand the case of England truly are of opinion that this great work of the conversion of our country will advance nothing at all, and never be achieved, and that the abuses and inward impediments which have hitherto chiefly hindered the same will rather grow and encrease daily, as by experience we see they doe.

The lack of direct episcopal government in England was the cause of 'intolerable abuses'. Some priests 'have come into England, and have practised their priestly function without a lawfull mission. Others have practised beyond the extent of their faculties. There are divers particular religious men here that do acknowledge no superiour in England. Some have committed notorious and daungerous indiscretions. Some live scandalously, and the like.'[5]

A great deal of the anxious concern which was being exuded here was polemically driven. But there was enough evidence of the *ad hoc* nature of the arrangements resorted to by the religious orders, and of the lack of proper authority structures to regulate the lives of their personnel, to allow Smith and his friends to make a convincing prima facie case that episcopal regulation would be positively beneficial for the whole English Catholic community.[6] In this context it was tempting and easy to argue that the disciplinary faults and failings to which the religious orders were allegedly prone made them beware the institution of episcopal authority for fear of having their sins discovered and corrected.

Among the polemical anecdotes which the secular clergy supporters of Bishop Smith collected were several stories that the religious interfered in marital disputes and broke up Catholic gentry families, and that they engaged themselves in the administration of 'temporal estates'.[7] It was possible to claim that the indiscipline of the regulars caused public scandal, turned Catholics against each other and impeded the 'conversion' of England.

This, we may be sure, was an analysis with which Smith's critics did not agree.[8] In return they accused him not just of personal tyranny and vindictiveness but also of claiming an authority which he did not possess and which Rome had decided not to grant him. Like his predecessor, William Bishop, he was not, they asserted, invested with ordinary jurisdiction. His

---

[5] AAW, A XX, no. 102, p. 354.
[6] T. McCoog, 'The Religious Life of the English Jesuits' (forthcoming); Lunn, 'Opposition', 4–6; Lunn, *EB*, 147.
[7] AAW, A XXI, no. 49, p. 175.
[8] One can read the English Jesuits' Annual Letters for this period (some of which are reproduced in Henry Foley's *Records of the English Province of the Society of Jesus*) as an attempt, under cover of a formal administrative report, to reply to some of their enemies' claims that the Society did more harm than good.

powers were only delegated ones. He could not, therefore, act as a Catholic bishop would in a country which was in communion with the see of Rome. They rejected both his formal claim to be able to approve the faculties of missionary priests in England and all the pendant powers which, they knew or suspected, Smith and his friends wanted to exercise – for example the authority to intervene in marriage and probate disputes.[9] To Smith's opponents, the demand for approbation must have resembled the subscription campaigns that had caused such dissension in the Church of England when launched against separatist and various lesser kinds of puritan nonconformity in Elizabeth's and early in James's reign. Inevitably it raised the question of what Smith thought the full extent of his authority was, and how far he was going to make alterations to the way that discipline was exercised over Catholics in England.

Arguments over the extent of Smith's powers were located primarily in the intricacies of canon law. However, the dry formality of those arguments was transformed by the semi-public circulation of them, usually dressed up with a good deal of scandalous retort and personal vituperation.[10]

These attempts to open up the debate to a wider public inevitably drew in the clergy's patrons. They were called upon either to endorse or to condemn the bishop's exercise of his authority. Smith accused his opponents of courting popularity in their circulation of petitions against him around the houses of the aristocracy and gentry. But his own supporters clearly employed exactly the same tactics. Benedict Jones OSB complained in September 1628 to his confrère Robert Haydock that 'the seculars did goe from place to place and shewed . . . to divers Catholicks' copies of a document, an open letter of November 1627, calling on Smith to justify, if he could, his claim to authority. The letter was signed by three distinguished Catholic laymen – Sir Basil Brooke (formerly one of Smith's patrons, but now his enemy),[11] the lawyer Francis Plowden and Sir Thomas Brudenell. (The document was known as the 'letter of the three gentlemen'.[12]) The secular priests did this, said Jones, 'to the end that' Catholics 'should disclaime it at least and so informe (as they have done and therby much prevailed) what a great multitude of Catholikes disavowed that lettre and that it was published in the name of the Catholikes by falshood and imposture'.[13]

Although Brooke, Plowden and Brudenell were acting as front men for many of Smith's clerical critics they were also raising issues which were of

---

[9] For the complexities of the approbation controversy, see Allison, QJ; Hughes, *RCR*, 347–9.
[10] See M. Questier, 'The Politics of Episcopacy in the Later Jacobean and Early Caroline Catholic Community: The Approbation Controversy in Context' (forthcoming).
[11] Allison, QJ, 120–1, 141; AAW, A XXVII, no. 58, p. 224; CRS 1, 100.
[12] The promoter of the letter, behind the scenes, was Sir Tobie Mathew.
[13] AAW, A XXII, no. 131, p. 579.

great concern to the lay patrons who supported the Catholic clerical network in England. They wanted to know, for example, not just whether Smith intended to go on visitation but also whether 'lay men . . . [were] bound to provide competent and sufficient temporall meanes and maintenance for the bishop as the times are now?' What was the bishop's record-keeping going to be like? Would he retain 'any catalogue of the names of the laity that are reconciled and of the priests that reside with them as also of marriages, christenings . . . [and] gossips by whom and before whom the saied marriages and christenings are made?'

The crunch point, however, was the looming threat of the bishop's 'tribunal'. The 'erecting of a tribunall for administration of anie course of justice, either distinct or contrary to our lawes, is an offence of high treason'. Necessarily it followed that 'all who submitt and conforme therunto may be drawenne within compasse therof, misprision of treason or premunire'. The operation of such a tribunal could not possibly be kept secret, and it would provoke the present regime into a severe retaliation. Even the most moderate Stuart monarch was not going to tolerate this. Smith's judicial machinery was the beginning of what might become a kind of State within a State. So the petitioners politely but threateningly enquired – would 'the conforming to this tribunal be a necessary act of faith'? Did Smith not think that this was a grievous affliction of the Catholic who perforce was obliged at the present time to serve two masters and was threatened with total forfeiture as a result? Was it really likely that the pope intended 'in such a time as we live to cast the Catholickes into such perplexities'? What, for heaven's sake, would happen if the bishop's tribunal gave one answer in a particular case, and one of the parties to the suit went off and got a different decision from a Church-of-England court? The whole thing was a nonsense and completely unworkable.[14]

In other words, the approbation controversy reignited all the fury and antagonisms of the appellant dispute. But now there was, in some ways, more to play for – both a more realistic prospect of tolerance for Catholics from a regime which was so different from its predecessors, and the chance to operate a fully functioning hierarchical Catholic structure. While Smith's enemies claimed that such a hierarchy would transgress the royal supremacy and bring the revenge of the State down on the Catholic clergy and Catholic laity alike,[15] Smith and his friends argued that, on the contrary, the reinstitution and function of episcopacy among English Catholics could not but bring the community and its Church into alignment, in this respect at least, with the Church of England which was also an episcopal Church. And thus

---

[14] AAW, A XX, no. 99, pp. 343–5; Allison, QJ, 117–19; AAW, B 48, no. 25.
[15] CRS 22, 156–7.

the Catholic community would be more acceptable to the Caroline State and regime.

Smith declared that he was an essential bulwark of the regime and State against any disorderly spirits within the Catholic community who might be so bold as to range themselves against the king's authority. He would also be able to position English Catholicism more effectively against the crown's puritan critics and opponents in England who were, as Catholics had often asserted, more of a threat to royal authority than Catholics could ever be.

Smith and his patrons enthusiastically recited the Jacobean royal maxim of 'no bishop, no king'. Smith argued that his own determination to exercise episcopal jurisdiction among and over English Catholics would help to guarantee order and stability in the realm; for he had King James's own assurance on this point. Smith remembered that James, at the Hampton Court conference,

in his wisdom . . . saied . . . no bishop, no king; which though he meant [it] of Protestant bishops yet in some degree it is true of Catholics; for, if we had had a Catholic bishop at the time of the powder treason, it is very like that [it] had never bin. For it is very like they would have consulted [about] it with the bishop whoe doubtlesse would have hindered it.[16]

There was no surer security for the State from an ill-intentioned Catholic than the maintenance of the authority of a quiet-minded Catholic bishop.

These points were echoed and amplified in Matthew Kellison's defence of Smith, his *Treatise of the Hierarchie*. Kellison drew a picture of the Catholic past in which Catholic religion and Catholic bishops in England had been a force for political order, holding the fort against the disruptive effects of noble dynastic ambition. 'As the Catholique Church and her religion is no enemie to temporall States, but rather hath conserved them in a temporall felicitie, so the goverment of this Church by Catholique bishops hath always been a strenght [*sic*] and defence unto the kingdome.' It was 'heresie, not the Catholike faith, that causeth garboiles, tumultes, divisions, rebellions and warres'. Some ill-intentioned people argued that 'Catholique religion and her bishops and priests cannot but be enemies to the State . . . now that England is not Catholique'. But the truth was that 'although the Catholique faith be opposit to heresie, yet it is not opposite to [the] State, as appeareth by so many States that have been and still are conserved by our religion, Church and pastours'. For 'in that it is an enimie to heresie, it is a freind and favourer of [the] State which rather tottereth than standeth under heresie'.[17]

---

[16] AAW, A XXI, no. 101, p. 417; CRS 22, 151–2. For the significance of the Gunpowder plot in the thinking of Smith and his leading supporters, such as Baron Arundell, see Allison, JG, 55, 58, 59; AAW, A XXIII, no. 132, p. 479, XIV, no. 87, p. 363.

[17] Matthew Kellison, *A Treatise of the Hierarchie and Divers Orders of the Church against the Anarchie of Calvin* (Douai, 1629), 395, 396, 397–8.

Smith was holding out to his patrons the prospect that they might become not just tolerable but actually *persona grata* to the State. The episcopal project, Smith promised his patrons, could turn into reality the enduring Catholic fantasy of reversing the statutory legal proscription of Catholicism. Those Catholics who opposed him were, by implication, enemies of the good of the Catholic community and not much better than the puritans who, Protestant conformist polemicists had always argued, were a dire threat to the commonwealth. Provocatively Smith was attributing to the religious all the faults which Catholic polemicists detected in contemporary puritanism.[18]

This was also the opportunity, implied Smith and his friends, for prominent Catholic laymen such as the second Viscount Montague, by supporting the episcopal project, to place themselves at the forefront of the Catholic community and to represent themselves to the State as the community's natural leaders.

Ironically, as the approbation controversy was in full swing, the regime decided to spin the opening of the 1628 parliament by appropriating some of the rhetoric of anti-popery. It was at this point, in mid-March 1628, that Sir John Coke decided to break up the Jesuit novitiate in Clerkenwell. Coke wrote up his account of the search and used the incident in parliament on 24 March 1628 to urge a grant of supply to the crown.[19] Of course, Coke's attack was not targeted exclusively against the Jesuits. In a Commons' committee on 26 March which dealt with the recusant problem, Coke referred to the 'hierarchy which is already established in competition with their lordships'. Smith and his 'vicars-general, archdeacons, rural deans, apparitors and such like' were not 'nominal or titular officers alone, but they all execute their jurisdictions and make their ordinary visitations through the kingdom, keep courts and determine ecclesiastical causes'. And, what was worse, thought Coke, 'they keep ordinary intelligence by their agents in Rome, and hold correspondence with the nuncios and cardinals, both at Brussels and in France'.[20]

Coke was here trotting out, in effect, some of the regulars' own rhetoric against the seculars. But the fact was that it was a Jesuit residence which had been unearthed in Clerkenwell. And the discovery connected nicely with standard contemporary tropes, subscribed to by both Protestants and also by some Catholics, about Jesuit scheming and ambition. The event was

---

[18] This line was spun out in much greater detail by Matthew Kellison. Kellison's *Treatise of the Hierarchie* attacked Calvinists as the principal opponents of the divine principle of unity fostered and promoted in episcopacy, and in the sovereignty of the pope and other monarchs. But since his book was clearly a product of the approbation controversy, his critique of presbyterian Protestantism inevitably acted also as a censure of Smith's Catholic enemies (principally the Jesuits).

[19] *CSPD 1628–9*, 53–6; Foley I, 97–141.   [20] Foley I, 99–100.

further publicised by the circulation of a fake letter, allegedly discovered in the search. It was addressed to the Jesuit rector at Brussels, and it rehearsed fantastic details of a Jesuit conspiracy to undermine the State. Since the letter described Buckingham as 'our furyous enemy' it was not unnatural for some to conclude that Buckingham's supporters had concocted it, though Buckingham apparently took extreme exception to the letter.[21] But the main point of the letter was the claim that the Jesuits had furthered the calling of the parliament in order to foment discord within the body politic. The letter rehearsed how many 'emynent statesmen' since the start of the 1620s had promoted the Spaniards' interests and how, 'nowe wee have planted that soveraigne drug Arminianisme', this would 'purge the Protestants from their heresie'. 'For the better prevention of the puritans, the Armynians have already blocked upp the duke's eares, and wee have those of our religion whoe stand continuallye at the duke's chamber to see whoe goes in and out.' The Jesuits, the letter said, hoped to profit from the ill humours in the commonwealth, of which Arminianism was only one. There were also the 'projectors' and 'promoters' whose activities would cause dissension between king and parliament. They would tell the king how he might 'rayse a vaste revenew and not be behouldinge to his subjects, which is by way of impositions and of excise'. To the arguments of the Arminians and 'promoters', various 'Church Catholiques' were adding their voices, showing 'the meanes howe to settle this excise'. The revenue raised would fund a levy of foreign mercenary troops who would ravage the realm. Either there would be a rebellion against the hardship, and the troops would 'subjugate' it, and be paid out of sequestrated rebels' property, or the soldiers would mutiny. Either way, the Jesuits would inherit the remains of whatever was left of the kingdom. For, in despair, the 'Protestantes as well as the Catholiques' would 'welcome in a conquerour', namely the Spanish king who would restore the Catholic Church in England.[22]

These rumours were, however fanciful, not unwelcome to Smith and his supporters. Thomas White was informed by a letter of 4 April 1628 that 'it is in many mens mouths that the Jesuits were houlding their parlament at Clarkenwell whiles the States of the kingdome were meeting in parlament at Westminster'.[23]

. But the discovery of approbation controversy papers among the clutch of things seized at the Clerkenwell house was the icing on an already potentially magnificent cake. News of these items came to the notice of the public. (Coke's own narrative of the discovery relates how the Jesuits planned not just to withdraw Catholics from their allegiance to the king but also, as the seized manuscripts demonstrated, 'by a faction against the secular priests,

---

[21] *Ibid.*, 116 (n. 29), 121–2.   [22] *Ibid.*, 116–21.   [23] PRO, SP 16/100/41, fo. 63r.

they labour to divide the papists amongst themselves and to suppress all those that will hold any conformity to the State'.[24])

A delighted William Harewell noted that 'the best learned of those that were taken in the house' were 'saide to be' the earl of Shrewsbury's clients (the Clerkenwell house was Shrewsbury's property); and they were 'then actually employed in writing against the bishop of Chalcedon, as the very Protestants themselves reporte, who are not like to faine it but to speake out of their writings [which] they sawe amongst the reste that were taken'. Harewell understood this from the letter of a 'Protestant minister to his friend'. The letter related that 'wheras the beste schollers of the Jesuites were assembled (as it is reported) to the number of ten in a house neare S. Johns gate to write new thinges against their bishop who (as men saye) is too good a man for such subjectes, they were all apprehended etc.'. And, said the minister's letter, 'this is the third knocke the Jesuites have had from heaven'. Harewell evidently endorsed the minister's interpretation of the Clerkenwell event as a providential blow to rival the discovery of the Gunpowder plot of November 1605 and the notorious Blackfriars disaster of October 1623. The minister was pleased to say that 'this laste is a third business which will frette them to the bones, for, as it is thought, the bishop prayeth well when God spoiles all his enemies of their armes'. Harewell recorded that other 'moderate Protestantes impute this misfortune of the Jesuites to the resistance of authority and liken them to puritanes who can not' abide 'the name of a bishop'.[25]

The question was, how far would Bishop Smith's patrons support him? What, in particular, would the second Viscount Montague and his family do? Would he accept Smith's case and champion him as he had championed George Birkhead during the mid-Jacobean period? Or would he endorse the line put by Smith's opponents that the new bishop had gone too far?

THE SECOND VISCOUNT MONTAGUE'S ROLE
IN THE CONTROVERSY

Professor Bossy's astute conclusion concerning the approbation controversy was that the entry into the lists by laymen such as Sir Basil Brooke was a crucial factor in defeating Richard Smith's pretensions.[26] I want to enlarge,

[24] See *CSPD 1628–9*, 55; PRO, SP 16/99/1, documents S i and ii (the 'letter of the three gentlemen' in Latin and English); Foley I, 114.

[25] AAW, A XXII, no. 42, p. 219. For the Blackfriars disaster, see Foley I, 76–97. Although, as we have seen, Shrewsbury's residence at Grafton was, initially, on Richard Smith's episcopal circuit, the earl was a prominent opponent of Smith in 1627. John Price SJ was one of Shrewsbury's chaplains, and in *c.* 1630 Richard Blount SJ was noted to be resorting to him, PRO, SP 16/178/43, fo. 149r. See also PRO, SP 16/111/67, fo. 137r; B. FitzGibbon, 'George Talbot, Ninth Earl of Shrewsbury', *BS* 2 (1953–4), 96–110, at pp. 96, 99, 100.

[26] Bossy, *ECC*, 56.

if I can, on Bossy's account by looking at the part played in this dispute by the second Viscount Montague, as an aristocratic patron, and by drawing some general conclusions about the significance of lay patronage here.

We might imagine that Montague's role in all this would have been rather formal. Why should he not just have let it be known that he supported the secular clergy in the same way as he had, during Birkhead's archpresbyterate, endorsed their reform programme and, during William Bishop's short-lived episcopate, shown great enthusiasm for the restored episcopal jurisdiction among English Catholics?

But, as we have already briefly noted, during the intervening years Montague had not simply continued to sponsor and endorse, unquestioningly, his secular clergy friends. He seems to have had his doubts about some of the secular clergy's projects, even though he had welcomed William Bishop when he arrived in England in 1623. Richard Smith, we know, at some point early in Charles's reign was able to include Cowdray among the houses of the aristocracy where he could stay. But it is not clear from exactly what point he was able to do this. For, even in 1626, it appears that the secular clergy leadership had some real cause to worry about Montague. In May of that year we find Benjamin Norton extremely perturbed to note how all was not harmonious within the Cowdray household. He remarked to Smith, 'nowe my good lord, if I shoulde tell your good lordship howe matters goe in my greate neighbors howse, it woulde aske an other sheete of paper'. 'In sum thearefore I saye thatt all goeth ill.' The second viscount was himself afflicted with not just a fever but also 'other malonchollye humors'. Norton believed that 'havinge made and setled his estate after some sorte uppon his sonn, hee woulde not-twithstandinge goe on in all or most thinges as beefore'. Most regrettably, he had ordered his son 'to putt awaie his true frende' Edward Kenion, the senior secular clergyman and long-term stalwart of the pro-episcopal lobby. 'The 3de of Maye the sonn, onelye to contente his father, yeelded.' Kenion was supposed to clear out on the next day. But, when Norton arrived at Cowdray on 4 May, 'the sonn tolde mee thatt hee in noe case woulde doe itt . . . for in deed hee seemeth to affecte' Kenion a great deal 'and to bee as constant unto him as hee maye withoute his fathers displeasure'. Norton was determined to support Kenion. He went to Montague 'twise and was with him more than an hower att a tyme'. But the atmosphere was so tense that Norton dared not broach the matter and the viscount did not mention it either.[27]

We do not know why Montague decided to eject Kenion. But Montague admitted, in his 'Apologeticall Answere' of 1628, the massive manuscript tract which he wrote in defence of Richard Smith (having, by this date,

[27] CRS 5, 397.

swung behind Smith), that he had never harboured any ingrained prejudice against any of the regular clergy. He stressed 'verely how intensively I have settled and ingaged my selfe upon the fathers of the Societie now for divers yeares'. God himself could witness 'how willingly I should have not only adventured but should have also actually given my life (at the least) for honor of them'.[28] Montague was a patron also of the Benedictines. In fact he had had to strive to prevent his 'intensive love to those religious fathers of the Society' from prejudicing and preventing 'an appretiative love of blessed St Benedict his order from whence by meane[s] of holy and greate St Gregory I have my Christianitie'.[29] It was common knowledge that, since the early 1620s, if not before, he had had Benedictine chaplains in his entourage. As late as 14 November 1627, when the approbation controversy was already raging, he had arranged 'before divers chosen freindes, to make such a festivall kinde of intertainment as I could to all the Benedictines I could gett together'.[30]

As we rehearsed in chapter 11, Montague admitted that he and Smith had had a serious falling out over Smith's presumption in gadding off in the mid-Jacobean period in order to follow the bishop of Luçon (the future Cardinal Richelieu). It was a

certaine and knowne truth that for some fourteene yeares since, I tooke a discourtesie from him (a discourtesie I say for I doe by noe meanes pretend any injury in it) the cause of the which discourtesie hath neither bene to this day in matter of argument cleered nor could welbe in matter of fact discontinued. It was about retorninge from the then bishop of Luson in France, who now is the most reverend and illustrious Cardinall Ritchlieu, to live with me, as he had formerly done, and as I much desired.

The years went by, and 'it grew into a habit in mee . . . that, not reckoninge him among the number of my speciall and peculiar freinds, I cast myne expectacions and conjoyned curtesies upon them from whom I might in probability finde usefull and desired correspondence', in other words, the regulars. The rift seemed almost total and 'after divers yeares, returninge into this land', Smith 'expected (as to me itt seemed) to have had some conveniency by mee, which I could not performe without the inconvenience of others that I was ingaged unto; the which I suppose he tooke unkindly, though his greate modesty' meant that 'by mee it could never be discerned'. Although, said Montague, neither of them were really to blame, they were definitely not talking to each other very much.

---

[28] The correspondence of the Jesuit general, Vitelleschi, shows that in early 1625 he was writing letters of gratitude to Montague, and even issuing letters patent (i.e. documents which the Society used to record its gratitude to its benefactors) to Montague's son Francis, ARSJ, Anglia MS 1/ii, fos. 214r, 215v, 218v.

[29] AAW, A XXII, no. 65 (draft of one section of Montague's 'Apologeticall Answere'), p. 333.

[30] AA, 461.

Montague had previously also fallen out with the third archpriest, William Harrison. Montague did not say what the reason was, but it was serious; and he 'saw little cause of that inward repose in them which I had formerly expected', although he kept some of the secular clergy with him 'according to my meanes', and had 'care to use others according to charitie'.[31]

The second viscount also confessed that he had, at the time of the first dissemination of the 'letter of the three gentlemen', even quarrelled with the priest John Southcot. Southcot was one of the principal linchpins of the pro-episcopal lobby. 'In the satisfaction of some demaunde of mine', said Montague, 'something was imparted unto me, whereby I, induringe nothinge but in favour of the Societie . . . did growe into a lesse conten[t]ment towardes' Southcot 'in respect of somethinge which I supposed to have passed on his parte otherwise than I (for favour of the Societie) could have wished'.[32]

At the same time, Montague had consulted Lawrence Anderton SJ about the letter. Montague claimed that he regarded Anderton with affection and admiration and held him to be 'unto my [me] (as it were) pignus amoris, frome the Societie, which I farr more than myne owne life esteemed'. Initially Montague believed that Anderton was likely to be even-handed and impartial in sorting out the dispute.[33] As late as the end of November 1627 Anderton was still in fact part of Montague's household, and 'his chamber . . . was', said the viscount, 'the next to myne owne' (apparently in Drury Lane).[34]

In his 'Apologeticall Answere', Montague unambiguously declared that, up until the time that the epistolary indictment of Smith started to circulate, he was very 'farr frome beinge his lordships especiall freind' and he would 'hardly at anie tyme indure that my lord bishop would have made use of anie of my house[s] in London – whereby they might remaine the more free and unincumbred for the fathers of the Societie'. For, he said, 'it is well knowne that my condition doth not beare to have anie great adherence either of inferiour followers, or of my equalls, and those I had were (in a manner all) . . . the freinds of the religious'.[35]

We have no independent evidence that any of this was really true, certainly not of any bad feeling between Montague and Harrison. Harrison, who died in 1621, had been resident with Lady Dormer, Montague's aunt. And it is extremely unclear, in Montague's account of the controversy, at what point, apparently during 1627,[36] he finally decided that Smith's stance and cause were justified. As we shall see in our narrative of the controversy, it appears that Montague's determination to support Smith emerged a lot

---

[31] AAW, A XXII, no. 65, pp. 335–6; AA, 596–9.   [32] AA, 447, 449–50.
[33] *Ibid.*, 452–3.   [34] *Ibid.*, 467–8.   [35] *Ibid.*, 445–6, 591–2.
[36] Montague himself claimed in his 'Apologeticall Answere' that it was the sight of the 'unreverend letter' (of 25 November 1627) written against Smith by 'A.B.' which first provoked him to action.

earlier during 1627 than the viscount himself acknowledged. (Montague's palace of Cowdray had, after all, been on Smith's itinerary from the time that the new bishop arrived back in the country.[37]) So Montague may well have been overdoing the former hostility between himself and Smith in order to make himself look even more the kind of honest broker and impartial arbitrator who was required to settle the community's discontents.

On the other hand, Montague had indeed taken Benedictine chaplains, and was on good terms with the Society. Not only was Anderton actually resident with him, but other Jesuits were not infrequently to be found in his household. For example, Montague casually remarked that when Smith had gone about, in formal manner at Montague's house in Drury Lane at the end of the first week of February 1628, to declare his authority again, in response to the regulars' challenge that he was concealing the papal breve by which he was appointed, that very morning Thomas Curtis SJ came by merely on the off chance, clearly in the belief that he was welcome there.[38] Montague recalled that on the day when he received Smith's gracious acceptance of his own offer to defend Smith from the 'ruffenesse' of the 'three gentlemen' and their unpleasant open letter, Richard Blount SJ was staying in Montague's house. The viscount approached him for his advice and even asked him to refute the letter![39] An informer's report of 1628 claimed that Montague was at that time playing host to 'Mr [John] Huddlestone, Mr [Andrew] White, [and] Mr [Andrew] Barker', who were all Jesuits.[40] Sir Tobie Mathew, the promoter of the 'letter of the three gentlemen', thought it was at least worth canvassing Montague for his support for the anti-Smith position.[41]

In addition, the style of the 'Apologeticall Answere' is sufficiently pompous to make it credible that its author, a relatively minor south-coast noble, should have taken umbrage in the 1610s that his chaplain, Smith, should have been so bold as to want to switch his loyalties and service to that complete nobody, the bishop of Luçon, the future cardinal-duc de Richelieu!

Nevertheless, at some point, despite his elaborate posturing and his claims to be even-handed, Montague dramatically decided to reverse himself and to weigh in wholeheartedly in support of the man whom, whatever their previous differences, he could with some justification have regarded as 'his' bishop, a man who had formerly been one of his household chaplains. Montague claimed that he was deeply shocked when the letter appeared, 'falselie attributed unto laie Catholickes, strikinge unto the verie bowells of the spouse of Christ', evidently 'countenanced by some regulars'.[42]

Montague seems to have calculated that his role as a patron (and, as we have seen, in his young years, he harboured some very large-scale ambitions as a clergy patron) meant that it was worth his while to perform a virtual U-turn and actively to sustain and champion again those secular priests whose cause he had in the past, from time to time, supported vigorously. Now, it seems, he decided to back Smith in the same way that he had shown support for William Bishop in 1623. We may speculate that, seeing Smith so desperately in need of a powerful patron to protect him, Montague envisaged a role for himself which brought him and Smith together properly for the first time since the mid-1610s. It would again be possible for the viscount to assert some kind of leadership over the community. His patronage would, in symbiotic alliance with prominent Catholic clergymen such as Smith, allow him to influence the way in which the Catholic community was organised and governed.

When Montague started to signal that he was prepared to re-direct his patronage, the pro-episcopal lobby raised the stakes by trying to turf the Benedictines out of Montague's household and favour. In late March 1627, Benjamin Norton, at Cowdray, waved in front of Montague's face a copy of *Romani Pontificis Providentia*, a bull issued by Pope Pius V. This decree categorically affirmed that, without the approbation of the ordinary of the diocese, confessions made to the religious were not valid.[43] Montague either was, or affected to be, much troubled by it. He immediately felt the need to summon his Benedictine chaplain Edward Ashe. Ashe could not satisfactorily answer him on this point. Then Richard Smith appeared at Cowdray, as if by magic, a few days later. Montague decided to ask him about it. Smith admitted that he too had been sorely troubled but, with great modesty and charitable circumspection, confessed that he feared provoking a controversy. (Something of a thespian culture clearly prevailed at Cowdray.) Montague then directly challenged Ashe and ordered him to ask Smith for approbation. Ashe buckled and duly complied.[44]

On 16 April 1627 John Cape wrote on Montague's behalf to Francis Cape, and told him that 'my lord is now this Munday evening in bedd' in his palatial Sussex residence, afflicted (predictably) with 'a fourth fitt of a tertian ague'. Montague was also 'infinitely afflycted about this matter of approbacion', in spite of 'the mutuall satisfaction that hath bene formerly taken by my lord bishop, by my lords ghostly father and by my lord himself'. One of the Benedictines, 'Mr Bennet', i.e Benedict Jones, had tried to satisfy the

---

[43] See Hughes, *RCR*, 349; AAW, A XXII, no. 65, p. 306. The Council of Trent's decree on approbation had been temporarily rescinded, allowing the regulars' own superiors to grant a form of approbation. But in 1570, by the bull of Pius V, the original Tridentine ruling was reinstated.

[44] Ashe had said that an (admittedly provocative) sermon delivered by Smith on Palm Sunday (18 March) 1627, concerning the nature of true obedience, 'savoured of heresie', AAW, A XX, no. 159, p. 601.

distressed viscount on this issue but to no avail. Montague was, allegedly, in a real tizz that he might have to make another 'generall confession'. What with such 'difficultyes of memory', it would be a great 'perplexitie' for him. But he would not go against the judgment of the Holy See.[45] Another clergyman, who was not a Benedictine, had instructed him 'not to stand upon these approbacions'. But Montague had piously expressed the wish that he might expire before he should do 'anything as to disobey the Church', in spite of 'his particular inclinacions to devote him selfe more to the religious than to the seculers'. He hoped that either Jones could 'restore him where my lord bishop', Richard Smith, 'left him with his old and most beloved religious ghostly father; or else' that some regular could 'shew him a sufficient release of the aforesaid apostolicall restriction, either from the same or from any succeeding vicar of Christ'. For to Montague's mind it seemed 'not undenied that this approbacion' was 'of practice in Catholicke countryes generally' even if other arrangements were necessarily in force for England 'dureing the soe long tyme of episcopall vacancye'. Should anyone doubt his impartiality and good faith, Montague was still happy to 'beare the testimony of his owne conscience that he' was 'mainely a devote of the religious'. In case anyone should think that this was some dark lay supremacist plot, Cape witnessed that 'my lord hath never conferred with [any] lay man in any parte of this busines but with two, who both spake of it first to him'. This account was endorsed 'indited from my Lords owne mouth in his bed at Cowdry'.[46]

Smith now agreed to meet with some of the leaders of the religious in London (Richard Blount SJ and Mark Crowder OSB).[47] It seems that they were prepared to cooperate, with conditions, on the approbation issue. But Smith's high-handed demeanour, presumably strengthened by the knowledge that Montague was now prepared to support him, persuaded them that a deal could not be done with the bishop.[48] Smith certainly said that they had hidden their true intentions from him and had temporarily duped him. For 'after they had asked and obtained his approbation' they 'impugned both his authoritie of approbation and his episcopal authoritie over the laicks' and 'stirred up certaine lay gentlemen their adherents for to make certaine captious interrogatories' which questioned his government.[49]

---

[45] *Ibid.*, no. 73, p. 257.   [46] *Ibid.*, pp. 257–9.

[47] In a letter of 22 April 1627 to an unnamed Catholic peer, who was almost certainly Montague, Blount said he was 'sorie to see the peace of your lordships mynd troubled abought the matter of approbation', but, whatever Smith's exact canonical status, 'their can be noe doubt but the confessions formerly made be verie sufficient, and I thinke none will denie it', *ibid.*, no. 96, p. 333.

[48] Lunn, 'Opposition', 7–8. Subsequently, it was alleged, Blount denied that he had ever sought approbation and regretted that 'any of his in the contrey hath asked [for] it', AAW, A XXI, no. 43, p. 157.

[49] AAW, A XXI, no. 32, p. 103. For the 'interrogatories', see AAW, A XX, no. 99.

Anyway, Montague undoubtedly started to make his opinions known to the regulars. Francis Cape described in a letter of 1 February 1628 an incident, involving David Codner OSB, which probably took place on or just after 14 November 1627. On that day, as we have already mentioned, Montague gave a 'festivall kinde of intertainment' for the Benedictine clergy whom he knew. While they were there he criticised their opposition to Smith. This evoked a hostile response from Codner. At this time or just after (suggests David Lunn), the viscount found Codner in the room of his own chaplain, Ashe. 'After some speeches had past between them', Montague called Cape in and, in earshot of Cape, 'sayd that if the house were absolutely his owne' (which it was not because he had partially ceded his estate to his son Francis) 'he would wish Don David to forbeare it'. Codner was not having this, and 'with a light posture of his body . . . not so well becoming one of his profession, declared what favours he had don to his lordships sonne'. He also said quite a lot else, though Cape alleged that he could not remember it. Montague suggested that Codner 'should forbeare the house'. Codner became, to put it mildly, upset. He 'flung out of the chamber'. Montague bowed to him, but Codner exclaimed 'nay, if you will not suffer me to be in your house, I will not give you my blessing'. 'In all which passadge' Cape 'could not observe in his lordship any want of respect or reverence towards' Codner.[50]

By the time that the 'letter of the three gentlemen' was being publicly hawked about, the viscount was regarded by the secular clergy leaders as unequivocally on their side. On 27 November 1627 Edward Bennett informed Smith that 'the noble vicount hath disclaymed from' the 'three gentlemen' (Brudenell, Plowden and Brooke), 'as you will understand by some thing I shall send you'. (Here Bennett may be referring to a manuscript tract entitled 'The Disclaim of Divers Lay Catholics', the production of which Montague seems to have organised.[51]) Bennett enthused that Montague 'deserveth much of the English hierarchy. I pray God blesse hym. Twise he was with me, and once I was invited to hym wher', in the presence of the Jesuits Lawrence Anderton and Thomas Poulton, 'he disclaymed from the letter' of Brudenell and the others, 'and desired me to doe hym justice', and 'to inform you that he had no part, nor would not, in this letter'. John Southcot 'was ther alsoe when I first came, in whose presence he did disclayme from this letter. Well, by his own letter you shall easily perceave how muche we ar bound unto hym.'[52]

Montague continued studiously to pose as a moderate. In his 'Apologeticall Answere' he recalled how, at some point before November 1627, Smith's

[50] AAW, A XXII, no. 14, p. 97; Lunn, *EB*, 157–8; CRS 5, 397.
[51] Allison argues that 'it was probably written, or at least put together by . . . Montague', Allison, QJ, 124.
[52] AAW, A XX, no. 177, p. 663.

agent in London had described the regulars as 'barking' against Smith, which the regulars took to mean that Smith's men regarded them as 'doggs'.[53] This was what caused the Benedictines, and particularly the future martyr Alban Roe OSB, to retaliate with the slander that Smith had played 'the divell at Cowdrie' with them.[54] Smith had sounded off about it in the presence of Montague and his Benedictine chaplain Ashe. Nevertheless Montague piously regretted the whole incident. He remembered that he had gone so far as to write, on All Saints 1627, to Matthew Kellison at Douai 'in as constructive termes of that matter, and concerninge that person, as my poore witt and invention could reach unto'. This letter was 'left open' and was 'subscribed under an notaries hand'. It was given to Benedict Jones OSB with Montague's seal so that the Benedictines could see and read it before sending it to Kellison.[55] Kellison, who was shortly to come out in print in defence of Smith, replied in January 1628 with a paean of praise to Montague's moderation, a 'sainte-like' letter according to the delighted viscount.[56] Montague's missive was most welcome, said Kellison, 'as well for the respect I have ever borne to your Honour, as allsoe for your zele to the common cause'.[57]

Montague also ticked off his relative Baron Arundell of Wardour for not being irenic enough on these issues. Arundell had written a letter, of 25 November 1627, attacking the 'letter of the three gentlemen'. This diatribe was itself addressed to Montague. It contained such strong terminology that Montague himself claimed to find it unacceptable as it stood. (Arundell, however, refused to moderate his language, and Montague resorted, in the end, to burning his relative's letter.)[58]

Arundell does seem to have been more aggressive, certainly in public, than Montague. A manuscript in the secular priests' Roman agent's papers, described as the 'advice of a noble man' and endorsed 'I think, my Lord Wardour', is very blunt. Though Arundell pretends that the episcopal issue is far above his comprehension, he then says that his letter, which Montague criticised, was not uncompromising enough. For 'though in my letter which bredd so great offence I have delivered my opinion from which I see no cause to vary', nevertheless, 'to give satisfaction, I will a little further explaine my selfe'. Seeing that the regulars object principally only to two things – the bishop's tribunal and approbation – which were in themselves entirely

---

[53] AA, 325–6.
[54] *Ibid.*, 464–5, 328–9. Montague said that the Benedictines' claim that Smith had played 'the devil' at Cowdray helped turn him into one of Smith's supporters, *ibid.*, 464–5.
[55] *Ibid.*, 333–4, 460.   [56] *Ibid.*, 334.
[57] Kellison's letter is written in a fine hand, not in Kellison's normal scrawl, which suggests that this letter was intended for circulation, AAW, A XXII, no. 4, p. 9.
[58] See AAW, A XX, nos. 166, 178. See also AAW, A XXI, nos. 9, 16.

unobjectionable, he had only this to say about their 'unfitting' speeches: 'mutiny is never satisfied with reason'. Referring to his soldiering career, he said 'I know by experience (who have seen some mutinies in armies) that mutine[e]rs the more gently they are dealt with [and] the more they are persuaded with reason, the more insolent they grow.' Arundell was implying that the only way to deal with the religious and the 'regulared' laity was to shoot or hang them (this would at least teach them some manners) though, modestly, he added that, as for 'the remedy', he would 'leave [it] to the higher powers'.[59]

Now, it is possible that Montague genuinely felt, as he himself claimed, that the more aggressive tones adopted by people such as Arundell were not conducive to the sort of atmosphere in the English Catholic community which he, as a leading Catholic patron, wished to see. On the other hand, this may well have been some kind of 'good cop, bad cop' routine to make it seem to the authorities in Rome that the principal lay patron of the new bishop was essentially moderate and irenic in such matters, a man on whose word they could rely. And, in fact, Montague himself immediately retaliated against the 'three gentlemen' with the 'Disclaim' which made essentially the same case as Arundell had done.[60]

On 13 December 1627 Montague penned or authorised a letter to the cardinals of the Inquisition stating that he had been lately asked to sign a lay declaration against the authority of the bishop of Chalcedon, namely the 'letter of the three gentlemen'. He had refused point-blank. But, hearing that the declaration would probably be sent to the pope and would be alleged to represent the sentiments of the English Catholic laity, he decided to intervene early in order to register how much he disapproved of the whole sorry episode and to refute the document point by point.[61] Montague's heir, Francis Browne, had written letters to the same effect on 8 December to Cardinals Francesco Barberini and Lorenzo Magalotti.[62]

The religious, particularly the Benedictines, did not cease to angle for Montague's goodwill. Benedict Jones OSB wrote to 'Monsieur Cape' (probably William Cape, Montague's servant) at the end of November 1627 that, 'though you have much of a Frenchman, and I soe much of a Catholike Spaniard, as remaining still a true Britton . . . yet I hope your charitie will soe much corre[c]t the malignancie of the French humors as to give you leave

---

[59] AAW, A XXIII, no. 132, p. 479. Arundell had been confronted, while he was colonel of the English regiment in Flanders, with what he considered to be a mutiny. As he wrote to the earl of Salisbury in 1606, his enemies had 'suborned the sergeant-major', Sir Thomas Studder, 'against me . . . in . . . foul treasons and mutinies', *HMCS* XVIII, 376. See D. Lunn, 'Chaplains to the English Regiment in Spanish Flanders, 1605–06', *RH* 11 (1971–2), 133–55, at p. 148.
[60] AAW, A XX, no. 173.   [61] AAW, A XXI, no. 7, pp. 29–30.   [62] *Ibid.*, nos. 3, 4.

to doe me a good office with my lord'.[63] Jones had been at the house of Sir
Henry Browne, Montague's uncle, on 19 August 1627 when Smith testified
that he had not cast any doubt on confessions made to regular clergy before
the approbation issue was raised.[64] Jones apologised now for his 'absence
to his lordship' in London, although this was merely because he was 'not
willinge to appeare in those parts in the day tyme'. Jones admitted that he
had been discouraged when he heard 'that my lord is exasperated against
the regulars as if they were factiously disobedient to the Sea Apostolike, a
fault worthily odious to my lords Catholike spirite'. Jones, however, hoped
that 'this is a mistakeinge, and that my lords charitie will not permitt him
to thinke that so manie modest, pyous, learned men would putt themselves
in the least morall danger of being guiltie of soe foule a fault'. Jones trusted
that Montague would understand that the Benedictines had no choice but to
proceed as they did. 'We owe this fidelitie to our orders, we owe this obedience to the sacred canons and to the Sea Apostolike; we do not onely pretend
the name of obedience, we are not counterfaits, wee are not hipocrits.' And
so the Benedictines desired 'the continuance' of Montague's 'good grace'
and sincerely intended 'to do him all faithfull service'. In fact, 'our poore
bodie hath (as he knowes) chosen him for our speciall patron; he hath (as
wee thinke) received us into his protection'. It was 'therfore now his office
to patronise us and to preserve us from dissolution and ruin, which wee
assure our selves this new pretended authoritie, if it prevaile, will in short
tyme cause'. Jones reiterated: 'Master Cape, if the bishop of Chalcedon be
declared ordinarie of England, with true canonicall power and jurisdiction
in foro enterno, which bishops have in Catholik cuntries, the regulars must
quickly goe seeke an other beinge.' Jones believed that this was 'farr from'
Montague's 'desires'. He hoped that the viscount would 'consider the case
of his poore clients'.[65]

Others, however, were less restrained. Indeed, David Codner OSB wrote
to Montague on 25 January 1628 at his Drury Lane residence blaming him
for the bust-up between them. Montague replied on 30 January that he was
fed up with Codner.[66] The Jesuit Thomas Poulton came on 6 March 1628 to
have a set-to with Montague about the bishop's authority and the contents
of the 'letter of the three gentlemen'. (William Harewell was called in to
record, in a notarial capacity, what was said.)[67]

[63] AAW, A XXII, no. 1, p. 1. As Montague acknowledged in his 'Answer' of 19 June 1628,
the letter 'though not dated, yet written about the end of November last' was written to 'a
servant of myne (or rather to my selfe for whom it was intended)', *ibid.*, no. 65, p. 356.
[64] Lunn, 'Opposition', 8–9; PRO 31/9/129, p. 149 (VA, Barberini MS 8619, cvii, 6).
[65] AAW, A XXII, no. 1, p. 1.   [66] *Ibid.*, no. 5, pp. 13–14, 15.
[67] *Ibid.*, no. 34, p. 191. For a letter of 14 June 1628 from Smith's vicars-general to the Jesuit
general complaining that Poulton had been dispersing the 'letter of the three gentlemen',

Montague's Drury Lane house was now being used by Smith as a base from which to pump out justifications for his stance. Montague testified how 'one tyme since Christemasse last [1627]' Smith 'in verie full termes expressed at my house in Drury Lane, before a solemne audience both of preists', including John Jackson, John Gennings and William Case, 'and of lay men of very principall quality', his views on the topic of approbation.[68] As we have already briefly mentioned, in February 1628, Montague's Drury Lane residence was the venue for an effort to get the Benedictines to acknowledge Smith's appointment. A meeting was set up at which a representative of the Benedictines could witness the official reading of the breve by which Smith was appointed. But it was a failure. Montague recalled the incident in detail in his 'Apologeticall Answere'. He averred that Smith 'did publishe his briefe before manie persons of severall qualities at his first comminge in and hath also done the like at other tymes afterward'. And following a request, made soon after Michaelmas 1627, by Lawrence Anderton SJ and Benedict Jones for a sight of the breve, Smith alerted Montague to his intention to bring an authenticated copy of the same to Montague's 'lodginge at Drury Lane'. Smith turned up 'about Candlemasse', 'against which tyme' Montague had, at Smith's request, 'sent for [the] father provinciall of the Benedictins and for the reverent provinciall also of the Societie' but 'could not procure soe much as a message to be delivered' to either of them, nor could he get hold of Anderton or Jones, though they were both then in London. Evidently they did not want to see it. Jones was 'by his owne servante . . . notified to have bene in the house of his residence when my servante came to seeke him', said Montague.[69] Smith, however, on 5 February 1628 at Montague's house in Drury Lane, in the sight of various people, including 'a gentleman of approved vertue' who was in line to inherit a peerage (presumably Francis Browne, Montague's son and heir), John Gennings (Montague's friend and superior of the Franciscans), John Jackson, John Southcot and Thomas Middleton (the superior of the Dominicans), deposited the copy of his breve so that anyone who wanted to view it could simply drop in and do so. He also 'made a new publication of his authoritie'. He passed the breve under the nose of Edward Ashe, Montague's chaplain, so that the Benedictines could not claim that it did not exist or that Montague was concealing it.[70] Montague noted that on the morning of 6 February, when Smith again proclaimed his authority at Drury Lane, the bishop gave 'the holly sacrament

---

see *ibid.*, no. 64. See also AAW, A XXIV, no. 45, p. 143 (a 'defence' of the bishop of Chalcedon's proceedings in 'shewing' Poulton's letter). Poulton was temporarily dismissed from the Society for casting aspersions on Cardinal Richelieu, Smith's patron and protector, ARSJ, Anglia MS 1/ii, fo. 319r; CRS 75, 271.
[68] AA, 146.   [69] *Ibid.*, 367, 368, 374ff, and esp. 383ff.
[70] *Ibid.*, 384–7, 393f; Dockery, *CD*, 36.

of confirmation unto' Elizabeth Cary, 'my Lady Faukland a viscountesse of
Scotland and unto sundrie others then assembled'. This was clearly some
kind of pre-arranged propaganda stunt to upstage the religious, for Paulinus
Greenwood OSB was the 'usuall ghoastlie father of the Lady Faulkland', herself a notable convert of the Benedictines. Greenwood was in the house at the
time. And when, said Montague, 'my lord bishop made a new publication
of his authoritie in the presence of my selfe and the rest of the companie',
with Greenwood actually in the room, Greenwood 'went out smilinge', i.e.
smirking, 'and [would] not stay, though moved thereunto'.[71]

Here, then, to the seculars' immense satisfaction, was evidence of serious,
indeed virtually unprecedented, friction between Montague and the regular clergy who opposed Smith. The clerical client's special status was not
supposed to be questioned by his patron (as Montague's false politeness to
Codner indicated), but equally the client was supposed to respect the superior
social position of the patron – which Codner, in Montague's case, did not.

In order to defend Smith, Montague wrote the massive polemical
manuscript work which we have already frequently cited, 'An Apologeticall Answere of the Vicount Montague unto Sundrie Important Aspersions',
drafts of or extracts from which now rest in the secular priests' Roman agent's
archive.[72] This narrates in vast detail the quarrel between Smith and the religious over the issue of approbation. Smith described it in 1631 as the book

[71] AA, 389–90; Lunn, 'Opposition', 11–12. William Harewell, the notary who was always on
hand to set down and certify every little tiff that the seculars and the religious had with each
other, drew up an 'authenticall relation' of the whole event (though he omitted the bit about
Greenwood's alleged smirk), dated 5 and 6 February 1628, AA, 390. Lady Falkland had been
converted to Catholicism by *inter alia* Benedict Jones OSB and Leander Jones OSB, Lunn,
EB, 176. In January 1629 John Jackson referred to the rumours spread by the religious that
Smith had refused to make public the text of his breve of appointment. Jackson claimed
that this had arisen merely because of a misunderstanding with the Jesuit Richard Blount.
Blount had asked to see it and, on being told that it was not immediately available, appeared
satisfied, and so Smith went off on visitation. Blount then 'divulged as if he [Smith] had
refused to shew his breve'. Smith sent an authenticated copy to Jackson who 'went often
to meet with Father Blount and often inquired after him' with the intention of shoving the
breve in front of his eyes. He also 'did shewe it to Father Gray alias Anderton a principall
Jesuit under Father Blunt'. And he was 'asked' by Jones, 'bluntly before the Lord Mountague
and Sir Tobie Mathew', whether he would show it to them, and Jackson willingly agreed.
Allegedly they then refused to read it (principally because Jackson would not allow them to
make copies of it) and it was apparently averred that Blount had said 'in effect that he cared
not a strawe for the sight therof'. Montague, ever the self-conscious promoter of peace and
harmony, chipped in that 'perhaps . . . he used not the word straw but some other to that
effect'. And subsequently the regulars had had the gall 'to make use of my Lord Mountague
his testimonie at Rome, that he thinks my lord bishop to have been backward in shewing the
said breve' whereas, said Jackson, Montague's 'meaning' was 'only that he was not forward
in giving them copies', PRO, SP 16/133/7, fo. 10r.
[72] The 'Apologeticall Answere' was dated 30 October 1628. For two long extracts in the
Roman agent's papers, which were incorporated in the final work, see AAW, A XXII, nos.
65 (19 June 1628), 66.

'by my Lord Montacute which cleareth me from invalidating confessions and other false assertions'. (Smith hoped that the Roman curia would allow it to be published.)[73] It was never printed, probably because it was basically unreadable rather than merely because of the length or because no printer could be found. This tract was clearly a product of Montague's own mind. It is excruciatingly turgid – phenomenally wordy and syntactically challenged, pedantic, prolix and in many places utterly obscure. For the average reader, Montague's English is on the same plane of comprehensibility as many of his chaplains' Latin. Smith evidently retained and valued the book less for what it said than because it was written by a great Catholic layman.[74]

At the start of his tract Montague announces that he has decided to answer the letter of the 'nameless author, covered under the letters A.B.' in part because he took, or believed people could take, the letters 'A.B.' to refer to him (i.e. Anthony Browne). 'It is covered under the letters of my name, and . . . in my house (as I may terme it) . . . some thinges must be supposed to have beene done wich be unjustly and untruly imputed unto his lordship [Smith]. For the better discerninge whereof and for evidence of that plaine dealing wich . . . I meane to use', Montague announces that he will go through the controversy in some considerable detail.[75] He notes also that his

antagonist is an individuum vagum, an unknowne person, to whome noe man can resort either for redresse of grivance or for resolution in matter of doubt; whereas I am (by Gods good guifte) the Viscounte Montague, a noble man in this land, who am and will be (God assistinge mee) ever readie and willinge to anie man, upon anie resonable demaunde, to give just and reasonable satisfaction . . . in all thinges accordinge to the qualitie and condition of the person by whome I shall be demaunded.[76]

On the other hand, behind all the verbiage, Montague's opinion about whose side should be taken in the approbation controversy is clear enough. He cites at length from correspondence which had passed from supportive and sympathetic curial officials in Rome to both William Bishop and Richard Smith, and he made an outwardly moderate but nevertheless unequivocal case for the claims to ordinary jurisdiction which Smith was now asserting.

Montague's own 'Disclaim' had exposed the lobbying by Sir Tobie Mathew and his friends. The viscount said that they had come to him to get him to side with them against Smith. Montague had flatly refused and informed Smith that he had done so.[77] Montague even repeated some of the points made by Arundell. Arundell had said that Sir Tobie (this 'wimble-minded

---

[73] AAW, B 27, no. 134, cited in Allison, RSGB, III, 203.
[74] When in July 1636 George Con passed through Paris on his way to London, Smith lobbied him on behalf of himself and his friends, and 'shewed him my Lord Montagues book', AAW, A XXVIII, no. 140, p. 471.
[75] AA, 6–7.   [76] *Ibid.*, 589; AAW, A XXII, no. 65, p. 332.   [77] Allison, QJ, 124–5.

politician') 'will rather sett a schisme in the Church than reconcile his hart to obedience'.[78] Montague similarly said that questioning Smith's authority would cause a schism.[79]

Though Montague refuses to endorse some of Smith's more extreme claims, such as that the religious were deliberately ordering their lay patrons and ghostly children to withhold obedience, virtually all of his reasoning is drawn from the standard maxims of the pro-episcopal lobby. It would definitely not have found favour with Smith's opponents. Montague, like Smith and his clerical officials, deftly skated over the fact that Smith had not been granted the ordinary jurisdiction which he craved. 'When the authoritie of a superior is literally expressed in his . . . commission', with 'nothing therein contradicting or derogating from the literall sence', 'then wee thinke that the graunt is evident and out of controversie, and consequentlie all subjects whome it doth concerne are bound soe to understand it and obey it'. Montague reiterated Smith's frequent claim that he, as a bishop, knew best how to use his new powers.

Montague also rejected the notion that Smith's exercise of his authority would imperil the lives and goods of lay Catholics:

our bishops ordinary authority hath noe externall action belonging to it, the end or object whereof may justly irritate and displease, but rather please and benefitt the State, for the true end and object thereof is the peace and good government of the Catholickes to keepe them in order and due obedience, both to theire temporall and spirituall superiors, whereby the State cannot bee impeached but rather furthered and assisted.

If the regime still had reservations about Smith's presence in the kingdom, Montague claimed that this was simply out of a dislike of Catholicism rather than specifically because of the recent institution of episcopal authority among English Catholics.

So, said the viscount, the difference between the presence of priests in the kingdom and the presence there of a bishop was being ridiculously overstated by the bishop's enemies. Smith's authority was only 'in aedificationem'. He could not damage the structure of English Catholicism. What, therefore, was all this fuss about the bishop's jurisdiction as expressed through a form of tribunal?

What daunger or inconvenience had it beene to have ended such controversies by a private triall before the ordinary which Catholicks have beene enforced to referre unto private trialls by particular priests or particular umpires? Or, if through defect of coercitive authority in such umpires the administration of justice could not proceed nor controversies bee ended, why is not the coercitive power of an ordinary to bee wished for in this case?

[78] AAW, A XX, no. 166, p. 636.   [79] *Ibid.*, no. 173, p. 653.

Could lay Catholics really wish to take their suits and cases before a Protestant tribunal instead, 'which neverthelesse is subject to such scandall and daunger that fewe or noe instances can bee alleaged of such appeales'? 'The like [is] to be said of all other causes incident unto spirituall courts, as administracions, controversies of tithes, contracts, marriages, divorces, alimony, bastardy, sclaunders etc.'

Some issues, of course, necessarily had to be brought before the relevant Church-of-England authority: with

other causes that are in use with Catholicks, some of them may have apparent necessity of the publicke Protestant Arches, at least wise in some particular cases, as suing out of administrations, or perhaps alsoe proving of wills, in which cases when there shall appeare any necessity of reference to the publicke Arches, the Catholicke ordinary must needes leave them to the publicke court.

But all the other aforementioned suits ('contracts, marriages . . .' etc.) could not

for scandall and daunger bee referred to the publicke court, and have most convenient meanes of remedy by the Catholicke tribunall, for want of which either justice is not administered at all, or else it is referred to voluntary trialls, which might bee as securely, and more authentically, declared juridically by the ordinary, as by such voluntary and insufficient meanes.

So 'there are not above two [eventualities] at the most, viz proving of wills and suing of administrations, which have any necessity of reference to the publicke Arches, and these not in all cases neither'.[80]

Therefore, the authors of the 'letter of the three gentlemen' were just plain wrong. It was ridiculous to allege that there was 'any offence or daunger of incurring praemunire by a publicke tribunall for the administration of justice in these matters, for noe lawe to this purpose hath beene made since the authority was claimed; and the lawes against innovation of tribunalls made in Catholicke times were never intended against the tribunalls of ordinaries but rather against the extraordinary tribunalls of delegates, and were made in favour of the ordinary Catholicke tribunalls heere'. The 'Disclaim' rejected also the idea that secrecy and discretion were impossible to maintain. 'Noe more daunger of concealment can bee imagined in this than when twenty or thirty persons (whereof many are women and children) are admitted to heare Masse.' And if it were alleged, as indeed it was, that confusion would result if one sentence were obtained from Smith's episcopal court and a contrary one from a Church-of-England tribunal, well, Catholics should not be attending on a Protestant tribunal in the first place. And if they do so, 'the sentence of the former court is either irremediably contemned, or the bishop himselfe

---

[80] *Ibid.*, pp. 654–5.

giveth way to the appeale, and soe the sentence of the one never resisteth the other'.[81]

Others from Montague's circle and kin network started to make their views similarly felt. Among the papers of the Roman agent is a letter addressed to 'their very loving cosin Sir John Gage baronett at his lodging in London' by Edward Gage, George Smith and Edward Smith. The letter noted that Sir John had desired 'to know' whether the views expressed in the notorious 'letter of the three gentlemen' were 'indeed the sense of the laye Catholiks of the countie of Sussex or no'. The letter returned answer that no 'lay Catholik in this countie . . . did ever knowe or alowe of the sayd letter, but do[es] utterly' reject it and 'much dislik som thinges therin as nott beseeminge good Catholiks'.[82]

But it is Montague's 'Apologeticall Answere' which shows how far the head of the Browne family and his immediate circle had been reorientated by the controversy over Richard Smith. Magnificently, Montague announces that the cause is urgent, namely 'the necessarie defence of our holy mother the Church violated in the most reverend person of one of her prelates'. In these circumstances, Montague's duty was clear and transcended all personal likes and dislikes.[83] He replies block by block to specific sections of the letter of 'A.B.'. His basic point is that Smith 'did not at the first move anie question at all of the invaliditie of mens confessions. I am absolutely assured uppon my owne particular knowledge, and that for divers monethes succeedinge, hee did not.' Of this, Montague was 'morally certaine'. So the regulars were responsible for starting the controversy, even if, Montague admitted, it was possible that 'the change of tymes and the change of circumstances' might have caused a 'change of oppinion in his lordship'.[84] Montague noted how Benjamin Norton 'had shewed me the briefe of Pius Quintus . . . and, havinge imparted the same to that good Benedictine, who is my ghostly father', Montague 'could not finde anie satisfaction against soe maine authoritie'. Any further doubts which he had were settled easily by Smith, who also argued over the same point 'with an aunciient servant of myne', William Cape, 'a man much knowne and estimed of many for his intire pietie, and for many yeares, and even then, much favoured by his lordship'.[85] Montague was now convinced that Smith meant no harm to the regulars, and indeed had been seeking only to underpin canonically the spiritual chaplaincies of all the clergy by regularising the authority by which

---

[81] *Ibid.*, p. 655.   [82] AAW, A XXI, no. 14, pp. 55–6.
[83] *Ibid.*, no. 65, p. 336.   [84] AA, 16; AAW, A XXII, no. 65, p. 306.
[85] AA, 16–17, 18; AAW, A XXII, no. 65, pp. 306–7. For Smith's 'argument' with William Cape at Easter 1627, see *ibid.*, no. 91.

they heard their penitents' confessions. Anyone who said otherwise was just trying to stir up envy against Smith.[86]

In the body of the tract Montague affirms at incredible and mind-numbing length, and often in *ad hominem* mode against his adversary, the canon law authorities on which Smith relies. He refutes his opponent's opinion that the 'Councell of Trent is not heere received, and consequently doth not binde'.[87] He deals scornfully with Smith's opponents' claim that, even if the decrees of Trent are to be accounted as having been received in England, the regulars are in some sense pastors in England, 'and that as much as secular preists'. He denies that all those who hold a pastoral benefice are exempted from seeking approbation (in the sense that the pope had effectively become their ordinary – himself being 'the ordinary of ordinaries' – and that England was simply one large parish; or perhaps that they had already received approbation from a bishop beyond the seas, an approbation which they could carry with them). Montague recited, however, that Smith had acknowledged that, if any of his opponents could show that they had received personal approbation from the pope, he would gracefully concede.[88]

At this point Montague also raised the issue of who in fact gave better pastoral care. He adverted to the recent plague epidemic. The seculars had themselves made quite extensive efforts to broadcast how pastorally dutiful and charitable they had been during the course of the crisis.[89] Of the regulars he asked, 'will they yet be pastours cum honore with the exemptions and priviledges thereof; and not cum onere, with the burthen and charge thereunto belonginge'? Who, asked Montague, 'did in the tyme of the last plague discharge the tender care of pastours to the sicke and whole in this towne, concear[n]inge the sicke'? Smith had made 'charitable provision'. And 'noe smale charge' was 'undertaken by one of the archdeacons with an other of the [secular] cleargie, and one only Benedictine whose labours for about five monthes were exceedinge greate in that good worke, without any healpe of the fathers of the Societie, notwithstandinge promis [was] made for two of them to helpe in this kinde' (though Montague admitted that he had got this information from Richard Smith and one of his archdeacons). There was also a charitable and good-hearted Carmelite who was involved in the business.[90] Other regulars had 'left the poore infected persons in theire soe great extreamitie'. Smith's archdeacon 'was inforced severall tymes to ride into the cuntrie to visite the infected there who were under the charge of the fathers of the Societie'.[91] Montague almost admits that Smith's men

[86] AA, 17. [87] *Ibid.*, 61. [88] *Ibid.*, 121ff, 131ff.
[89] See Anstr. II, 103–4. [90] AA, 127. [91] *Ibid.*, 128–9.

were prepared to go round forcing their way into pestilence-infected gentry houses in order to score one over the opposition.

In reply to the regulars' accusation that Smith was going to start soaking up the already scarce financial resources that the English lay Catholics channelled to their clergy, a scandalised Montague protested that 'I meselfe doe knowe that, out [of] nyne hundred poundes which he [Smith] brought out of France as the fruites of soe many yeares laboures, he hath alreadie in the onely common affaires of his charge spent full seven hundred poundes thereof, never having taken the value of one penny to his owne private use out of those exceedinge smale portions' which he obtained from domestic resources in England.[92] Montague denied also that Smith had any immediate plans to start exacting tithes or proving wills.[93] He refutes the allegation that Smith had not made public the breve by which he had been appointed.[94] He runs through the unsurprisingly uniform opinions of Smith's vicars-general (John Colleton, Richard Broughton and the rest) showing how they all support the bishop's line. Montague even cites passages from their correspondence.[95] He concludes by giving a brief account of the chronology of the dispute up to the time that he finished his 'Apologeticall Answere'.

Montague also wrote a series of supporting letters which were enclosed with the packets of memoranda and other documents sent to Rome at this time by the pro-episcopal lobby. (As we noted above, he had written to the Inquisition cardinals on 13 December 1627.) A dispatch to the secular clergy's agent in Rome in January 1628 noted how on the 18th of the month there had been 'sent unto you', among other items, a letter which Montague had penned to Cardinal Barberini on 20 December 1627.[96] On 28 July 1628 Montague wrote directly to Pope Urban VIII to refute the current rumours that English lay Catholics were opposed to Smith's jurisdiction. A few Catholics who were devoted to the regulars had resisted Smith and had drawn many after them but, without doubt, the majority adhered to their bishop.[97] This letter was enclosed in one of 2 August 1628 to Barberini and the cardinals of the Inquisition. Montague expressed the wish that Barberini would restore the splendour of the ecclesiastical authority which had been somewhat obscured among the English Catholics 'ex quorundam adversus episcopum nostrum insurrectione'. He enquired whether his letter of 13 December 1627 had reached the Inquisition cardinals. He mentioned that John Bosvile, the new secular clergy agent, was carrying a duplicate for

---

[92] *Ibid.*, 354.   [93] *Ibid.*, 359ff.   [94] *Ibid.*, 367, 368, 374ff.
[95] *Ibid.*, 605ff, 619; AAW, A XXII, no. 65, p. 340ff.
[96] PRO, SP 16/133/12, fo. 17r; AAW, A XXI, no. 11; PRO 31/9/129, pp. 149–54 (VA, Barberini MS 8619, cvii, 6).
[97] AAW, A XXII, no. 100, p. 495.

them to read.[98] Another of his letters, of 6 August 1628, presumably also carried by Bosvile, was addressed to the Jesuit general Muzio Vitelleschi, for whom the English pro-episcopal lobby did not reserve quite the same hatred which they harboured for many others of his order. Montague said that he had nothing against the Society personally. Some of his best friends were Jesuits, and he would be the last person in the world to deprive them of their just rights and privileges. But some Jesuits, notably Richard Blount and Lawrence Anderton, were behaving very badly, particularly over the issue of the Council of Trent's decrees concerning clandestine marriages.[99]

In his screed of 6 August 1628 Montague complained also that the English Catholic laity who followed the Jesuits neglected their duty to come to be confirmed by the bishop, and treated the sacrament itself with contempt. In his missive of 28 July Montague had protested to the pope that a letter, under an assumed name (Charles Scott), was circulating which accused Smith of polemically manipulating the sacrament. Montague averred that he himself, 'qui sacrae illi actioni saepe saepius interfui', i.e. who had frequently attended Smith's conferral of the sacrament, never heard Smith say (as Scott affirmed) that the unconfirmed were only 'half-Christian'. What he did hear the bishop say more than once was that they were not as yet 'perfect Christians'.[100]

On 26 October 1628 came another letter from Montague to Barberini, begging him to pay attention to the issues which Bosvile would raise with him – the deplorable chaos among English Catholics and the attacks on the bishop of Chalcedon. In particular, Montague slated the Benedictines'

---

[98] *Ibid.*, no. 116, p. 539. See also *ibid.*, no. 93. When John Bosvile was given his instructions as to the contacts he should make when he journeyed across Europe to Rome to take up the post of secular clergy agent there, he was told to show to the English secular priests at Douai, among other documents, 'my Lord Mountague his letter to the Inquisition which begins Non patitur, 13 December 1627'. The letter was to be shown also to Pierre de Bérulle in Paris. Once Bosvile was in Rome he was to 'shew the copie of my Lord Montague his letter to the Inquisition to as many as you can . . . but beware there be no coppies taken of it', *ibid.*, no. 93, pp. 469, 471. Bosvile arrived in Rome in early 1629, closely followed by a written denunciation from David Codner, accusing Bosvile of immorality and of laxity over the oath of allegiance, Hughes, *RCR*, 359; Lunn, 'Opposition', 13.

[99] AAW, A XXII, no. 121, p. 553; AAW, OB I/ii, no. 112, fo. 217r–v; CRS 22, 161–5; Hughes, *RCR*, 362. In his 'Apologeticall Answere' Montague claimed that it had 'beene resolutely urged by Father Laurence Anderton in my hearinge, wich I understand to be much disseminated and particularly amonge woemen, that by admittinge the Councell of Trent our children are concluded to be bastardes', AA, 82–3. For Vitelleschi's dismay at Montague's 'accusations', see ARSJ, Anglia MS 1/ii, fo. 285r.

[100] AAW, A XXII, no. 100, p. 495. Matthew Kellison argued that 'without a bishop you can be no perfect Christians' since 'confirmation (which ordinarilie you cannot have without a bishop)' is the sacrament 'which maketh you men in a spirituall life'. So, 'without a bishop you cannot hope to have . . . that speciall and abundant grace to professe your faith in tyme of persecution with an undaunted courage'. Confirmation was 'the ordinarie meanes by which it is given'. For want of this sacrament the heretic Novatus 'fell . . . as perchaunce many in our countrie have fallen', Kellison, *A Treatise of the Hierarchie*, sig. b7v–8r.

principal and printed assault on Smith, Barlow's *Mandatum*. From this text
Montague quoted a long passage in which, Montague alleged, the Benedictines threatened a schism in England if Rome's decision went against them.
He also quoted a long extract from a document known as the 'letter of the
three regulars'.[101] Their intention was, he said, to make the laity judges in
ecclesiastical matters and thus obtain authority over the Catholic Church in
England. They disparaged papal authority in some respects. And they argued
in bad faith on the issue of whether the Council of Trent's decrees were bind-
ing in England. Montague added that the Franciscans, the Carmelites and
the Minims abstained from hostility to the bishop.[102] If Montague had been
lukewarm at one time on the episcopacy issue, he was more than making up
for it now with a veritable flurry of petitions and memoranda to the Roman
curia.

DENOUEMENT

Richard Smith's cause, however, foundered. In the end, Rome refused to
support Smith unequivocally. Whereas in June 1627 the Congregation for
the Propagation of the Faith had instructed Smith to examine ('recognoscere')
the faculties of priests in England, the curial cardinals subsequently refrained
from backing him to the extent that he demanded.

In December 1627 the Inquisition made the first of a number of decisions
on the issue – or rather, came up with a classic curial administrative fudge.
In early January 1628, Peter Biddulph (in Paris) reported to Smith the burden of the curial ruling, in a letter the reading of which must have been as
pleasant and easy for Smith as swallowing sandpaper. The Inquisition and
the Holy Father had 'presently sent hether ther opinion and determination
in this matter to the most illustrious nuncio, who hath given me order to signifie it unto your lordship, that you may put it in execution as coming from
your own motion'. The 'holly congregation' desired that 'you should shew
as favorable' a countenance 'as may be to the regulars, especially in these
tymes, for to avoyd all occasion of complainte and difference'. Biddulph had
been ordered to command Smith not to summon 'missionaries to present
themselfes before you, or your viccars, to take approbation for to confess

---

[101] In *c.* August 1627 an attack on Smith's strategy had been penned by Thomas Preston OSB
under the name of the Benedictine David Codner. It was delivered in November to John
Jackson by a committee consisting of Mark Crowder OSB, the Dominican George Popham
and Lawrence Anderton SJ, and so came to be known as the 'letter of the three regulars',
Lunn, 'Opposition', 10; AA, 78–9 (Montague dated the letter, however, to 10 November
1627).

[102] AAW, A XXII, no. 141, pp. 611–18. Yet another petition, from Montague to the pope,
dated 25 July 1629, appealed for the confirmation of ordinary jurisdiction in England,
AAW, A XXIII, no. 123.

seculars, but to leave them to ther liberty'. Nor should Smith noise it about that confessions were void 'for want of' his 'approbation'. The pope advised that Smith should stop insisting on 'this question: whether you be ordinary or no'. Smith should be satisfied with 'delegat jurisdiction, because this is certayn and sur'. The pope admitted that Smith had 'the right' but commanded him to 'conforme . . . [him] self to the difficulty of the tymes . . . [rather] than soe rigorously demand' his 'right'. It can have come as little comfort to Smith to be told that the pope thought that 'as for the administration of baptisme, marriage and extreme unction . . . the regulars' were 'bound to come to take' his 'approbation'. 'And if the tymes were better, as ther was appearance the last year, his Hollines would not only be most redy to give' Smith 'the foresayd jurisdiction to approve regulars, but also what other facultie soever which in this tyme can not be executed'.

What the curia really wanted, quite naturally, was that the warring parties in England should simply shut up. Biddulph noted that it was the will of the pope and the Inquisition that they wished their 'determination' to be notified to Smith 'without making any decree'. Smith should, 'without any noise at all, according to the sayd directions . . . end this bussines quietly and peasibly with the regulars'.[103]

In all likelihood, this would not have settled very much, and in any case, according to Viscount Montague, the text of the decision went astray before reaching England. So the two sides were left relying on second-hand evidence about what had been decided. Consequently they still refused to give an inch.[104]

The nuncio in Paris, Guido del Bagno, instructed Smith to get on with giving approbation to the regulars. Smith finally conceded on 7 February 1628. But clearly neither he nor his opponents thought that the controversy was over. Smith's letter which issued the stipulated approbation noted that it was given 'only *lite pendente*, for the time the controversy of approbation hangs undecided by his Holiness'.[105]

Initially, after the duke of Buckingham's assassination, Smith seemed likely to regain some lost ground. Benedict Jones reported on 5 September 1628 that 'a generall peace is now more probable'. An end to the current military conflict with the French 'will much animate Chalcedon against us, and we understand that his Holinesse greatlie labours that peace as beeing little affected to the House of Austria'.[106]

---

[103] AAW, A XXII, no. 7, p. 19. See AAW, A XXI, no. 17 (December 1627) for Rome's decision that the bishop of Chalcedon did not have ordinary jurisdiction and was not to compel approbation from the regulars. For the Jesuit general's joy at this decision, see ARSJ, Anglia MS 1/ii, fo. 267v.

[104] Lunn, 'Opposition', 11, 19 n. 116; AA, 646–7.

[105] Lunn, 'Opposition', 11; AAW, A XXII, no. 18, p. 107; *CSPD 1627–8*, 550.

[106] AAW, A XXII, no. 131, p. 580; PRO, SP 16/107/105, fo. 207v.

But the secular clergy now told a story that the anti-episcopal agitators were putting their case against Smith directly to the Stuart regime. John Southcot narrated, in a letter of 19 December 1628 to Thomas White, how 'some of the hoatest among the laity ([Francis] Ployden being thought to be the cheefest of them) have put up a kind of petition to the king in the name of all Catholickes, wherin they do disclaime from the bishops power'. Southcot understood that they had informed Sir John Coke 'of no less [*sic*] than nine probates of wills made by this bishop or by his authority (which is altogeather false) and hereupon the said secretary at the councell table very lately produced this information, the king him self being present'. Allegedly Charles flew off the handle, followed by the lord keeper, and 'nonn durst open their mouths to excuse or mollify the matter any thing at all'. Charles 'threatned that he would hang the bishop if he could catch him by any meanes'. Southcot believed that this course had been encouraged by Barlow's *Mandatum*, for a copy of the book had been presented to Archbishop Abbot 'who urged this matter very far also at the councell table, since his late calling therunto by the king'. This was the cause of the 'very sharp proclamation' which was now issued for Smith's arrest, a copy of which Southcot enclosed in his missive to White.[107] The proclamation (issued on 11 December 1628) denounced Smith as a traitor for persuading the king's subjects away from their allegiance, for usurping 'to himself episcopall jurisdiction from the Sea of Rome' and exercising it within the realm, and for holding continual intelligence with the king's enemies.[108]

Southcot knew that this was largely show on Charles's part, 'for, when these matters were in hoatest treaty, the State was certainly informed where the bishop was and could have then apprehended him if they had meant it really'. As Coke had made clear when he addressed the March 1628 recusancy committee, the regime was well aware of both what Smith was doing and what his enemies said he was doing.[109] Southcot said that 'the lord that was known ordinarily to harbour him had express warning sent him by the king to look to him self'. In other words, Charles was trying to head off the inevitable stream of anti-popish agitation which would start when parliament assembled. (It was scheduled to meet on 20 January 1629.) He was also, speculated Southcot, trying 'to terrify the French' in the run up to the

---

[107] AAW, A XXII, no. 154, p. 665. John Bosvile reported the incident to the cardinals of the Congregation for the Propagation of the Faith, and accused Sir George Calvert, Baron Baltimore of being the instigator of the petition, Allison, QJ, 126.
[108] AAW, A XXII, no. 153, p. 663; Larkin, *SRP*, II, no. 104.
[109] AAW, A XXII, no. 154, p. 665; Allison, QJ, 127; cf. Lunn, 'Opposition', 14, 20 n. 163. Allison argues that the charges against Smith may have been laid in two stages – by Calvert in March 1628, and then by Plowden in November 1628, Allison, QJ, 127.

negotiations for the 'treaty of peace which is now at hand, the king being informed that the bishop hath ben a dependent of Cardinal Richelieu'.[110]

On the other hand, not only Coke but other members of the regime were, it seems, still far from happy about Smith's apparent encroachments on the king's authority. Southcot's letter notes that the king's and the lord keeper's vitriolic remarks about Smith were 'seconded' by others. As we saw in the previous chapter, efforts had been made to arrest some of Smith's leading officials. Then, on 28 August 1628, Edmund Arrowsmith (who, although he was a Jesuit, was one of Smith's officers) was executed,[111] and George Fisher believed that he was going to suffer the same fate.

But the storm passed. Arrowsmith's execution was, itself, hardly an example of joined-up government. According to the diarist Walter Yonge, it was the angry presiding judge Sir Henry Yelverton who was determined that the priest should die. Apparently, after the jury returned its verdict against him, Arrowsmith produced 'a letter to the judge from the duke of Buckingham' (whose own death, at the hands of John Felton, was only a few days away) in Arrowsmith's favour. Yelverton 'tolde him that publike affayers were to bee preferred before private letters'. At this, Arrowsmith brought out 'a kynde of pardon from the queene', but Yelverton replied that 'hee was to take notice of the kings proclamacion', of 3 August 1628, 'for execution of lawes against such persons, which proclamacion bore date 2 dayes after the pardon'. Arrowsmith's final throw of the dice was a letter from Charles himself, but Yelverton 'tolde him that the lawes and statutes of the kingdome must bee . . . respected or preferred before letters, and soe gave judgment'. But Yelverton still had to bully the 'popishly affected' sheriff before the local authorities would agree to slaughter Arrowsmith according to custom.[112] The trial and execution of the priest would hardly have done anything for the king's reputation as a convinced anti-popish Protestant.

And, indeed, as we know, Charles was unable to live up to the expectations of the anti-papists in the 1629 parliament, just as he had failed to satisfy them in the 1628 session. It is clear from the hostile members' speeches about the crown's record against popery that the failure to proceed harshly against the Jesuits arrested at Clerkenwell was one of the things which drove

---

[110] AAW, A XXII, no. 154, p. 665.
[111] For the accounts of Arrowsmith's martyrdom collected by the secular clergy, see *ibid.*, nos. 129, 143, 156. The Jesuits also wrote eulogies of Arrowsmith, ARSJ, Anglia MS 1/ii, fos. 284v, 285r, 290r, 295v. According to William Hargrave, a Jesuit version of Arrowsmith's misfortunes was 'sett forth . . . in French' at Liège, AAW, A XXII, no. 156, p. 672.
[112] BL, Additional MS 35331, fo. 24v. I am very grateful to Thomas Cogswell for this reference. For the proclamation, see Larkin, *SRP*, II, no. 96.

the Commons into paroxysms of fury, though it was not just royal leniency towards Catholics which had distanced the king from many of his subjects.[113]

Smith back-pedalled furiously now on the scope of the jurisdictional authority which he claimed. He claimed that his authority in no way prejudiced that of the crown. He denied that he had set up a 'new tribunal' for proving wills, or 'any other kind of tribunal than St Paul did when he excommunicated the incestuous Corinthians, or regular superiors do when they correct their brethren, neither have I all these four years exercised any authority at all over any lay person'.[114] He also denied that he was a lackey of the French Court. He had been a pensioner of Richelieu but, since arriving in England, he said, he had not taken a penny from the cardinal. Nor had he received any missive from him nor written to him more than once or twice 'since the French departed from your Majesty'. And, before that, he wrote to him for no other end than to move him to intercede with the French king that Catholics might enjoy that quietness which they hoped had been agreed upon and guaranteed in the treaty of marriage. Nor had he corresponded with Marie de Médicis.

Although Smith's 'new' thoughts on his authority were widely circulated, and his officials seemed on the verge of fixing up some sort of accommodation or *modus vivendi* with his critics, this prospective *détente* failed because Smith's opponents demanded that Smith go on the record and make a public statement about his acceptance of the limits on his power. And this was something which he refused to do.[115]

A second royal proclamation was now issued against Smith – on 24 March 1629. This was clearly intended to answer some of the criticisms levelled at the crown in the recently dissolved parliament.[116] However, no effective attempt was made to arrest Smith himself. There is a famous story, retailed by the papal agent Gregorio Panzani, that, around the time that the proclamation was issued, Charles wrote to Smith privately concerning a dispensation for Henrietta Maria which would permit her not to keep the rules on fasting while she was pregnant![117] But repeated public denunciations for treason hardly did Smith's credibility any good.

There were other bids to shore up Smith's position, and he drew on all the resources that Viscount Montague's entourage gave him. An attempt was made in summer 1629 to organise a conference between him and his

---

[113] See BL, Additional MS 35331, fos. 26r, 27r; Foley II, 420, I, 102–3, 104. George Fisher spent his time in prison busily writing up a terrifying account of his ordeal. But his sentence was commuted to one of life imprisonment, and he was soon, in effect, at liberty, Anstr. II, 106–7; PRO, SP 16/147/12, fo. 22r.

[114] AAW, A XXII, no. 154, p. 667. Smith asserted later, in a letter of 31 December 1629 to an unnamed lady at Court, that his authority was only spiritual. See Allison, QJ, 128–9.

[115] Allison, QJ, 131–2.

[116] Larkin, *SRP*, II, no. 109; AAW, SEC 16/1/4.   [117] Allison, QJ, 132; Hughes, *RCR*, 370.

opponents. As Smith wrote to Edward Bennett on 1 August, asking him to come up to London for the event, the conference was likely to be held in front of the French ambassador. Smith's friend, the Carmelite Thomas Dawson, had come to the capital and had spoken with the ambassador. Anthony Shelley was already there and John Colleton was expected. Smith suggested to Bennett, 'in order that you may be here the safer, I wish you [to] bring up your hostesse', Lady Dormer, 'as my Lord Gerard is comen, and she may come upon good pretense of seing' her nephew 'my Lord Montague before he goe over' (on a trip to the Continent to visit the English College at Douai), 'and also his daughter [Frances] Blomer who is brought to bed of a sonne'. They would have to summon all their reserves of patronage power because 'the Jesuits noble[men] and gentlemen are come to speake against the bishop from al partes of England'.[118]

Thus the last and desperate battle which Smith fought in England against his Catholic enemies took the form of a clash of patrons as much as a polemically informed debate merely between clerics. By now, however, Smith had been driven to take refuge in the French embassy. Secretary Coke was still issuing warrants to informers to procure Smith's arrest.[119] Finally, in 1631, Smith stormed off into exile in France, and resigned his episcopal title in what appears to have been an ill-judged fit of pique. This was, at least for the time being, the end of Smith's claim to the overarching power within the English Catholic community which he and his friends had craved.

THE VISIT TO DOUAI

Let us backtrack briefly to what was in effect the second Viscount Montague's ecclesiastical swan song – his visit to the college at Douai in autumn 1629 (Montague's first ever overseas journey). It was an important public demonstration of his goodwill towards and patronage of the secular clergy leadership's vision for the future of English Catholicism.[120] The second viscount was showing that, even in his last days, he was still prepared physically to turn out for the cause. One of Thomas White's correspondents

---

[118] AAW, A XXIII, no. 126, p. 455.

[119] BL, Additional MS 64901, fo. 108r (a warrant to John Fincham to apprehend Bishop Smith, 18 November 1630).

[120] An unsigned undated draft letter in the English secular clergy's Roman agent's papers, assigned to 1628 and addressed to Montague, proclaims that 'I have often understood from Doctor [Matthew] Kellison what an honourable friend your lordship hath been' to Douai. Douai had not received its 'accustomed pension from Spaine for these eight yeeres space nor from Rome these twelve monethds'. But others had relieved and sustained the college, 'amongst whome your Honor most worthely deserves the first place and therefore doubt not but that almighty God will give you the best reward'. His benefaction was 'an addition to your other good works, to which your glorie will be correspondent', AAW, A XXIII, no. 77, p. 295.

Figure 29.   Miles Pinckney, founder and chaplain of the English Augustinian convent at Paris.

told him that the 'little noble man our frend' had set out on 22 August on a journey to visit the college. The college diary for September 1629 records Montague's visit. On 1/11 September Matthew Kellison sent Miles Pinckney (see Figure 29) 'ad osculandum manus illustrissimi Domini D. Antoniae Mariae, Vicecomitis Montis Acuti eumque nomine reverendi domini praesidis [Kellison] ac totius domus ad collegium nostrum invitandum'. Kellison set out to meet Montague on 2/12 September accompanied by Robert Blundeston and others.[121] Montague was received into the college in fine style: 'ingressus est aulam domini praesidis, scholaribus convocatis, nomine totius collegii a Joanne Floyed paucis carminibus salutatus est'. Then he went to visit both the church and the hospital: 'ingressus est ecclesiam ubi Litaniae B. Mariae Virginis canebantur in gratiarum actionis [*sic*] pro faelici ipsius adventu, dein ductus est ad novum valetudinarium ubi cum suis hospitatus est'. On the next day Montague was honoured with a public disputation held in front of him. The 'defender', Richard White, dedicated his effort to him. Then in the refectory a play about St Ignatius of Antioch was performed: 'exhibita fuit . . . tragicomoedia de reditu sancti Ignatii episcopi et martyris ab exilio'. This was an obvious piece of propaganda on Richard Smith's behalf. It made all the standard points about the connection between episcopal rule and the promotion of true religion.

The viscount stayed until 18 September when, in front of him and the entire college, William Hargrave pronounced an oration 'in laudem vicecomitis progenitorumque ipsius' (particularly his grandfather, Sir Anthony Browne, the first Viscount Montague). When Hargrave had finished, Montague made a gracious reply, demonstrating his affection for the college 'ac clerum Anglicanum'. 'The words of your Reverence', Montague proclaimed,

spoken in reference to my grandfather, I acknowledge, and for them I thank you. But at the part which refers to my self I am confused, for I feel that the qualities for which you have been at pains to praise me are indeed far from me. I pray God that they may be fulfilled in me. But this I profess, that I have always wished to be a son of the Catholic Church and, please God, I always shall be. I assure you that the whole reason for turning off my journey from Calais, from the way which leads to Paris, was respect for this holy community.[122]

He then left for Brussels with Kellison and Pinckney. Just as the congenial little expedition to Douai was the occasion for a set of performances which would demonstrate to the eye of an important section of the Catholic community that this powerful lay patron still stood four-square behind the

---

[121] Blundeston, who had been at the Collège d'Arras, had set out for England, from Douai, on 5/15 May 1628. He was arrested at Dover where he refused the oath of allegiance, Anstr. II, 30–1. It is possible that his trip was connected with the subsequent visit of the viscount to Douai.

[122] CRS 10, 278–9, 419.

bishop, so the journey of Kellison and Pinckney to Brussels with the viscount was not merely to keep him company. A paper in the secular clergy's archives witnesses that Pinckney certified that at Brussels, in September, he was deputed to hear what a nun, Sister Ursula Hewicke, had to say in front of Henry Caleras, archpriest and visitor of the monastery of the Blessed Virgin at Brussels. She testified, in Montague's presence, that she had, back in October 1620, seen Richard Smith's arch-enemy Sir Tobie Mathew saying Mass.[123] The knowledge that Mathew was a secret cleric was one of the few weapons available to Smith to strike back at Mathew. (Smith referred contemptuously to Mathew as 'a cheef stickler'.[124]) As Montague travelled back to England, he still had both the time and the inclination to witness his clerical friends' efforts to collect the dirt on their Catholic enemies![125]

The second Viscount Montague expired on 23 October 1629. One of his attendants, his priest William Wright, testified in a note to Smith on the day of Montague's death that 'the last full period that ever he made to me (I meane the Right Honorable Vicount Mountacute) was: recommende me to my lord bishop and tell him that, as I allwaies were, so I die his devote and obedient child'.[126]

CONCLUSION

We can see here that the approbation controversy was in some sense a continuation of the political passions aroused by the dynastic marriage negotiations, during the early 1620s, between the Stuart regime on the one hand and the Spaniards and the French on the other – not so much because Catholics were factionally divided into Hispanophiles and Francophiles but because the opportunity for changing their political state and status had been raised by the prospect of one dynastic match, with Spain, and was then, at least temporarily, realised by a completely different treaty, i.e with the French. In the process this fractured the Catholic community much more seriously than if the accommodation with the State, for which, in theory, all Catholics hoped, had been achieved more quickly and decisively. Inevitably both the attempt to change the Catholics' political position and the new authority claimed by Bishop Richard Smith came to be seen as an adjunct of the alliance with France and of a royal foreign policy which, in spite of the military hostilities against Louis XIII in the later 1620s, was increasingly seen as a betrayal of the pan-European 'Protestant cause' – and, also, by many Catholics, as a betrayal of the Spaniards who alone, those Catholics claimed, had the

---

[123] CRS 22, 176.   [124] AAW, A XXI, no. 101, p. 406.
[125] At some point on his journey, Montague also made time for an interview with Richard Blount SJ who was in Flanders, ARSJ, Anglia MS 1/ii, fo. 307v.
[126] AAW, A XXIII, no. 146, p. 521.

true interests of English Catholicism at heart. The French by contrast (or so it could be argued) were more cynical, politically manipulative and self-interested than the Spaniards.

Later, in September 1631, George Leyburn wrote to Smith that '4 or 5' of his principal enemies had gone to 'satisfy the Spanish agent in whom the Jesuits information hath made great impression'. The agent was saying that

> the Spanish divines hath [*sic*] declared against you; secondly that you have a pension of the Cardinal Richlieu; thirdly that you . . . make a faction amongst Catholics, having been sent for their comfort; fourthly that you have been . . . [Richelieu's] chaplain; fifthly that your controversy is a . . . plot devised by the French to hinder the increase of Catholics for their own politic ends or at least to Frenchify them and avert them from Spain, and that you are an instrument of theirs for the compassing of their designs.[127]

So much, then, for the aristocratically sponsored attempt to unite the English Catholic community under the leadership of a priest in episcopal orders! But in the years after Bishop Smith's somewhat ignominious retreat to France and into the bosom of his favourite cardinal, and even after the death of his friend the second Viscount Montague, the political logic of the developments of the early 1620s, and of the pro-episcopal lobby's and its patrons' subsequent attempts to capitalise on those developments, continued to work itself out, generating in the process a great deal of both public and private comment about Catholicism in England. In the next chapter this is what we shall be looking at – the consequences of the politico-ecclesiastical Catholic quarrels of the 1620s.

And we shall attempt to look at these developments by reference to the reactions which the disagreements about episcopacy evoked among the leading aristocratic members of the English Catholic community. Although we have done our best to recover as much as we can about the Browne family, one of the infuriating things about the patronage and kinship networks among the upper echelons of English Catholicism during this period is that, for the most part, we really know so little about them. We can point to a significant number of peers and gentry who were identified by contemporaries as Catholics. But for most of the period we have no archival sources to turn to in order to find out what these people thought about specific politico-ecclesiastical questions, or to identify those with whom they discussed them, or to ascertain how they made the weight of their opinions felt.

Not the least significant aspect of the approbation controversy and its aftermath, therefore, is that the battle between the different clerical factions brought their patrons temporarily out into the open. In other words, at various points in the later 1620s and during the 1630s, the radical reforms

---

[127] AAW, OB I/ii, no. 121 (printed in CRS 22, 176).

of the community which had been proposed by Bishop Smith and his friends (including the second Viscount Montague and his circle) expose to our view several other aristocratic entourages and allow us to see the potential size and power of the aristocratic underpinnings of early Stuart Catholicism. This unusual, in some ways unique, view of the patronage structure of Caroline Catholicism afforded us by this dispute also reveals to us how far, in spite of the failure of Smith's project, the relationship between Catholicism and the early Stuart State had been transformed. In addition, it allows us to glimpse how the extended Catholic discussions of the virtues and values of hierarchy might allow a significant section of the Catholic community to allege that it was strongly in sympathy with what many contemporaries regarded as a new ethos within the Caroline Church of England.

14

Catholicism, clientage networks and the debates of the 1630s

'BUSTLING CHALCEDON IS DEAD IN THE NEST'[1]

The second Viscount Montague died while his chaplains and relatives were fully engaged in an apocalyptic struggle with their enemies. This was a battle which, as we have seen, they lost. Bishop Richard Smith's opponents settled with him by denouncing him to the regime. After two proclamations, in 1628 and 1629, which pronounced him to be a traitor, Smith was forced to take refuge at the French embassy in London.[2]

The enemies of the secular clergy leadership now gathered to press home their advantage. Sir George Calvert, Baron Baltimore, returned from his Newfoundland colony in 1630, and took control of the anti-Smith brigade. He raised again the issue and text of the 'letter of the three gentlemen'. In March 1631 it was put out again – under a new title: 'The Declaration of the Lay Catholics of England'.[3] It was shown to the Catholic ambassadors resident in London and, in April, to Carlos Coloma as he was returning to Spain through Brussels. Coloma signed a statement which guaranteed that the documentation presented to him was accurate.[4]

Smith's supporters struck back, mainly by trying to exploit their French contacts. The French ambassador Fontenay was, at first, reluctant to help them. But in late June 1631 he agreed to sign an amended version of a screed of 31 May[5] which ended up being printed at Paris under the title *Général*

---

[1] AAW, A XXIV, no. 45, p. 158 (reported comment of Thomas Poulton SJ on Richard Smith).
[2] See ch. 13, pp. 464, 466 above; *NCC*, 3–4.
[3] AAW, A XXIV, no. 77. See also *ibid.*, nos. 72, 78, 85, 86, 155; ch. 13, p. 437 above (for the origins of the 'letter of the three gentlemen').
[4] *The Attestation of . . . Don Carlos Coloma* (St Omer, 1631); ARCR II, no. 191; Hughes, *RCR*, 382, 384; Allison, QJ, 134.
[5] Entitled 'Abrenuntiatio Catholicorum Laicorum Anglice in Declarationum quandam sub ipsorum nomine false editum', AAW, A XXIV, no. 98.

Désadveu des Catholiques Lais d'Angleterre, contre une Déclaration qui a esté faussement publiée à leur nom.[6]

Nevertheless, Smith's position had become virtually impossible. With the breve *Britannia* (29 April/9 May 1631), the papacy finally came down on the side of his critics. Smith left the country on 24 August 1631, never to return. George Leyburn conducted him as far as Calais before coming back to London.[7]

Smith got to Paris and huffily resigned his episcopal title. He seems to have believed that, by doing this, he could cajole the pope into appointing another bishop, or possibly more than one.[8] The pope accepted Smith's resignation but did not replace him. Smith realised he had miscalculated, and tried to withdraw his resignation, but by then it was too late.[9]

Now the *post mortem* started. What had the English Catholic community really thought about Smith's claims? How far was it divided on the principal issues which had arisen among them in the early Stuart period and which had crystallised in the later 1620s during Smith's bid for dominance? How much of an *entrée* did Smith have within the other Catholic aristocratic entourages? And what was the situation at Court? Henrietta Maria and the French ambassador, predictably, came out in support of Smith. Probably there were many lay Catholics willing to do the same. Smith's enemies retaliated, however, by compiling, in October 1631, a 'Protestatio Declaratoria' which claimed that the English Catholic nobility almost all opposed Smith.[10]

But this was the point. How exactly did you measure Catholic opinion here? As in the appellant dispute, the various factions all claimed to represent the true sense of the Catholic community. After Smith went into exile a good deal of the argument revolved around who, exactly, could be said to have supported him and who had not. Affidavits and attestations were collected from prominent members of the community, in particular from the aristocracy.[11]

This brings us back to one of the issues which has been central to this book – namely the clientage networks which the clergy inhabited among their principal Catholic patrons, and how they functioned during this period. (In the 1630s we find the seculars compiling extensive surveys of the Catholic

[6] Fontenay reacted badly when Baltimore and Lord Somerset came to complain about it, Allison, QJ, 134–5; AAW, A XXIV, no. 99, p. 401; ARCR I, no. 362.
[7] Anstr. II, 193.
[8] See ch. 13, p. 467 above; AAW, A XXIV, no. 179.
[9] See AAW, A XXIV, no. 214 (Richard Smith to Pope Urban VIII, 8/18 December 1631, explaining that he had not intended absolutely to resign his jurisdiction); AAW, A XXVI, nos. 21, 29.
[10] NCC, 6; see below in this chapter.   [11] NCC, *passim*.

nobility.[12]) These nobles' entourages were one of the prime locations for these pitches for recognition, patronage and influence. And although we have seen that the Catholic episcopal project was vitiated because it was not sufficiently centrist, and not fully accepted by many major patrons in the Catholic community (even the second Viscount Montague's renewed support for Richard Smith in the controversies of the later 1620s may have come relatively late in the day), the fact was that the rhetoric which was used by each side to describe what good order, discipline and authority actually meant in these circumstances was designed to recruit support from as wide a section of the community as possible. These were values and ideals to which all patrons should, in both theory and practice, have subscribed. As we have seen, leading secular priests, including some of those whom we have discovered close to the centre of the Browne family, were well positioned to exert influence and to lobby in various locales and situations for what they wanted. These clergy continued their pitch- and case-making during the 1630s, trying to recruit support and mould opinions among the eminent Catholic families to which they had access.

It is worth reviewing how this struggle was conducted, for it reveals not just the range of opinions in the upper ranks of the Catholic community about controverted questions of Church government but also how fluid such opinion was, and how noble benefactors of the clergy could fluctuate between support for one side and for the other.

This battle for influence came out into the open with the aforementioned 'Protestatio Declaratoria' of October 1631 against Smith. The 'Protestatio' was intended by its promoters to be the final devastating blow to the bishop and his party. It was dispatched to Rome with additional documentation, including lists of names of Catholic nobles. Twelve had signed the protestation itself. Five had said that they agreed with it; but they had not actually put their signatures to it.[13] Of the other Catholic nobles, two (John Paulet, marquis of Winchester and Sir Thomas Arundell, Baron Arundell) were alleged to be for the most part favourable to the bishop, though they were said to

[12] See e.g. AAW, A XXVIII, no. 3, pp. 13–18, part of a review (dated 31 January 1635) of the state of Catholicism in England.
[13] According to Peter Biddulph, in April 1632, the witnessing of the document 'was done before a notarye whom the Jesuitts caused to come out of the Low Countryes', AAW, A XXVI, no. 49, p. 149. The nobles who signed were John Talbot, earl of Shrewsbury; Henry Somerset, earl of Worcester; Thomas Darcy, Earl Rivers; James Touchet, earl of Castlehaven; Lord William Howard of Naworth; Thomas Somerset, Viscount Cashel; Edward Somerset, Lord Herbert; Sir Henry Neville, Baron Abergavenny; Thomas Windsor, Baron Windsor; William Petre, Baron Petre; Sir Thomas Brudenell, Baron Brudenell; and Sir George Calvert, Baron Baltimore. Those who gave their assent, without signing, were Richard Burke, earl of St Albans; Sir Thomas Savage, Viscount Savage; Ulick Burke, Viscount Tunbridge; Henry Parker, Baron Morley and Monteagle; and Edward Vaux, Baron Vaux.

think that it was not now the right time to restore Catholic episcopal jurisdiction in England.[14] Two others (Francis Manners, earl of Rutland and Francis Browne, Viscount Montague) were not absolutely committed to one side or the other. Only one (Sir Henry Constable, Viscount Dunbar) supported the bishop wholeheartedly.[15] The same document also claimed that 300 gentry had allowed their signatures to be appended to it, and others had given their assent to it.[16]

As John Southcot described it, this document was 'composed' by Francis Plowden, Sir Basil Brooke and 'other their complices'. 'By the Jesuitts them selves' it was 'carried up and down all England' and shown to 'all Catholickes they could meet withall, whose consents, sometimes by persuasions, sometimes by threatnings, and alwaies by deceipt and cosenage, they extorted from divers as some of them have witnessed'.[17] Southcot informed Peter Biddulph in May 1632 that 'I heare my lord of St Albans gave his voice against my lords ordinariship not in writing but by word of mouth, but it was by importuning of Lord Baltimor, misinforming him about tribunals etc. The like importunity he used with others, being the Jesuitts chief instrument in this buissenesse, but', Southcot enthused, 'God rewarded him soon after with an untimely death'. 'His memory is and wilbe hateful for this action, as it is ridiculous', thought Southcot, for his clandestine marriage to his chambermaid.[18]

Southcot also fumed that Lord Brudenell 'sought to draw in my Lord Morley by . . . misinformation, telling him' scandalous stories of Smith's ambition, and in particular that he really had intended to set up a dictatorial tribunal to enforce his own brand of episcopal justice. Southcot had asked Leyburn 'to whom my Lord Morly discovered the matter afterward . . . to sett it down particulerly'. Southcot hoped that he would 'do it also in his letter to you', so that the nuncio in Paris 'may have a scantling of their dealings, and know in what manner they have (probably) wrought with the rest' of the Catholic aristocracy. Southcot feared that they had not 'been ashamed to use' the name of the marquis of Winchester, probably the most socially exalted Catholic patron of the period, 'in this kind, bycause I know he was sett uppon particulerly at his last being in town by my Lord Baltimore, Sir Basil [Brooke] and Mr George Gage in my Lord Rivers his house'. Southcot planned to cause Robert Floyd, a physician, who was one of Richard Smith's friends, 'to ask my lords of Abergavenny and Vaux what they have donn in the same kind'.[19] The pro-episcopal lobby was desperate to claim

---

[14] Baron Arundell's opinions are undoubtedly being misrepresented here. For Arundell's vitriolic denunciation of the 'Protestatio Declaratoria', see AAW, A XXIV, no. 87.

[15] The views of the remaining Catholic nobles were not stated. See Hughes, *HSJ*, 224–7.

[16] See Allison, *QJ*, 139; AAW, A XXIV, no. 73 (an English translation of the text of the 'Protestatio Declaratoria' with a different series of signatures).

[17] NCC, 109.   [18] *Ibid.*, 86.   [19] *Ibid.*, 79–80.

Winchester for themselves. (He was the brother-in-law of the second Viscount Montague's daughter Mary, whose first husband, William Paulet, Lord St John had died in 1621.) The secular priest William Case was, apparently, chaplain to Winchester's wife. Winchester was close to what remained of the Buckingham clan, and was thought by these Catholics to be an influential voice in and around the Court.[20]

Southcot was, in fact, quite optimistic that 'many of our nobility will be wonne to exclame from the late protestation. I have my lord marquis['s] hand and my Lord Morlys alreadie and I have writen' to the priest Thomas Martin 'for my Lord Sturtons, unto my cosen [Richard] Broughton for his lord', i.e. the earl of Rutland, 'unto Mr Rogers for his lord', to Cuthbert Trollopp 'for the Lord Euers, and here we shall have my Lord Arundelles especially and my Lord Mountagues', while George Fisher 'undertaketh for [the earl of] Casle Haven'. Southcot enclosed a 'forme' to which he intended to 'obtayne the cheef gentrys handes'. Via the queen's chaplain Robert Philip's means, 'I have imployed a very powerfull friend to my Lord Harbert to see if it be possible to make him disclayme.' The 'cardinalls of Propaganda Fide' should be told that shortly they would be receiving 'a generall disclame with the true handes of nobility and gentry'.[21]

Certainly, the principles and programme of the Catholic hierarchalists attracted a great deal more support from some sections of the community than Smith's enemies let on. The 'Protestatio Declaratoria' was palpably inaccurate when it claimed that the third Viscount Montague was uncommitted, or that Baron Arundell thought that it was not a fit time to consider restoring local Catholic episcopal jurisdiction, or even that the marquis of Winchester had rejected Smith.[22] George Leyburn protested to Biddulph that 'my Lord Herbert' had said 'that he never did subscribe to any writing whatsoever, and the Lord Vaux protesteth as much as for my Lord Arundell of Wardor, my Lord Viscount Mountegue, my Lord Morley, [the] earle of Rutland, my Lord Viscount Dunbar, [and] the marquis of Winchester'; and these nobles desired 'nothing more' than 'the returne of our bishop; and my Lord Rivers Viscount Colchester is muche offended that it should be sayd that he did subscribe'.[23]

---

[20] For the marquis of Winchester, see *ibid., passim.*   [21] *Ibid.*, 113–14, 115.

[22] John Southcot reported to Smith on 7 August 1632 that the marquis of Winchester was 'netled' about this matter, 'and so is my Lord Arundell also and I hope they will both do somwhat to vindicat them selves', AAW, A XXVI, no. 107, p. 300. Smith's supporters insisted that Francis Browne, third Viscount Montague was firm in their cause. The secular clergy's *c.* 1635 account of the Catholic peerage named him first among those who were well affected to the pro-episcopal lobby, AAW, A XXVIII, no. 3, p. 15. As we saw in ch. 13 (p. 451) above, he had written to Rome in favour of Smith in late 1627.

[23] AAW, A XXVI, no. 129, p. 355. According to John Southcot, Lord Herbert had protested that 'he gave not his hand to any paper, but only that he went to the French ambassador to tell him of the difficulties of the practise of the authority here in these times', *ibid.*, no. 107, p. 300.

Whatever these noblemen actually said when they were besieged and badgered for their opinions and support by leading clergy on both sides, Smith's supporters may well have been right to think that things were much more evenly balanced than the 'Protestatio Declaratoria' claimed, and that, if Smith were restored, or another came as a bishop in his place, many of those who opposed him would desist from their refusal to accept episcopal jurisdiction.[24]

In March 1632, for example, Thomas Longueville was able to report that there had been a major reorientation of opinion in the Stourton family. 'Divers, as you knoe, have theare been given up by our adversaries as to have subscribed against our maister my lord bishop wherof one was my Lord Stourtons eldest sonne and heyre Sir William Stourton.' But whereas Smith's enemies had already done their best to turn Lord Stourton and had failed, now the heir, Sir William, Longueville's own patron, had had second thoughts about opposing Smith. Although 'true it is he did subscribe', nevertheless 'you must knoe that now he hath cast of[f] the monke whoe then lived in his house', Smith's bitter enemy, David Codner, 'whose continual table talk was against my lord bishop, and now he hath taken a secular priest wholy depending upon him'. Longueville added that

by manie discourses which I have had with Sir William Stourton concerning this busines he hath sufficiently manifested how he wisheth he had never subscribed, and divers and sundrie times he hath told me how with all his hart he desireth a bishop in England, yea both Sir William and his brother in law Sir Edward Suilliard, whoe alsoe subscribed against our bishop, have told me that the regulars their ghostly fathers, whereof the formers was a monke, the others was and yet is a Jesuit, secured their conscience in the buisnes, otherwise they never would have done what they did.[25]

These battles confirm just how fluid Catholic opinion was on these bitterly controverted topics. The protagonists in these factional battles were intensely aware how easily slippage could occur between one position and another. As a result, these spats and disputes, however pernickety, petty and tedious they look, and however few people seem to have been directly and immediately involved in them, were one of the central processes by which Catholicism was identified, defined and redefined, and its meanings and significance hammered out, during this period. And they constituted one of the mechanisms by which certain strands of early seventeenth-century Catholicism came into contact with controversial new ecclesiastical aspects of the

---

[24] William Case claimed in February 1634 that such an opinion had been expressed by, among others, Viscount Savage and Earl Rivers, AAW, A XXVII, no. 131, pp. 407–8.

[25] AAW, A XXVI, no. 41, p. 129. Longueville had been involved in the student rebellion against the Jesuit authorities at the English College in Rome in 1623. He had actually been to Newfoundland with Lord Baltimore in June 1627, but returned shortly thereafter, Anstr. II, 202.

early Stuart State. For, as we know, the Caroline Church was also racked by dissent about the necessity of conformity and the dangers of nonconformity. Catholics were well aware that the battles within their own community over this issue were analogous to some of the discontents within the established Church. And this allowed some of these Catholics to represent themselves to the Caroline regime, and particularly to prelates such as William Laud, as friendly spirits and worthy of the State's tolerance if not, in fact, of its positive recognition and enthusiastic approval.

PATRONS AND PRIESTS IN THE 1630S: ENGLISH CATHOLICISM REDEFINES ITSELF

Looking at the scattered and shattered remains in 1631 of the Smitheian episcopal pretension, it would still be easy to conclude that those who had fronted and supported the Catholic episcopal reform project were effectively finished, embarrassed and humiliated, undoubtedly to the delight and satisfaction of many of their critics. Possession was nine-tenths of a credible claim to ecclesiastical authority. And Smith was no longer in possession. One could be forgiven for thinking that this was the time when 'Bossyworld' emerged finally, fully and gloriously into the light, with the English Catholic community largely politically quiescent, composed primarily of seigneurial chaplaincies and dominated by the laity. This was a situation which was far more to the liking and convenience of the religious orders, who thrived in such circumstances, i.e. when they were left largely to themselves, not disturbed by attempts to bring them under some pointless and unsuitable overarching system of episcopal discipline. And, indeed, a substantial number, probably a majority, of the leading Catholic patrons, particularly among the nobility, were sympathetic to the religious. Only a minority were ready completely to countenance the seculars' schemes to take the regulars' pride down a peg or two. A brief survey of the letters, papers and discourses of the pro-episcopal lobby in the 1630s sometimes gives the impression that this crowd of seventeenth-century Catholic hierarchalist 'moaning minnies' had, for the foreseeable future, completely lost out.

Yet to leave it at this, and to say that the projects for reform sponsored by the kinds of aristocratic patronage structures which we have been reviewing up to this point had come to nothing would be misleading. For I want to argue here that a great deal of what is typically taken for 'English Catholicism' in the 1630s was being generated, in fact, by our hierarchalist clerical friends and their patrons. And their vision of what that Catholicism, and its relationship with the State, should be like, and how it was possible for them to share certain clerical and ecclesiological ideals (especially of conformity and hierarchy) with particular Church-of-England men, were absolutely crucial in defining the Catholic experience in the 1630s even if they were in many ways not exactly 'typical' of all the people whom, in the 1630s, we might want to label as 'Catholics'. Here, then, we see again the essential rightness and relevance of John Bossy's account of English Catholicism in this period as, in a very important sense, defined by patronage, particularly the relationships between clergy clients and gentry and aristocratic patrons, though clearly the political and other effects of that Catholicism were not confined within such patronage nexuses. Indeed, the clerical clients of these families, men who were Richard Smith's leading supporters and the essential mainstays of what we have been referring to as the pro-episcopal lobby (e.g. John Southcot, George Leyburn, Richard Broughton, Peter Biddulph, Henry Holden and Thomas White), were themselves tied together in an elaborate kinship nexus.[26]

The reason that all of this may be important in national political terms is quite obvious. There is a general acceptance among historians that Catholicism (sometimes described as 'popery') was central to the collapse of the Caroline regime in and around 1640. As Caroline Hibbard has argued, there appeared to be convincing proof of a 'popish plot' to subvert substantial areas of the law and the right direction of foreign policy as well, of course, as the government of the Church of England.[27] As Kevin Sharpe has it, 'what perhaps alone served to connect the religious issues of 1640–2 with Laud and the Caroline regime was the fear of popery'.[28] For Sharpe, however, this was 'paranoia'. It is, in fact, faintly ridiculous even to think that William Laud was a crypto-Catholic or that actual Catholics were plotting the overthrow of the realm. Perhaps all such allegations of popish infiltration were coded language which was deployed in order to attack the regime on other issues. Such allegations do not, in themselves, explain why Catholics of the kind whom we have been studying should have been considered a credible cause of the breakdown of trust in royal government. But one feasible explanation of this phenomenon is that what these Catholics were aiming to achieve bore more than a family likeness to the new styles of ecclesiastical governance, sometimes referred to by historians as 'Laudianism', which provoked such opposition during the 1630s. We have already hinted more than once at this. Naturally, one does not want to make some simplistic equation of Laudian reforms with certain styles of early seventeenth-century Catholicism. (As is well known, Laud was always fairly uniformly hostile to the Church of Rome.) Nor do I want to repeat or plagiarise the research done by a variety of scholars, and notably Anthony Milton, on the links during this period between the Church of England and the Church

---

[26] For the kin relationships between these priests, see *NCC*, *passim*.
[27] Hibbard, *CI*.   [28] Sharpe, *PR*, 938.

of Rome;[29] or to paraphrase the splendid and groundbreaking work of Professor Hibbard which has restored a proper political perspective to the phenomenon of Court Catholicism in the decade before the civil war.

But there were several very obvious points of comparison and even contact. Indeed, the structure of political conflict within the English Catholic community invited Smith and his friends to perceive correlations between their position and ideals and those of the Church-of-England clergymen who were trying to bring about extensive changes in discipline in the established Church. Certainly, several contemporary Catholics' accounts, which describe the Church-of-England clerics of whom they most approved, look very close to the modern historiography of the ruction-causing, mould-breaking Laudian experiment.

Now, Catholics who claimed that this was true were themselves making a polemical case. But it was one which they expected contemporaries (and not just Catholic ones) to recognise. For some time, Catholic polemics had been stressing that there was an ideological meeting point between the monarchical principles which underwrote the papacy and those which sustained the Stuart regime. Matthew Kellison stressed, in his defence of episcopacy (*A Treatise of the Hierarchie and Divers Orders of the Church*) against 'the anarchie of Calvin', that 'nature and naturall reason seeme to pleade for a monarchie in which one soveraigne swayeth all', rather than for aristocracy or democracy. Even 'in man's bodie' proclaimed Kellison, 'there is a kinde of monarchie, in which the head is monarch that ruleth the rest of the members'. In 'man's soule' also there is 'a monarchie, of which the understanding is prince, who ruleth all the inferiour powers, and appeaseth unrulie and mutinous passions when they rebel against reason'. 'Nature sheweth this world to be governed by monarchie and to have one God.' For 'if there were manie Gods and governours', there would be 'confusion' rather than 'harmonie' and 'order'.[30]

These sentiments were, in themselves, perhaps nothing out of the ordinary. But they directly associated the Catholic campaign to restore episcopacy over English Catholics with support for the Stuart regime. And they echoed the Laudians' own excoriation of puritan nonconformity as a politically disruptive force, disobedient to both God and the sovereign. Much of Kellison's book defended the papal primacy. But Kellison's take on the topic

---

[29] Anthony Milton has demonstrated how many of the disputes and debates within the Church of England at this time took the Roman Church as a focal point. Those who wanted to put an anti-Calvinist or avant-garde conformist case naturally played up certain positive aspects of the relationship between the two Churches which much English Protestant polemical thought had previously denied, Milton, *CR*.

[30] Matthew Kellison, *A Treatise of the Hierarchie and Divers Orders of the Church against the Anarchie of Calvin* (Douai, 1629), 49–50.

was a radically different one from that of the Elizabethan polemical Catholic tracts in which defences of papal authority had been used to threaten the queen's sovereignty. Kellison concentrated now on the pope's power over other churchmen, particularly bishops in national Churches. The papacy's claims to authority over princes seem, for the time being, to have receded into the middle distance.[31]

Caroline Hibbard has stressed how significant the links between English Catholicism and the Caroline Court were. She argues that contemporary perceptions that popery was invading the Court were constructed not just around the shifts in Caroline foreign policy during the 1630s but also through knowledge of how informal channels of advice allowed a few favoured Catholics at Court to influence royal policy-making. She deftly analyses the means by which courtier Catholics, mainly in Henrietta Maria's entourage, were able to gain access to the king.[32]

As Hibbard argues, many of the courtier-Catholic activists and engagés, such as Sir Tobie Mathew, were not in any real sense 'typical'. But the issues which occupied the minds of courtier Catholics and which figured in their conversations and negotiations with the regime (such as, for instance, the possibility of toleration) were also hot topics of discussion within the wider Catholic community. These issues created channels of communication between the Catholic community and the Court.

With these thoughts in mind I propose to look now primarily, though relatively briefly, at the early to mid-1630s, before the period which is the subject of Hibbard's magisterial analysis and narrative (i.e. from 1636 onwards, starting with the well-known agency to the Stuart Court of George Con).[33] And I wish to look at the ecclesiastical politics of these years through the eyes of those Catholic clergy who had come out of the patronage networks which had been built up by aristocratic families such as the Brownes.

During the 1630s several of these clergymen reflected on and glossed the kinds of religion which they saw being practised in the Church of England. And they weighed up and evaluated different factional clerical interests, the rise and fall of particular groups, not just for the fun of seeing who was in and who was out but also as a means of measuring what they began to describe as a more fundamental shift in the exercise of the royal supremacy and the prevailing liturgical and theological culture of the English Church.

Now, it is no huge revelation to say that the 1630s saw a number of ecclesiastical developments which some contemporaries claimed were out of step with extant Church-of-England tradition. It is also no great secret that the

---

[31] *Ibid.*, ch. 4, pp. 106–7. There was also a significant difference here from the line and tone of Kellison's own *The Right and Jurisdiction of the Prelate and the Prince* (Douai, 1617).
[32] Hibbard, *CI.*   [33] *Ibid.*, 38–9.

law on conformity was now being enforced in a way which marked a break with the past.[34] As Peter Lake comments, while many bishops would wink at modified forms of subscription in order to allow tender consciences to remain within the Church of England, 'to Laudians formal subscription unaccompanied by honest, punctilious, indeed zealous obedience to the canons and formularies of the Church, seemed if anything even more dangerous, because more difficult to root out, than overt non-conformity'.[35]

Those Catholics who commented favourably on the Laudian experiment with conformity (as well as theology, liturgy and so on) were making a statement about the, by inference, acceptability to the State of their own proposals for reforming and governing Catholicism in England. At many points, the priests whom I have loosely termed 'hierarchalist', or 'pro-episcopal', emphasised how close they were to the Church-of-England clergymen of whose ecclesiastical and theological style they most approved.

We can see this in their accounts of high-profile Court conversions to the Church of Rome. Previously, the dominant discourse in describing those English Protestants who converted to Rome had been an essentially apocalyptic one. They were typically said to have abandoned heresy. Now we sometimes find accounts of these conversions, written by hierarchalist clergy, being toned down. Many of them no longer thought it was essential for the proselytisation process, which was supposedly a central part of all the Catholic clergy's ministry, to be predicated on the belief that the Church of England was an entirely false Church. Here it was possible to fix upon and exploit the ideas of certain Church-of-England clergymen who were using, as e.g. Richard Montagu famously did, a style of moderate rhetoric about the Church of Rome for their own polemical purposes against their enemies in the Church of England.

Thus, although Court conversions to Catholicism were nothing new, they could now be inflected with new emphases, particularly if it could be shown that the king was not really hostile to them. Edmund Price, a royal chaplain (and formerly a chaplain to the duke of Buckingham), was received, just before his death, into the Church of Rome by an English secular priest. John Southcot reported that the physician Robert Floyd had been 'questioned by the king this Christmasse' about the conversion. (Price and Floyd had been friends.) Floyd answered very discreetly and Charles went so far as to say that he did not personally abhor Roman Catholics.[36] A later account by Southcot

---

[34] N. Tyacke, *Anti-Calvinists* (Oxford, 1987), 224.
[35] P. Lake, 'The Laudian Style: Order, Uniformity and the Pursuit of the Beauty of Holiness in the 1630s', in K. Fincham (ed.), *The Early Stuart Church, 1603–1642* (1993), 161–85, at p. 182.
[36] *NCC*, 48; Albion, *CI*, 197; K. Fincham, 'William Laud and the Exercise of Caroline Ecclesiastical Patronage', *JEH* 51 (2000), 69–93, at pp. 80–1.

of the conversation between Floyd and Charles argued that the encounter with Floyd turned on Charles being informed that at least this conversion was not induced by overt and evangelical Catholic proselytising (typically associated with the Jesuits) to which practice he was evidently as averse as ever. Charles was reassured when Floyd phrased the event as an exercise in merely expressing distance from Calvinism. Charles had asked Floyd 'whether he brought any priest to Dr Price'. Floyd denied it but admitted that he had seen him 'in the compaghnie' of Catholic clergy often, though he thought none had performed 'any priestly function about him at his death'. As for whether 'he died a papist', Floyd answered 'that he thought he had because he had often heard him say he would saile to eternity rather in St Peters shipp than in John Calvins boat'. This evidently struck a chord with the king. Charles brightened up considerably and 'replied in these words: so had I to[o]. For we do not hould that Calvin could not err as you doe that the pope cannot.' Sensing the possibility of a real *détente* here, Floyd said 'that he did not hould that the pope (scilicet as a private man) could not erre, but ecclesia non errat, that the Church did not err'. 'So do I hould to[o]', exclaimed Charles in delight. For good measure, Charles 'saied further that he neither hated the papists nor their religion, and would be as gratious and mercifull to them as to his other subjects'.[37]

George Leyburn retailed another story from Court with a similar moral. A brother-in-law of one of the female attendants in the royal nursery had been reconciled to Rome just before his death. The man, one Mr Godbolt, had come home from overseas where he had been set upon and robbed. He was in such a bad way that he was unlikely to live. His brother, the husband of the nursery attendant (both of them good Catholics), tried to persuade him to embrace the religion of the Church of Rome. But the dying and very Protestant man refused outright, saying that he could never accept the doctrine of the real presence. His Catholic brother gave it up as a bad job. Then the woman who was attending on the dying Godbolt, herself a Protestant, decided to make absolutely sure that he should expire within the religion of the Church of England (as if he needed any encouragement that way). The 'better to confirme him, she gott one of the 2 ministers of the chappell at St James to come unto him'. This proved something of a mistake, for when the sick man started to complain how his Catholic brother had had the nerve to persuade him 'that the body of Christ was really in the sacrament', 'the minister replyed that it was very true doctrine and that he was bound to believe it, and withall he added that the Catholike religion was a good religion'. According to Leyburn, this came as such a shock to the sick man that 'he presently sent for his

[37] *NCC*, 48.

brother, desired a priest, was reconsiled and immediately after departed this life'.

Leyburn commented 'I doe assure you unfainedly that I am of opinion that we shall see shortly an other face of religion in this country', particularly since William Laud, Richard Neile and 'divers others who run with them . . . which are many' (because Laud 'haith very great power with our king') found 'that ther predecessors have been much defective in 3 poynts'. 'The first' was that 'they did abandon confessions, the second that they did reject all ceremonyes without which ther Church is without majesty, and the third' was 'that they did take away all kinde of worship and honour to pictures'.[38]

It is in this context that the paeans of praise lavished by these Catholics on Charles's natural clemency and tolerance make most sense. They knew quite well that Charles's attitudes were not in fact simply irenic. As Southcot expressed it in March 1633, 'I understand for certaine by one that hath many times privat conference with the king that he is well persuaded of all the Catholic tenets, but when he talketh with any Protestant minister or other he is presently drawne off againe.' The issue for clergy such as Southcot was really whether Charles would drop his opposition to some form of episcopal structure among the English Catholics. Southcot reported that 'the same party saieth' that the king 'is not against bishops and might be soon persuaded to admitt of them and to think them convenient for the government of his Catholic subjects'.[39]

This was what made it possible to enthuse about Charles's mild, moderate and merciful spirit and to pass over such things as, for example, the trial and execution in 1633 of the Irish friar Arthur McGeoghan.[40] The Venetian ambassador reported in December 1633 that the hapless friar 'suffered the extreme penalty two days ago'; he had returned from Spain where he had been overheard to say that he would not come into the realm 'unless it was to assassinate the king'.[41] Richard Smith was remarkably unsympathetic. He observed that the odd martyrdom did no harm; and, anyway, recently a privy councillor had promised to deal with the king to show him (yet again) what a good thing a Catholic bishop in England would be.[42]

Charles's own general line was, and not all that unreasonably, that he had not one whit varied from the formulae which his father, James of blessed memory, had used in order to discuss the niceties of religious division. Like James, Charles would talk endlessly about how he hated puritans and Jesuits equally. Like James he would not dismantle the formal structures of the

---

[38] *Ibid.*, 160.   [39] *Ibid.*, 157.
[40] See *ibid.*, 28, 205, 211, 294.   [41] *CSPV 1632–6*, 172.   [42] AAW, B 27, no. 113.

justice system by which priests were arrested and prosecuted. But, like James also, he would generally prevent the full penalties of the law being inflicted. He said, as his father did, that he would not have blood shed for cause of religion only; and he believed that the 1606 oath of allegiance could be taken as an oath of temporal loyalty, something which did not touch the pope's spiritual jurisdiction.[43]

However, Charles's approach to the Catholic issue was often subtly distinct from James's. During the 1630s there were several attempts by Catholics, particularly by the papal agent George Con, to secure a modification of the oath of allegiance. These proposed modifications came to nothing (at least before 1639),[44] but the tone of Charles's pronouncements on the nature of the loyalty oath was noticeably different from James's more strident account of what constituted political loyalty.

In the minds of the Catholic clerical observers of the Court there was a clear connection between Charles's ability to talk the irenic talk and the observable fact during the 1630s that a style of *de facto* tolerance was being established via the implementation of the compounding commissions which dealt with Catholic recusants. This is not to say that the whole structure of pecuniary mulct for nonconformity simply ceased to operate. In fact, many recusants continued to pay hefty sums to the crown. But the deal which they were offered was that, if they compounded in full for their recusancy debts, they would be released from the petty harassments and bullying inflicted on them by the pursuivants and other officials of the high commission and other agencies which traditionally had been charged with suppressing recusant separatism.[45]

Of course, making this accommodation work was not always going to be easy. And, certainly, in the early 1630s Catholics continuously griped that the arrangement was simply not working. During 1632 Southcot more than once bluntly stated that the pursuivants were still busy, and that many recusants' compositions had not yet been sorted out.[46] Some Catholics even said that Sir Thomas Wentworth, who took over the northern compounding commission in 1629, showed himself to be a barbarous tyrant towards the region's Catholics.[47] But increasingly during the 1630s there was a consensus among Catholics that the composition scheme was taking effect and that many Catholics would now be largely left alone. As a result, the pro-episcopal lobby could claim that the circumstances of the English 'mission' had changed, that persecution had abated and that the time was right for

[43] Albion, *CI*, 243–4, 244–5, 259, 267, 280; Hibbard, *CI*, 23.
[44] Hibbard, *CI*, 118–20.   [45] See *NCC, passim.*   [46] See e.g. *ibid.*, 59, 110, 133.
[47] AAW, A XXVI, no. 105 (a report by George Warwick in the form of a letter to Pope Urban VIII, 3 August 1632).

the return of a fully functioning episcopal system of government for English Catholics.[48]

By June 1633, Southcot was insisting that there was a genuine *de facto* toleration (though, he claimed, the Jesuits would try to deny it). All commissions for searching Catholic property had been taken away before the king had left for Scotland in March of that year. Now 'all publick chappells are mightily frequented without disturbance' by Catholics who wanted to hear Mass, and 'prisoners goe freely abroad without restraint'. The religious themselves, he said, were benefiting from this relaxation of the law, and they ought to be grateful. Thomas Middleton, superior of the Dominicans, was 'particulerly warranted to go freely where he will', and the secretary of State, Sir Francis Windebank, 'charged his keeper to give him this freedom'. It was, therefore, 'a shame we should be so ungratefull to his Majesty and the State when the favours are so manifest. Neither are compositions' for recusancy 'so intolerable as they seem'. For, 'wheras they report that the king taketh a full third part' of their estates, 'it is nowhere true, but at the most, of some few, a fo[u]rth and generally a fift part who by the law might take two parts from all convicted recusants'.[49]

Southcot had also heard 'nothing to any purpose donn by the judges in their circuitts this summer against recusants or priests'. 'A little before they began their circuitt[s]', the Jesuit Alexander Baker, who had been the subject of furious parliamentary protests in 1625, 'being taken openly in the street and committed to Newgate, was within few daies delivered by my Lord Chief Justice Richardson him self, at the queens entreaty, to whom meanes was made for it'.[50] In October 1633 Richard Smith believed that the New Prison was 'quite emptied'. In fact any imprisoned priest in London who wanted his liberty could have it.[51] In mid-December 1633 Southcot recorded that 'within this fortnight I heare there are 4 prisoners released upon bond, videlicet Mr Henry More, a Jesuit, out of the New Prison, and Mr Tres[h]ame, agent for the Benedictines, out of the same prison, Father Bonaventure [Jackson], Franciscan, out of Newgate, and a fourth whose name I know not. By this it may appeare that the report which is . . . given out' in Rome 'of persecution is not so true'. The earl of Argyll had been pursued by an informer who intended to 'sue the law for placing his daughter in a nunnery at Bruxelles, but . . . the king will have him to desist, and to lett fall his sute' against the earl. 'Neither are the pursevants very buissy in searching and when they do search they do it but slightly and nothing

---

[48] See also William Prynne, *The Popish Royall Favourite* (1643), for transcripts of royal warrants, issued during the 1630s, which guaranteed immunity from the recusancy statutes. Some of those named on these warrants were from the group of families related to the Brownes (including the Dormers, and the Arundells of Wardour), *ibid.*, 8–9, 12.

[49] NCC, 182.   [50] *Ibid.*, 198.   [51] AAW, B 27, no. 131.

so vigorously as heretofore.' The ungrateful Jesuits were so desperate when they saw their vision and version of a persecution (resisted manfully, they said, only by themselves) becoming unsustainable that, according to Smith, they 'do shew the [secular] clergies information touching the calmnesse of these times presented at Rome' and they had the nerve to 'say that it causeth the encrease of persecution here, but how impudently and foolishly they say soe, any wise body may judg[e]'.[52] As in the past, the only reason the Jesuits were spouting this nonsense was to persuade Rome that no Catholic bishop should again come to reside in the realm.

This new official tolerance was not the same as the full legal toleration which had been the stated aim and objective of much Catholic agitation during the period. As late as May 1636, a report compiled for the secular clergy's Roman agent, or for him to translate to show to the curial cardinals, admitted that Charles's 'wantes indeed doe in some sort compell him to take money of Catholiques by way of composicion for their recusancy'; and 'these paiments are commonly racked very high by the diligence of the comissioners, partly out of aversion in some of them from religion, but principally out of a desire in all of them to advance the kings profitt'. In addition, 'besides this generall molestacion' of the composition payments, 'there are many particular men and women in severall shires molested by informers, some also questioned (though not many) for marrying, and some for christning. The penalty of 12d a Sunday is also in some places exacted.' All this was done, however, by the 'officiousnes, covetousenes or malice of some inferiour officers' rather than 'by order from the State, which cannot be allwayes prevented while the lawes remayne in force'.[53]

To us, it has to be said, the secular clergy look a tad smug whenever we find them breezily opining that, however harsh the law was, the laity could take it – and indeed should regard themselves as fortunate to be suffering, or at least experiencing inconvenience, for the faith. The point here, however, is not so much whether there *was* a toleration or not (however one might measure that – and Catholics had been arguing about precisely that issue for years), but, as much as anything, which Catholics were likely to win out in the struggle to interpret and gloss the new directions in crown policy towards Catholicism. It was imperative, thought priests such as Southcot, to characterise the compounding policy as lenient even when certain recusants were having to fork out quite large sums for the privilege of being left alone. Thus in April 1633 Southcot glossed the new era of goodwill as follows: 'as for that report which the Jesuits do there give out of persecution, it is false

---

[52] *NCC*, 209–10.

[53] *Ibid.*, 278. The crown's income from compositions with recusants during the 1630s is the subject of research currently being undertaken by Simon Healy.

in all particulers, excepting only compositions; which, although they be high racked, yet are not so intolerable as they make them; and Catholickes had rather have them at any rate than loose their lives and liberties'.[54] And again, in the same month,

> as for that report which the Jesuits give out there of persecution, it is more than they dare avouch openly, and the truth is far otherwise in all respects, having only the compositions, which although they be high in many, yet in others they are reasonable, and in none, that I heare of, so great as to undo them utterly. The king is nothing inclined to use severity, but rather clemency, as all the world knoweth, and the times ar now very calme which maketh more freedom than hath bin seen a great while. The king and currant of the State is [sic] wholy now antipuritan, and tends [sic] to a moderation both in opinions and practise.[55]

And, in mid-June 1633, 'for persecution we have as great a calme as ever we had, God continew it long'.[56] Again, in July 1633, George Leyburn insisted that 'the pursivants have donn little in the country as yet (saving only in one or two houses in Norfolk) and lesse in London. And generally it is confessed that we never had' so great a calm 'since the queene came in than now. God continew it. The compositions go on slowly. Some are strained high, but they are such as can pay well, and it is not any desire of persecution but only the kings waunt that enforceth it.'[57]

Sometimes, in the later 1630s, the pro-episcopal lobby sensed that they might be winning out in this interpretive battle over whether the Caroline State was demonstrably more tolerant than its predecessors, or even itself in the early years of Charles's reign. Leyburn's opinion in February 1637 was that the Jesuits' tune was finally changing. 'Before, in their speeches . . . noething was soe frequent in their mouthes as persecution, hard conditions of Catholiques, and the kings rigour against them; but now they sing a contrarie song.' Richard Blount SJ himself, in his attempt to placate the king over the recent publication of an offensive polemical book by Matthew Wilson SJ, extolled 'the kings clemency, and preacheth much of the ease and quietnes which Catholiques now enjoye in respect of former tymes'.[58]

THE KING, THE LAUDIANS, THE PURITANS AND THE CATHOLICS

In April 1633, as we have just seen, John Southcot described the whole drift of Charles's policy as 'anti-puritan'. He added a story which he had got from George Leyburn (reported by one of the queen's servants) that 'the king him

---

[54] *Ibid.*, 168.   [55] *Ibid.*, 175.   [56] *Ibid.*, 186.   [57] *Ibid.*, 192.
[58] *Ibid.*, 307; Matthew Wilson, *A Direction to be Observed by N.N.* (St Omer, 1634).

self, before some of his own domesticall servants, spake very Catholickly both of the use of the Inquisition' as well as of 'the popes pardons . . . by occasion of a book that was read unto him by a bedchamber man while he had his picture drawen, wherin were taunts against both'. Charles seems to have imagined that dissent within the Church of England might be dealt with effectively by the Inquisition's procedures. Of the Inquisition 'he saied thus: "it is a good thing, and it were to be wished that it were in all places of Christendom to bridle mens tongues"; and then, turning to the reader, he saied "you and I might be long enough in Spaine without feare of the Inquisition if we held our peaces and spake nothing in matters of religion"'.[59] As Charles went off to Scotland in March 1633, Richard Smith, who had heard this same story, remarked that the king had discoursed favourably on the 'severitie of the Inquisicion'.[60]

All through the 1630s Smith's friends collected and recorded the headline-grabbing incidents which demonstrated the regime's anti-puritanism – the cases of Henry Sherfield, William Prynne, John Bastwick, John Burton, the feoffees for impropriations and so on.[61]

A famous public occasion on which Catholics detected royal anti-puritanism was the visit made by the king and queen to Oxford in 1636. George Leyburn recounted on 3 September what he had seen there. On the outskirts of the city, the royal party had been met by local bigwigs, university dons and others, and in particular by the chancellor, Laud himself, and all proceeded in front of the royal coach to 'Christ Church Colledge wher they were lodged, and after supper intertayned with a new comedy called the Passions Calm'd, or the Floating Iseland'. This was presented by the public orator, William Strode. It had been written at Laud's own prompting. Here was 'represented a king whos name was Prudentius (you may imagine our most prudent prince) and an Intellectus Agens a person active and wise (you may imagine his Grace of Canterbury)'. By the passions, Leyburn said,

you may understand the puritans and all such as are opposit to the courses which our king doth run in his goverment. Thes passions were very unrulye and disobedient unto Prudentius['s] goverment in soe much that they resolved noe longer to suffer him to be their king, which, the Intellectus Agens perceaving, persuaded Prudentius to yeeld his crowne quietly, which he did.[62]

This play seems to have been based rather loosely on the plot of William Shakespeare's *Measure for Measure* (with verbal echoes of Shakespeare's *Twelfth Night* and Ben Jonson's *The Alchemist*). A ruler, Prudentius,

[59] NCC, 176.   [60] AAW, B 27, no. 117.   [61] NCC, 31, 116, 150, 153, 158, 316.
[62] *Ibid.*, 288. For the text of the play, see B. Dobell (ed.), *The Poetical Works of William Strode . . . to which Is Added The Floating Island a Tragi-Comedy . . .* (1907), 137–263.

surrenders the reins of power to the 'passions', a series of vices whose ill humours could easily be linked with contemporary puritanism. In this play, however, the passions are already actively conspiring to take the crown from Prudentius at the time that he hands over authority to them. (One of them, the ear-less Malevolo, a 'malicious contriver', is a figure for William Prynne; and there are references also to the feoffees for impropriations. Undoubtedly to Leyburn's delight, another of the passions, Irato, subscribing to the contemporary association of Jesuits with puritans, says, as they plot against Prudentius, 'I begin / To think on St Raviliack, and St Garnett'.[63]) With the lunatics now firmly in charge of the asylum, they decide they want an elective monarchy. 'Thes disordered passions, having now the crowne, consulted together on whom they should bestowe it, and election was made of Lady Fancy.' This was a disaster, for she abrogates the rule of law and decrees that all should follow their lusts. The result is chaos. Under her 'goverment they fell into bitter discords and discentions amongst them selves, plotting to kill each other'. 'At length beeing wearie of thes differences they resolved to aske counsell of Desperato what to doe, who would make noe answere but presented unto them many naked knyfes and roapes', and also quantities of poison. The passions are thus on the verge of carrying out a mass suicide pact, organised by the Calvinist mountebank physician Desperato, when Intellectus Agens intervenes and invokes Prudentius's authority to restore all to order. They

thought good to advise with [the] Intellectus Agens who persuaded them to submitte them selves unto Prudentius and returne the crowne agayne unto him, which counsell, beeing in this extremity, they did willingly embrace. Prudentius receaved the crowne agayne from the passions and accepted of their submission with an acknowledgement of their foule error and made a speech unto them full of sweetnes, signifying that the courses which he ran in his goverment

were 'for their good'. And, Prudentius added for good measure, 'as for the navy it was to defende them and the kingdom'.[64] This was a sharp dig at those who were already criticising the Ship Money levies. Elsewhere in the play Prudentius declares that he levies taxation only to benefit the commonwealth.[65]

At least one contemporary account claimed that some of the spectators found the production rather a bore.[66] But Leyburn noted that 'their Majesties laughed hartely' at the figure of the openly puritan Malencholico: 'ther was represented a puritan minister who made very good sport'. Malencholico 'was marryed to Concupiscence'. When 'he came with the passions to tender

[63] *Ibid.*, 148, 186, 153.   [64] NCC, 288–9.   [65] Dobell, *The Poetical Works*, 162.
[66] K. Sharpe, 'Archbishop Laud and the University of Oxford', in H. Lloyd Jones, V. Pearl and B. Worden (eds.), *History and Imagination* (1981), 146–64, at p. 151.

his submission to Prudentius, he kneeled doune and sayd O King, I kneele not to thee but to the [*sic* for thy] power, neither doe I adore thee'.[67]

Royal revenue was an issue which this brand of hierarchalist Catholicism could exploit in order to draw a contrast between their own loyalism and the alleged disloyalty of puritan opponents of the crown. Picking up on the religious overtones of the quarrels in the later 1620s' parliaments about the extent and limits of royal revenue-raising powers, some Catholics intimated that a loyalist Catholic bishop would side with the king in such disputes. In one position paper of 1634, alongside all the good 'commonwealth' effects which it was alleged a Catholic bishop would have (everything from the suppression of 'excesse drinking' to the prevention of 'inordinat recourse to forreine ambassadours'), it was added that 'a Catholick bishop, being toler-ated by the State, by his gravity and authority may perswade Catholickes, more forcibly than any other can, to graunt extraordinary contributions or benevolences when they shalbe required for the supply of his Majesties occasions'.[68]

This type of loyalist Catholic discourse was never quite as innocent as it seemed. Though the pro-episcopal lobbyists did their best to conceal it, it must have been obvious to many how ambitious some of these Catholics' schemes for a 'tolerated' Catholic episcopal presence in England actually were. One of the assurances which the pro-episcopal priests had given dur-ing the first half of the 1620s, as they manoeuvred to get William Bishop and then Richard Smith into office, was that a Catholic bishop in England would not style himself bishop of any of the established English sees. (This was part of the lobby's claim that they were interested in spiritual issues alone, and that they were in no way challenging the crown's authority in ecclesiastical matters as far as the Church of England was concerned.)[69] But in the 1630s they were now considering having bishops who *would* use the names of established English sees for their titles. They even planned to call one of them the archbishop of Canterbury. As Southcot mused to Biddulph in January 1632, 'why might not my lord of Chalcedon or some other be made archbishop of Canterbury and reside ordinarily in Rome as the Irish metropolitan doth', and 'then some other two bishops more be made with subordination to him to reside in England?'[70]

To those on both sides of the confessional divide who looked askance at the secular clergy leadership's plans to re-install Catholic episcopal authority in England, this was all the proof that was needed to show that the hierar-chalists' public minimalism was nothing but a blind, a front to conceal their

---

[67] NCC, 289; Dobell, *Poetical Works*, 235.   [68] NCC, 239.
[69] See Kellison, *Treatise of the Hierarchie*, 410–11.   [70] NCC, 45.

plans for a fully fledged spider's web of malign clerical officialdom which would spread out across the kingdom. In June 1633 Southcot reported to Rome that 'our antibishopists are much terrified with the newes of 3 or 4 bishops and they labour all they can to hinder it'.[71] (In the same month, Smith's friends were thinking that he might be made a cardinal, for which favour they had petitioned Richelieu, though Smith himself concluded that it would be interpreted as a sign of ambition and that he should delay accepting any such honour until more English bishops had been appointed by Rome.[72]) It was certainly believed that the religious were loudly talking up the pro-episcopal lobby's plans in order to alarm the State. As Biddulph was told by Southcot at this time, 'here the regulars give out that we shall have 3 bishops and an archbishop'; and 'a certaine Jesuit priest demanded of an other priest that had ben a Jesuit (hearing that we were to have more bishops)' whether 'it were a mortall sin to seek to hinder it by meanes of the State, by which it appeares how these men are minded and how . . . they are bent against episcopall power'.[73]

Southcot would, however, have done nothing to allay the regulars' suspicions when he added that 'perhaps in time and by degrees we shall come to have' these bishops, and 'no doubt it were needfull for the good government of this Church that so many were made', and then 'neither the regulars nor the State would . . . have any hope to suppresse episcopall authority'. With the 'faculties of missionaries being once well ordered, they would quickly bring all thinges here to a good passe and the laity to some conformity and unity of mindes who are now pittifully divided amongst them selves by reason of their ghostly fathers differences'.[74]

Now, none of this would exactly have been music to the ears of, for example, William Laud. But this did not prevent these Catholics from pressing their case even to the archbishop himself. They had for years been working to turn *détente* with the State into actual *entente*. As we remarked above, they could discern analogies between their own case and that of the more enthusiastic enforcers of conformity in the Church of England. According to John Southcot in February 1633, John Colleton had been told that Laud had

saied openly to some freindes of his not long since that, if he were the king, he would rather have the Catholickes governed by a bishop than otherwise, or than by the Jesuitts (for I heard it both waies reported), and he gave this reason, bycause, saieth he, if the bishop be a quiett man and a lover of his country, the king may be the securer by his government of all his Catholick subjectes.[75]

[71] NCC, 187.   [72] NCC, 180; AAW, B 27, no. 133.
[73] NCC, 179, 182–3.   [74] *Ibid.*, 180.   [75] *Ibid.*, 149.

Richard Smith, for one, believed that he could appeal to Laud and endorse the series of ideological positions and tenets which Laud might be thought to hold and represent.

In a letter of 26 March/5 April 1635, Smith directly approached the archbishop. (Smith knew that he was not the only Catholic talking to Laud. The monk Leander Jones discussed the issue of the oath of allegiance with the archbishop in the mid-1630s to see if some sort of compromise was possible. The Benedictines evidently intended to undercut the seculars' own pitch to the regime on this issue.[76]) Smith wrote that

it is not unknowne unto your Grace how much I have bin opposed theise many yeares lately past by some domesticke (as I may terme them) adversaries of myne, antihierarchists, and no frends to bishops, who have sought not only to disgrace me in forraine parts but to make me suspected and hatefull to my king and country at home by casting most injurious aspersions both upon my person and clayme.

Smith denied that he was a French stooge; Charles was his true sovereign. And

as for the claime of that episcopall authority which hath bin conferred upon me for the good of English Catholicks, your Grace well knoweth how conformable it is to the practise of our religion in all places, and how necessary for the preservation of peace and holy discipline, both among preists and laicks, which cannot but by consequence redownd to his Majesties greater service.

He claimed, probably with a good deal of truth, that he admired Laud's 'great and magnanimous exploytes' hitherto 'achived to the admiration of the Christian world, both in advancing the universall good of the English nation, and his Majesties service generally, as most particularly in the suppressing or reducing to dew obedience the refractory spirits of those who have ever bene noted to be disloyall both to the Church and State'.[77]

Laud's answer does not appear to have survived, but Southcot wrote to Smith on 27 July that, although Laud's response was not so good as had been hoped, Smith still had the opportunity to acknowledge his favour, which 'by the advise of freinds here is thought will better be expressed in a particuler letter to Mr Doctor [Brian] Dupper'. Duppa was tutor to the young Prince Charles, and was a creature of Laud. He seems to have been well disposed towards the secular clergy leadership.[78]

---

[76] Albion, *CI*, 146, 256–7. In May 1635 Leyburn reported that 'the munckes now doe carie ther heads high, relying upon ther power with the bishop of Canterbury', *NCC*, 254–5.

[77] *NCC*, 253–4.

[78] *Ibid.*, 259–60. An undated letter from Gregorio Panzani to Urban VIII noted that Smith had written to Laud to offer that his jurisdiction should be modified. According to Panzani, Laud had gone so far as to say that he actually admired Smith, and that he had shown Smith's missive to Charles, Dockery, *CD*, 44–5. In April 1634 Leyburn had been delighted by a Good Friday sermon preached by Duppa in front of the king. Duppa 'tooke occasion

Thus, the empathetic link between Laudianism and a certain strand of contemporary Catholicism was more than some simple common admiration for the 'beauty of holiness', though many Catholics did observe the modifications made to the interiors of churches, particularly the changed position of the communion table, with considerable interest. What was just as, if not more, important here was the likeness between Laudian rhetoric and the distinctive discourses used by this fraction of the Catholic community, a fraction which claimed to speak on behalf of the majority of English Catholics.

Richard Smith and his friends frequently asserted that their own Catholic critics, particularly the Jesuits, were alienating moderate Protestants through their own theological and rhetorical intemperance. For example, in November 1636, George Leyburn read Matthew Wilson SJ's *A Direction to be Observed by N.N.*, a tract which was penned in defence of Wilson's own *Mercy & Truth. Or Charity Maintayned by Catholiques. By Way of Reply upon an Answere Lately Framed by D. Potter to a Treatise Which Had Formerly Proved, that Charity was Mistaken by Protestants: With the Want Whereof Catholiques Are Uniustly Charged for Affirming, that Protestancy Unrepented Destroyes Salvation.* Leyburn commented that Wilson had indeed been uncharitable and that his 'booke hath given great disgust to the State and will doe the Jesuistes more hurt than they can imagine'. Sir Francis Cottington had 'delt with' the papal agent George Con 'about it who doth much condemne' Wilson 'for his indiscretion'.[79] Christopher Potter's book, *Want of Charitie*, had itself been a reply to the Jesuited Sir Tobie Mathew's *Charity Mistaken* of 1630. The seculars knew that Potter was one of Laud's favourites.[80]

It was axiomatic among the pro-episcopal lobby that their quarrels with the Jesuits could be assimilated into the current controversies between the Society and its enemies in Europe, particularly in France. During the pamphlet war over Matthew Kellison's *Treatise of the Hierarchie*, Smith received a great deal of support from his French friends, especially the Abbé de St Cyran (who wrote under the pseudonym of Aurelius). Smith appealed to the Sorbonne and to the French bishops. They responded by condemning

to speake of the breache or seperation made by Harry the Eight from the Sea of Rome, and he did call it an unhappie breach, and wished the king to take into his consideration the reuniting of this kingdome with the Romaine Church. And also he tooke occasion to speake of the Catholiques of this country and he sayd that many of them were very good and did instance . . . the bishop of Calcedoine who, when the queen was first with child, caused a prayer to be generally sayd for her safe delivery', and 'also commanded all Catholiques to praye' for Charles's 'prosperity, for which act the Jesuists did complaine of him at Rome', *NCC*, 251.

[79] *NCC*, 301; Hibbard, *CI*, 67–8.
[80] Milton, *CR*, 155–7; *NCC*, 196–7; Sir Tobie Mathew, *Charity Mistaken, with the Want Whereof, Catholickes Are Uniustly Charged* (St Omer, 1630).

Kellison's Jesuit antagonists (Matthew Wilson and John Floyd). As Antony Allison comments, Smith was championed by 'extreme Gallicans in France who used' the issue 'to attack the Jesuits and, through them, the papacy. It is impossible properly to understand the conflict in the Catholic Church in England unless we see it in relation to the wider struggle in Europe.'[81]

It was quite obvious to contemporaries that there might also be an empathy between moderate Church-of-England men and French Catholic churchmen who expressed quasi-'Gallican' sentiments about the role of episcopacy in strong national Churches.[82] Indeed John Southcot noted how Christopher Potter had used French authors to reply to Sir Tobie Mathew's *Charity Mistaken*. Sir Toby's 'little book' claimed to prove that 'it is not against charity for Catholics to say that Protestants remaining such cannot be saved'. But an answer had come out 'by one Doctor Potter, chaplaine to his Majesty, wherin (although the matter be but poor otherwise) he laies load upon the Jesuitts', and cites, among others, 'for proofes against them in divers things', the Abbé de St Cyran.[83] The publication of Protestant tracts was not, of course, in itself a good thing. Irenicism could be taken too far. Potter's book was, after all, a persuasion to remain Protestant.[84] But the Jesuits were at fault for attacking the wrong Protestants. They were also impeding the progress of toleration. In June 1637 Leyburn was delighted to be able to tell Smith that George Con had 'had an order from Rome . . . to suppresse . . . [Wilson's] booke as also to correct him; and he hath delt with the [Jesuit] provinciall about both'. The provincial had 'written a circular letter unto all the Jesuists to suppresse the booke' and had ordered Wilson to keep away from London.[85]

It is in this context, perhaps, that one should read the streams of Catholic comment during the mid-1630s about the theological and sacramental changes which underpinned the Laudian concept of 'the beauty of holiness'.[86] Some of these innovations persuaded some Catholics that there was even the possibility of a reunification of the Church of England and the Church of Rome. We know that, for instance, the papal agent Gregorio Panzani and Bishop Richard Montagu discussed this topic.

However, it is the Catholic hierarchalists' characterisation of the puritanism of the Caroline Church which is really the key to their comments

---

[81] Allison, RSGB, I, 330.   [82] Milton, CR, 264–9.
[83] NCC, 204–5.   [84] *Ibid.*, 213.
[85] *Ibid.*, 316. This was not always an easy case for Smith's friends to make. This was because authors such as Wilson were making favourable comments about Laud which were very similar in some ways to the anti-Jesuit secular clergy's observations about him, Hibbard, *CI*, 68; Wilson, *A Direction*, 22–3.
[86] See Lake, 'The Laudian Style', 164–8. For a long report, compiled by the Catholic secular clergy in 1636 on the condition of the Church of England, describing these alterations, see NCC, 272–9. For a Catholic account of the lavishness of Richard Montagu's chapel, see AAW, A XXVII, no. 182.

about the changes in sacramental and liturgical culture which they observed there. As Peter Lake and others have argued, Laudian ideologues chose to define their religious style against an image of puritanism which was in some respects new – although the origins of such an image can be discerned in, for example, the thought of Richard Hooker. As Lake writes, 'it is only when the Laudian project', in the sense of its positive liturgical and other claims and innovations, 'is set over against this polemically constructed image of puritan deviance and subversion that the full polemical and political resonance of the Laudian project can be recovered'.[87] In a probably conscious mimicry of contemporary Laudian discourses, Catholic hierarchalist clergy put out a similar analysis.

Nowe the puritans who dissent from the Protestantes both in doctrine and discipline doe utterly condemn all the aforesaid doctrines and practizes of superstition, idolatry and the like, bearing noe lesse (if not more) aversion and malice against this sort of Protestantes than they doe against the Catholiques. And these being in number most (because all citties, townes and corporacions are generally full of them, in minde refractory, and in power mighty) it is evident that one of the greatest impedimentes to the foresaid union or reconciliation

between the Church of England and the Church of Rome 'proceedeth mainely from them'; and, if the strength of the puritans were to be diminished, 'there would bee farr better hopes not only of effecting this union both sooner and easilier, but also . . . Catholickes would in the meane tyme be gentlyer dealt withall by the State'.[88]

Perhaps we should not be entirely surprised by this. For many years, Catholics had declared that there were fatal fissures within the Church of England. But in the context of the 1630s such claims took on a completely new significance. Whether there was any real prospect of an ever closer union between the two Churches was not really the issue for the most thrusting and politically savvy of the Catholic clergy who meddled on the fringes of the Court and had access to the queen and to a number of cardinals and nuncios in mainland Europe. What animated them was the impact of Laudian ideas about the enforcement of conformity and about the definition of orthodox belief in the English Church. They could, they thought, now assert that they were attuned to the programme of the new men in the established Church. On this basis they could assert also their own leadership of the Catholic community, for they were, so they said, best placed to effect a necessary and long overdue reconciliation between Catholics and the State.

We can see here, then, how a series of issues and concerns, spawned and fuelled by organisational and political problems among English Catholics,

---

[87] Lake, 'The Laudian Style', 180. See also *NCC*, introduction.
[88] *NCC*, 274–5.

could mesh with concerns and problems outside their community. What I hope this chapter has demonstrated is that the growth of Catholic clerical and ecclesiastical structures within the entourages of lay patrons (in particular, aristocratic patrons) contributed, during the 1620s and 1630s, to the formulation of a coherent set of ideas about how English Catholicism could be reformed and regulated so as to make it more acceptable to the Caroline regime. This was a high-stakes game which could, in theory, end in a complete reversal of the legal and political orthodoxies which had framed the Reformation settlement.

15

Epilogue: the civil war and after

The story of how the political difficulties of the crown were exponentially increased in the later 1630s and the early 1640s by Catholicism and Catholic activism has been told a number of times, and notably by Caroline Hibbard. Professor Hibbard has shown how the papal agent George Con, almost from the first moment that the Scots rebelled, manipulated the breakdown of proposals for an Anglo-French alliance. He contrasted loyal Catholic subjects with rebellious (Scottish) Protestants, and suggested that papal authority might be called upon to prevent foreign intervention in Scotland. Con's activities were a prime source for the formulation of contemporary 'popish-plot' conspiracy theories, as was the involvement of Catholics (predominantly Irish and Scottish, but also some English and Welsh) in the attempt to put down the Covenanters.[1] When Scottish Catholic peers were heavily involved in grossly unsuccessful but high-profile attempts in Scotland to take on the Covenanters,[2] and when English crypto-Catholic peers such as the earl of Arundel were prominent among those leading the king's forces up country to confront the Scottish rebels, neither the rank and file nor even the officer corps had to be predominantly professing papists to excite the kind of widespread popular hostility which manifested itself in the riots and disturbances charted so well by Robin Clifton.[3]

There has, however, been a debate about the extent of Catholic involvement in the war. It was axiomatic among pro-parliament propagandists that royalist forces were riddled with Catholics, even dominated by them. Royalist apologists (such as Clarendon) utterly denied it. During the Interregnum, Catholics themselves, for obvious political reasons, claimed that if Catholics had been found within the royalist garrisons it was because they had been hunted and harried there, and some scholars have accepted their accounts

---

[1] Hibbard, *CI*, 94–5.   [2] *Ibid.*, 115, 152–7, 180.
[3] R. Clifton, 'The Fear of Catholics in England 1637 to 1645' (D.Phil. thesis, Oxford, 1967). For the Catholics, especially Catholic peers, who either joined or contributed financially to the campaign, see Hibbard, *CI*, 101.

of their actions.[4] Some historians have suggested that the vast majority of Catholics had no love for either side and desperately wanted to keep out of the fighting.[5] Anthony Fletcher argues that in East Sussex 'the recusant gentry . . . contributed little to the royalist cause'.[6] He claims that 'in Sussex as in other counties there was . . . a strong tendency for recusants to remain neutral', and he cites the flight abroad of leading Catholics, such as Francis Browne, third Viscount Montague, to France, where he stayed for much of 1643 and 1644.[7] Keith Lindley cites Paul Hardacre's estimates that only 'a seventh or an eighth of all' subsequently 'sequestered Catholics supported the king in some way', while Lindley himself estimates that between a fifth and a sixth did so, though his figures seem to indicate considerably greater involvement in some social groups than in others.[8]

In fact, Lindley's figures, incorporating a range of types of involvement, from active military engagement to mere moral support (all drawn from the not necessarily entirely reliable investigative work carried out by parliamentary commissioners for compounding who dealt with royalist delinquents), can be used to support either a thesis of limited Catholic involvement, or of extensive Catholic commitment (above a certain social level) to the royalist cause.[9] Not surprisingly, the surviving records do not contain evidence of marauding hordes of armed plebeian Catholics. On the other hand, the further up the social scale one goes, the more pronounced, it seems, that royalist sympathies among Catholics turn out to be, at least in some areas.[10] There must be a suspicion here that what we are seeing is not actual royalism but *detected* royalism. Active royalism among the Catholic gentry seems to have been quite extensive.[11] Considering Lindley's premise that Catholics had been so badly treated by Charles, and had little to gain by going out on a limb for him (particularly in areas which were unsympathetic to him), the surprising thing is not that sometimes, in certain counties, only a small percentage of Catholic gentlemen were identified as active royalists, but rather that *any* were! And Peter Newman's work has shown that the research of

---

[4] See K. J. Lindley, 'The Part Played by Catholics', in B. Manning (ed.), *Politics, Religion and the English Civil War* (1973), 126–76, at p. 128. Brian Manning argues that 'just as puritans were attacked by anti-puritan mobs and by the king's soldiers, and were forced to take refuge in parliament's garrisons and armies, so Catholics were attacked by anti-popery mobs and by parliament's soldiers, and were forced to find shelter in the king's garrisons and armies', B. Manning, 'Preface', in Manning, *Politics, Religion and the English Civil War*, 126.

[5] Lindley, 'Part Played'; B. Manning, 'Neutrals and Neutralism in the English Civil War 1642–1646' (D.Phil., Oxford, 1957).

[6] A. Fletcher, *Sussex 1600–1660* (1975), 281.   [7] *Ibid.*, 284.

[8] Lindley, 'Part Played', 127–8, citing P. H. Hardacre, *The Royalists during the Puritan Revolution* (The Hague, 1956), 8, 60.

[9] For the commissioners' dealings with Francis Browne, third Viscount Montague's estate in Sussex, see HEH, BA 60/1555.

[10] Lindley, 'Part Played', 136, 139, 140.   [11] *Ibid.*, 174–5.

Lindley and others underestimates the number of Catholics who, during the war, held military commissions from the crown. A significant proportion of royalist field commanders were from Catholic families.[12]

As Lindley himself notes, after 1660, Catholics were determined to prove how far they had risked all for the royalist cause.[13] William Blundell insisted that 'as soone as his Majesties pleasure was knowne . . . a very great number (in . . . proportion to the whole) of his English Catholick subjects repayred to his collours; wher they made no sparing sacrifyse . . . of their lyves and fortunes'. Blundell thought that perhaps a fifteenth of all the English gentry in 1642 were Catholics, and 'it hath bene lykewaies supposed that a third or 4th part of the English gentlemen that fought for their Majestyes here consisted of their Catholick subjects', while in the 'northern countyes . . . the proportion of Catholicks' was in all probability 'much greater than this'. And Blundell claimed that he did not 'remember . . . any one English Catholick, eyther poor or rich, that hath served in the late war at any tyme on the rebels part'.[14]

Of course, many Catholics were prevented from serving in royalist armies. Not all were of military age or capable of fighting. Also, some royalist commanders thought that it would be a public relations blunder if they directly recruited known Catholics to staff the royalist officer corps (though that evidently did not stop Catholics from holding royal commissions). At the same time, the fact that particular Catholics did not actually hold commissions from the king to fight for him did not bar them from involvement in local military conflict. They were more than likely to become caught up in the fighting if, for example, their property was targeted by parliamentarian forces.

It may well be worth seeing, briefly, what happened to the group of Catholic families which we have pursued all the way through this book, and which, we have observed, functioned as patrons to some of the principal ideologues of the Catholic movement in this period. Some sense of how

---

[12] See P. R. Newman, 'Catholic Royalists of Northern England, 1642–5', *Northern History* 15 (1979), 88–95; *idem*, 'Roman Catholic Royalists: Papist Commanders under Charles I and Charles II, 1642–60', *RH* 15 (1981), 396–405; *idem*, *Royalist Officers in England and Wales 1642–1660: A Biographical Dictionary* (New York, 1981); A. Hopper, '"The Popish Army of the North": Anti-Catholicism and Parliamentarian Allegiance in Civil War Yorkshire, 1642–46', *RH* 25 (2000), 12–28; *A Most True Relation of the Present State of his Majesties Army* (1642). See also, for English Catholic royalist banners, bearing a range of political messages, P. M. Daly, A. Young and B. C. Verstraete (eds.), *The English Emblem Tradition* (4 vols., Toronto, 1993–8), III, 5, 8, 40, 88, 50, 57, 92, 95, 135, 197, 206, 207, 210, 211, 216, 241. I am very grateful to Richard Cust for this reference.

[13] Lindley, 'Part Played', 128, citing Roger Palmer, *To All the Royalists that Suffered. . . . The Humble Apologie of all the English Catholics* (n.p., 1666).

[14] Lancashire Record Office, DDBl. acc. 6121. Box 2 (The Blue Book), fo. 7r–v. I am extremely grateful to Geoff Baker for this reference.

far these families were caught up in the conflict would help to contextualise the contemporary analyses of the part played by Catholics generally in the period immediately before the outbreak of hostilities and during the civil war itself.

Even in the late 1630s, Catholic clergy who inhabited the series of aristocratic and gentry entourages which we have been exploring were positioning themselves so that, should the political ante be upped, they would be able to exploit the conflict between the crown and its critics.

The clergy, including some on the fringes of the Brownes' entourage (such as Anthony Champney) who organised the well-known 1639 Catholic financial aid to the revenue-starved royal military machine, saw the crown's political difficulties as an opportunity to offer the kind of support which the Catholic community could loyally provide. As Gordon Albion points out, Cardinal Francesco Barberini himself informed George Con how anxious he was that English Catholics should both enlist for service and stump up cash to crush the heretics in Scotland.[15] Champney, now dean of the secular clergy's episcopal chapter, drew up a circular letter in January 1639 to all English Catholics, encouraging them to offer assistance to their embattled king:

> you may understand that, hearing dailie the common reports of the discontentments in Scotland, wee were advised by some frends about the Court, upon whom wee have reason to relie . . . in such affaires, that it would bee expedient for us in this present occasion to make some expression of our readinesse to serve his Majestie in such manner as might bee suting with our profession; wherupon this common letter, which goeth heerwith, was conceived; and beeing communicated with the same frends, and by them approoved, it was allsoe made knowne to Mr Secretarie Sir Francis Windebanke, and by him to the kinge who (as Mr Secretary tould us) liking well the contents said: that if occasion should bee . . . wee should know his further pleasure therin, which now wee have latelie understood from the said Mr Secretary.

Champney therefore advised the clergy recipients of this letter that they should

> make it knowne unto all those that are in your charge or district, exhorting them to the carefull performance of that which is proposed therin . . . and consequentlie to resist the attempts of such as would withdrawe themselves from the subjection due unto their soveraynes, who therfore never drawe the sword which God hath putt into their hands more justlie than against such subjects as seeke to shake off the yoake of their subjection.

This was a wonderful opportunity for a magnificent gesture, refuting so many years of puritan slanders that Catholics were fundamentally disloyal.

---

[15] See Albion, *CI*, 334.

Champney added a postscript reiterating how far this was a Court-based initiative. He emphasised that

the queene hath been acquainted with this common letter, and her Majestie doth not onlie approove it but allsoe most earnestlie desireth that it may bee efficaciouslie sett forward; which shee would not doe but that shee knoweth how much good this expression of our dutie at this time would worke upon the kinge his most clement disposition towards his Catholicke subjects.

Secondly, 'the kinge himselfe will expect our readinesse heerin'. 'Some Catholickes' had 'allreadie offered theyr service to his Majestie (which hath been well taken)'. But 'if the rest should not doe the like, the affection of the Catholickes in generall towards his Majesties service wooould not appeare soe manifestlie as it should doe'. Thirdly the king himself had approved the letter 'and therfore will expect such effect of it as may testifie our true affections towards his service'. Fourthly, it was in all Catholics' interests to stir themselves in the cause of the Stuarts.

The proper interest of the Catholickes themselves in this cause ought to moove them; the businesse importeth them chiefelie, for if the faction of those rebellious spiritts should prevaile (which God forbide) the Catholickes doubtlesse will feele the ill effects of it more than others, and therfore they ought . . . to engage themselves farr rather than hazard an evill event in a businesse

of such moment.[16]

On 4 April 1639, at the direction of the queen, in a convention of Catholic laymen and clergymen assembled at the house of the papal agent, a list of collectors for the cash in question was compiled. Not all Catholics were particularly keen to contribute. Some even said that since the realm was at peace there was no need. But what was significant was that Con believed that the alternative to such a contribution was a reimposition of the full financial penalties for recusancy (as the government thrashed about for any kind of financial supply without having to go to parliament for it). In other words, here was a stark choice, clearly understood by leading Catholics. They were faced by two alternative scenarios – a manifestation of their loyalism and continued royal tolerance of them on the one hand, or, on the other, a refusal to step forward and a knee-jerk return to the bad old days of continuous mulcts, or worse. Neutralism was hardly an option here.[17]

---

[16] AAW, A XXIX, no. 36, pp. 145–6. For Henrietta Maria's own letter of 17 April 1639 to the English Catholics inviting a financial contribution from them, see AAW, A XXIX, no. 78. For the mechanics of trying to effect the contribution, see Hibbard, *CI*, 102–4; *idem*, 'The Contribution of 1639: Court and Country Catholicism', *RH* 16 (1982), 42–60; *CSPV 1636–9*, 535, 545. In the Long Parliament it was noted by Alexander Rigby, a Lancashire MP, that Champney and the papal agent Carlo Rossetti had ordered a 'fast among the papists towards the queen's pious intentions', Hibbard, *CI*, 173–4.

[17] Albion, *CI*, 335–6.

A significant number of the Browne family and its kin network intervened in some manner on behalf of the royalist cause, or at least against the parliamentary one. In fact, taking into account that a fighting role in the civil war was conditioned by both age and opportunity, the extent of the Browne family's and its kin's participation in the war is astonishing. Cowdray was occupied by Sir William Waller's parliamentary troops in 1643 after Sir Ralph Hopton's royalists had been thrown out. In the same year, the third Viscount Montague's estates were sequestrated, though a proposal of the local parliamentary county committee to demolish Cowdray altogether was shelved in September 1644, technically on the grounds that it should continue as a parliamentary fortification but perhaps also because of a fear of offending local opinion. Instead it was garrisoned 'for the keeping under of the ill-affected party, which we hear is too great in those parts'.[18] The third viscount's eldest son, Anthony, was wounded at York in 1644. Anthony's father-in-law was killed at Marston Moor.[19] Sir Peter Browne, the son of Sir Henry Browne (the second Viscount Montague's uncle), was mortally wounded at Naseby.[20] The second Baron Arundell of Wardour was wounded at the battle of Stratton and died subsequently, at Oxford, on 19 May 1643. William Arundell's son, Charles, the second Viscount Montague's grandson, was slain at Worcester in 1649. William Arundell survived the war, but his wife, Mary (the second Viscount Montague's daughter) was ensnared at Woodhouse Farm in the village of Horningsham in Wiltshire and, allegedly, escaped by having herself carried away in a coffin.[21]

The Arundells' castle of Wardour was the site of a famous siege in May 1643. It was commemorated in Catholic rolls of honour as much as in royalist historiography. Here Blanche Arundell, the second baron's wife, set a heroic example. A messenger from the parliamentary commander, Sir Edward Hungerford, was rebuffed with 'I know no parliament army; troops of rebels are there in the field, enemies alike to their royal master and to his loyal subjects. I will treat with none of these.' The messenger was allowed a brief view of the interior because Lady Arundell wanted to deceive him into thinking that she had many more armed men than she actually possessed. Catholic liturgical rituals punctuated the bouts of fierce and desperate fighting. The castle was damaged by the detonation of gunpowder in one of the

---

[18] Hope, *Cowdray*, 24–5. For the sequestration, see *ibid.*, 25. A significant number of the inhabitants of Midhurst had balked at signing the parliamentary Protestation of May 1641 when it was offered to them in early 1642, T. J. McCann, 'Midhurst Catholics and the Protestation Returns of 1642', *RH* 16 (1983), 319–23; D. Cressy, 'The Protestation Protested, 1641 and 1642', *HJ* 45 (2002), 251–79, at p. 273.

[19] Hope, *Cowdray*, 25.

[20] B. Stapleton, *A History of the Post-Reformation Catholic Missions in Oxfordshire* (1906), 11.

[21] J. A. Williamson, *Catholic Recusancy in Wiltshire 1660–1791* (1968), 229.

service tunnels running under the walls and in one of the drains. It was surrendered on 8 May 1643.[22] In mid-March 1644 the third Baron Arundell (having besieged Wardour Castle for three months) finally fought his way back into his ancestral home. In the final stages of this second siege, Arundell placed a considerably larger quantity of gunpowder under the castle. The detonation (whether deliberate or, perhaps, by accident) of the gunpowder on 14 March, and then the preparation of yet another mine, forced the parliamentary defenders, led by Edmund Ludlow, to surrender, but Lord Arundell's victory was gained only at the expense of reducing the family residence to a ruin.[23] (See Figure 14.)

Another celebrated siege, in which many of the defenders were Catholics drawn from among the families which have figured prominently in this book, occurred at Basing House in Hampshire. John Paulet, fifth marquis of Winchester, a colonel of horse and foot, led the defence of Basing from July 1643 until it was finally taken in October 1645.[24] The marquis's wife, Honora, was a daughter of Richard Burke, fourth earl of Clanrickard. (The Clanrickard family had a house in Kent which almost certainly served as a point of contact between this Irish family and some of the clergy who served the Sussex Catholic gentry.[25]) She recruited Sir Henry Gage (son of John Gage of Haling and Margaret Copley) to help fight off the besiegers of Basing, which he did (twice – in September and November 1644).[26] Two other defenders from the Hampshire Catholic gentry who had links with many of the families within the Brownes' kin network were Major John Cuffauld (killed in the final assault) and his brother Lieutenant Francis Cuffauld.[27]

William, eleventh Baron Stourton, who, as we saw in the previous chapter, was lobbied so hard in the early 1630s by the secular clergy to support Bishop Richard Smith, did not personally engage in hostilities but his residence,

---

[22] Foley III, 527–32; Wiltshire and Swindon Record Office, MS 2667/22/4/1.

[23] *VCH Wiltshire* XIII, 222; B. K. Davison, *Old Wardour Castle* (1999), 31–3. Lord Arundell's brother-in-law Francis Cornwallis was a royalist cavalry commander, Newman, *Royalist Officers*, 86.

[24] G. N. Godwin, *The Civil War in Hampshire (1642–45) and the Story of Basing House* (revised edition, 1904), 353–4.

[25] See *NAGB*, 45, 211.

[26] Sir Henry Gage became the governor of Oxford and was fatally wounded at Culham Bridge in January 1645.

[27] R. Ryden, 'Catholic Royalists at the Siege of Basing House', *Catholic Ancestor* 4 (1993), 227–31; Berry, *Sussex*, 294; see also HEH, BA 67/14 (a lease, dated September 1652, of property at Battle, granted by the third Viscount Montague to Francis Cuffauld). (There perished, 'slain . . . in cold blood', at Basing one Captain Edward Wyborne, probably from the Kentish recusant family of that name, Newman, *Royalist Officers*, 410; *The Royal Martyrs* (1663), 5.) For Sir Henry Gage's participation with Edward Somerset, Lord Herbert of Raglan in the scheme in 1644–5 to land Irish troops in Wales to aid the king against parliament, see Hibbard, *CI*, 226. William Gage, of Bentley in Sussex, was lieutenant colonel of horse in the regiment of Thomas Culpeper, Newman, *Royalist Officers*, 147.

Stourton House, like Wardour Castle, was appropriated by Edmund Ludlow. Stourton's eldest son, Edward, died serving his royal master at Bristol. Another son, William, was involved in Penruddock's rebellion in 1655.[28]

The second Baron Dormer (by now, the first earl of Caernarvon) was killed at the first battle of Newbury on 20 September 1643.[29] The first Viscount Dunbar (son of Sir Henry Constable and Margaret Dormer) was killed while defending Scarborough Castle in 1645.[30] John Stradling, a grandson of the Elizabeth Gage (sister of the George Gage of Spanish match fame) who married Sir John Stradling of St Donats, was a royalist major-general who died whilst interned in Windsor Castle.[31] The Somerset family, led by Henry Somerset, first marquis of Worcester, suffered huge losses in the king's cause. The marquis (who was the third Viscount Montague's father-in-law) died in prison after the surrender of Raglan.[32]

And so, if we had time, the list would go on. Others have picked out similar patterns of royalism within other Catholic kin nexuses. For example, among the relations of Lord William Howard, as H. S. Reinmuth remarks, Howard's fourth son, Thomas, died at Piercebridge in December 1642, while a son of Sir Francis Howard, also called Thomas, was slain at Atherton Moor in 1643. Sir Francis's brother-in-law, William Widdrington, was killed in the 1651 attempt to restore Charles II.[33]

Reinmuth comments on this display of Catholic royalism that 'it is a heart-breaking story of those who had never enjoyed more than a grudging and partial toleration from Charles I'.[34] It is perhaps also an account of how much Catholics thought it was worth investing in this proffered opportunity to barge their enemies out of the way in both a local setting and on the wider national stage. A tract entitled *The Royal Martyrs*, printed in 1663, listed the names of 'the lords, knights, officers and gentlemen that were slain (by the rebels) in the late wars in defence of their king and country'. It asserted that of the 'neer five hundred persons of condition' who were killed in the royalist cause 'about three hundred were Protestants' and 'one hundred and fiftie' were 'Roman-Catholicks'.[35] Another pamphlet, published at the Restoration (*A Catalogue of the Lords, Knights and Gentlemen (of the Catholick*

---

[28] Williamson, *Catholic Recusancy*, 210.

[29] Newman, *Royalist Officers*, 113. Henry Huddlestone, a grandson of the first Baron Dormer, became a lieutenant colonel of dragoons, and surrendered at Worcester in 1646, *ibid.*, 202. Dormer's banner carried a depiction of five dogs (representing the Five Members), each with the word 'Pym' coming from their mouths, attacking the royal lion, Daly, Young and Verstraete, *The English Emblem Tradition*, III, 210.

[30] Newman, *Royalist Officers*, 81.

[31] Traherne, *SC*, xxii; Newman, *Royalist Officers*, 359–61.

[32] Newman, *Royalist Officers*, 350–3.

[33] H. S. Reinmuth, 'Lord William Howard (1563–1640) and his Catholic Associations', *RH* 12 (1973–4), 226–34, at p. 231.

[34] Reinmuth, 'Lord William Howard', 231–2.   [35] *The Royal Martyrs*, 14.

Religion) that Were Slain in the Late Warr, in Defence of their King and Countrey), commemorated just those Catholics who perished in the conflict. Like *The Royal Martyrs* it makes an extraordinarily clear statement of the Catholic understanding of what it meant to fight for the king.[36]

For Catholics whose political traditions had always involved support for the Stuarts, the opportunity to fight against the parliament undoubtedly represented the logical culmination of the Catholic struggle for respectability and acceptance ever since the mid-Elizabethan period. P. R. Newman makes a most apposite point when he remarks that 'almost 87% of Catholic field officers had no experience whatsoever of secular office holding before 1642'. They were, he observes, 'the faceless Catholics' of the anti-popery tracts, and when they came forward to raise troops and fight for the king, they were, perhaps rightly, 'seen as dangerous men whose hour had come'.[37] For some of those in the Brownes' kinship group, as indeed, one suspects, for many royalist Catholics, the war seems to have offered a chance to recover the status that some of their forebears had once enjoyed as servants of the crown – a return almost to the good old days before their place in political society was undermined by the ridiculous innovations of the Reformation and the zealotry of 'Protestant-cause' attitudes to Europe.

The Restoration period would probably have persuaded them that they had been right all along. The crown's attempts to formulate and enforce legislation against Catholics generated criticism from angry Protestants that it was being half-hearted, just as Charles I had been criticised during the later 1620s and in the 1630s. The crown appeared still to be shielding Catholics from the full force of the law.[38] After the dissolution of the Oxford parliament in March 1681, quite naturally, there 'began a period which was free from . . . anti-Catholic enactments'. In Charles II's last years, Protestant Dissenters, in some counties, figure more frequently than Catholics in the exchequer's recusancy rolls.[39]

In the second half of the seventeenth century we can find leading Catholics from our clutch of interrelated families interfering on behalf of their co-religionists.[40] Even during the Interregnum, Henry Arundell, third Baron Arundell, and his cousin Francis Browne, third Viscount Montague, had continued to represent the community. In 1653 they, with Sir Thomas Brudenell,

---

[36] A manuscript copy of this list (recycled in James II's reign) is filed among the draft martyrologies which are preserved in Bishop Richard Challoner's working papers, AAW, B 28, no. 15 (described as 'faithfully transcribed from a Catholick Almanack for the year 1686'); T. H. Clancy, *English Catholic Books 1641–1700: A Bibliography* (Chicago, 1974), no. 183.

[37] Newman, 'Roman Catholic Royalists', 402.

[38] Williamson, *Catholic Recusancy*, ch. 1; J. Miller, *Popery and Politics in England, 1660–1688* (Cambridge, 1973).

[39] Williamson, *Catholic Recusancy*, 32, 33.

[40] At the start of Charles II's reign there were approximately thirty Catholic peers, *ibid.*, 183.

first Baron Brudenell, had petitioned Oliver Cromwell for favour to be shown to Catholics. In 1660 a flood of Catholic petitions was directed to the House of Lords, and one of them was submitted by Baron Arundell. Arundell played an active part in parliament in the 1660s and 1670s. He was one of the signatories of the secret Treaty of Dover. He, with other Catholic peers, was caught up in the Popish plot. He was imprisoned in the Tower but was never brought to trial. He occupied his time posing as a martyr suffering for his faith, and trusting in providence, and he set down his thoughts on these topics in verse.[41]

Under James II some of these Catholics moved into high-profile public offices. Arundell served on James's privy council and was lord keeper of the privy seal.[42] His cousin Francis Browne, fourth Viscount Montague became lord lieutenant of Sussex in January 1688. (As Victor Stater points out, thirteen Catholics were appointed lords lieutenant by James when he restructured the lieutenancy between August 1687 and March 1688.[43]) Among the fourth viscount's deputy lieutenants were Sir John Gage, Sir John Shelley and Richard Caryll.[44] And Francis Browne's brother, Henry, the future fifth viscount, became a commissioner for the customs in 1687–8, and subsequently served James II as one of his secretaries of State in exile at St Germain-en-Laye.[45] The Caryll family supplied another of James's secretaries in his early years abroad, namely John Caryll, first Baron Caryll.[46] As Paul Monod observes, a disproportionate number of those Catholics who accompanied James into exile after the Revolution were southerners.[47] Howard Erskine-Hill notes that the Jacobite nonjurors among the clergy included the minister of the Brownes' parish of Midhurst who was 'bound over to assizes for drinking to King James and the prince of Wales'.[48] Monod's excellent study suggests that 'John Bossy's depiction of the English Catholics as a religious community centred on the gentry' helps us to understand 'the survival of recusant Jacobitism'. It is clear that the English Catholic community, which moved into open support for the Stuarts before and during the civil war and in the Restoration period, subsequently supplied much of the personnel and ideological impetus for Jacobitism.[49]

---

[41] *Ibid.*, 1, 185–6.   [42] *Ibid.*, 187.

[43] V. Stater, *Noble Government* (Athens, Ga., 1994), 167, 172.

[44] Stater, *Noble Government*, 171. In Wiltshire, the fourth viscount's relatives Sir Anthony Browne and William Browne were in 1688 recommended as suitable for service as deputy lieutenants and JPs, Williamson, *Catholic Recusancy*, 230.

[45] T. J. McCann, 'On the Alleged Murder of his Chaplain by Henry Browne, 5th Viscount Montague of Cowdray', *SAC* 131 (1993), 126–8.

[46] H. Erskine-Hill, 'John, First Lord Caryll of Durford, and the Caryll Papers', in E. Cruickshanks and E. Corp (eds.), *The Stuart Court in Exile and the Jacobites* (1995), 73–89.

[47] P. K. Monod, *Jacobitism and the English People, 1688–1788* (Cambridge, 1989), 135–6.

[48] Erskine-Hill, 'John, First Lord Caryll of Durford', 146.

[49] Monod, *Jacobitism and the English People*, 135.

Also, the clerical and ecclesiastical issues which internally politicised the Jacobean and Caroline Catholic community lost none of their vigour and intensity after 1660. Ideologically, as Eamon Duffy has demonstrated, the questions which split the community during the 1620s and 1630s were so much part of mainstream Counter-Reformation culture and debate that they were never likely to have been resolved and buried by the defeat and departure of Bishop Smith. As Duffy comments, the secular clergy's 'obsessive hierarchalism' can be 'amply paralleled in Counter-Reformation Europe', notably in Holland. Their continuing insistence that they were the 'only persons . . . that by divine institution and the principal design of their vocation are entrusted with the care of souls' was rooted firmly in 'Bérullian and Borromean thinking'.[50] After 1660 the seculars' episcopal chapter carried on its pre-civil-war campaigns with enthusiasm. It indulged in the same kind of propagandistic activities as before, even down to the publicisation of the assistance which secular priests rendered to plague victims.[51] After James II's accession in February 1685, Rome acted swiftly to restore episcopal government among and over English Catholics. To govern in the long-deceased Richard Smith's place (but now with the title of bishop of Adrumetum), the Roman curia chose, in August 1685, John Leyburn, nephew of George Leyburn and former tutor to the fourth Viscount Montague.[52]

At the end of the seventeenth century the clergy were still fighting the battles that we have seen them engaged in before the civil war. As Duffy shows, even in the early eighteenth century they were in conflict over the membership and function of confraternities. Gerard Saltmarsh believed in 1712 that unless the seculars obtained their own store of spiritual privileges to dispense to the laity 'they may pack up shop and be idle, or turn regulars, for the Dominican draws by rosary indulgence, the fryer by cords, the Carmelite by scapulars, and now, as the good fathers of the Society have order'd matters, they carry away all the rest by *bona morte* privileges and indulgences'. (In 1698 a draft petition to Rome scornfully mentioned the encroachment of 'i banditti Gesuitici' in the competition for places in gentry households.)[53]

In a list of Catholic 'persons of quality' and their chaplains, drawn up between 1704 and 1706, we can see how the struggle for patronage which had raged ever since the late sixteenth century was even now in full swing. While some families retained the allegiances which they had professed in the earlier part of the seventeenth century, others had clearly changed sides.

---

[50] E. Duffy, 'The English Secular Clergy and the Counter-Reformation', *JEH* 34 (1983), 214–30, at pp. 217–18, 221.
[51] Williamson, *Catholic Recusancy*, 97, 103; P. Hughes, 'The Return of the Episcopate to England', *Clergy Review* 10 (1935), 197–201; ch. 13, pp. 459–60 above.
[52] Anstr. II , 196.   [53] Cited in Duffy, 'The English Secular Clergy', 220–1.

Thus, among those who took their chaplains from among the secular clergy, we find, perhaps predictably, the fourth Viscount Montague and the third Viscount Dunbar. But now, surprisingly, so did the third Baron Baltimore and the eighth Baron Teynham. Among those who 'depend on the regulars' we have the fourth Baron Arundell. The thirteenth Baron Stourton, by contrast, 'keeps to none, but his tenants are helped by a [secular] clergyman'. The Cottons at Watergate in Sussex were now looking to the seculars for spiritual assistance, while the Carylls in Sussex were still firmly wedded to the regulars.[54]

We could also try to recount and document the Catholic contributions to the Jacobite risings of the eighteenth century although they, and in fact the whole of post-1660 Catholicism in Britain, are really the subject of another study altogether.[55] But what our account of the Browne entourage's involvement in seventeenth-century politics perhaps shows is that only on one level will the decline of Catholicism work as a major narrative element of the period between the Reformation and 1642. If the meaning of post-Reformation Catholicism is restricted to an essentially medieval liturgical pattern of sacrament and ritual, then, clearly, Catholicism in England suffered a swift and catastrophic decline very soon after the 1559 settlement came into force. But if we understand Catholicism as a fluid political issue, which created powerful patronage nexuses and bodies of opinion about major points of crown policy (ecclesiastical and religious uniformity, the succession, foreign political and especially dynastic alliances and so on) then it is arguable that the 'decline' thesis does not work. While peers such as the Viscounts Montague, and indeed many of those in the upper echelons of the Catholic community, often look rather inactive, particularly since they were largely excluded from local and national office, an account of Catholic kin and patronage networks shows that their influence was not as circumscribed as we might at first think. This may help to explain why such people might have been so readily comprehended in the language of anti-popery used by so many Protestants in the later sixteenth and seventeenth centuries. Even if the Brownes' entourage, particularly its clerical wing, consciously distinguished its own Catholicism from the alleged extremism of the Society of Jesus, this did not mean that they faded into the background, becoming less offensive and less popish as a result.

---

[54] J. A. Williamson, 'The Distribution of Catholic Chaplaincies in the Early Eighteenth Century', *RH* 12 (1973), 42–8. A list of those who were maintained as chaplains at Wardour from the 1680s down to the nineteenth century is solidly Jesuit, Williamson, *Catholic Recusancy*, 243–4.

[55] The research of Gabriel Glickman, of Pembroke College, Cambridge, looks set to transform our understandings of Catholic Jacobitism.

It is possible to argue that Catholics such as the second Viscount Montague and his relatives, friends and chaplains, misread a good deal of the contemporary political scene. They may have defined their Catholicism too strictly. They perhaps took their recusant nonconformity and their attitudes to the issues defined by the 1606 oath of allegiance too seriously. They were undercut by other clergy who were more casuistically flexible on such things. Their attempt to represent Rome in England was perhaps too ambitious. Certainly this is what emerges from the story of Bishop Smith's attempts to exert ecclesiastical dominance over the English Catholic community.

On the other hand, the style and public impact of the Catholicism which we have identified among (even if not exclusively among) these people was very considerable. Within it we can detect many of the classic articulations of what is generally recognised as mainstream English Catholicism in this period. On several of the key contemporary issues which defined the division between Catholics and Protestants (over allegiance and conformity, for example) many of the leading Catholic statements and positions were enunciated by precisely these people. They were also heavily involved at some of the key moments when toleration appeared to be a real possibility. Now, obviously, they were not the only ones who postured and politicked over such themes and issues, and what we know about them is to some extent dictated by the chance survival of records. Had similar material produced by other factions and groups survived in greater abundance, then the picture which I have tried to draw might well need to be modified. But making allowance for all this, we can say that, by identifying, as we have done in this study, certain patterns of patronage and clientage within the Catholic community, we may have stumbled upon a crucial image-making and opinion-forming machine and a nexus of political views and interests within that community which, if rescued from the rather narrow historiographical channel into which they have usually been forced, certainly help to explain the relationship between Catholicism and its critics in the period leading up to the civil war.

———— Appendix 1 ————

The Brownes in town and country

The foundation of the Brownes' estate in Sussex was Battle Abbey,[1] which was granted in August 1538 to Sir Anthony Browne three months after it ceased to be a religious house.[2] After moving in, the new owner proceeded to demolish what was not required for domestic contentment and display, and indeed anything which might spoil a good view of the garden. That included the abbey church, which was therefore levelled with the earth. (By contrast the kitchen building was kept on for the new owner's use, and was taken down only in 1685.[3]) The Brownes lived in the Abbot's House which formed the left side of the cloister.[4]

Browne added (by royal grant in 1544) the property of St Mary Overy in Southwark to his haul of former monastic assets.[5] The Fitzwilliam estate, which came to him in 1542, also contained its share of former monastic possessions – Easebourne Priory Waverley Abbey,[6] Calceto Priory and lands previously in the possession of Newark Priory and Syon Abbey. In particular it contained Cowdray palace, part of the manor of Midhurst.[7]

---

[1] *VCH Sussex* IX, 106.

[2] In 1539 Sir Anthony Browne purchased several of Battle Abbey's attached manors, Bindoff, *HC*, I, 521. For his previously rather limited property portfolio, see *ibid.*

[3] *VCH Sussex* IX, 104.

[4] *Ibid.* Sir Anthony added 'a new west front to the abbot's great chamber, with an octagonal turret at the north-west angle', and subdivided parts of the house into rooms for living accommodation. For building works at Battle, including the guest-range (of which only the twin octagonal towers survive), see *ibid.*, 105; BL, Additional MS 33508, fo. 23r; J. G. Coad, *Battle Abbey* (English Heritage, third edition, 1994), 12–13.

[5] Bindoff, *HC*, I, 521; LMA, P92/SAV/1953. Other property in Southwark was acquired by Sir Anthony subsequently. See e.g. BL, Additional MS 31952, fos. 146v, 147v.

[6] *VCH Surrey* II, 623.

[7] The names, for the manor, were interchangeable. See R. B. Manning, 'Anthony Browne, 1st Viscount Montague: The Influence in County Politics of an Elizabethan Nobleman', *SAC* 106 (1968), 103–12, at p. 104; *VCH Sussex* IV, 74–80. Fitzwilliam's Sussex property had been settled on a trustee, his nephew, in 1538, for him, his wife and his lawful issue and, in default, his half-brother. His widow inherited a life interest, but Sir Anthony evidently moved in before her death, Hope, *Cowdray*, 21–2.

As well as these large holdings of property, the Brownes' estates in Sussex came to incorporate the following: Cocking Manor which the first Viscount Montague bought from Lord Lumley in 1584,[8] some sort of manorial estate in Todham,[9] Heyshot Manor which the earl of Northumberland had sold to Sir Anthony Browne in 1534 and which Montague sold to the earl of Bedford in 1577,[10] Lodsworth Manor (a grant of which was made to Sir Anthony Browne in June 1547),[11] Selham Manor which came to the family through Sir Anthony's father's marriage to Lucy, daughter of the marquis of Montague,[12] Westbourne Manor which came to the family via the same route,[13] Stedham Manor which was acquired by the first viscount from the Dentons (William Denton served as steward to Sir Anthony Browne and the first viscount; his grandson, the second viscount, sold Stedham to the Coldhams, a well-known recusant family),[14] Ashcombe Manor,[15] a moiety of the manor of Clayton (acquired from Richard Culpeper),[16] Poynings Manor and Fulking Manor (in Poynings parish),[17] the church and the so-called manor of Hastings, and chantry land in Winchelsea (all in grant to Sir Anthony Browne),[18] which so-called manor had several impropriate livings,[19] Northeye Manor in Bexhill which Viscount Montague acquired by purchase in 1566,[20] Barnehorne Manor,[21] Wartling rectory (until 1586),[22] Peasmarsh Manor (another grant of 1547 to Sir Anthony Browne but sold off in 1557),[23] Brede Manor (by grant in 1541),[24] Maxfield Manor,[25] and the manor of Sedlescombe (a grant made to Sir Anthony Browne in 1542).[26] There were further land purchases in Sussex by Viscount Montague from the 1560s to the 1580s.[27]

[8] *VCH Sussex* IV, 45. For the transfer of Cocking and other property from Lord Lumley in trust for Montague to two of Montague's servants, Anthony Garnett and Thomas Churchar, see SRS 19, 107. See also PRO, C 2/James I/K6/35.

[9] *VCH Sussex* IV, 52, notes that Todham is in Easebourne parish, but because of a 'complex of subenfeoffments it is difficult to say what constituted the manor of Todham, held of Viscount Montague in free socage, of which Richard Knight died seised in 1584'. George Dennis, who was one of the Brownes' friends, purchased the estate from Richard Knight's son, John, in 1587.

[10] *Ibid.*, 61.   [11] *Ibid.*, 73.

[12] *Ibid.*, 80. Selham was part of the second viscount's mother's jointure.   [13] *Ibid.*, 130.

[14] *Ibid.*, 82; SRS 20, 416.   [15] *VCH Sussex* VII, 34.   [16] *Ibid.*, 141.

[17] *Ibid.*, 209–10, 201.

[18] *VCH Sussex* IX, 17, 20, 75, 81, 246, 249; ESRO, RAF 3/4, fos 2r, 6r.

[19] The Manor of Hastings is, in fact, the Free Chapel of St Mary in the Castle.

[20] *Ibid.*, 121. This manor became part of the second Viscount Montague's daughter Frances's dowry on her marriage to John Blomer, *ibid.*; ESRO, RAF 3/4, fo. 22v.

[21] *VCH Sussex* IX, 118.

[22] *VCH Sussex* IX, 141; PRO, C 66/1303, mem. 23a; ESRO, RAF 3/4, fo. 7r.

[23] *VCH Sussex* IX, 157; SRS 20, 343; cf. ESRO, RAF 3/4, fo. 6v.

[24] *VCH Sussex* IX, 169, 181; Manning, *Religion*, 234; SRS 19, 61.

[25] *VCH Sussex* IX, 180; SRS 20, 294.   [26] *VCH Sussex* IX, 278.

[27] See e.g. SRS 19, 33 (the purchase of Bepton Manor in 1568); SRS 19, 105 (the purchase of Clayton Manor in 1588); BL, Additional MS 31952, fos. 153v–154r, 152r; SRS 19, 286; BL,

The Brownes also built up extensive estates in Surrey, in addition to their large ex-monastic estate in Southwark. In April 1566 by way of exchange and purchase Montague obtained the 'lordship and manor of Pytfold Dertford, otherwise Highe Pitfolde'.[28] The Waverley property, noted above, constituted a considerable part of Montague's land holding in this county, and comprised, *inter alia*, Dockenfield Manor,[29] Oxenford Grange (which passed to Sir Henry Browne who sold it to Sir George More of Loseley in 1609)[30] and Wanborough Manor.[31] Montague also held Down Place Manor in Compton parish,[32] Godalming Manor (of which Montague became steward rather than owner),[33] Shalford Clifford Manor (which Sir Anthony Browne had obtained from the earl of Cumberland in January 1544 to add to Shalford Bradestan Manor, the other half of the original estate),[34] and Effingham East Court Manor.[35] There was also the manor of Henley. Henley Park became the residence of the first viscount's brother Francis Browne.[36] Montague enjoyed some form of tenure of the manor of East Horsley, where Thomas Cornwallis (the queen's groom porter) and his wife Katherine resided. Katherine Cornwallis was the youngest daughter of Sir Thomas Wriothesley, first earl of Southampton.[37] (Montague's son Anthony regarded Thomas Cornwallis as his 'dere frende'.[38]) West Horsley Manor had been granted to Sir Anthony Browne in 1547. Thereafter it was held by his widow for her life, and then went to Viscount Montague, who died there.[39] Sir Anthony Browne had also

Additional MS 31952, fos. 154v, 157v. For other manors and associated property in the first viscount's possession at the time of his death, see WSRO, SAS/BA 67 (in particular, in Sussex, the farm of Chinting Poynings, 'the capital messuage and mansion house in the park called River Park', the manors of Shulbread, Willinchmere and Verdley, Northolt Farm, Bayham Manor, Lynch Manor and Levenshothe Manor in Kent; and Neatham Manor in Hampshire).

[28] *VCH Surrey* II, 612.

[29] *Ibid.*, 614. This property was mortgaged in 1614 by the second viscount.   [30] *Ibid.*, III, 65.

[31] *Ibid.*, 374. In 1579 Montague sold Waverley House in Southwark, part of the abbey's property, to Thomas Cure, MP for Southwark (in 1563, 1571 and 1586), I. Darlington, *Bankside: The Parishes of St Saviour and Christchurch, Southwark* (Survey of London, 22, 1950), 83.

[32] *VCH Surrey* III, 19; BL, Additional MS 31952, fo. 128r.

[33] *VCH Surrey* III, 31; Loseley MSS, 654; BL, Harleian MS 6990, no. 27.

[34] *VCH Surrey* III, 108. See BL, Additional MS 31952, fo. 125v.

[35] *VCH Surrey* III, 322.   [36] *Ibid.*, 342.

[37] Mott, HR, 124. She had formerly been fiancée to Sir Matthew Arundell, whose son Thomas's marriage to Mary Wriothesley she promoted, *ibid.*, 126. Katherine was an uncompromising recusant but enjoyed *de facto* toleration from the crown, HMCS VIII, 541; cf. Cockburn, *Surrey Assizes: James I*, nos. 53, 91, cf. nos. 756, 1039, 1178, 1285, 1345, 1610, 1658, 1673, 1753; Hyland, CP, 209.

[38] SHC, LM 6729/8/122.

[39] *VCH Surrey* III, 353–5. A lease of West Horsley Manor was acquired in August 1601 by Lord Buckhurst for twenty-one years, PRO, PROB 11/113, fo. 7r–v (for which reference I am grateful to Rivkah Zim.) See, however, *VCH Surrey* III, 355, remarking that West Horsley Place 'appears to have been largely rebuilt in the early seventeenth century' by the second Viscount Montague, 'who resided there. The two wings formerly projected farther than they do now; foundations exist outside them.' In all probability, the viscount 'built the gallery in the west wing'.

obtained the manors of Pirbright, Send, Jury, Worplesdon and Byfleet (where Sir Anthony was keeper, and built the manor house, a favourite residence where he ended his life, and from which his funeral cortege travelled back to Battle).[40] In Mary's reign, Stockwell Manor in Lambeth was granted to Viscount Montague by the crown as also was Estham Manor.[41]

Montague House in Southwark was the Brownes' principal London residence (until the mid-Jacobean period), though technically, of course, it was in Surrey.[42] The priory of St Mary Overy, granted, as we saw, to Sir Anthony Browne, was structurally altered to create the building which was then known as Montague House.[43] Since Montague House and its immediate environs were themselves eventually demolished (in 1828),[44] description of it is necessarily somewhat perfunctory. Montague Close (which had been part of the priory – its cloisters) surrounded the residence on two sides. To the west was Long Southwark and to the east lay Winchester House and Primrose Alley. After the Dissolution, the Close was leased to tenants. Jeremy Boulton notes that 'Montague House continued to be occupied by the heirs of Lord Montague until its conversion into tenements in 1612.'[45] This decision to lease Montague House was taken after the second viscount was heavily fined for his refusal in 1611 to take the oath of allegiance, though the fine was paid in fact out of the proceeds of the sale of Wanborough Manor.[46] In November 1625 the second viscount sold his remaining property rights in both Montague House and the Close to Robert Bromfield and Thomas Overman. Bromfield started re-developing and improving the area.[47]

[40] *VCH Surrey* III, 364, 366, 368, 392, 401, 402.

[41] *Ibid.*, IV, 57, 222; PRO, SP 46/13, fo. 144r; PRO, SP 46/17, fo. 54r.

[42] See F. T. Dollman, *The Priory of St. Mary Overie, Southwark* (1881).

[43] *Ibid.*, 29. cf. Darlington, *Bankside*, 43, noting that 'Montague Close covers the site of the cloisters and conventual buildings of St Mary's Priory', and that the family probably lived in what had once been 'the house of the prior of St Mary Overy'. Cf. Mott, HR, 473, for an account of the organisation and plan of Southampton House.

[44] Dollman, *The Priory of St. Mary Overie, Southwark*, 29.

[45] J. Boulton, *Neighbourhood and Society: A London Suburb in the Seventeenth Century* (Cambridge, 1987), 174, citing Darlington, *Bankside*, 43–4; *VCH Surrey* IV, 129.

[46] See ch. 11, p. 359 above; *VCH Surrey* III, 374.

[47] Boulton, *Neighbourhood and Society*, 175, citing LMA, P92/SAV/1336, 1333. Viscount Montague and William, Baron Petre sold 'Montague House and all' Montague's 'messuages, wharves and ground "in the close of St Mary Overies between the middle gate of the Close and the outer gate next unto Southwark" to Robert Bromfield and Thomas Overman'. Bromfield had leased a nearby wharf in 1601. Once in possession of the Close he started building works, upgrading the buildings to make them suitable 'for men of better ability', Darlington, *Bankside*, 43–4; PRO, C 54/2637/17. Robert Bromfield sat as MP for Southwark in 1621 and 1624. Sir Edward Bromfield was master of the Leathersellers' Company in 1625–6, sheriff in 1626–7 and mayor in the later 1630s, when he proved a strong supporter of crown taxation policy, and was, apparently, an anti-puritan. He was attacked in the Long Parliament, V. Pearl, *London and the Outbreak of the Puritan Revolution* (1961), 293–4. Robert Bromfield was named as a tenant in the Close in the chancery suit brought by William Arundell against Hugh Cressey in October 1622, PRO, C 2/James II/A1/5, mem. 1a. See also LMA, P92/SAV/450, pp. 422, 449, P92/SAV/192, p. 18, P92/SAV/201, p. 31.

Montague House directly adjoined the parish church, St Saviour's, which lay directly to the south,[48] and was also very close to the Clink, 'a gayle or prison for the trespassers in those parts, namely, in olde time', as John Stow says, 'for such as should brabble, frey or breake the peace on the said banke, or in the brothell houses'.[49]

In the first Viscount Montague's will, of July 1592, it was specified that the viscountess, Lady Magdalen, should have the mansion house of St Mary Overy 'with all the stables, wharfs, gardens and other appurtenances' with the 'use of the household stuff', except that the heir, Anthony Maria Browne, should have, at the age of twenty-one, possession of the 'long stable with lofts over', and 'the great vault forthright against the porter's lodge, with the way through the wharf to the water bridge', and control over the 'jewell howse otherwise called the evidence howse', the keeping of which was entrusted to the executors of the will until the heir reached his majority.[50] Richard Smith's biography of the viscountess mentions that Montague House 'was a common retire for priests coming in and going out of England, and also a refuge for such as resided in London; wherein also one priest had his residence, to minister the sacraments to such Catholics as resorted thither'.[51]

Boulton comments that 'Roman Catholics made up less than one per cent of communicants in 1603' in Southwark, but that 'these few were mainly concentrated in Montague Close'. He says that 'only nine householders can be identified positively as Catholics between 1618 and 1624'.[52] But detection of nonconformists in this area was patchy. As Boulton observes, 'frequent attendance at church by the whole population of the parish every Sunday could not be enforced in St Saviour's'. The church simply was not big enough, and 'no administrative system was developed . . . to ensure a good regular attendance'. In consequence, 'presentments for such dereliction were . . . rare and normally confined to papists or separatists'.[53] But, by the same token, the few who were presented must have stood out as seriously and offensively obstinate. So their Catholicism cannot be gauged purely numerically. At the same time, we know from the Southwark sacramental token books that

---

[48] By a statute of 32 Henry VIII the Southwark parishes of St Margaret and St Mary Magdalene 'were united and the priory church of St Mary Overy became the parish church under the new name of St Saviour's', Darlington, *Bankside*, 6–7; John Stow, ed. C. L. Kingsford, *A Survey of London* (2 vols., Oxford, 1908), II, 53, 59.

[49] Stow, ed. Kingsford, *Survey*, II, 55–6. For the position of the Clink prison, south of Clink Street and west of what is now Stoney Street, see Darlington, *Bankside*, plate 1.

[50] WSRO, SAS/BA 67.   [51] Southern, *ERH*, 42.

[52] Boulton, *Neighbourhood and Society*, 284. As Boulton notes, the records of the archdeaconry of Surrey are missing for this period. They would have been extremely useful for a view of whom the Church court officials considered to be nonconformists in the area. We are therefore reliant on the assize records (*ibid.*, 7) and to a lesser extent on the Southwark sacramental token books.

[53] *Ibid.*, 286.

some members of the Browne family, who on most tests were Catholics, were sufficiently conformable to take communion at St Saviour's.[54]

Within the Close there was, at times, a great deal of Catholic activity. On 8 November 1605, shortly after the Gunpowder plot came to light, one of the regular purveyors of news to the regime about the Brownes' Catholic establishment in London, John Bird, claimed that 'weekly Masses are' said 'in the old lady's house', i.e. Lady Magdalen's rooms in Montague House, for 'the . . . Brownes and their adherents'. In one 'assembly or conventicle' there were some 'laical sorts out of London', especially three uncles of the second viscount (presumably Sir George, Sir Henry and one of the other children of Lady Magdalen by the first viscount), and 'as fish or fowl in nets' they 'may be there surprised', by which means 'that cursed fraternity may be broken, and by an exemplary punishment many hundreds of pounds may be drawn into his Majesty's purse'. According to Bird, Montague House was full of 'secret oratories for massing, vaults, and places for all their books, church ornaments for closets and chambers for all festivals, saints' days, Sundays and working days in costly workmanships of gold upon velvet and silks, chalices, pipes, silver implements, beads well stored with valuable stones and gold, [and] private letters of advertisements of foreign occurrencies and domestical' from the Catholic clergy.[55]

As we have observed, Montague House was close to the Clink prison. Particularly in the early seventeenth century there were many Catholic clergy incarcerated here. These were often quite prominent and ideologically committed men, for example Thomas Preston, the monk and political theorist, who wrote tracts justifying the regime's general stance on the duty of loyalty required from Catholics. The archpriest George Blackwell was held there, after his arrest in 1607, not many yards from Montague House where, as archpriest, he had spent some of his time, especially in the company of the second Viscount Montague's steward John Loane.[56] Former appellant priests detained in the prison included the furiously anti-Jesuit Robert Charnock and Anthony Hebburn. There were other clerical inmates of the Clink, however, such as John Colleton who, though they had attacked the Jesuits during the appellant controversy, were absolutely unyielding on the question of the Jacobean oath of allegiance. So there was something of an ideological ferment going on inside the gaol. At the same time, the prison was noted for

---

[54] LMA, P92/SAV/186–201. By late 1628, when a survey was done by Surrey JPs of who was recusant in the county near to London, they could name only ten people for St Saviour's parish, and only three (a 'girdler', his wife and their son) specifically living in Montague Close, PRO, SP 16/122/54, fo. 84r. Of course, this may well have been because the second Viscount Montague had long since left the Close and had moved west (and north of the river) to Drury Lane.

[55] *HMCS* XVII, 475.   [56] See ch. 10, p. 319 above.

its remarkable laxity. For those such as Preston who were in favour with the regime, it was essentially a form of lodgings in London. This meant that close to one of the principal sites of aristocratic Catholicism in the metropolis, Montague House, there was, in effect, also a clerical college, virtually a think-tank for defining Catholic answers to key questions about the relationship between the regime and its Catholic subjects, questions on which the second viscount held strong opinions (though, of course, he vacated Montague House in the middle of James's reign).

Undoubtedly, from time to time, the Catholics in Southwark, as in other parts of London, must have felt quite embattled. The second viscount was involved, up to 1605, in a series of tithe disputes with the churchwardens of St Saviour's parish.[57] There seems to have been a succession of puritan clergy at St Saviour's, in the shape of lecturers appointed there by the vestry.[58] We should, however, not imagine that Catholics were completely excluded from all aspects of local life and activity. Even the contemporary debates about popular 'moral' issues, such as theatres, might involve Catholics living in Southwark. The Globe, for example, was very close. There was in the mid-1610s a fierce debate among the priests in the Clink about the issue of theatre-going, which activity some of the clergy there relished as a pleasing diversion from the tedium of being locked up with other, often tetchy, Catholic clergymen. But John Colleton regarded their pleasures, and also their (allegedly) unseemly modes of dress, as a scandal to their profession.[59] In St Saviour's this was undoubtedly a hot topic for discussion. The St Saviour's lecturer, Thomas Sutton, elected in February 1615, was a well-known puritan foe of the theatre.[60]

The Brownes' widely dispersed estates not only gave them influence in more than one county but also allowed them a presence in the capital which was very different from their influence in the country. Montague House and the surrounding Close were open to a large number of people, in the context of a London socio-cultural and political scene (close to the Court, Paul's Cross and other London pulpits, the theatres and so on) which was a world away from Cowdray and Battle in the Brownes' home county of Sussex. The reports of the goings-on in Montague House from informers such as John Bird are rarely paralleled by similar accounts from the Brownes'

---

[57] See LMA, P92/SAV/450, pp. 343, 351, 361, 369, 390.

[58] A lectureship had been founded in the parish by 1578, P. Seaver, *The Puritan Lectureships* (1975), 124. For the lecturers there, who were often of a strongly Protestant or puritan persuasion, see *ibid.*, 106, 150, 214, 217, 224, 234, 236.

[59] P. Lake with M. Questier, *The Antichrist's Lewd Hat* (2002), 267; Folger Library, MS V a 544; A. J. Cook, *The Privileged Playgoers of Shakespeare's London, 1576–1642* (Princeton, 1981), 143; I. J. Semper, 'Jacobean Playhouse and Catholic Clerics', *The Month* NS 8 (1952), 28–39.

[60] *CSPD 1611–18*, 419.

Sussex estates. Looking at the presence and activities of the Browne family in Southwark demonstrates to us how London would have transformed and magnified the impact of their distinctive religious and ideological positions and why they, with other Catholic aristocratic and gentry families in the capital, would have been, to many Protestants, a convincing instance of the growth of popery, something which was not so readily evident in the provinces. It certainly helps us to make sense of the vociferous parliamentary calls in this period for Catholics to be excluded from London.

Appendix 2

The families of Browne, Dormer,
Gage and Arundell

THE FAMILY OF BROWNE (Viscounts Montague of Cowdray)

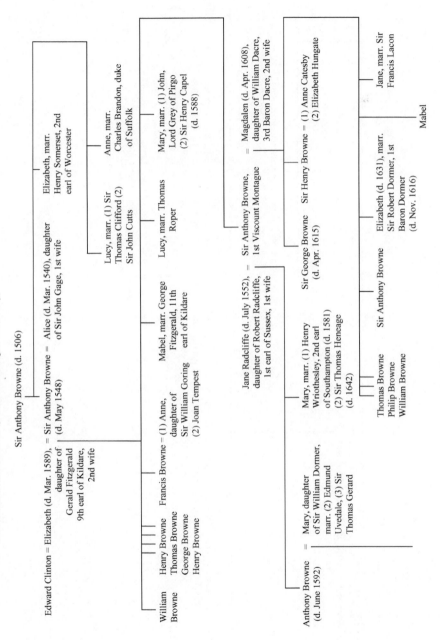

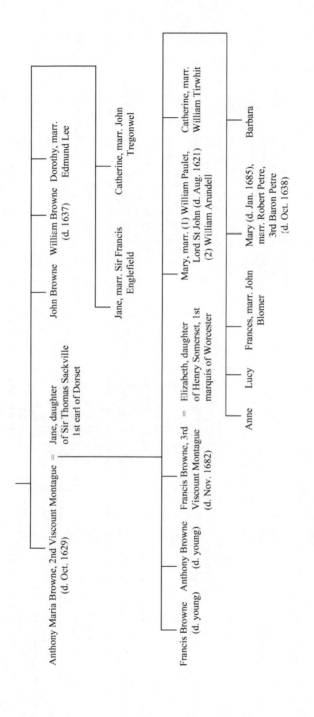

Anthony Maria Browne, 2nd Viscount Montague = Jane, daughter
(d. Oct. 1629)   of Sir Thomas Sackville
                                                  1st earl of Dorset

John Browne   William Browne   Dorothy, marr.
               (d. 1637)   Edmund Lee

Jane, marr. Sir Francis   Catherine, marr. John
Englefield   Tregonwel

Francis Browne   Anthony Browne   Francis Browne, 3rd   =   Elizabeth, daughter
(d. young)   (d. young)   Viscount Montague   of Henry Somerset, 1st
                                    (d. Nov. 1682)   marquis of Worcester

Anne   Lucy   Frances, marr. John   Mary, marr. (1) William Paulet,   Catherine, marr.
                Blomer   Lord St John (d. Aug. 1621)   William Tirwhit
                                       (2) William Arundell

                                       Mary (d. Jan. 1685),   Barbara
                                       marr. Robert Petre,
                                       3rd Baron Petre
                                       (d. Oct. 1638)

THE FAMILY OF DORMER (Barons Dormer of Wing)

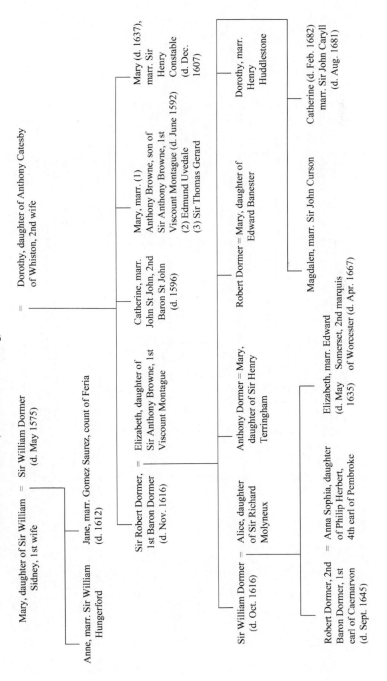

THE FAMILY OF GAGE (of Firle)

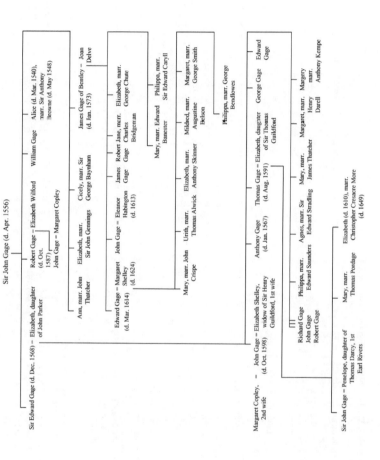

THE FAMILY OF ARUNDELL (Barons Arundell of Wardout)

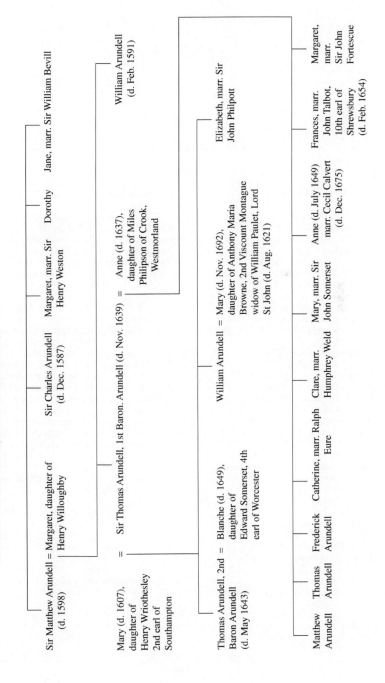

INDEX

Titles in the series

13381829R00343

Printed in Great Britain
by Amazon.co.uk, Ltd.,
Marston Gate.